The Reluctant Land

The Reluctant Land

Society, Space, and Environment in Canada before Confederation

Cole Harris

With cartography by Eric Leinberger

UBCPress · Vancouver · Toronto

16 15 14 13 12 11 10 09 08   5 4 3 2 1

Printed in Canada on acid-free paper.

Library and Archives Canada Cataloguing in Publication

Harris, R. Cole
The reluctant land: society, space, and environment in Canada before Confederation /
Cole Harris; with cartography by Eric Leinberger.

Includes bibliographical references and index.
ISBN 978-0-7748-1449-2 (bound); ISBN 978-0-7748-1450-8 (pbk.)

1. Canada – History – To 1763 (New France) 2. Canada – History –
1763-1867. 3. Canada – Historical geography. I. Title.

FC161.H37 2008   971   C2008-900648-8

Canadä

UBC Press gratefully acknowledges the financial support
for our publishing program of the Government of Canada through the Book
Publishing Industry Development Program (BPIDP), and of the Canada Council
for the Arts, and the British Columbia Arts Council.

This book has been published with the help of a grant from the Canadian Federation
for the Humanities and Social Sciences, through the Aid to Scholarly Publications
Programme, using funds provided by the Social Sciences and Humanities
Research Council of Canada, and with the help of the K.D. Srivastava Fund.

UBC Press
The University of British Columbia
2029 West Mall
Vancouver, BC V6T 1Z2
604-822-5959 / Fax: 604-822-6083
www.ubcpress.ca

In memory of Louise Dechêne

Contents

Maps and Figures / IX

Preface / XV

Acknowledgments / XXI

1 Lifeworlds, circa 1500 / 1

2 The Northwestern Atlantic, 1497-1632 / 20

3 Acadia and Canada / 52

4 The Continental Interior, 1632-1750 / 92

5 Creating and Bounding British North America / 117

6 Newfoundland / 137

7 The Maritimes / 162

8 Lower Canada / 231

9 Upper Canada / 306

10 The Northwestern Interior, 1760-1870 / 377

11 British Columbia / 416

12 Confederation and the Pattern of Canada / 448

Index / 476

Maps and Figures

MAPS

1.1 Distribution of population, northern North America, 1500 / 2

1.2 Physiographic regions, northern North America / 4

1.3 Vegetation regions, northern North America / 4

1.4 Economies, northern North America, 1500 / 6

1.5 Seasonal round of Algonquian groups north of Lake Huron / 8

2.1 Cartographic understandings of North America, early sixteenth century / 22

2.2 Eastern North America, Pierre Desceliers, detail of world map, 1550 / 25

2.3 Sixteenth-century European place names, Avalon Peninsula / 26

2.4 Part of America, Luke Foxe, 1635 / 28

2.5 New France, Samuel de Champlain, 1632 / 30

2.6 The inshore and banks fisheries / 32

2.7 European inshore fisheries, 1500-1600 / 37

2.8 Basque whaling stations, Gulf of St. Lawrence / 38

2.9 Port of Tadoussac, Samuel de Champlain, 1613 / 39

2.10 Peoples, trade routes, and warfare around the St. Lawrence Valley, c. 1600 / 42

3.1 Acadian marshland settlement, 1707 / 58

3.2 Acadian farms near Port Royal, modified from Delabat, 1710 / 59

3.3 Louisbourg Harbour, 1742 / 64

3.4 Distribution of population in Canada, 1667 and 1759 / 66

3.5 Quebec in 1759 / 70

3.6 Farm lots conceded near Quebec by 1709 / 75

3.7   Settlement patterns near Montreal, c. 1760 / 77
4.1   Jesuit missions around the Great Lakes before 1650 / 94
4.2   Settlement around and beyond the Great Lakes, late 1650s / 96
4.3   Trade and settlement around and beyond the Great Lakes, 1670 / 99
4.4   Settlement around and beyond the Great Lakes, 1685 / 101
4.5   Settlement around and beyond the Great Lakes, 1701 / 103
4.6   French and British territorial claims after the Treaty of
      Utrecht / 105
4.7   Settlement around and beyond the Great Lakes, 1750 / 107
4.8   Distribution of Native groups northwest of the Great Lakes,
      1720-60 / 113
5.1   France in North America, c. 1750 / 118
5.2   Geopolitical claims to North America, 1763-83 / 122
5.3   Quebec after the Royal Proclamation, 1763 / 124
5.4   Western British North America after the Convention
      of 20 October 1818 / 130
5.5   The bounded space of British North America / 133
5.6   Population density of British North America, 1851 / 134
6.1   French and English fisheries in Newfoundland, c. 1600 / 138
6.2   Inshore fishing ships and winter residents, c. 1675 / 141
6.3   Winter population, 1766 and 1784-85 / 144
6.4   Trinity, 1801 / 148
6.5   Population, 1836 / 152
7.1   Land capability in Greater Nova Scotia / 163
7.2   Loyalists in the Maritimes, 1785 / 168
7.3   Distribution of population in the Maritimes, 1800 / 174
7.4   Population of New Brunswick, 1851 / 185
7.5   Sawmills and settlement, a hypothetical landscape / 190
7.6   Acadian settlements in New Brunswick / 193
7.7   Settlement along the lower Miramichi, 1851 / 194
7.8   Plan of Lord Selkirk's estate at Point Prim, lots 57 and 58,
      c. 1803 / 197
7.9   Distribution of population, Prince Edward Island, 1833 / 198
7.10 David Ross farm, lot 34, 1841 / 199
7.11 Origin of the island population, by township, c. 1851-81 / 201
7.12 Landholding in Middle River / 204

7.13   Hardwood Hill / 213

7.14   Shipyards, St. Mary's Bay / 214

7.15   Distribution of population, Nova Scotia, 1851 / 216

7.16   Exports from Nova Scotia, 1854 / 218

7.17   Great roads and bye roads in Nova Scotia, 1851 / 219

7.18   Shipbuilding, 1870 / 220

8.1   Soil capability for agriculture, Quebec / 235

8.2   Seigneurial ownership, 1791 / 237

8.3   Rang settlement patterns: a) near Trois-Rivières; b) on a hypothetical seigneurie / 239

8.4   Villages in the seigneurial lowland, 1815 and 1851 / 241

8.5   Locations of case studies / 248

8.6   St. Lawrence transportation system, 1860 / 265

8.7   Origin of Canadian immigrants to Montreal, 1859 / 267

8.8   Value of industrial production, St. Lawrence corridor, 1871 / 273

8.9   Distribution of selected occupations in Montreal, 1861 / 274

8.10   Colonizing the fringe of the Canadian Shield / 279

8.11   District of St. Francis (detail), Canada East, 1863 / 293

8.12   Dams and manufactures along the Magog River, 1827-67 / 294

8.13   Free grants and Crown sales in Winslow Township, 1850-60 / 295

8.14   Distribution of population, Quebec, 1871 / 299

9.1   Soil capability for agriculture / 307

9.2   English origins by county, as recorded on gravestones in Peel, Halton, and York Counties / 313

9.3   Township surveys / 317

9.4   Distribution of population, 1825 / 321

9.5   Initial allocation of land in Essa Township, Northern Home District, c. 1821 / 325

9.6   Rural settlement near Peterborough / 326

9.7   Percentage of cultivated land per township, 1851 / 329

9.8   Wood production / 340

9.9   Population distribution, 1851 / 343

9.10   Population density, 1851 and 1871 / 349

9.11   Railways, 1860 / 357

9.12   Population distribution, 1871 / 359

9.13   Manufacturing establishments in Hamilton, 1860 / 361

9.14 Colonization roads in the Ottawa-Huron Tract / 368

10.1 French and British trade routes in the northwestern interior, 1755 / 380

10.2 Trade routes in the northwestern interior, 1774-89 and 1806-21 / 381

10.3 Fur posts in 1821 and 1825 / 383

10.4 Depletion of beaver in the Petit Nord / 386

10.5 Red River settlement, 1816 / 387

10.6 Distribution of Native peoples in 1821 and 1860 / 391

10.7 The establishment of missions / 396

10.8 Red River parishes and population, 1856 / 399

10.9 Distribution of population in southern Manitoba, 1870 / 404

10.10 Palliser's Triangle and the Fertile Belt / 407

10.11 Economic activities at Norway House, 1870 / 411

11.1 Principal European explorations in the Cordillera, 1774-1811 / 417

11.2 Smallpox epidemics, eighteenth century / 419

11.3 North West and Hudson's Bay Company posts in the Cordillera, 1805-46 / 426

11.4 Land surveys near Victoria, 1855 / 430

11.5 Gold rush transportation, 1865 / 436

11.6 Douglas reserves (1864) and reductions (1868) in the lower Fraser Valley / 438

11.7 Population in southern and central British Columbia, 1881 / 441

12.1 Making the Dominion of Canada, 1867-73 / 452

FIGURES

1.1 Late pre-contact Tsimshian village of Kitkatla / 12

1.2 The Draper Site, a sixteenth-century Huron village / 13

2.1 *Englishmen in a Skirmish with Eskimo* (detail), 1585-93 (artist, John White) / 27

2.2 Newfoundland fishing stations, 1772 / 33

2.3 Habitation at Port Royal, c. 1606 / 40

2.4 Habitation at Quebec, 1608-12 / 41

3.1 *Quebec as Seen from the East*, 1688 (artist, J-B-L Franquelin) / 69

3.2 The wooden house / 81

3.3 "Église Saint-Laurent, Île d'Orléans," c. 1870 / 84

6.1 Summer and winter populations, eighteenth century / 143

6.2   *The Town and Harbour of St. John's, 1831* (artist, William Eagar) / 153

6.3   *Bell Isle Beach, Conception Bay, Newfoundland* (detail), 1857 (artist, William Grey) / 156

6.4   *Harbour Breton, Newfoundland* (detail), n.d. (artist unknown) / 157

6.5   *Trinity Bay and Hearts Content* (detail), 1865 (artist, J. Becker) / 157

7.1   *Perspective View of the Province Building, Halifax* (detail), 1819 (artist, John Elliott Woolford) / 174

7.2   "Lumberman's Camp, Nashwaak River, New Brunswick," c. 1870 (photographer, William Notman) / 187

7.3   *View of Saint John, N.B., 1851* (detail) (artist, J.W. Hill) / 189

7.4   *The Green at Fredericton*, c. 1838 (artist, W.H. Bartlett) / 192

7.5   *River St. John from Forks of Madawaska, 1839* (artist, Philip J. Bainbrigge) / 194

7.6   *Sunny Side Stock Farm, Res. of Robt. Fitzsimons, Long River, New London, Lot 20, P.E.I., 1880* / 202

7.7   *Drying Codfish*, c. 1880 (artist, R. Harris) / 207

7.8   *Mining Scenes, Caledonian Mines, Cape Breton County*, c. 1880 / 208

7.9   *View from Retreat Farm, Windsor, N.S.* (detail), c. 1839 (artist, William Eagar) / 212

7.10 *The Town and Harbour of St. John, New Brunswick* (detail), 1866 / 221

8.1   *View from the Citadel of Quebec, 1838* (artist, W.H. Bartlett) / 236

8.2   *View of Château Richer, 1787* (artist, Thomas Davies) / 238

8.3   *The Village of Pointe Lévis, Lower Canada* (detail), 1838 (artist, H.W. Barnard) / 261

8.4   *Locks on the Rideau Canal, 1838* (artist, W.H. Bartlett) / 264

8.5   *Timber Depot near Quebec, 1838* (artist, W.H. Bartlett) / 269

8.6   *View of the Port and of the Rue des Commissaires, 1843* (artist, James Duncan) / 269

8.7   Housing in Montreal: a) fourplex and duplex; b) *St. Antoine Hall* / 275

8.8   *Canada Marine Works, Augustin Cantin, Montreal, Canada East, 1857* / 276

8.9   *The Habitant Farm,* 1856 (artist, Cornelius Krieghoff) / 286

8.10 Mill at Sherbrooke on the Magog River (artist, W.H. Bartlett) / 290

8.11 *Stanstead, Lower Canada* (detail), 1842 (artist, W.H. Bartlett) / 297

9.1   Emigration from the British Isles, 1815-65 / 310

9.2   Land prices in Essex County, 1800-50 / 319

9.3   *Road between Kingston and York [Toronto], Upper Canada* (detail), c. 1830 (artist, J.P. Pattison) / 323

9.4   *A Clearing, Upper Canada* (detail), 1839 (artist, Philip J. Bainbrigge) / 327

9.5   *First Home in Canada,* n.d. (artist, William Armstrong) / 328

9.6   *Adolphustown, Upper Canada,* c. 1830 (artist, John Burrows) / 328

9.7   *Grist Mill, Saw Mills, Etc. on the Nappanee River, at Nappanee Village* (detail), c. 1830 (artist, John Burrows) / 337

9.8   *Cobourg,* 1838 (artist, W.H. Bartlett) / 345

9.9   *Toronto, Canada West. From the Top of the Jail* (detail), 1854 (artist, Edwin Whitefield) / 346

9.10 Ontario house types (artist, Peter Ennals) / 350

9.11 Ontario barns (artist, Peter Ennals) / 351

9.12 *Reception of His Royal Highness the Prince of Wales by the Inhabitants of Toronto, Canada West, 27 Oct. 1860* (detail) (artist, G.H. Andrews) / 370

10.1 *Indians Completing a Portage, 1873* (detail) (artist, William Armstrong) / 378

10.2 *Half Breeds Travelling* (detail), 1848-56 (artist, Paul Kane) / 395

10.3 *Manitoba Settler's House and Red River Cart,* c. 1870 (artist, William Hind) / 402

10.4 *Blackfoot Indian Encampment, Foothills of the Rocky Mountains,* c. 1870 (artist, William Armstrong) / 408

10.5 *Main Street, Winnipeg,* 1871 (artist, E.J. Hutchins) / 409

11.1 *View of the Habitations in Nootka Sound* (engraving by Samuel Smith from drawing by John Webber, 1778) / 419

11.2 *View from Fort Langley,* c. 1858 (artist, J.M. Alden) / 425

11.3 *Fort Yale, British Columbia,* 1864 (artist, Frederick Whymper) / 433

11.4 "Gold Mining, Cariboo," n.d. (photographer unknown) / 435

Preface

Sprawled irregularly across a continent, and settled at different times by different peoples, Canada is not an easy country to know. French then British settler colonies were superimposed on Native peoples, and discontinuous patches of European settlement were bounded by rock, frost, and, eventually, the border with the United States. In various ways, Canada has been a reluctant creation. No European country has anything like its past, nor does its neighbour, the United States. The American past has to do with extension and abundance, the Canadian, slowly worked out near or beyond the northern continental limit of agriculture, with discontinuity, paradox, and limitations – with boundaries at almost every turn. There have been no a prioris, no master plans, no first principles. There has been an evolving patchwork of settlements, and in each of them an accumulating experience with the land and peoples nearby that eventually would be combined into a country.

Complicating the problem of knowing Canada is the widespread contemporary disinclination to write national histories. They are seen as hegemonic, as favouring the interests of some over others, and, at worst, as imposing a triumphant linear narrative on the intricate variety of the past. If national histories are viewed in this light, the challenge, obviously, is to deconstruct them. Yet, early in the twenty-first century it is far from clear what national history of Canada awaits deconstruction. There is no consistent, broadly accepted narrative of the Canadian past. Most of the country's historians work at a much more local scale, so much so that some of them lament the near demise of Canadian history. The Canadian public, for its part, is hesitant about the nature of Canadian identity and the meaning of being Canadian. In these circumstances, construction seems at least as important as deconstruction. It too can be sensitive to ambiguity, nuance, and difference. It need not treat a country's past as a stage for a well-programmed play any more than as an amalgam of changing places where lives were lived and events occurred, settlements were created or destroyed, and the land was etched with differently lived lives. Such is the past one wants to explore – not to promote, preach, or create a national vision but to understand and thereby bring into somewhat clearer focus what this country is and what it is not.

And so I return with a good deal of enthusiasm and a certain sense of urgency to an undertaking in which I have engaged before. In the late 1960s and early 1970s, John Warkentin and I wrote a general account of early Canada, *Canada before Confederation: A Historical Geography.* In the late 1970s and through much of the '80s, I edited another general account, the first volume of the *Historical Atlas of Canada.* The former, which was intended as an undergraduate text, served for a considerable time but has been superseded by new research, fresh ways of conceptualizing and theorizing the past, and the changing nature of Canada. The latter, to which many scholars contributed, has proved more resilient, but would be handled differently today. Moreover, its coverage was shaped by its cartographic emphasis, and ended, for the most part, at the beginning of the nineteenth century. It seemed clear, therefore, that a new account of early Canada was needed. *Canada before Confederation* was too dated to be revised. A different book was required, but only recently have I had time to review current literatures, think again about this country, and write. *The Reluctant Land* is the result. It is intended for students in history or historical geography and for all others – including scholars and the reading public – who seek a broad account of land and life in early Canada. I would like Canadians to know their country better.

Early Canada was a distinctive and changing human geography, and I have long assumed that my own field, historical geography, was particularly well placed to consider this mixture of people and land. Yet, some historians work with similar ingredients, and in this book I have sought to write an interdisciplinary account, at once historical and geographical, of land and life in early Canada between AD 1500 – when, five hundred years after the Norse, Europeans began to re-encounter a vast and diverse

Native land – and the Confederation years of the late 1860s and early 1870s. Except here and there where the discussion touches on my own research, I have relied on regionally and topically focused secondary literatures, the most relevant parts of which, for my purposes, are identified in the suggested readings that follow each chapter. The grist for a fresh, large account of early Canada lies in the rich body of detailed local research completed over the last thirty years and more; the orientation of such an account is inflected by contemporary Canada itself and, to some extent, by the currently available theoretical literature. It is a matter of absorbing these research findings, and then of musing about them in relation to each other, the country past and present, and the interpretative and theoretical frameworks at hand.

But one needs be cautious. There is no theoretical framework from which Canada can be deduced. Theory tends to abstraction and simplification; used deductively, it is inclined to strip away a country's complexity and individuality. If theory has the invaluable capacity to pose new questions and open new avenues of enquiry, it cannot provide a broad synthetic understanding of the intricate, variegated convergence of people and land out of which early Canada emerged. Marx's imposing analysis of early industrial capitalism, for example, catches some elements of early Canada while missing many others altogether. For the purposes of this book, he is a useful but partial resource. Similarly, though recent literatures in cultural theory and postcolonial studies have generated important enquiries into the interrelationships of culture and power, they have largely ignored other forms of power. Moreover, as many critics have pointed out, they tend to describe a generic colonialism, thus underplaying the variety and complexity of colonial experience, particularly as colonialism worked itself out in settler colonies. And so, though I draw on these and other theoretical literatures in various ways, readers will find, I hope, that *The Reluctant Land* is not dominated by them.

Rather, I have tried to work inductively with both Canada and theory – the former rather more than the latter. I largely agree with Harold Innis, still Canada's most distinguished economic historian, that the conceptualization of Canada must emerge in good part from within Canada itself. The country has been a particular creation. There are, however, patterns in this distinctiveness to which theoretical literatures can be some guide, but even more, I think, a steeping in the country's circumstances.

In a general book on early Canada, that steeping entails an immersion not in the archives, which (at the scale of the whole country) are simply too large and undigested, but rather in the archivally based research literature. The recent focus of most of this literature, whether written by historians, historical geographers, or historical sociologists, has been social or economic; it is this focus, coupled with my own inclinations, that orients much of the analysis in this book. I have taken a good part of the research literature of the last thirty years, my own writing on and experience with this country, and such elements of more general theory as seemed relevant, put them into a pot, and stirred – the recipe for this book. Although full of the changing local arrangements of this sprawled land and of my attempts to account for them, it is also intended as a step towards the clearer conceptualization – in the loosest sense, the incipient theorization – of the background of the country as a whole.

Given its scale and objectives, *The Reluctant Land* omits far more than it treats. These pages contain next to nothing of biography or of political, institutional, or religious history. Many people appear, but few individuals. Stories are few, although perhaps the whole book is a story. Rather, there are accounts of the changing arrangement and interactions of people and land in early Canada and of the humanized spaces of early Canadian life. *The Reluctant Land* looks less at individuals than at these frames within which their lives were situated, and does so because they largely shaped early Canada and remain, I think, the point of departure for thought about this country. A good part of contemporary Canadian life – much of our politics and creative writing, for example – still revolves around them.

I begin with an overview of settlement patterns in northern North America in AD 1500, just as Europeans were beginning to re-establish connections across the North Atlantic. Such a point of departure permits a description of pre-contact Aboriginal lifeworlds without requiring an explanation – unnecessary for the purposes of this book – of their origins. Chapter 2 deals with European explorers and cartography, with fishers and fur traders, and with the possible sixteenth-century introduction of European diseases. From there, Chapter 3 turns to the French settler colonies in Acadia and Canada, following them to the mid-eighteenth century. Chapter 4 treats the continental interior and the turbulent mix of Native peoples, introduced diseases, missionaries, French and English fur traders, and soldiers that emerged there during the seventeenth and first half of the eighteenth centuries. The fifth chapter is geopolitical; it considers the wars, treaties, and boundary settlements out of which British North America emerged, and in so doing establishes the geographical framework for the rest of the book. From this point, my treatment is regional because in these years British North America was, essentially, a set of separate colonies and regions. Chapter by chapter, I consider Newfoundland, the Maritimes, Lower Canada (Quebec), Upper Canada (Ontario), the northwestern interior, and British Columbia. In each, to put it baldly, I explore the changing interrelations of society, space, and land. In Chapter 12, I summarize the Confederation agreements, and then, more generally and abstractly than elsewhere in this book, consider the patterns of land and life on which they were superimposed. This leads me, finally, to reflect on some of the implications of Confederation and its long North American past for Canada as we know it today.

A note about the word "Canada," which has not always meant what it does today. During the French regime it referred either to the French colony along the lower St. Lawrence River or (frequently interchangeably with "New France") to the large French position in northeastern North America from the eastern Gulf of St. Lawrence through the Great Lakes. After the conquest, and particularly after the Quebec Act of 1774, the term was replaced by "the Province of Quebec," then was revived after the Constitutional Act of 1791 in the terms "Lower Canada" (today, southern Quebec) and "Upper Canada" (southern Ontario). There, with the modification in 1841 to "Canada East" and "Canada West," this toponymy rested until Confederation. The Atlantic colonies were not part of Canada. Nor was the West. Nor, for a good time, were all the inhabitants of Lower Canada Canadians. Long after 1760, Canadians were the French-speaking people whose ancestors had settled along the lower St. Lawrence during the French regime. Others there – Scots, Irish, English, Americans – were newcomers. In this book I use the word "Canada" in three different senses: to refer, anachronistically, to the whole territory of modern Canada, as in the subtitle; to refer to the French colony along the lower St. Lawrence; and to refer to the territories variously called Canada between 1791 and Confederation. I use the term "Canadian" as it was employed during the French regime and long thereafter: to identify the French-speaking inhabitants of Canada. I do not refer to "French Canadians" or "English Canadians" until the 1850s and 1860s, when these identifications became more current.

Finally, a few words about Louise Dechêne, to whom this book is dedicated. She was a committed and exemplary scholar; her best-known book, *Habitants et marchands de Montréal,* published in 1974, remains by far the outstanding work on Canada during the French regime – rivaled only by a manuscript on the state and warfare that she left unfinished at her death and is soon to be published. She poured talent and energy into her writing, her students, and her collaborations (volume 1 of the *Historical Atlas of Canada,* for example). She had a deep, abiding respect for careful, archival scholarship, and, through her own such work, for the ordinary people of early Canada, knowing as she did the difficulty of most of their lives. She was a friend who put her views strongly and would probably have disagreed with parts of the analysis that follows.

Acknowledgments

The Reluctant Land grows out of the detailed scholarship on early Canada completed over the last long generation, the impetus given North American historical geography by Andrew H. Clark at the University of Wisconsin, and the book, *Canada before Confederation,* that in the late 1960s he encouraged John Warkentin and me to write. Some years later, the *Historical Atlas of Canada,* the first volume of which I edited, assembled an enormous body of considered information, to which this book is greatly indebted, about the spatial organization of early Canadian society. More recently, Donald Meinig's monumental study, *The Shaping of America: A Geographical Perspective on 500 Years of History,* has encouraged me to persevere with this more modest synthesis.

As chapters were written, I sent them to friends and regional specialists. They, of course, did not always agree with me on important points or find their advice always taken, but their comments invariably improved the manuscript. All of them have my warm thanks: Jean Barman, Ted Binnema, Will Castleton, John Clarke, Daniel Clayton, Serge Courville, Julie Cruikshank, Denis Delâge, Catherine Desbarats, Gerhard Ens, Matthew Evenden, Derek Fraser, Robert Galois, Allan Greer, Naomi Griffiths, Paul Hackett, Gordon Handcock, Douglas Harris, Matthew Hatvany, Conrad Heidenreich, Stephen Hornsby, Keith Johnson, Diane Killou, Anne Knowles, Michel Lavoie, Jack Little, Richard Mackie, Elizabeth Mancke, John Mannion, Larry McCann, Jamie Morton, Carolyn Podruchny, Maurice Saint-Yves, Seamus Smyth, Laurier Turgeon, Peter Ward, John Warkentin, Wendy Wickwire, and Graeme Wynn. Two anonymous reviewers for UBC Press were also exceedingly helpful.

Although I did not ask the Social Sciences and Humanities Research Council to support this book, the council's generous assistance for the *Historical Atlas of Canada* and for my two subsequent books on British Columbia has allowed me to develop many of the ideas and understandings on which *The Reluctant Land* is based. Eric Leinberger, the brilliant design cartographer who prepared the maps, has been a great pleasure to work with. The heads of my department while this book was being written, Graeme Wynn and Michael Bovis, offered encouragement and a corner of indispensable office space for a retired professor. At UBC Press, my principal thanks are due to Jean Wilson (for good sense and wisdom throughout), Holly Keller (for the efficient management of flows), Deborah Kerr (for impeccable copy editing), and David Drummond and Irma Rodriguez (for design). Over the years my wife, Muriel, a more rigorous scholar than her husband, has provided the support, criticism, and home that underlie all my scholarly endeavours.

The Reluctant Land

1
Lifeworlds, circa 1500

When Europeans began to re-establish contact with North America, almost five hundred years after the brief Norse encounters, virtually all the continent had been occupied for thousands of years. The last major migration into unoccupied space had occurred about 2000 BC as Palaeo-Eskimos spread eastward across the High Arctic from northern Alaska. Much earlier, big-game hunters entered most of the territory that is now Canada not long after the retreating Wisconsinan ice sheets vacated it some twelve thousand to eight thousand years ago, and both the archaeological record and oral tradition concur that they tended to settle down after the initial migrations. Different cultures emerged in different environments. In 1500 most people lived approximately where their ancestors had lived for dozens, even hundreds, of generations – from time immemorial their present-day descendants would say. Ideas moved more readily than people. The idea of pottery diffused into what is now Canada about 1000 BC from both the northwest (Siberia–northern Alaska) and southeast; the idea of the bow and arrow diffused somewhat later, reaching the northern plains in the second century AD. Cultures adjusted as new ideas were introduced, but people tended to remain where they were. The land became intimately known through generations of experience, and lifeworlds depended on a fine balance of technology, environmental knowledge, and population. In 1500 no one could have imagined North America, but at more local scales people knew the land intimately and, within the limits of their technologies, used it as intensively as they could.

We do not know how many people inhabited what is now Canada in 1500 or precisely how this population was distributed. In 1910 an American scholar, James Mooney, estimated that at the time of Columbus 1,150,000 people lived in North America north of the Rio Grande, 220,000 of them in Canada. Thirty years later the distinguished American anthropologist Alfred Kroeber considered Mooney's estimates rather too high. Since then, however, most pre-contact population estimates for other parts of North America have been revised upwards as the impact of introduced infectious diseases has become clearer. Some scholars now estimate that considerably more than 220,000 people lived in coastal British Columbia alone. But there is no certain evidence, and the matter comes down to educated (and often politically inflected) guesses. A total of 500,000, suggested by the historical geographer Arthur Ray, seems a reasonable contemporary estimate for the population of what is now Canada in 1500. Map 1.1 suggests its approximate distribution at that date.

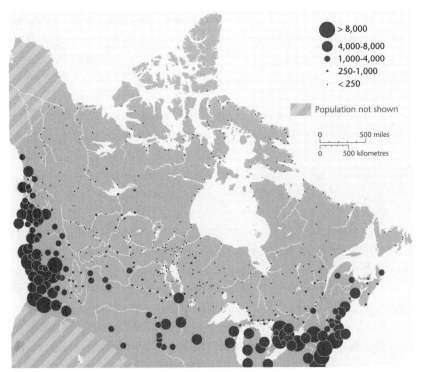

MAP 1.1   Distribution of population, northern North America, 1500 | Adapted from C. Heidenreich, in *Historical Atlas of Canada,* vol. 1, *From the Beginning to 1800,* ed. R. Cole Harris, cart. Geoffrey J. Matthews (Toronto: University of Toronto Press, 1987), plates 18 and 69.

This map is a drastic cartographic aggregation of many complex and now largely unknown distributions. Its details are questionable, but its general patterns reflect fundamental realities. Throughout most of what is now Canada, the population density was exceedingly low, seldom more than one hunting band (usually some thirty people) in some two thousand square miles. In only two or perhaps three regions were densities markedly higher: the St. Lawrence and eastern Great Lakes lowlands, the Pacific coast, and perhaps the northern plains.

At the most basic level, these distributions are explained by the biological yield of the land. In the absence of long-distance food transfers, the lower the biological yield, the less human food was available. The areas of highest biological yield – the Pacific coast, the eastern Great Lakes lowlands – were where population densities were also highest. A vast expanse of land was dominated by long, bitterly cold winters. In approximately half of what is now Canada, the topsoil was underlain by continuous or scattered permafrost (permanently frozen ground), and lakes were frozen for more than half the year. Few places remained untouched by a June or September frost. Summers were short. A huge crescent of land – almost the whole northeastern quadrant of North America – comprised the ancient, ice-scoured, granitic mass of the Canadian Shield, an environment of rock, swamp, acidic soils, and innumerable lakes and rivers. The southern margins of the Canadian Shield were covered by a mixed coniferous-deciduous forest, the northern reaches by lichen woodland diminishing into tundra. Between them, stretching from Labrador to the Mackenzie Valley, lay a vast boreal forest dominated by spruce, balsam fir, and pine. Maps 1.2 and 1.3 show some of these defining characteristics of the land with which, in intricate local ways, the people inhabiting northern North America were closely bound.

Five hundred years ago, this vast and generally lean land supported many complex, culturally diverse societies. Overall, they are very imperfectly understood and are usually represented, as in the following account, by simplifying generalizations. The common category "hunters, fishers, and gatherers," for example, includes many different societies and economies. Some of them tended wild plants and, in so doing, blur the boundary between farmer and non-farmer. For their part, "farmers" also hunted, fished, and gathered. Yet, when knowledge is limited and summary accounts are required, generalization is unavoidable. This chapter provides

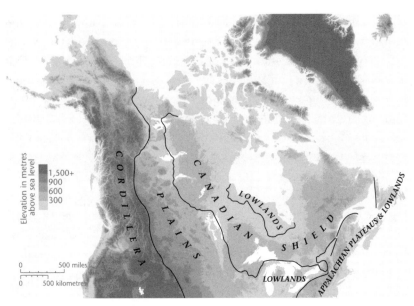

Map 1.2   Physiographic regions, northern North America

Map 1.3   Vegetation regions, northern North America

such an account of hunting, fishing, and gathering societies and also of farming societies in northern North America five hundred years ago. Then it discusses some common understandings of the world around them held by these diverse North American peoples.

HUNTERS, FISHERS, AND GATHERERS

In about AD 1500, as long before and since, hunting, fishing, and gathering was the dominant economy across most of northern North America. Agriculture dominated the economy only in the eastern Great Lakes and St. Lawrence lowlands, where a system of corn-based farming of Central American origin had been introduced almost a thousand years earlier. Along the west coast, rhizomes cultivated in intertidal gardens supplemented food supplies, some of the peoples around the northern perimeter of the eastern Great Lakes and St. Lawrence lowlands farmed intermittently, and here and there a few others grew tobacco. Everywhere else, people depended entirely on hunting, fishing, and gathering.

Map 1.4 generalizes their main hunting, fishing, and gathering strategies. Such economies, which relied on the wild, fluctuating return of the land, modified their environment slightly (principally by burning and by the selective hunting of animals), and never produced enough food to sustain people permanently in one place. An adequate food supply was distributed over a considerable area and was always subject to factors beyond human control, such as cyclical fluctuations in the populations of small animals. In such circumstances, resource procurement strategies that depended on specialization and immobility would fail; hunting, fishing, and gathering economies were necessarily mixed and mobile. People moved through known territories to known seasonal resource procurement sites, were familiar with different ecologies, and knew the ways of many species of animals and plants. Being mobile and travelling under their own power, usually in canoes in summer and on snowshoes in winter, they lived with few possessions, most of them quickly made from local materials. With simple (if often ingenious) tools and tool kits, only their accumulated generational experience with and knowledge of the land enabled them to live in harsh environments. The anthropologist Robin Ridington suggests that the technologies of these cultures are best thought of as systems of knowledge rather than inventories of artefacts. Given the resources available to them and the necessities of mobility and of travelling light, they had long since worked out the most efficient way – often the only way – of living where they did.

Such economies could often satisfy needs with less than full-time labour, thus creating a good deal of leisure time. However, because the supply of wild food was inherently uncertain, starvation remained a

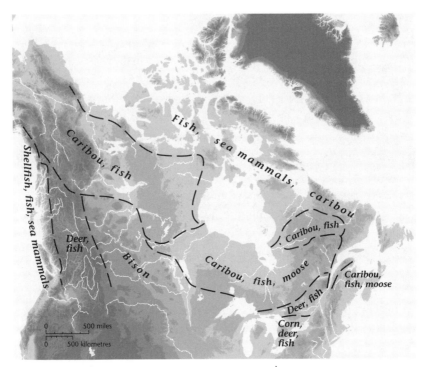

Map 1.4 Economies, northern North America, 1500 | After C. Heidenreich and J.V. Wright, in Harris and Matthews, *Historical Atlas of Canada*, vol. 1, plate 18.

possibility; a challenge for all hunting, fishing, and gathering economies was to minimize this risk as much as possible. In different environments different strategies had been worked out to do so. Throughout the vast extent of the boreal forest, people lived for most of the year in mobile hunting bands of approximately thirty members – a specialized strategy adapted to a particular environment but one that reveals characteristics of all hunting, fishing, and gathering societies.

The hunting bands of the boreal forest were mobile because locally available resources would soon be depleted by sedentary populations; they were small because more people would overreach even dispersed food supplies, but not too small, because the band could not rely on only one or two providers whose incapacity would threaten its survival. Successful hunters shared food among the families of the band, a practice that was reciprocated and that distributed risk. Moreover, the hunting band always had the capacity, when large ungulates such as moose, woodland caribou, or deer were scarce, to take smaller animals and fish. They too were shared.

In emergencies, gathering usually yielded some food, but not enough to sustain people for long. As long as big game were available, hunting was much the most efficient way to obtain the four to five thousand calories a day that each adult needed to get along in winter. The resources taken at particular sites were often owned, but the territories of hunting bands were seldom precisely defined, and bands rarely claimed exclusive right to them. A needy band could usually hunt, therefore, in neighbouring territory, yet another form of reciprocal risk aversion. The hospitality, generosity, and sharing that characterized many of these societies were all at some level strategies to avoid risk.

The hunting band was a mobile unit of knowledge intimately adapted to its circumstances. Its members could make snowshoes, canoes, and shelters, as well as the tools required to obtain and prepare food. They knew where and when to find particular foods, and had the skills to obtain them. By drying, smoking, or freezing, or by mixing pounded meat with fat (to make pemmican), they could preserve some of them. Work and space were largely gendered, the women managing the camp, preparing food, and making clothing, the men hunting and fishing, though, when necessary, women hunted and fished. The camp tended to be associated with women and families, the bush with men and the animals they hunted. Otherwise, work was unspecialized. People had many skills, which sustained a way of life. Centuries later, when an Indian reserve commissioner in northern British Columbia asked a chief what work he did, the chief replied that he did not work. His father and uncles had taught him how to live, and he would teach his children.

The hunting band was not self-sufficient in several critical ways. It could not produce many acceptable marriage partners (incest taboos were rigorously enforced), the trade goods required for the manufacture of some tools or coveted as luxuries, the labour for specialized, labour-intensive tasks, or settings for making or affirming alliances (often by marriage). The yearly round required, therefore, concentration as well as dispersion, and included at least one period when several hunting bands came together. In much of the boreal forest, they assembled in summer at superior fishing sites where labour was usually pooled to build fishing weirs. Trade and courting took place, and people feasted, danced, gambled, competed in games, exchanged information, and cemented alliances. Soon enough, however, local food supplies would decline, and the hunting bands

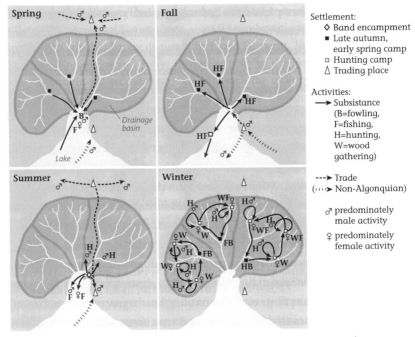

MAP 1.5   Seasonal round of Algonquian groups north of Lake Huron | After
C. Heidenreich, in Harris and Matthews, *Historical Atlas of Canada*, vol. 1, plate 34.

would disperse on their separate circuits. Map 1.5, which shows the seasonal round of Algonquian groups along the north shore of Lake Huron,
illustrates this pattern.

The basic unit of social organization throughout the boreal forest was
the family, and there was virtually no formalized coercive power above it.
Within a hunting band, one of the heads of its families was usually particularly respected, a chief of sorts whose advice was heeded, if not necessarily followed. At the summer gatherings one of these chiefs, by virtue of
eloquence, experience, or perceived wisdom, was usually accorded a particular hearing, but no one had the authority to speak for all those present
or to order them about. There was no overall chief. A hunting chief coordinated labour during a large hunt, but only for its duration. Some of
these dispersed low-density populations hardly engaged in warfare, and
even raids were usually revenge killings involving very few people. A larger
raid might have a temporary war chief. This diffuse social organization,

with a slight hierarchy of local power and no central point of command, was not held together from above. The social climate was egalitarian, and decision making largely by consensus. Stability came from below, essentially from the social relations surrounding families. Young people usually married outside their own hunting band, and, in this way, ties of kinship linked people in different hunting bands. A given nuclear family would not necessarily pass successive winters in the same band. People lived within intricate spatially extended genealogical networks within which, principally, they found their social bearings and, in many cases, their access to particular resources. This context, reaffirmed when hunting bands met, underlay the cooperation, mutual aid, and hospitality on which they depended for survival.

The hunting, fishing, and gathering societies of the boreal forest in 1500 made up an intricate mosaic of local knowledge fields within which there was almost no salience. No centralized authority organized space. It was organized, rather, by local experience, knowledge, and kin relations. People knew the local stories of how they came to be, and fashioned their lives around local spirit-beings. Theirs was a far more intimate knowledge of the land than any that would follow. When explorers arrived and wanted maps, these people sometimes drew maps for them – lines on the ground or on birchbark that occasionally found their way into European cartography. But the inhabitants of local knowledge fields did not need maps because the land, as they needed to know it, was embedded in their stories, place names, lore, and experience.

Beyond the boreal forest, people followed different seasonal rounds and developed somewhat distinct social structures, which in most cases, however, varied only in detail from those just described.

The peoples of the northern plains also spent most of the year in small mobile hunting bands with non-hereditary leaders and flexible memberships. In summer, hunting bands pursued bison on the open plains, but in 1500, long before the horse arrived on the northern plains, the principal communal hunts were probably in winter in the protected valleys of the parkland belt that rimmed the northern plains, and in the foothills of the Rockies. Bison went there for shelter, and people followed them, taking large numbers by driving them over cliffs (buffalo jumps) or into pounds, elaborate structures made of piled logs and posts bound together with leather thongs. Both hunting and meat processing required large pools of labour, and people over-wintered nearby in sedentary camps. If this model is correct, winter was their principal time for trading and socializing. Plains peoples were active warriors. War clubs appear in the archaeological record, and petroglyphs (pictures etched on stone) depict shield-bearing warriors in action. Some of this was posturing: when two war parties met, the warriors often settled behind their large bison-hide shields, shot some arrows, and dispersed when honours were assuaged. Yet raids on unsuspecting camps could be bloody. There may have been more warfare because different peoples were drawn together in search of bison, population densities were relatively high, and the control of favoured bison-taking sites conferred huge advantage. Fighting was usually led by a temporary war chief.

To the north of the boreal forest and west from Hudson Bay, the Chipewyan depended on barren ground caribou, large herds of which moved into the lichen woodland in winter and onto the open tundra in summer. The caribou were relatively dispersed in the woodland and on the tundra, then massed along their migration routes. The Chipewyan moved with the caribou, in so doing approximately reproducing their annual round of concentration and dispersion. The major kill sites were on the migration routes, where the Chipewyan gathered in early winter (November) or late winter (April-May) in regional bands of several hundred to as many as a thousand people. When they dispersed in local bands, each was characteristically considerably larger than the hunting bands in the boreal forest because of the labour required to build the chutes and pounds in which caribou were commonly taken. Smaller bands of two or three families scouted for caribou and, when positioned along the migration routes, formed extended lines of communication. As in the boreal forest and on the plains, ties of kinship extended across many bands, providing the basis for cooperation, sharing, and hospitality.

On the Pacific coast, where an abundance of marine and terrestrial resources was available, the pre-contact population density is estimated to have been in the order of two people per square mile, more than a hundred times that in the boreal forest and probably the highest of any hunter-gatherer peoples in the world. In fact, it is now clear that most northwest coast peoples practised a little agriculture in estuarine locations;

indeed, with their permanent villages, material wealth, and capacity to support an elaborate ceremonial and artistic life, they resembled settled agriculturalists more than hunter-gatherers. It has been said that they "farmed" the woods, the intertidal zone, the salmon rivers, and the sea. From late November until well into March, they lived in plank-house villages of as many as two or three thousand people (Figure 1.1). Then most of them dispersed to various resource procurement sites. In the early spring, many went to the eulachon fisheries (where these small oily fish were rendered); in the late summer and fall, even larger numbers travelled to the main salmon fisheries (where large quantities were cured by drying or smoking). Smaller numbers went to clam beds, berry patches, and other gathering sites. Some moved to hunting grounds, others to various fisheries. Back in the village for winter, they lived on stored foods and participated in many social and ceremonial activities. The village usually comprised several house (or lineage) groups, families that lived together in one or several longhouses, shared a common (often supernatural) ancestor, and had inherited rights to particular crests, songs, names, and resources. These were ranked societies. The house group comprised an elite, commoners, and slaves. The chief of a house group had the power to set the timing of the seasonal round, allocate and redistribute resources, exact tribute, and bestow names. Such chiefs met in a village council, and one of them was recognized as the head chief. In some places, particularly among the Nuu-chah-nulth on the west coast of Vancouver Island and the Tsimshian near the mouth of the Skeena River, the head chief apparently had considerable power.

Both surviving stories and the archaeological record attest to a good deal of warfare, not all of which was revenge-based raiding. Some wars were fought over territory, and some groups that lost were squeezed out of existence. With high population densities came pressure on resources – quite possibly as many salmon were taken in these fisheries as in the later industrial ones – for, amid general abundance, were times of dearth and starvation. One explanation for the ranked, hierarchical, status-conscious societies along the Pacific coast is that as the competition for resources increased and fighting became more intense, people traded, in effect, relative equality and family-centred autonomy for the security provided by a more elaborated social hierarchy dominated by a strong leader.

FIGURE 1.1   Late pre-contact Tsimshian village of Kitkatla (artist, Gordon Miller). Although there were different regional house types, all pre-contact peoples along the coasts of what are now British Columbia, Washington, and southern Alaska lived for several months each winter in large villages somewhat like this. | *Historical Atlas of Canada*, vol. 1, *From the Beginning to 1800*, ed. R. Cole Harris, cart. Geoffrey J. Matthews (Toronto: University of Toronto Press, 1987), plate 13.

FARMERS

As Map 1.4 shows, agriculture dominated the economy only around the eastern Great Lakes and in the St. Lawrence Valley. These people lived in villages occupied throughout the year and located on defensible sites accessible, as historical geographer Conrad Heidenreich has shown, to both water and well-drained sandy loams that could be worked with digging sticks. As many as two thousand people lived in the largest villages behind massive palisades made of several rows of posts, each up to a foot thick and fifteen to thirty-five feet high (Figure 1.2), but most villages were smaller, perhaps a thousand people on about four acres. Beyond the villages was a form of shifting cultivation on fields that the men had cleared and the women worked. Corn, the principal crop, was planted in hills together with kidney beans and squash – some twenty-five hundred hills to the acre apparently. Sunflowers and tobacco were grown in other fields. Every six to twelve years, depending on the application of ash, worn-out fields were abandoned and others cleared and planted. Where villages and fields were concentrated, the population density may have been as high as fifty or sixty people per square mile. These people hunted, fished, and gathered, but agriculture was the mainstay of their economy. Their human landscapes were like no others in northern North America.

Within a village, to judge by early seventeenth-century evidence, several extended families lived together in a single longhouse, but the basic unit of political organization was the clan segment, people who claimed descent from a common female ancestor and lived in the various villages of the tribe. Within most villages were several clan segments, each with a civil and a war chief, the former responsible, in consultation with heads of households, for maintaining law and order, coordinating group activities, and diplomacy; the latter was responsible for military matters. Beyond the clan segment was the village. The civil chiefs of each clan segment in the village attended a village council presided over by the most respected civil chief; the war chiefs attended another similar council. Beyond the village was the tribe and a tribal council that, apparently, all chiefs of clan segments were entitled to attend. One of the attending chiefs

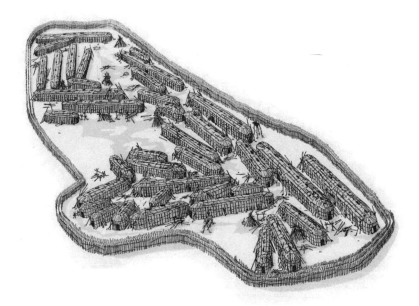

FIGURE 1.2   The Draper Site, a sixteenth-century Huron village. The thirty-eight longhouses in this farming village on a four-hectare (ten-acre) site east of Toronto housed perhaps two thousand people. | J.V. Wright, "Iroquoian Agricultural Settlement," in Harris and Matthews, *Historical Atlas of Canada*, vol. 1, plate 12.

was recognized as head chief of the tribe with power to make treaties and to grant permission to cross tribal territory but not to interfere with the internal affairs of any clan segment other than his own. And beyond the tribe was the confederacy and its associated confederacy council, to which each village in the confederacy could send its clan segment chiefs, one of whom spoke for the others. The business of this council seems to have been to determine how best to support the confederacy and its allies and to weaken its enemies. At this, as at all other levels of political organization, decision making was apparently by consensus, and equality and local autonomy were accepted ideals. The anthropologist Bruce Trigger finds an unresolved paradox in these agricultural societies between such ideals and their tendency to accumulate power and prestige.

As on the plains and along the Pacific coast, warfare was common. In this case the motive for most of it seems to have been revenge and, for young men, the winning of prestige. Raiding was common, but large war parties sometimes attacked villages and, especially if they gained entry by stealth and had the advantage of surprise, killed or captured most of the inhabitants. If the palisades were torched and the enemy emerged, the two sides would fight a pitched battle – one that often ended when the attackers withdrew after a few deaths on both sides. Prisoners were the great prize, a source of prestige for the warriors who captured them and of satisfaction for the villagers, men and women, who either adopted them into a clan segment or tortured and killed them.

Lifeworlds

However the economy and social life were organized, a broadly common understanding of the world around them characterized all these societies. That world was not quite as it seemed. Everything that existed – people, plants, animals, rocks, places, the wind, the rain – was animate and sentient. People and elements of what modern Western culture considers nature interacted as common thinking and feeling beings. Moreover, the same being could inhabit different shapes. A bear might be a warrior's ghost; the rain might be a dead mother, weeping. There were no boundaries between the living and the dead, the animate and the inanimate, the human and the natural. In many accounts, the world had been made as it was by a transformer figure – Gluskap, the mighty warrior, for the Mi'kmaq

in Nova Scotia, Coyote, the trickster, for the peoples of the interior plateau of British Columbia – who would eventually return to set things right.
In the meantime, people had to get by in worlds full of helpful and ma-
levolent spirit-beings. They could hope to placate some of them, and to
acquire their power, by gifts and sacrifices, by adhering to taboos, and by
prayer often associated with fasting and purification rites in vision quests
intended to reveal guardian spirit-beings. Shamans, people with particular abilities to communicate with the surrounding world of spirit-beings,
were powerful figures in these societies but were to be treated warily. Used
for good, their powers made them healers and seers, used for ill, sorcerers
and witches.

The beliefs of all the northern North American peoples had this much
in common, but the details of particular being worlds varied greatly. Particular local beings, for example, inhabited particular features of local landscapes. Historian Leslie Upton notes that the Mi'kmaq propitiated with
gifts particular waterfall, cove, or river beings. Bruce Trigger makes the
same point about the Huron, one of the agricultural peoples north of
Lake Ontario, who associated both friendly and hostile beings with many
individual landscape features, and sought to propitiate them or to secure
their aid with offerings of tobacco left nearby or thrown on campfires.
Robin Ridington's studies of the Dunne-za, or Beaver people, of the Peace
River Valley show how intimately their dreams and spirit-beings were
bound up with the land, such that Dunne-za knowledge of the land, spir-
ituality, and the land itself formed a seamless whole. Susan Marsden, a
student of the Tsimshian, the people of the lower Skeena River and the
adjacent British Columbia coast, has explored the Tsimshian concept of
spanaxnox (variously, the homes of spirit-beings or those spirit-beings
themselves). In the Tsimshian view, the spanaxnox inhabited an organized
underwater society, parallel to the Tsimshian's own. The realms of humans
and spanaxnox were accessible to each other: people and underwater
beings could interact – as when a whirlpool swept a chief's daughter down
to a spanaxnox village in which she married, bore a son, and eventually
was returned to her own people where her son, both human and spanaxnox,
became a great chief. And so, when the Tsimshian travelled they moved
not only through landscapes accessible to the senses, but also through the
territories of their underwater counterparts the spanaxnox, who, rather

like the spiteful Greek sea-god Poseidon, would work their vengeance if not properly approached and propitiated.

The local knowledge fields within which people lived comprised, therefore, a good deal more than ecological or social information. That information was embedded in an animate world of spirit-beings that inhabited all things, shaped events, and, together with the stories the elders told and retold, gave meaning to the world. In these societies, ecological, social, and what modern Western culture would call supernatural information were components of the same knowledge field. People who lived within such knowledge fields held an intricate, coherent, holistic, and experience-based knowledge of particular places. Such knowledge was overwhelmingly contextual and radically unspecialized. Unlike the specialized knowledge that enables those who have it to accomplish the same task almost anywhere, these were fields of knowledge that enabled those who possessed them to live in particular places.

The German philosopher Jürgen Habermas has argued that such a lifeworld, as he called it, supplies its members "with unproblematic, common background convictions that are assumed to be guaranteed." In pre-modern societies, he maintains, people lived "within the horizon of their lifeworld" and could not reach beyond its preinterpreted understandings. In other words, they could interpret and communicate the world only within their own terms of reference. This argument is challenged, both by those who maintain that all people are able to think beyond their own lifeworlds and by those who hold that none are. However these arguments are resolved, it is clear that radically different lifeworlds began to interact in northern North America some five hundred years ago and had great difficulty making sense of each other. The Europeans brought a more wide-ranging geographical experience of the world and with it a category – savages – that they could apply to the indigenous people they met. This, however, was a category of their own making, one deeply embedded in a literary and philosophical tradition and not easily transcended even by the contrary evidence of local experience in New World settings where, often, Europeans did not seem particularly civilized or non-Europeans particularly savage. A convenient label laden with cultural and political power, it would tend to validate the European presence and to enhance the difficulty of reaching beyond European lifeworlds to begin to understand non-European societies, economies, and habits of mind.

There are few records of the reaction of indigenous people to the first Europeans in the northeast, though there are stories that the first encounters were foretold in dreams and that people were intensely curious about the newcomers. Around the Great Lakes in the early 1630s, Jesuit missionaries were initially assumed to be Manitous, non-human beings. In the west, where first contacts occurred much later, more indigenous accounts of them have survived. To judge from these, the people of Nootka Sound on the west coast of Vancouver Island were at least as terrified as curious when, in 1778, Captain Cook's ships arrived. Some thought they were propelled by Haitetlik, the lightning snake; others thought they were salmon and the crew "a fish come alive into people." An old man said that the moon had come, using a sea serpent for its canoe. Thirty years later, when the fur trader Simon Fraser and some twenty men descended the Fraser River, many people thought that Coyote, the transformer, had returned, bringing with him sun, moon, morning star, and others who had participated in the making of the world. Their return had been generally foretold; with it the remaking of the world was at hand. In the Arctic half a century later, explorers looking for the lost Franklin expedition met Inuit who had never seen, or apparently never heard of, white men. "Where," they asked, "did you come from? Is it the sun or the moon?" Given the world as these Inuit knew it, theirs was a real question.

In these examples, people interpreted the new and strange within their own terms of reference. Initially, they could hardly do otherwise, as there was no other source of understanding to draw on. When they began to recognize the otherness of Europeans, they still faced the immense challenge of understanding it, just as Europeans faced the challenge of understanding them. Entirely different lifeworlds had met, and, whether or not Habermas is strictly correct, the problems of understanding were formidable. As time went on, the difference, perhaps, was not so much that different lifeworlds had different capacities to understand, as that they had different opportunities to ignore. The people who had always lived in northern North America could hardly ignore the increasingly aggressive presence of Europeans among them, whereas Europeans would increasingly devise means to possess and organize the land with little or no reference to those who had long preceded them. Europeans – many of them – could be oblivious to Native people in a way that Native people could not be oblivious to them.

Habermas thought it a characteristic of modernizing societies that lifeworlds were increasingly invaded by specialized, rationalized, and institutionalized systems of thought. He called this the systems penetration of the lifeworld, and considered that it broke local ways out of the horizon of the lifeworld and reshaped societies around the logics of specialized systems. In so doing, system and lifeworld were uncoupled. His is a European philosopher's thoroughly abstract analysis, but it may not be entirely irrelevant to the chapters that follow, which explore the changing face of northern North America as capital, missionaries, settlers, and the accoutrements of colonial governments moved this vast territory out of the many local knowledge fields that characterized it five hundred years ago.

BIBLIOGRAPHY

The most accessible summary of the prehistory of northern North America is still found in *Historical Atlas of Canada*, vol. 1, *From the Beginning to 1800*, ed. R. Cole Harris, cart. Geoffrey J. Matthews (Toronto: University of Toronto Press, 1987), plates 1-18. Also useful are Arthur J. Ray, *I Have Lived Here since the World Began: An Illustrated History of Canada's Native People* (Toronto: Key Porter Books, 1996), chaps. 1-3; and Olive Patricia Dickason, *Canada's First Nations: A History of Founding Peoples from Earliest Times* (Toronto: McClelland and Stewart, 1992), chap. 4.

On hunter-gatherers, I have relied generally on Allen W. Johnson and Timothy Earle, *The Evolution of Human Societies: From Foraging Group to Agrarian State* (Stanford: Stanford University Press, 1987), particularly chaps. 2 and 7; Robin Ridington, *Little Bit Know Something: Stories in a Language of Anthropology* (Vancouver and Toronto: Douglas and McIntyre, 1990); and Edward Rogers and James Smith, "Environment and Culture in the Shield and Mackenzie Borderlands," in *Handbook of North American Indians*, vol. 6, *Subarctic*, ed. June Helm (Washington DC: Smithsonian Institution, 1981), 130-45.

More specifically, on hunter-gatherers, consult Robin Ridington, "Beaver," and James G.E. Smith, "Chipewyan," both in Helm, *Handbook of North American Indians*, vol. 6, 350-60 and 271-84. See also Hugh A. Dempsey, "Blackfoot," in *Handbook of North American Indians*, vol. 13, *Plains*, ed. Raymond J. DeMallie, part 1 (2001), 604-28; and Philip K. Bock, "Micmac," in *Handbook of North American Indians*, vol. 15, *Northeast*, ed. Bruce G. Trigger, (1978), 109-22. Leslie Upton, *Micmacs and Colonists: Indian-White Relations in the Maritimes, 1713-1867* (Vancouver: UBC Press, 1979), chap. 1. Also on the Blackfoot and other groups on the northern plains, see Theodore Binnema, *Common and Contested Ground: A Human and Environmental History of the Northwestern Plains* (Norman: University of Oklahoma Press, 2001), chaps. 2

and 3. Recent work on agriculture practised by the predominantly fishing-hunting societies along the Pacific coast is reported by Douglas Deur, "Rethinking Precolonial Plant Cultivation on the Northwest Coast," *Professional Geographer* 54, 2 (May 2002): 140-57. William Cronon provides an accessible account of the economies and ecologies of both hunter-gatherers and farmers in *Changes in the Land: Indians, Colonists, and the Ecology of New England* (New York: Hill and Wang, 1983), chap. 3.

On the Huron, see particularly Bruce G. Trigger, *Children of the Aataentsic: A History of the Huron People to 1660* (Montreal, Kingston, and London: McGill-Queen's University Press, 1976), chap. 2; and Conrad Heidenreich, *Huronia: A History and Geography of the Huron Indians, 1600-1650* (Toronto: McClelland and Stewart, 1971), particularly chap. 8. Heidenreich's essay "Huron," in DeMallie, *Handbook of North American Indians,* vol. 13, 368-88, is also exceedingly useful.

On the Tsimshian spanaxnox, see Susan Marsden, "Adawx, Spanaxnox, and the Geopolitics of the Tsimshian," *BC Studies* 135 (Autumn 2002): 101-35. On the reaction to the arrival of Captain Cook, refer to Daniel W. Clayton, *Islands of Truth: The Imperial Fashioning of Vancouver Island* (Vancouver: UBC Press, 2000), chap. 2. On the reaction to Simon Fraser, see J.A. Teit, "Mythology of the Thompson Indians," in *The Jesup North Pacific Expedition,* Memoirs of the American Museum of Natural History, vol. 8, part 2 (New York: G.E. Stechert, 1912), 416; and also Wendy Wickwire, "To See Ourselves as the Other's Other: Nlaka'pamux Contact Narratives," *Canadian Historical Review* 75, 1 (1994): 1-20.

The relevant writing by Jürgen Habermas is *The Theory of Communicative Action,* vol. 2, *Lifeworld and System: A Critique of Functionalist Reason* (Boston: Beacon Press, 1987), part 6.

2

The Northwestern Atlantic,
1497-1632

At the end of the fifteenth and the beginning of the sixteenth centuries, the human societies in the eastern and western hemispheres began to be reconnected, and, as they were, two theatres of European activity emerged in the western Atlantic. One began in the Caribbean in 1492 and quickly spread into Central and South America. The other began in Newfoundland in 1497 and spread hesitantly westward. Most of the coast between the two was reconnoitered in the 1520s, then largely ignored for much of a century.

The northern theatre touched a deeply indented, rocky, ice-scoured coast dominated by a severe continental climate that froze many harbours for at least a month a year. Yet Europeans soon explored this inhospitable coast, in so doing reporting, renaming, and mapping it in ways that they could understand. As soon as it became evident that a valuable resource – an apparently endless supply of codfish – had been located, European commercial capital arrived. From the beginning of the sixteenth century, fishing ships came annually from Europe. The northeastern edge of a previously invisible continent came into European focus, some of its products entered European economies, and it began to figure in the geopolitical calculations of European courts. Its peoples may have experienced the effects of introduced infectious diseases. In such ways, the separation of the two sides of the Atlantic ended, and the momentum of change along this edge of North America became increasingly European.

Imagining and Claiming the Land

Before many Europeans could operate along the northeastern fringe of North America, the European imagination had to make some sense of it, less, perhaps, to establish "what was there" than to arrange and order the land in terms that Europeans could understand. Otherwise, it was bewildering and profoundly disorienting. The process of ordering New World space, and thereby of making it knowable, continues to the present, but for some time after initial contact, explorers' reports and maps were the principal means of bringing this space into some preliminary focus. Reports, based on fleeting observation and self-serving promotions, were usually tantalizing exaggerations. The maps that explorers and cartographers produced were egregious abstractions that represented endless complexities by a few lines. Yet these words and lines enabled Europeans to know and think in certain ways – ways embedded in systems of power that allowed them to begin to possess spaces they hardly knew.

Explorers' reports and the maps they and European cartographers produced were means of translation and simplification. They rendered the myriad voices of new lands in an accessible European language. Once translated into this language, the land could be communicated, and then could be argued and strategized over from afar. Moreover, to the extent that this language enabled Europeans to orient themselves in a space about which they knew little, it allowed them to ignore indigenous voices situated in intricate but, from a European perspective, essentially alien systems of knowledge. A few lines on a map served to eviscerate the land of its indigenous knowledge, thus presenting it as empty, untrammelled space available for whatever the European imagination wished to do.

The process of translation and simplification began as soon as Europeans came into regular contact with the northeastern corner of North America. Its modern European discovery began, as far as we know, in July 1497, when the Genoese explorer-merchant John Cabot, sailing with the financial backing of merchants in Bristol and the permission of the English Tudor king Henry VII, reached coastal Newfoundland or Nova Scotia. He found a bleak coast, waters teeming with fish, and some prospect of a sea route to China, for which he received £10 from Henry VII and support from his backers to outfit five ships for a voyage the next year. One of these ships soon returned, storm-damaged, but the other four never did. In 1499 a Portuguese, João Fernandes, reached at least Greenland (which he named Tiera de Lavrador, a name that would migrate west); a year later another Portuguese, Gaspar Corte-Real, also authorized by King Manuel of Portugal, sailed as far as Greenland. He was back in 1501 and continued

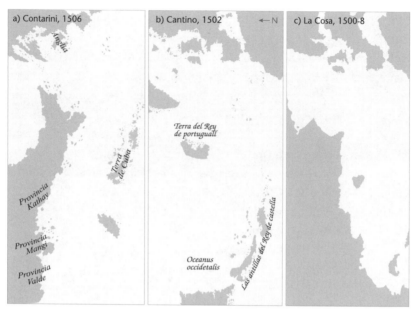

a) Contarini, 1506

Anglia

Terra de Cuba

Provincia Kathay

Provincia Mangi

Provincia Valde

b) Cantino, 1502   ← N

Terra del Rey de portuguall

Oceanus occidetalis

Las antillas del Rey de castella

c) La Cosa, 1500-8

MAP 2.1   Cartographic understandings of North America, early sixteenth century |
Reproductions of the original maps are in Derek Hayes, *Historical Atlas of Canada: Canada's History Illustrated with Original Maps* (Vancouver and Toronto: Douglas and McIntyre, 2002), 16, 19, and 21.

to Newfoundland, but then was lost at sea, as was his brother Miguel who sailed to look for him. These precarious probes into the northwestern Atlantic had found and reported land, but what land? Cabot and his backers thought he had reached a northeastern peninsula of China, an assumption represented on several early sixteenth-century maps (Map 2.1a). Fernandes and Gaspar Corte-Real thought they had found an island (Map 2.1b). The conceptual discovery of North America apparently had not been made, although a remarkable map by the Spaniard Juan de la Cosa and variously dated from 1500 to 1508 suggests that it might have been (Map 2.1c). La Cosa's map shows a continuous coastline between the Spanish discoveries in the Gulf of Mexico and English discoveries, marked with flags, far to the north. It is the first representation of the east coast of North America. Some hold that La Cosa, who was in the Caribbean in 1499, could have got this information only from John Cabot, who, according to this interpretation, charted the coast and somehow communicated his findings to La Cosa before he and his ships disappeared.

Whatever the case, most European cartographers did not accept anything like the continental outline on the La Cosa map until the late 1520s. By this time the Florentine Giovanni Verrazano, sailing for France, and the Portuguese Estévan Gomez, sailing for Spain, had charted the east coast of North America between Newfoundland and Florida. With a fairly continuous land mass established, the eastern edge of North America was coming into focus, and exploration turned to other questions: how to get around or through this obstruction on the route to China, or whether profit might be derived from it. Verrazano had reported what he took to be open ocean beyond an offshore bar along the coast of the Carolinas. In the north, the Gulf of St. Lawrence was not yet known, nor was Newfoundland again understood as an island.

By the 1530s, bullion from the Spanish conquests of the Aztecs in Mexico, the Maya in Guatemala, and the Inca in Peru was flowing to Spain, and the prospect of finding and looting other empires became as enticing as a short route to China. In this climate of speculative imperialism, François I, king of France, commissioned Jacques Cartier, a Breton master-mariner from St-Malo, to enter a reported strait beyond the Baye des Chasteaulx (the Strait of Belle Isle, between Newfoundland and Labrador). Cartier sailed in April 1534, and before his return in early September had explored most of the Gulf of St. Lawrence, taken possession of the land in the name of the French king, and captured two St. Lawrence Iroquoians whom he took to the French court. These achievements earned him a second commission, and he was back the next year with three ships and 112 men. Directed by his two captives, Cartier sailed up the St. Lawrence River as far as his larger ships could navigate. From there he explored west to Montreal Island, where he found a large well-palisaded village (Hochelaga) comprising, he reported, some fifty houses, each about fifty paces long and twelve to fifteen wide. Returning to his ships, he spent a harrowing winter of unanticipated cold, scurvy (a quarter of his men died), and increasing Native hostility before capturing ten villagers including the local chief (Donacona) and getting away to France. But he had found, as he reported to the king, "the largest river that is known to have ever been seen," flowing through well-inhabited "lands of yours" of great fertility and richness. He also brought reports of a kingdom of the Saguenay, one moon's journey beyond Hochelaga, where he had been told "there are many towns and ... great store of gold and copper." Such reports, embellished by

Donacona in France, drew an expedition in 1541 of some five hundred men. Headed by a French nobleman, Jean-François de la Roque, sieur de Roberval, this was intended less to find a route to China (which now seemed unlikely via the St. Lawrence) than to establish a colony and exploit the riches of the Kingdom of Saguenay. Almost everything went wrong. Cartier and Roberval were at odds, diamonds and gold sent back to France turned out to be quartz crystals and iron pyrites, the Kingdom of Saguenay was not found, and scurvy and Native attacks decimated the colonists. Roberval and the last of the survivors left in July 1543. The French would not be back on the St. Lawrence for almost forty years.

Cartier's explorations – and particularly the colonization venture with Roberval – had much in common with those of the Spaniards Coronado (with three hundred men) and De Soto (with six hundred), who at approximately the same time were drawn by tales of kingdoms and treasure into lands far north of the Gulf of Mexico. None of them found what they sought while traversing huge territories that Europeans had never seen before. In fact, Cartier had accomplished a great deal, although his politics had antagonized the St. Lawrence Iroquoians, the principal reason, probably, for the French withdrawal from the river. He had brought the Gulf of St. Lawrence and the St. Lawrence Valley into a European field of vision, had taken possession of them in the name of the king of France, and had transformed the cartography of northeastern North America. Cartier's own maps have not survived, but cartographers in Dieppe drew on his discoveries to produce several magnificent maps. Part of one of them, drafted by Pierre Desceliers in 1550, is reproduced in Map 2.2. Newfoundland is shown detached from the mainland, the islands in the Gulf of St. Lawrence are approximately in place, and the St. Lawrence River is drawn to and somewhat beyond its confluence with the Ottawa.

Wherever Europeans had been, the map is strewn with names. Along the Atlantic coast, it includes but a few of the many names associated with the inshore fishery (see below). Map 2.3 shows more of them: the place names on sixteenth-century maps that can be located precisely on modern maps of Newfoundland's Avalon Peninsula, a small fraction of the names that, undoubtedly, were then current in the largely oral world of the inshore fishery. Even within R de sam Joham (St. John's Harbour), there must have been dozens of place names in several European languages. Further west on Desceliers' map, the place names are either

MAP 2.2   Eastern North America, 1550. The map is oriented with south at the top; the peninsula at upper right is Florida. | Cartographer, Pierre Desceliers. For a large colour reproduction, see Hayes, *Historical Atlas of Canada*, 29.

gallicized renderings of Amerindian words or French names given by Cartier. All these names, superimposed on older namings in languages Europeans did not know and could not pronounce, served to make the land accessible to Europeans. It was acquiring an outline they could visualize and names they could recognize. Place names were a means of erasure: the name "Terre des Bretons," for example, obscured the Mi'kmaq and other Native peoples who lived there and other European fishers who came there. A few of them suggest a tentative hybridity as some Native words were rendered in European phonologies.

Desceliers' 1550 map, like other small-scale maps of the day, was not for general distribution. He intended it primarily for Henri II, then the king of France, and not simply for the king's pleasure. It showed the territory discovered and claimed for France by a French explorer commissioned by the king, and situated this territory in a continental geography, as then understood. Such maps were statements of possession and geopolitical

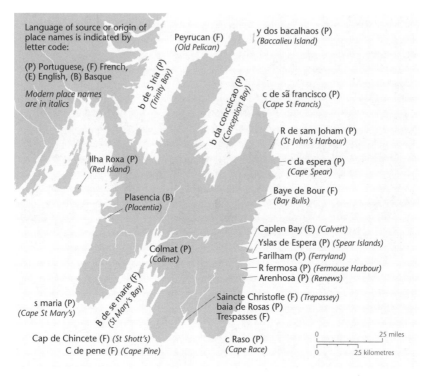

Language of source or origin of place names is indicated by letter code:

(P) Portuguese, (F) French, (E) English, (B) Basque

Modern place names are in italics

b de S Iria (P) *(Trinity Bay)*

Peyrucan (F) *(Old Pelican)*

y dos bacalhaos (P) *(Baccalieu Island)*

b da conceicao (P) *(Conception Bay)*

c de sã francisco (P) *(Cape St Francis)*

R de sam Joham (P) *(St John's Harbour)*

Ilha Roxa (P) *(Red Island)*

c da espera (P) *(Cape Spear)*

Plasencia (B) *(Placentia)*

Baye de Bour (F) *(Bay Bulls)*

Caplen Bay (E) *(Calvert)*

Colmat (P) *(Colinet)*

Yslas de Espera (P) *(Spear Islands)*
Farilham (P) *(Ferryland)*
R fermosa (P) *(Fermouse Harbour)*
Arenhosa (P) *(Renews)*

s maria (P) *(Cape St Mary's)*

B de se marie (F) *(St Mary's Bay)*

Saincte Christofle (F) *(Trepassey)*
baia de Rosas (P)
Trespasses (F)

Cap de Chincete (F) *(St Shott's)*
C de pene (F) *(Cape Pine)*

c Raso (P) *(Cape Race)*

0   25 miles
0   25 kilometres

MAP 2.3   Sixteenth-century European place names, Avalon Peninsula | After S. Barkham, in *Historical Atlas of Canada*, vol. 1, *From the Beginning to 1800*, ed. R. Cole Harris, cart. Geoffrey J. Matthews (Toronto: University of Toronto Press, 1987), plate 22.

tools. In effect, they were a means to transfer a few bits of information, real or fanciful, about a distant place to what the French sociologist Bruno Latour calls a centre of calculation where this spare information could be put to work. In this case it entered the diplomatic channels of French geo-politics. So recontextualized, bits of information from maps or reports could be transformed into territorial claims that, from the perspective of the peoples inhabiting the territory, seemed to have dropped from the blue. When, in 1569, Gerard Mercator first engraved and printed a map of the world in the projection for which he became famous, he identified the lands on either side of the St. Lawrence River as Nova Francia.

The reports and maps generated by Cartier's voyages and the French claims to the St. Lawrence had the effect of shifting northward the search for a passage to China. Magellan had found a southern passage; surely

FIGURE 2.1   *Englishmen in a Skirmish with Eskimo* (detail), 1585-93 (artist, John White). A fight on the south shore of Frobisher Bay, Baffin Island. Result: five or six Inuit dead, one of Frobisher's men seriously wounded, and an Inuit woman and her son captured. | British Museum, 00026164001, © The Trustees of the British Museum.

God, in his wisdom, had also created a northern one. Most of the effort to find it was English. Beginning in the 1570s with three expeditions led by Martin Frobisher, continuing in the 1580s with John Davis, and ending in 1616 with William Baffin and Robert Bylot, the search between Greenland and Baffin Island reached the extraordinary latitude of 77°45'N. It produced several ceremonial possession takings of land, fighting with the Inuit (Figure 2.1), black gold ore mined in Frobisher Bay (it turned out to be highly metamorphosed igneous rock), and harrowing reports of ice – on which Coleridge probably drew for "The Rime of the Ancient Mariner" – but no passage. South of Baffin Island, Henry Hudson followed a strait into a huge chamber of the sea that became known as Hudson Bay, where he and his men over-wintered in 1610-11. After the ice finally broke up the following June, most of his crew mutinied and abandoned him. Other explorers followed: William Button in 1612-13; the Dane Jens Munk in

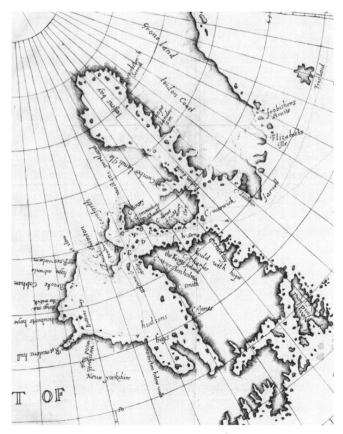

MAP 2.4   Part of America, Luke Foxe, 1635 | British Columbia
Archives, 1-61569.

1619-20; and in the early 1630s Luke Foxe, backed by London merchants,
and Thomas James, backed by a rival group in Bristol. With the technology of the day, the passage they sought did not exist to be found. But these
voyages into Hudson Bay as well as those into Davis Strait and Baffin Bay
had transformed the cartography of far northeastern North America. Luke
Foxe's map, published in 1635 (Map 2.4), shows what had been accomplished. There were still a few holes in the cartographic coastline that might
lead to passages, but after so much negative information investors were
no longer willing to assume the cost of probing them. Although they had
no return to show for investments spread over fifty years, the English had
acquired experience with arctic navigation and knowledge of Hudson Bay,

and both would be drawn on when an English fur trade began later in the century.

By this time there had been French settlements on the St. Lawrence for more than two decades, and the fur trade (discussed below) was well in train. In 1632, near the end of his life, Samuel de Champlain, the explorer/trader/cartographer who had established the French on the St. Lawrence, published his final cartographic synthesis of the regions in which he had spent most of his adult years. This remarkable map (Map 2.5) shows the Atlantic coast with fair precision, identifies three of the Great Lakes – Lac St. Louis (Lake Ontario), Mer Douce (Lake Huron), and Grand Lac (Lake Superior or Lake Michigan) – and suggests Lake Erie. Champlain's cartography had reached with some accuracy far into the continental interior, well beyond territory that any European had seen.

The map suggests just how far the venture on the St. Lawrence had drawn the French towards the continental interior and into contact with Native peoples. To a considerable extent, Champlain had reproduced Native geographical knowledge while, like other European cartographers, simplifying and decontextualizing it. He could not reproduce the intricate textures of Native environmental knowledge, and the edges of that understanding that he did reproduce were detached from their cultural context. The pictorial representations of Native settlements on Champlain's map include elements of Native architecture while resembling European peasant villages (Map 2.5). Much of the map simply creates blank space. At the same time, it produced a type of information that, at the scale of northeastern North America, Native knowledge could not match. It had shifted the land into a different category of information, one that Native people did not need, but that Europeans did, for it allowed them to visualize space and, however approximately, to get their bearings. Ironically, the Native information that Champlain incorporated in his map became a means of enabling Europeans to reconceptualize Native space in European terms. Like Desceliers' before it, Champlain's map enabled the French Crown to claim territory, and in so doing to ignore Native possession while asserting its own interests. A rudimentary knowledge of the land, made available in Europe, became a considerable source of European power – a cartographic equation of power and knowledge that would be repeated across the continent.

Map 2.5   New France, Samuel de Champlain, 1632 | Library and Archives Canada, NMC, 51970.

THE SIXTEENTH-CENTURY FISHERIES

While this process of discovering, naming, reporting, and claiming was going on, European capital and labour mobilized to exploit a major new world resource. John Cabot had found an abundance of codfish; virtually as soon as this resource was known, portions of European offshore fisheries moved to exploit it. Years ago Harold Innis, Canada's most distinguished economic historian, argued that the early Canadian economy turned around the export of slightly processed primary resources – staple trades, he called them – of which the first was the cod fishery. As far as the sixteenth century is concerned, he was right on both counts.

The transatlantic cod fishery grew out of an international fishery conducted by French, Basque, Portuguese, and English fishers in waters off southern Ireland, one of several offshore European fisheries established long before 1500 in response to declining inshore fish stocks. Ships and fishing technologies, experienced labour, sources of supplies, lines of credit, insurance, and investors were at hand. So were markets, especially among the growing urban population of the relatively well off, for a suitable food for the many fish days – 153 a year in France, Spain, and Portugal – prescribed by the church. Whereas European inshore fisheries were often local extensions of peasant economies, the offshore fisheries were complex commercial systems driven by experienced, profit-seeking commercial capital. When John Cabot and his successors reported new fish stocks, portions of this well-established commercial system swung westward to connect one of the world's largest supplies of edible fish to European markets. The Portuguese were there first, followed quickly by Normans and Bretons, and in the 1520s by French and Spanish Basques.

Although this fishery had reached a rock-bound – and, in winter, icebound – coast, one of the least hospitable in the midlatitudes on earth, it relied entirely at first on inshore waters for fish and on-shore installations for processing them. In this inshore fishery, fishing took place from small boats, not from the ship that had crossed the Atlantic. It depended, therefore, on suitable sites ashore that were accessible to the fishing grounds. Captains sought out harbours where their ships could be safely anchored or moored, and where there were beach cobbles (rather than sand) for drying cod, room for landing stages and cabins, wood for construction and repairs, fresh water, and (less certainly) cloudy, windy weather for

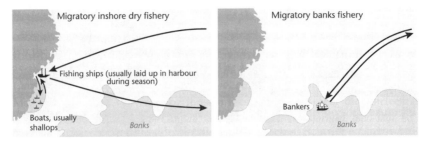

MAP 2.6   The inshore and banks fisheries | After cartograms by G. Head, in Harris and Matthews, *Historical Atlas of Canada*, vol. 1, plate 21.

drying. Such harbours were identified, named, and returned to year after year. After midcentury, another fishing strategy appeared as some captains began to make directly for the offshore banks, fish there from aboard ship, and return to Europe without landing in the New World – a strategy provoked, perhaps, by climatic deterioration with the onset of the Little Ice Age and the migration of cod to deeper waters offshore. Thereafter, inshore and banks fisheries (depicted schematically in Map 2.6) would have a long coexistence.

Both fisheries were labour-intensive. On the banks, fishermen used baited hooks and weighted hempen lines, often of fifty metres or longer. The cod they laboriously hauled on board were headed, gutted, and boned at tables on the deck, and the fillets preserved in the ship's hold between layers of salt, a "wet" (or "green") cure. In the inshore fishery, landing stages and cabins had to be built or repaired, and boats (usually prefabricated in Europe) assembled, work that occupied the better part of a month after the ship arrived. During the fishing period, usually lasting some six weeks, crews of three fished with hook and line in small boats close to shore and, at the end of each fishing day, unloaded their catch at a landing stage. There the cod were dressed as in the offshore fishery, then lightly salted and piled for several days, then washed, then put out to dry (Figure 2.2). In good weather, this dry cure took about ten days, during which the cod were spread out, skin down, at dawn, turned at midday, and piled at night – drying that moved each piece of cod some thirty times. Some three months after it had arrived, when all of this was accomplished, the ship had to be loaded and readied to sail. All work was manual. When fish were abundant, the specialized division of labour on the landing stages was, essentially, an unmechanized assembly line that worked around the clock. The largely unskilled work of washing and drying began at dawn, about 3:00 a.m., and continued until dark. The fish boats, usually carrying one experienced fisherman (always a man) and two novices, also left at dawn for long days on choppy waters with hempen lines, five-pound

FIGURE 2.2   Newfoundland fishing stations, 1772. Particular building techniques, even particular methods of piling fish, were associated with fishers from different parts of Europe. The upper illustration depicts a Basque operation. The cannon in the lower picture (probably on the Labrador shore) was intended to ward off the Inuit. | M. Duhamel du Monceau, *Traité générale des pêches* (Paris: Saillant et Nyon, 1772).

weights, and heavy cod. Many workers, relentless toil, little sleep – such was life at a shore installation.

This labour had to come from somewhere, and there were two options: to bring it from Europe or to recruit it overseas. The latter was tried, not always unsuccessfully, but there were basic problems. Along most of the coasts frequented by the transatlantic inshore fishery, the indigenous population was too small and too dispersed to provide more than occasional supplementary labour. Moreover, relations between Europeans and Natives had soon soured. Some Native women were raped, some Native people killed. In much of Newfoundland, the Beothuk avoided the coasts when the Europeans were there, then ransacked their landing stages and cabins for iron when they were not. The Thule Inuit, more formidable warriors, drove inshore cod fishers off the Labrador coast, killing some in the process. From the fishers' perspective, civilization had encountered savagery. Hostility, then, rather than accommodation or interdependence, soon characterized race relations in this fishery. Shore workers rarely saw a Beothuk, and usually tried to shoot the few they did see. Captains at shore installations in northern Newfoundland mounted cannon on their landing stages to fend off the Inuit (Figure 2.2). South of Newfoundland, Mi'kmaq families occasionally assisted with drying, but, overall, the labour force of the sixteenth-century fishery came, year after year, from Europe.

Large numbers of ships, men, and boys were involved. In 1578 an English merchant, Anthony Parkhurst, estimated that 350 to 380 ships and eight to ten thousand men were sent out each year; there is growing evidence that Parkhurst's figures are too low. The historian Laurier Turgeon reports that three French ports – Rouen, La Rochelle, and Bordeaux – sent 156 ships in 1565, and estimates that by 1580 there were 500 ships from France alone, most of them small unspecialized vessels of forty to a hundred tons. Although a less spectacular enterprise than the Spanish sailings to the Caribbean and Gulf of Mexico, the Newfoundland cod fisheries involved several times as many ships and far more people. They took back an enormous amount of food, as much as a million hundredweight (some fifty thousand tons) of processed cod in 1615. Green cod went to northern ports, and dried cod, with better preserving qualities, to more southerly ports, many of them in the Mediterranean. The historian D.B.

Quinn suggests that, year in and year out, Newfoundland cod may well have been as valuable as the gold and silver from New Spain.

The installations created by the inshore fishery were seasonal work camps, the oldest type of European settlement in Canada, and a type that survives to the present. They were starkly utilitarian places organized around the processing of a resource for shipment. A landing stage, an oil vat, a washing cage, perhaps low platforms (flakes) for drying cod, rough cabins (often roofed with sails) for officers and crew: these were the constructions at a fish camp. Its inhabitants were a detached segment of European society with, in the sixteenth century, no option but to return to Europe. The land around was forbidding; there was no alternative employment. In these circumstances, European wage rates held, just as they did in the offshore fishery, which did not touch the New World. The social structure of the camp, dominated by the captain, reflected the hierarchy of work, which in turn reflected something of the social structure of the ports of embarkation. The officers were of higher social standing at home than the fishermen and shore workers, most of whom came from the landless, mobile poor in the hinterlands of the ports. For such people the fishery, hard as it was, offered relatively attractive employment, far less killing, for example, than a voyage to the Caribbean. Insurers assumed that no more than 3 to 4 percent of the fishing ships would be lost in any given year, and there was less disease than on more southerly voyages. A fish camp also reproduced something of the cultural localness of sixteenth-century Europe. Its people had come from the same local region and shared elements of a local culture: accent, clothing, food preferences, building technologies, perhaps even ways of baiting hooks and drying fish. Essentially, the camps were thin seasonal offshoots – expressing sharply defined but truncated social hierarchies and selected elements of distant local cultures – of the complex social hierarchies and regional cultures from which they had sprung and to which they remained attached. The families of these fishermen were on the other side of the Atlantic.

Because it generated wealth and particularly because it provided a nursery for seamen for royal navies, the transatlantic cod fishery was watched from the courts of Western Europe and figured in geopolitical and military calculations, particularly when English fishermen began to frequent Newfoundland waters in the 1570s. The English arrived partly because the Danes had pushed them out of Icelandic waters but also, as historical geographer Stephen Hornsby has shown, because English merchants who had begun trading in the Iberian Peninsula and throughout the Mediterranean for local goods and other goods from the Levant and the Indies, turned to the Newfoundland fisheries to find additional means to pay for their Mediterranean purchases. A triangular trade soon linked English ports in the West Country, the Newfoundland fisheries, and Mediterranean markets. This English presence in the fishery developed shortly before warfare broke out between England and Spain for the control of the Atlantic. For both powers, their fisheries provided seamen for navies, but when the Spanish Armada of 1588 was harried by the English navy and wrecked by gales, when two subsequent armadas also failed, and when English privateers raided with increasing success around the peripheries of the Spanish Atlantic – including driving both the Spanish and Portuguese off the east coast of Newfoundland's Avalon Peninsula – the balance of sea power turned to the English. Behind English sea power lay the offshore fisheries, dominated increasingly by Newfoundland.

At some point in the sixteenth century, most European ports from Bristol to Lisbon had participated in this fishery. By 1600 the Spanish and Portuguese fisheries were in sharp decline, a result of royal exactions of capital and men to finance and man the armadas, rising outfitting costs (as bullion from New Spain drove up Iberian prices and made it difficult for Spanish and Portuguese fishermen to compete with the French and English), and English privateering. Map 2.7 shows the coasts frequented by fishermen of various nationalities throughout the sixteenth century. By the end of the century the picture had simplified: English fisheries dominated in eastern Newfoundland between Cape Race and Bonavista, and French fisheries almost everywhere else.

Basque whaling operations along the south coast of Labrador closely followed the beginnings of the cod fishery. An experienced whaling fleet had long operated out of the Basque ports in northern Spain, and with reports of bowhead whales along the Labrador coast a portion of it crossed the Atlantic to exploit them. The first Basque whaling stations on the Labrador coast of the Strait of Belle Isle appeared in the 1530s; by the 1570s at least twenty to thirty large whalers, many of them of four to six hundred tons' burden and carrying at least a hundred men, arrived each year. The whaling stations were another form of sixteenth-century work

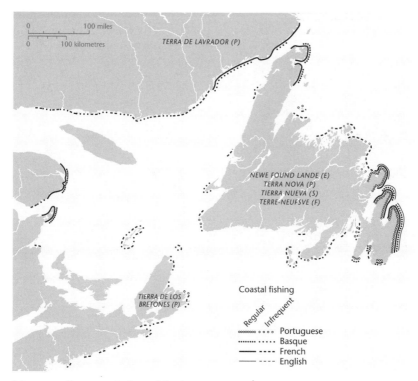

MAP 2.7 European inshore fisheries, 1500-1600 | After J. Mannion, in Harris and Matthews, *Historical Atlas of Canada*, vol. 1, plate 21.

camp focused, in this case, on rendering blubber into train oil. Again, seasonal European labour comprised the principal workforce, although much more Native labour was used than in the cod fishery – Laurier Turgeon reports an English navigator, Richard Whitbourne, who said that Natives assisted the Basques "with great diligence and patience to kill, cut up and boil the whales to make train oil." In the 1570s, whales were becoming scarce along the Strait of Belle Isle, perhaps because of over-hunting but quite possibly because of climate change. By the early 1580s some of the Basque whalers shifted westward towards the mouth of the Saguenay River (Map 2.8), where several recently excavated whaling stations reveal that they also employed Native labour and traded for furs. Like the Basque cod fishery and for many of the same reasons (plus, perhaps, the depletion of bowhead whales), Basque whaling in the Gulf of St. Lawrence declined precipitously in the late 1580s and ceased in the 1630s.

MAP 2.8   Basque whaling stations, Gulf of St. Lawrence | After L. Turgeon, "French Fishers, Fur Traders, and Amerindians," *William and Mary Quarterly* 55, 4 (1998): 592.

THE EARLY FUR TRADE

As early as the 1530s, a few fishermen also traded for furs, but by the 1550s and 1560s some Norman vessels and others from La Rochelle were outfitted exclusively for the fur trade. Most of them made for the coasts of Cape Breton Island, peninsular Nova Scotia, and the Gulf of Maine. This trade virtually stopped in the 1570s, a consequence, apparently, of religious wars in Europe, but resumed in the 1580s and focused increasingly on the gulf and estuary of the St. Lawrence. Many of the Basque ships in the Gulf of St. Lawrence engaged in both trading and whaling; a few may have come only to trade. Laurier Turgeon has found notarial records in Bordeaux of twenty Basque ships outfitted for fur trading between 1580 and 1600. At the same time, Breton merchants from St-Malo became interested in the fur trade. A small trading ship from St-Malo reached the St. Lawrence in 1581, and several more over the next few years. The impetus to trade came from the growing demand in Europe for broad-brimmed beaver felt hats and, fortuitously, from the disruption of Russian fur supplies after Swedes captured the Baltic port of Narva in 1581. Basques and Bretons competed in this trade, sometimes violently, offering copper kettles, iron axes and knives, beads, cloth, and clothing for beaver pelts, and also for marten and otter. Trade goods from the 1580s appear in archaeological sites around the eastern Great Lakes (earlier trade goods, entering from the Gulf of Maine in the 1550s and 1560s, appear in Iroquoian sites south of Lake Ontario). The trade slackened in the 1590s, partly because access to Russian

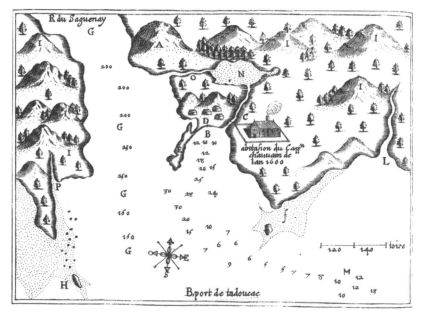

Les chifres montrent les braffes d'eau.

A Vnemontaigne ronde fui le bort de la riuiere du Saguenay.
H Le port de Tadouffac.
C Petit ruiffeau d'eau douce.
D Le lieu ou cabannent les fauuages quand ils viennent pour la traicte.
F. Maniere d'ifle qui cloft vne partie du port de la ri-

uiere du Saguenay.
F La pointe de tous les Diables
G La riuiere du Saguenay.
H La pointe aux alouettes.
I Montaignes fort mauuaifes, remplies de lapins & boulleaux.
L Le moulin Bode.
M La rade ou les vaiffeaux

mouillent l'ancre attendant le vent & la maree.
N Petit eftãg proche du port.
O Petit ruiffeau fortant de l'eflãg,qui defchai ge dans le Saguenay.
P Place fur la pointe fans arbres, où il y a quantité d'herbages.

MAP 2.9   Port of Tadoussac | Samuel de Champlain, *Les Voyages du sieur de Champlain* (Paris: Jean Berjon, 1613), 172.

supplies had been re-established through the arctic port of Archangel, then resumed at the end of the century.

In 1599 the French king, Henri IV, awarded a Huguenot, Pierre de Chauvin de Tonnetuit, a trading monopoly and required him to "inhabit the country and build a lodging there" (habiteroient le pays, et y feroient une demeure). Chauvin built a fort well up the St. Lawrence at Tadoussac at the mouth of the Saguenay River – a minuscule palisaded European space in Native territory – and maintained it through the winter of 1600-1, the first European trading post in Canada (Map 2.9). He died in France early in 1603. Later that year his successor, Aymar de Chaste, sent three ships to the St. Lawrence, on one of which was Samuel de Champlain,

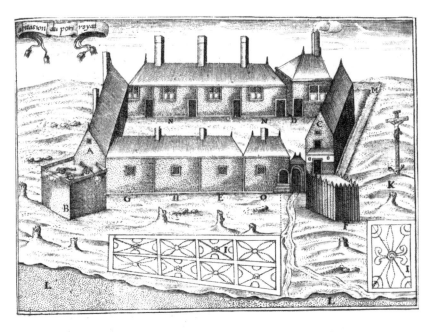

A Logemens des artifans.
B Plate forme où eſtoit le canon.
C Le magaſin.
D Logemét du ſieur dePontgraué & Champlain.
E La forge.

F Paliſſade de pieux.
G Le four.
H La cuiſine.
O Petite maiſonnette où l'on retiroit les vtanſiles de nos barques ſque de puis le ſieur de Poitrincourt ſit

rebaſtir, & y logea le ſieur Boulay quand le ſieur du Pont s'en reuint en France.
Q Le cemetiere.
R La riuiere.

N ij

FIGURE 2.3   Habitation at Port Royal, c. 1606. Champlain's base for exploration and trade in what is now the Bay of Fundy. | Samuel de Champlain, *Les Voyages du sieur de Champlain* (Paris: Jean Berjon, 1613), 99.

apparently as an observer. Champlain, then in his midthirties, was an experienced cartographer and navigator; as historical geographer Conrad Heidenreich has pointed out, he learned more about the river and its tributaries that summer than had all those who preceded him. He was the first systematically to gather information about the interior from Native informants, the first to recognize the potential of the birchbark canoe as a vehicle for exploration. He also participated in the ceremonial ratification of an alliance between a large group of Innu (Montagnais) and Algonquin assembled near Tadoussac and François Gravé Du Pont, commander of the expedition and representative of Henri IV. In return for a military alliance, the Innu and Algonquin allowed the French to settle in the St. Lawrence Valley – an understanding Henri IV had made the year before

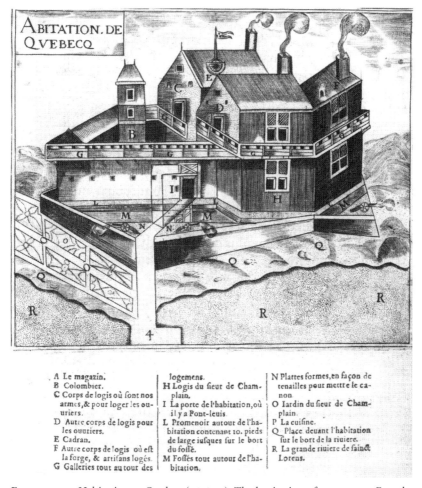

A Le magazin.
B Colombier.
C Corps de logis où font nos armes,& pour loger les ouuriers.
D Autre corps de logis pour les ouuriers.
E Cadran.
F Autre corps de logis où eft la forge, & artifans logés.
G Galleries tout autour des logemens.
H Logis du fieur de Champlain.
I La porte de l'habitation,où il y a Pont-leuis.
L Promenoir autour de l'habitation contenant 10. pieds de large iufques fur le bort du foffé.
M Foffés tout autour de l'habitation.
N Plattes formes,en façon de tenailles pour mettre le canon.
O Iardin du fieur de Champlain.
P La cuifine.
Q Place deuant l'habitation fur le bort de la riuiere.
R La grande riuiere de faind Lorens.

FIGURE 2.4   Habitation at Quebec (1608-12). The beginning of permanent French settlement along the lower St. Lawrence. | Champlain, *Les Voyages*, 187.

with two Innu whom Chauvin had taken to France. In 1604 Champlain was in the employ of Pierre du Gua, sieur de Monts, who had acquired Chauvin's monopoly. De Monts opted for a settlement south of the Gulf of St. Lawrence in the Bay of Fundy (Figure 2.3) where, again, Champlain sought out Native informants and conducted the first detailed survey of the Atlantic coast southward to Cape Cod. Back on the St. Lawrence to stay in 1608, Champlain established a fort at Quebec (Figure 2.4), near where Cartier had over-wintered in the 1530s, a shrewd selection of a commanding site on the principal Atlantic entry to the continental interior.

He intended it as a base for inland exploration and as a focus of potential colonization, but immediately as a fur trade post in a promising area where competition could be controlled.

The fort at Quebec placed Pierre de Gua's trading venture deep in the continental interior and amid the complex array of Native peoples shown in Map 2.10. Champlain understood that further exploration and successful trade depended on Native good will, on alliances with particular Native groups, and on Native technologies of travel and survival. He sent a

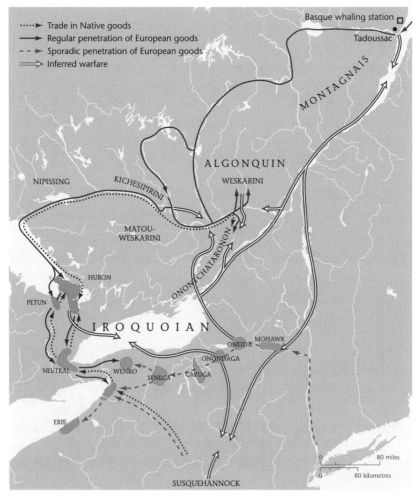

MAP 2.10   Peoples, trade routes, and warfare around the St. Lawrence Valley, c. 1600 | After B.G. Trigger, in Harris and Matthews, *Historical Atlas of Canada*, vol. 1, plate 33.

French boy (Etienne Brûlé) to live with the Huron, and accepted in return a Huron lad (Savignon), that each might learn the other's language. He expanded the alliance of 1603 to include the Huron, and was well aware that in so doing he had entered a military alliance against the Iroquois League. To solidify the alliance, in 1609 he ascended the Richelieu River with a party of Huron and Algonquin and raided a Mohawk village, members of the most easterly tribe in the Iroquois League (Map 2.10). In 1613 he travelled some 250 kilometres up the Ottawa River until stopped by the Kichesipirini, an Algonquian-speaking people. Two years later he got through to the Huron settlements at the foot of Georgian Bay and participated in a Huron raid into Iroquois territory south of Lake Ontario before returning to Huronia for the winter. Champlain had solidified the Huron-Algonquin-Innu alliance, brought the Huron directly into the fur trade, and acquired much information about the lands and peoples around the eastern Great Lakes.

With Huron participation in the fur trade, the well-established Huron trading networks shown in Map 2.10 became the framework within which furs were collected and French trade goods distributed throughout the eastern Great Lakes. Increasingly, the Huron obtained furs from more inland peoples and traded them to the French along the lower St. Lawrence for durable, useful goods such as axes, knives, kettles, and cloth (but rarely for firearms, which the French were reluctant to trade), in so doing displacing the Algonquian-speaking traders in the Ottawa Valley. As the Huron consolidated their position as middlemen, they prevented French traders from operating west of Montreal Island, and also traders from more inland peoples such as the Nipissing, Petun, and Ottawa from reaching the French. By the late 1620s, a competing alliance of Mohawk and Dutch emerged along the Hudson. As it did, the Mohawk resumed their northward raids. Although French fur traders were hemmed into the St. Lawrence Valley, their trade produced twelve to fifteen thousand beaver pelts a year by the mid-1620s.

In these years Quebec was a fur trade post. Barely twenty people might be called settlers. In 1627 Cardinal Richelieu, the French minister responsible for commerce and colonies, awarded a trading monopoly to the Company of One Hundred Associates, a broadly based, well-financed group that, in return for its monopoly privileges, assumed a charter obligation to found a colony. The next year the company sent four hundred colonists in four ships, which were captured in the gulf by an Anglo-Scottish force also bent on trade and colonization in the St. Lawrence Valley. At Quebec, Champlain was starved into submission. However, England had no prior claim to the region, and France regained it by the terms of the Treaty of Saint Germain-en-Laye in 1632. Father Le Jeune, the Jesuit priest who accompanied the French back to Quebec, reported that only one French farming family had survived the Anglo-Scottish years.

Although by this date an autonomous fur trade was little more than fifty years old, some of its enduring qualities were already apparent. It was entirely dependent on Native labour to gather and prepare furs, and on Native traders to barter them for European goods. The most common focus of interaction between European and Native traders was the fur trade post, a palisaded and otherwise fortified site where European traders in Native territory felt relatively secure. The fur post was linked on the one hand to Native sources of fur, on the other to European suppliers and markets. Extended lines of transportation provided these connections: on the European side, a transatlantic voyage, and on the Native side, canoe trips of many hundreds of kilometres. Considered in its most abstract geometry, the fur trade was emerging as a system of nodes (forts) and circuits (routes of transportation and communication) that connected European and Native worlds.

The speed with which the French fur trade on the St. Lawrence bypassed the Kichesipirini and other groups in the Ottawa Valley, and then with which the Huron drew on trading connections around much of the northern Great Lakes, is an early indication of its capacity for territorial expansion. The resource itself was widely distributed, and the incentive to exploit it was driven by the Native demand for European goods and by European traders' interest in profit. There is no clear evidence at this early date that resource depletion was driving expansion. As historical geographer Arthur Ray has suggested, it is more likely in these years that traders sought to bypass middlemen so as to get at cheaper furs and the people who wore them. Coat beaver – beaver pelts worn as coats to wear off the long guard hairs – were particularly sought. As one coat comprised five to eight beaver pelts, and as two or three years of winter wear were required to remove the guard hairs from these pelts, a substantial trade in coat beaver required access to a good many people. Ray suggests that the early trade expanded towards people (coat wearers) as much as towards beaver populations.

As the fur trade moved into Native territory and away from Europe, it began to merge, somewhat, Native and European cultures. Early portents of this hybridity can be seen in Champlain's geopolitical dealings with Native peoples, his winter in Huronia, his maps, his appreciation of the birchbark canoe, and in the speech-making and present-giving that accompanied trade at Quebec.

THE EUROPEAN IMPACT

By the early 1630s, some 130 years after Cabot's landfall, the northeastern corner of North America was considerably changed. European explorers had reconnoitered its difficult coastline, and their maps and reports had made it well known in Europe. Along the axis of the St. Lawrence River and northern Great Lakes, French geographical knowledge extended deep into the continental interior. Both France and England laid claim to this territory: the English along the east coast of Newfoundland and in the north, the French everywhere else. European commercial capital pursued a transatlantic cod fishery that was now more than a century old, and was rapidly establishing a viable fur trade operating out of the St. Lawrence. Native lives were altered by European introductions.

Although the cod fishery and the fur trade both drew European capital to New World resources and depended on transatlantic connections to European markets, the nature and location of the resources they exploited and the means they used to do so created radically different spatial economies. The one was tied to the Atlantic coast, the other moved quickly inland. The one drew almost all its labour from Europe, the other depended largely on Native labour and required very few Europeans. The cod fishery tended, therefore, to brush Native people aside, whereas the fur trade depended on them. The pattern of one was somewhat radial (its hub a rocky New World coast and adjacent fishing grounds, its rim a long European coast punctuated by fishing ports, and its many spokes the voyages between), and the other strikingly linear, tied to the river. A somewhat radial system favoured an international trade that was competitive rather than monopolistic (there was no point at which the whole system could be controlled), whereas linearity encouraged monopoly. Eventually, the fur trade would expand across the continent, in so doing altering the lives of all Native peoples with whom it came in contact. The cod fishery would remain fixed along the seacoast, to which for almost three hundred years it would transport most of its labour across the Atlantic.

The early effects of the fur trade and cod fisheries on Native livelihoods and cultures are now exceedingly difficult to discern. The Beothuk people of Newfoundland undoubtedly coveted European goods, particularly iron, which they usually obtained by pillaging shore installations after the fishermen had left for the season. Well-made iron arrowheads turn up in archaeological sites. Such introductions made Native life easier. On the other hand, as fishermen took over the coasts, Native bands often were forced away, and livelihoods that had depended on both the interior (in winter) and the coast (in summer) were undermined. This seems to have been the fate of the Beothuk, who, increasingly cut off from the coast, would eventually starve in the interior. On much of the Labrador coast the Thule (Inuit) drove off Europeans, although interactions between the Innu (Montagnais) and Basque whalers along the south coast of Labrador west of the Strait of Belle Isle were common and peaceful. As European goods entered Native economies, and as Native groups vied with each other to acquire them, there is reason to suppose (but no evidence) that the intensity of intergroup warfare increased and that groups well placed to obtain these goods would either dominate those that were not or would be displaced by more powerful groups. The fur trade also encouraged Native economic specialization, as the early emergence of middlemen, first in the Ottawa Valley and then among the Huron, suggests.

But the most important question about the changing character of Native life, and one that still cannot be conclusively answered, is whether European infectious diseases had diffused among the Native peoples of northeastern North America at this time. The coming of Europeans had broken millennia of biological isolation during which highly infectious diseases such as smallpox and measles had emerged in agricultural populations living in close association with domestic animals. These diseases had become endemic in Europe and Africa, where, over the centuries, populations developed some genetic immunity. When Europeans and Africans began to cross the Atlantic, their diseases accompanied them and diffused among people who had no genetic resistance to or cultural experience with them. The effects were catastrophic. Mortality rates from virgin-soil epidemics of smallpox (that is, among populations with no previous exposure to the disease) were characteristically in the order of 50 to 75 percent, sometimes higher. Growing evidence from around the western hemisphere suggests that a hundred years after the first epidemics reached a given area, it seldom had more than 10 percent of its pre-epidemic population. In the long run there was no escaping these inadvertent introductions. They would diffuse everywhere. But had they diffused into northeastern North America during the first long century of European activity there?

The strongest evidence that they had is a statement from the Jesuit father Biard in 1611. Writing about the Mi'kmaq, Biard said: "They are astonished and often complain that since the French mingle with and carry on trade with them they are dying fast and the population is thinning out. They assert that ... all their countries were very populous, and they tell how one by one different coasts, according as they have begun to traffic with us, have been more reduced by disease." There is also the puzzling disappearance of the St. Lawrence Iroquoians, the people whom Jacques Cartier encountered in the 1530s in several villages near Quebec and at Hochelaga on Montreal Island. When the French returned to the St. Lawrence in the 1580s, these people were gone. The lower St. Lawrence Valley was sparsely inhabited by Innu in the east and Algonquin in the west; the tribes of the Iroquois League, the Iroquois tribes living south of the St. Lawrence and of Lake Ontario, considered the St. Lawrence Valley as well as the land immediately north of Lake Ontario to be their hunting territory. For want of other evidence, the current tendency is to discount Biard and to assume that the St. Lawrence Iroquoians were dispersed by warfare instigated either by the Huron or by members of the Iroquois League (most likely the Mohawk). The motive for such attacks, many have argued, may have been access to the European goods that were beginning to enter the St. Lawrence Valley. Possibly so, but given the number of men crossing the Atlantic each year, the shortness of the voyage under favourable conditions (well under a month to eastern Newfoundland), and the long incubation period of smallpox (seven to eighteen days) during which the disease is neither apparent nor infective, it is clear that a disease such as smallpox could readily have crossed the Atlantic. It reached York Factory on Hudson Bay in 1720 after a sea voyage of two months. Basque voyages into the Gulf of St. Lawrence were much shorter than this, and at some whaling stations Basques and Native people worked side by side. There is evidence that St. Lawrence Iroquoians traded with Europeans as far east as the Strait of Belle Isle. Quite possibly Father Biard should be taken at his word; quite possibly the St. Lawrence Iroquoians were dispersed by warfare after being decimated by disease. Elsewhere on the continent, epidemics commonly upset balances of power and led to heightened warfare. The fact of the matter, however, is that until more evidence appears, no firm statement can be made about sixteenth-century disease in northeastern North America.

Environmental impacts are also difficult to assess, although, as environmental historian Richard Hoffmann has pointed out, the general pattern is clear enough. Europeans were externalizing their own demands in distant ecologies, an "ecological footprint" that only a handful of them would ever see. The products of these activities – in the fishery, dried or salted pieces of cod – were standardized and decontextualized wares, substitutes in the European market for many species of increasingly scarce local fish. Environmental effects were displaced and were either invisible or, because so distant, inconsequential.

There is no doubt about the impact of the inshore fishery on the coasts behind it. Shore installations required a great deal of wood, and as early as 1622 an observer noted that "the woods along the coasts are so spoyled by the fishermen that it is a great pity to behold them, and without redress undoubtedly will be the ruine of this good land. For they wastefully bark, fell and leave more wood behind them to rot than they use about their stages although they employ a world of wood upon them." Forest fires may have been even more damaging and have ranged farther inland. The extent to which fish stocks were affected is unclear. These were hook, line, and bait fisheries, the production of which, large as it was, pales by twentieth-century standards. Yet, there is medieval evidence that similar technologies depleted cod stocks in European waters. In addition, historical geographer Grant Head has found the following in a 1683 Colonial Office document regarding the somewhat later inshore Newfoundland fishery:

> Though there be Harbours and conveniences on shoare for the making
> of Fish there is not fishing ground or can constantly be fish enough for
> so many Boates as they have kept, as is evident, for they seldom make

good Voyages above once in three Years, whereas were there but half so many Boates fisht there, they could not make so great a Destruction One Year as to prejudice the next yeares fishery.

Although the evidence is equivocal, sixteenth-century whaling may have depleted the population of bowhead whales along the coast of Labrador.

The fur trade also externalized demand for a denatured product, in this case dried and cured beaver pelts, but no reliable information about its environmental impact exists at this time. There is no evidence that the members of the Iroquois League had begun to raid northward because beaver were depleted in their territories. In the longer run, the spatial organization of the fur trade itself – its permanent settlements, regional economic specialization, routes of long-distance transportation, and capacity to distribute provisions – would make it an ecological system that differed radically from the older Native systems on which it was superimposed.

In sum, European influences acquired a considerable momentum in northeastern North America in the sixteenth century. The coastline and the principal Atlantic entry to the midcontinental interior were explored, mapped, and claimed. The cod fishery and the fur trade drew European capital far ahead of European agricultural settlers, perched European men in tiny camps – a fishing installation, a fur post – surrounded by alien land, and created systems for negotiating New World space and exploiting New World ecologies. Around the fishery, Native people recoiled somewhat. The fur trade, however, drew Europeans into the continent and towards Native people, in so doing locating patches of land that would prove suitable for agricultural settlement.

BIBLIOGRAPHY

For a summary of sixteenth-century exploration, see Richard Ruggles, "Exploring the Atlantic Coast," in *Historical Atlas of Canada,* vol. 1, *From the Beginning to 1800,* ed. R. Cole Harris, cart. Geoffrey J. Matthews (Toronto: University of Toronto Press, 1987), plate 19. For a short discussion of the early voyages, consult John L. Allen, "From Cabot to Cartier: The Early Exploration of Eastern North America, 1497-1543," *Annals of the Association of American Geographers* 82, 3 (1992): 500-21; and for a more extended discussion, refer to Samuel Eliot Morison, *The European Discovery of America: The Northern Voyages* (New York: Oxford University Press, 1971). For a survey of sixteenth- and early seventeenth-century cartography that includes fine reproductions of the principal maps, see Derek Hayes, *Historical Atlas of Canada: Canada's History Illustrated with Original Maps* (Vancouver and Toronto: Douglas and McIntyre, 2002), 7-56. For the principal documents relating to explorations before 1612, consult D.B. Quinn, *New American World: A Documentary History of North America to 1612* (New York: Arno Press, 1979). For Champlain's exploration and cartography, see Conrad Heidenreich, "The Beginning of French Exploration out of the St. Lawrence Valley: Motives, Methods, and Changing Attitudes towards Native People," in Germaine Warkentin and Carolyn Podruchny, eds., *Decentering the Renaissance: Canada and Europe in Multidisciplinary Perspective, 1500-1700* (Toronto: University of Toronto Press, 2001), 236-51; Heidenreich, with Edward H. Dahl, "La cartographie de Champlain (1603-1632)," in Raymonde Litalien and Denis Vaugeois, eds., *Champlain: La naissance de l'Amérique française* (Sillery: Nouveau Monde and Septentrion, 2004), 312-32; and Heidenreich, "Early French Exploration in the North American Interior," in J.L. Allen, ed., *North American Exploration*, vol. 2, *A Continent Defined* (Lincoln and London: University of Nebraska Press, 1997), 65-148. On maps and power, consult Bruno Latour, *Science in Action: How to Follow Scientists and Engineers through Society* (Cambridge, MA: Harvard University Press, 1987), chap. 6; and J.B. Harley, "Maps, Knowledge, and Power," in Denis Cosgrove and Stephen Daniels, eds., *The Iconography of Landscape: Essays on the Symbolic Representation, Design and Use of Past Environments* (Cambridge and New York: Cambridge University Press, 1988), 277-312.

A good general understanding of the sixteenth-century fishery can be obtained from the following: the essay "The Atlantic Realm" and plates 21 and 22 in Harris and Matthews, *Historical Atlas of Canada*, vol. 1; Laurier Turgeon, "French Fishers, Fur Traders, and Amerindians during the Sixteenth Century: History and Archeology," *William and Mary Quarterly* 55, 4 (1998): 585-610 (for a fine summary of recent evidence and understandings); and Richard C. Hoffmann, "Frontier Foods for Late Medieval Consumers: Culture, Economy, Ecology," *Environment and History* 7 (2001): 131-67 (for an analysis of ecological strategies embedded in the fishery). The European importance of the cod fishery is assessed in D.B. Quinn, "Newfoundland in the Consciousness of Europe in the Sixteenth and Early Seventeenth Centuries," in G.M. Story, ed., *Early European Settlement and Exploitation in Atlantic Canada* (St. John's: Memorial University of Newfoundland, 1982), 9-30.

For those wishing to go farther, the magisterial work on the early French fishery is Charles de La Morandière, *Histoire de la pêche française de la morue dans l'Amérique septentrionale*, 3 vols. (Paris: Maisonneuve et Larose, 1962-66). The equivalent on the early English fishery is Gillian T. Cell, *English Enterprise in Newfoundland, 1577-1660* (Toronto: University of Toronto Press, 1969). The early English fishery is more generally situated in the economy and geopolitics of the North Atlantic world in Stephen J. Hornsby, *British Atlantic, American Frontier: Spaces of Power in Early*

Modern British America (Hanover, NH: University Press of New England, 2004). The eighteenth-century fishery in Newfoundland is explored in Grant Head, *Eighteenth Century Newfoundland: A Geographer's Perspective*, Carleton Library No. 99 (Toronto: McClelland and Stewart, 1976).

On the beginnings of the fur trade along the St. Lawrence, see Harris and Matthews, *Historical Atlas of Canada*, vol. 1, plate 33; Laurier Turgeon, "Les français en Nouvelle-Angleterre avant Champlain," in Litalien and Vaugeois, *Champlain*, 98-114; Bruce G. Trigger, *Children of the Aataentsic: A History of the Huron People to 1600* (Montreal, Kingston, and London: McGill-Queen's University Press, 1976), chaps. 5 and 6; Conrad E. Heidenreich, "History of the St. Lawrence-Great Lakes Area to A.D. 1650," in Chris Ellis and Neal Ferris, eds., *The Archaeology of Southern Ontario to A.D. 1650*, Occasional Publication of the London Chapter, Ontario Archaeological Society No. 5 (London: Ontario Archaeological Society, 1990), 475-95; and José António Brandão, *"Your Fyre Shall Burn No More": Iroquois Policy toward New France and Its Native Allies to 1701* (Lincoln and London: University of Nebraska Press, 1997), chap. 5. Although written years ago, Harold A. Innis, *The Fur Trade in Canada: An Introduction to Canadian Economic History* (New Haven: Yale University Press, 1930; repr. with an introduction by Arthur. J. Ray, Toronto: University of Toronto Press, 1999) remains impressive. Chaps. 1-3 are relevant here.

For excellent summaries of the vast literature on the introduction and effects of epidemic diseases, refer to Robert T. Boyd, *The Coming of the Spirit of Pestilence: Introduced Infectious Diseases and Population Decline among Northwest Coast Indians, 1774-1874* (Vancouver/Seattle: UBC Press/University of Washington Press, 1999), chap. 1; Paul Hackett, *A Very Remarkable Sickness: Epidemics in the Petit Nord, 1670 to 1846* (Winnipeg: University of Manitoba Press, 2002), Introduction and chap. 1; and William Denevan, "Native American Populations in 1492: Recent Research and Revised Hemispheric Estimate," in William Denevan, ed., *The Native Population of the Americas in 1492*, 2nd ed. (Madison: University of Wisconsin Press, 1992), xvii-xxix. For an assessment of the evidence of disease in Atlantic Canada in the sixteenth century, see Ralph Pastore, "Native History in the Atlantic Region during the Colonial Period," *Acadiensis* 20, 1 (1990): 200-25.

3
Acadia and Canada

Early in the seventeenth century, the French Crown began to attach the responsibility for colonization to the monopolies it granted to fur traders. French settler colonies began to appear and with them farms and towns, new forms of European settlement in northeastern North America. At first these were proprietary colonies chartered by the Crown and administered privately. Canada, the colony along the lower St. Lawrence River, was Crown-granted to the Company of One Hundred Associates (the Company of New France) in 1627 and obligated by its charter to bring four thousand colonists in fifteen years. In Acadia, the colony around the Bay of Fundy (La Baie Français), trading privileges were also coupled with the responsibility to colonize. However, colonization and fur trading were not complementary activities, trading companies never met their charter responsibilities, and in 1663 a young Louis XIV and his ministers revoked the charter of the Company of One Hundred Associates. Canada then became a Crown colony administered by government officials. At this date, the English held Acadia, but when France got it back in 1670, it too became a Crown colony.

  With the creation of colonies, women began to cross the Atlantic in some number; as they did French settlement in northeastern North America became permanent. Unlike the migratory workforce of the fishery, some of the immigrants to Canada and Acadia stayed. They were not numerous. In Canada perhaps a thousand immigrants, many in families, arrived and settled during the tenure of the Company of One Hundred Associates; another eight or nine thousand came and left descendants during the years of royal government from 1663 to 1759 (many more came and left or died in the colony without issue). Acadia drew only a trickle of immigrants who settled and left descendants, probably not many more than three hundred. A few families had come before 1654, when the English captured the colony, and hardly a hundred immigrants, almost all of them men, came after 1670. Most of the men were soldiers, indentured servants *(engagés),* or fishermen who had managed to quit the fishery for a marshland farm and an Acadian woman. In both colonies after the early years, most immigrants were single, young, and from urban backgrounds.

These immigrants reached places associated with fur trade economies that depended on Native labour. For most of them, farming at the edge of a mixed coniferous-deciduous forest and near the northern climatic limit of agriculture was their only possible livelihood. Plantation crops were out of the question. Only the hardier crops and livestock of northwestern France could be raised, and then only after farms had been hewed out of the forest or made by diking and draining marshes. Markets for farm produce were few and hard to reach. In these circumstances, family farms began to spread along the St. Lawrence River and on the marshes around the Bay of Fundy. In Canada, the small town of Quebec had emerged by the 1680s and Montreal shortly thereafter, each in a countryside stretched along the river. Port Royal, the largest centre in Acadia, was never more than a village – a small garrisoned fort, a warehouse, a couple of stores, a church, and a scatter of houses and barns.

Tucked away in the continental interior some twelve hundred kilometres from the open ocean, Canada was not easily taken, especially after its towns were walled and garrisoned, a military alliance was in place with Native groups around the Great Lakes, and the Canadian militia emerged as a mobile, forest-experienced fighting force. The colony was in French hands from 1632 to 1759, and during these years the French state often administered it more closely than any province in France. Open to the North Atlantic and situated in the borderland between the French and English positions in North America, Acadia was administered much more irregularly. The colony fell to the English in 1613, 1628, and 1654, and was not restored to France until 1670. Twenty years later, during another French-English war (the War of the League of Augsburg, 1689-97), an expedition from Massachusetts again captured Port Royal; Acadia would not be fully recognized as a French possession until 1697. In 1710 Port Royal fell yet again, this time to a force of two thousand English marines and New England militiamen. Three years later the Treaty of Utrecht (ending the War of the Spanish Succession, 1701-13) confirmed the loss; the Acadians, French-speaking and Roman Catholic, found themselves in an English colony that did not know quite what to do with them. More often than not in these fluctuating circumstances, they were hardly governed.

Settled by similar people, largely dependent on mixed family farming, and very differently served by the state, these early French colonies raise fundamental questions about the transferability of society and culture from one place to another. Their settlers were no longer in a country of twenty million people living on scarce, unevenly distributed land, and within a mosaic of local cultures and steep hierarchies of social and political power. That France was an ocean away and, for the illiterate majority of immigrants, soon out of reach. At hand were a forest, a few Native people, and elements – more here, less there – of French power. Migration had left a great deal behind, subjected immigrants to new experiences, and, overall, changed the context of their lives. But what were the leading edges of change, and how substantial and how influential were they? Is it possible to generalize about the nature of social and cultural change in European settler colonies overseas? Over the years, a large and contentious literature has emerged around these questions. It has been possible to argue, as in their very different ways did early nineteenth-century political economists, Karl Marx, and the American frontier historian Frederick Jackson Turner, that the changing relative cost of land and labour reorganized settler societies overseas. Others have suggested that settler colonies became, in a sense, refugia where particular clusters of European ideas flourished and extended their lifespans. Among these scholars are the English historian Arnold Toynbee, who held that European religions tended to fossilize in colonies overseas, and the American political scientist Louis Hartz, who posited that only fragments of European cultures emigrated overseas, where, no longer checked by competing interests, they reproduced and expanded. Early Canada and Acadia, two small colonies settled in somewhat different circumstances by immigrants of the same national background, most of whom became family farmers, pose these larger analytical questions with particular clarity.

ACADIA

Partly because the Acadian settlements around the Bay of Fundy were shattered by deportations that began in 1755 and systematically depopulated the region over the next several years, a huge literature has accumulated about them. For the French historian and Christian moralist Rameau de Saint-Père, writing in Paris in the 1870s, Acadia was a feudal colony in which seigneurs provided leadership for a Catholic people of simple wants, high moral purpose, and the French, Catholic instincts of civility and progress. For Francis Parkman, prominent nineteenth-century American historian, the Acadians were a poverty-stricken Catholic people living in a rough, poverty-induced equality. For Émile Lauvrière, a French historian writing in the 1920s, Acadian society was "une sorte de communisme spontané," made possible by the abundance of land and selfless moral virtues. For Andrew Clark, an American historical geographer writing in the 1960s, the Acadians were sharp traders – as shrewd as the Yankee merchants with whom they dealt – linked to the North Atlantic trading system. Myth succeeds myth, and Acadia has become, in effect, a moral and social primal variously constructed by those who have written about the colony.

That said, much about Acadian life is fairly securely known, especially since the 2005 publication of historian Naomi Griffiths' monumental book *From Migrant to Acadian*. For example, it is known that, from its small beginning, the Acadian population grew rapidly, largely by natural increase, and that the Acadians found niches for a mixed crop-livestock agriculture, derived from northwestern France, on the marshes created by the great tidal range of the Bay of Fundy. By the 1650s, if not before, the Acadians were diking these marshes, fitting the dikes with sluice gates (*aboîteaux*) and clapper valves to allow fresh water to drain and exclude the sea. Land so diked and left for a few years to freshen made excellent arable (ploughland) and pasture. It is known that there was no agricultural export staple and very little local market beyond the garrison, whether French or English, at Port Royal, and also that Acadians traded with New England and, after 1717, with Louisbourg. English officials at Port Royal in the 1730s worried that as many as six to seven hundred cattle and two thousand sheep were exported to Louisbourg each year, although the Louisbourg records show few such imports, and it is far from clear how large this trade actually was. The volume of Acadian trade with New England, which was illegal when the French controlled Acadia, cannot be established precisely but certainly was larger than that with Louisbourg. From time to time, merchants from Boston operated stores at Port Royal or sent trading ships to the Acadian settlements farther up the bay (primarily to obtain furs). For their part, small Acadian-built ships traded in Boston, occasionally even in the Caribbean.

It is also clear that colonial state administrations, whether French or British, impinged weakly on Acadian lives. In the 1630s and 1640s, at the beginning of continuous Acadian settlement, feuds between the holders of different royal commissions left the few Acadian settlers largely to their own devices. Between 1654 and 1670, when Acadia was in English hands, English control was confined to the forts; the Acadians fended for themselves on their marshland farms. In 1670, when the French regained control of Acadia, it became a royal colony defended by French troops and administered by a governor sent from France and an intendant in Canada (an Acadian governor complained that it was easier to communicate with France than with Canada). At this point, the official regulation of Acadian life increased. Titles to large undeveloped seigneuries were rescinded, and smaller seigneuries were conceded. Attempts may have been made to organize local militias. *Corvée* labour probably was demanded for public projects, and troops probably were billeted in peasant households. A royal warehouse was built at Port Royal, and, in principle, trade was more regulated. But by this time settlement was dispersed on marshes around the Bay of Fundy, and just how far such organization reached into the countryside is impossible to say. Probably not very far. With eleven different governors or deputy governors between 1670 and 1710, there was little administrative stability, and there was never enough money to create an efficient bureaucracy. Officials complained that the Acadians were independent and ungovernable. An illegal trade with New England continued. In any event, Acadia was a royal French colony for only forty years, during eight of which an English force occupied Port Royal. After 1710 the British again controlled the forts but struggled to administer a countryside inhabited by unfamiliar French-speaking people whom, as Catholics, English law excluded from public office and jury duty. Acadians cooperated with the new colonial administration in various ways – repairing the fortification at Port Royal (renamed Annapolis Royal), piloting British ships in the Bay of Fundy, selling foodstuffs for the garrison, and providing some liaison with the Mi'kmaq, the Native people of the area. Elected Acadian deputies served on a council appointed by the governor; the minutes of the council at Annapolis Royal suggest that they acted as channels of communication for council orders and proclamations, as some approximation of a rural police force, and as adjudicators (drawing on jumbled elements of French civil and English common law) of civil and, more rarely, criminal disputes. The deputies were also expected to oversee the maintenance of roads and to collect quit rents (a small charge intended less as a source of revenue than as a measure of the authority of the British Crown). The Acadians cooperated with a British colonial administration in these ways, but the British state was hardly a burden on them: it neither maintained local militias nor recruited troops; nor (apart from the nominal quit rent), did it tax this countryside. For the most part, the Acadians looked after their own lives and maintained their neutrality in the face of confrontations between Britain and France. When, in 1730, most of them swore an oath of allegiance to Britain, they did so with qualifications: as long as they remained British subjects on British soil, they would not take up arms with the French.

It was in the context of rapid population growth, available marshland that could be turned to a northwestern European crop-livestock combination, limited markets, uncertain geopolitical control, and weak or erratic interference from above that the Acadians took up land around and eventually beyond the Bay of Fundy. From a base on the marshlands at Port Royal, their settlement spread to all major marshes around the bay (Map 3.1). By the 1730s, as marshland became scarce, more families turned to the uplands, principally by moving to Île Saint-Jean (Prince Edward Island). In 1750 there were at least ten thousand Acadians, virtually all living on family farms and descended from a small number of immigrants.

The family farm was the basic unit of production and the primary locus of sociability. At the intersection of strikingly different ecologies, it provided subsistence for a family and, eventually, some modest surplus for sale, basic peasant goals everywhere. Acadian farmers raised principally wheat, peas, and hay on the diked marshland (also some oats, rye, barley, and flax), and pastured their cattle there. In kitchen gardens or fields on higher ground near the farmhouse at the edge of the marshland, they grew the hardy vegetables of western France, particularly cabbages

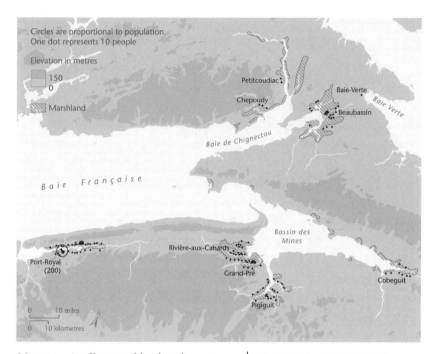

MAP 3.1   Acadian marshland settlement, 1707 | After J. Daigle, in *Historical Atlas of Canada*, vol. 1, *From the Beginning to 1800*, ed. R. Cole Harris, cart. Geoffrey J. Matthews (Toronto: University of Toronto Press, 1987), plate 29.

and turnips, and also a few fruit trees, apples primarily but pears and cherries as well. Most farmers kept a few hogs, sheep, and poultry; by the early eighteenth century, many of them had a horse or two. With the forest (and therefore wood, berries, and game) and the Bay of Fundy (and therefore fish) as well as diked marshland and a kitchen garden all at hand (Map 3.2), the Acadian farm provided the large portion of a family's domestic needs in return for the consumption of virtually all of its labour.

Groups of such farms constituted a countryside that depended on broad grass-covered dikes some two to six metres high. Behind the dikes were fields of wheat, peas, and hay; behind these diked fields at the edge of the upland were farmhouses, gardens, some upland fields, and small farm buildings. In some places the farmhouses were considerably isolated from each other, in others grouped in hamlets (usually of close kin), in yet others scattered in irregular lines above the marsh. These buildings were wooden (often on stone sills), of various forms of log or post-and-beam construction, and usually whitewashed. Roofing consisted of thatch, bark, or board.

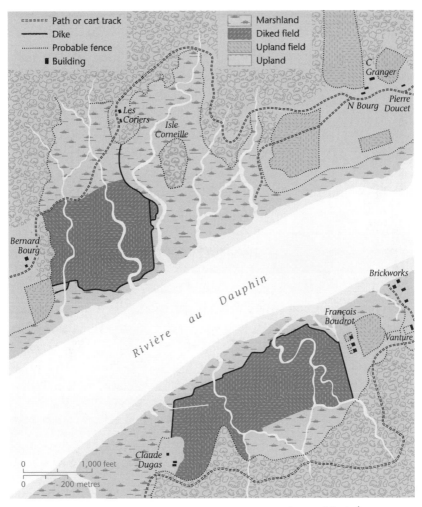

MAP 3.2 Acadian farms near Port Royal, 1710 (cartographer, Delabat) | After J. Daigle, in Harris and Matthews, *Historical Atlas of Canada*, vol. 1, plate 29.

Beyond the dikes at low tide were tidal mud flats, at high tide the sea. Behind the upland buildings and gardens was a dark, predominantly coniferous forest. It was a strikingly distinctive landscape, like no other anywhere. Within it were the local services required by a peasant society: small grist- and sawmills, a blacksmith, a wheelwright, a cooper, occasionally a merchant (most tradesmen were also farmers). There were also small churches, which at least one French observer likened to barns. This was a reproducible countryside that first emerged along the Rivière au Dauphin at Port Royal and then spread, with some variation, as Acadian settlement expanded. It became the local context of Acadian life.

That context provided relatively well for the ordinary peasant family, as the rapid growth of the Acadian population, virtually entirely by natural increase, attests. For all the work of building and maintaining dikes, farmland was far more accessible than in France, and, as a result, the subsistence needs of farm families were more easily met. As long as land was available, the means of social reproduction was at hand. In these circumstances, Acadian women married at an earlier age, on average, than French peasant women; their children, better fed than their equivalents in France, were much more likely to reach adulthood. Families with ten or twelve surviving children were common. Close relatives often lived on adjacent farms (perhaps on divided parental land), and hamlets of close kin seem to have been a common form of Acadian settlement. The work of building and maintaining the dikes was probably shared among such relatives. Beyond these local kin groups were more extensive ties of consanguinity. After a time, most people in each settlement were related to each other, and blood ties linked all the Acadian settlements – as would be expected given a small founding population and few incoming marriage partners. In this sense, the Acadians were soon a people constructed around nuclear farm families and their myriad genealogical extensions.

The question, then, is what lay on top of these peasant families? The answer, apparently, is not very much. Of the powers that bore directly on the French peasantry, the church appears to have survived best. The Acadians were erratically served by resident or itinerant priests responsible to the bishop in Quebec. The priests were supported either by an annual "pension" or by a tithe introduced, with some resistance, in the 1680s and fixed, on instructions from Quebec, at one twenty-sixth of the grain harvest. When Acadia became a British colony, the priests remained and were supported by the Acadians but viewed suspiciously by a colonial administration convinced, not without cause in some cases, that they conspired with the French. Besides performing their religious functions, priests often arbitrated civil disputes. A few itinerant or parish priests and a distant bishop were, however, a very lean slice of the hierarchy of the Catholic Church in France.

A feudal regime seems to have fared even less well. In France almost all land was held from the Crown in seigneuries, and seigneurs were expected to subgrant it through a descending hierarchy that eventually reached the peasant landholding (the *roture* in French legal terminology), for which annual rents were due and that required tenants to use, and pay for, a variety of seigneurial services. A few seigneuries were granted in Acadia, most of them by the Crown after 1670, but the extent to which seigneurial rights were ever exercised is very unclear. Early Acadian seigneurs were usually fur traders for whom a seigneurie was a means of acquiring a trading monopoly. One or two may have organized the initial settlement of their seigneurie (dikes, land allocation), and probably the basic seigneurial charges were collected for a time here and there. A few seigneurs drew up notarized deeds for the land they conceded to tenants *(en roture)*. A notary established for a time at Port Royal followed the Coutume de Paris, the codification of French customary law used in much of northern France. One surviving deed, issued in 1679 for land near Port Royal that the tenant had already farmed for some years, describes the holding in a system of metes and bounds (an irregular survey sensitive to local physical features). Metes and bounds were probably the rule, but most farmers probably never held a notarized deed from a seigneur for their land or paid any seigneurial dues. Acadian settlement was not far from squatting, with some leaven – more or less in different places – of seigneurial control. After 1713 the legal status of seigneurial tenure was as much in doubt as its practice had always been. Occasionally, British colonial officials did report that seigneurial dues as well as quit rents were being collected here and there. Whatever the law, from the seigneur's perspective the management of a seigneurie in a sparsely populated colony without an export staple was hardly a paying proposition.

Acadia was, overwhelmingly, a peasant society. Its land, more available than land in France, had provided the opportunity for a few people to create farms and reproduce peasant families through several generations. The economy, never strong except during the early years of the fur trade, had deflected capital. The smallness of the population, the low return from rent, and the legal confusion following conquest had deterred seigneurial management. France and England both claimed sovereignty over Acadia, and the Acadians could not avoid some effects of the wars between these powers, but they were largely free of the annual state exactions that, in France, were another heavy burden on the peasantry. A few settlers were not worth the expense of close administration. One might think of Acadia as a peasant "fragment" of France, but not (as Louis Hartz would have had it) because peasants had settled there. The majority of immigrants to Acadia came from urban backgrounds. Acadia was a peasant society because land that provided fairly generously for peasant households did not provide much support for the hierarchy of power that, in France, sat upon the peasantry. There was little inducement for these elements of French rural society to come to Acadia; if they did come, there was little to sustain them.

What, then, can be said about social power and culture within this peasant society? The records are exceedingly thin. It was not an egalitarian society. There was no wealth, but some of the farmer-merchants who operated small ships out of the Bay of Fundy must have been comfortably off and probably provided much of the Acadians' political leadership. A favourable inheritance, an advantageous marriage, and perhaps a particular shrewdness allowed a few farmers to own as many as forty to fifty head of cattle and to plant almost fifty *arpents* (one arpent equals five-sixths of an acre) of field crops each year. The largest holdings at Beaubassin and Chignecto, settlements at the foot of the bay, were on this scale, and may have belonged to farmer-merchants. Near Port Royal, a French immigrant who arrived some time before 1715 and married into a well-established Acadian family owned a good deal of land, two gristmills, a sawmill, and two small trading vessels – a fortune by Acadian standards. Most families had far less but seem to have had enough to get by. Excavations of an Acadian house near Port Royal reveal imported iron tools and kitchen crockery, purchases that sales of farm produce allowed. There was no reason for healthy young people to be landless, although the dikeable marshlands were taken up by the 1730s, and some young families had to move to Île Saint-Jean. Overall, the social range in the Acadian countryside was slight compared to that of French peasant societies, but presumably in Acadia, as in other societies where the social range was narrow, fine differences were particularly remarked within intricate, closely read, local hierarchies. Most of such detail cannot now be recovered, although it is known that, caught as the Acadians were between French and British spheres of influence, allegiances even within families to one or the other were often sharply divided.

Acadia did not reproduce any of the many French peasant cultures. Acadian culture merged the various local ways that immigrants carried in their minds across the Atlantic with the common experience of marshland life around the Bay of Fundy. People from different regional backgrounds in western France mixed and married in Acadia. Their progeny further mixed the brew. Not all the remembered French ways survived; even in the immigrant generation, a selection was being made based on the relevance of particular memories to the circumstances of marshland life and, to some extent, on the number of people sharing them. French pasts were being recomposed and recontextualized in a different setting on the other side of an ocean. To this was added the experience of the marshlands and some contact with the Mi'kmaq – in at least five of the seventy-odd households at Port Royal in 1671, the wife was Mi'kmaq – contacts that were close in the early years and then increasingly distant as the needs of settler and of hunter-fisher-gatherer societies diverged. After a time, a way of life emerged that, though French in most details, did not correspond to any particular French rural culture. The Acadians spoke, for example, a distinctive dialect of French; indeed, the whole Acadian way of life might be thought of as a distinctive dialect of French peasant culture that reflected more of its particular New World context and less of its diverse French inheritance with each generation. The regional cultural variety within this way of life cannot now be recaptured, but given the small number of immigrants to Acadia, the blood relations that ran through its society, the common marshland experience, and fairly easy travel by water and eventually by trail between settlements, there is reason to surmise that Acadian culture was fairly homogeneous.

The marshlands and the family farms made from them, the keys to the Acadian world, were far more attractive to some elements of French society than to others. Essentially, they provided a type of access to land that rewarded the labour of the peasant household. In terms of political economy, the entry costs of land were too low to allow for the reproduction of the social hierarchy of the European countryside. Moreover, the mixing of peoples of different French regional backgrounds, the selective retention of former ways, and the ongoing experience with the marshlands prevented the replication of any particular French peasant culture. The distinctive French peasant society that emerged in Acadia was the product, essentially, of these circumstances. In this reading (as mythic as many others?), the terms of access to land were as critical as, in their very different ways, the political economists, Marx, and Turner held. If it is useful to think of Acadia as a refugium of a variant of French peasant culture, this was not so much because a few French peasants had settled there as because, within the technologies and possibilities of the day, the Bay of Fundy context in which settlers found themselves had largely eliminated any other option.

A few Acadians, more of them women than men, moved to Louisbourg, the French fortress town on Île Royale built to protect the entrance to the Gulf of St. Lawrence after the loss of Acadia and Newfoundland under the terms of the Treaty of Utrecht (1713). In so doing they entered a drastically different society. Fishing installations lined Louisbourg Harbour (Map 3.3), but the rocky, often fogbound land behind barely permitted gardening. An opportunity for the generational reproduction of farm families did not exist. Rather, the town of Louisbourg was the largest military fortification of its day in North America, a centre of the French cod fishery, and a major North Atlantic port. Its massive walls enclosed a grid of streets and a society dominated by rank in the colonial administration or the

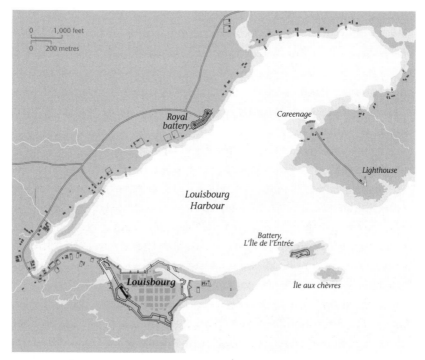

Map 3.3   Plan of Louisbourg Harbour, 1742 | Cartographer unknown. After K. Donovan, in Harris and Matthews, *Historical Atlas of Canada*, vol. 1, plate 24.

military, merchant power, and wage relationships. The town provided the trades and services of a military base and a port; manufactured goods were imported. Its population was exceedingly diverse, the women usually born in the New World, the men coming from all French provinces and a few from elsewhere in Europe. Its society was stratified and hierarchical. A French garrison town and port perched at a western edge of the North Atlantic, yet connected administratively, commercially, and personally to France, Louisbourg was, in many ways, the diametric opposite of the peasant farming societies the Acadians had created on the marshes around the Bay of Fundy. Historians John Reid and Elizabeth Mancke hold that it represented "an abandonment of Acadia as a colonial endeavour and the development of Île Royale as an extension of metropolitan commercial, military, and political interests."

CANADA

As Acadia was dominated by the Bay of Fundy, so Canada was dominated by the St. Lawrence River and its valley. The colony was on the principal Atlantic entrance to the continental interior, well inland from the open North Atlantic. The river connected it in both directions, and the valley provided land suitable for farming. To the north, not far from the river, lay the granite edge of the Canadian Shield; to the south, only somewhat less confining, were the most northerly ridges of the Appalachian Highlands. Between was a plain laid down by the Champlain Sea in immediate postglacial times and covered, when French settlers encountered it, by a thick and largely deciduous forest. The river cut through this plain, its banks high and steep near Quebec and becoming steadily gentler farther west.

When French settlers began to take up land in this valley, far fewer Native peoples lived there than when Jacques Cartier had arrived in the 1530s (Chapter 2). They were primarily or exclusively fishers, hunters, and gatherers (Chapter 1), mobile Algonquian-speaking people who inhabited the valley seasonally and whose imprint on the land was slight. For the purposes of French exploration and trade, they were necessary allies, but, unlike the St. Lawrence Iroquoians of Cartier's day, they had neither the capacity nor perhaps, given the alliance of 1603 (Chapter 2), the desire to fend off French settlement. In the eyes of French immigrants, they were hardly there, and most of them probably left the valley as French settlement advanced. The approximately nine to ten thousand immigrants during the French regime who stayed and left descendants rarely competed with them for land. Four-fifths of these immigrants were male, the great majority young and unmarried, but otherwise they were a fairly representative sample of French society, excluding the *grande noblesse*. In the early years, most were Normans; later they came principally from a broad belt of western France north of the Garonne. They quickly created the two basic elements of the human geography of France: towns and

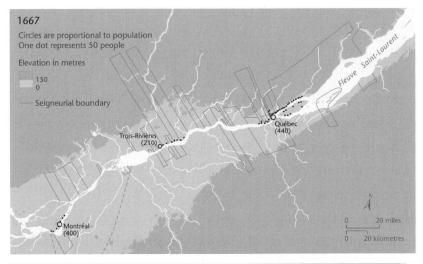

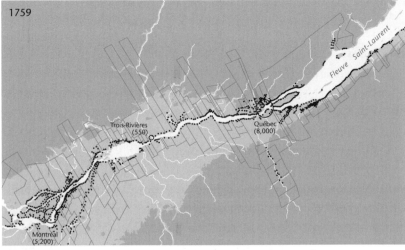

MAP 3.4   Distribution of population in Canada, 1667 and 1759 | After R.C. Harris, *The Seigneurial System in Early Canada: A Geographical Study* (Madison: University of Wisconsin Press, 1966), 90-91 and 102-3.

countryside. Settlement spread along the St. Lawrence River from fur posts and incipient towns until, by the end of the French regime, two narrow bands of settlement, with some extensions inland along tributaries, stretched from well below the town of Quebec to a short distance above Montreal (Map 3.4). At this date a resident Canadian population of some seventy thousand expressed far more of French life than had ever been possible in Acadia.

The Towns

The towns were the centres of power, although the countryside was where most people lived. Quebec began as a trading post in 1608 and Montreal as a mission in 1642, but other functions were soon added, and before the end of the seventeenth century both places became small administrative, military, and commercial centres that could be called towns. Their existence reflected the needs of a French government that sought to centralize its colonial administration and concentrate its soldiers in a few well-defended sites, of religious orders for administrative headquarters for their work, and of merchants for permanent bases of operations at crucial break-of-bulk points in extended transportation systems. As these functions concentrated together, they drew shopkeepers, artisans and tradespeople, domestic servants, labourers, and a certain amount of manufacturing. Overall, by the early eighteenth century almost a fifth of the Canadian population was urban. Quebec had a population of more than two thousand in 1717 and of almost five thousand in 1744. Montreal was about half as large, whereas Trois-Rivières, established as a trading post at the mouth of the St. Maurice River in 1617, was hardly more than a village at the end of the French regime.

When Canada became a royal colony in 1663, Quebec, the colony's deep-sea port and point of transition between ocean and river shipping, became its capital. It received a new governor, an intendant (the official in charge of civil affairs), their staffs, and a complement of troops. Administratively and militarily, Quebec was the principal locus along the St. Lawrence River of French imperial power, both aspects of which grew and increasingly merged over the years. Like the colonial administration, several religious orders established their Canadian headquarters in Quebec. The fur trade, which dominated the town's exports, required no more than a couple of ships a year. Shipping expanded, however, when French imports increased, as they did whenever the threat of war loomed and particularly during the last two war-troubled decades of the French regime. Most ships left in ballast for want of cargo. To these functions, the town added the tradespeople associated with a port, with construction and transportation, and with the considerable purchasing power of royal officials and prosperous merchants. In 1739 royal shipyards began making ships-of-the-line in Quebec.

At Montreal, the point of contact with the continental interior, the small ships and riverboats that plied the lower St. Lawrence gave way to the canoes that carried the fur trade farther inland. European manufactures and foodstuffs from local farms were shipped inland, the former as trade goods, the latter to feed canoe crews and provision fur posts. The principal fur merchants maintained establishments in the town, managing a trade that drew furs from deep in the continental interior, warehoused them, then shipped them to Quebec for export to France. With much less purchasing power than Quebec, Montreal supported a smaller and less diverse group of artisans. Yet it was a regional centre of colonial administration, and several religious orders including the Sulpicians, seigneurs of Montreal Island, maintained establishments there. In 1688 the town was enclosed by a wooden palisade for protection against the Iroquois, and in the eighteenth century by stone bastions and a wall. With a sizable garrison, it was another strong point in France's defence of Canada and her North American empire.

To a considerable extent, Quebec and even Montreal were creations of the French state. The fur trade did not require a large urban base, and there was no other secure export staple. The import trade was primarily controlled by French merchants, some of whom placed agents in Canada. Although Canadian merchants dominated the export trades in wood and foodstuffs to Louisbourg and the French West Indies, these trades began only in the 1720s and were never large or continuous. In these circumstances, only a few Canadian merchants prospered. Essentially, the urban economy expanded when the French state invested in these towns – sending troops, building fortifications or ships in royal shipyards – and languished when it did not, fluctuations tied primarily to the expectation of war. When state investment receded, times were hard in the towns; when a depressed economy coincided with crop failures and rising grain prices, officials distributed relief to prevent starvation.

FIGURE 3.1   *Quebec as Seen from the East,* 1688 (artist, J-B-L Franquelin). The commercial lower town and institutional upper town (vertical scale much exaggerated) are clearly apparent. | J-B-L Franquelin, *Carte de l'Amérique Septentrionale* (cartouche), 1688, Library and Archives Canada, C-016091.

In layout and appearance, Quebec and Montreal resembled in a general way the pre-industrial coastal towns of northwestern France. In Quebec, the common European distinction between a lower town given to commerce and an upper town dominated by administration and the military emerged early and clearly, as a considerably exaggerated cartouche on a 1688 map shows (Figure 3.1). Jammed between cliff and river, the lower town was a place of narrow streets and contiguous stone buildings. By the mid-eighteenth century almost all of them were stone structures; many were three storeys high, with well-proportioned shuttered windows on spare facades and small narrow dormers on steeply pitched roofs with massive chimneys at either end – the domestic urban architecture of the day in northwestern France. Prosperous merchants and their families lived in such houses, but the lower town also supported the tradespeople, shopkeepers and innkeepers, labourers, clerks, and many others who made their livings from the activities of a port. The upper town was much

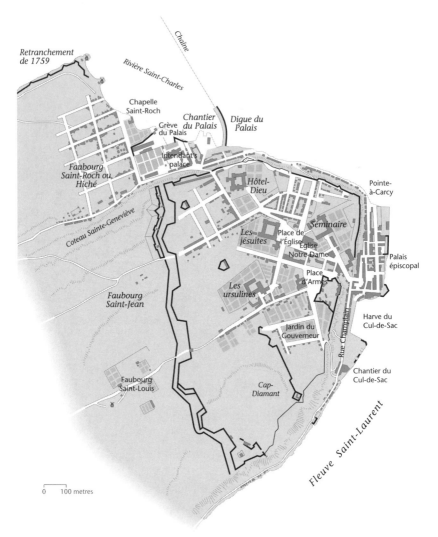

Map 3.5   Quebec in 1759 | Cartographer unknown. After M. Lafrance and
A. Charbonneau, in Harris and Matthews, *Historical Atlas of Canada*, vol. 1, plate 49.

more spacious, especially in the seventeenth century, a place of massive
military fortifications, handsome institutional buildings in French baroque
styles, residences of royal and clerical officials, orchards, and geometrical
gardens. In the eighteenth century the upper town became more crowded
as much of its open space was subdivided into lots and sold or rented to
people driven out of the lower town by the cost of property there (Map
3.5). Just outside the wall at the northwestern corner of town, a suburb,

Saint-Roch, emerged in the 1740s to house artisans and labourers who worked in the royal shipyards nearby. Saint-Roch became a place of small wooden houses, high population densities, and high land costs (per unit area). In Montreal, where the topography was much less abrupt, the organization of urban space was essentially similar: commerce dominated the waterfront (the lower town), institutional buildings were set well back from the river (the upper town), and many of the poor lived in small wooden houses at the city's margins.

Urban society was sharply stratified by income and occupation, and by many fine social distinctions, as it was in France and elsewhere in Europe. Especially in the lower towns, people of differing occupation, income, and social standing lived side by side, as they did in similar settings throughout the towns of pre-industrial Europe. In Montreal, as in Quebec, the stone houses of the well-to-do were clustered in the lower town, but artisans and their families lived close by in smaller houses of wood or stone, as did some poor families who could afford no more than the rent for a room. Others, who could afford less, begged. And, like French and other European towns of the day, Quebec and Montreal were exceedingly unhealthy. Historian Yvon Desloges estimates that two-thirds of the children born in Quebec died before their fifteenth birthday. Nor did the towns retain enough of their surviving young to maintain their populations. Throughout the French regime, young people raised in the towns tended to move to the countryside. The towns depended, therefore, on immigrants, some from scattered locations in France, others from the Canadian countryside. Their populations were culturally diverse (more so than in the smaller French towns, which usually reflected the populations of adjacent countrysides) and exceedingly mobile. Most people rented, characteristically for no longer than two years in any location. Apparently, many who held land in a rural parish nearby moved to Quebec or Montreal when work could be found there and went back to the countryside when it could not. Such geographical mobility in and out of town may well have been more common than in France and appears to have encouraged far more occupational mobility. Trades were much less defined in Canada; in varying circumstances, a man might be either a cabinetmaker or a carpenter, a blacksmith or a locksmith, a stonecutter, a carter, or a mason.

However, as Louise Dechêne has suggested, the principal difference between Quebec and Montreal and their counterparts in northwestern

France may well have been associated with the particular strength, and increasingly militarized character, of the French state. Governors in Canada wielded more power than those in French provinces; the intendants, unlike their French provincial counterparts, tended to become military managers and, bypassing the courts, final arbiters of civil disputes. Their ordinances fixed the price of foodstuffs, regulated weighing and measuring, set the time that goods could be displayed in the market, and admonished the young for their improprieties. Tradespeople complained that their activities were more circumscribed than in France. There was no municipal government apart from the state; the assemblies of resident freemen that had been established at the beginning of the towns were abolished in the 1670s. Troops conducted the nightly watch and functioned as a sort of urban police, as to a much lesser extent did urban militias. In Dechêne's view, state regulation and surveillance hung over the towns, the principal loci of a system of state power that in Canada over the years became more pervasive and militarized than in France. The accretion of state authority in Canada may be tied to the relative weakness of alternative sources of power – creating, therefore, a vacuum for the state to fill – but principally, Dechêne argues, to the succession of wars with Native groups and the British for control of North America in which the colony was caught up. War, she suggests, militarized Canada to the point that the whole colony became virtually a garrison during the last two decades of the French regime.

The Countryside
In 1667, during the fourth year of royal government, the approximately four thousand French-speaking people living in Canada were distributed along the St. Lawrence River as shown in Map 3.4. At the end of the French regime, when seventy thousand people lived in the lower St. Lawrence Valley, the river remained the axis of settlement along which, for some four hundred kilometres, towns and countryside were arranged. The eastern end of the axis opened into the Gulf of St. Lawrence where Canadian or French merchants operated cod-fishing stations. The western end opened towards the continental interior, its indigenous peoples, and the fur trade. Some young men living east of Quebec were employed seasonally in the fishery; others, living near Montreal, were hired as voyageurs (canoe men). Although the fur trade recruited some four to five hundred

voyageurs a year by the 1730s, most of these men would eventually turn their fur trade earnings into the development of a farm along the lower St. Lawrence. Indeed, the overwhelming majority of the people who grew up on farms in the St. Lawrence Valley became members of farm families themselves. The land accommodated them and the population grew rapidly, largely by natural increase. With a birth rate in most years of over fifty per thousand people, and a death rate usually under thirty per thousand, it doubled approximately every twenty-seven years. Farms spread along the lower St. Lawrence, and the people who lived on them comprised some four-fifths of the Canadian population.

All rural settlement in Canada took place within seigneuries. The French axiom *"nulle terre sans seigneur"* (no land without a seigneur) was observed, and the seigneurial system provided the framework of settlement in the Canadian countryside. A settler who took up land in the St. Lawrence Valley either acquired it directly from a seigneur or seigneurial agent, or obtained it from someone who held land from a seigneur. The Company of New France granted about fifty seigneuries, some very large, with the intention that the seigneurs it had created would be active colonizers. Very few were, and when the Crown took over Canada, it made many more grants, generally smaller, and itself assumed much of the responsibility for colonization, for a few years sending regular contingents of settlers. Long before the end of the French regime, all potential agricultural land along the lower St. Lawrence had been conceded *en seigneurie.* The holders of these grants were expected to subgrant land without initial charge. A settler who approached a seigneur for land would receive a notarized contract describing the land in question and specifying the annual charges for it: a *cens,* a token payment identifying a property that could not be subgranted (in French legal terminology such land was held *en censive* and its holder was a *censitaire*); and a *rente,* a more substantial payment in kind or cash intended to be a real source of seigneurial revenue. There were also banal charges (for services the seigneur provided), of which the gristmill banality (one-fourteenth of the grain ground) was the most important. The seigneur could levy a mutation fine *(lods et ventes)* on the sale of the property (one-twelfth of the sale price), reserve some timber, and retain fishing privileges. As long as these charges and reserves were complied with, the concession (the roture) could be worked, inherited, or sold without seigneurial interference – but subject to the protections for members of the family built into the Coutume de Paris, the French civil code followed in Canada. If seigneurial charges were not met, the seigneur could repossess the property. Legal historian John Dickinson makes the important argument that in this new setting where the slate was clean and the terms of access to land were defined by legal contracts, the rule of law tended to replace the older and less defined rights of French regional custom (also in this connection, Chapter 9).

Seigneurs organized the geographical distribution of lots within their seigneuries. Settlers could not take up isolated lots or survey lots as they wished. Rather, the allocation of land followed an ordered progression, usually lot-by-lot along the St. Lawrence and then, when the riverfront in a given seigneurie was allocated, in fairly ordered rows behind. A lot so obtained was bounded by two parallel lines and had a characteristic length-to-width ratio of about ten to one. This cadastral system, introduced from Normandy, where it had been used in medieval colonization schemes, was employed at the beginning of Canadian settlement and remained the Canadian norm throughout the French regime. In a colony in which the river was the highway, it had many advantages: it was quickly surveyed yet allowed families to live on their own farms with easy access to neighbours, differing soil and vegetation types (usually aligned parallel to the river), and to river (and eventually road) transportation. A lot of fairly average size was some eighty to a hundred arpents, but there was a good deal of variation. Map 3.6, which shows the cadastral survey near Quebec and includes the surveys for nucleated villages that Intendant Jean Talon initiated in the late 1660s (plans that were neither successful nor imitated), suggests the flexible geometry that this system imposed on the Canadian landscape.

Such lots became the homes of farm families; like marshland farms in Acadia, they provided for most of the subsistence needs of the families that worked them. The agricultural individualism and crop-livestock combinations of northwestern France (quite unlike the collective constraints associated with open field villages in northeastern France) had been introduced, although because the cost of labour had risen drastically in relation to land, agricultural practices shifted to emphasize land and conserve labour. Farmers lived on their own land and made their own agricultural decisions – but within constraints of environment, custom, and economy that shaped a fairly common set of agricultural practices throughout the

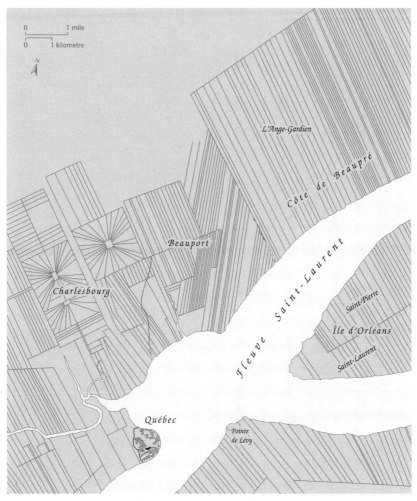

MAP 3.6 Farm lots conceded near Quebec, 1709 | Cartographer, le Sieur de Catalogne. After Harris and Matthews, *Historical Atlas of Canada*, vol. 1, plate 52.

colony. Wheat, the principal field crop, was commonly raised in a two-course rotation of wheat and fallow, occasionally in a three-course rotation. Peas, oats, and barley were also field crops. Most farmers kept a few cattle, sheep, pigs, and poultry, and usually one or two horses, used for hauling. Manure went into the kitchen garden, where most of the common vegetables and fruits of northwestern France were grown. Farm buildings, of log, timber-frame, or (less commonly) stone construction and usually roofed with thatch, were made from local materials, as, mostly, were furniture and tools. The forest provided winter fuel and the river often provided fish. When thirty or forty arpents were cleared, such a farm went a long way towards meeting the basic requirements of peasant agriculture: as much self-sufficiency as possible and some surplus for sale. Essentially, a European ecology based on landed property rights, fixed boundaries, both ploughland and pasture, and northwestern European crops and livestock had been transferred to the banks of the St. Lawrence. There, forests gave way to fields.

A farm was not easily made, of course. Lives went into clearing, grubbing, and building. The forest yielded, but, as elsewhere in northeastern North America, the pioneer struggle to subdue it was protracted and often killing. A poor immigrant just off a ship from France could not acquire a farm lot and expect to survive on it for the several years required to bring forested land into some agricultural production. Wage work would usually be sought for a time and savings accumulated. The children who grew up on farms fared better. Farmers sought to establish as many sons as possible and often acquired additional lots for this purpose. Many younger sons began to clear their own farms while still living at home before they married (one son would take over the family farm). In a system of partible inheritance (equal division among children), they could expect to inherit a fraction of the value of the parental farm (a debt the son who had taken on the family farm assumed towards his siblings). Daughters, who usually received household furnishings and animals in lieu of land, moved to their husbands' bush farms when they married. In such ways pioneering began and farms and farm families reproduced themselves.

The peasant family (in Canadian terminology, the *habitant* family), the primary unit of production and socialization in rural Canada as in Acadia, was situated within a local society structured by ties of kin, neighbourhood, and need. There was a good deal of mutual aid, a sustaining local economy, and relatives and friends nearby who shared a family's achievements and griefs. The family farm could hardly exist – nor did people want to live – without this socio-economic infrastructure. Young people stayed as close as they could to an established settlement when they began to farm. Families that did not produce enough grain to feed themselves until the next harvest often relied on loans from those that

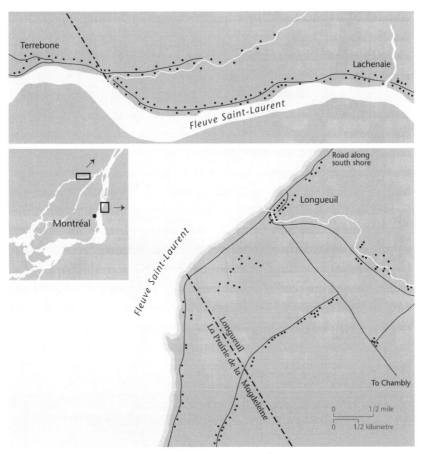

MAP 3.7   Settlement patterns near Montreal, c. 1760 | After Harris, *The Seigneurial System in Early Canada*, 155 and 158.

did. There was a constant local barter of goods and services. The boundaries of this local geography of peasant life in Canada cannot be precisely established, however, because rural society was never precisely bounded. The *côte*, a somewhat detached line of farmhouses, each on its own long-lot farm and fronting on river or road (Map 3.7), was certainly a neighbourhood and a locus of mutual aid. Often, most people in a côte were related to each other. The parish, usually more extensive than a côte, was also a social unit. People met each other at mass and other religious ceremonies, and the young tended to find marriage partners within the parish. On the other hand, except at the beginning of settlement and then in a small minority of cases, the seigneurie was never a framework of peasant economy or society. Medieval feudalism was not re-created along the St. Lawrence, if by that is meant a seigneur and peasantry in close symbiotic relationship. Farmers in a given seigneurie obtained their own flour from the seigneurial mill(s), paid the cens et rentes to the same seigneur (or agent), and dealt with the same seigneurial restrictions, but from the peasants' point of view the seigneurie itself was not a unit of rural economy or sociability. Blacksmiths and other tradesmen were scattered along the lines of settlement without regard to seigneurial boundaries. If there were a village nearby (rare during the French regime), several tradesmen and a merchant probably operated out of it. Kin often lived close together – a côte might be dominated by a few family names, a parish by not many more – but some kin were widely scattered. Peasant society comprised all these interactions in a variety of geographical spaces and scales.

The peasant family also existed within a local hierarchy of social power. The local elite comprised the seigneur (if he or she lived nearby), then the parish priest, then the militia captain, then prominent tradesmen and perhaps merchants. In a few seigneuries, particularly some of those held by religious orders, seigneurial courts dealt with civil disputes and were vehicles, as Colin Coates has shown in a study of a Jesuit seigneurie near Trois-Rivières, for the consolidation of elite, and particularly of seigneurial, power. Local militia captains, who were appointed by the governor, were responsible for drilling the local militia (infrequently, apparently, in times of peace), and, more basically, for maintaining the rules and authority of the state in the countryside. They publicized official edicts and ordinances respecting road and bridge construction and the maintenance of ditches, and were expected to recruit labour for work on fortifications in the towns, arrange for the billeting of troops, report to the intendant those who sold alcohol without a permit, and help track down and arrest army deserters. Usually respected older men in their communities, the militia captains were the common link between rural society and the state. Louise Dechêne suggests that, given the rarity of seigneurial courts and the absence of legally constituted rural communities, they made an essentially military organization, the militia, a means of filling a relative administrative void in the countryside.

Habitant families were also situated at the northern climatic margin of North American agriculture and in a rural economy that did not produce an agricultural export staple. Given the long Canadian winter, farmers could work the land for just over half the year only, a severe constraint in a system of production that depended on labour-intensive technologies and family labour. Wheat was the principal Canadian crop, but in most years some two-thirds of the colony's annual wheat production was required for food and seed in the countryside itself. Such surplus as the countryside produced found small diversified markets in Quebec and Montreal and, by the 1720s, some outlet in Louisbourg and the French West Indies. In these circumstances the long-term price of wheat declined slightly in the seventeenth century, stabilized between 1700 and 1735, and then rose sluggishly, the reflection of an agricultural depression that the colony could not shake and, as the price of wheat in France followed a different trajectory, of the detachment of the Canadian rural economy from the French.

Whether the availability of land, a depressed agricultural economy, and partible inheritance created a relatively egalitarian peasantry is a much-studied question. It is apparent that the availability of land was tempered by the enormous labour of developing it, and that an ordinary farm, when finally established, was rarely divided among heirs (unless the initial concession had been unusually large) or sold outside the family. One son would take it over, together with debts to his brothers for their shares of its value. If possible, they would be established nearby. In this way the parental farm subsidized the expansion of settlement, while concern to establish as many sons as possible diffused the accumulation of wealth. At the same time, a sluggish economy, coupled with the domestic orientation of peasant production, constrained economic opportunities. Even so, some families provided relatively abundantly for their children, initial advantages that tended to carry through lifetimes and generations. There is now ample evidence that prosperity and poverty coexisted within the Canadian peasantry. There were peasant farms in Canada with seventy or eighty arpents of cleared land and sizable surpluses for sale; other farms had little cleared land and little margin, especially in years when harvests failed, between meagre subsistence and starvation. But egalitarian societies are imaginary constructs, and it is more instructive to compare inequality in the Canadian and French countrysides. For all the regional variation in France, and pending more work on the matter in Canada, the following generalizations will probably hold: the most prosperous Canadian peasant families were less well off than the most prosperous French peasants, the bulk of Canadian farm families lived more comfortably than the bulk of the French peasantry, and the desperate poor were less common in the Canadian than in the French countryside. Compared to its French equivalent, the peasant social gradient flattened in Canada during the French regime.

There was also what might loosely be called a habitant culture, although it would seem to have been much less homogeneous than its counterpart in Acadia. People from diverse French regional backgrounds met and married in Canada, and different families faced similar demands of pioneering on forested lots in the St. Lawrence Valley. Both the mixing inherent in migration and the new material circumstances inherent in pioneering exerted strong selective pressures on memories of French ways. Immigrants who, for example, had lived in France in houses of many different types constructed with many different materials, built wooden houses along the lower St. Lawrence using construction techniques – usually timber frame with squared-log infill (Figure 3.2) – that had been rare in France since the clearing of the medieval forest. Yet some immigrants knew these techniques, and because they were suddenly relevant they again became common. In many other ways, details of French peasant cultures were being discarded or recomposed. Succeeding generations continued the process, mixing people while exposing them to broadly similar material settings. The generational movement of young people to new farms that, as local populations grew, were often well removed from the parental farm, gave this recalibrated peasant culture a good deal of geographical momentum. Yet, as the historians Jacques Mathieu and Alain Laberge have shown, a great deal of local variation existed. By the early eighteenth century in some areas of older settlement, all land was taken up, farms were cleared, there were virtually no incoming families, many of the young were forced to leave, and most of the people who remained were related – prime conditions for the emergence of local subcultures. In areas of newer settlement, the population was more diverse, clearings were smaller, and blood relationships beyond the family were less established. The fur trade at the western end of the colony and the cod fisheries at the eastern end imparted some cultural shading, as did initial concentrations of people from particular regions of France. Within the common geography of long-lot farm in the St. Lawrence Valley, there was, clearly, a great deal of local

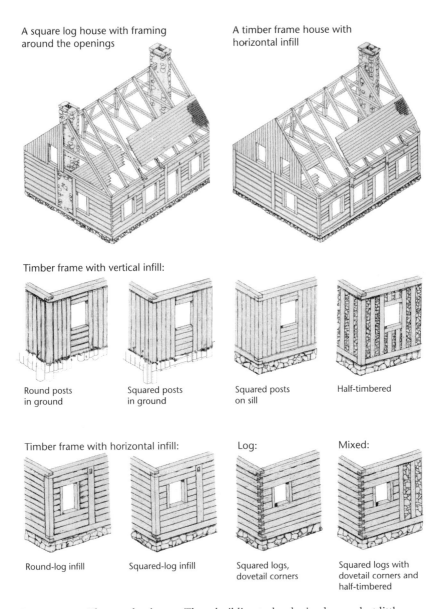

A square log house with framing around the openings

A timber frame house with horizontal infill

Timber frame with vertical infill:

Round posts in ground

Squared posts in ground

Squared posts on sill

Half-timbered

Timber frame with horizontal infill:

Round-log infill

Squared-log infill

Log:

Squared logs, dovetail corners

Mixed:

Squared logs with dovetail corners and half-timbered

FIGURE 3.3 The wooden house. These building technologies, known but little used in seventeenth-century France, became common in a colony where wood was widely available. | After G-P Léonidoff, "The Wooden House," in *Historical Atlas of Canada*, vol. 1, *From the Beginning to 1800*, ed. R. Cole Harris, cart. Geoffrey J. Matthews (Toronto: University of Toronto Press, 1987), plate 56.

cultural variation, a reflection of particular founding populations, patterns of subsequent migration, and local economic emphases. In detail, most of this variety cannot now be recovered.

Nor is it altogether clear what charges burdened the Canadian peasantry, or to what effect. Certainly the Canadian peasantry was far less detached than the Acadian from the sources of external power that weighed on the French countryside. Seigneurial charges in Canada are commonly estimated at 5 to 10 percent of an established farm's gross product, a lower percentage than in most of France. However, historian Allan Greer has argued that the burden of these charges is more realistically appreciated if seen as a percentage of farm surplus, of which he suggests they averaged some 50 percent. Others consider this figure too high, though agreeing that seigneurial charges comprised a substantial drain on peasant production. There is evidence that seigneurs were lenient (or perhaps negligent) when pioneer settlers had little to pay and sparsely settled seigneuries were unprofitable, and that their demands stiffened as farms became established and seigneurial populations rose. Overall, the religious orders managed their seigneuries most carefully, but many lay seigneurs were also careful managers, especially when thirty or forty censitaires were established and a seigneurie began to be a paying proposition. Censitaires rarely escaped seigneurial charges altogether and, if they did, only for a time. Records were kept, and sooner or later debts had to be paid. A censitaire who had not paid for years risked the loss of a roture. As in France, peasants procrastinated as they could, but eventually paid. A regime of property had been put in place, and its charges, superimposed on peasant economies oriented towards domestic self-sufficiency and producing only modest surpluses for sale, could be heavy burdens. Many censitaires were chronically in debt to their seigneur. Yet, compared to that of France, this regime of property did not produce wealth. There were neither enough censitaires nor a buoyant enough rural economy to generate it. There were no châteaux, no grand manor houses.

The habitants faced other demands from above. The first settlers in many areas were served by missionary priests, but as the local resident population grew the bishop invariably established a resident parish priest (a *curé*). The common Canadian tithe became one twenty-sixth of the grain harvest, lower than most tithes in France, but not as low, apparently, as those in areas of recent French settlement. Early in the 1660s the bishop (Monseigneur Laval) sought to impose a Canadian tithe of one-thirteenth, which settlers refused to pay; over the years there was an immediate reaction whenever a priest tried to collect at this higher rate. In France a state tax, the *taille,* was usually the heaviest single charge on the peasantry, averaging some 12 to 15 percent of the peasant harvest. The taille was never assessed in Canada, initially to encourage settlement and then, apparently, because officials considered it too difficult and costly to collect. However, men were expected to serve in the militia and to provide labour (several days a year) for roadwork (the *corvée royale*) and military construction (the *corvée militaire*). Many families near Quebec and Montreal were required to billet troops. All these exactions of the state, as Louise Dechêne has shown, increased in times of crop failure or warfare; then the market for wheat was controlled, and wheat and other farm products were taxed and even requisitioned. The merchants who bought grain and sold manufactured goods in the countryside were more regular conduits between farm and town. They were also moneylenders, their loans guaranteed by land and earning interest at 5 percent. An elder son who had taken over the parental farm might borrow, for example, to settle his brothers' shares of the inheritance. Many habitants were in debt to these merchants; some debts led to confiscations. Merchants, therefore, were also landholders, although, compared to merchant holdings in France, the amount of rural land that they controlled was small in Canada. The overall burden of these various external charges is difficult to assess, but in peaceful times probably amounted to a good 15 percent of the annual product of a midsized farm. In France the figure was almost certainly higher, 20 percent at least, in places as much as 40 percent. When war loomed in Canada, the state could requisition this much and more.

An outline of the geographical context of peasant life in Canada emerges from all of this. The Canadian countryside was not the Acadian, and certainly not any countryside in France. At its heart was the long-lot farm, usually fronting on the St. Lawrence River and backing into the forest. On such a farm, commonly towards the river, was a small house, usually log or timber frame and thatched, with farm buildings behind, a kitchen garden, and fields dominated by wheat and fallow. Similar farms lay on either side, separated from each other by split-rail fences. Adjacent farmhouses sat about one or two hundred metres apart. They were part of a range of long-lot farms and of a line of farmhouses, the côte, the immediate neighbourhood of the peasant households that lived there. Not far off were a parish church (Figure 3.3) and, perhaps, a seigneurial manor, usually little larger than the farmhouses nearby. A gristmill (wind or water powered) and miller as well as other rural tradesmen were commonly within two or three miles. In a few places, small villages had appeared, the location of the parish church, tradesmen, and perhaps a merchant or two. Many kin were near at hand, both in the immediate côte and beyond. Ties of blood, friendship, mutual aid, and economic dependence ran through this local fabric of settlement. Farther away were the towns, perhaps not visited very often but well known as seats of authority. Colonial administrations, high courts, and garrisons were there. So were the houses, hospitals, and convents and seminaries of the religious orders, as well as market days and merchants. In front of the parish church, militia captains read and posted the edicts and ordinances emanating from a town, troops might come from the town, and merchants in the fall. Often the seigneur lived in Quebec or Montreal, perhaps leaving an agent in the seigneurie. In such ways

FIGURE 3.3 "Église Saint-Laurent, Île d'Orléans," c. 1870 (photographer unknown). Demolished more than 140 years ago, this church, among the most beautiful buildings ever erected in what is now Canada, was fairly representative of the larger parish churches along the lower St. Lawrence during the French regime. | Library and Archives Canada, C-014123.

the power that concentrated in the towns reached into the countryside. The towns boasted some fair measure of the elegance of the French elite – the mannered ways and styles of architecture that, in the countryside, peasants glimpsed only in the baroque interiors of their parish churches. Much farther way, and indistinctly remembered, were France and increasingly distant relatives with whom an illiterate peasantry had long since lost touch. The fur trade into and beyond the Great Lakes and the cod fisheries in the gulf had become much more real.

This was a countryside that, as in Acadia, tended to favour the peasantry. The land-labour ratio had turned considerably in their favour, the underlying reason why seigneurial charges on the Canadian peasantry were lower than those on French peasants. The availability of land permitted the reproduction, generation after generation, of the farm family; long-lot farms provided most of the subsistence needs of the families that worked them. As in Acadia, a high rate of natural population increase was a measure of this landed opportunity. However, the larger networks of power within which the French peasantry lived had not dissolved in Canada. Canada was administered as a province of France, and especially when the colony was at war, the state appropriated much of the labour and produce of the countryside. Seigneurs held land from the king, and censitaires held farms from seigneurs, as in France. If seigneurial charges had declined somewhat in Canada, they were still burdensome. A bishop, subject to Rome, was established in Quebec, and his priests were in the countryside, supported by well-defined tithes. Merchants were there too, especially from the 1730s when agricultural exports increased and the rural economy picked up a little. To be a peasant in Canada was to live within the demands of these networks of power but, at least in peacetime, to be less burdened by them than in France.

COMPARATIVE REFLECTIONS

France did not, and could not, reproduce itself precisely in either Acadia or Canada. Yet even in Acadia, where there were no towns, and after 1710 no French administration, many elements of French peasant life survived. The level of reproduction was much higher in Canada, where towns as well as countryside emerged, the former housing a complex apparatus of state, ecclesiastical, and commercial power. The differences between the two colonies stemmed in good measure from the different purchase of the French state: secure in Canada and tenuous or absent in Acadia. But underlying the many differences between Canada and Acadia was a common tendency that, years ago, the political economists identified in settler societies. Compared to that of rural France in the seventeenth century, the relative value of land and labour had shifted in both Acadia and Canada to the advantage of labour. This was the essence of the peasant opportunity in these colonies. Peasants possessed labour, and relatively low entry costs to land gave them the opportunity to use their labour to create new family farms. They did so, generation after generation. There was nothing mystical about this process, nor was it novel. European peasants found themselves relatively advantaged, for similar reasons, in the century after the Black Death (because the population had suddenly dropped), and in areas of expanding settlement even in the seventeenth century.

If opportunity in the countryside stemmed from the low cost of land relative to labour, in Canada that opportunity existed within a system of power that included both towns and countryside, as it did in France. Because Acadia was townless and external power sat weakly on its settlements, the Acadian peasantry was, at once, unusually autonomous and particularly vulnerable. Its very detachment from the spatial configuration of power in seventeenth- and early eighteenth-century European societies would underlie the tragedy of deportation. In the France of the day, towns and countrysides contained separate, although interrelated, societies. The towns were relatively literate and mannered, the principal loci of refined culture. They were also commercial centres, and nodes in a system of sovereign power extending outward from king and court. Countrysides were more oral, vernacular, and local. They supported the elites in the towns and in the châteaux the elite maintained in the countryside because peasants could be made to pay, but the towns could not begin to control the everyday details of rural life. Nor had they any interest in doing so, and readily ignored the peasantry as long as it furnished revenue and recruits for the army. The French social philosopher Michel Foucault held that sovereign power, emanating from the towns, controlled life but not bodies. It could send out soldiers to quell a peasant uprising or make a spectacle of punishment to instill fear and secure compliance. It could kill, and did so as need arose (the control of life). But it could not control bodies; that is, it could not control the details of individual lives. The disciplinary mechanisms of such power were still lacking, and most of them, Foucault thought, would emerge later in association with the project of modernity. It is instructive in this regard that there was no official bureaucracy in seventeenth- and early eighteenth-century France to collect even the taille; the job of doing so was farmed out to thousands of local collectors who wrung what they could from recalcitrant peasantries. As yet, there was no bureaucracy to standardize power, no schools with standard curricula, no academic disciplines with theories of normative behaviour. Undoubtedly Christianity exerted a far more normative influence on peasant lives than did the state, but not even Christianity had effaced the localness of the pre-modern countryside.

Thus, even when most of the machinery of French power came to a settler colony, as it did in Canada, the countryside retained a considerable autonomy. People drawn from France to the edge of a New World forest were considerably on their own, not only, or even primarily, because of their distance from France or the novelty of their environment, but also, and perhaps most significantly, because of the spatial limitations inherent in the power structures of the day. In France as in Canada, peasants were left to work out the details of their lives. When communication was still substantially blocked by distance, as it was, the result was a diversity of local rural lifeways. In both Acadia and Canada, there were French traditions to go by, but peasant life in Acadia and Canada was a product of novel admixtures of French backgrounds in new settings. It discarded some traditions, rearranged others, and added new elements. In Canada there was a full complement of French legal and administrative structures, but they were far from the sum of peasant life. As the historical geographer Serge Courville has pointed out, the local spaces remained to be filled in, peasants did so themselves, and a distinctive countryside emerged. The regionally varied peasant culture in Canada was new in the sense that there was no other quite like it, but it was nestled within traditional systems of power that allowed a great deal of latitude for local cultural variety. In this sense, the creation of a distinctive peasantry reproduced a French countryside that, itself, produced diversity. It is in this sense that the countrysides of both Canada and Acadia may be thought to have contained distinctive French peasant cultures.

On the other hand, although Montreal, Quebec, and Louisbourg differed in some ways from French towns of their size, the similarities are much more remarkable. Considering that these towns were far from France, a high level of urban social and cultural reproduction overseas might not have been anticipated. Apparently, according to the social theorists, French expectations about both society and space were successfully transplanted to these towns. But why, especially when expectations for the transplantation of French countrysides were less realized? Essentially, French towns were reproduced overseas because the powers that underlay urban life in France could be and were relocated. The administrative and military apparatus of the state, ecclesiastical administrations, and commercial capital: these sources of power focused on the towns and drew townscapes and social formations in their train. Among them, the emphasis shifted towards the state. In the countryside, the hold of French power was less comprehensive, principally because the technologies of European power available in the seventeenth and early eighteenth centuries controlled countrysides less well than towns, but also because the relative availability of land and high cost of labour in Canada and Acadia favoured the peasantry and tended to discourage a landed elite. Peasants found more space in such a society, but so, in Canada, did the state.

BIBLIOGRAPHY

Acadia

The works referred to by Rameau de Saint-Père, Parkman, and Lauvrière are E. Rameau de Saint-Père, *Une colonie féodale en amérique, L'Acadie, 1604-1881*, 2 vols. (Paris: Librarie Plon, 1889); Francis Parkman, *A Half-Century of Conflict* (Boston: Little, Brown, 1892); and Emile Lauvrière, *La tragédie d'un peuple* (Paris: Bossard, 1922). Rameau de Saint-Père published several important documents that are not easily available elsewhere.

For a more contemporary introduction to the Acadians, see Jean Daigle, "Acadian Marshland Settlement," in *Historical Atlas of Canada*, vol. 1, *From the Beginning to 1800*, ed. R. Cole Harris, cart. Geoffrey J. Matthews (Toronto: University of Toronto Press, 1987), plate 29. Although probably exaggerating the extent of Acadian commerce, A.H. Clark, *Acadia: The Geography of Early Nova Scotia to 1760* (Madison: University of Wisconsin Press, 1968), is the most thorough account of Acadian settlement and economy. A short and more political account by Naomi Griffiths is *Contexts of Acadian History, 1686-1784* (Montreal and Kingston: McGill-Queen's

University Press, 1992). Griffiths' most recent and imposing book, *From Migrant to Acadian: A North American Border People 1604-1755* (Montreal and Kingston: McGill-Queen's University Press, 2005), is also primarily a political history but includes a wealth of social and economic information and fascinating accounts of the relationships between the Acadians and the various colonial administrations that attempted to govern them. See particularly chaps. 6, 7, 11, and 12. On Mi'kmaq-Acadian relations, consult William C. Wicken, "Re-examining Mi'kmaq-Acadian Relations, 1635-1755," in Sylvie Dépatie, C. Desbarats, D. Gauvreau, M. Lalancette, and T. Wien, eds., *Vingt ans après Habitants et marchands: Lectures de l'histoire des XVIIe et XVIIIe siècles canadiens* (Montreal and Kingston: McGill-Queen's University Press, 1998), 93-114. On Acadia in its imperial context, refer to Elizabeth Mancke and John G. Reid, "Elites, States, and the Imperial Contest for Acadia," in J.G. Reid, M. Basque, E. Mancke, B. Moody, G. Plank, and W. Wicken, *The 'Conquest' of Acadia, 1710: Imperial, Colonial, and Aboriginal Constructions* (Toronto: University of Toronto Press, 2004), 25-47; Elizabeth Mancke, "Imperial Transitions," in ibid., 179-202; and on Acadian political culture, Maurice Basque, "Family and Political Culture in Pre-conquest Acadia," in ibid., 48-63. There is no better short introduction to Louisbourg than Kenneth Donovan, "Île royale, Eighteenth Century," in Harris and Matthews, *Historical Atlas of Canada*, vol. 1, plate 24.

Canada

For a substantial introduction to early Canada, see plates 45-56 and "The St. Lawrence Settlements," the essay preceding them, in Harris and Matthews, *Historical Atlas of Canada*, vol. 1, 113-17. The far larger, and still the key work on both the economy and society of early Canada, is Louise Dechêne, *Habitants et marchands de Montréal au XVIIe siècle* (Montreal and Paris: Plon, 1974); and, in translation, *Habitants and Merchants in Seventeenth Century Montreal* (Montreal and Kingston: McGill-Queen's University Press, 1992). My own earlier book, R.C. Harris, *The Seigneurial System in Early Canada: A Geographical Study* (Madison: University of Wisconsin Press, 1966), was largely superseded by Dechêne's analysis, and most of the studies that followed her work have filled in the picture she painted.

An analysis of the scale and background of French immigration to Canada is provided by Leslie Choquette in *Frenchmen into Peasants: Modernity and Tradition in the Peopling of French Canada* (Cambridge, MA, and London: Harvard University Press, 1997). For important reviews of the literature on the rural economy, see Catherine Desbarats, "Agriculture within the Seigneurial Régime of Eighteenth-Century Canada: Some Thoughts on the Recent Literature," *Canadian Historical Review* 73, 1 (1992): 1-29; and Louis Michel, "L'économie et la société rurale dans la vallée du Saint-Laurent aux XVIIe et XVIIIe siècles: bilan historiographique," in Dépatie et al., *Vingt ans après,* 69-89. Also Sylvie Dépatie, "La Structure Agraire au Canada," *Historical Papers/Communications Historique* 18 (1986): 56-85. Thomas Wien,

"Les travaux pressants. Calendrier agricole, assolement et productivité au Canada au XVIIIe siècle," *Revue d'histoire de l'Amérique française* 43, 4 (1990): 235-58; and Louis Michel, "Un marchand rural en Nouvelle-France, François-Augustin Bailly de Messein, 1709-1771," *Revue d'histoire de l'Amérique française* 33, 2 (1979): 215-62. Although most of Allan Greer's *Peasant, Lord, and Merchant: Rural Society in Three Quebec Parishes, 1740-1840* (Toronto: University of Toronto Press, 1985) treats a later period, chaps. 1-5 should be consulted.

On rural society, see Sylvie Dépatie, "La Transmission du patrimoine dans les terroirs en expansion: un example canadien au XVIIIe siècle," *Revue d'histoire de l'Amérique française* 44, 2 (1990): 171-98; Christian Dessureault, "L'égalitarisme paysan dans l'ancienne société rural de la vallée du Saint-Laurent: elements pour une re-interpretation," *Revue d'histoire de l'Amérique française* 40, 3 (1987): 373-408; Jacques Mathieu, "Mobilité et sédentarité: stratégies familiales en Nouvelle-France," *Récherches sociographiques* 18, 2-3 (1987): 211-27; Jacques Mathieu and Alain Laberge, "La diversité des aménagements fonciers dans la vallée du Saint Laurent au XVIIIe siècle," *Historical Papers/Communications Historique* 21 (1989): 146-66; and by the same authors, "L'expansion de l'écoumène," in Serge Courville, ed., *Atlas historique du Québec: Population et territoire* (Sainte-Foy: Les Presses de l'Université Laval, 1996). Also in this regard, see Serge Courville's important work on villages: *Entre ville et campagne: l'essor du village dans les seigneuries du Bas-Canada* (Sainte-Foy: Les Presses de l'Université Laval, 1990). More recently, Colin Coates provides a broad analysis of economic and social landscapes in several seigneuries near Trois-Rivières in *The Metamorphoses of Landscape and Community in Early Quebec* (Montreal and Kingston: McGill-Queen's University Press, 2000).

On the state in the countryside, see Catherine Desbarats, "Les deniers du Roi dans l'économie canadienne du XVIIIe siècle," in Dépatie et al., *Vingt ans après,* 189-207. However, the dominant work on this important and, until recently, under-examined topic is Louise Dechêne, *Le Partage des subsistances au Canada sous le régime français* (Montreal: Boréal, 1994). Dechêne's even more important book on the organization of political and military power in Canada is not yet published (as of September 2007). This huge, complex study was not quite complete when she died in 2000. It has been edited by Hélène Paré, Sylvie Dépatie, Catherine Desbarats, and Thomas Wien, and will be published as Louise Dechêne, *Le peuple, l'État et la guerre au Canada sous le régime français* (Montreal: Éditions du Boréal). My comments on the organization of state power are drawn principally from this remarkable work.

Serge Courville treats the spaces of cultural reproduction and change in early Canada in "Espace, territoire, et culture en Nouvelle-France: une vision géographique," *Revue d'histoire de l'Amérique française* 37, 3 (1983): 417-29; and in English translation, "Space, Territory, and Culture in New France: A Geographical Perspective," in G. Wynn, ed., *People, Places, Patterns, Processes: Geographical Perspectives on the Canadian Past* (Toronto: Copp Clark Pitman, 1990), 165-76.

The towns figure obliquely in much of the above, but there are more focused treatments in the following. On Quebec: John Hare, Marc Lafrance, and David-Thiery Ruddel, *Histoire de La Ville de Québec, 1608-1871* (Montreal: Boréal/Musée canadien des civilizations, 1987); Yvon Desloges, *Une ville de locataires: Québec au XVIIIe siècle* (Ottawa: Service des Parcs, Environment Canada, 1991); and Serge Courville and Robert Garon, eds., *Atlas Historique du Québec: Québec, ville et capitale* (Sainte-Foy: Les Presses de l'Université Laval, 2001), parts 1 and 2. On Montreal: Jean-Claude Robert, *Atlas Historique de Montréal* (Montreal: Art Global, Libre Expression, 1994), parts 2-4; and Daniel Massicotte, "Stratification sociale et differenciation spatiale en milieu urbain pre-industriel: le cas des locataires Montrealais, 1731-1741," *Revue d'histoire de l'Amérique française* 44, 1 (1990): 61-83. Two useful comparative articles on artisans in Quebec and Montreal are Jean-Pierre Hardy, "Quelques Aspects du Niveau de Richesse et de la Vie Matérielle des Artisans de Quebec et de Montreal, 1740-1755," *Revue d'histoire de l'Amérique française* 40, 3 (1987): 339-72; and Dominique Bouchard, "La Culture Matérielle des Canadiens au XVIIIe siècle: analyse du niveau de vie des artisans du fer," *Revue d'histoire de l'Amérique française* 47, 4 (1994): 479-98.

4

The Continental Interior,
1632-1750

In the years between the return of the French to the St. Lawrence in 1632 and the fall of New France in 1760, the population of the vast continental interior around and west of the Great Lakes remained almost entirely Native. Late in the 1750s there were probably not two thousand people of European ancestry in this huge territory, although the fur trade, new infectious diseases, missionaries, horses, and European imperial ambitions had profoundly affected its Native societies.

Most of these introductions came from the east via the St. Lawrence or Hudson Rivers and the eastern Great Lakes, or from the north through Hudson or James Bay. The first tentative influences from the east, associated with fishermen in the Gulf of Maine and whalers and fur traders along the lower St. Lawrence in the 1580s, strengthened after 1608 when Champlain established a permanent trading post at Quebec (Chapter 2). The English touched the shores of Hudson Bay early in the seventeenth century but began to exert a sizable influence inland only in the 1670s when the Hudson's Bay Company (HBC) began to establish bayside posts. Horses arrived early in the eighteenth century, following the grassland northward from New Spain.

THE ST. LAWRENCE–EASTERN GREAT LAKES ENTRY, 1632-70
After three years of Anglo-Scottish control, the French returned to the St. Lawrence in the summer of 1632. Samuel de Champlain, who resumed command of the French position on the St. Lawrence, quickly re-established the alliance with the Algonquin and Huron that Henri IV had begun almost thirty years before (Chapter 2). He well understood that this was a

military as much as a commercial alliance, and that it pitted the French against the Iroquois League, a traditional enemy of the Huron and Algonquin. By the early 1630s the Iroquois were backed by the Dutch on the Hudson River. In geopolitical terms, a northern Huron-Algonquin-French alliance based on the St. Lawrence confronted a southern Iroquois-Dutch alliance based on the Hudson.

The Huron and Algonquin quickly found that an influential component of the French alliance was the arrival of black robes – missionary priests – in their settlements. In these years of the Counter-Reformation, Catholic missionary zeal ran high, the Jesuits had friends at court, and the missionary enterprise in New France was placed in their hands. Like missionaries elsewhere, the Jesuits argued that their missions should be shielded from the unmanageable and potentially damaging influences of other whites, particularly of dissolute male traders. As earlier in Paraguay, they wanted the interior, its peoples, and their converts to themselves. This arrangement also suited Native traders (who anticipated less competition) and colonial administrators (who favoured a managed trade on the St. Lawrence). It became official French policy to allow only the Jesuits, their servants, and eventually a few soldiers into the interior. French traders were forbidden to venture inland; rather, Native allies of the French were to bring furs to the St. Lawrence. Trading and proselytizing were accorded different spaces; it was within this spatial politics that, in 1634, the Jesuits opened their first permanent mission among the Huron, while the Company of New France opened a new trading post at Trois-Rivières, on the St. Lawrence west of Quebec.

Over the next twenty years, this arrangement was destabilized and then destroyed by disease and warfare. There is no doubt that epidemic diseases – measles, influenza, smallpox, and perhaps others – accompanied the Jesuits inland. Many Huron, thinking that the Jesuits had spread them deliberately, wanted to kill the priests and terminate the French alliance. Terrifying and lethal as these virgin-soil epidemics were, others argued that the alliance had become necessary for Huron survival in the face of attacks from the Iroquois League. The Jesuits remained. By 1641 when the epidemics had run their course, they had killed about half the people around the eastern Great Lakes, particularly the young and elderly. The Huron population plummeted from some twenty thousand to about nine thousand, a death rate similar, probably, to that among all the other

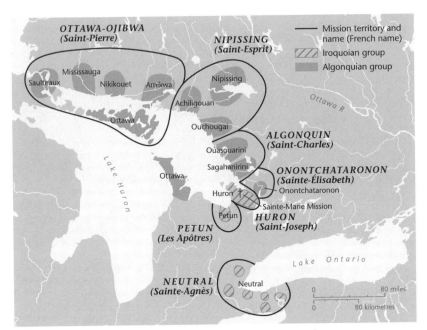

MAP 4.1   Jesuit missions around the Great Lakes before 1650 | After C. Heidenreich, in *Historical Atlas of Canada*, vol. 1, *From the Beginning to 1800*, ed. R. Cole Harris, cart. Geoffrey J. Matthews (Toronto: University of Toronto Press, 1987), plate 34.

Iroquoian and Algonquian peoples in the region, including the five tribes of the Iroquois League. Throughout this carnage the Jesuits began to win more converts. In 1639 they established a central fortified mission, Sainte-Marie, and began to place parish priests, and even to build churches, in the principal Huron villages. They opened missions to Algonquian groups north of Huronia, to the Petun just to the west, and to the Neutral to the south (Map 4.1). Where they had baptized before the epidemics struck, they thanked God that the souls of the dead were in heaven.

Overriding even these horrendous epidemics was an increasingly violent confrontation between the two European-Native alliances. In the 1630s, during the worst of the epidemics, the Iroquois raided sporadically northward. Although the Huron-Algonquin-French alliance barely held together during this time, each year some Native traders made their way down the Ottawa River to Trois-Rivières or Quebec. In 1641 the most easterly of the tribes in the Iroquois League, the Mohawk, attempted to negotiate a peace treaty with the French. The Mohawk wanted muskets and pressed the

French to terminate their alliance with the Algonquin and Huron, terms the French could not accept. Influenced by the Jesuits, the French had not to this point traded muskets with their allies, yet relied on them for furs. When the French established a fort (Fort Richelieu) well west of Trois-Rivières at the mouth of the Richelieu River and, in 1642, a mission at Montreal – both in territory the Mohawk considered part of their hunting preserve – the Mohawk unleashed a flurry of attacks on these positions and on the trade routes to them. They dispersed some of the Algonquin groups in the Ottawa Valley and for several years prevented furs from reaching the St. Lawrence. In 1645 the French managed to negotiate a peace with the Mohawk; Huron and Algonquin middlemen brought a flood of furs that year and the next, but the peace ended abruptly late in 1646 when several Mohawk murdered the Jesuit priest (Father Jogues) sent to establish a mission among them. The Mohawk accused the Jesuit of causing an epidemic and crop failures but may have killed him because their peace with the French was opposed by other Iroquois tribes and had not worked out as intended.

The scale and intensity of Iroquois raids increased after 1646, when the Huron and other peoples in the Jesuit sphere of influence were split into Christian and pagan factions and shorn, after the epidemics, of much of their leadership. By this time, the French had begun to trade muskets to their allies, but in limited numbers and only to Christian converts, whereas the Iroquois were now well armed by the Dutch. In 1646-47 Iroquois war parties dispersed the remaining Algonquin groups in the Ottawa Valley. In 1648 a war party of Mohawk and Seneca overwhelmed two villages in eastern Huronia, taking seven hundred captives. In March 1649, a thousand well-armed warriors destroyed the remaining Huron villages and killed, captured, or dispersed the Huron. Similar fates soon befell the Petun, Neutral, and Nipissing. Other groups fled. The missionary enterprise collapsed. The Jesuit *Relations* (their accounts sent back to France and published there) recount the horrors of priests tortured and killed. By 1653 the peninsulas of southern Ontario and Michigan were deserted, and clusters of refugees gathered near Quebec, south of Lake Erie, and west of Lake Michigan. The human geography of the whole Great Lakes region had been reconfigured (Map 4.2).

The cause of the Iroquois wars has been much debated. For years the prevailing assumption has been that these were economic wars driven by

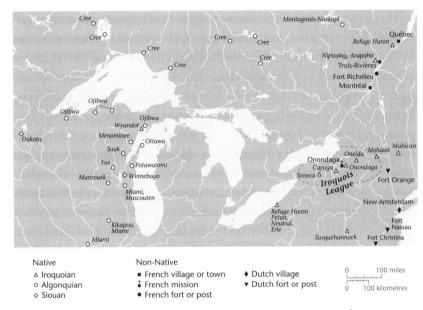

MAP 4.2   Settlement around and beyond the Great Lakes, late 1650s | Adapted from C. Heidenreich, in Harris and Matthews, *Historical Atlas of Canada*, vol. 1, plate 37.

the Iroquois' need to obtain furs after they became dependent on European goods and beaver were depleted in their territories. The historian George T. Hunt developed this case in an influential book *(The Wars of the Iroquois)* published in 1940, and the anthropologist Bruce Trigger, author of a major study of the Huron published in 1976 *(Children of the Aataentsic)* has largely supported it, as, recently, has the ethnohistorian Roland Viau in a study of war in Iroquois culture *(Enfants du néant et mangeurs d'âmes).* However, the historical geographer Conrad Heidenreich and the historian José Brandão have shown that the Iroquois were not yet dependent on European goods (except perhaps on firearms to wage war), and almost never raided to obtain furs. The Iroquois were still motivated, they argue, by the honour and prestige traditionally attached to warfare, and they sought to defend their traditional hunting territories (important for game as much as for furs), bring their Iroquoian neighbours into the Iroquois League, and use captives to rebuild their depleted populations. In many Iroquois villages by the 1650s, more than half the villagers were Iroquois by adoption. With an imbalance of weaponry in their favour and a weak and divided enemy leadership, they were in a position to achieve these ends. Essentially, Heidenreich and Brandão argue that, far from adopting practices associated with European markets, the Iroquois were traditionalists seeking in changing circumstances to maintain their values, territories, and (with captured peoples) populations. This may be the dominant current understanding of the causes of these horrific wars, which killed or maimed so many, forced huge adjustments on survivors, and drew French traders away from the lower St. Lawrence and deep into the continental interior.

In the aftermath of the Iroquois wars, most refugees were located in a triangle of land south of Lake Superior and west of Lake Michigan (Map 4.2). There, the Iroquois harassed them from the east, while the Dakota Sioux, on whose hunting territory they were now impinging, began attacking from the west. People concentrated for safety in patches of dense settlement – some twenty thousand in the villages around Green Bay (Wisconsin) alone. In these villages were displaced, mixed populations with, often, little more in common than their displacement. Fear held them together. Culturally and politically, lives were in flux, circumstances precarious. Moreover, defensive concentrations of people created ecological problems. All the refugee centres were at sites adjacent to major fisheries and to land suitable for corn cultivation. But corn in these settlements was grown at the climatic margin, and fisheries were pushed to their capacities. One or other frequently failed. Game animals within any reasonable range of these settlements were hunted out. People were caught between the conflicting spatial pressures of war (concentration) and famine (dispersion). Concentration and malnutrition created conditions ripe for epidemic diseases – smallpox, measles, and others that cannot now be identified. Historian Richard White considers that these refugee settlements comprised "a desperate world," "a world of horrors."

For several years the Iroquois wars completely disrupted the fur trade and pushed the tiny colony of Canada to the brink of ruin. The trade resumed, hesitantly, only in 1654 after the French concluded a shaky peace with the Iroquois, and 120 Native traders from the refugee settlement west of Lake Michigan arrived at Montreal. They wanted muskets, powder, and shot. When they left, the governor allowed a French trader, Chouart des Groseilliers, to accompany them – the first French trader permitted west of Montreal. After two winters in the refugee settlements, Groseilliers returned to Montreal in 1656 with a large contingent of Native traders and favourable reports of the trading potential around the western Great Lakes. Some ninety Native canoes arrived in Montreal the following year, but in 1658 the peace with the Iroquois collapsed and Iroquois raids resumed into the Ottawa Valley and to the margins of Canada. In 1660 an Iroquois war party killed Dollard des Ormeaux, commander of the garrison at Montreal, and sixteen men on the Ottawa River near Montreal. In these perilous circumstances, the fur trade was again reduced to a trickle, although in 1659 a few Mississauga (eastern Ojibwa) got through to Montreal. When they left, Groseilliers and his brother-in-law Pierre Esprit Radisson slipped away with them. Over the next year Radisson and Groseilliers explored the south shore of Lake Superior and beyond, probably to the Mississippi, entered into alliances with Native groups, and gained some sense of the vast fur-bearing territories west and north of Lake Superior. Unlike the Jesuits, who sought to remake Native cultures, they adopted many Native ways and traded, as historian Martin Fournier has shown, within Native protocols. They returned to Montreal accompanied by many canoes and a wealth of furs, for which, as this trade was illegal, Groseilliers was briefly imprisoned. However, Radisson and Groseilliers had identified a sizable commercial opportunity, and illegal French traders (coureurs de bois) backed by merchants in Montreal increasingly operated in the interior. By the late 1660s, after the French had forced another peace on the Iroquois (this time by sending a regiment of six hundred soldiers – the Carignan-Salières – to burn the Mohawk villages), there may have been one or two hundred coureurs de bois around and beyond the western Great Lakes, most of them trading out of huts. The still official policy of allowing trade only along the lower St. Lawrence and of forbidding French traders to travel inland – reiterated in France by Jean Baptiste Colbert, Louis XIV's powerful intendant – had collapsed in practice.

The Jesuits also heeded Radisson and Groseilliers' discoveries, and in the early 1660s again began to establish missions. Each was much smaller, however, than the expensive, failed Huron missions, usually just a priest and servants. By 1670 there were three missions around the western Great Lakes, all in established refugee centres (Map 4.3). In this year a trading post, Fort de la Baie-des-Puants, was built on the west shore of Lake Michigan at Green Bay, the first such post west of the lower St. Lawrence. Many

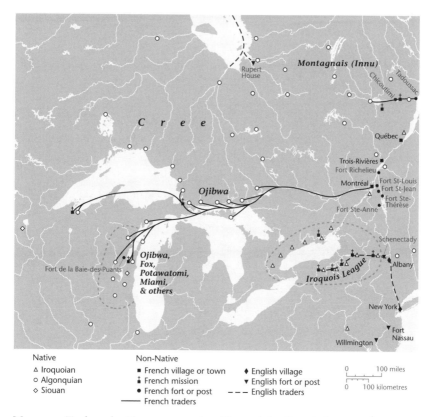

MAP 4.3   Trade and settlement around and beyond the Great Lakes, 1670 | Adapted from C. Heidenreich, in Harris and Matthews, *Historical Atlas of Canada,* vol. 1, plate 38.

of the Ojibwa, previously scattered south of Lake Superior, returned to their former territories north of Lake Huron after peace was secured with the Iroquois.

In these years, the Native response to missionaries and fur traders seems to have been essentially pragmatic: both were useful for specific purposes. The missionaries were welcome if they could heal, win battles, and secure food supplies. When they could not, support for them ebbed. In the politics of conversion, if Christ rather than a Manitou brought the sturgeon, then, when the sturgeon failed, so had Christ. It was always risky, as Richard White has noted, to link the power of Christ to the mating habits of a large fish. Essentially, he suggests, the Jesuits found themselves in a world where Christ and God were becoming Manitous. French fur traders found that the refugees' basic needs were for food and defence, and that they would hunt beaver to trade only if these needs were supported. They undertook the long journey to Montreal when food supplies were ample and there was little threat of Iroquois raids. The most effective inducement to trade was the threat that, if refugee traders did not supply beaver skins, the French would take their trade elsewhere, leaving the refugee villages, deprived of muskets, powder, and shot, defenceless against the Iroquois and Sioux. In making this claim, the French began to reposition the fur trade within a military alliance, which from the perspective of the refugee peoples around the western Great Lakes was a major reason for trade. In 1670 they were at war with the Dakota Sioux across a broad front from Lake Superior to the Illinois country southwest of Lake Michigan. As in Huronia some twenty years before, French arms had become essential to their survival.

CONTINENTAL GEOPOLITICS, 1670-1713

Rebuffed by the French, Radisson and Groseilliers took their vision of the fur potential of the lands north and west of Lake Superior to Boston, and eventually to London where they told the Stuart court of Charles II that the northern fur trade could be exploited at great profit through Hudson Bay. Well before this date, English explorers had mapped the circumference of the Bay and the route to it (Chapter 2), and in the late seventeenth century English commercial and geopolitical theorizing stressed the importance of balancing northern and southern territories and economies. A probing voyage to Hudson Bay in 1668 returned handsome profits, and in 1670 the Hudson's Bay Company, backed by some of the most powerful men in Restoration England, received a royal charter for the "sole Trade and Commerce" of all the lands draining into Hudson Bay. The new company opened three posts at the bottom of James Bay in the 1670s (Rupert House, Moose Factory, and Fort Albany) and a post on Hudson Bay at the mouth of the Hayes River (York Factory) in 1682. Immediately, Cree in the hinterlands of these posts began trading there, as, at Fort Albany and York Factory, did Assiniboine traders from well south and west of Lake Winnipeg.

This English presence to the north, coupled with the southward drain of furs to the better prices offered by English merchants at Albany on the Hudson River, forced the French fur trade inland. Even the governor, Louis

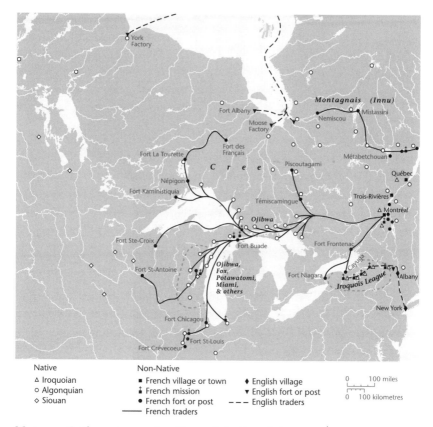

MAP 4.4   Settlement around and beyond the Great Lakes, 1685 | Adapted from
C. Heidenreich, in Harris and Matthews, *Historical Atlas of Canada*, vol. 1, plate 38.

de Buade, comte de Frontenac, established two illegal posts on Lake Ontario in the 1670s and authorized the explorations of his favourite, the cavalier de la Salle, which would lead to the creation of several posts west of Lake Michigan. Officials in Canada estimated that as many as three hundred coureurs de bois were in the west by the late 1670s, all of them operating illegally and many trading with the English. Recognizing that this interior trade could not be stopped, Intendant Colbert finally legalized it in 1681, in so doing pardoning the coureurs de bois and instituting a system of trading permits *(congés)*. Henceforth, twenty congés, each of which entitled its holder to take a canoe-load of trade goods into the interior, would be issued each year. Effects of the opening of the interior to legal trade and the introduction of the congé system were almost immediate: a rapid increase in the number of fur posts (Map 4.4), the end of the

Montreal fur fairs and the emergence of major entrepôts in the interior to replace them, the beginning of an oversupply of beaver, and even (to increase the value of a congé) the construction of larger canoes.

After fifteen years of relative peace, the Iroquois wars resumed just as Colbert's policies were being put into effect. In the early 1680s, the Iroquois encroached on Miami and Illinois hunting territories south of Lake Michigan, and fighting broke out there. The Miami and Illinois were French allies, yet the French were unable to assist them. French attempts to appease the Iroquois with presents failed, an Iroquois war party pillaged Fort Frontenac on Lake Ontario, and the French were forced into an ignominious agreement to abandon the Miami and Illinois. The French-Native alliance, a bulwark of the French defence against both Iroquois and English, was deeply compromised. A governor, de La Barre, was recalled, and another governor, Brisay de Denonville, was sent out with five hundred troops to subdue the Iroquois. His first action, however, was northward. In the spring of 1686 he sent 105 men – French soldiers and Canadians – overland from Montreal to take the English posts on James Bay. It is a measure of the growing Canadian experience with inland travel that this apparently impossible expedition succeeded: the three posts were captured and fifty thousand prime beaver skins taken. The next year, de Denonville led a mixed force of French troops, Canadian militia, and Natives recuperated into the French alliance against the Seneca, a member of the Iroquois League, and succeeded in burning villages and cornfields. In 1689, when the Iroquois responded with devastating raids against the French settlements near Montreal, France and England were at war – war that would last for most of the next twenty-four years (the War of the League of Augsburg, 1689-97; the War of the Spanish Succession, 1701-13) and would include a transatlantic struggle to control the continental interior of North America.

There, in the 1690s, the French had the better of it. Canadian militia and Native allies raided frontier settlements in the English colonies, and weather and French troops held off counterattacks by land and sea. The French-Native alliance finally overcame the Iroquois after raids in 1693 and 1696 destroyed the villages of the Mohawk, Onondaga, and Oneida. When, the next year, France and England signed what proved a temporary peace and the English abandoned the Iroquois, they were a spent force. In 1701 they and more than thirty other Native nations came to Montreal to

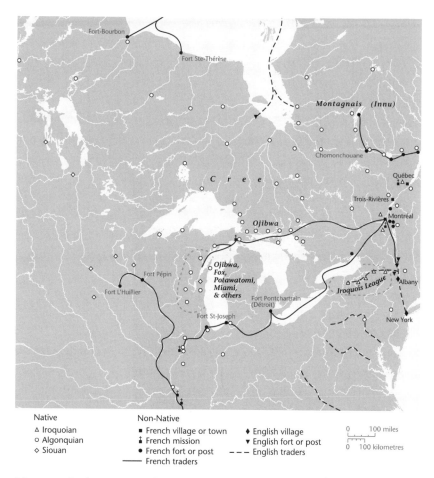

MAP 4.5   Settlement around and beyond the Great Lakes, 1701 | Adapted from C. Heidenreich, in Harris and Matthews, *Historical Atlas of Canada,* vol. 1, plate 39.

negotiate peace. In the ensuing treaty the Iroquois gave up claims to western land and agreed to remain neutral in any future conflict between the French and English. For the first time in almost a century, Canada's southern flank was relatively secure.

At the end of the seventeenth century, with the English almost eliminated from Hudson Bay and the Iroquois no longer threatening, the French were in position to feel confident of their hold on the continental interior. This, plus an oversupply of beaver, the expenses of warfare, and the urgings of the Jesuits, led the Crown to the decision, late in 1696, to close most of the interior posts. The old spatial model of trade was to be re-established.

Native traders were again to come to Montreal – a policy that infuriated fur merchants in Montreal and many Native traders, some of whom said that their father, Onontio (the governor in Quebec), had abandoned them and that they would never trade with the French again. It also left some two hundred coureurs de bois in the interior illegally. However, the Crown persisted. The ban on interior trading had become situated within a continental geopolitical strategy: to build forts on the Gulf of Mexico, establish a chain of garrisoned forts and encourage the opening of missions in the huge reach of land between the Gulf of Mexico and the Great Lakes, extend the French-Native alliance throughout this territory, and, in doing all of this, contain the English east of the Appalachians. Map 4.5 shows the results of these policies at the beginning of the eighteenth century. Detroit, established in 1701, was intended to be one of the strong points in the chain between Canada and the mouth of the Mississippi.

What the French had created, however, was a vacuum in the continental interior, which English influences began to fill. The coureurs de bois could now obtain trade goods from the lower Mississippi and, cut off from Canada, increasingly traded with the English. The founding of Detroit was probably a mistake as it drew Native groups southward towards easier contact with the Iroquois and the English traders who were beginning to infiltrate the Ohio Valley. The demand that Native traders make the long trip to Montreal, coupled, as the French dealt with a glut of beaver skins, with efforts to reduce the price of furs, strained the French alliance to the breaking point. Conditions at Detroit were particularly turbulent. In 1712, fighting erupted there between the Fox and a group of Ottawa-Potawatomi; when the French sided with the latter, they found themselves at war with the Fox. The interior was not peaceful, the French were not in control, and the fur trade was slipping out of their hands. The policy of withdrawing traders from the west and of containing English expansion by creating a buffer of garrisoned posts, missions, and a French-Native alliance was failing. In these circumstances, the Treaty of Utrecht of 1713, which ended the War of the Spanish Succession, was a final straw. It awarded the lands around Hudson Bay to the English ("British" after the 1707 Act of Union between England and Scotland), gave them "dominion" over the Iroquois, and declared the eastern Great Lakes and Ohio Valley a free trade zone. Had there been any doubt before, it was now abundantly clear to officials in both Canada and France that the geopolitics of the previous fifteen

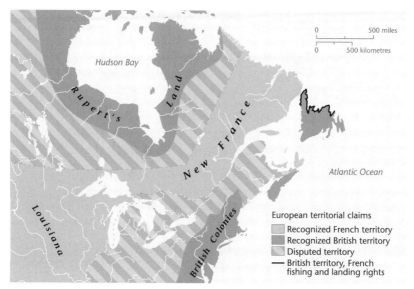

MAP 4.6   French and British territorial claims after the Treaty of Utrecht | After C. Heidenreich, in Harris and Matthews, *Historical Atlas of Canada*, vol. 1, plate 40.

years could not be sustained. In pinching New France between defined British positions east and north, the Treaty of Utrecht left France with little option but to occupy the interior aggressively so as to resolve on the ground the control of a vast territory on which radically different British and French claims were now superimposed (Map 4.6). Although the Treaty of Utrecht called for a joint commission to resolve these differences, it met belatedly and achieved nothing.

THE FUR TRADE IN NATIVE SPACE, 1713-50

After the Treaty of Utrecht, the French Crown lifted the ban on interior trade, and traders from Canada reoccupied the interior. Within a few years, they re-established former posts and then moved into new territory beyond. By the 1720s they were well established on the Missouri River; in the 1730s they built posts on the Red River south of Lake Winnipeg. When they reached the Saskatchewan River in the 1740s, they encircled most of the major drainages into Hudson Bay. Moreover, in 1717 the Crown granted a merchant company a trading monopoly on the lower Mississippi, in return for which it was to establish a colony, Louisiana, where, the next year, the company founded New Orleans. At about the same time, French agricultural settlement began south of Lake Michigan: at Vincennes on the lower Wabash River and at Kaskaskia on the upper Mississippi. For its part, the Hudson's Bay Company reoccupied all but one of its former posts, and in 1717 built a major new post, Fort Churchill, northwest of York Factory at the mouth of the Churchill River. The company explored inland but built only one inland post, Henley House, constructed in 1743 on the Albany River above Fort Albany. After Native allies of the French sacked it in 1755, HBC employees refused to return there. Overall, the company did not expand inland, because its bayside trade was highly profitable. In the south, Anglo-American traders continued to infiltrate the Ohio Valley, many of them bringing pack horses, trading for a few days, and leaving. Their first temporary posts in the upper Ohio Valley were built in the 1720s; they opened a more permanent post, Fort Oswego at the southeastern corner of Lake Ontario, in 1726. Such, briefly, was the evolving geography of Anglo-French commercial rivalry in the continental interior in the years after 1713.

Map 4.7 depicts these patterns as they were about 1750. In the north at this date, the Hudson's Bay Company operated five river-mouth posts around the perimeter of Hudson and James Bays and Henley House in the interior. The flow of goods to and from these posts reached far inland where, eventually, it met and competed with the French. The French trade flowed along a divided east-west axis from Montreal and a north-south axis on the Mississippi. A southern route from Montreal followed the St. Lawrence River and Lakes Ontario and Erie to a major entrepôt at Detroit, where trails connected it to the Mississippi watershed. A more northerly route followed the Ottawa River and Lake Huron to Michilimakinac, the northern counterpart of Detroit. From there a branch turned south into Lake Michigan and beyond to the Mississippi; another turned west to Lake Superior, and then, by many portages, to Lake Winnipeg and the Saskatchewan River beyond. Most of the Great Lakes basin, the Mississippi Valley, and much of the huge territory northwest of Lake Superior were within the orbit of the French fur trade. In the southeast, however, Anglo-American traders were active in the Ohio Valley where, in 1750, they had several posts. A French military expedition the year before to clear them out had not been successful (Chapter 5). All of this was superimposed on territory that Native people occupied and understood to be theirs.

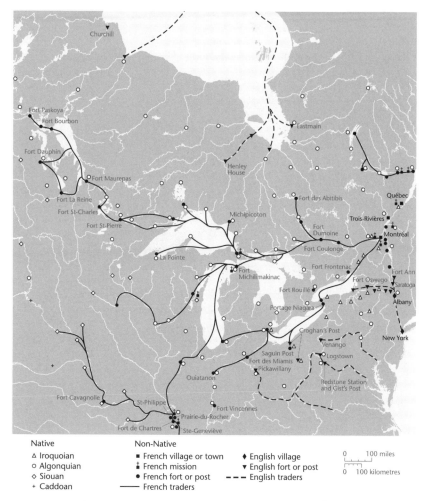

MAP 4.7 Settlement around and beyond the Great Lakes, 1750 | Adapted from C. Heidenreich, in Harris and Matthews, *Historical Atlas of Canada*, vol. 1, plate 40.

The land the fur traders actually controlled was, in fact, severely limited, hardly extending beyond the palisades of their forts. The forts were defensive sites as well as loci of trade. Many were garrisoned. Cannon stood at embrasures in the walls, gates were barred by night (and often by day), and watches were posted. There was a rigid hierarchy of command. There was often a central parade ground with buildings ordered around it. The forts have been likened to military outposts or even, in the rigidity of their discipline and the isolation of their "crews," to ships at sea. The historian

Jennifer Brown, writing about the HBC "factories" or "houses," as they were often known, suggests that over the years they acquired many of the characteristics of large English households in which the householder and his family, servants, and apprentices lived in sharply stratified proximity. All these analogies emphasize the fact that the forts were loci of external power. They were also sites of hybridity, partly because the men employed there often came from diverse cultural backgrounds, but principally because Native women, who provided sexual companionship, much useful labour and skills, as well as connections with Native societies beyond the walls, also lived there. The fur trade could hardly function without them. Because they were in the forts, Native as well as European languages were spoken, and the traders' involvement with the Native world went far beyond the ceremonial requirements of trade.

Away from the forts, their immersion in Native worlds only increased. Especially in the French trade and in the years when the interior trade was illegal, the coureurs de bois usually operated where there was no fort nearby. They were in Native villages, far beyond the protection of cannon and palisade, even farther from the laws and monopoly of violence associated with the state. They lived by their wits, their adaptability, and, often, the relationships with Native women that gave them a place, and eventually kin, in Native society. Many of them spoke a Native language and, when long away from the French settlements along the lower St. Lawrence, dressed and ate much as Native people did – at a time when trade goods and other external influences were altering Native ways. In these circumstances, the boundary between Native and non-Native blurred. This is Richard White's middle ground, space that was always negotiated and over which negotiation frequently collapsed. When it did, life beyond the protection of a fort was perilous. In 1684, the one year for which such data exist, Natives killed thirty-nine French traders.

Damaged as it often was, the French-Native alliance also reached into Native space and provided the political and military framework within which the French fur trade usually operated. After the Treaty of Utrecht, the British traders on Hudson Bay hardly required an alliance; their forts were militarily secure and the rivers draining into the Bay usually brought a profitable trade. The French and the Natives with whom they traded were more vulnerable commercially and militarily, and both sought the protection and security of an alliance. As it evolved, the alliance became a sort of diplomatic middle ground dependent on many Native understandings. In Native eyes, the governor in Quebec, Onontio, was the head of the alliance, and Native people were his children. A good father looked after his children: he assisted in their wars, mediated their internal disputes, covered (provided compensation for) their dead, gave generous presents, and supported them in times of particular need. When the French behaved in these ways, the alliance worked. There were indirect French precedents – in French customary law a seigneur was expected to look after his tenants as would "a good father of a family" – but the system was costly and cumbersome, and the French often tried to streamline it. Whenever they did, former Native allies turned sullen and uncooperative. Because many officials in Quebec and Paris considered that both the defence of New France and the viability of the fur trade turned on the health of the alliance, they usually managed to cobble it together. When it worked, the alliance was a presence in the village societies west of Lake Michigan and afforded some protection for French traders there.

As French traders travelled inland, and especially as the coureurs de bois established direct trading contacts in Native villages, they displaced most of the specialized Native middlemen who, before the collapse of Huronia, had linked Native hunters and trappers to the French. Although a few Native middlemen continued to trade at Montreal after 1681, and local middlemen systems must have emerged around French posts inland, the dominance of Native middlemen in the French trade diminished in direct proportion to the number of French traders in the interior. On the other hand, as the Hudson's Bay Company traded almost entirely at bayside, its connections inland depended on middlemen; in this respect its trade closely resembled by the early eighteenth century the French trade on the St. Lawrence a century earlier. In the early days of the HBC, Native traders from the grassland – Mandan from the Missouri Valley, Gros Ventre from southern Saskatchewan – had traded at the posts on Hudson Bay. By 1720, however, Cree and Assiniboine traders located between the Bay and the grassland had consolidated their position as middlemen; as they did almost no others ever reached a bayside post. These middlemen were specialized traders who used the goods they acquired for a year or two, then passed them on at large markups to more inland groups in return for furs. Historical geographer Arthur Ray has shown that the competitive disadvantage of grassland traders involved more than Cree and

Assiniboine reluctance to let them through: their access was impeded by the prohibitively long trip to the Bay, the short time (given freeze-up dates) in which it had to be accomplished, the limited cargo capacity of canoes for provisions, the difficulty of obtaining meat en route (grassland people disliked fish), and even, towards the middle of the eighteenth century, the diminished canoeing skills of increasingly equestrian peoples.

Native people sought European goods for their symbolic value, their utility, and their pleasurable and addictive qualities (tobacco and alcohol). Although they did need guns to fend off enemies so armed, little evidence indicates that they were yet dependent on other European goods. Ways employed for dozens of generations were not forgotten and could be returned to if need be. Yet, the fur trade had inserted new goods into local, consensual Native lifeworlds in which livelihoods were based on economies of multiple occupations, the acquisition of material wealth was only an encumbrance, and prestige accrued from giving rather than accumulating. In these circumstances, the social significance of goods changed, and trade itself took on new meanings. Briefly put, a market economy had fallen into un-European space where the laws of supply and demand hardly seemed to apply.

The degree to which European market principles explain Native trading practices has been debated for many years. Fundamental issues are at stake, and the matter remains unresolved, although the polar positions are now largely rejected. In a series of major studies extended over many years, Arthur Ray offers a qualified economic analysis of Native trade at Hudson Bay. In his view, Native middlemen were shrewd traders who had a fine appreciation of the quality of the goods offered to them, rejected those with minor defects, played off English and French traders against each other, and never sought to encumber trade with political-military alliances. To some extent, their trade was divided by relative shipping costs – which were higher to Montreal than to the Bay – with the more valuable furs going to the French in exchange for lighter more expensive goods, and heavier lower-value furs going to the British in exchange for heavier items such as kettles and guns. He admits, however, that European market economics do not entirely explain this trade. It was always preceded by elaborate ceremony that included the smoking of the calumet (pipe) and the exchange of presents. Otherwise, trade would not take place. Moreover, the Native demand for European durable goods was inelastic. If the price of furs rose, Native traders would reduce the supply because they acquired the goods they needed with fewer furs. Such demand inelasticity appears to have been related partly to the limited carrying capacity of canoes, but probably more to the irrelevance of material wealth to status or need in mobile hunting-fishing societies. It posed problems for European traders, however, to which their most common solution was to rely on addictive non-durables, principally tobacco and alcohol. As French and British competition intensified in the interior, both were lavishly used. The British trade, it was said, depended on Brazilian tobacco and rum, the French on brandy.

On the other hand, while observing that the French fur trade connected Native societies to the world economy, Richard White stresses its non-economic character. For him, the trade, as Native peoples understood it, was primarily about relationships and needs rather than profits; he argues that even the French, because of their dependence on the Native alliance, were drawn towards this understanding. In this view, trade took place between friends and entailed social responsibilities, particularly to satisfy needs. The more the buyer's need, the greater the seller's responsibility. Trade was framed in terms of gifts, and gift goods were ritual as well as utilitarian objects that flowed through social channels, incurred reciprocal obligations, and created bonds between societies. They bought influence and prestige, and generated respect. In this conception of trade, the value of goods was customary. It did not change. If the French gave more, Onontio, the governor in Quebec, was shown to be a kind and generous father, but if he gave less the alliance would shudder. Onontio no longer loved his Indian children. It is possible of course that, as the fur trade developed differently in varying contexts, each of these analyses could be correct in different circumstances.

However Native people responded to it, the fur trade had introduced the world economy to the continental interior. It also introduced infectious diseases, and its trade routes became vectors of disease diffusion. In the mid- to late seventeenth century, smallpox, measles, and probably influenza and other infectious diseases circulated among the refugees west of Lake Michigan, but at this time may not have spread farther inland. Smallpox was certainly at York Factory in 1720, brought by ship. Its more widespread occurrence, as historical geographer Paul Hackett has shown, was in 1737-38, when it broke out in Boston, spread to the settlements along the lower St. Lawrence, and then entered the fur trade. Its expression in the northern interior was patchy, but it is known to have been along the waterways between Lake Superior and Lake Winnipeg, around much of Lake Winnipeg, and on the Hayes River at York Factory – all routes of the fur trade. Through much of this trajectory it was a virgin-soil epidemic.

The horse was another introduction, this one from the south and unconnected with the fur trade. Horses were in Santa Fe (New Mexico) by 1600, where they had been introduced from Mexico City. As horse stealing became an art, they spread northward, reaching the headwaters of the Missouri, Shoshone territory, by approximately 1720. Horses conferred a huge military advantage, of which, by the 1740s, the Shoshone were taking full if short-lived advantage. They were raiding northward, pushing the Blackfoot and Gros Ventre, peoples of the northwestern plains, towards the North Saskatchewan River. However, they could not prevent horses from reaching their enemies who, from both the St. Lawrence and Hudson Bay, began to be supplied with muskets, to which the Shoshone had little access. With these introductions, the balance of power shifted towards the Blackfoot and Gros Ventre.

As the early Iroquois wars had shown so dramatically, the differential possession of firearms disrupted former balances of power, often with lethal consequences. The carnage and displacements in southern Ontario in the 1640s would be approximately repeated as firearms diffused westward. As long, for example, as the Cree and Assiniboine controlled the flow of arms into the interior, their relative power was greatly enhanced. In the north, intense fighting erupted along the Cree-Chipewyan border. James Knight, a Hudson's Bay Company trader, reported that six thousand men, mostly Chipewyan, had been killed. Undoubtedly Knight exaggerated, but it is clear that the military situation stabilized only after 1717 when, with the establishment of Fort Churchill, the Chipewyan gained direct access to firearms. In the south, fighting erupted between the Assiniboine and the Dakota Sioux. In this case, the French supported the Sioux; when the French held York Factory but did not restock it with firearms for several years, the Assiniboine's supply of arms failed and the Sioux massacred them. A trader suggested that they had lost the ability to defend themselves with bows and arrows. In the southwest, the Assiniboine warred with the Gros Ventre, Blood, and Blackfoot; in the northwest, the

Cree forced their way into Beaver territory. All this fighting around a Cree-Assiniboine perimeter ringed with bloodshed was encouraged and intensified by the differential introduction of firearms.

Displacements and relocations of people were both causes and effects of warfare, as the migrations of refugee Huron, Petun, Ojibwa, and others to the west of Lake Michigan had shown. Displaced themselves by warfare, these refugee peoples endured the consequences of their relocation – long wars with the Fox and Dakota Sioux. Throughout the continental interior, warfare and disease shifted the location of Native groups, and in so doing increasing the instability of changing lifeworlds. Depopulated territories were reoccupied by others, as when, early in the eighteenth century, eastern Ojibwa (Algonquian speakers) moved into Upper Canada (Chapter 9). Almost everywhere, tribal territories shifted. Map 4.8 shows the changing distributions of the peoples of the northern continental interior between 1720 and 1760. The Assiniboine and Cree had expanded slightly westward, while losing territory southeast of Lake Winnipeg to the western Ojibwa, who occupied the relative vacuum created by the Sioux wars and smallpox. In the north, the Chipewyan, now well armed, advanced some way into Cree territory.

At a much more local scale, the fur trade encouraged economic specialization. Many Native economies now revolved around it. The Cree bands that had settled near the HBC posts on the Bay (the Homeguard Cree) lived off the provisioning trade and depended on firearms, cloth, and leather obtained at the posts. Other Cree, and some of the Assiniboine, had become specialized traders. The seasonal rounds of most of those who hunted and trapped had been adjusted to allow more time to take

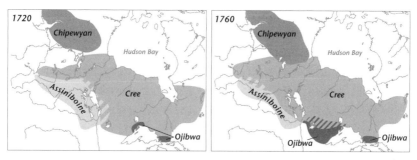

MAP 4.8   Distribution of Native groups northwest of the Great Lakes, 1720-60
After A.J. Ray, in Harris and Matthews, *Historical Atlas of Canada,* vol. 1, plate 60.

beaver and marten, the principal trade furs. As Native economies focused on these animals, their relationship with them and with the land changed. Hunters became more territorial, defending their right to take these animals in their territories and to exclude other hunters. They could still hunt there for food, but not for the animals that entered the fur trade.

Finally, it needs to be remembered that, for all of these changes, in 1750 the continental interior remained Native space within which British and French trading posts were pinpoints of European control. Yet, clearly, the lives and livelihoods of all the Native peoples of the continental interior had been deeply affected by the fur trade. It was not so much that European trade goods, or even the fur trade itself, had transformed Native ways, as that the fur trade had introduced a set of demographic, geopolitical, cultural, and economic changes that, in sum, drastically recontextualized Native life. Populations plummeted and in some cases recovered. Peoples were relocated. Balances of power shifted; warfare became more intense. Economies became more specialized. Talk of a Christian God was in the air. Many new goods were available, and although they were invested with Native meanings, they also carried voices from the distant societies in which they had been made. The overriding picture is of tumult and change, of peoples and places in flux. Yet the fur traders, French and British, had come to extract commodities, not to acquire land, and if European states claimed vast stretches of land, most of which no European had ever seen, these were abstract geopolitical visions entertained from afar. Within the continent, and for all the changes in their lives and livelihoods, Native peoples remained the owners and occupiers of the land.

BIBLIOGRAPHY

Again, the place to start is an intricate series of maps by Conrad Heidenreich depicting changing patterns of settlement, trade, and warfare around and beyond the Great Lakes basin, in *Historical Atlas of Canada,* vol. 1, *From the Beginning to 1800,* ed. R. Cole Harris, cart. Geoffrey J. Matthews (Toronto: University of Toronto Press, 1987), plates 35 and 37-41. See also "Inland Expansion," the essay that introduces this section of the atlas, and on French exploration, Conrad Heidenreich, "Early French Exploration in the North American Interior," in J.L. Allen, ed., *North American Exploration,* vol. 2, *A Continent Defined* (Lincoln and London: University of Nebraska

Press, 1997), 65-148; and W.J. Eccles, "French Exploration in North America, 1700-1800," in ibid., 149-202.

On the Iroquois wars and the dispersion of the Huron, consult the following: Bruce G. Trigger, *Children of the Aataentsic: A History of the Huron People to 1660* (Montreal, Kingston, and London: McGill-Queen's University Press, 1976). Bruce G. Trigger and Gordon M. Day, "Southern Algonquian Middlemen: Algonquin, Nipissing, and Ottawa, 1550-1780," in Edward S. Rogers and Donald B. Smith, eds., *Aboriginal Ontario: Historical Perspectives on the First Nations* (Toronto and Oxford: Dundurn Press, 1994), 64-77. Conrad E. Heidenreich, "History of the St. Lawrence-Great Lakes Area to A.D. 1650," in Chris Ellis and Neal Ferris, eds., *The Archaeology of Southern Ontario to A.D. 1650*, Occasional Publication of the London Chapter, Ontario Archaeological Society No. 5 (London: Ontario Archaeological Society, 1990), 475-95. José António Brandão, *"Your Fyre Shall Burn No More": Iroquois Policy toward New France and Its Native Allies to 1701* (Lincoln and London: University of Nebraska Press, 1997). Roland Viau, *Enfants du néant et mangeurs d'âmes: Guerre, culture et société en Iroquoisie ancienne* (Montreal: Boréal, 1997). The different positions on the Iroquois wars, discussed above, are represented in this literature.

On the refugee populations west of Lake Michigan and their relationships with the fur trade and the French alliance, the chapter depends on Richard White's commanding analysis in *The Middle Ground: Indians, Empires, and Republics in the Great Lakes Region, 1650-1815* (Cambridge: Cambridge University Press, 1991). On Radisson and Groseilliers in the Lake Superior region in the 1650s, see Martin Fournier, "Le Voyage de Radisson et des Groseilliers au Lac Supérieur, 1659-1660; un événement marquant dans la consolidation des relations Franco-Amérindiennes," *Revue d'histoire de l'Amérique française* 52, 2 (1998): 159-87. Still important on French policy in the region is W.J. Eccles, *Canada under Louis XIV, 1663-1701* (Toronto: McClelland and Stewart, 1964).

The chapter's analysis of Native relations with the Hudson's Bay Company relies largely on writings of Arthur Ray, namely, *Indians in the Fur Trade: Their Role as Trappers, Hunters, and Middlemen in the Lands Southwest of Hudson Bay, 1660-1870* (1974; repr. with a new introduction, Toronto: University of Toronto Press, 1998); "Indians as Consumers in the Eighteenth Century," in Carol M. Judd and Arthur J. Ray, eds., *Old Trails and New Directions: Papers of the Third North American Fur Trade Conference* (Toronto: University of Toronto Press, 1980), 255-68; "Buying and Selling Hudson's Bay Company Furs in the Eighteenth Century," in Duncan Cameron, ed., *Explorations in Canadian Economic History in Honour of Irene M. Spry* (Ottawa: University of Ottawa Press, 1985), 95-115; and "Some Thoughts about the Reasons for Spatial Dynamism in the Early Fur Trade, 1580-1800," in Henry Epp, ed., *Three Hundred Years: Henry Kelsey's "Indian Country of Good Report"* (Regina: Canadian Plains Research Center, 1993), 113-23. For Jennifer Brown's discussion of post society, consult *Strangers in Blood: Fur Trade Company Families in Indian Country* (Vancouver: UBC Press, 1980).

For the Shoshone and the geopolitical advantages of the horse, refer to Theodore Binnema, *Common and Contested Ground: A Human and Environmental History of the Northwestern Plains* (Norman: University of Oklahoma Press, 2001). On the provenance and routes of the early epidemics, see Paul Hackett, *A Very Remarkable Sickness: Epidemics in the Petit Nord, 1670 to 1846* (Winnipeg: University of Manitoba Press, 2002).

5
Creating and Bounding British North America

While French settlement expanded along the lower St. Lawrence and around the Bay of Fundy and two fur trades reached into the continental interior, England and France contended for North American dominance. At its height, the French empire in North America comprised, cartographically, a vast crescent of land extending from Île Royale (Cape Breton Island), at an eastern corner of the Gulf of St. Lawrence, through the Great Lakes to the Gulf of Mexico (Map 5.1). After France lost this position during the Seven Years' War and Britain lost her thirteen seaboard colonies during the American Revolution, the geopolitical struggle resumed, with a more northerly focus and less intensity, between the United States and Britain. By 1846, after years of geopolitical manoeuvring and some fighting, the present border between Canada and the United States was established. A political space had been defined, British North America, within which modern Canada would come to be. There was nothing preordained about this space – the great French geographer Elisée Reclus considered it a geographical absurdity. It was a historically created political geography that, having been brought into being, profoundly affected the societies and economies within it.

CREATING BRITISH NORTH AMERICA
In 1750 some ten thousand people of French ancestry lived in Acadia (most of them in British territory), barely sixty thousand such people resided in Canada, perhaps two thousand in Louisiana, and another thousand (settlers, traders, and soldiers) in the vast territory between. In the thirteen British colonies along the Atlantic seaboard, the population was some

MAP 5.1   France in North America, c. 1750 | Adapted from *Historical Atlas of Canada*, vol. 1, *From the Beginning to 1800*, ed. R. Cole Harris, cart. Geoffrey J. Matthews (Toronto: University of Toronto Press, 1987), plates 25, 30, and 40.

thirty times greater. Moreover, after the Treaty of Utrecht (1713), by the terms of which France ceded Newfoundland, Acadia, and the lands around Hudson Bay to Britain, the Atlantic entry to New France was closely bounded. British claims were established to Hudson Bay, the principal island at the entrance to the Gulf of St. Lawrence, and the whole Atlantic coast of North America between Cape Breton Island and Florida. Canada was accessible through narrow straits overlooked by land ceded to Britain, possessor of the most powerful navy on the North Atlantic. Moreover, on the ground rather than on European maps, most of the French empire in North America was Native territory over which French control was disputed and tenuous.

Anchoring the French position in North America were, towards its seaward extremities, garrisoned forts and towns, and, deep in the continental interior, a shifting and always somewhat precarious alliance with Native groups. Louisbourg, the massive fortress town on Île Royale that an Anglo-American force captured in 1745 and the British government returned in 1748, was the strong point in the northeast. Quebec and Montreal, on the lower St. Lawrence, were also walled and garrisoned towns, foci of imperial defence, as farther inland were the large, well-garrisoned forts at Detroit and Michilimakinac. Far to the south, the town of New Orleans and Forts Natchez and Arkansas were their smaller counterparts on the Mississippi. Militarily important as these places were, many officials in Canada considered that the French alliance with Native groups around the western Great Lakes was the key to the defence of New France. Pitting the French and their Native allies against the Iroquois and the British, it provided, when it worked, a bulwark against English expansion into the Ohio Valley and southern Great Lakes. As historian Richard White has shown, the alliance operated in a middle ground between French and Native, binding the village world of Native society and the ambitions of imperial France. Native members of the alliance conceptualized the governor in Quebec – Onontio – as the father of his Indian children, a mediator of their disputes, a provider of presents and trade goods at a reasonable and reliable price, and a participant in their wars. The alliance was always fragile, however, and never drew all the Native groups that had collected west and south of Lake Michigan into its orbit.

By the mid-eighteenth century, a hundred years after the devastating Iroquois wars that had depopulated the eastern Great Lakes basin (Chapter 4), a variety of Native peoples had repopulated the Ohio Valley. Most of them, hostile to the French alliance, traded with the English. At the same time, some of the seaboard colonies, most notably Virginia, claimed trans-Appalachian territory. In 1749, the governor in Quebec (de La Galissonière), convinced that the Ohio country was the key to the French position in North America, sent a small army to subdue the region and bury lead plates to mark this boundary of New France. Neither was effective. More was needed, and as both the French and the British sent troops into the area, the military engagements began that anticipated the Seven Years' War between France and Britain (1756-63) and led to the fall of New France.

Initially, the French were the more successful. In 1752, their Native allies captured Fort Pickawillany, the most westerly of the British forts in the Ohio Valley. The next year two thousand French troops invaded the Ohio country and built four forts there. In 1754 French soldiers defeated George Washington and four hundred American troops at Fort Necessity; the following year Native warriors and a few French soldiers and Canadian militiamen routed General Braddock and some fifteen hundred British and American soldiers near Fort Duquesne (Fort Pitt, later Pittsburgh). In so doing, the French virtually eliminated the British from the Ohio Valley and revitalized the French-Native alliance. However, the Native peoples of the Ohio Valley viewed the alliance primarily as a means of protecting their land, which they now perceived to be threatened by settlers and land claims originating in the British colonies. Some of them sought to use the French to defeat the British, after which they would drive out the French. The French alliance itself, a means rather than an end, was expendable. In 1758, when British ships blocked the entrance to the Gulf of St. Lawrence and reduced the French supply of trade goods, disgruntled Native leaders turned to the British who, in a peace treaty signed at Easton, Pennsylvania, in October 1758, agreed to renounce all claims to lands west of the Appalachians. Assuming that their land was protected, the former Native allies of the French laid down their arms, leaving the French exposed and vulnerable. In November, a massive British force, almost seven thousand strong, captured Fort Duquesne, now defended by only three hundred French troops. Without Native allies, the French were forced to withdraw from the Ohio Valley.

In the east, British successes came earlier. In 1749 the British established Halifax, a major garrison town built to counter Louisbourg after its return to the French the year before, and brought in several thousand Protestant settlers from the British Isles or the Rhineland to strengthen their hold on a colony inhabited largely by French-speaking Catholics whose loyalty they had long suspected. In 1755 more than two thousand American militia plus a few British troops captured Fort Beauséjour at the northern end of the Bay of Fundy. In the same year, and without consulting London, colonial British officials began the deportation of the Acadians. British shipping blocked the mouth of the Bay of Fundy and the Acadians were detained – at Grand-Pré they were ordered into their churches – and shipped south to the British colonies. Over the next several years, most of those who had escaped the first roundup were pursued, captured, and shipped away. Their going sundered families and emptied the marshlands. A sizable enclave of French settlement in North America was obliterated, an instance of total war that recast the human geography of the region.

In the spring of 1758, a massive British deployment of ships and men converged on the Gulf of St. Lawrence. Louisbourg fell in July 1758, after a six-seek siege mounted by thirty-nine warships and thirteen thousand troops. Six weeks was the time that the marquis de Vauban, the French military engineer who designed Louisbourg, had calculated that one of his forts could withstand a sustained, skilful assault. Quebec fell the next year after a summer-long bombardment and a battle outside the walls on hummocky terrain known as the Plains of Abraham. Military historians judge that the British general, Wolfe, made a grave tactical error in drawing up his troops on the Plains of Abraham, that the French general, Montcalm, erred in attacking them there, and that, with an elite French force from Montreal only two hours' march away, the commandant in Quebec, de Ramezay, surrendered the city too quickly. For all these compounded errors, the British had taken Quebec, and when British ships arrived the following spring, the capture was confirmed. In early September 1760, as seventeen thousand British troops approached Montreal, its governor, Rigaud de Vaudreuil, had no choice but to surrender. When the news reached officers in the interior, some burned and abandoned their posts. Others awaited the peace treaty that, they anticipated, would return New France to France.

However, to the dismay of many, including many former Native allies of the French, the loss was confirmed by the 1763 Treaty of Paris. France retained fishing rights in northern Newfoundland and acquired two small islands, Saint-Pierre and Miquelon, off southern Newfoundland (Map 5.2a). Otherwise, she relinquished all territory east of the Mississippi, with the exception of the town of New Orleans. In the secret Treaty of San Ildefonso the year before, she had already transferred New Orleans and all French territory west of the Mississippi to Spain. Some French officials calculated that these losses were to France's advantage because they would encourage the English colonies to revolt. Certainly, European claims to North America – superimposed on land that Native people considered

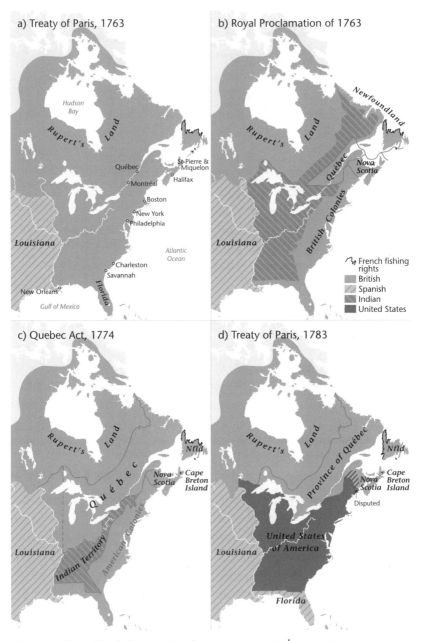

MAP 5.2   Geopolitical claims to North America, 1763-83 | After W.J. Eccles, in Harris and Matthews, *Historical Atlas of Canada*, vol. 1, plates 42 and 44.

theirs and largely controlled – had been greatly simplified: Britain held the eastern half of the continent, Spain most of the southwest, and, except for the concessions around Newfoundland, France had been eliminated.

Later in 1763, and in response to Native unrest around the southern Great lakes as Anglo-American traders, land speculators, and settlers poured into the Ohio Valley (ignoring the Treaty of Easton) and as officials in Quebec prohibited the distribution of presents (a central practice in the French-Native alliance), the British government issued a Royal Proclamation with the intent of separating Britain's eastern North American colonies from Indian lands to the west. To this end, the boundary of Canada – or, as it was known in the Royal Proclamation, the boundary of the Government of Quebec – was narrowly and hastily drawn (Map 5.2b, Map 5.3). The northern boundary was a convenient line through territory the British government knew nothing about. The southern, which followed the 45th parallel of latitude from the St. Lawrence to the height of land between the St. Lawrence and the sea as far as Chaleur Bay, bore some relationship to the contested and never precisely defined boundary between the former French position on the St. Lawrence and the English position on the Hudson. The land to the east and south of this narrow trapezoid (the present Maritime provinces) became the enlarged colony of Nova Scotia. The land to the west and south was reserved "under Our sovereignty" for the "Indians." Settlers there were to leave, prior grants and surveys were disallowed, trade could take place only under licence, and the Crown alone could purchase land. The British government did not intend to seal off the interior so much as to manage the interior trade and provide for the orderly acquisition of Native land. It intended to establish settlements around the interior posts and in the Illinois country, and to negotiate with the Iroquois for the division of the Ohio Valley although, as legal historian John Weaver has shown, British officials never prosecuted more than a handful of the speculators, squatters, and surveyors who continued to operate there. The Royal Proclamation did mean that, in British law, Canada (Quebec) had no more claim to the continental interior than did any other British colony.

However, the Royal Proclamation accorded ill with reality and did not stop a Native uprising against the British (Pontiac's "rebellion"). The St. Lawrence had been the principal eastern gateway to the continental

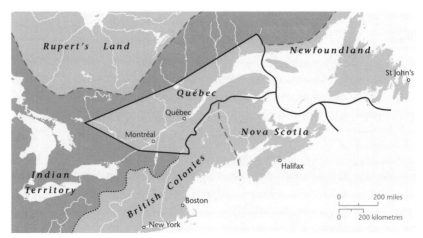

MAP 5.3   Quebec after the Royal Proclamation, 1763 | After D.G.G. Kerr, ed., *A Historical Atlas of Canada* (Toronto: Thomas Nelson and Sons, 1961), 31.

interior, and for many Native people the governor of Canada had been the father of a crucial alliance. An effect of Pontiac's uprising, during which Native warriors captured all but three of the western posts, was to force the British to adopt some of the ways of the French in the interior and to reconcile Native leaders to the reality of the British presence. The governor in Quebec, now British, was again Onontio. But if the alliance was somewhat re-established, the French settlers at Detroit and in the Illinois country were now officially in "Indian" country, beyond the reach of British law or government. At the other end of the colony, the Royal Proclamation transferred gulf fisheries that operated out of the port of Quebec to the jurisdiction of Newfoundland. Within the colony, it made no provision for Roman Catholicism or for French law, in principle preventing the ordination of clergy and invalidating almost all property rights. In practice, governors worked around a proclamation that did not fit colonial realities.

This awkward, ill-fitting proclamation was replaced by the Quebec Act in 1774. It enlarged the boundaries of Quebec in the east to include much of the gulf and Labrador, and in the west to include the Great Lakes and much of the Ohio Valley (Map 5.2c). In a sense, the settlements along the lower St. Lawrence had been reattached to the Great Lakes basin and the Illinois country, although by this date some fifty thousand American settlers lived west of the Appalachians, most of them squatters beyond the control of any government. Armed bands of Virginians and Pennsylvanians fought each other and "Indians" in the upper Ohio Valley. The Quebec Act had revised the map, creating a political space that British authority had little capacity to manage. Within Quebec, it granted Catholics "free exercise" of their religion and adopted French civil and English criminal law. The reasons for these important changes – variously interpreted as measures of remarkable tolerance, as components of a subtle politics of assimilation, or as attempts to forestall the Americans in the Ohio Valley – and their effects on French speakers in Quebec, have been long debated. Here it is sufficient to point out that the Quebec Act officially reconnected the St. Lawrence settlements to much of their traditional hinterland and incurred the wrath of American politicians, settlers, and land speculators who, coveting western land and wanting no truck with papists, considered it another of the "intolerable acts."

In 1775, early in the American Revolution, the Continental Congress authorized the invasion of Canada. A two-pronged attack, one via the Hudson and Richelieu Rivers and the other via the Kennebec and Chaudière, converged on Quebec and began a winter-long siege that was lifted only in May 1776, when the vanguard of the British fleet arrived. The Americans had expected the habitants to rally to the republican cause, whereas, after the Quebec Act, British officials anticipated the opposite. Although some habitants, particularly along the south shore below Quebec, where British troops had burned more than a thousand farms in the summer of 1759, supported and even fought for the Americans, the great majority remained neutral. In the east, American privateers raided almost all coastal settlements in Newfoundland and Nova Scotia, seizing more than two hundred ships in Nova Scotia alone. Most of the Maliseet, the Native people of the Saint John Valley, supported the revolution; the Mi'kmaq remained neutral. Many settlers in Nova Scotia, most of them recently arrived from New England, sympathized with the Americans, but British sea power, which concentrated in Halifax and increasingly controlled the coasts, secured the region. In the trans-Appalachian west, the *pays d'en haut* of the French regime, atrocities committed by American Indian-haters turned many Native groups towards the British and to an approximation of the older alliance. By 1781-82 the British and their Native allies dominated much of the pays d'en haut. Overall, however, the British had concluded that they could not win a war waged against a dispersed, hostile settler population. Following the peace negotiations of 1782-83, a newly independent nation, the United States of America, came into being. The territory draining into Hudson Bay, Newfoundland, and the old French colonies of Canada and Acadia remained British. In the starkest military terms, as historical geographer Stephen Hornsby has suggested, Britain had lost a continental war but had held colonies she could defend by sea. Thereafter, he points out, a maritime British empire expanded into the South Pacific while a continental American one expanded across a continent.

The Treaty of Paris of 1783 drew the border between British North America and the new United States of America. In Britain, political opinions regarding it had been sharply divided. Tory politicians argued to contain the United States by holding on to as much territory and as many strong points as possible, thereby, they thought, reducing American independence to a hollow achievement. Whig politicians, some of them influenced by the political economy of Adam Smith and the doctrine of free trade, argued that the American Revolution had shown colonies to be expensive liabilities, and that negotiations with the Americans should seek amity and commercial opportunity rather than territory. When the Treaty of Paris was negotiated, the Whigs were in power. British negotiators were not averse, initially, to American suggestions that in the interests of friendship and trade Britain should cede both Quebec and Nova Scotia. Eventually, there seemed reason to retain these colonies: the Loyalists could be accommodated with land, supplies of naval stores for the Royal Navy and foodstuffs for the British plantation islands in the Caribbean would be protected, and, most compelling, the St. Lawrence route to the continental interior would probably draw much of the commerce of the Illinois country and Mississippi basin. Trade, rather than territory, was the prize; to this end a preliminary agreement, signed in October 1782, gave British and American ships free, equal access to ports, harbours, and rivers anywhere in the United States or the British empire. However, such an agreement contradicted the Navigation Acts, which protected British carriers of colonial commerce, and the final draft of the Treaty of Paris protected open navigation only on the Mississippi. Other matters were left for a subsequent treaty. Bargaining for commercial rather than territorial advantage, Britain had ceded land in return for the prospect of free trade.

Map 5.2d shows the border created by these negotiations. South of the lower St. Lawrence, it followed the boundary established by the Royal

Proclamation of 1763; immediately to the west of it as far as Lake Erie, it followed the boundary established by the Quebec Act. Thereafter, it followed the middle of the Great Lakes (excluding Lake Michigan) to a point on the northwest shore of Lake Superior, and on through a named but non-existent lake on the Pigeon River through the Lake of the Woods to its northwestern corner. From there (not shown on Map 5.2d) it ran due west, hypothetically to the Mississippi (which did not extend so far north). In the east, it followed the St. Croix River from its mouth on the Bay of Fundy to its source, and then, along a line to be marked out by a commission, northward to the height of land. As it turned out, there were ambiguities at either end of this line. It was not altogether clear which river, precisely, was the St. Croix, or where it arose. The location of the border between Lower Canada, New Brunswick, and the state of Maine would not be finally settled for almost sixty years (the Webster-Ashburton Treaty of 1842). At the western end, there were the problems created by non-existent lakes and by the fact that the Mississippi River was not where it was supposed to be. These problems apart, the Treaty of Paris of 1783 established a border between British North America and the United States across approximately half a continent.

Britain had turned over most of the pays d'en haut, or as the Americans knew it, the Old North West, to the United States, and with it the sites of most of the inland posts of the Montreal fur trade, including Michilimakinac, Detroit, and Grand Portage (the point of access from Lake Superior to the northern plains), as well as the connection to the Mississippi via Lake Michigan. Fur merchants in Montreal and London, furious at the loss of trading territory and facing, they argued, the impending collapse of the fur trade, proposed a boundary running west from Lake Erie to Lake Michigan. Some officials, tuned to the ways of the alliance, urged the retention of posts until ample territory had been permanently set aside for Native people and even assured them that the king would not cede what he did not own and would never abandon his Native children. In large parts of the pays d'en haut, the British stayed at their posts. The legal writing, however, was on the wall; the Treaty of Paris of 1783 had awarded the new United States a huge inland territory – twice the territory, according to the surveyor/geographer David Thompson, that it could justly claim. It had not been kind to the fur trade, nor to the Native allies of the British. But it had protected the gateway to and the principal population centre of the old French empire in North America. In this was the abiding spatial irony of the previous twenty-five years. Britain had acquired the heart of the French position in North America while losing her own.

By the early 1790s, it had become clear that a line running west from the Lake of the Woods would not strike the Mississippi River, and, therefore, that this portion of the border needed to be renegotiated. Moreover, British traders had not vacated American territory. These matters were partially resolved by Jay's Treaty in 1794. Britain, still intent on securing the interior trade and on making Montreal rather than New Orleans the port for the upper Mississippi country, proposed a boundary from the western end of Lake Superior to the Red River (thought to flow south) or an even more southerly boundary to intersect the Mississippi south of the present city of St. Paul. The Americans accepted neither proposal. Jay's Treaty left aside the location of the boundary west of the Lake of the Woods until a joint survey established the course of the Mississippi – a survey never made. In deference to British interests in free trade, the treaty allowed traders and peltries free passage across the border of 1783 and unimpeded access to rivers and portages. However, it did not exclude the imposition of duties on imported goods, and when, about 1800, American customs officers arrived to collect them, most British traders withdrew from American territory. The British had finally quit almost all of the pays d'en haut. Their Native allies had been abandoned. Without British support, Native chiefs ceded much of the pays d'en haut to the Americans in the Treaty of Greenville and guaranteed them military reservations in the rest.

There matters sat until June 1812, when the United States, provoked by British interference with American maritime commerce, support for western Indians, and meddling in Spanish Florida and Texas, and well aware of Britain's military preoccupation with France, declared war on Great Britain. An early American objective was the annexation of what is now southwestern Ontario, where, in July, an American force invaded from the west, anticipating local support. The War of 1812 was a strange affair. New England never supported it. Settlers in British territory did not rally to the Americans, and American invasions were repulsed. Eventually, British warships controlled the sea, and the American ships Lake Erie. Early in the war, British forces captured Michilimakinac and Detroit, and later Prairie du Chien on the upper Mississippi. At the end of the war, the

Americans captured New Orleans. When the war ended late in 1814, Britain held a good deal of American territory: much of what is now Maine and upstate Michigan, almost all of what is now Wisconsin. However, by the terms of the peace treaty, signed at Ghent in December 1814, the boundaries specified in the Treaty of Paris of 1783 were restored. The duke of Wellington had argued that, in any larger sense, the United States was neither conquered nor readily conquerable. Britain was tired of war. The alliance of British and Indians in the pays d'en haut, the successor to the French-Indian alliance that began with Champlain, had collapsed for the final time, and with it the capacity of surviving Native groups to resist the expansion of American settlement. In Richard White's terms, the days of the middle ground in the pays d'en haut had come to an end.

The Treaty of Ghent referred a number of outstanding issues, including boundary problems, to commissions. One was the precise location of the boundary between Lake Superior and the Lake of the Woods, about which there would be intermittent negotiations for years and a final settlement only in 1842 (the Webster-Ashburton Treaty). Another was the boundary west of the Lake of the Woods. A century before, during the negotiations between the British and French following the Treaty of Utrecht, Britain had claimed the 49th parallel as the southwestern boundary of her territories around Hudson Bay. Many eighteenth-century maps represented this boundary. When, in 1803, the Americans purchased Louisiana from the French (to whom it had been recently retroceded by the Spanish), this northern boundary was assumed. As an American diplomat averred, it was already on the map! The British, who still believed that the Mississippi rose farther north, also favoured it, assuming that it would give their traders unimpeded access to the river. And so, in a Convention of 20 October 1818, and with remarkably little fuss, the 49th parallel was fixed as the boundary between British North America and the United States between the Lake of the Woods and the continental divide. None of the signatories of this convention had a clear idea about what, precisely, was on either side of the line they had selected. As it turned out, the headwaters of the Mississippi arose just to the south of it, the Missouri drainage basin was also to the south, and the drainage towards Hudson Bay, with the exception of part of the Red River, lay to the north. So did most of the fur posts established by the North West and Hudson's Bay Companies (Map 5.4). Historical geographer Daniel Clayton has pointed out that

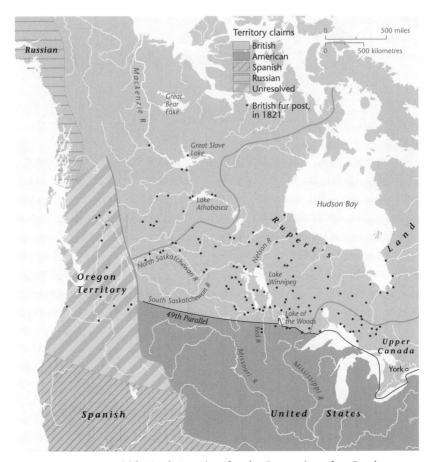

MAP 5.4   Western British North America after the Convention of 20 October
1818 | Adapted from D.W. Moodie, V.P. Lytwyn, B. Kaye, C. Heidenreich, and R. Galois,
in Harris and Matthews, *Historical Atlas of Canada*, vol. 1, plates 62 and 69.

the boundary negotiators had reduced the complexity of western exploration and settlement "to a simple set of geopolitical coordinates and precedents." And so they had. But if a single straight line were to be drawn
west across the plains, this one probably accorded better with prior experience than any other they could have chosen.

Unable to agree on a line west of the continental divide, the boundary
negotiators created the Oregon Territory, a huge space between Spanish
Mexican claims to the south and Russian to the north that would be open
to British and American traders. In 1819 the Americans concluded a treaty
with the Spanish, and in 1824 one with the Russians, that fixed the southern

and northern boundaries of the Oregon Territory at 42°N and 54°40'N respectively. Within this territory, the resolution of the boundary between the United States and British North America was left for later.

British and American diplomats unsuccessfully negotiated the matter in 1826. The Americans attached most importance to first discovery (the maritime fur trader Grey, at the mouth of the Columbia in 1792) and the natural contiguity of Oregon with inland American settlement (an early form of manifest destiny). The British emphasized scientific discovery at the behest of the Crown (Cook and Vancouver) and the fact of occupancy (Hudson's Bay Company traders and posts throughout and beyond the Columbia basin). When negotiations resumed in the early 1840s, the political temperature had risen sharply. The Oregon Trail had opened; American settlers were taking up land in the Willamette Valley. Oregon had entered the American imagination, a place of agricultural settlement, competitive markets, and individual liberty rather than, as apparently under the Hudson's Bay Company, of ossified and rapacious monopoly. All of Oregon, President Polk affirmed, rightly belonged to the United States. In Britain, feelings about the arrogant belligerence of American democracy ran high, and mutterings of war sounded on both sides of the Atlantic. But there were good reasons not to fight. The British government was preoccupied with the Irish potato famine and with bitter arguments over the Corn Laws; the American government was at war with Mexico and concerned about Britain's reaction to American expansionism. The British foreign secretary, Lord Aberdeen, promoted a secret press campaign representing the uselessness of Oregon, a place that British national honour need not defend. In the end, the two governments compromised. The Oregon Treaty of 1846 extended the border along the 49th parallel to the Pacific and assigned Vancouver Island to Britain. Like the border settlement through the Great Lakes in 1783, this one also undermined the established spatial logic of the fur trade. Again fur traders protested vehemently.

THE SPACE MARKED OUT BY AN ANTECEDENT BOUNDARY

In these ways, a long geopolitical process had reached a measure of resolution. French claims to North America had been virtually eliminated, the Spanish claim confined to the southwest, and Britain and the United States had divided most of the continent between them. Two transcontinental political spaces – the United States of America and British North America – had been created, and would endure. But did the space that had become British North America, and eventually became Canada, make any historical-geographical sense? As noted above, Elisée Reclus thought not, a judgment that reflected both his assessment of a long-antecedent boundary (one that preceded the emergence of the society that would justify it) and his suspicion, as an anarchist, of large states. Somewhat similarly, Goldwin Smith, Oxford-educated classicist, journalist, and influential Toronto intellectual at the end of the nineteenth century, held that British North America contradicted the north-south grain of the continent and the unity of the Anglo-Saxon race. He favoured a continental union with the United States. On the other hand, in the 1930s Harold Innis maintained that Canada had grown out of the fur trade – a northern staple trade – anchored in the Canadian Shield and in the transportation routes that spread a French, then a British, presence across much of a continent.

These are both arguable propositions. For years after the border was finally drawn, most people in British North America lived within local frames of reference – a village, a parish, a valley, at most a colony – in relation to which British North America was a distant abstraction. For those close to the border, as most were, social and economic relations were usually closer with adjacent American settlements than with remote, largely unknown, and culturally different parts of British North America. For many of them, the grain of the land and of social and economic interaction ran north-south. On the other hand, from the very beginning of the French presence on the St. Lawrence, Champlain's alliance with the Huron and Algonquin pointed the French fur trade towards the northwest, and this edge of a much broader trade survived, barely, the border settlement of 1783. Eventually, the fur trade spread a British presence across a continent, linked this trading territory to London and empire, and provided some check to American continental ambition.

Both propositions are underlain, of course, by a vigorous geographical determinism. According to the first, Canada will fragment or merge with the United States because the border is long, artificial, and a priori, or (in other variants of this position) because it contradicts the natural north-south grain of continental topography and the natural unity of the Anglo-Saxon race. According to the second, Canada is a logical, even inevitable, creation because the border is the outgrowth of a northern geography based on the Canadian Shield and the fur trade. But perhaps the border did no more than create a political space encompassing certain possibilities and certain limitations. Perhaps neither are people determined by the spaces they inhabit, nor is the character of these spaces determined by the people they contain. Perhaps, in the language of social theory, the one is constitutive of the other; perhaps they exist in ongoing reciprocal interaction. Perhaps, in this light, British North America is best thought of as a created space in which certain things would happen, none of them inevitable, but all of them affected by the space in which they took place and that they, in turn, adjusted. Perhaps, out of these myriad interactions would eventually emerge Canada as we know it. So conceptualized, the space that became British North America is embedded in the fabric of Canada, but in ways that have been worked out over the years in innumerable undetermined imbrications of people and land.

As Map 5.5 shows, the border had been drawn near and in many places well beyond the northern limit of agriculture. Even along the border, much of the land was too rocky, too cold, or, in the Cordillera, too steep to farm. Three hundred kilometres north of the border, virtually all of it was. If, after Innis, rivers and canoes facilitated westward commercial expansion, the land blocked and contained agricultural settlement. After the border agreements, the unblocked continental interior lay south of the border – the Illinois country and beyond, west and south – to which the French had come, but neither French arms nor British diplomacy had held. This was the land in which the American historian Frederick Jackson Turner could plausibly describe a broad frontier crossing the whole length of the

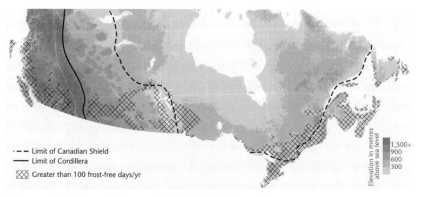

MAP 5.5   The bounded space of British North America

MAP 5.6   Population density, British North America, 1851 | Adapted from J. Mannion, G. Handcock, B. Osborne, J-C Robert, and D. Sutherland, in *Historical Atlas of Canada,* vol. 2, *The Land Transformed,* ed. R. Louis Gentilcore, cart. Geoffrey J. Matthews (Toronto: University of Toronto Press, 1993), plates 8 and 10.

Appalachians and moving west in a succession of stages while, at the edge of frontier expansion, American culture continuously re-created and reinvigorated itself. South of the border, the settlement experience with the land encouraged this powerful spatial metaphor as, north of the border, it did not. Huge as it was, British North America disappeared northward into rock, muskeg, and barrenness, and along the border in the south presented only patches of land that would attract settlers. As drawn, the border would separate two landed experiences, one essentially generous, the other pinched.

Moreover, diplomatic arguments and military manoeuvring had sidelined the issue of Native title while creating a bounded space, British North America, the overwhelming majority of which was still possessed by Native people. The more than 2 million people of European background who lived there in the middle of the nineteenth century, some two-fifths of them French-speaking, were almost entirely confined to the St. Lawrence Valley and the peninsula of southern Ontario, or to patches of land in New Brunswick, Nova Scotia, Prince Edward Island, and Newfoundland (Map 5.6). Everywhere else, except in the small agricultural settlement at Red River, Natives were the predominant or only population. The land, in their view, was theirs. The fur trade had brought new goods, adjusted seasonal rounds of hunting and fishing, encouraged economic specialization, intensified warfare, and relocated many groups. Epidemic diseases had decimated many populations, some of which had rebounded fairly quickly, others not. Except, perhaps, in a few corners of the High Arctic, Native life had changed, but the fur trade, dependent on Native labour rather than on Native land, had not dispossessed Native people. If the epidemics had thinned memories and reduced the intensity of local land use, they had not emptied the land that, although population densities were low – lower, often, than they had been for centuries – remained inhabited and owned.

This huge, thinly populated, and, in European terms, largely barren territory had become the space left to British North America. It was the product of a considerable history and of a complex, evolving array of powers, although it was only an outline, an anticipatory geography that, in itself, had little meaning. Yet, it existed on paper and in law, a space for governments and imaginations to work with.

BIBLIOGRAPHY

There are large literatures on the wars, treaties, and enactments mentioned in this short chapter. The following are a few works that bear particularly on the border.

For cartographic treatments of the evolving border and of some of the military engagements that influenced them, see the following: Norman L. Nicholson, *The Boundaries of Canada, Its Provinces and Territories,* Geographical Branch, Mines and Technical Surveys, Memoir 2 (Ottawa: Queen's Printer, 1964), 13-31. D.G.G. Kerr, ed., *A Historical Atlas of Canada* (Toronto: Thomas Nelson and Sons, 1961), especially 26-40. *Historical Atlas of Canada,* vol. 1, *From the Beginning to 1800,* ed. R. Cole Harris, cart. Geoffrey J. Matthews (Toronto: University of Toronto Press, 1987), plates 42-44. *Historical Atlas of Canada,* vol. 2, *The Land Transformed, 1800-1891,* ed. R. Louis Gentilcore, cart. Geoffrey J. Matthews (Toronto: University of Toronto Press, 1993), plates 21 and 22.

Two old but still useful accounts of late eighteenth-century trade policies and boundaries are Gerald S. Graham, *British Policy and Canada 1774-1791: A Study in Eighteenth-Century Trade Policy* (London and New York: Longmans, Green, 1930), chap. 4; and S.F. Bemis, "Jay's Treaty and the Northwest Boundary Gap," *American Historical Review* 17, 3 (April 1922): 465-84. An efficient account of British property rights and of their application in the Ohio Valley after 1763 is in John C. Weaver, "Concepts of Economic Improvement and the Social Construction of Property Rights: Highlights from the English-Speaking World," in John McLaren, A.R. Buck, and Nancy E. Wright, *Despotic Dominion: Property Rights in British Settler Societies* (Vancouver: UBC Press, 2005), 79-102. Detailed accounts of border negotiations and adjustments in the east after the Treaty of Paris of 1783 are in Francis M. Carroll, *A*

Good and Wise Measure: The Search for the Canadian-American Boundary, 1783-1842 (Toronto: University of Toronto Press, 2001). The ambiguities and illusions surrounding the St. Croix border are discussed by David Demeritt, "Representing the 'True' St. Croix: Knowledge and Power in the Partition of the Northeast," *William and Mary Quarterly*, 3rd ser., 54 (1997): 515-48. Much the most penetrating account of the emergence of the border in the west is Daniel W. Clayton, *Islands of Truth: The Imperial Fashioning of Vancouver Island* (Vancouver: UBC Press, 2000), chap. 12.

Richard White situates the geopolitical struggles for the control of North America within the shifting pattern of European-Native alliances in *The Middle Ground: Indians, Empires, and Republics in the Great Lakes Region, 1650-1815* (Cambridge and New York: Cambridge University Press, 1991). Stephen J. Hornsby offers a broad analysis of the spatial implication of the Seven Years' War and the American Revolution in *British Atlantic, American Frontier: Spaces of Power in Early Modern British America* (Hanover, NH: New England University Press, 2004), chap. 6.

On space, time, and society, see for a start Anthony Giddens, *The Constitution of Society: Outline of the Theory of Structuration* (Berkeley and Los Angeles: University of California Press, 1984), particularly chap. 3 and 355-72.

6
Newfoundland

Newfoundland's uninviting land, at or beyond the margin of North American agricultural possibility, was balanced by abundant maritime resources that commercial capital had begun to exploit at the beginning of the sixteenth century and would long continue to do so. Over time, however, the spatial strategies of resource exploitation changed. In the sixteenth century, capital and labour were drawn seasonally from Europe, and the axis of exploitation was transatlantic: a European port of embarkation, a seasonal fishing harbour somewhere on the coast of Newfoundland (Chapter 2), a return voyage, usually to a different port, to market the cod. In the seventeenth century, planters (fishing proprietors), their servants, and often their wives began to over-winter in Newfoundland; by the early nineteenth century both management and labour were primarily located there. Over the years, the axis of exploitation had become coastal, comprising a few major centres where the merchants maintained their principal establishments and a scatter of smaller coastal settlements (outharbours/outports) where most fishermen and their families lived. At one end of this coastal axis was the larger economy of the North Atlantic, at the other end the extreme localness of outport life, embedded as it had come to be in kin relations, local environmental knowledge, and elements of peasant culture transplanted from England or Ireland.

THE SEVENTEENTH CENTURY
At the beginning of the seventeenth century, the English and French dominated the Newfoundland fishery. The English were concentrated along

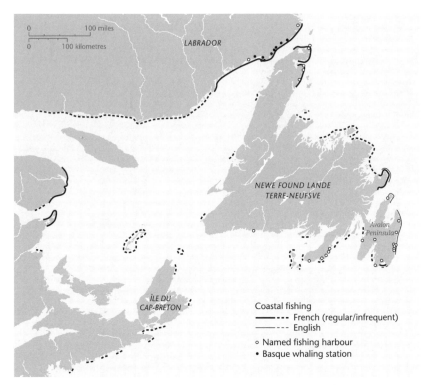

Map 6.1   French and English fisheries in Newfoundland, c. 1600 | Adapted from
J. Mannion and S. Barkham, in *Historical Atlas of Canada*, vol. 1, *From the Beginning to 1800*,
ed. R. Cole Harris, cart. Geoffrey J. Matthews (Toronto: University of Toronto Press, 1987),
plate 22.

the east coast of the Avalon Peninsula and on the outer headlands of Conception and Trinity Bays, whereas the French fishery ranged more widely
around the gulf, the Labrador shore, and the coasts of Newfoundland (Map
6.1). These were migratory fisheries. There was no year-round European
settlement. Early in the seventeenth century, however, several English
groups developed schemes to challenge the migratory fishery by establishing proprietary colonies. Private ventures with royal charters, they were
intended to establish settlers, develop mixed economies based on agriculture, mining, and lumbering as well as fishing, and turn a profit for their
investors. In 1610 a London-Bristol joint stock company (the Newfoundland Company) obtained a royal charter and planted a settlement on the
western shore of Conception Bay; in the 1620s and 1630s George Calvert
(later Lord Baltimore) and after him David Kirke (who had ousted
Champlain from Quebec in 1629) attempted to establish colonies south of

St. John's around Ferryland; and there were other less prominent schemes. Women were sent to these settlements, and agriculture was attempted. A little lumber was cut, minerals sought, and residential fisheries created. Except for Kirke's establishment at Ferryland (which, recent archaeological investigations have shown, adapted to the fishery and prospered through much of the seventeenth century), none of these ventures were profitable; their proprietors soon gave up. Newfoundland winters had proved more daunting than anticipated, and all attempts to establish viable commercial economies other than fishing failed. Later in the century – in 1662 – the French Crown established a garrison and civil administration at Plaisance (Placentia), the principal French fishing port in southern Newfoundland where by that date there was some year-round settlement.

These various plans and settlements were situated in a long debate in both England and France about the feasibility and desirability of settling Newfoundland. Those who argued against settlement (who tended to be successful West Country merchants in the migratory fishery) held that the island was uninhabitable. If it could be settled, residents would undermine the migratory fishery by destroying shore installations, taking the best fishing sites, debauching seamen, and (by reducing the labour pool) driving up wages. The mother country would lose seamen for her navy; her merchants would lose trade to foreigners. The counter to these arguments was that Newfoundland was indeed habitable, that by extending the fishing season and reducing the expense of annual building, settlement would create a more efficient fishery, and that a resident population would forestall the French – or the English. Throughout the seventeenth century, neither argument prevailed. Neither government encouraged or forbade settlement, and as the century progressed the advantages of some settlement became increasingly apparent even to the merchants who controlled the migratory fishery. At the same time, a niche opened for small fishing proprietors ("planters" in English, "*habitants-pêcheurs*" in French) operating from a residential base in Newfoundland. The result was the beginning of a process of relatively invisible settlement without the fanfare of royal charters, the expense of colonization schemes, or, probably, any expectation of permanence.

From the merchants' point of view, there were advantages to leaving caretakers in Newfoundland to mind the wharves (stages), drying platforms (flakes), and cabins required by the inshore fishery and vulnerable, when untended, to rival fishing interests and to Beothuk people in search of iron. Moreover, a few men left behind to cut lumber and build fishing boats enabled those brought over in the spring to turn quickly to fishing. The cost of keeping men in Newfoundland through the winter was approximately the same as transporting them across the Atlantic and back; therefore, when one ship in a given fishing harbour left men behind, others there tended to follow suit or risk competing poorly the next year. At the same time, some men with inadequate capital to outfit a ship for a transatlantic fishing season but able to acquire a few boats and hire their crews (three fishermen and two shore workers per boat), began to operate in Newfoundland. Of these small entrepreneurs there were two types: residents, who lived in Newfoundland for some years, and migrants (byeboatmen), passengers on fishing and sack (trading) ships, who came out for the season, operated boats, and hired labour. In either case, they depended for provisions, labour, and markets on sack or fishing ships from England or France, or on coastal traders from New England. For the merchants who owned the fishing ships, the sale of passages to Newfoundland became a source of revenue on outbound voyages.

Most over-winterers in Newfoundland were young, single men – mostly eighteen to twenty-five years old – who had been recruited in the hinterlands of the principal ports of embarkation: le Havre, St-Malo, and Les Sables d'Olonne in France; Dartmouth, Bideford, and Plymouth in England. Many of them worked for the planters/habitants-pêcheurs; a few had been hired by the ship merchants as caretakers, woodcutters, and boatbuilders; and some had been left behind, to survive a Newfoundland winter as best they could, by captains who did not want the expense of transporting them back to Europe. By the 1670s there were also some 160 planters along the English shore, about half of whom were heads of households. Their wives and daughters made up most of the white, female population of Newfoundland. A few women came as domestic servants and, much in demand in a young, overwhelmingly male society, usually married as soon as their terms of service expired – although an Anglican chaplain, visiting in 1680, complained that people "live like heathens in a licentious and lawless incestuous manner." About a dozen habitant-pêcheur families lived in Plaisance. Map 6.2, based on English data for 1675 and French data for 1687, shows the distribution of these residents along the French and English shores. The map also indicates the distribution of

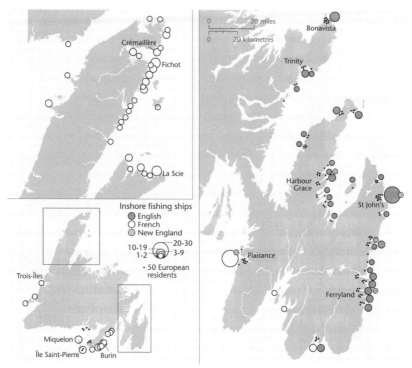

MAP 6.2 Inshore fishing ships and winter residents, c. 1675 | After J. Mannion and G. Handcock, in Harris and Matthews, *Historical Atlas of Canada*, vol. 1, plate 23.

inshore fishing ships – that is, the ships that had arrived that year (1675) in various harbours to pursue the inshore boat fishery. In the late seventeenth century the migratory fishery, much as described in Chapter 2, still dwarfed the residential.

In a major study of the English fishery, historical geographer Gordon Handcock has emphasized the fluctuating and inherently temporary nature of most seventeenth-century settlement in Newfoundland. He has shown, for example, that there is almost no surname continuity between a nominal census of 1708 (which names household heads) and similar censuses taken some thirty years earlier. More recently, Peter Pope, a historical archaeologist who has excavated parts of the Kirke settlement in Ferryland, has established that Ferryland was a major, continuously occupied settlement from its founding in the 1630s until a French force from Plaisance sacked it in 1696. At Ferryland, at least, descendants of some of the colonists established in the 1630s lived there in the 1690s. Moreover,

Pope notes that the censuses did not record women unless they were widowed heads of households, and argues that women were the stabilizing element in Newfoundland's seventeenth-century residential population, a point with which Handcock would agree. The question, then, is whether the experience at Ferryland was representative. Handcock suggests that it was not, but does note that there were descendants in eighteenth-century Newfoundland of families who had lived around Conception, Trinity, and Bonavista Bays, and at St. John's in the seventeenth century. The argument turns, perhaps, on the frame of reference. If, for example, one compares seventeenth-century settlement in Acadia (Chapter 3) with that in Newfoundland – the one an isolated and genealogically connected population tied to marshland farms around the Bay of Fundy, the other fishing families living on a rocky coast within the transatlantic dynamic of the fishery – then the contrast between continuity and transience is striking.

THE EIGHTEENTH CENTURY

At the beginning of the eighteenth century, the French and English fisheries in Newfoundland were located approximately where they had been a century before. This, however, war would soon change. Through most of the 1690s and the first decade of the eighteenth century, England and France were at war (the War of the League of Augsburg, 1689-97; the War of the Spanish Succession, 1701-13), and fighting spread to Newfoundland. Since the 1660s, the French had maintained a fort and garrison at Plaisance, and in the early 1690s the English built and garrisoned a fort at St. John's. It did them little good. In the winter of 1695-96, a French overland force made up largely of Canadian militia and Native allies destroyed almost every English settlement in Newfoundland, in the process killing some two hundred people and taking seven hundred prisoners. Ten years later a similar campaign achieved a similar result; even St. John's was destroyed, although the fort held out. It fell in 1708 during yet another French attack in which the French took eight hundred prisoners, sent the captured English garrison to Quebec, and again burned the settlement. But as none of these winter victories were stabilized by summer naval support, the English returned and rebuilt. Eventually, the control of Newfoundland was settled in Europe where the War of the Spanish Succession had not gone well for France. In 1713 the Treaty of Utrecht awarded Newfoundland to Britain, while according French fishermen the right to catch and cure fish, but not

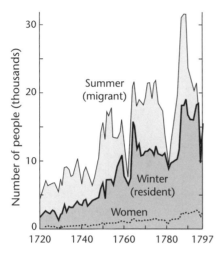

FIGURE 6.1 Summer and winter populations, eighteenth century. Note the growing relative importance of residents and the virtual elimination of migrants by the end of the century. | After J. Mannion, G. Handcock, and A. Macpherson, in *Historical Atlas of Canada*, vol. 1, *From the Beginning to 1800*, ed. R. Cole Harris, cart. Geoffrey J. Matthews (Toronto: University of Toronto Press, 1987), plate 25.

to settle, in northern Newfoundland. After Utrecht, the habitants-pêcheurs at Plaisance moved their families and operations across Cabot Strait to Île Royale (Cape Breton Island).

At the beginning of the eighteenth century, perhaps four thousand people over-wintered along the English shore. The great majority were servants; fewer than two hundred were women. At Plaisance, the principal French settlement on the island, where there were some forty families, the population may have been more balanced. Over the next few years, warfare reduced these numbers; then, after 1713, almost all the French residents left. Thereafter, the French fishery concentrated in the north and became entirely migratory, a seasonal inshore fishery that, year in and year out, brought hundreds of ships and as many as ten thousand men across the Atlantic. The British fishery remained both residential and migratory, and through the rest of the eighteenth century the summer and winter populations associated with it fluctuated as shown in Figure 6.1. The proportion of over-winterers grew over the years, but even in the 1790s, when there were some fifteen to twenty thousand of them, about half were servants who would leave Newfoundland when their terms of work expired. The ratio of resident men to women was some five to one.

Almost all these over-winterers had come from one of two small regions in Britain: southwestern England (more particularly, the hinterlands of Poole, Plymouth, Dartmouth, and Exeter) and southeastern Ireland (particularly the hinterland of Waterford). Most of the merchants who controlled the Newfoundland fishery in the eighteenth century operated out of these ports and recruited labour nearby. Often, ships from the English ports called at Waterford en route to Newfoundland to take on provisions (salted pork, beef, and butter) and cheap Irish labour. In time, Irish merchants themselves engaged in these trades. For most of the recruits, the fishery offered welcome employment. In Ireland, where crop failures, high food prices, and famine recurred in the eighteenth century, the fishery was, for some, an alternative to starvation, for others a means to pay an Irish rent. Few recruits had previously fished; they came from farms, from small trades, from among those who hardly had an occupation and sought day labour where they could, or were lads from parish poorhouses whom overseers of the poor placed with fishing masters. In Newfoundland these two ethnic groups, one Protestant, the other Catholic, met in almost all settlements, although the English predominated along the northeast coast and the Irish to the south (Map 6.3). Some of the Irish spoke no English.

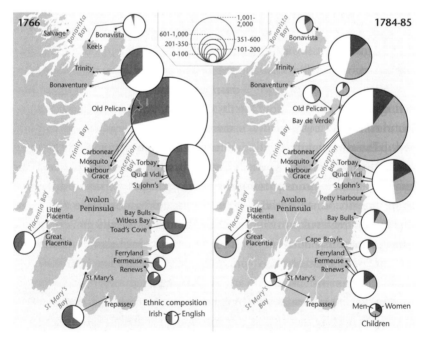

MAP 6.3   Winter population, 1766 and 1784-85 | After J. Mannion, G. Handcock, and A. Macpherson, in Harris and Matthews, *Historical Atlas of Canada,* vol. 1, plate 25.

Small boats, operating within three or four kilometres of the harbours where their catches were cured, continued to take most fish, and some early eighteenth-century observers held that inshore waters were being over-fished. Historical geographer Grant Head has suggested that declining inshore fish stocks may have provided the impetus for the development of a Newfoundland-based banks fishery. Perhaps for this reason, some planters began outfitting schooners for the banks, where the catch was salted down and then brought ashore for drying, which because of the quantity of fish involved took place on far larger drying platforms (flakes) than had previously been built. Some British ships also began to fish the banks; most of them also finished the cure ashore. The product, low-quality dried cod, was often marketed as slave food in the West Indies. Particularly along the northeast coast of Newfoundland, and later in the century in Labrador, salmon fisheries, sealing, and even trapping became important commercial activities. Easily taken by weirs or nets in spawning rivers or by gillnets set along the shore, salmon were salted and barrelled. Seals, taken in midwinter by nets strung across narrow ocean passages, were rendered into oil. A few trappers operated well inland in winter along frozen rivers. In these ways the Newfoundland economy diversified a little, and in a few places, particularly along the north coast and in Labrador, both frontiers of eighteenth-century British expansion, salmon fisheries and sealing predominated. Overall, Newfoundland's export economy remained almost as dependent on cod as since the earliest days of the fishery.

Apart from the fishery, local economies were exceedingly weak and almost entirely oriented towards subsistence. There was virtually no commercial agriculture, although most families grew potatoes, turnips, and cabbages in kitchen gardens and kept a few livestock. In 1750 there were only some fifty acres of improved land near St. John's; in the early 1770s there were only seventeen hundred such acres on the whole island, most of them in grass. The cultivated acreage increased during the American Revolution, when imports of foodstuffs were interrupted, but however much people relied on fish the island never came close to feeding itself. Lumber was cut here and there, and almost all boats and smaller craft were built locally from local wood. The cutting of firewood, ever more arduous as the coastal forest receded, provided some employment. Often, it was easier to move in winter into the forest, where fuel was at hand. Most of the inhabitants of Trinity, the largest settlement on Trinity Bay, apparently did so, living in wooden huts (tilts) made of small logs placed vertically with an end sharpened and driven into the ground. In such circumstances, hunting and even trapping became important, other means of eking out livelihoods.

The fishery, however, was a huge source of wealth, and was situated in a complex matrix of trade. It required large quantities of salt, naval stores (including turpentine, wood tar, and cordage), and fishing gear. The construction of settlements required building supplies, and both residents and migrants required foodstuffs. Almost all manufactured goods had to be imported. Throughout much of the seventeenth century, English or French ships had carried most of this trade, but before the end of the century ships from the British seaboard colonies to the south were becoming increasingly successful interlopers in a trade that merchants in Britain would much rather have controlled themselves. These colonial competitors broke open what had been a closed trading system, lowering some commodity prices, providing an outlet for disaffected workers (thereby increasing the price of labour), and flaunting Navigation Acts and customs regulations, both of uncertain application in Newfoundland because the island, though recognized as British, was not a colony. The cod these ships carried away went primarily to Mediterranean or Iberian ports (where salt was obtained) or to the West Indies. Rather than cod, some British-American traders sought bills of exchange, which they would redeem with British goods. Trading patterns were intricate and shifting, even at the scale of a single firm, and were always affected by wars, politics, and fluctuations in price. In general, the dried cod produced by the migratory French inshore fishery went principally to markets in southern France, and the wet (green) cod produced by the French banks fishery went to northern France. Most of the dried cod produced by the British fishery went to Mediterranean or Iberian ports, but some low-quality product went to the West Indies. Bread, flour, lumber, staves, and naval stores came increasingly from the English seaboard colonies, and rum, sugar, and molasses from the West Indies, trades carried almost entirely by American ships. Salted pork, beef, and butter came from Ireland, and most other imports came from southwestern England. In the early 1770s goods from Ireland, New England and the Middle Colonies, and the West Indies accounted for 80 percent of the value of imports at St. John's.

The merchants engaged in these trades were the links with the planters and bye-boat keepers who, through most of the eighteenth century, accounted for more than half of the cod produced by the British fishery. Often, these links were made by the captain of a sack ship, in which case the British merchant firm in question made no infrastructural investments in Newfoundland. But as the century advanced and the complexity of dealings with many small fish merchants as well as with ship and bank fisheries increased, many firms located agents, clerks, bookkeepers, tradesmen, and even boat crews in Newfoundland. They built wharves and stages, warehouses, stores, and substantial residences there. In so doing they created sizable merchant establishments, to which some merchants and merchant families moved, the beginning of a shift in the location of management that, at the end of the century, became prevalent. In the eighteenth century, most of these establishments were in St. John's, Carbonear, Harbour Grace, or Trinity. The commercial ascendancy of St. John's was not yet fixed, and each of these ports dominated a local coastal trade.

Map 6.4 shows Trinity as it was at the end of the eighteenth century and identifies the merchant firms operating there. The largest of them was Benjamin Lester and Co., a Poole firm that maintained a large merchant house, substantial wharves and warehouses, and a shipyard. The firm also kept five agents in settlements around Trinity and Bonavista Bays, and had stores, cooperages, cookhouses (bunkhouses), salt houses, and warehouses in many of the settlements in these large bays. It sent out bankers, operated inshore boat fisheries on its own account, and traded with planters. As operations such as Lester and Co.'s developed, the inport-outport system that would dominate nineteenth-century Newfoundland emerged. Places such as Maggotty Cove and Pease Cove (Map 6.4), essentially outports located close to an inport (Trinity), were sites of resource production; merchant firms in Trinity and places like it supplied the outports and took their fish. As the system developed, planters in the outports organized production, and merchants in the larger centres organized trade. Although the two were interdependent, power lay with the merchants, who set the prices of supplies and fish. The planters required the external connections the merchants provided, and also the merchant credit that tided them over the inevitable fluctuations of the fishery. Almost no money changed hands; cod were traded for provisions (truck) at

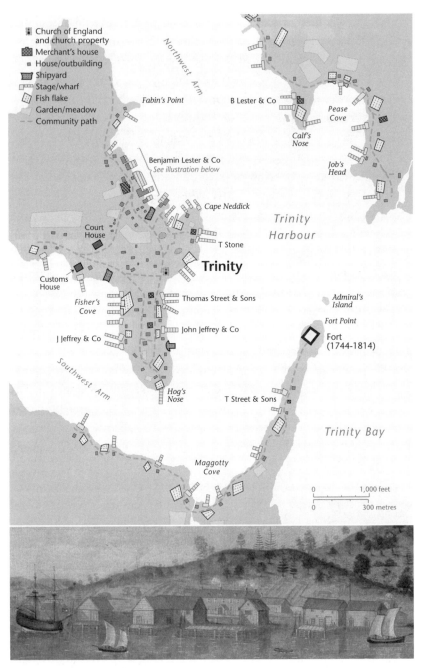

Map 6.4   Trinity, 1801 │ After G. Handcock, in Harris and Matthews, *Historical Atlas of Canada*, vol. 1, plate 26.

rates the merchants controlled – the truck system as it was known in New-foundland. The system spread debt throughout the outports, but histor-ian Keith Matthews has argued that there was rarely another buffer against misfortune: no parish or government relief, and little capacity in tiny com-munities for local charity or mutual aid. When merchant firms collapsed, as they frequently did, people in the outports could be left destitute. Mer-chant credit filled a gap of sorts while embedding ties of dependency and debt in Newfoundland's settlement pattern and in the spatial structure of the island's society and economy.

Map 6.4 shows a court house, customs house, and fort in Trinity, insti-tutions that raise the question of how state power was deployed along an increasingly settled coast that was not a colony. In 1697 an Act to Encour-age Trade to Newfoundland – popularly, King William's Act – confirmed the old custom that the first English captain to arrive in a harbour was its admiral for the fishing season, with power to judge disputes involving fishery personnel and property. Those suspected of serious criminal of-fences were to be returned to England for trial. The alleged venality and corruption of these admirals has become part of Newfoundland mythol-ogy, but recently a legal historian, Jerry Bannister, has shown that the ad-mirals were preoccupied with fishing and rarely judged, and that judicial authority passed to the commodore of the naval squadron sent to patrol in Newfoundland waters each summer. The Royal Navy was a regular pres-ence. As many as twelve warships operated seasonally off Newfoundland and in wartime escorted fishing ships in convoy; after 1729 the commo-dore of the Newfoundland squadron was also the island's governor. The squadron left in the fall, after which the island's growing residential popu-lation was left to its own devices, but by the 1750s a system of civil magis-trates and local courts was well in place. Before the end of the century Newfoundland was administered much like an English county: justices, constables, sheriffs, courts of session, a grand jury, customs officers. Ban-nister shows that the island's law became an amalgam of English statutes, common law, and local custom that served full well to protect the interests of the powerful – the merchants and planters who owned property and employed people. Newfoundland was not unregulated space; the island, said one high British official, had become "a sort of colony." The spectacle of gallows, whipping post, and stocks was at hand, backed by the ships of

the Royal Navy that patrolled offshore. This legal-military equipme ᵗ f᧐-
cused on centres such as Trinity and must have been more attenuated in
the outports.

THE EARLY NINETEENTH CENTURY

Except for residential fisheries on the small islands of Saint-Pierre and
Miquelon (ceded to France by the Treaty of Paris, 1763), the nineteenth-
century French fishery remained migratory and focused on the northern
peninsula, where it had largely been since 1713. On the other hand, the more-
than-two-hundred-year-old British migratory fishery collapsed. In 1790 it
accounted for some 55 percent of British cod production in Newfoundland, in 1810 for barely 5 percent. The bye-boatmen disappeared. Among
the reasons for the collapse of the migratory fishery are overproduction
and declining fish prices in the 1780s and early 1790s, which put many
merchants out of business; in addition, the Napoleonic Wars greatly increased the difficulties of supplying and managing transatlantic fisheries
from Britain. Moreover, families in Newfoundland tended to remain there
in wartime conditions, and as more young, island-born women reached
marriageable age, more men were inclined to stay. Nor were conditions in
southwestern England and southeastern Ireland conducive to their return.
In Devon and Dorset prices for land and food were rising (advantageous
for landlords but not for the poor); "improving" landlords were consoli-
dating landholdings, in so doing replacing tenants with improved farm
technologies; and cottage industries, particularly in textiles, were giving
way to factory production. In southeastern Ireland conditions were fairly
similar: severe overpopulation was driving up land values and depressing
wages, landlords were refusing to sublet or to renew long-term leases, and
domestic crafts were less and less able to compete with machines. Management also relocated, although less completely. By 1810 most British firms
involved in the Newfoundland fishery had agents and accountants in St.
John's. In the span of some twenty years, the long dominance of the British
migratory fishery had come to an end, and Newfoundland itself became
the primary locus of the labour and a good deal of the management on
which its fisheries depended.

At almost the same time, two new shorter-range migratory fisheries
developed along the northeast coast of Newfoundland and the Labrador
shore: the first, a seal fishery in which seal oil and skins were procured and

whelps (newborns) were taken on broken ice floes, operated from late winter to early spring and was exceedingly dangerous; the second, a summer cod fishery, was confined to inshore waters along the Labrador coast (the Labrador floater cod fishery). These were schooner fisheries, prosecuted principally from ports around Conception Bay and St. John's. They combined urban merchant capital and outport labour, and well before the mid-nineteenth century each of them involved hundreds of ships and thousands of men, many of whom participated in both fisheries. For some of these men, they replaced the schooner fishery to the banks; indeed, a principal impetus for the Labrador floater fishery may have been poor catches on the banks. Together, these new fisheries became essential components of the economy of northeastern Newfoundland, tying it to distant as well as local resources and supporting high population densities (Map 6.5). Because seals could be taken cheaply in nets or traps close to shore, sealing, like inshore cod fishing, was also a local outlet for family labour. At midcentury seal oil and skins comprised some 30 percent of the value of exports from Newfoundland.

As the mercantile control of the British fishery shifted across the Atlantic, it concentrated principally in St. John's. With some five thousand residents in 1810, St. John's, now larger than Poole or Dartmouth, had quickly become the dominant settlement in Newfoundland. It was no longer primarily a fishing port. Although many bankers and boats were still based there, its economy in 1810 was dominated by the almost four hundred ships that came to trade, bringing most of the island's imports and taking about half of its exports. St. John's was Newfoundland's only town, its dominant central place. The wharves and warehouses of some fifty merchant firms lined its waterfront, and shops, public houses, and residences lined the long street behind. Artisans associated with the activities of a port – carpenters, coopers, sailmakers, and so on – lived there in considerable number. Some of its merchants were still junior partners of British firms, but many operated independently. They supplied and provided credit for a growing share of the island's outports, and established agents in many of them. They outfitted dozens of ships for the spring sealing fleet or for the Labrador floater cod fishery. Across the Atlantic, they dealt increasingly with Liverpool, Bristol, Greenock, and London rather than with the British ports of the eighteenth-century fishery (Figure 6.2).

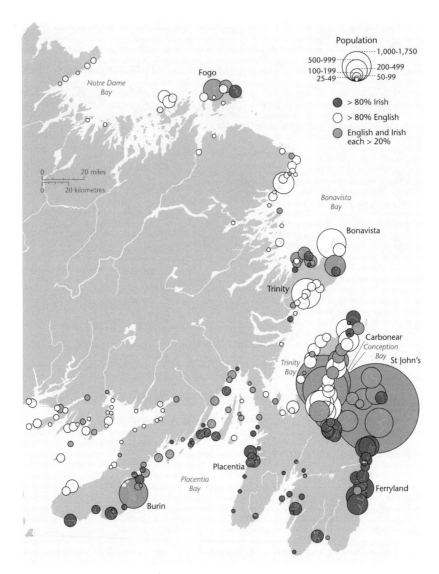

MAP 6.5   Population, 1836 | After J. Mannion and G. Handcock, in *Historical Atlas of Canada*, vol. 2, *The Land Transformed*, ed. R. Louis Gentilcore, cart. Geoffrey J. Matthews (Toronto: University of Toronto Press, 1993), plate 8.

The growth of St. John's was but part of the rapid early nineteenth-century increase in the resident population of Newfoundland, which more than tripled from fewer than twenty thousand people in 1800 to some seventy thousand by 1835. Immigration accounted for most of this growth;

FIGURE 6.2 *The Town and Harbour of St. John's,* 1831 (artist, William Eagar). Note the wharves that were the focus of Newfoundland's import and export trades, the more institutional town behind (including, upper right, the new Government House), and the farmland (the largest patch in Newfoundland). The Battery in the foreground protected the harbour's entrance. | Library and Archives Canada, 1970-188-1508.

some thirty to thirty-five thousand immigrants probably arrived between 1800 and 1835, the great majority of them young, single men, and almost none married couples or children. The old migration fields established by the migratory fishery held: immigrants still came from southwestern England or southeastern Ireland. Some arrived as indentured servants, but others had simply purchased the cheapest possible passage to North America. Apparently, few of them returned, and probably most moved on to other North American destinations. Enough stuck, however, so that the older areas of settlement in eastern Newfoundland became increasingly crowded, and settlement expanded westward along the northeast and south coasts. Map 6.5 shows the distribution of population and also of Irish and English (close correlates for the distribution of Catholics and Protestants) in 1836. St. John's had become a town of some fifteen thousand, and there were now many small settlements along the south and northeast coasts. The Irish still predominated from St. John's south and westward to Placentia Bay, the English almost everywhere else. By this date the preponderance of males to females had declined to about two to one, a reflection of the growing availability of wives among young, Newfoundland-born women.

After 1835, the rate of immigration rapidly declined, eventually to a trickle. Following the reorientation of merchant firms in Newfoundland towards Liverpool, Bristol, and London, the origins of these later immigrants were more diverse, but as there were few of them the ethnic composition of the Newfoundland population hardly changed. As immigration declined, population growth became increasingly dependent on natural increase. The rate of population growth slowed, the gender imbalance diminished further, and the percentage of island-born increased. By 1870 they accounted for almost 95 percent of a population that in the previous thirty-five years had doubled to about 145,000. Different regional demographies emerged. By the 1840s or even earlier in the long-settled outports along the coasts of the Avalon Peninsula, there was no space for newcomers (unless they married into an established family), or even for all progeny of established families. The fishery was fully taken up, there was virtually no agricultural hinterland, and only sealing provided some alternative seasonal employment. In these circumstances, the marriage age rose, the birth rate declined, and out-migration began. To the immediate west, in Placentia, Trinity, and Bonavista Bays, these effects of disappearing niches for family livelihoods were felt ten to twenty years later. Farther west again, in Notre Dame Bay and along the south coast, resource development was taking place, the marriage age was lower than elsewhere in Newfoundland, and in-migration was still occurring as late as 1870.

Although sealing expanded rapidly, particularly between 1820 and 1860, accounting in some years for as much as a quarter of exports, the Newfoundland economy remained dependent on the cod fishery. Except for the banks and Labrador floater fisheries, it continued to be prosecuted by families living in the outports and managed by merchants in the major centres, principally St. John's. There was this significant change: whereas in the eighteenth-century planters and bye-boat keepers in the outports hired seasonal and usually migratory labour, in the nineteenth century inshore fishing and curing became almost entirely the undertakings of resident families. Planter-families organized production and depended on credit from merchant firms to whom they became indebted. Men fished, men and women cleaned the fish, and women and children cured them. Women and children worked around the flakes: turning the cod, taking it in when it rained, piling it when dried. In effect, these families were small-scale farmers of the sea who also gardened (this, too, was women's work), gathered, and here and there, conditions permitting, farmed a little on the land. In some respects, they were a peasantry – a peasantry beholden not to landlords for the rent of land but to merchants for supplies. In time, groups of families in isolated outports became enmeshed in kin relations. A young woman usually moved to an adjacent outport, her husband's home, when she married. Otherwise, there was little population movement except when, for want of local place, a son left for distant parts. The historical geographer Alan Macpherson has shown that in Bonavista Bay on the north coast of Newfoundland, settlement expanded not in response to the plans of merchants but as groups of related families sought out and occupied new locations (on this phenomenon in Lower Canada, see Chapter 8).

For immigrants from England and Ireland, fishing was a learned activity, as were the forms of hunting and gathering in which they engaged. On the other hand, gardening and farming, such as they were, depended on transferred crops, livestock, tools, and practices. In outports settled by the Irish, as the historical geographer John Mannion has shown, ridged and trenched potato patches (lazy beds) appeared, as did many Irish peasant tools. In Ireland, such ways faced pressures from the agricultural improvers, but in Newfoundland, where agriculture was overwhelmingly a subsistence activity and therefore largely immune from modernizing pressures, they would have a long life. Much the same was true of dialects. Because immigrants came from various villages and townlands, outport Newfoundland did not reproduce the micro-dialects associated with particular settlements in southwestern England or southeastern Ireland, but an isolated outport, where almost everyone hailed from one or other of these regions and had little contact with the outside world, would reproduce a more generalized regional dialect, which then would have a long life in Newfoundland. Similarly, it has been argued that in the process of migration Irish Catholicism tended to lose its local saints and superstitions and become more homogeneous – although many leprechauns may be suspected in Irish outports. Migration had shuffled the deck, diminishing the legacy of Old World localities while creating another form of locality in the outports of Newfoundland.

In these isolated places, where there were paths but no roads to adjacent settlements, and external contacts were largely by sea, people fashioned meagre livelihoods out of the local sea and land (Figures 6.3, 6.4,

Figure 6.3   *Bell Isle Beach, Conception Bay, Newfoundland* (detail), 1857 (artist, William Grey). The basic ingredients of a well-established residential family fishery: a wharf (stage), a drying platform (flake), a small house, an enclosed garden plot. | William Grey, *Sketches of Newfoundland and Labrador* (Ipswich, UK: S.H. Cowell, 1857), The Rooms Provincial Archives, Newfoundland, VA 39A.7.

and 6.5). They came to read the inshore waters for signs of fish, acquire a vernacular knowledge of local marine ecologies, learn the means of coaxing crops from recalcitrant land, and know when and where to gather berries or eggs and how to hunt and trap – particular forms of the local knowledge characteristic of most peasantries. Coming from stone or wattle-and-daub building traditions, they learned to build with wood, much if not all of it unmilled. Within the system of the cod fishery, local lifeworlds and knowledge fields emerged. Compared to those left behind in England or Ireland, these lifeworlds were relatively egalitarian, with neither the poorest of the poor nor the comfortably fixed. Families lived on their own land, they all fished, and most of them gardened or farmed a little. As Mannion puts it, "there were no landlords, middlemen, strong farmers, traders, artisans, cottiers, or landless labourers." But if some of

FIGURE 6.4 *Harbour Breton, Newfoundland* (detail), n.d. (artist unknown). An isolated fishing village on the rocky, treeless south coast of Newfoundland. | Library and Archives Canada, 1969-25-2.

FIGURE 6.5 *Trinity Bay and Hearts Content* (detail), 1865 (artist, J. Becker). The houses in the foreground, pioneer homesteads of resident fishing families, suggest the early nineteenth-century circumstances of many Newfoundlanders. | *Frank Leslie's Illustrated Newspaper,* 9 September 1865.

these categories had been eliminated, others had been relocated. In the nineteenth-century spatial economy of Newfoundland, the merchants, middlemen, artisans, and most of the landless labourers were in the centres, and fisher-farmers in the outports. At the scale of the island, as historian Sean Cadigan has shown, the social hierarchy was simple and steep: a merchant class in the towns, a class of small producers in the outports.

At the scale of an outport, people lived in a rough equivalency that included their common dependence on cod, on whatever crops and livestock they managed to raise, and on merchants. When any one of them failed, as they often did, there could be famine in the outports.

In 1820 the governor of Newfoundland informed the Admiralty that the island "might be more properly termed a colony than a fishery plantation." Its people, he said, had become landsmen. So they had. In St. John's, where the first newspaper appeared in 1807, some among the professional class began to agitate for constitutional government and elected assemblies. The island's governors and officials in Britain were more likely to maintain that Newfoundlanders were too uneducated and primitive to govern themselves, and to wonder how legislators could assemble on an island where there were few roads, harbours were icebound in winter, and almost everyone was preoccupied with the fishery in summer. Some of them expected the migratory fishery to return. Yet Newfoundland increasingly attracted the attention of political and moral reformers in Britain (those seeking to extend the suffrage and concerned about human rights – in this case, about abuses in the courts and excessive corporal punishments). In 1824, after treating Newfoundland as little more than an elaborate fishing station for most of the previous 250 years, the British government promulgated laws that, in effect, recognized it as a colony, and in 1832 provided for an elected assembly based on what, for the day, was a broad suffrage: men twenty-one years of age and older who could show that they had occupied a building of any description for at least a year. Largely invisible in the background of this emerging colony was an opposite trajectory: in the 1820s the members of the last bands of Beothuk people, pushed off the coast by fishermen and increasingly threatened in the interior by hunters and trappers, died of starvation along the Exploits River in northcentral Newfoundland.

With the inception of the new colony, its governor built a mansion – Government House – the better to express the dignity of his office, but in the outports, where the potato crop had failed and fishing was poor, there were reports of starvation. In January 1832, some two thousand fishermen assembled near Harbour Grace in Conception Bay to protest the truck system, which they saw as the source of their poverty. They wanted cash for fish, as did sealers for seals. The sealing fleet did not sail that year until this demand was met. Conditions were desperate, and the dispersed labour force scattered in the outports was beginning to organize in self-defence. The next year a reluctant governor and magistrates provided relief – thought to discourage initiative and encourage dependence – when it became clear that the poor had eaten their seed potatoes and had nothing to plant. Relief was little enough: a third of a pound of bread per day to those with access to fish and half a pound to those without. Clearly, the new colony was sharply divided by class as well as by religion and ethnicity. In St. John's, Carbonear, and Harbour Grace, there was a measure of expatriate wealth: a merchant, administrative, and (particularly in St. John's) military elite lived with servants and English furniture and sent their children across the Atlantic to English schools. The hard-scrabble lives in the outports were another world, although, difficult as life was there, outporters were probably a little better off, year in and year out, than the poor they had left behind in the West Country or southern Ireland. To be sure, the fisheries on which they depended were not inexhaustible; as the resident population rose in the early nineteenth century, fish production declined, probably from over-fishing. The forest had been pushed farther from the coast, making the gathering of wood, which was essential to outport life, ever more laborious. People lived on meagre land between the sea and the forest, in patchy, discontinuous coastal settlements that by the early nineteenth century reached around much of Newfoundland. Human landscapes, fashioned largely from local materials, were handmade, improvised, and ingenious, the work in difficult environments far from home of people with little economic margin and no external regulatory constraints. To outsiders they seemed a clutter of small irregularly placed buildings, flakes, gardens, small fields, fences, and wandering cattle; to insiders they were ordered by local knowledge about the rights of particular families and their kin. People had combined what they could take from sea and land, obtain from merchants, learn from earlier immigrants, and remember from home into modest livelihoods. Usually they managed to get by. The Beothuk were gone and Newfoundland was resettled. Although St. John's and the other centres were the loci of power, most Newfoundlanders lived in the outports, their accents identifying their origins in southeastern Ireland or southwestern England, and their ways of life considerably reworked in Newfoundland.

Bibliography

For the seventeenth and eighteenth centuries, the place to start may be plates 23 and 25-28, plus the relevant parts of the essay "The Atlantic Realm," in *Historical Atlas of Canada*, vol. 1, *From the Beginning to 1800*, ed. R. Cole Harris, cart. Geoffrey J. Matthews (Toronto: University of Toronto Press, 1987), 47-51. For the nineteenth century, see *Historical Atlas of Canada*, vol. 2, *The Land Transformed, 1800-1891*, ed. R. Louis Gentilcore, cart. Geoffrey J. Matthews (Toronto: University of Toronto Press, 1993), plate 8. For a fuller historical background, see Keith Matthews, *Lectures on the History of Newfoundland, 1500-1830* (St. John's: Breakwater Books, 1988); and, although largely a narrative political history, Patrick O'Flaherty, *Old Newfoundland: A History to 1843* (St. John's: Long Beach Press, 1999).

On the early seventeenth-century colonization schemes, see Gillian T. Cell, *Newfoundland Discovered: English Attempts at Colonisation 1610-1630* (London: Hakluyt Society, 1982). For a more recent work, consult Peter E. Pope, *Fish into Wine: The Newfoundland Plantation in the Seventeenth Century* (Chapel Hill: University of North Carolina Press, 2004). See also his "Scavengers and Caretakers: Beothuk/European Settlement Dynamics in Seventeenth-Century Newfoundland," *Newfoundland Studies* 2, 2 (1993): 279-93. Also see James A. Tuck, "Archaeology at Ferryland, Newfoundland," *Newfoundland Studies* 9, 2 (1993): 294-310.

Recent work on the eighteenth century began with Grant Head, *Eighteenth Century Newfoundland: A Geographer's Perspective* (Toronto: McClelland and Stewart for the Carleton Library, 1976); and has been followed by W. Gordon Handcock, *Soe Longe as Their Comes Noe Women: Origins of English Settlement in Newfoundland* (St. John's: Breakwater Books, 1989); and by Jean-François Brière, *La Pêche Française en Amérique du Nord au XVIIIe Siècle* (Montreal: Éditions Fides, 1990). More recently, Jerry Bannister has published an admirable legal history: *The Rule of the Admirals: Law, Custom, and Naval Government in Newfoundland, 1699-1832* (Toronto: University of Toronto Press for the Osgoode Society for Canadian Legal History, 2003). A shorter version of some of Bannister's principal arguments will be found in his article "The Fishing Admirals in Eighteenth-Century Newfoundland," *Newfoundland Studies* 17, 2 (2001): 166-219. On more specialized eighteenth-century topics, see John Mannion, "Irish Migration and Settlement in Newfoundland: The Formative Phase, 1697-1732," *Newfoundland Studies* 17, 2 (2001): 257-93; and Alan G. Macpherson, "A Modal Sequence in the Peopling of Central Bonavista Bay, 1676-1857," in John J. Mannion, ed., *The Peopling of Newfoundland: Essays in Historical Geography* (St. John's: Institute of Social and Economic Research, Memorial University, 1977), 102-35.

There are huge gaps in the study of nineteenth-century Newfoundland. There is not, for example, a good analysis of St. John's, and more general accounts by historians and historical geographers often end in the 1830s. In these circumstances, the above account relies principally on works already cited plus the following: Sean T. Cadigan, *Hope and Deception in Conception Bay: Merchant-Settler Relations in Newfoundland, 1785-1855* (Toronto: University of Toronto Press, 1995); Michael Staveley, "Population Dynamics in Newfoundland: The Regional Patterns," in Mannion, *The Peopling of Newfoundland,* 49-76; Chesley W. Sanger, "The Evolution of Sealing and the Spread of Settlement in Northeastern Newfoundland," in ibid., 136-51; Patricia Thornton, "The Transition from the Migratory to the Residential Fishery in the Str. of Belle Isle," *Acadiensis* 19, 2 (1990): 92-120; Shannon Ryan, *The Ice Hunters: A History of Newfoundland Sealing to 1914* (St. John's: Breakwater Books, 1994); John Mannion, "Old World Antecedents, New World Adaptations: Inistioge (Co. Kilkenny) Immigrants in Newfoundland," *Newfoundland Studies* 5, 2 (1989): 103-75; and Mannion, *Irish Settlements in Eastern Canada: A Study of Cultural Transfer and Adaptation,* Research Publication No. 12 (Toronto: University of Toronto Press, 1974).

7
The Maritimes

After the deportation of the Acadians and the fall of Louisbourg in 1758, the territory that came to be called Nova Scotia and today comprises the Maritime provinces of Canada was exceedingly sparsely populated and of dwindling strategic significance. War had moved to another theatre, the St. Lawrence Valley, leaving only some ten to twelve thousand people, including Native groups, in the whole territory. The population of the garrison town of Halifax declined from approximately six thousand in 1752 to fewer than two thousand in 1759. The British forts around the Bay of Fundy were maintained with small garrisons. Most of the British and foreign Protestants whom the British government had sent to Halifax in the early 1750s to provide a buffer between New England and New France had left the colony or lived in coastal settlements south of Halifax: some fifteen hundred near Lunenburg and perhaps another thousand in settlements along the South Shore. Most of them depended on government rations. The Acadian marshlands were almost deserted, although some Acadians – perhaps a thousand or more – still hid in the forest. The Mi'kmaq and Maliseet (the Native people of the Saint John River Valley) were there too, their circumstances equally precarious. They had fought with the French against the British, and still maintained territorial control over most of Nova Scotia. On several occasions officials in Halifax, with whom the Mi'kmaq and Maliseet now had no choice but to deal, had resolved to destroy them.

Forests covered this largely depopulated land. On the harshest sites coniferous forests resembled those farther north, and on the most benign sites primarily broadleaf deciduous forests resembled those farther south.

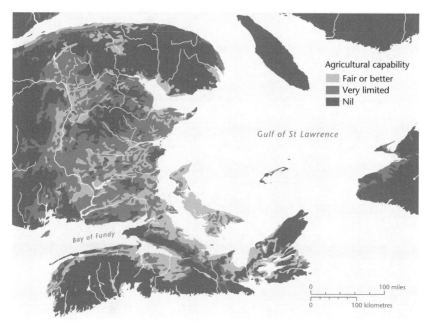

MAP 7.1   Land capability in Greater Nova Scotia | After Canada Land Inventory, Soil Capability for Agriculture, Atlantic Provinces.

The mixed coniferous-deciduous forests that predominated elsewhere included mature stands of white and red pine. The land underneath the forest, a northern extension of the Appalachian Highlands, was rough and glaciated. Much of it was upland, the soils rocky, thin, and acidic, and the growing season short. In lowland pockets along the coast and in the river valleys, the land was better and the growing season longer, but the lowlands were bounded and discontinuous. No large sweep of potential agricultural land existed. The outer Atlantic edge of this Nova Scotia was particularly barren, except in relation to the fishing grounds. The Acadians had demonstrated that the crops and livestock of northwestern Europe could be raised on the marshlands around the Bay of Fundy and on the Island of St. John (Prince Edward Island), but the agricultural potential of most of the rest was little known. It would prove to be modest. Map 7.1, derived from modern land capability surveys, shows that much of this large territory, now the Maritime provinces, had no agricultural potential, and that the potential of most of the rest was limited. Compared with the best land in the English colonies to the south or in the French settlements southwest of Lake Michigan, there was no outstanding agricultural land.

Deeply indented by the sea, Nova Scotia was maritime territory jutting into the western North Atlantic and was exposed, as for many years past, to the pressures and demands of the outside world. The relative vacuum that it had become in the late 1750s would soon draw in people, institutions, and circuits of power of the day. To the south were rapidly expanding and land-hungry settler colonies; across the Atlantic were peoples seeking some escape from enclosures, industrialization, and increasingly aggressive market economies. Commercial capital would seek profitable new resources; industrial capital would create new demands and, by the 1830s, would begin to export the industrial system itself. The legal-managerial-normalizing apparatus of the state would expand. These pressures were at hand, and Nova Scotia would respond to them in its fashion. In the late eighteenth century, that response was primarily framed by war, in the early to mid-nineteenth century by industrialization in the British Isles.

THE LATE EIGHTEENTH CENTURY: THE CONSEQUENCES OF WAR

Immigration

Of the two main streams of immigration to Nova Scotia during these years, one came from the south, the other from the British Isles. They brought different peoples and usually placed them apart.

The larger of these streams, the former, came in fits and starts. The collapse of French power in North America during the Seven Years' War had suddenly opened a broad swath of land from northern New York through northern New England to Nova Scotia for settlement, land that land-hungry New Englanders almost immediately sought. In the five years from 1759 to 1764, sixty thousand people – "planters" in the language of the day – moved north into this former geopolitical buffer zone, some eight thousand of them into Nova Scotia. The incentive to move to Nova Scotia was partly the developed farmland on the vacant Acadian marshlands, partly the favourable terms that the governor of Nova Scotia, Charles Lawrence, was offering: a hundred acres to each family head and fifty acres for each member of the household (soon generalized to five hundred acres per family) within townships of 100,000 acres, and no quit rents for ten years. He intimated, but did not guarantee, that New England's institutions of local government would be respected. Moreover, he said, the government would subsidize immigration by providing transportation and food (promises not always kept). For young families in crowded New England townships, these terms were enticing. The New England town meeting, which provided a framework for a rapid response to them, would discuss the move, establish the number of families interested in relocation, and appoint a management committee. It would hire the agents to negotiate the terms of a land grant and, in some cases, a lot-layer to survey it. With new land secured in this way, potential emigrants would then be in a position to move. Often the men went first to draw lots for land (distribution was to be as equitable as possible) and prepare for their wives and children. In this ordered fashion, several hundred people could leave one township and relocate in another within a year.

Officials in the colony of Nova Scotia quickly alienated a great deal of land. Initially, no individual was to receive more than a thousand acres, no family more than five thousand acres, and grantees were to improve one-third of their holdings each decade. By 1764, however, the British government considered this too restrictive. Concerned about the reaction in New England and the Middle Colonies to the Royal Proclamation, which closed the Ohio Valley to land speculators and settlers (Chapter 5), it permitted the governor to grant land in any quantity in response to any plausible proposal to settle it. In total some 5.5 million acres were virtually given away before 1783, most of them before the end of 1765. Quit rents were never collected. On the other hand, the colonial administration did not allow the level of township autonomy that the planters believed they were promised. In the 1760s, the government took the surveying of local land and the appointment of local officials (constables, overseers of the poor, fence-viewers, dike commissioners, and the like) away from the townships and reduced their representation in the Nova Scotia assembly – moves, historian Jack Bumsted has pointed out, that were consistent with the prevailing British view that New England town-meeting democracy risked unbalancing and destabilizing the British constitution.

The influx of planters from New England almost doubled the population of Nova Scotia and reshaped its ethnicity. Broadly, the old Acadian lands became a northern extension of New England, although group migration produced patches of somewhat differently minded people. The township of Truro, at the eastern end of Minas Basin, was settled by New

Hampshire Presbyterians of Scots-Irish background; the township of Horton, fifty miles to the west, was settled by Congregationalists from Connecticut; the fishing townships along the rocky South Shore were settled from coastal Massachusetts. As the grantees initially controlled land division within townships, different land systems emerged. In some townships, grantees acquired land in a single block of five hundred acres; in others they acquired parcels of different categories of land scattered through the township. In most of the fishing townships along the South Shore, little land was surveyed; rather, fishing families divided the beach among themselves. Considered as a whole, the New Englanders who acquired land in Nova Scotia in the early 1760s were mobile in pursuit of opportunity; though vigorous defenders of local democracy and local autonomy, they were probably less committed to the collective institutions of township life as ends in themselves than as means to family-centred achievement. Many grantees never turned up in Nova Scotia. Others soon left. In the agricultural townships, there was much buying and selling of land, the accumulation of which seems to have been a central preoccupation. Many grantees were speculators; all were well attached to market economies. Such values, coupled with distrust of distant government, appreciation of local democracy, and rock-ribbed religious conviction within a variety of Protestant denominations, reoccupied the former Acadian lands around the Bay of Fundy, the seasonal Acadian fishing ports along the South Shore, and accompanied the very few New Englanders who went to Cape Breton Island, the Island of St. John, or the Saint John Valley.

The planter migrations petered out almost as quickly as they began. The Royal Proclamation had not effectively closed off the Ohio country; backcountry settlers and speculators operated there, and in 1768 the Treaty of Fort Stanwix, between the Iroquois (who neither controlled nor owned this land) and the British (who were in the same position), apparently legitimized their presence. For some, western lands were more enticing than Nova Scotia; others returned whence they came. By the end of the decade, more New Englanders were quitting Nova Scotia than going there, a state of affairs that probably did not change until the American Revolution.

That long struggle, which culminated in the Treaty of Paris of 1783 and the separation of the United States of America from British North America, produced another surge of immigration from the south, this time a mass movement of political refugees. These were the Loyalists, as the British called them, people unwilling to trade their allegiance to Britain for citizenship in a new republic. Some thirty-five to forty thousand of them fetched up in Nova Scotia, most of them in 1783, an assisted evacuation, funded by the British government and transported in British warships, of a politically favoured population that had to be looked after, at least for a time. It descended upon a small, overwhelmed colonial administration and quickly spun off two new colonies: New Brunswick, created after a group of prominent Loyalists with aristocratic dreams of a hierarchical society run by gentlemen lobbied the British government to separate the land north of the Bay of Fundy from Nova Scotia; and Cape Breton Island, formed when officials in London accepted the bizarre argument that the island would attract five thousand Loyalists from Quebec if it became a colony. Each of these small administrations struggled to accommodate the Loyalists. Officials withdrew (escheated) some 1.5 million acres from the more prodigal of the grants made in the 1760s but could not immediately meet the demand for land. The Loyalists who poured into Halifax, Annapolis Royal, and the new Loyalist towns of Shelburne and Saint John lived in churches and stores, on overcrowded ships, or in huts or tents. They were quick to criticize, and probably about a fifth of them left almost immediately. Stretched colonial governments did what they could to provide lumber, tools, provisions, and free land in grants of a hundred to a thousand acres, some of them within large blocks of land that the Loyalists then surveyed into lots.

Map 7.2 shows the distribution of Loyalists in 1785. Their coming bid up the price of land in the established agricultural townships, but, except in the southern Annapolis Valley, few settled there (the Scots-Irish in Truro supported the American Revolution and would not admit Loyalists). Their principal settlement in Nova Scotia was at Shelburne, an instant Loyalist town that briefly had ten thousand people. There were perhaps twelve hundred Loyalists in Halifax, and others scattered along the coast. In New Brunswick, the Saint John Valley became predominantly Loyalist, as did the settlements around Passamaquoddy Bay in the new colony's southwestern corner. The few Loyalists on Cape Breton were in or near Sydney, the capital of this colony. The few on the Island of St. John acquired land from the proprietors to whom, in the mid-1760s, the whole island had been granted.

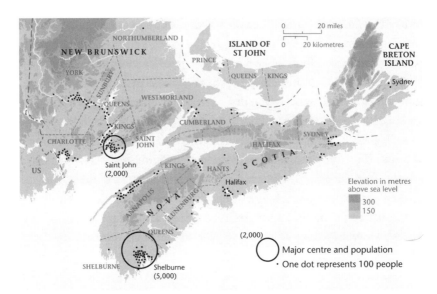

MAP 7.2   Loyalists in the Maritimes, 1785 | After G. Wynn, in *Historical Atlas of Canada*, vol. 1, *From the Beginning to 1800*, ed. R. Cole Harris, cart. Geoffrey J. Matthews (Toronto: University of Toronto Press, 1987), plate 3.

Most of the Loyalists came from the former Middle Colonies. Some of them had been successful merchants or prominent landowners, and some were well educated, but most were ordinary folk with backgrounds in trades or farming. Given the circumstances of their coming, a good many were destitute. Most of them came in nuclear families – the wives coming, whatever their own views, because of decisions their husbands had taken. Single men were likely to be soldiers from disbanded Scottish regiments. Some 10 percent were blacks attracted to the prospect of equality in a colony they hoped was free of slavery. Probably considerably more than 10 percent had not been born in the Thirteen Colonies. Not many had prior experience with pioneer farming. Yet almost all of them were political refugees, and their expectations, as historian Neil MacKinnon has pointed out, were less those of pioneers than of Loyalists seeking restitution and the triumph of their cause. Some thought they were laying the foundations of a new empire in "a place chosen by the Lord's elect." Many brought a hatred of republican America ("Satan's Kingdom" according to one), some because of the treatment they had received there as opponents of the revolution, others because they believed in the institution of the monarchy and admired ordered, deferential societies. In other respects they were much like the planters who had come to Nova Scotia before them: keen to get ahead, attentive to the marketplace, and resolute in defence of their and their families' interests. As they had not come in small organized groups, unlike the planters, they were less attached to particular local institutions.

Fate and dreams had brought the Loyalists to Nova Scotia, but the land hardly held them. The king's bounty looked after them for a time, but ended in 1787. Those clearing land soon realized how little good land was available, and how far a few cleared acres were from a viable commercial farm. Visions of landed estates and country mansions were soon thwarted by high labour costs and weak markets. Merchants anticipated taking over the carrying trade with British islands in the West Indies (after 1783 the Navigation Acts excluded American shipping) but had trouble raising local cargoes. The black refugees found themselves free but unequal and racially stigmatized. When they were offered free passage to Sierra Leone, and free land and racial equality there, about a third of them left for this new "promised land." In different ways, expectations far outran realities, and Loyalist misgivings soon turned on local officials, British policies, prior planter societies, and, as they competed for scarce resources, other Loyalists. The place favoured by the Lord's elect began to seem "an ungrateful place," and, as the passions of war softened, some returned to the new country they had fled. By 1790 two-thirds of the buildings in Shelburne were empty.

Eighteenth-century migration from the British Isles, which was smaller and later, came mostly from Yorkshire in northeastern England and from the Western Highlands of Scotland. In the early and mid-1770s about a thousand immigrants arrived from Yorkshire. Most of them came in families; many had been substantial farmers or tradespeople in Yorkshire who had been driven to leave by escalating rents charged by landlords bent on building and furnishing mansions. They settled on the tidal marshes and adjacent uplands around Chignecto Bay in the northwestern corner of the Bay of Fundy. There were somewhat more Scots, at least three thousand of them, a late eighteenth-century vanguard of a much larger Scottish migration early in the next century. The population in the Western Highlands was rising rapidly, a consequence of the widespread adoption by 1770 of the potato, more effective inoculations against smallpox, and the rapid growth of a commercial kelp harvest. At the same time, the large landowning families, which controlled all the land in the Western Highlands and from whom all farmers held tenancies or subtenancies, sought to benefit from the agricultural improvements of the day and the growing industrial demand for wool by increasing productivity on and rents from their lands. They began converting tenancies into sheep runs, which they could readily do because almost all their tenants held land on short lease. Some landlords simply increased the duration and price of leases, intending thereby that the cost of land would force a tenant – often an outsider familiar with new agricultural methods – to cultivate it more intensively. Such changes destroyed the old mixed agricultural economy of the Western Highlands, with its commercial emphasis on black cattle sold to drovers (to pay the rent) and its largely subsistent cultivation of oats, barley, and potatoes. People were forced to abandon their villages (clachans) in the interior and settle along the coast on small lots (crofts) that the landlords laid out for them. There they farmed a little and paid the rent by gathering kelp, burning it, and selling the ash (used to manufacture soap) to their landlords or to a merchant. This income enabled them to pay the rent for their crofts, and their landlords to acquire, in effect, their labour for nothing. In the eyes of most landlords, economists, and planners, the destruction of the clachans and of the traditional rural economy of the Highlands was an inevitable and necessary adjustment to changing economic opportunities. Many of them advocated relocating the dispossessed in new industrial towns in the Lowlands or in the similar towns envisaged for the Western Highlands, and strongly opposed emigration, which in their eyes drove up the price of labour.

In these circumstances, most of those who left could afford to pay the some £3 per adult and £10-£12 per family for a transatlantic passage – some £30 for both passage and start-up funds for farming. A few indentured servants apart, they were among the better off tenant farmers, and they left to avoid the future that the landlords, economists, and planners envisaged. Their motives, Jack Bumsted has shown, were deeply conservative: they sought to preserve their mixed pastoral-arable farming, their Gaelic language, their religion, and their clan ties. They migrated in families and settled in isolated locations on the Island of St. John, visited by only a few ships a year, or on the north shore of Nova Scotia, from where there was barely a trail to the south. A few of them moved on to the west coast of Cape Breton Island. Their hand implements – spade, *cas chrom* (wooden hand-plough), and hoe – were more efficient tools in stumpy, semi-cleared fields than animal-drawn ploughs and harrows, which they did not know and had never used in Scotland.

In the background of these migrations was a trickle of returning Acadians. In 1764 they were officially allowed to resettle, provided they took the oath of allegiance and dispersed in small groups. Some Acadians emerged from the forest, some walked back from Massachusetts, and some returned in small boats from the seaboard colonies to which they had been sent. As their former lands were now occupied by others, they settled principally on Cape Breton Island, in the Halifax area, in the southwestern corner of Nova Scotia (where they were granted land on St. Mary's Bay in 1768), in the Saint John Valley, at the north end of Chignecto Bay, in isolated settlements along the north coast of New Brunswick, and on the Island of St. John. They too were refugees, but with none of the support the Loyalists received. Most of them squatted; when lands they occupied were allocated to others, as when the Loyalists arrived in the Saint John Valley, they were forced to move again. They wished, one of them then told the authorities, to move north to the Madawaska Valley where they could live undisturbed and "retain the customs, language and religion of their ancestors." By this time, there was some official sympathy for the Acadians and some interest in settling a contested border area (Map 7.6). Acadian families wishing to move to Madawaska were granted two hundred acres there. For the most part, however, the Acadian migrations hardly registered with colonial officials, and it is impossible to be very precise about the numbers involved. Perhaps there were two or three thousand people seeking a place to be.

The Economic Underpinnings

All of these different peoples participated, however indirectly, in an economy driven less by resource development and manufacturing than by immigration and government spending. Agriculture was possible but constrained by the limitations of soil and climate and the lack of an export staple. Fishing, which dominated the economy along the Atlantic face of Nova Scotia and Cape Breton Island, yielded bare livings for fishermen and wealth for a few merchants but never more than a small fraction of the return of the Newfoundland fisheries. Lumbering was important for local use, and some squared timber, lumber, and masts were exported, particularly from the coastal borderlands of New Brunswick and Maine. Small ships were built in several harbours, some for the local carrying trade, some for export. But none of these activities, or all of them together, added up to a robust regional economy. It is quite likely, as the economic historian Julian Gwyn has argued, that in these years the economy of the region had more to do with war than with anything else.

All the migrations had been affected by war: the planters coming to land made available by the deportation of the Acadians at the beginning of the Seven Years' War, and the Loyalists coming as refugees after the American Revolution. Scottish migration stopped during the American Revolution; after 1792 it was curtailed by war with France. In wartime the British government was loath to lose Highland Scots, whom it considered its best soldiers. Moreover, colonies assumed more strategic importance in wartime, and annual British public spending on them increased. Administrations were expanded, fortifications improved, and garrisons enlarged. Coin imported to pay troops circulated in the economy. Merchants positioned themselves to benefit from government spending, particularly in the provisioning trades associated with the garrisons, in the process enriching themselves while having little impact (they dealt largely with imports) on local rural economies. In new colonies with weak economies, this British investment was critical. In Britain, liberal politicians derided the profligate expenses generated by backward colonies.

Entailed in the settlement process itself was a more indirect form of subsidy. Many of the planters brought some capital. As they acquired land and speculated in more, they borrowed against the security of their land grants, raising mortgages from more prosperous local planters or from merchants in Halifax, Saint John, New England, or even England. Some of the funds so raised circulated in rural economies. Many Loyalists also brought capital, a fact reflected in the sharp rise in prices with their coming. Some of the Yorkshire immigrants bought and established substantial farms quickly, using funds earned on one side of the Atlantic to subsidize a beginning on the other, as on a more modest scale did some of the Highland Scots. Retired army officers received pensions, of which some £200,000, historical geographer Graeme Wynn has calculated, was paid to residents of Nova Scotia or New Brunswick. Payments by the British government to Loyalists in these colonies for losses sustained during the revolution amounted to even more, some £270,000, much of which also entered local economies. Many of the supplies that the Loyalists received from the government were purchased locally from merchants, farmers, or fishermen. In all these ways, much of the cost of pioneering and the vitality, such as it was, of local economies relied on external capital. Those, like the Acadians, without access to such capital depended on subsistence agriculture supplemented, if they could find it, by wage labour.

The Region in 1800

Map 7.3 shows the distribution of the some seventy-five to eighty thousand people who, at the beginning of the nineteenth century, lived in the British colonies of Nova Scotia, New Brunswick, Cape Breton Island, and Prince Edward Island. There were three towns: Halifax with some eight thousand inhabitants, Saint John with twenty-five hundred, and Shelburne with two thousand. Fredericton, the capital of New Brunswick, Charlottetown, the capital of Prince Edward Island, and Sydney, the capital of Cape Breton Island, were villages. At this time Halifax and Quebec were the two largest towns in British North America, and were much of a size. Structurally they were also similar, two sharply stratified urban societies dominated by government administration, military spending, and commerce. Halifax was a major military base, had the largest colonial administration in the region, received and redistributed the lion's share of regional imports (many associated with Halifax's administrative and military functions), and controlled most of the export trade in fish. Wharves lined the waterfront, but the British imperialism that had created Halifax in 1749 still dominated it fifty years later (Figure 7.1). The Church of England, the official colonial church and the religion of the elite, stressed the virtues of an ordered, "well formed" society and of loyalty to empire. Prince Edward, duke of Kent, commanded the town's troops and capped a social hierarchy that, at its upper end, included a round of balls, formal dinners, and elegant entertainments in the Georgian parlours of fine inner-city houses. Living close to the wharves at the other end of the social scale were stevedores and labourers, prostitutes, and blacks. Saint John, with its garrison largely transferred to Halifax with the 1792 resumption of war between Britain and France, its location less advantageous for Atlantic trade, and the capital of New Brunswick upriver at Fredericton, was a port for the Saint John River and the Bay of Fundy. With neither an agricultural hinterland nor much external trade, Shelburne was a fading relic of Loyalist

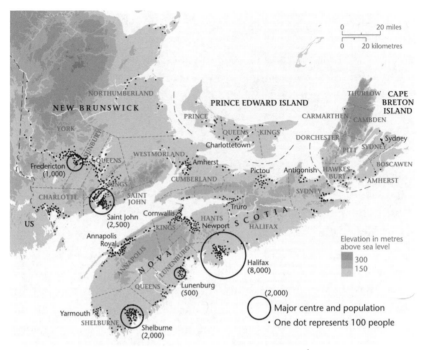

MAP 7.3   Distribution of population in the Maritimes, 1800 | After G. Wynn, in Harris and Matthews, *Historical Atlas of Canada,* vol. 1, plate 32.

FIGURE 7.1   *Perspective View of the Province Building, Halifax* (detail), 1819 (artist, John Elliott Woolford). The British administrative presence and the expatriate values of an urban elite dominate this and other paintings of late eighteenth- and early nineteenth-century Halifax. | Library and Archives Canada, 1993-335-3.

settlement. Fredericton, Charlottetown, and Sydney had little economic base; their garrisons and colonial administrations were tiny, as was their trade. Fredericton, the largest of them, had almost one thousand, Sydney some two hundred, and much of its classical revival arrangement of streets and parks had become cow pasture.

Cod was the region's principal export, although the volume of trade was only about a ninth of Newfoundland's. Three quite different fisheries operated off the Atlantic coast of Nova Scotia and around Cape Breton Island: a transatlantic migratory fishery that brought a seasonal workforce and was controlled by merchants based in the Channel Islands, a New England fishery that exploited both the offshore banks and inshore waters, and a resident fishery controlled by local merchants and operated out of many small ports. By 1800 the transatlantic migratory fishery was a fraction of its former size, but where it survived – at Arichat and Chéticamp on Cape Breton Island – it produced large unmechanized but factory-like operations for processing fish. As for centuries past, the cod were caught from small boats (shallops) in inshore waters. Although primarily a schooner fishery to the offshore banks, the New England fishery also brought small boats to fish inshore waters, often relying on residents to cure the catch. The resident fishery, much like its counterpart in Newfoundland, depended on local fishermen and on a chain of small-to-middling merchants – the smallest in some of the outports, the most substantial in Halifax – who advanced supplies and credit and took cured fish. Relatively egalitarian kin-based societies emerged in the outports where virtually every family depended on fishing, a cow or two, a kitchen garden, and a little pasture amid the rock. Almost all of them were indebted to a merchant. There were paths but no roads between most settlements. Life was hard, people were poor, and buildings spare and utilitarian: sheds and drying platforms (flakes) along the beach and weathered dwellings and sheds behind, their arrangement ordered more by kin and local topography than by geometry.

Wood was also exported, though in small quantities. Many small water-powered sawmills served local settlements, and small ships were built in many harbours, but bulk wood exports came mainly from the accessible coastal forests of southwestern New Brunswick. By 1800 about two thousand tons of squared timber, 4 million board feet of lumber, and some four thousand masts and spars were exported annually, the lumber and squared timber principally to the West Indies, the masts and spars to British naval shipyards. A few mills equipped with several "gangs" of reciprocating saws were able to cut several boards at once, and a few lumberers owned the dozen or more teams of oxen required to haul the largest masts – huge "sticks" of white pine up to thirty-five metres long – to a river. In such ways, the forest was being nibbled at some of its edges.

Most settlers depended primarily on farming indifferent soils near the northern climatic limit of agriculture. As the Acadians had discovered long since, only the hardy crops and livestock of northwestern Europe, for which there was little export market, could be raised. At the end of the eighteenth century, the region was a regular net importer of foodstuffs, particularly of wheat and flour. However, there were local markets, principally in the towns. Where soils were fair and settlers had brought some capital, as in the planter settlements around Minas Basin, the Yorkshire settlements at Chignecto Bay, or some of the Loyalist settlements in the Saint John Valley, there were farms with more than a hundred acres of cultivated land and pasture as well as sizable herds and flocks. The Yorkshire settlers sent almost a thousand cattle and as many small barrels of butter to Saint John and Halifax each year. Using the account books of a general store in Horton, a planter settlement on Minas Basin, historian Elizabeth Mancke has shown that in the exchange and largely cashless economy of the store, men sold barrels, boards, flour, fish, oats, potatoes, bricks, wheat, and a variety of other goods to the store; women purchased many of the goods sold by the store to facilitate their own domestic production. They bought raw cotton, for example, and cotton-carding brushes, so they could spin and weave cotton at home, making cloth and clothing, most for their families but some to be sold back to the store. In such ways, Mancke suggests, commercial and subsistence economies were intertwined to the point that, in a place such as Horton, a subsistence economy detached from the commercial world never existed. Nor were settlers particularly prosperous: Horton may have boasted a few substantial American Georgian houses (with a central hall, two chimneys, and several bedrooms on the second floor), but a study of probate records (wills) shows that at this time the average house in the area consisted of two to four small sparsely furnished rooms.

In the heart of the former Acadian marshlands, Horton was one of the most prosperous agricultural areas in the region. Most farmers elsewhere were much less well off. Graeme Wynn estimates that an average farm in the Saint John Valley consisted of some twelve cleared acres; Stephen Hornsby, another historical geographer, describes average clearings on Cape Breton Island at the time that were even smaller. In many places, the common dwelling was a shanty, its log walls cross-notched at the corners, its single-slope roof covered with sod or bark, and its floor dirt. This was pioneer farming at its most difficult, conducted, in the case of most of the Highland Scots, by people accustomed to hardship but not to the unremitting labour of making a farm in a forest. There was no margin on such farms; sickness or an accident could destroy them. When tiny clearings could not support a family, men took such other work as they could find: fishing, hunting, trapping, cutting sawlogs, working for other farmers, hauling. No families lived completely self-sufficiently, but on these frail pioneer farms money was rare, purchases were few and far between, and the whole family effort was bent towards producing the goods essential for survival.

The map of population distribution in 1800 (Map 7.3) can be interpreted in the light of these different economies: fishing accounted for most of the settlement on Cape Breton Island and along the Atlantic coast of Nova Scotia, lumbering for some of the settlement in southwestern New Brunswick and along the Miramichi, and farming for almost all other rural settlement. Because the region had been settled by different peoples who had fetched up in different places, the map can also be read ethnically. In general, southern Nova Scotia and southwestern New Brunswick had been settled from the south; these areas were English-speaking and Protestant. More northerly areas were settled from the British Isles or by returning Acadians; there, Gaelic and French were more common than English, Catholics more common than Protestants. Within these general patterns, the grid of ethnicity and religion was finely calibrated as, often, people in adjacent settlements spoke different languages and adhered to different Christian faiths. The Scots in northern Nova Scotia segregated themselves: the Presbyterians in Pictou, the Catholics fifty kilometres away in Antigonish. Because settlements were usually closely bounded by rock and water, and connections between them were often difficult, ethnic/

religious isolation in scattered settlements became a normal condition. In such circumstances, there would be few outsiders, and descendants of the founding population would be increasingly related. A few surnames dominated the Yorkshire settlements; among the Acadians on Cape Breton Island, bloodlines were so intertwined that missionaries requested special dispensations to marry kin.

Class differentiation in these rural societies was much less than many prominent landholders had anticipated. The proprietors who held all the Island of St. John in twenty-thousand-acre lots intended to rent land to tenants and create a stratified, class-conscious, and semi-feudal society. Some Loyalists, particularly in the Saint John Valley, held similar views, and received official support for them. But to imagine such societies was one thing, to create them another. Planter society – even considerable elements of Loyalist society – was far more democratic and far less deferential than English society; even the evangelical fervour that caught up many planters emphasized an individual's relationship with God and the irrelevance of government and social position. Yorkshire and Scottish settlers had come to escape landlords and the rents they charged. In these circumstances, there was little disposition towards gentility. More basically, the relative availability (and hence cheapness) of land and the relative weakness of the markets, compared to anywhere in rural Britain, had tended to favour those who worked the land and to discourage those (such as landlords) who profited from it. The social range in some rural settlements was very small – everyone was poor. Other settlements contained both prosperous and poor. Evidence shows that the social range was growing in the planter settlements as the percentage of landless men increased, but at the end of the eighteenth century there was probably no wealth. For people in these rural settlements, most of whom had a lively sense of sin, Halifax and Saint John constituted different and dangerous worlds. There one could find ostentation and pretension, theatres offering dubious entertainments, grog shops, and brothels. In the case of Halifax, there too was colonial political power and officials who, advised from London, had shifted political authority from local to central administrations.

Increasingly ignored in the background of these developments were the Mi'kmaq. In 1726 the British had negotiated a treaty that granted them proprietary rights over their fishing, hunting, and plantings, and, in the

Mi'kmaq understanding, exclusive right to their land. The Mi'kmaq probably perceived a treaty of 1761 – in which the British monarch offered friendship and protection, and chiefs and colonial officials buried a hatchet to symbolize peace – to be a reaffirmation of the earlier treaty. But, as historian William Wicken has pointed out, treaties were both oral and written agreements with very different connotations in Native and European cultures. What was said and what was written were unlikely to be the same. Moreover, as time passed Native memory focused on the oral account and colonial officials on the written. As written, the treaties were full of ambiguities and therefore open to reinterpretation favourable to a settler colonial society bent on the acquisition of Native land. In these circumstances, Mi'kmaq power as an autonomous people persisted through the American Revolution (when they were courted by both sides) but collapsed when they were no longer militarily useful and the Loyalists arrived. Historian Leslie Upton notes that in all the correspondence about the settlement of Loyalists there is no word about the dispossession of Native people. Eventually, a little land was licensed (reserved) for their use: some sixty thousand acres in New Brunswick and a third as much in Nova Scotia, although the best of it was subsequently occupied by settlers. Native people were being detached from the resources on which their livelihoods depended. Often, they could not get at the coast, and in the interior game had become scarce – in one year white hunters killed nine thousand moose for skins on Cape Breton Island. In these circumstances malnutrition bordered on starvation in Native communities, diseases such as measles, whooping cough, scarlet fever, and croup (respiratory ailments) were endemic, and outbreaks of smallpox and typhus were frequent. Sickness reduced mobility, further narrowing opportunities to earn a living and increasing poverty. A little later, a Mi'kmaq chief described the situation: "My people," he said, "are poor. No Hunting Grounds – no Beaver – no Otter – no nothing. Indians poor – poor for ever. No Store – no Chest – no clothes. All these Wood once ours. Our Fathers possessed them all. Now we cannot cut a Tree to warm our Wigwaum in Winter unless the White Man please." On the far side of the continent not many years later, other chiefs would say almost exactly this (Chapter 11). Settler colonialism repeats itself, as do its effects. Settlers want Native land; settlers and colonial governments have the physical power to take it and the capacity to legalize the taking. They live within taken-for-granted discourses about the location of civilization and savagery and about progressive and wasteful land uses that legitimate dispossession while giving it a veneer of altruism.

THE EARLY NINETEENTH CENTURY: THE CONSEQUENCES OF INDUSTRIALIZATION

Whereas in the late eighteenth century, war dominated the settlement and economy in the Maritime colonies of British North America, in the early nineteenth century the region responded more to the profound reorganization of British life associated with industrialization. Although weakly industrialized itself, it could not escape the effects of British industrialization on the location of people and on assumptions about markets, trade, and the colonial system. At one basic level, what was happening was this: As custom-built factories and growing fixed capital costs became more common from the 1790s, the location of production began to centralize. It was shifting – more rapidly in some sectors of the economy than others – from many small producers in the countryside to factories, which increasingly were located in cities. As this happened, the bonds of tradition and custom that had regulated rural economies and tempered the effects of the market were weakened or sundered, and many local communities, shorn of their means of support, were uprooted. In Marxian terms, people were being deterritorialized (that is, detached from prior bonds between people and place) and reterritorialized in relation to the requirements of capital (that is, to land conceived as resources and freed from the restraints of custom, and to labour detached from land). They were being separated from their own means of production (from the land and the use value of their own labour on it) and were being transformed into free (unencumbered) urban wage labourers dependent on the social relations of capital.

At the same time, the economic momentum of the factory system slowly shifted power away from the old landed elite. More than any other work, Adam Smith's *Wealth of Nations,* published in 1776, was the bible of this transformation. Smith argued for the vitality and benefits of the unregulated market, an increasingly appealing argument in a country that was the first to industrialize and was confident of its ability to produce and sell. The debate in Britain was protracted and intense, but by the 1840s the free traders had won. The tariff on foreign timber was reduced by more than half in 1841-42, the Corn Laws (which had protected British agriculture) were repealed in 1846, and the Navigation Acts (which had favoured colonial shipping) were repealed in 1849 and 1850. The old mercantilist empire, premised on protected trade between colonies and mother country, and castigated in *The Wealth of Nations,* was gone; markets were less regulated in mid-nineteenth-century Britain than ever before or since. The rights of private property were established in common law to the point that William Blackstone, the most read commentator on the law, held that private property rights were vested in "the immutable laws of nature."

The collapse of the mercantile system, the advent of free trade, and the domination of laissez-faire economics raised basic questions about the value of colonies themselves. The midcentury defence of them offered by Earl Grey, secretary of state for the colonies, was tepid at best: colonies, he argued, had prestige value for a great power, and the Colonial Office had responsibilities to settlers and Native people. The honour of the Crown, he said, was at stake – not an argument that easily moved the British treasury. In such circumstances, the Colonial Office sought to turn over most of the cost and administration of colonies to the colonies themselves. It favoured responsible government, although a few years earlier Herman Merivale, for years the under-secretary in the Colonial Office, had argued that the interests of settlers and of Native people were fundamentally opposed (both wanting the same land), and that if executive power (ultimately, the Colonial Office) were not interposed between them, the former would exterminate the latter. By midcentury such arguments counted for little with a British government dominated by the doctrine of laissez-faire, preoccupied with India and Ireland, uncertain about the imperial value of small colonies at the edge of the northwestern Atlantic, and anxious to divest much of the responsibility for them to colonists clamouring for responsible government.

These British developments reshaped the context of the Maritime colonies under consideration here, most immediately because they brought tens of thousands of new immigrants, some from England but more from the Western Highlands of Scotland or from Ireland.

In the Western Highlands, the clearance of peasant farmers from the clachans and the settlement of most of them in small crofts along the coast were followed, after a generation or two, by another clearance, this time of the crofts themselves. As long as the price of kelp held up, crofting (based on subsistence farming, gathering, and sales or wages from kelping) was a marginally viable way of life. In these years, the landlords did what they could to discourage emigration – including lobbying for improved conditions (and therefore higher fares) in the emigrant ships. Although the increasing availability of foreign alkalis and the use of chemical substitutes depressed kelp prices after the end of the Napoleonic Wars, kelping continued, and most of those leaving before 1825 could afford to pay for their passage. Then, in 1825, when the government removed a tax on salt, the price of kelp collapsed. The kelp industry ended; without it, the crofting economy failed. Crofters could not pay their rents, and landlords sought to replace them with sheep. A few crofters were resettled on new crofts on rocky land, some found their way to Glasgow or another industrializing city, but many emigrated. Now eager to rid themselves of a redundant peasantry, the landlords often forgave arrears, and some even paid for passages, a generosity they could easily afford from the rents they obtained from sheep farmers. The numbers involved cannot be established precisely: at a very rough estimate, perhaps twelve to fifteen thousand Highlanders arrived in the British Atlantic colonies between 1800 and 1825, and perhaps forty thousand between 1825 and 1845 when, in response to potato blight and famine in the colonies, this migration stopped. Throughout, this was a migration of families, kin groups, and communities, and usually went where relatives or friends had gone before. Overall, those arriving before 1825 were a good deal better off than those who came after, some of whom were destitute.

In Ireland in the early nineteenth century, the population was rising at a rate of about 1 percent a year, the cost of land was increasing in response, and prices of domestic manufactures were declining. In the broadest terms, the Irish peasantry was caught in a cost-price squeeze that made it harder and harder to get by. For many, especially in Ulster, the combination of small-scale farming with spinning and weaving had served since the mid-eighteenth century, the women spinning and the men weaving in the interstices of the seasonal routines of farming. But, as farms became smaller upon being divided among children (usually the two eldest sons) or as parts of them were let to subtenants, and as machines replaced some domestic trades and reduced the value of others, the struggle to make ends meet only increased. With the mechanization of cotton spinning in Belfast in the 1770s, there was a short opportunity for hand weavers of cotton until they were displaced by the textile mills of Lancashire. The spinning of flax was not mechanized until 1825, and the hand weaving of linen survived longer, but at prices depressed by the availability of cotton. And so it went. Weavers worked longer hours for lower returns. Those who could not grow flax on tiny holdings contracted with a merchant to supply a product at a fixed price in return for an assured supply of yarn – a "putting-out" system that turned formerly independent farmer-weavers into something more akin to a rural proletariat. Poverty dominated these countrysides, and for a great many people the margin of survival was exceedingly small. By the early 1840s the potato was virtually the only food of a third of the Irish people and the principal food of more than half of them. When a potato blight – a fungus that quickly killed the plant and rotted the potatoes – struck in 1846 and virtually eliminated the crop for several years, a million people died, most of them from diseases associated with severe malnutrition, poor hygiene, and completely inadequate measures of public health.

These conditions produced two large and different nineteenth-century migrations. Between 1815 and 1845 about a million Irish people made their way to North America, almost two-thirds of them to the British North American colonies. Then, between 1845 and 1855, there was a panic-stricken exodus of more than 2 million people, the great majority of whom went to the United States. The first migration was made up of people who had decided to leave, usually because economic prospects were dim, but sometimes because of sectarian violence. They usually had the funds to cross the Atlantic and begin elsewhere – the continuation, in larger numbers, of a century-old migration to the American colonies (the "Scotch-Irish"). Considerably more than half of them were from Ulster, and Protestants outnumbered Catholics by approximately two to one. The famine migrants were poorer on average than their predecessors, although the poorest usually stayed put or went to Liverpool, and a larger proportion of them were Catholic. They came from all parts of Ireland, including the Gaelic-speaking areas of the west. The proportion of these migrations that fetched up in the Atlantic colonies of British North America was small, but large enough to have a profound local effect, particularly in New Brunswick. In 1851 a third of its population was Irish.

With these migrations, the various peoples who, even today, comprise the bulk of Maritime Canada's population, were in place. Although none of them were detached from the larger changes of the early nineteenth century, there seemed an opportunity – which many had sought – in the crannies of this sea- and rock-bound region, to deflect or somewhat postpone the changing nineteenth-century world. In the Maritimes as elsewhere, most immigrants sought to re-establish a measure of the land-based and family-centred security they had known (or imagined) before war or industrialization got in the way. Most of them came to farm, but, in this patchy, interrupted land settled by different peoples and penetrated by different economies, few would escape either the limitations of the land or the reach of industrial civilization.

New Brunswick

Between 1800 and 1851 New Brunswick's population grew from some 25,000 to almost 200,000, and in the latter year was distributed as shown in Map 7.4. Since 1800 (Map 7.3), much land had been taken up and settled, and at the mouth of the Saint John River there was a sizable urban population, the largest in the Maritime colonies. These changes reflected the reach of commercial and, increasingly, of industrial capital into the forests of New Brunswick and also of settlers looking for agricultural land and a rural haven from an industrializing world – which the spare land of New Brunswick provided in measured amounts.

The interest of capital in New Brunswick grew with the British demand for timber. When, in 1806, Napoleon blockaded the continent, including most of the Baltic ports, to British shipping, British imports of squared timber and lumber from the Baltic declined rapidly, and Britain turned to her North American colonies for the wood on which the Royal Navy and a burgeoning industrial economy depended. Exports of ton (squared) timber from New Brunswick increased from some 2,000 tons in 1800 to 60,000 tons in 1810 to an annual average of more than 240,000 tons in the 1820s and 1830s. Exports of lumber (deals, planks, and boards) grew more slowly, but by the 1840s they rivalled the importance of ton timber. Until the early 1840s, this trade was protected by tariffs, which gave colonial wood a decisive competitive advantage, after freight, in the British market.

Moreover, during many of these years capital enjoyed a virtually unregulated access to the forests. In the early years, the Crown reserved all timber suitable for naval purposes; after 1816 the colony introduced a system of timber licences intended to specify the area and amount of cut and

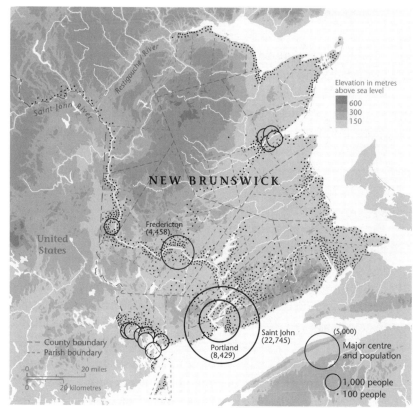

Elevation in metres
above sea level

600
300
150

NEW BRUNSWICK

Restigouche River

Saint John River

Fredericton
(4,458)

United
States

County boundary
Parish boundary

0   20 miles
0   20 kilometres

Portland
(8,429)

Saint John
(22,745)

(5,000)

Major centre
and population

1,000 people
· 100 people

MAP 7.4 Population of New Brunswick, 1851 | After G. Wynn, *Timber Colony:
A Historical Geography of Early Nineteenth Century New Brunswick* (Toronto: University
of Toronto Press, 1981), 151.

to raise revenue for forest management by a levy of a shilling per ton. But
managing a vast and largely unknown forest that had suddenly come within
reach of the North Atlantic economy posed daunting problems. British
experience provided few guidelines. It was far from clear what should be
done, and when laws were enacted, the surveillance of timber operations
scattered across tens of thousands of square kilometres was virtually impossible. For the most part, the forest was open to those with means to cut
it. Then, in 1827, the Colonial Office accepted the argument of British political economists that free land in settler colonies served only to increase
the price of labour (because potential labourers could acquire land), discourage investment by people of means (who would be faced with exorbi-
tant labour costs), and produce a social rabble (because the economic basis

of an ordered, hierarchical society had been undermined). Henceforth, land was to be sold by public auction at an upset price of three shillings an acre. But if, as the political economists claimed, free land encouraged a rabble, this policy, which permitted up to twelve hundred acres to be purchased at once, encouraged timber speculators. When a few years later the government began to auction five-year licences for large blocks of land, critics complained that such a system would progressively eliminate small operators and create monopoly, which to a considerable extent it did. In 1846 fourteen timber concerns held over 5 million acres of licensed Crown land in New Brunswick.

Logging itself was pre-industrial manual work that was easily learned, widely dispersed, and entered into in many ways. Located within four or five kilometres of watercourses large enough to float timber during the spring freshet, it was a winter activity pursued when sap was out of the trees and snow was on the ground. The trees were felled and cut into lengths, roughly squared with broad axes if intended for ton timber, and hauled by horses or oxen over rough roads to a stream bank where they were piled to await the spring thaw. Near the settlements, two or three farmers working in partnership might cut timber on or near their own farm lots and live at home; in more remote locations, groups of as many as twenty men lived in roughly constructed logging camps and worked for wages under a "master lumberer" (Figure 7.2). To prepare for the spring drive, obstructions were removed from the local watercourse, bush cleared from its banks, dams constructed to raise water levels, and sluices built to carry timber around them – increasingly expensive activities that favoured the larger operators. Wood often jammed, nor was always recovered. Eventually, most of it, a jumble of logs and "sticks" (squared timbers) belonging to many different owners, reached a main river. There it was usually sorted and built into rafts. The squared timber went directly to a river-mouth port where it was often squared again, then loaded for shipment overseas. The logs went to a sawmill where they were cut into lumber and then rafted or boated to a port. The ports were the hinge-point between the interior and the Atlantic, the rivers the main routes inland, and their tributaries a dendritic system that, the various river basins considered together, gave access to much of New Brunswick's forest.

This trade, as Graeme Wynn has shown in considerable detail, was coordinated by merchant-wholesalers based mainly in the port towns. They

FIGURE 7.2   "Lumberman's Camp, Nashwaak River, New Brunswick," c. 1870 (photographer, William Notman). Work camps like this were common in the pine forests of New Brunswick and in the fringe of the Canadian Shield north of the St. Lawrence River and Lake Ontario. The bunkhouse (the building with the smoking chimney) was known as a *cambuse* in Lower Canada. | Library and Archives Canada, PA-112117.

relied on transatlantic contacts with British import-export agencies or timber firms for information about the British timber market and for the purchase and shipment of British merchandise. In the other direction, the merchant-wholesalers supplied merchandise and credit to country store-keepers who, in turn, supplied local farmers, farmer-lumberers, and small logging and sawmilling operations. The country storekeepers were as cru-cial in their sphere as the merchant-wholesalers in theirs. Operating in a largely barter economy dependent on credit, they took in the local surplus of farm and forest, and relayed it to the ports. Some of them organized and financed small timber operations, and where the supply warranted it rafted timber downriver either to be sold on their own account or delivered to a merchant-wholesaler. As time went on and lumbering moved farther in-land, timber brokers, essentially agents of the merchant-wholesalers in the interior, became more common. More specialized than storekeepers, they supplied provisions to storekeepers, lumberers, and sawmillers, and organized the purchase and driving of wood on a merchant-wholesaler's account. In such ways, the commercial system connected the remotest lumber camp with the centres of British finance.

The ports were the principal foci of transshipment and information gathering along this commercial axis. Unlike Fredericton (site of the colonial capital and of the principal British garrison in the colony) or the early towns along the St. Lawrence, they were overwhelmingly commercial and, eventually, industrial centres – products of capital. With more than thirty thousand people in 1851, the urban concentration of Saint John and Portland at the mouth of the Saint John River was by far the largest in the colony (Figure 7.3). "Whatever Saint John is," one observer noted, "it must be admitted that shipbuilding and the timber trade have made it." It exported wood and imported a great variety of goods, in so doing maintaining a larger fleet of sailing ships than any other British North American port and equipping itself with banks and insurance firms. With the advent of steam power in the 1830s and 1840s, which detached sawmilling from waterpower sites and allowed it to concentrate at the ports, Saint John and Portland became major centres of sawmilling. The twenty-six sawmills there in 1851 employed almost eight hundred men. More men, tradesmen of various stripes, worked in shipyards that, as historian T.W. Acheson has pointed out, were essentially expanded artisans' workshops. Urban societies in these places were sharply stratified by work and wealth. Merchant-wholesalers, manufacturers, or some combination of the two, lived in fine Georgian townhouses and dominated the social structure. Smaller ports tended to become the commercial-industrial fiefs of one entrepreneur. Joseph Cunard's steam sawmill in Chatham near the mouth of the Miramichi River employed some eighty men. Much of their wages went for clothes and provisions at Cunard's store. Others worked in Cunard's shipyard. Cunard was also the local justice of the Court of Common Pleas. Chatham was his town, much of the timber along the Miramichi was under his control, and as the years passed those who worked for him increasingly comprised an industrial proletariat.

The timber trade was a risky business, even from the perspective of capital. The resource on which it relied became less accessible as the forest was thinned or burned. Although the demand for wood became less selective – at first the finest white pine for masts and spars, then slightly smaller pines for ton timber, then smaller pine and spruce for lumber –

FIGURE 7.3 *View of Saint John, N.B., 1851* (detail) (artist, J.W. Hill). Note the smokestacks (upper left) from steam-powered sawmills. | Library and Archives Canada, 1997-112-1.

the cut moved steadily inland and costs rose. At the other end of this commercial axis, prices fluctuated in the British market, and there was the long, worrying debate about free trade. After the colonial timber preference was reduced in 1842, exports of ton timber fell over the next two years by 50 percent, and of lumber by almost 20 percent. After a brief recovery, a further reduction of timber duties in 1846, followed by a deep recession in Britain, left a glut of wood in British ports and depressed wood prices throughout British North America. In general, the smaller timber concerns were particularly vulnerable. Regulations concerning timber access, the increasing isolation of merchantable timber, the advent of steam-powered sawmilling, and the ability to ride out low prices for wood exports all favoured large operators, although even they were not safe. Joseph Cunard's enterprises on the Miramichi failed in 1848 and drew many of his creditors with him.

Most immigrants, however, came to New Brunswick with the intention of farming. Until 1827 heads of families could acquire a hundred acres plus fifty more for each child; recipients of more than two hundred acres were to pay five shillings for each fifty acres over two hundred. Quit rents were stipulated but not collected. Any loyal subject of the Crown thought fit to cultivate and improve land could expect to receive, virtually free, a forested lot in New Brunswick. By 1827, when the price of land was raised to a minimum of three shillings an acre, most of the good farmland in New Brunswick had been alienated.

In fact, farming was a less autonomous activity than most intending settlers had imagined. For indigent immigrants, work loading the timber ships or in the forest was a means of earning the capital without which it was virtually impossible to start a farm. For those with pioneer farms, seasonal employment in the woods was a means of getting by. For those with larger farms and a surplus to sell, the logging camps and timber ports were accessible markets for hay, oxen, and foodstuffs. For many small sawmillers, local farmers were the principal market for their lumber. Timber duties, such as they were, helped finance the construction of public roads on which farmers depended. In such ways, lumbering and farming were interdependent, as Map 7.5 suggests. It was often alleged that logging led to dissipation and debt, and farming to stable communities; the full-time farmer, it was said, would become prosperous, whereas the farmer-logger would sink into debt. Agrarian ideology was in the air, but it underestimated the interdependence of the two economies and fit the

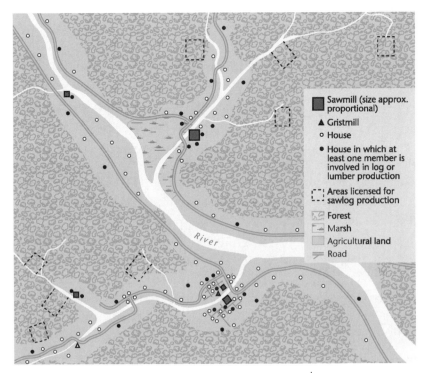

MAP 7.5   Sawmills and settlement, a hypothetical landscape | After Wynn, *Timber Colony*, 99.

colony only in patches. Many farmers had no choice but to be involved with the timber trade, and in so doing to be drawn towards an increasingly capitalized and industrialized economy.

Although New Brunswick imported wheat and flour, and exported almost no agricultural produce, there were local markets in the towns, the logging camps, and among the considerable rural population that did not raise enough to feed themselves. Farm families produced for their own consumption but also, when they could, to supply these markets. In general in this region of long winters and short growing seasons, their cleared land was in meadow and pasture; their ploughed land in oats, buckwheat, sometimes wheat, potatoes, and roots; and their emphasis on livestock, usually cattle. There was some regional market specialization. Farmers on the Tantramar Marsh in northeastern New Brunswick shipped hay, meat, and oxen to the lumber camps along the Miramichi. Many of those in the Kennebecasis Valley near Saint John sent meat, hay, grain, and butter to the city, a hinterland that by 1850 extended some 150 kilometres northeast of Saint John to and beyond the Petitcodiac River. Many in the upper Saint John Valley sold oats and hay to the logging camps. There were also prosperous and poor farmers, as T.W. Acheson and others have convincingly shown. Agricultural society was not egalitarian. The largest farms had more than a hundred cleared acres and raised considerable surpluses; the smallest had only a few cleared acres and did not support a family. In areas farmed for two or three generations, half or more of the farms were usually well-established commercial operations, whereas in more recently settled areas (commonly on poorer land) most farmers relied on off-farm work.

Over the years, access to both forest and farmland became steadily more difficult. As the cut moved inland and the scale of operations increased, it became harder to combine farming and logging. Working away in the timber camps and then on the drives, or closer at hand in the sawmills, many men were becoming, in effect, loggers or mill hands. Moreover, by midcentury the opportunity to acquire a successful farm was largely restricted to those who inherited such a farm or could afford to purchase it. In the old established agricultural areas, farmland was expensive, little unoccupied land was suitable for farming, and a growing percentage of the working population were tenants, labourers, or servants. In the newer areas, land was cheaper but poorer. It offered a family little more than a

FIGURE 7.4   *The Green at Fredericton,* 1838 (artist, W.H. Bartlett). A landscape
of privilege and power in the heart of the colonial capital. | *Canadian Scenery,* vol. 2
(London: Nathaniel Parker, 1842), facing p. 102.

subsistence plus, if it could be found, some off-farm work. Compounding
these difficulties, the fungus that wreaked havoc in Ireland a year later
destroyed the potato crop in 1845 and for several years thereafter. On many
small farms in New Brunswick, only hunting, fishing, gathering, and accumulating debt averted starvation. The inducements to leave farm and
debts behind were strong. Along the Miramichi, talk of Wisconsin was in
the air, and many farms were abandoned.

   Political and cultural power, the principal axis of which ran through
the Saint John Valley, were superimposed on all of this (Figure 7.4). The
valley was Loyalist territory, and in the early nineteenth century many
immigrants from Ulster were added to the Loyalist stock. The two were
mutually reinforcing: both Protestant, loyal, and British. In their eyes, *they*
were respectable New Brunswick, the bastions of its economic and social
order, and they wielded political power. Until well after 1850 they excluded
Roman Catholics from almost all important public offices.

   For others in New Brunswick, the mannered ways of the elite in
Fredericton, the political power of Protestantism, and racialized judgments
about the inferiority of Acadians and Irish Catholics were only oppres-
sive. The Acadians, almost 15 percent of the population of New Brunswick
in 1851, had been shunted to land around its margins (Map 7.6, Figure 7.5).
In their settlements along the gulf, they were primarily fishers who grew

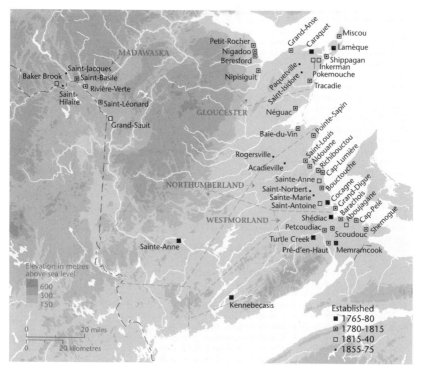

MAP 7.6 Acadian settlements in New Brunswick | After R. Brun, *De Grand-Pré à Kouchibougouac: L'histoire d'un peuple exploité* (Moncton: Les Éditions d'Acadie, 1982), 38-39.

some potatoes and supported a few cattle on saltmarsh hay – a recipe as elsewhere for poverty and debt to fish merchants. They lived in small thatch-roofed houses built of squared logs, occasionally of wattle and daub (poles interlaced with branches and covered with clay), and in villages where, frequently, everyone was a relative. The settlements at the mouth of the Miramichi were composed largely of southern Irish or Highland Scots (Map 7.7) who worked small farms or in the mills or shipyards. They too tended to settle with others of their kind, live within extended families, and speak a language other than English. Economically, few of them were better off than the Acadians; nor, as most were Roman Catholics, did they have more access to the levers of power. From all these gulf shore settlements, Fredericton was a world away.

Isolated as they were, these people were less threatening to the Protestant, British ascendancy in New Brunswick than the famine Irish who poured into the towns of the Saint John Valley in the 1840s. From the

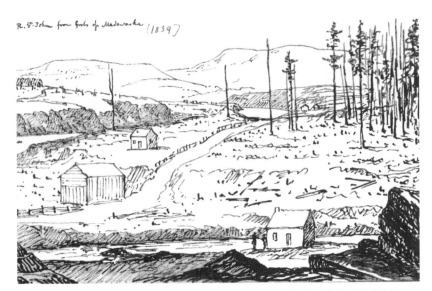

FIGURE 7.5   *River St. John from Forks of Madawaska,* 1839 (artist, Philip J. Bainbrigge). Here, near the junction of the Saint John River (background) and the Madawaska, the settlers were Acadians, and the rough pioneer landscape was the obverse of *The Green at Fredericton* (Figure 7.4). | Philip J. Bainbrigge, "Journal," 79, Library and Archives Canada, C-049610.

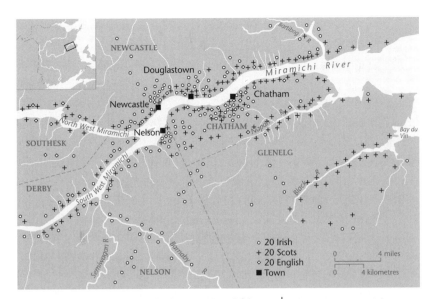

MAP 7.7   Settlement along the lower Miramichi, 1851 | After J. Mannion, *Irish Settlements in Eastern Canada: A Study of Cultural Transfer and Adaptation* (Toronto: University of Toronto Press, 1974), 25.

perspective of most older settlers in the valley, these Irish were undesirable on many counts: they were health hazards, they were threats to public order and to the wages of respectable working men, they were not loyal British subjects, most of them were Catholics, and they were altogether too numerous. In Saint John, a third of the population was Irish in 1851. With their arrival, the number of Loyal Orange Lodges in New Brunswick increased rapidly. The Orange Order, an ultra-Protestant and defensively British organization that had emerged out of Catholic-Protestant feuding in late eighteenth-century Ireland, had come to New Brunswick with immigrants from Ulster. In its rituals, its many secret signs, its initiation rites and oaths, and its parades, the order bespoke an aggressively triumphant British Protestantism. In the Saint John Valley in the late 1840s, it drew adherents from all Protestant classes and ethnicities and, with support in high places, became, virtually, a paramilitary extension of the government. Its parades on 12 July to celebrate the 1695 victory of the Protestant William of Orange over the Catholic James II at the Battle of the Boyne were intended to demonstrate Protestant power – its symbolic control of the streets and the city – and to provoke Catholics. They did both very effectively. There were bloody, deadly riots in Saint John in 1847 and again in 1849 as Orange parades wound through the dense local networks of tenements, slaughterhouses, wharves, warehouses, and shipyards where most of the Catholic Irish lived. On these occasions the city was a stage for the performance of a play with a set cast and a familiar outcome. The Protestants, better organized and equipped and backed by the constabulary and the courts, would win. The ascendancy of Protestantism and of the established order would be affirmed. The world was shown to be more nearly as it should be, although the Catholic Irish, some much bloodied, remained. The historian Scott See interprets these riots as manifestations of nativism (the negative reaction of the established to newcomers) and, to the extent that the Orange Order took social control into its own hands, as examples of vigilante justice.

Basically, the riots would seem to reveal something of the tensions in an increasingly class-divided society in the throes of early industrialization and faced with a finite resource base as the accessible forest was cut over and the limits of agricultural land were reached. Nor were they unrelated to the loss of the imperial preference, a deep transatlantic recession, and the mixing on one side of the Atlantic of ancient antagonisms from the other side. Peoples of differing ethnicities and conflicting religious prejudices contended for recognition, employment, and power in a changing economy in bounded space with limited opportunities. As See points out, those who considered themselves the founding and essential population (ignoring the Mi'kmaq and Maliseet) were more than prepared to keep others at bay.

Prince Edward Island

Beneath the forests of the Island of St. John, or Prince Edward Island as it was renamed in 1799, was more contiguous, potentially arable land than anywhere else in the Maritimes. As it was taken up, the island became, and long remained, overwhelmingly rural. The fishery was small, lumbering more important, and wooden shipbuilding more important yet, but the island never developed an overriding staple trade comparable to the timber trade in the Saint John and Miramichi Valleys or the fishery along the outer Atlantic coast. Yet it grew from some four thousand inhabitants in 1800 to eighty thousand in 1861 and attracted, and in these years largely held, a mix of peoples: Acadians, Loyalists from the United States, Highland Scots (two-thirds of them Protestant), English (particularly from north Devon), and southern Catholic Irish. Most of them intended to farm in a place where, compared to anywhere in Britain, the cost of land was low and that of labour was high – and where hewing a farm out of a forest with hand tools and a horse or a brace of oxen consumed enormous amounts of labour. As elsewhere in the Maritimes, winters were long, growing seasons short, and agricultural markets local or regional. Within approximately these circumstances, most of Prince Edward Island slowly became countryside in the early nineteenth century.

In the 1760s the island had been divided into sixty-seven lots of approximately twenty thousand acres each and allocated to proprietors who, by the terms of their grant, were to pay an annual quit rent to the Crown, bring out within ten years at least one Protestant non-British settler for every two hundred acres of the proprietorship, and lease farm lots to them. Although no proprietors met these terms, the system was still in effect in the early nineteenth century and, for all the attempts of settlers and island politicians to abolish it, remained so until 1875. Characteristically, proprietors (or their agents) leased land in approximately hundred-acre parcels for 999 years at an annual rate of £5, which was usually waived for the first

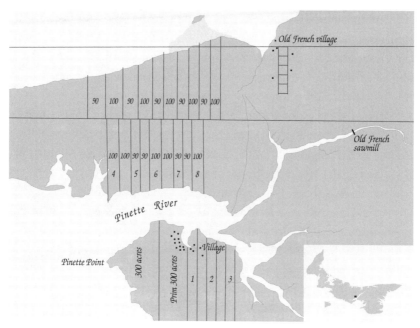

MAP 7.8   Plan of Lord Selkirk's estate at Point Prim, lots 57 and 58, c. 1803 | After M. Hatvany, "Tenant, Landlord, and the New Middle Class: Settlement, Society, and Economy in Early Prince Edward Island, 1798-1848" (PhD diss., History, University of Maine, 1996), 146.

three or four years to allow settlers to establish themselves. Although this was about a twentieth of the per-acre cost of leasehold in Scotland, it was more than the cost of Crown land elsewhere in the Maritimes, and some early Scottish settlers, their experience with landlords fresh in their minds, removed to Cape Breton or mainland Nova Scotia to acquire freehold. The lots themselves were long narrow strips laid out perpendicular to the coast (Map 7.8), much like the long lots along the lower St. Lawrence (Chapter 3) and for approximately the same reasons: ease of surveying, access within one lot to different soil and vegetation types and to the main transportation artery (river or sea). When the waterfront was taken, long lots in the interior were laid out at right angles to roads.

Although many of the more prosperous farmers eventually purchased freehold, these terms of access to land hardly changed over the years. Nor, essentially, did the demands of pioneering: the need for provisions to tide over a family for several years until a forested lot began to resemble a farm; the essential tools and animals required for pioneering; and the relentless work of clearing, grubbing, building, and then of planting and harvesting. By some estimates, it cost well over £100 and four or five years of unremitting family labour to establish a farm that might begin to support a family. On such a farm, women cleared, planted, and harvested almost as much as did men; the image of the farm wife tending the household, kitchen garden, and cows fits later, more prosperous times. But if rents and the demands of pioneering remained fairly constant, the economic circumstances of the immigrants themselves and the timing of their arrival on the island did not. As elsewhere in the Maritimes, the early arrivals were, on average, better off than those coming later, and they had the pick of land. They resided in dispersed settlements along the coasts or rivers – each family on a long-lot farm – a location that gave them access to the outside world, to saltmarsh hay (an immediately available agricultural resource), and to some of the best soils on the island (Map 7.9). These were huge advantages. Immigrants arriving in the 1830s and 1840s, finding the front lands taken, settled in the interior where transportation costs were greater, there was no natural hay, soils were usually poorer, and there was no seaweed or mussel-mud (high in calcium, in which island soils were deficient) to improve them. If they had no capital, which few

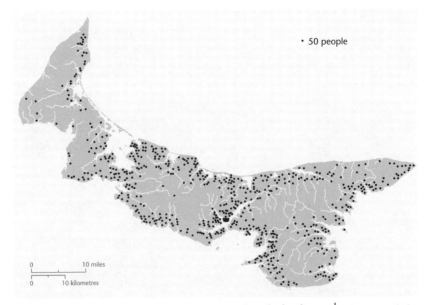

MAP 7.9   Distribution of population, Prince Edward Island, 1833 | After A.H. Clark, *Three Centuries and the Island: A Historical Geography of Settlement and Agriculture in Prince Edward Island, Canada* (Toronto: University of Toronto Press, 1959), 71.

did, they had no choice but to become indebted to a merchant for supplies and to seek off-farm work. Such farms developed slowly and carried heavy debts, first to a merchant, then to a landlord. Inequality, as historian Matthew Hatvany has shown, was built into the process of settlement itself.

Map 7.10, based on a settler diary and the 1841 census, is a schematic representation of what was probably a typical frontland farm in the early 1840s. Thirty-five acres were cleared and cultivated on this lot on the Hillsborough River near Charlottetown. Oats and potatoes were field crops, but more land was in meadow, pasture, or fallow. The cattle and pigs on such a farm foraged in the woods in the summer and were fed saltmarsh or farm hay or potatoes in winter. This was no longer a pioneer farm. It had a large kitchen garden, probably at least two horses as well as cattle, pigs, and perhaps sheep, and in most years produced some surplus of oats, potatoes, livestock, and butter for the Charlottetown market nearby. It relied on seasonal wage labour, most drawn from more inland farms, and it paid the rent.

In newer areas of settlement inland, the situation was rougher and more precarious. Clearings were smaller, fields stump-strewn, and as in

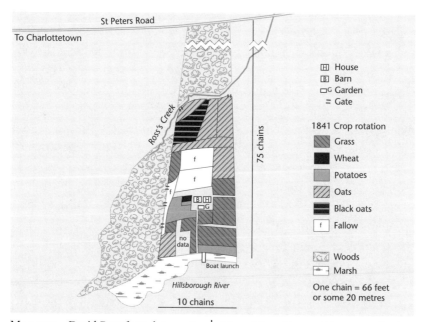

MAP 7.10   David Ross farm, lot 34, 1841 | Adapted from Hatvany, "Tenant, Landlord, and the New Middle Class," 249.

New Brunswick many men became, in effect, farmer-loggers whose winters were spent cutting, squaring, and transporting timber. In this way, some earned the means to establish a farm, but many others became steadily more indebted to a timber merchant who, as the local shopkeeper, bought timber and farm produce and sold imported goods. Where the merchant had a local monopoly, as was often the case, his power could be daunting. It was in poorer inland areas that agitation for the abolition of the landlord system was most intense and, as historian Rusty Bittermann has shown, drew farmers from all the island's ethnicities into a common defence of the rights of small property holders. Expecting that the land would be escheated (returned to the Crown), many settlers refused to pay their rents. Some drove off agents who tried to collect them. But when debts accumulated, the merchants were paid first. Hatvany suggests that an increasingly powerful merchant class hid its own growing influence and landholdings behind a politically motivated and widely popular denunciation of the proprietors.

The more important merchants operated within an intricate multi-scaled matrix of commercial relations. Locally, they maintained country stores, buying local products cheaply and selling imported goods at large markups. Regionally, they shipped island agricultural produce to lumber camps in New Brunswick and fishing settlements in Newfoundland, as well as to St. John's and Halifax where they were consumed or redistributed. They shipped timber to British markets, often in ships they had built on the island and would eventually sell in Britain. They imported British manufactures, including the metal parts, cordage, sails, and other equipment of the ships they built. Some of them owned a lot of land, held promissory notes to a good deal more, and acted as agents for absentee proprietors. The most successful of them, James Yeo, a Cornishman who settled at New Bideford in western Prince Edward Island, managed a fleet of transatlantic ships, built some dozen ships a year, established a son as agent and dominant merchant in the town of Appledore near Bideford, north Devon, and seems to have held a good fraction of the population of western Prince Edward Island in debt to him. People were afraid of Yeo, and with good reason. When he ran for election, they voted for him. Elections were not secret, and Yeo was explicit: he would call in the debts of any who voted against him, in which event many families would lose their farms.

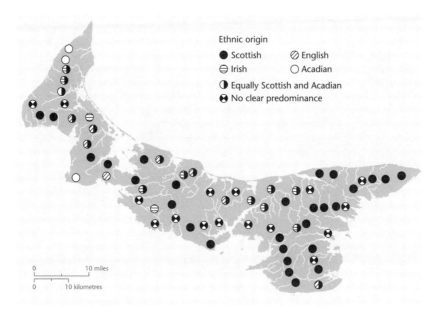

MAP 7.11 Origin of the island population, by township, c. 1851-81 | After Clark, *Three Centuries and the Island,* 90.

Map 7.11 suggests something of Prince Edward Island's ethnic diversity and reveals a pattern of settlement that, in basic ways, was much like that along the lower Miramichi (Map 7.7). In some areas different ethnicities mixed, but more frequently they did not. People characteristically lived in local rural communities with others of the same cultural background who, frequently, were kin. At a large scale, clusters of people with a common surname were typical components of the settlement pattern. To all intents and purposes, Catholics and Protestants did not intermarry, and there probably was little intermarriage between French-speaking Acadians and Gaelic-speaking Catholic Highlanders, or of either with Irish Roman Catholics, some of whom spoke Irish Gaelic. There was probably more mixing among Protestants, most of whom were English speakers. Overall, this was a society in which ethnic and religious divisions were sharp and consequential. Even crops reflected ethnic preferences, as the historical geographer Andrew Clark has pointed out: Acadians preferred wheat, Highland Scots oats.

An influential strand of the historiography of pre-Confederation Prince Edward Island pictures a largely egalitarian society of smallholders (if beset

"SUNNY SIDE STOCK FARM" RES. OF ROBT FITZSIMONS, LONG RIVER, NEW LONDON, LOT 20, P. E . I.

FIGURE 7.6   *Sunny Side Stock Farm, Res. of Robt. Fitzsimons, Long River, New London, Lot 20, P.E.I.,* 1880. A prosperous farm in a countryside of family farms that comprised the primary locus of social life on the island. | Library and Archives Canada, C-026597.

by distant proprietors) and a golden age of relative autonomy and self-reliance. The island's society was not egalitarian, and golden ages tend to be ideologically inflected social constructions, but the island during these years was remarkable nonetheless. In 1861, when well over 50 percent of the population in Great Britain was urban, Prince Edward Island was 92 percent rural. Charlottetown, the only town, was a small administrative and commercial centre. There were no factories and only a few small steam-powered mills on the island. Merchant shipbuilders were the largest employers of wage labour, their shipyards unmechanized seasonal operations employing perhaps thirty or forty men, most of them from farms nearby. Most of the many small manufactories on the island – gristmills, sawmills, cardingmills, blacksmith shops and foundries, tanneries, and the like – were operated by two or three people, usually a father and son(s). They were scattered throughout a countryside in which there was poverty but also a measure of comfort. Surveying the family years and stories, a good many farmers could only conclude that their own circumstances were vastly better than those their forbears had left behind. The Highlanders from the crofts on the Isle of Skye might have gone to Glasgow, but instead they chose Prince Edward Island, a decision that reverberated through succeeding generations. In Glasgow most of them and their descendants would live in brick tenements on working-class streets and labour in factories. In Prince Edward Island they became farmers and tradesmen in a society that was of the nineteenth century but detached from its urbanizing and industrializing momentum. People lived with kith and kin among other small farmers (Figure 7.6) in a countryside that was a haven of sorts from urban industrialization – a temporary haven, however, because the island was small and by 1861 much of it was already cleared and cultivated.

Cape Breton Island

Although Cape Breton Island was reunited with Nova Scotia in 1820, I treat it separately. It reveals more clearly than anywhere else in the Maritimes the effects of rapid early nineteenth-century immigration to a limited land.

At least twenty thousand Highland Scots arrived on the island between 1800 and 1845, most of them coming in the calamitous years following the collapse of kelping and the crofter economy in 1825. The relative few arriving before 1825 usually had paid for their passage and brought a little capital; many of those arriving after 1825 had been shipped overseas by improving landlords and were destitute on arrival. However they came, they transformed Cape Breton Island. Its population rose from fewer than three thousand people in 1800 to fifty-five thousand at midcentury and in 1871 to seventy-five thousand, about two-thirds of whom were of Scottish descent; the great majority were farmers.

These migrants had left one rocky, bounded land for another, with the substantial difference in Cape Breton that there were no great landlords. Before 1827 freehold grants of a hundred acres were available on the island for registration fees and survey costs amounting to £3-£5. The cost of acquiring freehold title to a forested hundred-acre lot on Cape Breton Island was approximately equivalent, Stephen Hornsby has pointed out, to the annual rent of a five-acre croft in Scotland. In 1827 the Colonial Office, responding to the arguments that led to similar changes in New Brunswick, directed the surveyor general of Cape Breton to charge at least two shillings and threepence an acre (£12 10s. for a hundred acres) payable in four equal, annual instalments beginning at the time of sale.

These charges fell principally on the immigrants who could least afford them. The best land was in the valley bottoms along the rivers – intervale, as it was widely known – but intervale was always bounded by rocky, acid-soil uplands where the growing season was shorter and agricultural opportunities more circumscribed. Given the choice, immigrants

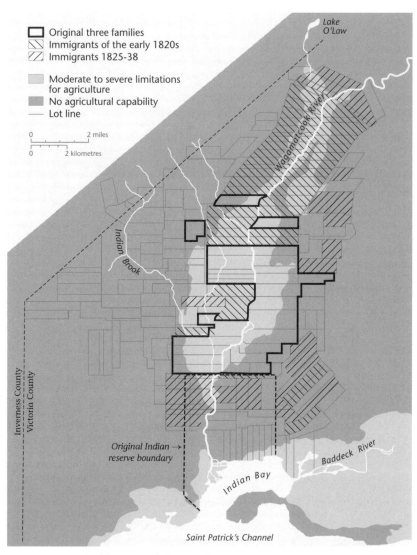

MAP 7.12 Landholding in Middle River | After R. Bittermann, "The Hierarchy of the Soil: Land and Labour in a 19th Century Cape Breton Community," *Acadiensis* 18, 1 (1988): 37.

would claim the intervale, as did the relatively prosperous Scots arriving before 1825. In Middle River, a valley in central Cape Breton, historian Rusty Bittermann has shown that the first three families (each with several grown sons) acquired four thousand acres, most of the best land in the valley (Map 7.12). Such were the advantages of arriving first and of having enough capital to purchase available land at low prices. Those arriving after 1825 had neither of these advantages, and the intervales were already taken. Most of them squatted on unsurveyed upland. They became "backlanders," a term, Bittermann suggests, that indicated both where they lived and something of their social standing.

Although settlers on the intervale – "frontlanders"– faced the relentless labour of clearing land, and although success was far from assured, there was some light at the end of the tunnel. Eventually, at least some of them created farms. The pioneer shanty was replaced by a one-and-a-half-storey log house, occasionally by a balloon frame house of the New England Cape Cod type. Some harvest labour was hired. These were mixed farms that grew potatoes, oats, barley, occasionally spring wheat, and some vegetables for domestic consumption, kept most of their improved land in meadow and pasture, and raised a variety of livestock. They sold cattle and sheep on the hoof as well as butter, cheese, and occasionally milk to buyers in local fishing and mining settlements, but their principal markets were in St. John's or Halifax, where they competed with farmers shipping from Prince Edward Island or mainland Nova Scotia. Frontland farms on Cape Breton Island were not large, nor were their markets, but a limited opportunity had been seized. Some frontland farmers owned forty to fifty cattle and almost as many sheep – approximately the holdings of the more prosperous Acadian farmers around the Bay of Fundy a century before (Chapter 3). Their lives had greatly changed: in the Highland crofts, they had been tenants; now they were landowners who had improved their standard of living. In the Scottish clachans (which few of these settlers had directly known), they had raised the same crops (for domestic consumption) and livestock (for sale); now, living where labour was required for clearing and building, and land was cheap, they cultivated land far less intensively and pastured their livestock on their own property rather than in communal pastures.

On the uplands, the result was very different. Destitute immigrants often worked for wages before they could begin to farm. Their clearings, when eventually made, were small and carried few livestock. Oats was the only grain that usually ripened. These were subsistence farms, from which a cow or two, a few hides, or a tub of butter were occasionally sold. Even at midcentury, most backlanders lived in one-room shanties with dirt floors. They had few tools and, as squatters rather than landowners, no access to capital. They relied on potatoes and negotiated a precarious line between barely getting by and not. A winter that outlasted hay supplies, or a frost that came too late or too early, was easily devastating. Only a few years after most of the backlanders had come, some of them were starving, and a reluctant government provided relief. By the mid-1840s the situation was worse. After the potato blight arrived in the summer of 1845, potato crops failed for several years; in these same years, particularly long winters killed many upland cattle. Although officials believed that aid sapped individual initiative and weakened moral fibre, the situation was desperate and they again provided relief. Mass starvation was averted, but it had become clear that the Cape Breton uplands, in themselves, were no alternative to destitution.

For most upland families, off-the-farm employment became a necessary survival strategy. The nearest and least dislocating employment was on the lowland farms, where there was seasonal harvest work for men and women, and a little year-round work building fences and clearing land. Some men found part-time employment carting or hauling, working for the local shopkeeper, or labouring at one of the many small manufactures in the countryside – smithy, gristmill, sawmill, tannery, and the like – although they were small family enterprises that rarely needed additional help. Some women sold yarn they had spun or cloth they had woven to the local shopkeeper.

The other principal sources of work on the island took men off for a time, and left behind women and children to tend upland farms. In 1851 fishing still supported about a quarter of the island's population and, after farming, was the most common occupation. It remained a deeply conservative activity, the cod fishery tied to technologies that had not changed for centuries, and newer mackerel, herring, and salmon fisheries equally pre-industrial and labour-intensive. All these fisheries relied on fishermen in small boats operating close to shore and on manual labour to process the catch (Figure 7.7). A small fraction of this workforce still crossed the Atlantic each season from the Channel Islands, but the rest was local – principally Acadians at Île Madame and the other Acadian settlements in the south or at Chéticamp in the northeast, or New Englanders and Irish along the southeast coast. At a few places on the west and north coast, and around Bras d'Or Lake, Scottish merchants had established small fisheries. They employed Scots, and some other Scots worked in other Cape

FIGURE 7.7 *Drying Codfish,* c. 1880 (artist, R. Harris). Clothing and buildings were different, but the technology of dry curing was unchanged since the sixteenth century. | G.M. Grant, *Picturesque Canada,* vol. 2 (Toronto: Belden Brothers, 1882), 821, Library and Archives Canada.

Breton fisheries. Overall, the sources of employment in the fishery were established and the fishery provided relatively few openings for upland farmers.

Coal mining provided more. Industrial coal mining began on Cape Breton after 1827 when a British company, the General Mining Association, acquired several pre-industrial coal mines near Sydney and undertook, essentially, a process of industrial colonization. Investing heavily, the company built a modern colliery, mining railways and wharves, rows of brick houses for miners and their families, and a company store. In effect, it built a company town, the first of its kind in British North America. Initially, it imported British miners, but in the 1840s began to hire locally. During the American Civil War, when American markets were open and the Cape Breton mines were exporting over 300,000 tons of coal annually, they employed more than fifteen hundred men and boys, of whom 60 percent were from Cape Breton. Not all of these employees were miners; nor were all of the Cape Bretoners Scots. Whoever they were, the Cape Bretoners who worked at the mines were entering a world dominated by the work discipline and time relations of industrial capitalism (Figure 7.8), a world that made little allowance for saints' days or the routines of farming. They began to encounter ethnicities they had never known before and found themselves in settings that were predominantly English-speaking.

FIGURE 7.8   *Mining Scenes, Caledonian Mines, Cape Breton County,* c. 1880.
A colliery pit head, not different from many of the day in the British Isles, the locus
of wage work under a foreman in an industrial environment. | Grant, *Picturesque
Canada,* vol. 2, 848.

They began to be involved in labour disputes, some of which would lead
to strikes. They were becoming miners, but with upland farms and the
minimal security they offered in reserve.

There were few other employments on the island. In 1851 over two
hundred small ships were under construction in Cape Breton, most of
them in Acadian areas on the south coast where, characteristically, they
were used in the fishery. The thousand seamen listed in the 1851 census
were largely from the Acadian settlements in the south or the New England settlements along the southeast coast. There were no cities to draw
people looking for work. Sydney, the largest centre apart from the colliery
towns, had six hundred inhabitants in 1851.

The other option was to leave, and after the potato blight and famine
in the mid-1840s it was increasingly exercised. In some cases families emigrated – in the 1850s almost nine hundred people, most of them in families, left for New Zealand – but this was largely a migration of young,
single adults. Their motives for leaving were many, and not all of them
can have been economic. Presumably, some left for adventure or to escape

parental control or sexual abuse, but probably most left either because they could not face a life of unremitting poverty, because their parents could no longer support them, or because they or their parents had decided that emigration, a job elsewhere, and money sent or brought home were essential means of family support. Some of these migrations were seasonal; many others were not intended to be permanent, although they often became so. Halifax was a major destination, Boston even more so, especially for women, most of whom entered domestic service. The destinations of the men were more scattered. Few went to the Canadas. A good many found seasonal work in lumber camps of the Miramichi, and many more fetched up across the northern United States, some even reaching California during the gold rush from where, a decade later, a few found their way north to the Fraser River. These migrations detached people from dense networks of kith and kin, and, in the case of many young Scots, from the Gaelic language. Their world had been intensely local, and suddenly they were in vast and unfamiliar space. Horizons, Stephen Hornsby notes, were very near and very far. "Where does this road go to?" an American traveller asked a Cape Breton girl. "It goes to the Strait of Canso, sir, and on to Montana – that's where my brother John is workin' on a ranch – and I don't know where else it goes."

Mainland Nova Scotia

Unlike New Brunswick, and to a lesser extent, Prince Edward Island and Cape Breton, mainland Nova Scotia had no dominant export staple. It was a net importer of agricultural goods, and its exports of timber, fish, and furs were small relative to those of other British North American colonies. Apart from timber, and that in declining supply, it had little to offer an industrializing Britain. As the nineteenth century advanced, it faced a declining market for fish in the West Indies and increasing American competition for the West Indian carrying trade. Tariffs largely excluded it from American markets for fish and wood. Yet Halifax merchants had long envisaged their port as a major centre of North Atlantic commerce, a rival to Boston and the metropolis of a region that would come to rival New England. When Britain was at war, as she was early in the nineteenth century (with France and with the United States during the War of 1812), and British military and naval spending poured into the city, this vision almost seemed attainable. But the long peace that began in 1815 exposed the city's vulnerability – Halifax in peacetime, it was said, was like "a town at the close of a fair." The city was superimposed on a limited regional economy that expanded its production of goods and services roughly in proportion to the rate of population growth. In such circumstances, economic historian Julian Gwyn argues, capital is likely to be in short supply, income distribution to become increasingly uneven, and a large fraction of the population to be underemployed, underpaid, and unable to save.

Halifax merchants extended their commercial networks beyond the provisioning trades associated with the British imperial presence to include the British sugar islands in the West Indies. They assembled cargoes from agents in the fishing ports, lumber contractors, and rural storekeepers – or from New England traders of similar American goods – took fish, lumber, and provisions to the West Indies in ships usually built in Nova Scotia, and exchanged them there for sugar, molasses, rum, specie, and promissory notes. Characteristically, they then returned to Halifax, where some of the cargo was sold and the rest reshipped to other British North American colonies, or they sailed directly to Britain where the cargo and perhaps the ship would be sold. In either case, the West Indian trade paid for imports of British manufactures. To protect this trade, Halifax merchants lobbied the British government to exclude American traders from the British West Indies and to declare Halifax a free port open to American traders (who, in this view, would exchange fish, wood, and provisions for sugar and molasses – all to be carried to or from the West Indies in Nova Scotian ships). If the British government went along with these schemes, which occasionally it did, there would be a reaction from British sugar planters (who wanted access to American traders and their goods), from the American government (which quickly forbade imports of sugar and molasses from free ports), and from the growing body of British political opinion that favoured free trade and the repeal of the Navigation Acts. Moreover, when the British parliament abolished slavery in 1833, it undermined the labour force required for the British sugar plantations. Free labourers would not accept their former working conditions, and the slave-owning French and Spanish islands in the West Indies, to which merchants from Halifax had no special access, became the main suppliers of sugar and molasses, even to the British market. In these circumstances, the Halifax merchant lobby could not protect its old West Indian trade, which by the 1840s was in rapid decline. It was partially replaced by growing access to the American market as some American tariffs were reduced.

These difficulties came to a head in the 1840s, a time of particular hardship throughout Nova Scotia. The Atlantic economy was in one of the deepest recessions of the century. The old imperial trading economy had been effaced by free trade. The agricultural economy of Nova Scotia, never robust, had been weakened by failures of the wheat and potato crops. The carrying trade with the West Indies was failing. There were many business bankruptcies, and there was talk in some quarters of annexation to the United States. For Gwyn the whole longer period from 1815 to midcentury "brought severe stress and few prosperous years." Overall, he is probably right. The Nova Scotian economy was not industrializing, as was New England's, and did not begin to reproduce the spectacular growth that characterized the British economy at this time. Nova Scotia was a limited land jutting into a changing world that it could neither control nor avoid. Its merchants faced constraints they could not overcome, and many of its inhabitants got along by finding a variety of employments within what British historians would describe as economies of multiple occupations. According to Gwyn, "limited horizons and reduced expectations made Nova Scotia ultimately a noted exporter of human beings" – a harsh if essentially accurate judgment, yet one that underestimates the challenges and, in the face of them, the accomplishments of life in the colony.

Throughout these years, most Nova Scotians identified themselves primarily as farmers, and as the colony imported more foodstuffs (by value) than it exported, the failure of the agricultural economy is implied. But in Nova Scotia, as elsewhere in the Maritimes, there were many successful commercial farmers (Figure 7.9). There were also broadly successful farming districts, particularly in the Annapolis Valley, around Minas Basin, and along parts of the north shore. Farmers in the Annapolis Valley and Minas Basin supplied a great variety of farm products to Saint John and Boston and droved cattle to Halifax; those on the north shore, like the more successful farmers on Cape Breton Island, shipped to the timber camps along the Miramichi or to Newfoundland. There was also a substantial internal trade in farm produce, aggregate data for which are exceedingly difficult to obtain. This trade supplied timber shanties, pioneer farmers not yet producing enough to feed themselves, ship construction

FIGURE 7.9 *View from Retreat Farm, Windsor, N.S.* (detail), c. 1839 (artist, William Eagar). A prosperous farm, employing seasonal hired labour, on former Acadian lands at Minas Basin. Note the grain harvested with sickles and the absence of scythes and any mechanical equipment. | Library and Archives Canada, C-013365.

sites, local artisans, villages and small towns, and a good portion of the Halifax market. Yet, overall pioneering had been no easier on mainland Nova Scotia than anywhere else in the Maritimes; nor, somehow, was there less rural poverty or a more egalitarian countryside. Almost all farms contained subsistent and commercial elements, often in very different proportions. However, the essential purpose of farming was not to improve the colony's balance of payments, support non-farming populations, or generate individual wealth. It was to support farm families, and this, however unevenly, it usually did.

The mixed family farm with a kitchen garden, some land in grain but more in meadow and pasture, and a variety of livestock, was the basic unit of production and socialization in Nova Scotia, as elsewhere throughout the Maritimes, in the first half of the nineteenth century. The family farm was inserted in a matrix of other such farms, country roads, and rural tradespeople (smiths, millers, wheelwrights, and so on). Map 7.13, which shows an area known as Hardwood Hill, near Pictou in the heart of Scottish Presbyterian Nova Scotia, gives some sense of this matrix. Note the schools, church, and mills, all serving farm families nearby. The region supported a considerable population, the limits of which had almost been reached by midcentury. The 1851 census reveals a shortage of young adults;

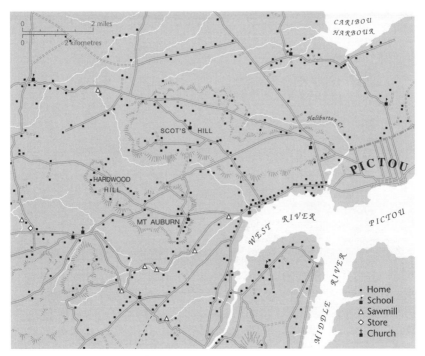

MAP 7.13 Hardwood Hill | After R. Bittermann, R. MacKinnon, and G. Wynn, "Of Inequality and Interdependence in the Nova Scotian Countryside, 1850-70," *Canadian Historical Review* 74, 1 (1993): 6.

young people who could not expect to inherit a farm or marry into one were already leaving. The problem was not want of enterprise but of land, and for this, within the technologies and institutions of the day, there was no remedy.

In Nova Scotia, as elsewhere in the Maritimes, few farms produced enough to provide for the families that lived on them. In such cases, people sought to supplement farm with off-farm work, a strategy that for some moralists smacked of irregularity and disorder, but which, when one economy was insufficient, was an essential means of survival. Year by year, people found such work as they could, rarely repeating quite what they had done the year before. Their work environment was fluid; jobs came and went and fit around the seasonal demands of farming. There was more off-farm work for men than for women, but women participated in this work regime, either by maintaining the farm while their men were away or by working on harvest crews, as camp cooks, or as domestic servants. The farm was the base, the point of departure, from which people reached out seasonally to virtually every corner of the Nova Scotian economy. Perhaps the most telling recent evidence of this process, in the work of historical geographer Larry McCann, comes from the shipyards in St. Mary's Bay in

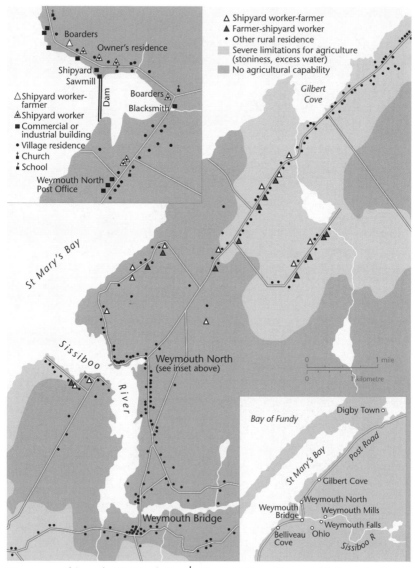

MAP 7.14   Shipyards, St. Mary's Bay | After L. McCann, "Seasons of Labour: Family, Work, and Land in a Nineteenth-Century Nova Scotia Shipbuilding Community," *History of the Family* 4, 4 (2000): 510.

southwestern Nova Scotia. As Map 7.14 shows, shipyards along St. Mary's Bay generated a sizable demand for labour, the most skilled of which – the master builder who organized and oversaw construction, and a core of shipwrights – were full-time tradesmen. Their work on one ship finished, they moved on to another. Less skilled workers, however, usually came from farms within three miles of the shipyard, the distance that men could reasonably walk to work. Characteristically, they were employed in the shipyard for about half the work days in a given month, and often for no more than two or three months at a time in an on-and-off-again pattern of work. Most shipyards closed, or greatly curtailed their activities, when farm work was pressing. In winter, men might work in a lumber camp in the interior, and in spring on the drives that brought wood to sawmills near the shipyards. Was this, as some would have it, proto-industrial work, an early stage of industrialization? It hardly fits the time discipline of industrial capitalism and seems to have been at least as tuned to the rhythms of farming. It always required the relentlessly manual demands of pre-industrial work and probably had much to do with age-old ways of recruiting labour to build wooden ships.

The only clearly industrial work on mainland Nova Scotia in the first half of the nineteenth century was in the coalfields. The same British company, the General Mining Association, that acquired mines and coalfields near Sydney on Cape Breton Island also obtained coal properties near Pictou and developed them much as its holdings on the island: a modern pit head, workers' housing, a company store, an iron foundry, a railway connecting mine and coal wharf. As much as at any colliery in the English Midlands, such a settlement was a product of industrial capitalism. There were not, however, other such investments in Nova Scotia at this time. British capital invested in textile and boot and shoe factories in New England, but not in Nova Scotia. There were dozens of small pre-industrial manufactures producing goods such as rope, nails, beer, spirits, leather articles, and even pianos, but there were no factories. Nor were there steam sawmills: in 1851 the 1,150 sawmills in Nova Scotia (including Cape Breton), all of them small and water powered, provided seasonal employment for only some eighteen hundred people. Why, then, this detachment from industrial processes, especially when consumer durable goods were being mass-produced in New England? As yet there are no conclusive answers, but it is likely that the reasons have to do with the scattered nature of the

Nova Scotian and larger Maritime markets, their low overall purchasing power, and the high transfer costs associated with reaching them along poor country roads. The low cost of shipping mass-produced goods across the Atlantic and the absence of tariffs on British manufactures (the New England factories were so protected) also were contributing factors. Merchants in Halifax were well aware of the problems, but solving them was another matter. In the 1840s, when the economy was at its worst, many of them became ardent boosters of railways, which seemed to offer a solution to the problems of scale that beset the city and region. A railway to Canada, some of them held, would break Halifax from its rock-bound space, open a large central Canadian hinterland, and allow the city, an ice-free port, to become *the* port of British North America.

The distribution of the Nova Scotian population (including Cape Breton) in 1851 is plotted on Map 7.15. People lived along the coast, or inland in the river valleys. Halifax, the seat of government, garrison, banks, the principal colonial merchants, and of many tradespeople and small

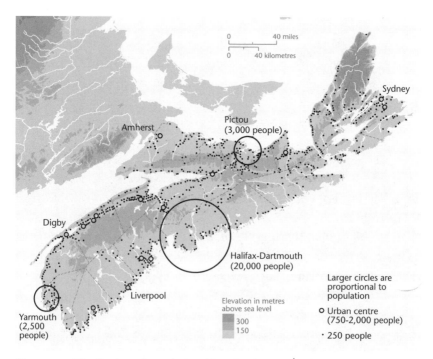

MAP 7.15   Distribution of population, Nova Scotia, 1851 | After R. MacKinnon, "Historical Geography of Agriculture in Nova Scotia, 1850-1950" (PhD diss., University of British Columbia, 1991), 17a.

manufacturing establishments, was a city of twenty thousand. The focus of imports and a major collecting point for exports, it was the metropolis of Nova Scotia. The next-largest places, Pictou with three thousand people and Yarmouth with twenty-five hundred, were regional centres, as were several other small central places with populations in the 750-1,500 range. Each county contained many smaller villages and hamlets, in each of which, usually, there was a general store, a saw- and/or gristmill, a smithy, a church, and perhaps a cardingmill. For most rural people, such a village was their principal point of off-farm contact. Life was still very rural; in 1851, 90 percent of Nova Scotians lived on farms or in nucleations with fewer than a thousand people.

Map 7.16, showing the distribution of Nova Scotian exports in 1854, implies that there was a good deal of regional economic specialization. As for centuries past, the Atlantic littoral remained primarily a fishing coast, with flakes, stages, and fishermen's huts on or just above cobbled beaches and patchy gardens and fields among the rocks behind. The overwhelming concentration of fish exports in Halifax is a measure of the merchant control of the fishery and, indirectly, of the patterns of debt and dependency that connected an inport, such as Halifax, with the many tiny outports along the coast. The export of wood from ports south of Halifax is a reflection of timber operations in the upper drainage basins of the rivers in the area, the location of the largest stands of white pine in Nova Scotia. Shipbuilding in St. Mary's Bay and elsewhere along the Bay of Fundy (manufacturing category) is underrepresented because ships built in Nova Scotia were characteristically sold elsewhere and were not recorded as exports. The relative agricultural productivity of the Annapolis Valley and southern Minas Basin is apparent. Gypsum was shipped from mines south of Truro, and coal from Pictou. The ports on Northumberland Strait west of Pictou exported wood; to the east, Antigonish exported a few agricultural products. But the larger part of the Nova Scotian economy was not oriented towards exports. It produced to feed farm families and to supply local markets, and in so doing generated more sameness than the export figures imply. The common core of the Nova Scotian economy consisted of the mixed family farm, with its emphasis on livestock, meadow, and pasture, and the economies of multiple occupations that circled around such farms. They sustained most Nova Scotians in the local communities where most of them lived.

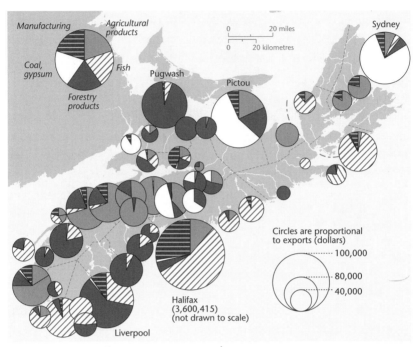

MAP 7.16   Exports from Nova Scotia, 1854 | After MacKinnon, "Historical Geography of Agriculture in Nova Scotia," 25a.

In 1851 some 280,000 people lived in Nova Scotia (including Cape Breton). Immigration had virtually stopped; the colony's agricultural land, such as it was, had been taken. Those of Scottish descent comprised just over a third of the population and, as fifty years before, were concentrated in the north. Another third, those of English (Anglo-American) descent, were primarily in the south. Acadians lived along St. Mary's Bay in the southwest and in several settlements on Cape Breton. The German-Dutch remained near Lunenburg, south of Halifax. The Irish, almost a sixth of the population, were more scattered. Mi'kmaqs were less than 1 percent of the population, and blacks, the colony's other severely racialized minority, were only slightly more numerous. All these people, in a sense, were Nova Scotians subject to the laws of the British colony in which they lived. Yet the capacity of a recently formed colonial state such as Nova Scotia to reach into the corners of its territory and instill a sense of common citizenship was extremely limited. There was no common system of public education, no common training or accrediting of teachers, no standardized school curriculum. Along the fishing coasts, few children attended school. The road network had improved greatly since 1800 (Map 7.17), but overland transportation was still slow, expensive, and, in spring and fall, often impossible. In 1851 a road trip from Halifax to Pictou or any other settlement along the north coast was still a major undertaking. In these circumstances, people lived with memories of where they or their ancestors had come from – memories that increasingly focused on a few symbolic markers – with information and ideas drawn from the larger Atlantic world and diffused from the ports, and with the people around them, most of whom shared their ethnicity and religion and were likely to be relatives. They knew they were part of the British empire, part of a specific British colony, part of the communion of a certain Christian denomination and of its dogmas and demons (the pope, for example, for many evangelicals), but in the countryside where most people lived, away from the professional and merchant elite in Halifax, the local church and local community were more real. Out of the vast displacements of people that had created Nova Scotia and all the other Maritime colonies had reemerged intense local attachments where most people found the principal meanings of their lives.

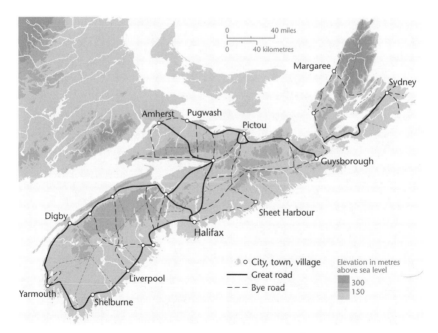

MAP 7.17   Great roads and bye roads in Nova Scotia, 1851 | After MacKinnon, "Historical Geography of Agriculture in Nova Scotia," 37a.

Summation: The 1850s and 1860s

The Maritime economy strengthened in the 1850s and 1860s as, once again, it benefited from war. Demands created by the Crimean War brought an abrupt economic upturn in 1854, and the American Civil War, coupled with a Reciprocity Treaty (partial free trade) between British North America and the United States (1854-66), created several years of prosperity in the early 1860s. Between 1851 and 1871, coal production expanded at three times the rate of population growth. Shipbuilding tonnage increased overall, particularly the tonnage of large vessels intended for international trade. The shores of the Bay of Fundy in the 1850s and 1860s became one of the world's major shipbuilding regions (Map 7.18), Saint John one of the world's major ship-owning ports. In both Saint John and Halifax, factories increasingly displaced workshops, in the former principally foundries, cotton and woollen mills, and footwear and clothing factories (Figure 7.10);

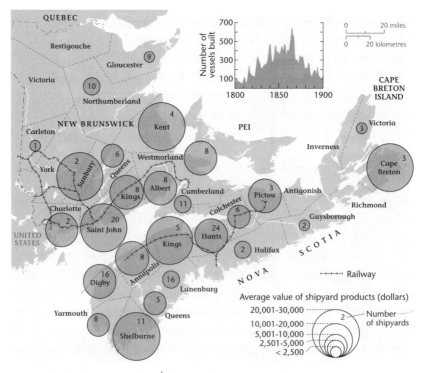

MAP 7.18   Shipbuilding, 1870 | After McCann, "Seasons of Labour," 491; and T. McIlwraith, in *Historical Atlas of Canada*, vol. 2, *The Land Transformed*, ed. R. Louis Gentilcore, cart. Geoffrey J. Matthews (Toronto: University of Toronto Press, 1993), plate 26.

FIGURE 7.10   *The Town and Harbour of St. John, New Brunswick* (detail), 1866.
Note the concentration of smokestacks and small factories in the foreground. |
Illustrated London News, 12 May 1866, 464, Library and Archives Canada, C-000737.

and in the latter food-processing industries, principally breweries, distilleries, and sugar refineries.

At the same time, the staple trades were in relative decline. Timber
prices fell throughout most of these years; forest products, some three-
quarters of New Brunswick's exports in 1850, accounted for barely half in
1870. The fishery was no healthier. New Englanders rather than Nova
Scotians exploited the offshore banks, and between 1850 and 1870 only
cod production increased more rapidly than the rate of population growth.
By this measure, the production of mackerel, herring, and salmon declined sharply. In these circumstances, Maritime merchants invested in
ships and profited from carrying trades. Low prices of wood coupled with
duty-free imports of ship fittings enabled Maritime shipbuilders to produce vessels at competitive prices, and the collapse of the American merchant marine (a consequence partly of the Civil War, of regulations
preventing the American registration of foreign-built ships, and of American tariffs on British manufactures) opened a commercial opportunity
for Maritime shipping. Whereas American ships had carried more than
70 percent of American imports and exports in the 1840s, they carried less
than 30 percent in the 1860s. Some Maritime merchants, owners of vessels, profited from carrying charges, whereas others, shippers of goods,
profited from buying low and selling high. In these years wooden ships

built and owned in the Maritimes operated throughout the North Atlantic and reached all of the world's major deep-sea ports. Yet their principal cargoes were rarely Maritime goods, and many of them rarely visited Maritime ports. As historians Eric Sager and Gerald Panting point out, merchant ship owners deploying capital overseas had done much to create a "golden age" of sail that, except for the returns of shipbuilding and the wages of a few seamen (most were picked up in ports around the world), increasingly bypassed the Maritimes.

It is hardly surprising, therefore, as Julian Gwyn has noted, that the distribution of wealth became even more unequal in the 1850s and 1860s. By his calculations, the richest 5 percent of the population of Nova Scotia controlled some 38 percent of its wealth in 1851 and almost 56 percent in 1871. The large well-appointed houses built in these years in Halifax and Saint John, and the sophisticated lives some led in these places, were tangible reflections of the concentration of wealth. On the other hand, real wages (adjusted for inflation) were falling: for agricultural labourers from about seventy-five cents a day in 1851 to about fifty cents in 1871, for washerwomen from twenty-five cents a day to eighteen cents. In these years, the population of the Maritime colonies rose by some 40 percent, almost entirely by natural increase. Although some Maritime boosters claimed that the region's unsettled lands were "as tempting to the settler as the prairies of the West," the limits of agricultural settlement had been reached and probably exceeded. Overall, the agricultural economy was not robust; even on Prince Edward Island, the average output per farm was far less than in Upper Canada. The fishery produced wealth for a few merchants and near destitution, commonly, for fishing families. Industrial manufacturing was just beginning to create employment. In these circumstances, there was a steady downward pressure on the value of labour, the principal corollary of which was emigration. Birth rates were high and the population was growing, but from almost everywhere in the Maritimes the seepage of young was under way. There was almost no immigration, some of the young were leaving, and as the years passed those who remained in any given patch of settlement became ever more interrelated. The region remained fragmented, an archipelago of scattered settlements that had been occupied by different immigrants, then socialized ethnically and religiously, then stabilized by the pattern of emigration.

Although Saint John and Halifax were much the largest cities, neither dominated the region or even a colony. Saint John was the port of the Saint John Valley and of the settlements around the Bay of Fundy – the principal areas of planter and Loyalist settlement and of Nonconformist religion (Baptist and Methodist). The reach of Halifax extended along the Atlantic coast of Nova Scotia and the south shore of the gulf – where Scots, Irish, and Acadians (most of them Presbyterians or Roman Catholics) were the principal settlers. Goods, information, and people circulated within these fairly discrete inter-colonial spaces. Railways, with their promise of modernization, diversification, and spatial hegemony, seemed to offer merchants in either city the opportunity to extend their sphere of influence and to consolidate colonial territories. By 1870 there were, in effect, two rail systems, one in New Brunswick, the other in Nova Scotia (Map 7.18), and in these years before the completion of the Intercolonial Railway from central Canada, they may have increased somewhat the internal economic integration of each colony.

The colonial state itself barely penetrated the localness of most Maritime life. Some politicians – the likes of Joseph Howe and others in the colonial capitals – spoke and wrote of common colonial identities that transcended religious and ethnic differences and the localism inherent in the pattern of settlement, but they were few. Arguments about railways, prohibition, or the land system engaged politicians of all stripes and, in colonies where most adult men could vote, probably contributed to the making of some cognitive political space at the scale of each colony. The infrastructure of these colonial states – the legislatures, sessions, courts, and grand juries – would have had a similar effect, as would the laws, for example about trespass on Crown lands by loggers or squatters, that central governments were increasingly able to enforce. Central governments also oversaw many local appointments and the distribution of patronage. However badly, because they did not have trained bureaucracies to fall back on, they conducted censuses. They were political and administrative realities, and the territories they represented acquired some coherence thereby. But how much? Was anything like the disciplinary societies that Michel Foucault associated with modernity – societies that invented normalcy and deviancy and devised many micro-technologies of power for securing the former and expunging the latter – in place in the Maritimes in the 1850s and 1860s? There were attempts. The lunatic asylums built in each colony taught habits of regular, disciplined work within organized routines; the insane were to be cured by system. Similarly, the impetus to create a normal school for the training of Nova Scotia teachers sought to develop a "uniform and systematic" teaching that would elevate, civilize, and standardize what educational reformers judged to be a diverse and largely backward countryside. Yet, when the Normal School Act passed in 1855, there was still no system of licensing, and local school boards continued to hire as they wished. The act had been watered down in deference to those who considered it a Presbyterian plot, and to those others who thought it would infringe on local and parental rights. Church officials and local boards remained staunch defenders of religious instruction, curricula, and minority languages. Overall, the weak capacity of the state to interfere in the conduct of ordinary lives is striking. Graeme Wynn suggests that in the Maritimes in these years religion and the local community had much more capacity to shape such lives than did the state. He would seem to be right. If some of this decentred power embodied elements of what Foucault understood by pastoral power, much more, probably, was the power of custom. People were not free agents. Their lives were situated within a multitude of understandings and prohibitions that operated at various scales and within various frameworks, the most important of which were probably family, local community, church, and ethnic group. For the most part, the colonial state had little influence on any of them. People knew who they were, but they were not Nova Scotians so much as Lunenburgers, or Acadians from Chéticamp, or Highland Scots from Antigonish.

Viewed from the more urbanized and industrialized parts of the British Isles, Maritime society in the 1850s and 1860s had organized land and life rather differently. Whereas British society had become primarily urban, that of the Maritimes was overwhelmingly rural. Whereas the British economy was heavily industrialized, the Maritime economy was beginning to industrialize in only a few centres. In the Maritimes, the standardizing, regulatory momentum of the state and the technologies of surveillance that accompanied it had relatively little purchase. Although most settlers had come from the British Isles, some of the most dynamic and disruptive changes in nineteenth-century Britain had expressed themselves weakly, a reflection, basically, of the relative availability of land (resources) for people of modest means. In the Maritimes, this was a limited and increasingly curtailed opportunity, but it had been enough, compared to Britain of the day, to underlie a very different human geography, one that held urban-industrial society somewhat at bay.

Whereas there had been only 10,000-12,000 people in the whole region in 1759, just over a century later there were more than 750,000. Out of a bounded forested land, immigrants had created work camps, countrysides, and towns, and in them well-established settler societies in which, hard as life often was, most people were getting by, some were comfortably off, and a very few were wealthy. In so doing, they had transformed the physical land. In many places, the forest was cleared; almost wherever it remained, it was altered, in some cases by fire, as by the great Miramichi fire of 1825, more often by logging. Over large areas, loggers had thinned the forest, taking most of the mature pine and spruce. Near the shipyards, the hardwoods had been cut. Near the towns, cordwood had become scarce and was supplied by coastal shipping. Overall, the region was still largely forested, but forests unaltered by recent human interventions survived only in its corners, well away from waterways. The rivers themselves were changed ecological systems. Sawmill dams had curtailed or eliminated many salmon runs; sawdust, slabs, and bark discarded from the mills piled up and rotted on former spawning grounds. Snags and brush were cleared for timber drives, decreasing feed and cover for fish. There was concern in the 1860s that the decline of fish habitat and spawning grounds in the rivers was affecting the natural food supply for cod and mackerel. Returns to individual fishers were declining along the Nova Scotian coast, partly because the Reciprocity Treaty had opened inshore waters to Americans, but also, some feared, because fish stocks were depleted. Nova Scotians began fishing in Labrador waters where they immediately incurred the hostility of Newfoundlanders who were already there. Ecological changes had many consequences, most of which were unknown and unconsidered, but the new human geography was tangible enough, a visible record of the progress of lives that migrations had re-established in new places.

This transformed land was, of course, the former home of the Mi'kmaq and Maliseet. It had been taken from them by a settler colonial society backed by a complex arsenal of power that, in the long run, Native people could not match. These powers defended the interest of capital and settlers in the acquisition of land, and hence the dispossession of Native people. The legitimation of dispossession – to the extent needed – was provided by a discourse that located civilization and savagery and identified the land uses associated with each. Following this appropriation of land by immigrants, only a few patches of reserve land were left to Native people; over the years even they were encroached upon when and where settlers found use for them. The Mi'kmaq and Maliseet predicament in the 1850s and 1860s was exactly what it had been in 1800: they did not have access to enough resources to secure adequate livelihoods. Many Maritimers had assumed that they would die out, but as Confederation approached they were still there, speaking their languages, practising elements of their cultures, hanging on in wretched conditions. It was easy to forget them; most Maritimers did, but they were of the land in a way no others were, and their land provided the basis for the opportunity that capital and settlers had seized. Settler colonialism has two faces. The Maritime region on the eve of Confederation was a complex creation, a product of the now largely invisible courage, fortitude, and talents of a great many people who, for the most part, moved there out of adversity and made lives for themselves and their progeny in exceedingly difficult circumstances. A new theatre of human life was their creation, but one built on the displacement of Native peoples and their ways. Intrinsic to settler colonialism, therefore, is a moral issue that the survival of the Mi'kmaq and Maliseet, precarious as it was, passed on to the future.

BIBLIOGRAPHY

1760-1800

General cartographic treatments of these years are in two plates by Graeme Wynn, Debra McNabb, and L.D. McCann in *Historical Atlas of Canada*, vol. 1, *From the Beginning to 1800*, ed. R. Cole Harris, cart. Geoffrey J. Matthews (Toronto: University of Toronto Press, 1987), plates 30 and 31. Complementing them are two articles, also by Wynn: "A Province Too Much Dependent on New England," *Canadian Geographer* 31, 2 (1987): 98-113; and "A Region of Scattered Settlements and Bounded Possibilities: Northeastern America 1775-1800," *Canadian Geographer* 31, 4 (1987): 319-38. For a summary historical account, refer to Margaret R. Conrad and James K. Hiller, *Atlantic Canada: A Concise History* (Don Mills: Oxford University Press, 2006), chap. 7.

On planter migration, see R.S. Longley, "The Coming of the New England Planters to the Annapolis Valley," in Margaret Conrad, ed., *They Planted Well: New England*

Planters in Maritime Canada (Fredericton: Acadiensis Press, 1988), 14-28; and Elizabeth Mancke, "Corporate Structure and Private Interest: The Mid-eighteenth Century Expansion of New England," in ibid., 161-77. On the Loyalists, consult Margaret Ellis, "Clearing the Decks for the Loyalists," *Canadian Historical Association Annual Reports* (1933): 43-58; Neil MacKinnon, *This Unfriendly Soil: The Loyalist Experience in Nova Scotia, 1783-1791* (Montreal and Kingston: McGill-Queen's University Press, 1986); Ronald Rees, *Land and the Loyalists: Their Struggle to Shape the Maritimes* (Halifax: Nimbus Publishing, 2000); and M.A. MacDonald, "Clash or Collaboration? Saint John Loyalists Meet the Planters and Others of the River, 1784-1785," in Margaret Conrad, ed., *Planter Links: Community and Culture in Colonial Nova Scotia* (Fredericton: Acadiensis Press, 2001), 174-88. On the Yorkshire migration, see Bernard Bailyn, *Voyagers to the West: A Passage in the Peopling of America on the Eve of the Revolution* (New York: Alfred Knopf, 1986), 407-29. On Scottish migration, a fine summary is J.M. Bumsted, "Scottish Emigration to the Maritimes, 1770-1815," *Acadiensis* 10, 2 (1981): 65-85; a more detailed account is in Bumsted's book *The People's Clearance, 1770-1815* (Edinburgh/Winnipeg: Edinburgh University Press/University of Manitoba Press, 1982). The documentation on Acadian migration and resettlement in this period is poor, and for all the writing on the subject there is no authoritative account.

For the overall regional economy during these years, I have relied on Julian Gwyn, "Economic Fluctuations in Wartime Nova Scotia, 1755-1815," in Margaret Conrad, ed., *Making Adjustments: Change and Continuity in Planter Nova Scotia, 1759-1800* (Fredericton: Acadiensis Press, 1991), 60-88.

My description of the region in 1800 depends on a variety of sources, beginning with Graeme Wynn, "The Geography of the Maritime Provinces in 1800: Patterns and Questions," in Conrad, *They Planted Well*, 138-50. Wynn also provides a view of New Brunswick in 1800 in *Timber Colony: A Historical Geography of Early Nineteenth Century New Brunswick* (Toronto: University of Toronto Press, 1981), chap. 1. Stephen Hornsby offers a similar cross-section of Cape Breton Island in 1800 in *Nineteenth Century Cape Breton: A Historical Geography* (Montreal and Kingston: McGill-Queen's University Press, 1992), chap. 1.

On the farming economy, see particularly Debra McNabb, "The Role of the Land in Settling Horton Township, Nova Scotia, 1766-1830," in Conrad, *They Planted Well*, 151-60; and Elizabeth Mancke, "At the Counter of the General Store: Women and the Economy in Eighteenth-Century Horton, Nova Scotia," in Margaret Conrad, ed., *Intimate Relations: Family and Community in Planter Nova Scotia, 1759-1800* (Fredericton: Acadiensis Press, 1995), 167-81. For rural culture, particularly in planter areas, refer to David Jaffee, "New England Diaspora: Village Culture in Post-revolutionary New Hampshire and Nova Scotia," in Conrad, *Planter Links*, 81-104; and J.M. Bumsted, *Henry Alline, 1748-1784* (Toronto: University of Toronto Press, 1971), chap. 1. On the Mi'kmaq and Maliseet, see L.F.S. Upton, *Micmacs and Colonists: Indian-White*

Relations in the Maritimes, 1713-1867 (Vancouver: UBC Press, 1979), chaps. 5-7; W.D. Hamilton, "Indian Lands in New Brunswick: The Case of Little South West Reserve," *Acadiensis* 13, 2 (1984): 3-28; William C. Wicken, "Mi'kmaq Land in Southwestern Nova Scotia, 1771-1823," in Conrad, *Making Adjustments*, 113-22; and by the same author, *Mi'kmaq Treaties on Trial: History, Land, and Donald Marshall Junior* (Toronto: University of Toronto Press, 2002).

1800-70

The literature on the British background of the early nineteenth-century migrations is vast, and I have found the following summary accounts helpful. On broad structural changes in the British spatial economy, see R.A. Dodgshon, "The Changing Evaluation of Space 1500-1914," in R.A. Dodgshon and R.A. Butlin, eds., *An Historical Geography of England and Wales*, 2nd ed. (London: Academic Press, 1990), 255-84. For the background of migration from the Highlands, consult Stephen Hornsby, *Nineteenth Century Cape Breton: A Historical Geography* (Montreal and Kingston: McGill-Queen's University Press, 1992), chap. 2. On Irish demography and migration, see L. Kennedy and L.A. Clarkson, "Birth, Death and Exile: Irish Population History, 1700-1921," and C.J. Houston and W.J. Smyth, "The Irish Diaspora: Emigration to the New World, 1720-1920," both in B.J. Graham and L.J. Proudfoot, eds., *An Historical Geography of Ireland* (London: Academic Press, 1993), 158-84 and 33-65. Líam Kennedy provides a fine account of Ulster's changing rural economy in "The Rural Economy, 1820-1914," in Líam Kennedy and Philip Ollerenshaw, eds., *An Economic History of Ulster, 1820-1939* (Manchester: Manchester University Press, 1985), 1-61. More focused is Peter Toner, "The Origins of the Irish in New Brunswick," *Journal of Canadian Studies* 23 (1988): 104-19.

Graeme Wynn, *Timber Colony: A Historical Geography of Early Nineteenth Century New Brunswick* (Toronto: University of Toronto Press, 1981), provides a framework within which much of New Brunswick can be considered. See also his essay "Moving Goods and People in Mid Nineteenth-Century New Brunswick," in D.H. Akenson, ed., *Canadian Papers in Rural History,* vol. 6 (Gananoque, ON: Langdale Press, 1988), 226-39. On agriculture in the colony, see T.W. Acheson, "New Brunswick Agriculture at the End of the Colonial Era," *Acadiensis* 22, 2 (1993): 5-26. On Saint John, the key work, also by Acheson, is *Saint John: The Making of a Colonial Urban Community* (Toronto: University of Toronto Press, 1985), particularly chap. 1. On sectarian violence, see Scott W. See, *Riots in New Brunswick: Orange Nativism and Social Violence in the 1840s* (Toronto: University of Toronto Press, 1993). For the relationship between violence and the urban geography of Saint John, consult Gordon Winder, "Trouble in the North End: The Geography of Social Violence in Saint John, 1840-1860," *Acadiensis* 29, 2 (2000): 27-57. On the Acadians, an angry account that contains much important detail about settlement and economy is Régis Brun, *De Grand-Pré à Kouchibougouac: L'histoire d'un peuple exploité* (Moncton: Les Éditions d'Acadie, 1982). On the Irish, refer to John Mannion, *Irish Settlements in Eastern Canada: A Study of Cultural Transfer and Adaptation* (Toronto: University of Toronto Press, 1974). Hard to obtain, somewhat folksy, and altogether intriguing is Joseph A. King, *The Irish Lumberman-Farmer* (Lafayette, CA: privately published, 1982).

For my purposes, the most useful work on Prince Edward Island in the first half of the nineteenth century is Matthew Hatvany, "Tenant, Landlord, and the New Middle Class: Settlement, Society, and Economy in Early Prince Edward Island, 1798-1848" (PhD diss., History, University of Maine, 1996). Andrew H. Clark, *Three Centuries and the Island: A Historical Geography of Settlement and Agriculture in Prince Edward Island, Canada* (Toronto: University of Toronto Press, 1959) provides much cartographic detail about settlement patterns and agriculture. Rusty Bittermann describes women's work on pioneer farms in "Women and the Escheat Movement: The Politics of Everyday Life on Prince Edward Island," in Janet Guildford and Suzanne Morton, eds., *Separate Spheres: Women's Worlds in the 19th-Century Maritimes* (Fredericton: Acadiensis Press, 1994), 23-38; and has recently published an important book on the escheat movement: *Rural Protest on Prince Edward Island: From British Colonization to the Escheat Movement* (Toronto: University of Toronto Press, 2006). On religious divisions, see Ian Ross Robertson, "Party Politics and Religious Controversialism in Prince Edward Island from 1860 to 1863," *Acadiensis* 7, 2 (1978): 29-59. For West Country merchants, and particularly James Yeo, consult Basil Greenhill and Ann Giffard, *Westcountrymen in Prince Edward's Isle,* 3rd ed. (Halifax: Formac, 2003), particularly chaps. 7 and 8.

The essential analysis of nineteenth-century Cape Breton is Stephen Hornsby, *Nineteenth Century Cape Breton: A Historical Geography* (Montreal and Kingston: McGill-Queen's University Press, 1992). On wage labour and farm life, see two important articles by Rusty Bittermann: "The Hierarchy of the Soil: Land and Labour in a 19th Century Cape Breton Community," *Acadiensis* 18, 1 (1988): 33-55; and "Farm Households and Wage Labour in the Northeastern Maritimes in the Early 19th Century," *Labour/Le Travail* 31 (1993): 13-45. Although primarily concerned with years beyond the scope of this chapter, Betsy Beattie, *Obligation and Opportunity: Single Maritime Women in Boston, 1870-1930* (Montreal and Kingston: McGill-Queen's University Press, 2000), is a sensitive treatment of an important and understudied topic.

Julian Gwyn, *Excessive Expectations: Maritime Commerce and the Economic Development of Nova Scotia, 1740-1870* (Montreal and Kingston: McGill-Queen's University Press, 1998), offers a thorough but severe analysis of Nova Scotian economic development. On agriculture, see Robert MacKinnon, "Historical Geography of Agriculture in Nova Scotia, 1850-1950" (PhD diss., University of British Columbia, 1991); Rusty Bittermann, Robert MacKinnon, and Graeme Wynn, "Of Inequality and Interdependence in the Nova Scotian Countryside, 1850-70," *Canadian Historical Review* 74, 1 (1993): 1-43; Robert MacKinnon and Graeme Wynn, "Nova Scotian

Agriculture in the 'Golden Age': A New Look," in Douglas Day, ed., *Geographical Perspectives on the Maritime Provinces* (Halifax: St. Mary's University, 1988), 47-60; and A.R. MacNeil, "Early American Communities on the Fundy: A Case Study of Annapolis and Amherst Townships, 1767-1827," *Agricultural History* 62, 3 (1989): 101-19. On urbanization and industrialization, see David Sutherland, "Halifax Merchants and the Pursuit of Development, 1783-1850," *Canadian Historical Review* 59, 1 (1978): 1-17; Danny Samson, "Industrial Colonization: The Colonial Context of the General Mining Association, Nova Scotia, 1825-1842," *Acadiensis* 29, 1 (1999): 3-28; L.D. McCann, "'Living a Double Life': Town and Country in the Industrialization of the Maritimes," in Day, *Geographical Perspectives,* 93-113; and McCann, "Seasons of Labour: Family, Work, and Land in a Nineteenth-Century Nova Scotia Shipbuilding Community," *History of the Family* 4, 4 (2000): 485-527. On the standardization of schooling, consult George D. Perry, "The Grand Regulator: State Schooling and the Normal-School Idea in Nova Scotia, 1838-1855," *Acadiensis* 32, 2 (2003): 60-83.

For overviews of the Maritimes just prior to Confederation, see Phillip A. Buckner, "The 1860s: An End and a Beginning," in Phillip A. Buckner and John G. Reid, eds., *The Atlantic Region to Confederation: A History* (Toronto/Fredericton: University of Toronto Press/Acadiensis Press, 1994), 360-86; and Carman Miller, "The Restoration of Greater Nova Scotia," in David Bercuson, ed., *Canada and the Burden of Unity* (Toronto: Macmillan, 1977), 44-59. For shipbuilding at midcentury, refer to Eric W. Sager and Gerald E. Panting, *Maritime Capital: The Shipping Industry in Atlantic Canada, 1820-1914* (Montreal and Kingston: McGill-Queen's University Press, 1990), chap. 5. For a consideration of the limited purchase of the state, consult Graeme Wynn, "Ideology, Society, and State in the Maritime Colonies," in Allan Greer and Ian Radforth, eds., *Colonial Leviathan: State Formation in Mid-nineteenth-century Canada* (Toronto: University of Toronto Press, 1992), particularly 307-22.

8
Lower Canada

The British conquest of Canada in 1759-60 repositioned the French-speaking people along the lower St. Lawrence in a British empire that had recently warred with France, would soon do so again, and was deeply suspicious of Roman Catholicism. Early British plans for this new colony, embodied in the Royal Proclamation of 1763 and the instructions that accompanied it, were explicit: a French colony was to be remade into an English one. English common law and land tenures would be introduced, and there would be a Protestant judiciary and an elected assembly for which only Protestants could vote or hold office. Catholicism would be tolerated but not supported. Rome would have no ecclesiastical jurisdiction in Canada, whose inhabitants would be induced to embrace Protestantism. But intentions are one thing and opportunities another. There were only a handful of Protestants in Canada. The first British governors – James Murray, then Guy Carleton – were more sympathetic to the Canadian elite than to the merchants and camp followers who had quickly established themselves in Quebec and Montreal.* In these circumstances, the exclusionary anti-Catholic and anti-French provisions of the Royal Proclamation were bent or disregarded. French civil law remained in force.

---

* The terms French Canadian and English Canadian emerge much later, when English-speaking settlers began to consider themselves Canadians. In the aftermath of the conquest, and until well into the nineteenth century, their use would be anachronistic. In this chapter, "Canadian" identifies French speakers whose ancestors lived in Canada during the French regime; immigrant English-speaking people are identified by language, religion, or ethnicity.

Plans for an elected assembly were put aside. Catholics were admitted as jurors and lower court judges. In a private chapel near Paris in 1766, a bishop of Quebec was quietly consecrated and allowed to return to Canada. Precedents for a qualified religious tolerance had been found in corners of the empire and accepted in London. Then, in 1774, the Quebec Act officially reinstated French civil law (thereby reconstituting seigneurial tenures as the basis of landholding), altered the oath of allegiance so that Catholics could hold public office, and allowed the church to collect tithes. English-speaking merchants were outraged, the Catholic clergy greatly relieved. In some ways, the colony had returned to what it was. Its mercantile economy was still attached to a transatlantic metropole. Quebec and Montreal remained small administrative, commercial, and military towns with steep social hierarchies. The countryside was almost entirely French-speaking. Of the some 100,000 people who lived along the lower St. Lawrence in the mid-1770s, hardly more than 1 percent (the garrisons apart) were English-speaking newcomers.

But, of course, power had changed hands. Colonial officials, officers and troops, and most of the principal merchants were now British. As power shifted to these English-speaking, almost entirely Protestant, and largely urban people, the older Canadian society along the lower St. Lawrence tended to focus on, and find its essential character in, the farms and villages in the seigneurial lowlands. For this society, control of the principal towns as well as access to the continental interior and to the North Atlantic had been attenuated or lost. Immigration from France had virtually ceased; commercial and administrative connections that had been with La Rochelle and Paris were now with Bristol and London. In the continental interior, the political boundary drawn in 1783 between British North America and the United States lopped off a great deal of the pre-conquest hinterland of Montreal, a loss consolidated by Jay's Treaty in 1794 (Chapter 5). The Constitutional Act of 1791, which created Upper and Lower Canada, drew a boundary along the Ottawa River; south and west of it, the French language, French civil law, and Roman Catholicism had no official protection. Most of what remained of the diverse westward connections that had characterized the French regime came to be controlled by the English-speaking merchants who now dominated the fur trade. This trade still drew young men west, but as its labour requirements were modest, a declining proportion of the rapidly growing Lower Canadian population had any experience with it. The great majority of Canadians, the French-speaking people of Lower Canada, would live out their lives within a wedge of land in the lower St. Lawrence Valley between the Canadian Shield and the Appalachian Highlands.

In these circumstances, relations with the external world largely shifted into the hands of British officials and merchants, most of whom were proudly attached to the British empire and took for granted an array of economic, cultural, political, and ideological connections that reached far beyond Quebec or Montreal, where characteristically they lived. There were also English-speaking settlers, most quite ordinary folk. Of the several thousand Loyalists who reached the St. Lawrence in the 1780s, about a thousand settled east of the Ottawa River: some five hundred in fishing villages around the Gaspé Peninsula and almost all the rest in Montreal or villages nearby. Americans, most of them farmers, came as land seekers in the early 1790s, when the government decided to divide Crown land beyond the seigneuries into townships and make it available in freehold. They settled southeast of Montreal in townships on or near the American border (the Eastern Townships), or in the Ottawa Valley. At the height of immigration from the British Isles between 1830 and 1855 (Chapter 7), some 800,000 immigrants arrived at Quebec, many of them destitute Irish. Most of this huge wave of poor and often desperate people carried on to Upper Canada or the United States, but perhaps forty to fifty thousand fetched up in the towns and townships of Lower Canada. By 1851 there were some 220,000 English speakers in Lower Canada (then Canada East), almost a quarter of the population. They were a majority in Montreal and close to a majority in Quebec. They dominated the Eastern Townships and the Ottawa Valley. A few settled on farms or in villages in the St. Lawrence lowlands.

Compared, however, to Upper Canada or the Maritimes, Lower Canada in the late eighteenth and early nineteenth centuries was not an immigrant society. Canadians remained the bulk of the population. After 1760 until approximately 1850, the Canadian birth rate held at just over fifty births per thousand people, the Canadian family averaged some seven children (over eight in complete families, that is, when both spouses lived through the woman's child-bearing years), and the death rate averaged about twenty-five per thousand until about 1840, when it declined somewhat. With an average annual population growth of over 2.5 percent, the population doubled every twenty-six or twenty-seven years and spread through the rural seigneurial lowland. In 1851, some 890,000 people lived in Lower Canada, more than 600,000 of them on farms or in villages in the lowlands. More than 90 percent of these rural people were Canadians.

Superimposed on the St. Lawrence Valley and the prior human geography of the French regime, these developments created a patchwork of local human geographies as diverse peoples in different places worked out their lives and livelihoods. Even the dominant narrative in Lower Canada during the century after the conquest – the story of the Canadian people – unfolded very differently in various places. There were other stories about other peoples. Difference was at hand, and the four broad and somewhat arbitrary regions within which I consider Lower Canada in this chapter reflect an attempt to capture as much of it as possible. I begin with the rural St. Lawrence lowlands because the colony's dominant population was there, and because, as Canadian lives turned inwards after the conquest, the rural lowland was their primal space. These people, who had lived in Canada for generations and shared the French language, a common religion, and a broadly similar historical memory and environmental experience, were then in Lower Canada, as now in Quebec, those around whom most of the rest have been arranged. I then turn to the principal towns – Quebec, Montreal, and, to a much lesser extent, Trois-Rivières – sites of rapid economic change and of mixed and largely segregated populations. Next, I examine the Shield fringe (including the Ottawa and Saguenay Valleys), and the incursions there of capital, labour, and subsistent farming. In a last major section, I treat the Eastern Townships, where initial American immigrants were followed, some two generations later, by Canadians and Highland Scots. I close the chapter with a few remarks about Lower Canadian stories.

THE ST. LAWRENCE LOWLANDS

Map 8.1 identifies the location, size, and something of the agricultural potential of the St. Lawrence lowlands. The boundary between agricultural and non-agricultural land north of the St. Lawrence marks the southern edge of the Canadian Shield, a granitic ice-scoured upland unsuitable for agriculture except on alluvial or lacustrine (lake) deposits in some valleys. Almost all the non-agricultural land south of the river is in the Appalachian Highlands. Valleys in the Appalachians are broader than in the

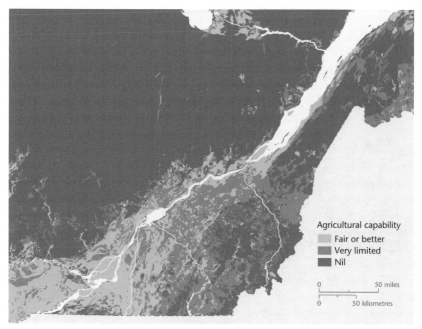

MAP 8.1   Soil capability for agriculture (Quebec) | Canada Land Inventory, Lands Directorate, Environment Canada. Also *Historical Atlas of Canada,* vol. 1, *From the Beginning to 1800,* ed. R. Cole Harris, cart. Geoffrey J. Matthews (Toronto: University of Toronto Press, 1987), plate 46.

Canadian Shield, and their agricultural potential is somewhat greater. Between these two uplands lie the St. Lawrence lowlands (Figure 8.1). Most of it could be farmed, although there are large swaths of land – usually moraines, or shorelines, dunes, or deltas associated with the arm of the sea (the Champlain Sea) that covered the lowlands after deglaciation – with little or no agricultural potential. By far the largest extent of fair to good agricultural land is in the southwest, on the Montreal plain.

These lowlands included most of the territory that had been granted en seigneurie during the French regime and was held within the terms of the Coutume de Paris, one of several codifications of French civil law (Chapter 3). After a fashion, both the seigneurial system and the Coutume de Paris survived the conquest. The articles of capitulation signed in Quebec and Montreal acknowledged prior property rights, and in 1762, Governor Murray granted two new seigneuries to British army officers. Although the Royal Proclamation of 1763 and its accompanying instructions were intended to introduce freehold tenures and British civil law,

FIGURE 8.1   *View from the Citadel of Quebec,* 1838 (artist, W.H. Bartlett). Note the Canadian Shield looming over a constricted valley, the lines of rural settlement, the lower and upper towns of the port of Quebec, and the British military presence. | *Canadian Scenery,* vol. 2 (London: Nathaniel Parker, 1842), facing p. 93.

thereby ending seigneurial grants, the Quebec Act of 1774, which restored French civil law, again made them possible. There were soon applications for new seigneuries, although, in the tumultuous circumstances surrounding the American invasion (Chapter 5), none were granted. A seigneurie conceded in 1788 on the south shore of the Gaspé Peninsula at the western corner of Chaleur Bay was the last seigneurial grant in Canada. Instruction from London accompanying the Constitutional Act of 1791 stipulated that Crown land was to be divided into townships and made available in freehold tenures. Henceforth, the seigneurial territory was fixed. Comprising approximately the St. Lawrence lowlands (with some extensions north and south), it was bounded by rock and, increasingly, by townships and freehold tenures.

During the French regime, seigneuries were held by religious orders, by the colonial nobility and their descendants, by merchants, and occasionally by ordinary settlers. After the conquest, the Crown expropriated some dozen seigneuries, most of them previously held by the Jesuits, and British army officers began to buy, or marry into, seigneurial estates, as did some British merchants. By 1791 more than a quarter of the seigneuries in Lower Canada, not counting those held by the Crown, were in the hands of British seigneurs (Map 8.2); by 1851 approximately half of them were. At the same time, an English common law emphasis on private property and individual rights worked some way into the law. Even the Quebec Act, which had reinstated Canadian civil law, allowed either Canadian or English law to govern inheritance. Debates about the civil law were intense, and positions changed over the years. Early in the nineteenth century, most of the Canadian elite defended the seigneurial system and Coutume de Paris as bulwarks of Canadian society, whereas British merchants and lawyers considered that the limitations they imposed on private property rights (the claims, for example, of widows and children that restricted the sale of property) were anachronistic impediments to a modern economy. Out of protracted debate emerged a confusion of law: part Coutume de Paris, part English statutes, and part judicial misinterpretation (by judges who read legal French with little sympathy or understanding). By the 1840s many of the Canadian political and legal elite favoured the liberalization of property and contract relations; some of them wanted to abolish the seigneurial system – George-Étienne Cartier, later one of the Fathers of Confederation, considered it "absurd." With declining support among the Canadian elite, the system was exposed and vulnerable; it was legally abolished in 1854. Former censitaires (tenants) could purchase their farms from

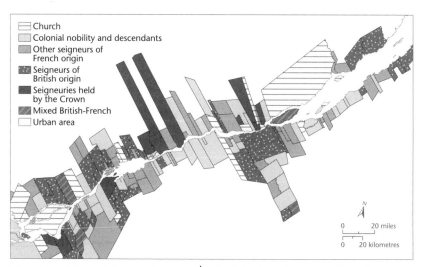

MAP 8.2   Seigneurial ownership, 1791 | After L. Dechêne, in Harris and Matthews, *Historical Atlas of Canada,* vol. 1, plate 51.

FIGURE 8.2   *View of Château Richer,* 1787 (artist, Thomas Davies). Note the Canadian Shield in the distance, the Île d'Orléans (right), the eel traps in the river, the dike separating marsh and farmland, and the row of farmhouses at the lower edge of the terrace. The stone house in the foreground, with its root cellar, barns, and gardens, was the home of a relatively prosperous farm family. | © National Gallery of Canada.

the seigneur or, as most of them did, continue to pay the rents (now the interest charged against the value of their property). The government compensated seigneurs for losses, and, as capitalists, they were free to develop their properties and speculate in land. The law had been changed to fit a market economy.

Yet the seigneurial lowland, considerably settled by French-speaking people when English-speaking immigrants began to arrive in the colony and subject to a version (however anglicized) of French civil law, deflected most potential English-speaking settlers (Figure 8.2). As the inhabitants of William Henry (Sorel), a Loyalist settlement at the mouth of the Richelieu, informed the governor, "If the cens et rents and lods et vents, etc. be enforced upon us, it will prevent many valuable members of society from settling among us, and in the end reduce the present flourishing Borough of William Henry to an obscure and ordinary Canadian village." Such attitudes secured the primary space – new farms in an expanding countryside – for a rapidly growing Canadian population.

The Spread of Settlement

As the population grew, settlement spread inland, away from the river. The row of farmhouses that, during the French regime, lined the river, became, more commonly, a row of farmhouses along a road. Local river traffic declined, carting became more important. Ranges *(rangs)* of long-lot farms were opened one behind the other, the ranges connected to each other by cross roads. In some cases, houses were on one side of the road and the back, or *trait carré,* of a row of previously conceded long lots was on the other (single ranges); in others (double ranges), houses were built on either side of the road (Map 8.3). Eventually, the cultivable land in a

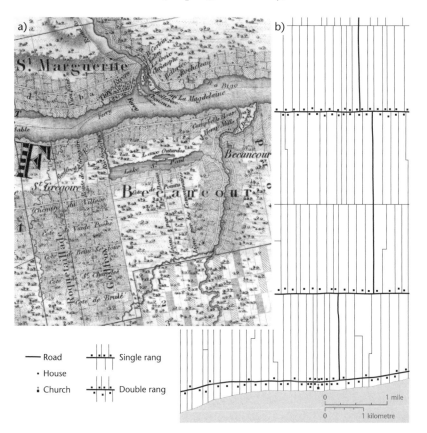

Road
• House
⚐ Church
Single rang
Double rang

0   1 mile
0   1 kilometre

MAP 8.3   *A Topographical Description of the Province of Lower Canada* (detail), 1815. Rang settlement patterns: a) near Trois-Rivières; b) on a hypothetical seigneurie. |
a) Joseph Bouchette, *A Topographical Description of the Province of Lower Canada* (London: W. Faden, 1815), UBC Library, Special Collections; b) After C. Harris and J. Warkentin, *Canada before Confederation: A Historical Geography* (New York and Toronto: Oxford University Press, 1974), 74.

given seigneurie was taken. Near Quebec, where seigneuries were closely bounded by the Shield or the Appalachian Highlands, all possible farmland was often taken during or shortly after the French regime. Then, people began to move farther afield, a few to seigneuries down the St. Lawrence towards Gaspé, but many more upriver towards the Montreal plain where most of the potential farmland in Lower Canada was available. There the ranges of long-lot farms spread farthest from the river. Overall, the expansion of agricultural settlement in the seigneurial lowlands after 1760 shifted the population inland from the river and westward.

Strategies for these movements and for the generational reproduction of family farms reflected the local availability of land. When potential farmland was available nearby, a father commonly applied for and obtained additional lots in anticipation of his sons' needs. He would pay the seigneurial charges until his sons took over the lots and began to farm. Both sons and daughters would provide free labour on the parental farm until they married (sons at an average age of twenty-five, daughters at twenty-two) and moved. Eventually one son, not necessarily the eldest, would take over the family farm in return for the obligation to care for aging parents and, in many cases, debt to his siblings for their shares of the inheritance. This system, prevalent throughout the French regime and dependent on the local availability of land, broke down when land became scarce. Then, the family faced the choice of selling the parental farm and moving, parents and children together, to a pioneer district where land was still available, or of maintaining the family farm while some, perhaps most, of its progeny moved away. The former option (which placed the cohesion of the family ahead of landed patrimony) was fairly common. Mobility within the St. Lawrence lowlands was not confined to the young. In some parishes, a third or more of the farms changed hands each decade, and farms held in the family line through many generations were unusual. Farms were sold for many reasons, but one, undoubtedly, was the desire of parents, born of affection and need, to live close to their progeny. Many parents, of course, did not move. Intricate networks of kin relationships characterized many older rural areas. Yet the price of stability, where land was scarce, was usually the departure of most children and reliance in old age on the son and his wife who had taken on the family farm.

In the early nineteenth century, some alternative to this centrifugal movement to new land was provided by the rapid growth of villages.

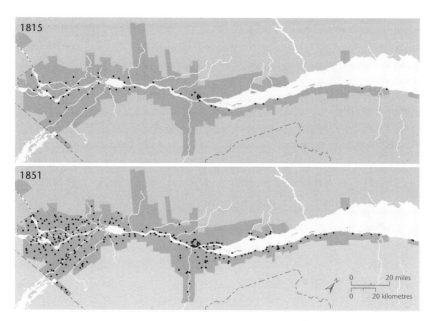

MAP 8.4   Villages in the seigneurial lowland, 1815 and 1851 | After Serge Courville, *Entre ville et campagne: L'essor du village dans les seigneuries du Bas-Canada* (Sainte-Foy: Les Presses de l'Université Laval, 1990), 36.

Because farms were rarely subdivided, the rural farming population in a given area was essentially static once all the local land had been taken up. The rural non-farming population was growing, however, at an average annual rate in the early nineteenth century of over 4 percent, well above the rate of natural population increase. The locus of this growth was the village. Historical geographer Serge Courville has identified some fifty villages in the seigneurial lowlands in 1815, two hundred in 1831, and over three hundred in 1851 (Map 8.4). In some cases a village appeared where a seigneur divided a portion of his domain or of a roture into village lots and, usually, laid out a market square and a rectangular grid of streets. More often, villages grew haphazardly along the road on either side of a church as farmers sold plots of land along the front of their farms. Occasionally the range thickened at a crossroads or near a grist- or sawmill. Often village location was caught up in the local politics of church location. Settlement expansion entailed the creation of parishes, and the location of new churches was always contentious – the prestige of a range, travel time, and commercial advantage were at stake. In settled countrysides, the bishop usually managed to locate new churches some eight to twelve kilometres apart. Many of these church sites became the focus of hamlets or villages. The few largest villages eventually supported many trades and small industries, as well as two thousand or more inhabitants. They were virtually small towns. In 1851, approximately eighty-eight thousand people lived in the villages of the rural seigneurial lowlands, 13 percent of the population. Although these villages attracted more Protestant, English-speaking (or occasionally Jewish) people than the surrounding farmland, some 85 percent of their inhabitants were Canadians. Of these, most had been born nearby; they were products of short migrations towards a non-farming occupation that offered an accessible, if partial, local solution to the recurrent family-centred challenge of establishing the next generation.

The Changing Economic Context

This rural society of farmers and villagers – the primal Canadian society throughout the century after the conquest – was situated within an economy that hardly favoured either labour or agriculture. Most basically, perhaps, the growth of population and intensifying pressure of people on land had increased the value of land in relation to labour. A context that, during the French regime, had favoured labour (the peasantry) had turned to favour land (the seigneurs and other large landholders). Moreover, by the early nineteenth century the agricultural economy of the St. Lawrence lowlands faced increasing competition from farmers farther west who benefited from higher yields on newly cleared and climatically more suitable land. There was also the endemic problem of markets. Canada had no firm agricultural export staple during the French regime; nor, although exports of wheat and horses increased in the late eighteenth century, did Lower Canada. The internal market provided many fewer mouths to feed than did the farming population itself.

During the French regime, seigneurs conceded farm lots without initial payment and for modest annual charges (Chapter 3). In an attempt to attract settlers, some of them deferred these charges for several years or even made small payments to new censitaires when they acquired a lot. The availability of such land, which provided an alternative to wage work, drove up the price of labour. But as population pressures rose, so did the cost of land, and as land became less accessible labour became more plentiful and cheaper. In these circumstances, seigneurs or, more usually, their agents became attentive managers of increasingly populous and profitable seigneuries. They conceded lots sparingly to selected censitaires, raised rates, and added new charges or restrictions. Some of them required a cash payment (in addition to the annual seigneurial charges) before they would make a grant; some accepted bribes. They kept close track of debts, and some of them sold their back rents to rent collectors. When accumulated debts approached the value of a farm, they were more likely to evict – and then to demand prior payment of the debts on the farm when they re-conceded it. Or they might rent such a farm, usually in some form of sharecropping, or sell it. In the latter case, the purchaser would make a down payment (usually 10 percent), pay the lods et ventes (a seigneurial sales tax of one-twelfth of the sale price), take out a mortgage on the remainder at 5-6 percent, *and* pay the annual seigneurial charges. As the timber trade developed, seigneurs usually reserved rights to the commercial exploitation of timber and to the expropriation of sawmill sites on farm lots. Because contracts of concession en roture were legal documents, and when they could be produced their terms held, these new or increased seigneurial charges tended to be levied on more recently settled land.

From a censitaire's vantage point, the rising cost of land only increased the difficulty of access to it. The cheapest land was a concession from a seigneur of a farm lot for no initial charge, then followed by the annual cens et rentes and such charges for services as the seigneur had imposed in the contract of concession. Yet, as settlement spread through the lowlands, such land was less and less available. Land could be rented from a censitaire (at higher rates than the annual seigneurial charges) or from a seigneur (usually in some form of sharecropping), and increasingly was. By the 1830s approximately 30 percent of the farms in the seigneurial lowlands were rented. It could also be purchased, but prices were high. And it could be inherited or deeded to a particular son before his parents' death, an increasingly common practice as land values rose. If landed inheritances were partible (divided) as stipulated in the Coutume de Paris and land prices were high, the debts incurred by the son who took over the family farm could become overwhelming. That son would assume debts to his siblings equal to the retail value of the property minus his fraction of the inheritance (given eight children, his legal debt was seven-eighths of the value of the inheritance). Such an inheritance usually entailed a mortgage and years of debt. In the mid-nineteenth century, a roture of ninety arpents on the Montreal plain, with a farmhouse and farm buildings and some thirty arpents cleared and cultivated, was worth about nine thousand French livres (£375 sterling or $1,500). Serge Courville calculates that to purchase such a farm (10 percent down payment) required annual payments equivalent to more than two hundred bushels of wheat, which the farm could hardly produce. Hence the drift towards wills, donations, and impartible inheritances that bypassed the protections for the family built into the Coutume de Paris. For those with farms, there were also the annual seigneurial charges, which prosperous farmers could easily pay, but which smaller largely subsistent farms, already burdened with debt, often could not. Many also owed debts to merchants and to priests for unpaid tithes. When harvests were good, farmers got by; in a succession of bad years they would borrow again, if they could, and their problems would be compounded. The number of landless would increase.

It is also clear that as agriculture expanded in Upper Canada and the Ohio Valley, as transportation systems improved, and as transfer costs to eastern markets and ports declined, farmers in the seigneurial lowlands, like their counterparts in New England and upstate New York, were in a weakened competitive position. Exports of wheat from the port of Quebec had increased in the late eighteenth century (to the West Indies, Spain, and Portugal, and then principally to Britain), reaching their highest level in 1802. For most of the next thirty years, there was a slight annual export surplus, but by the 1830s, and continuously thereafter, Lower Canada became a substantial net importer of wheat and flour. As economic historian John McCallum has shown, its farmers could not compete with wheat grown farther west on cheaper, recently cleared land (high yields on virgin soils) with longer growing seasons. At a continental scale and in an increasingly integrated market, wheat cultivation had shifted westward. In these circumstances, the only commercial agricultural option was to diversify production towards products that bulk or perishability protected from western competition – dairying or market gardening, for example. But as late as 1851, when there were barely 100,000 people in Quebec and Montreal and 88,000 more in lowland villages and small towns (where a good deal of food was produced), there were more than 500,000 people on lowland farms. The lumber camps took hay, oats, peas, and potatoes, but in small quantities in relation to the number of Canadian farms. Local distilleries and breweries took a little barley and rye. McCallum suggests that farmers in the seigneurial lowlands, like others in the northeastern United States, were caught in structural market problems that, for the most part, they could not solve. Cheaper western products had captured external markets, and internal markets were small. For many, the only rational solution was emigration. Farmers and their progeny from New England and upstate New York would move westward, a northern stream of American westward expansion. Canadians would move south to the textile towns of Protestant New England – two migrations propelled by similar economic circumstances, one of them a heroic exercise in transcontinental nation building, the other, according to many of the Canadian elite, a dire threat to the Canadian nation.

Arguments about Mentality

Beyond these economic considerations is an argument about culture and mentality that has simmered for almost two hundred years. Lord Durham, in Lower Canada in 1838 to report on and make recommendations about the Rebellion of 1837, thought he had found a conservative, inward-looking, unprogressive, and essentially feudal society. Its instincts, he concluded, were egalitarian and unenterprising, its agriculture "rude and unskilled" – "the worst form of small farming." Durham's views have made him and his report symbols, in Quebec, of English Canadian arrogance and assimilative ambition, but parts of his analysis have had a long academic life. In a monumental book, *Histoire économique et sociale du Québec, 1760-1850,* published in 1966, historian Fernand Ouellet argued that rural Canadian society in the early nineteenth century was in a state of accelerating crisis created, essentially, by a failure of production. He maintained that land was becoming scarce, farming methods and technologies were outmoded, and yields were falling on depleted soils. In the face of steady external demand, agriculture was becoming increasingly subsistent. A rural proletariat was emerging. A proliferation of artisans and shopkeepers, most of them operating near the bottom of the commercial hierarchy, did not save a situation for which, increasingly, the remedy was emigration to the United States. Rural Canada, he asserted, had become prisoner of its own defensive mentality, a mentality that was sustained, even encouraged, when land was available but that blocked progressive change when it was not. Arguing similarly a few years later, economic historian Albert Foucher attributed what he took to be the Canadians' lack of entrepreneurship to a church-dominated mentality that treated agriculture as a way of life rather than a source of revenue. Geographer Jean-Claude Lasserre posited that the Canadians had turned their backs on the river and its commerce, leaving them to the English.

More recently the argument has been given a different twist by historical sociologist Gérard Bouchard, who suggests in numerous articles and a remarkable book on the colonization of the Saguenay Valley, *Quelques arpents d'Amérique*, that peasant and capitalist economies in the Saguenay – and elsewhere in Lower Canada – were intertwined (a condition he calls *co-intégration*) but that their objectives differed. Peasant life, he suggests, depended on an economy of multiple occupations *(pluriactivité)* in which, often, both farm and non-farm work, and both subsistent and commercial activities, were essential. The farm family was an abundant source of labour, some of which (especially of young, single adults) was commonly deployed in a variety of off-the-farm pursuits. However, the purpose of this work was not personal enrichment: it was to support the family, particularly its generational replication. The family's very ability to accommodate itself to wage labour and the modern economy allowed it to preserve some of its most traditional ways: a high birth rate, a local family- and community-centred autonomy, a dated agricultural technology, a distrust of formal schooling. Canadian rural society, Bouchard maintains, drew on a capitalist economy as need be but adopted neither its spirit nor its structures. It should not be judged as a dysfunctional pre-modern economy but rather as "a social system that should be considered and interpreted in its own light and in relation to its own principal objective, family reproduction in a context of interdependence." Similarly, historian Allan Greer has suggested that though peasant economies (such as those he studied in the lower Richelieu Valley) always included subsistent and commercial elements, their objective was not the generation of individual wealth but the use of family labour to provide as much family-centred autonomy and security as possible.

Others maintain that Canadian farmers were profit-seeking participants in market economies. Economist Gilles Paquet and historian Jean-Pierre Wallot have argued that none of Ouellet's assertions about an agricultural crisis in the early nineteenth century hold. Land, they maintain, was not yet scarce. There is no evidence that yields were falling because soils were exhausted, no evidence that rural living standards were falling. The external demand for wheat and other agricultural products was not stable, nor, although it was growing rapidly, was the internal demand. Overall, production was more reliable than demand. Rural society was tuned to the market and made rational economic choices. The Canadians were not an anachronistic peasantry hostile to progress; rather, they were economic maximizers operating within a growing economy. When land was available and labour was required for clearing, an extensive agriculture with low inputs of labour per unit of land was a rational choice. So, when markets were uncertain, was a disinclination to invest in new technologies and methods that could well increase debts. Throughout North America, small farmers in such circumstances reacted similarly while participating in market-oriented, modernizing economies. Geographer Serge Courville used spatial evidence about rural economies on the Montreal plain to reach a similar conclusion. He has argued that, apart from the temporary advantage of high yields from previously uncultivated soils, the productivity of agriculture in the Eastern Townships (settled by Americans) and of Canadian agriculture on the Montreal plain was the same. Showing that a concentric pattern of agricultural production developed in response to the Montreal market, with more intensive land uses, such as market gardening and dairying, on relatively expensive land close to Montreal and less intensive land uses, such as wheat farming, on less expensive land farther from the city, he has taken this to be compelling evidence of an integrated market-oriented rural economy.

The Empirical Evidence

These matters are much debated, as, given their centrality to the interpretation of Quebec, would be expected. Only the careful accumulation of local evidence can hope to resolve this debate, and a good many such studies have been undertaken. The following examples, first from various locations on the Montreal plain and then from points farther east (Map 8.5), suggest the type of local evidence that is now available.

Sorel, Saint-Ours, and Saint-Denis (after Allan Greer)

On Sorel's sandy soils wheat yields were low, and most farmers did not participate in the growing late eighteenth-century export trade in wheat. Subsistence agriculture prevailed, and access to a market economy depended on the sale of labour. Montreal-based fur traders relied on young

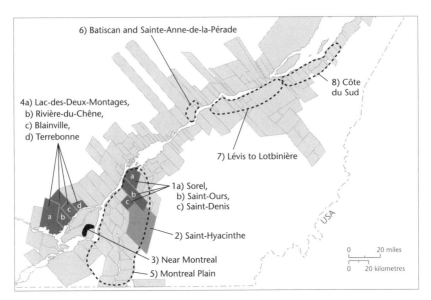

MAP 8.5   Locations of case studies

men from the seigneurie to paddle freight canoes to an entrepôt in the western Great Lakes. In Sorel the combination of subsistence farming and seasonal wage labour encouraged population growth and increased population density. In 1831 the mean cultivated land per farm was thirty arpents (one arpent equals five-sixths of an acre) in Sorel and seventy-nine arpents in Saint-Denis, a seigneurie a few kilometres to the south that was largely untouched by the fur trade. The marriage age was lower in Sorel, the birth rate higher. Farms there were being subdivided. An overcrowded countryside was increasingly vulnerable to any downturn in the labour market. Allan Greer notes that in eighteenth-century Europe the introduction of domestic industry into rural households had similar effects on farm size, fertility rates, and economic vulnerability.

In Saint-Ours and Saint-Denis soils were better, agriculture was the basis of the economy, and the emphasis on wheat held until the 1830s when the crop was decimated by wheat rusts and the Hessian fly. Greer finds no evidence of an earlier agricultural crisis. During the first decades of the nineteenth century, yields held up overall, agricultural equipment improved slightly, and the old agricultural economy remained intact. It relied, as it always had, on family labour to produce as many as possible of the goods on which the family depended, *and* some marketable surplus for sale. When the market for wheat improved late in the eighteenth century, farmers sold more wheat, but their mixed agricultural economy, dependent on family labour and producing primarily for the family, did not change. Almost all farms carried small numbers of horses, cattle, sheep, and pigs. None of them produced specialized commercial crops intended exclusively for sale. Except occasionally (as during harvests) none depended on non-family labour. This, Greer holds, was not a profit-maximizing economy, rather a typical peasant agriculture oriented towards the maintenance of the family and situated within a still somewhat feudal economy. The large villages of Saint-Ours and Saint-Denis served this rural world, providing professions (priests, notaries, surveyors, doctors), artisans (blacksmiths, wheelwrights, butchers, and so on), and manufacturers (mostly grist- and sawmillers).

After the end of the eighteenth century, the effects of population pressure became increasingly pronounced. The number of landless increased until, by 1831, more than half of all households were in this category. Almost a quarter of household heads were labourers, most of whom lived in the countryside. Renting and sharecropping became common. The rate of natural population increase (birth rate minus death rate) exceeded the rate of population growth; in expanding numbers, people were leaving Saint-Ours and Saint-Denis. Overall, rural society there was becoming increasingly differentiated, with prosperous farmers and their families on the one hand and households of labourers with crushing debts and few assets on the other. Within the landholding farming population, Greer identifies a strong tendency towards equality. Whereas the poor usually left their assets to one child, commonly a son, leaving the others to fend for themselves (because a meagre inheritance rarely could be usefully divided), the better off attempted to provide for as many of their children as possible. Within the family, theirs was an egalitarian ethic that, generation by generation, distributed assets among progeny and tended to prevent the accumulation of wealth. Greer holds that the farming population of Saint-Ours and Saint-Denis was not more stratified in the 1830s than it had been sixty to eighty years before.

Saint-Hyacinthe (after Christian Dessureault)
Sparsely settled in 1790, Saint-Hyacinthe was rapidly colonized over the next forty years, and, by 1831, with over fourteen thousand inhabitants,

had no more unconceded agricultural land. At that time, two-thirds of its family heads were farmers, and agriculture, particularly cereal cultivation, dominated the economy. Farms were largest, some over three hundred arpents, in the older settlements. As a group, farmers in the older settlements were better off than they had been forty years before; as in Saint-Ours and Saint-Denis, their farm equipment was slightly better, and more of them owned iron stoves and clocks. For them, there had been no early nineteenth-century agricultural crisis. However, on more recently settled land – "islands of poverty" Christian Dessureault calls them – farms were much smaller and estate inventories meagre, a reflection, presumably, of the growing cost and scarcity of land. He also finds an emerging proletariat of landless labourers (13 percent of household heads), a minority of whom lived in the seigneurie's several villages. This was not an egalitarian society. Apart from the seigneur, priests and merchants were its wealthiest members, followed by a group that included professionals (doctors, notaries) and the most prosperous artisans and farmers, all of whom lived in the villages or along the oldest ranges of settlement. Yet Dessureault estimates that about half the farms in the seigneurie, mostly in the newer settlements, hardly participated in a market economy. Families survived by combining subsistence farming with whatever non-farm work could be found and often were no better off than landless labourers, many of whom lived in squalor. Nor, in 1831, was it a proto-industrial society. Most of the artisans in the seigneurie (9 percent of households) provided goods and services for local consumption and worked in small shops, often with their sons.

Farming near Montreal (after Jean-Claude Robert)
Beyond the suburbs of Montreal in the 1820s and 1830s, Jean-Claude Robert finds a commercial market-oriented agriculture based on market gardening and livestock. Here farmers worked land intensively, and many of them depended on wage labour. They grew barley, rye, wheat, and peas, but principally potatoes, and kept sizable numbers of cattle and pigs. Most were Canadians; their farms, though commercial operations, were smaller and, on average, less than half as productive as those of British or American immigrants. Immigrants with capital had bought choice farmland near Montreal, and at least one of them, William Evans, was a widely read

agronomist, an active member of agricultural societies, and an agricultural writer of some note.

Lac-des-Deux-Montagnes, Rivière-du-Chêne, Blainville, and Terrebonne (after Serge Laurin)

In these four seigneuries, Serge Laurin finds a full-blown agricultural crisis in the 1830s and 1840s. His analysis is as follows: Wheat cultivation collapsed in these years; formerly the region's principal crop, it had almost disappeared by the mid-1840s, a victim partly of wheat rusts and insects but principally of overworked and exhausted soils. Usually it was replaced by oats, but yields of oats were low, as they were of potatoes. In most of the region, agricultural productivity, whether measured per person or per unit area, declined. The result was an impoverished and indebted peasantry, one increasingly inclined to seek off-farm work (usually in the timber trade), or to sell or abandon small indebted farms. Those who quit farming usually became day labourers – 34 percent of the working male population of Deux-Montagnes in 1851 – or left the region. Emigration from these seigneuries to the United States began in the 1830s. Locally, gristmills closed, the number of artisans declined, and some priests reported that their parishioners could not support them. On the other hand, the seigneurs prospered as a group, benefiting from the increasing population pressure on land and the commercialization of the forest. So did the merchants, many of whom were anglophones. As creditors, they were in a position to acquire land, as merchants, to hoard and sell when prices were high.

The Montreal Plain in 1831 (after Serge Courville)

In a countryside still dominated by a dispersed population of family farmers, Courville emphasizes the number of villages and rural industries, and the importance of an internal market in Montreal, in the villages, and in the rural industries themselves. Although most rural industries were small local establishments, some, more capitalized than the rest, regularly employed workers and shipped product away. Gristmills, sawmills, carding- and fulling mills, distilleries, breweries, tanneries, pot and pearl asheries, and other local industries were accessible markets for local farmers. While producing primarily for family needs, many farmers also sought to position themselves in relation to the market, growing rye, for example, near distilleries and practising relatively intensive land uses near Montreal. Specialization, Courville holds, is a reflection of a spatially integrated market-oriented economy in which even domestic crafts such as spinning and weaving often participated. In his depiction, the Montreal plain in 1831 was an integrated economic space containing both prosperity and poverty, as well as fairly sharp regional specializations that reflected local ecologies and different transfer costs to markets. In this countryside, the village was the point of transition between urban and rural, the place where many of the surplus farming population found employment, acquired new skills, and were increasingly equipped for urban life. In this countryside, two spatial orders, one traditional (internalized, local), the other modern (externalized, expansive), met and overlapped.

The following examples are from downriver, well east of the Montreal plain (Map 8.5).

Batiscan and Sainte-Anne-de-la-Pérade near Trois-Rivières
(after Colin Coates)
In these seigneuries in the late eighteenth and early nineteenth centuries, the rate of population growth slowed while the birth rate remained high (therefore, emigration), and wheat cultivation declined, giving way to less commercial crops such as oats, buckwheat, and potatoes. Holdings of livestock remained much as they were during the French regime. Colin Coates takes this to suggest shrinking agricultural opportunities and growing rural impoverishment, while noting an increasing level of social differentiation. A few farmers amassed considerable holdings of land and livestock, and merchants, notaries, militia captains, and prominent artisans comprised a growing petite bourgeoisie. Most farms, however, were subsistence operations supplemented, when possible, by off-farm work in local forests and sawmills, in the Batiscan iron works (built by British capital) that operated between 1799 and 1813 and hired unskilled local labour, and in smaller local industries. Coates' economic and social analysis ends in the 1820s, just before the advent of, as he puts it, an "increasingly capitalized forestry mixed with subsistence agriculture."

Lévis to Lotbinière (after Roch Samson et al.)

The population of these seigneuries grew five times between 1791 and 1850 (well above the rate of population growth for Lower Canada as a whole), and settlement spread to the limit of available land. In 1800 agriculture dominated a robust economy, and wheat, raised for both domestic consumption and sale, was the primary crop. Then, at the beginning of the nineteenth century, a series of disastrous harvests inaugurated a long and painful reorientation of agriculture away from wheat and towards oats, potatoes, hay, and eventually dairying. There were good years, but more that were not, especially from the late 1820s through most of the 1840s. In 1835 the Hessian fly arrived and decimated remaining wheat fields, and in 1843 the potato blight that, a few years later, would devastate Cape Breton Island and Ireland (Chapter 7). The spectre of starvation loomed in the countrysides between Lévis and Lotbinière. Priests reported that many farmers had no seed to plant and that the poorest had nothing to eat.

These conditions, coupled with alternative employments, shifted the economy away from agriculture. Whereas agriculture employed 74 percent of the population in 1831, it employed 43 percent in 1851. In these seigneuries with abundant forests close to Quebec, forestry became a major early nineteenth-century economy. Seigneurs contracted for the cutting and delivery of logs from their seigneurial backlands. Some of them constructed large modern river-mouth sawmills, laid out lots, and built small houses nearby, which they rented to workers, creating small industrial towns in the process. Some built and operated shipyards; all of them owned gristmills and retained some position in the grain trade. John Caldwell, the most prosperous of these seigneurs, lived above his mills in a manor that by Lower Canadian standards was a neo-classical mansion. Although few data survive regarding the conditions of work in the mills, there was, as noted above, a buyers' market for labour. A skilled labourer's wages could not support a family.

The Côte du Sud (after Alain Laberge)

After absorbing their own populations for generations, by the early nineteenth century the seigneuries along the Côte du Sud faced the effects of population pressure. Although settlement spread rapidly inland, the rate of population growth began to trail the rate of natural population increase. Two different agricultural economies emerged. Older, well-established farms close to the river produced sizable surpluses of wheat and subsequently managed, overall, the transition from wheat to oats, hay, and livestock. Seigneurs, most of them Canadians, experimented with new crops and methods, and participated in the formation of agricultural societies. Farmers, virtually all of them Canadians, adapted to changing markets and slowly adopted some agricultural innovations. After the Montreal plain, this was the most productive and prosperous agricultural region in Lower Canada. On the other hand, settlers who had been pushed into the backlands by population pressures created small subsistent farms on poor soils and eked out poverty-stricken lives. In these circumstances, the Côte du Sud began to export some of its young. Many of those who remained in the area found seasonal employment. Some were hired by the schooner cod fisheries that operated out of the small ports along this coast and made for Gaspé or the Strait of Belle Isle. Others – although this was not a major timber region – worked in lumber camps in the forests behind the seigneuries. Still others became day labourers (10-20 percent of the working population in most of these seigneuries by 1831), usually lived in one of the villages that had emerged in every parish, and found such employment as they could in small rural industries (grist- and sawmills, fulling- and cardingmills, tanneries) or as seasonal agricultural workers. As elsewhere in the St. Lawrence lowlands, rural society was becoming increasingly stratified: at the top the seigneur (when at hand) and the priest, then the village elite, then, less clearly, the range from principal farmers to landless labourers.

Interpreting the Evidence

What, then, is to be made of these different and in some cases contradictory interpretations, all of which offer careful, useful analyses of the varying realities they seek to describe? There are several fairly obvious conclusions.

In the first place, it is clear that rural society and economy in the seigneurial lowlands were far from homogeneous, that the geographical distribution of prosperity and poverty was very uneven, and that what one finds depends, in good part, on where one looks. That said, no generalized and systemic agricultural crisis occurred in the first two or even three decades of the nineteenth century. Individual years were bad, and pockets of acute rural poverty existed in every major sub-region of the lowlands, but there were also prosperous rural households and many more that were getting by. In well-established farming areas, particularly those on the Montreal plain, living standards probably rose a little during these years. If a generalized agricultural crisis did develop, it was in the 1830s and 1840s when wheat crops failed, rural living standards fell, and, among the most afflicted, the spectre of starvation loomed. For a great many rural families, these were exceedingly difficult years. They had been precipitated by crop failures caused by insects and rusts, and perhaps too by agricultural practices that had worn out soils. The extensive agricultural methods that had served when land was abundant (Chapter 3) were still practised; two- and three-course rotations remained common, and fields were not well manured (largely due to lack of livestock). Except on newly cleared land, seed-yield ratios were low – as they long had been along the lower St. Lawrence, and as they were on family farms throughout northeastern North America. As John McCallum has shown, the problem on which the crop failures of the 1830s and 1840s were superimposed was the emergence of western competition from farmers on new and often intrinsically more productive soils in climatically more favoured conditions. Moreover, if it is appropriate to speak of an agricultural crisis during these years, it should be kept in mind that there were still prosperous farmers and others who were getting along. The areas of most acute rural poverty lay in the newer settlements where, characteristically, the quality of the land (even allowing for high yields on newly cleared sites) was lower yet its cost was higher than in the older settlements, access to markets was more difficult, and (in pioneer conditions) there was relatively little cultivated land per farm. Along the older côtes and ranges, most farm households weathered the collapse of wheat cultivation; a few probably profited from it.

It is also clear that as the value of land increased in relation to labour, the countryside became a more differentiated social space. As a group, the seigneurs prospered. They had more dues-paying censitaires, charged more for land, and held valuable real estate. Forested backlands unsuitable for farming became assets with the growth of the timber trade. For many seigneurs (both Canadian and British), their seigneuries became, essentially, property investments that were managed by agents. Seigneurs in Lower Canada never amassed anything like the wealth of the great estates of pre-revolutionary France, but a considerable percentage of the product of the countryside accrued to them. Some of them invested in rural industries, around which villages often appeared – a common motor of village formation in the St. Lawrence lowlands. The farm on the seigneurial domain, characteristically operated by a manager and worked with hired labour, was usually much the largest farm in a seigneurie. The seigneurial manor, whether of the steep-roofed, narrow-dormered Canadian style or some variant of neo-classical architecture, was usually by far the largest house.

As a group, merchants and professionals also prospered. There had been merchants in the countryside since the seventeenth century, but as the rural population and economy expanded, the number of merchants increased. Like their counterparts in the Newfoundland outports, they traded local goods for imports, acquiring the one as cheaply and selling the other as dearly as possible. For the most part, transactions depended on credit and on payments in kind, and merchants often became substantial creditors who vied with the seigneur for the prior payment of debts. They were also members of the rural community, able to participate, if they wished, in its moral economy; undoubtedly some of them tided over desperate families, extending credit they knew would not be repaid. Alongside the merchants in almost every village were professional people – notaries, doctors, surveyors – most of whom were new to the countryside since the French regime and were among the most prosperous members of rural society. Not uncommonly, such men owned two or three farms.

The generational reproduction of a qualified equality among farm families became more difficult as land values rose. An increasing number of people became landless; some of them combined work on the family farm with intermittent off-farm work, some moved to a village and acquired a trade or got by on casual labour. A great many others, perhaps most farmers in the St. Lawrence lowlands, worked small farms that produced little more than subsistence livelihoods. Many of them also depended on seasonal off-farm employment to pay the seigneurial charges and purchase the short list of required goods that a subsistence farm could not provide. Yet other farmers, benefiting from rising land prices and local market opportunities, consolidated their position as substantial commercial producers. Some of these large farms belonged to notaries, innkeepers, or merchants, but most of them to prosperous farmers, some of whom were anglophones. There was now more potential to prosper – or to become impoverished – in one lifetime, and those who prospered were in a position to pass on their advantage. If, as Allan Greer has noted in Saint-Ours and Saint-Denis, prosperous Canadian farmers and artisans characteristically divided their holdings into as many parts as would make reasonably sized family operations (thereby securing livelihoods for as many of their progeny as possible), then, at least among Canadians, the accumulation of property would be checked generation by generation. If, on the other hand, prosperous anglophones passed their property to a single son, then, among them, inter-generational wealth would tend to accumulate. There is no comparative study, however, of inheritance patterns in Canadian and British families in the lower St. Lawrence countryside. It is clear that for all who lived there, the declining value of labour in relation to the value of land and the growing variety of employments and trades in an increasingly populous countryside had exerted a constant differentiating pressure. The social range was less in regions of recent settlement, where, typically, a common poverty prevailed, but the tendency everywhere was in the same direction.

Faced with the declining competitive position of wheat and with crop failures, the more prosperous farmers in an increasingly differentiated countryside were in a position to diversify their operations and maximize their sales. They had the capital to make agricultural improvements – new farm buildings, better quality stock – and to respond fairly quickly to changing markets. Their cultivation of oats, rye, and barley increased. Potatoes, rare during the French regime, became common. More land was put into meadow and pasture, and hay production increased. The orientation of many farms shifted towards livestock: meat or dairy cattle, sheep, horses, pigs. Collectively, these farms produced sizable surpluses, almost all of which went to Lower Canadian markets. Most farmers, however, had far less room to manoeuvre. A great many of them, deeply in debt, negotiated a perilous margin between getting by and not. In such circumstances, investments in agricultural improvements with uncertain outcomes often involved unacceptable risks: additional debt, less food for a family, the loss of a farm. They would shift away from wheat and towards other grains, meadow, and pasture, but more slowly than wealthier farmers. They might acquire a few more livestock, but their farming techniques and the quality of their livestock would hardly change. The circumstances of more and less prosperous farmers were different and so too their capacity to respond to a changing rural economy. By and large, the capacity to respond was concentrated near the markets in the older areas of settlement, particularly on the Montreal plain and along the Côte du Sud.

What, then, of the debate over mentality, particularly as it bears on attitudes towards market and family? It can be said, I think, that Canadian and at least some British farmers in the St. Lawrence lowlands approached farming out of very different backgrounds. Behind the Canadians lay a North American agricultural experience that was many generations old and, by and large, had been proved to work. It had supported their families. A few British farmers, on the other hand, were well acquainted with early nineteenth-century European agronomy. Some Canadian seigneurs also promoted agricultural improvements, but there was hardly an early nineteenth-century Canadian equivalent of William Evans, steeped as he was in the literatures of political economy and agricultural science. Such men organized and ran the major agricultural societies, promoting what they took to be the efficiencies of complex crop rotations, the selective breeding of livestock, and the regular manuring of fields. Probably it can also be said that some British farmers arrived with funds that few Canadians could match, which may largely explain the relative pre-eminence of British farmers near Montreal. Farmland near the city, though expensive, was judged a good investment and attracted a category of prosperous British farmer. Such men usually had some prior exposure to contemporary agricultural theory that, better than elsewhere in Lower Canada, fit the circumstances of expensive land close to a market. Moreover, their farms were larger than those of the Canadians. However, they were few, and their importance is easily exaggerated. William Evans was a critic of Canadian agriculture, but had he lived in the Maritimes he would have levelled the same critique at most of the farmers around him. By his standards, they too were wayward. Indeed, there is little to suggest that the mentality of Canadian and Maritime farmers differed very much, or that they responded differently to the market. In general, both practised a mixed agriculture oriented towards self-sufficiency, both made such market connections as they could (sales of farm produce, off-farm work), and probably both were more committed to family-centred well-being than to profit.

Gérard Bouchard has suggested that the concepts of co-intégration and pluriactivité (page 246) and the emphasis on the family fit many rural

North American societies, especially in areas of pioneer settlement. He is almost certainly right, although it could still be argued that these concepts have a particular relevance to rural Canadian society in Lower Canada. If that be so – if co-intégration, pluriactivité, and a primary emphasis on the family describe a Canadian mentality particularly well – then, I think, there are only two ways in which this case can be argued. One is to show that Canadians, given the opportunity, were particularly inclined to practise a form of partible inheritance. However, as pointed out above, that demonstration has not been made; moreover, inheritance in rural Upper Canada was similar to that in rural, French-speaking Lower Canada (Chapter 9). The other is to show that, hemmed in by an English-speaking and largely Protestant population, they were more inclined than most English-speaking settlers in North America to put up with economic hardship in situ. That is, more than others, they tended to sacrifice the prospect of economic gain elsewhere for the familiarity, and the cultural and social security, of known local worlds. Perhaps so, but given the mobility of Canadians within the St. Lawrence lowlands and, eventually, their massive migration beyond it, this is a difficult case to make. Nor has it been made. In sum, as there is now no evidence that mentality is a useful explanatory variable, it is best put aside. The circumstances in which people found themselves – the quality of the soil, the distance from market, the cost and availability of land, the length of settlement, and so on – had far more influence on economic performance than did differences in mentality. As has been shown, the circumstances of rural life varied enormously throughout the St. Lawrence lowlands.

The Cultural Landscape

If there was no distinctive Canadian mentality vis-à-vis the market, there certainly was a distinctive Canadian culture that found its reflection in the patterns of common speech, the stories told and songs sung, the historical memories shared, and the human landscapes of the seigneurial lowlands. At the heart of these landscapes was the long-lot farm. Narrow fields bounded by split-rail fences stretched back from river or road to the forest (now commonly a woodlot). Near the front of each farm was a cluster of buildings: a house with a stable, cow shed, and other farm buildings behind – or increasingly as the farm economy turned towards livestock and hay, a long, low barn with livestock kept on the ground floor and a side ramp to a hayloft above. Adjacent farmhouses were usually less than a hundred metres apart. Their styles had changed somewhat over the years: more gently pitched roofs with more pronounced and curved eaves, more windows (including dormers), often a front porch, and a main floor raised well above the ground. For the most part, these were adaptations to a northern continental climate. The overhanging eave protected the facade, and to some extent the porch, from rain, sleet, and snow; additional windows improved ventilation on summer days; and a cellar (a late addition to larger houses) served for storage in winter and as a summer kitchen. Their techniques of construction, on the other hand, had hardly changed since the French regime. Most houses were still wooden, their construction either timber frame (usually *pièce sur pièce en coulisse*) or log with dovetail corners (Chapter 3). Exterior walls were whitewashed. In more prosperous areas, stone houses were common, their walls usually also whitewashed. Here and there some of the ornamentation around windows and doors borrowed from the architectural styles of the day – a Georgian or neoclassical transom, Victorian gingerbread around dormers – but these were folk houses rooted in the French regime, and ultimately in France. As during the French regime, ties of neighbourhood, kin, and mutual aid organized primarily at the scale of côte, range, or parish laced the countryside together.

At intervals, the line of farmhouses and farm buildings that comprised a côte or range thickened into a village (Figure 8.3). There, lots were small and houses much closer together. A few village houses, the homes of the elite, were larger than any in the countryside, and village houses were more likely to be built of stone, but otherwise they and farmhouses were identical. Barns and other farm buildings were in the villages as well. It was as if the countryside had been squeezed to make the village. The parish church, which dominated the village, was the common hallmark in early nineteenth-century sketches and etchings of the rural Canadian landscape. Frequently located on a bluff overlooking the river, on a beach ridge of the former Champlain Sea, or at a bend in a road so as to give a terminal view of it from both directions, the church loomed over the village, its single, double, or occasionally triple spires making it visible for many kilometres. The parish contributed labour, money, and materials to the church, but architecturally it was only partially and, as time went on, indirectly a product of folk

FIGURE 8.3   *The Village of Pointe Lévis, Lower Canada* (detail), 1838 (artist, H.W. Barnard). Perhaps the most accurate surviving image of a sizable Canadian village in the 1830s. | Library and Archives Canada, 1961-081-3.

culture. The bishop usually provided the plans, and with the rise of Canadian nationalism in the early nineteenth century, these were intended to evoke the parish church of the French regime. Even Louis XVI classicism, introduced belatedly to Lower Canada in the 1820s by Jerome Demers, director of the Séminaire de Québec, and his protege Thomas Baillargé, blended with a concept of the traditional church.

Here and there in this countryside of common memories were other notes altogether. Some of the seigneurs, most of them British but some Canadian, built elaborate seigneurial manors in the British or American styles of the day. Some of them laid out gardens that reflected English picturesque or romantic tastes. Somewhat to his father's annoyance, even one of the sons of Louis-Joseph Papineau, leader of the Partie Patriote, wanted to create an English garden. At another scale, English-speaking farmers and villagers tended to reproduce their own aesthetic traditions, which, inserted in a countryside derived from the French regime, immediately stood out as places apart.

The State in the Countryside

Until the Rebellion of 1837 the British colonial state penetrated this countryside much less effectively than had the French state during the later years of the French regime (Chapter 3). After the Constitutional Act (1791) most rural men could vote for representatives of the House of Assembly, although its powers were severely circumscribed by a cautious colonial administration. The power of the British army, garrisoned in the towns, hung over the countryside – it was used to decisive effect during the Rebellion of 1837 – but the army had neither interest nor capacity to manage rural society. Although the rural militia, a legacy of the French regime, survived under the British, companies mustered only once a year in peacetime (to count and report members present); apparently, militia captains (unpaid) were less representatives of the state than respected local men to whom minor misdemeanours and disputes were often referred. In most parishes there was also a justice of the peace, a local legal office introduced after the conquest. Justices of the peace, commonly merchants, professional men, or seigneurs, were unpaid and usually little versed in the law. Members of local societies, they were not the law's disinterested purveyors. They left few records and it is hard to know precisely what they did – according to Allan Greer, the majority were corrupt or inactive. Even from the perspective of the colonial state, their doings seem to have been largely invisible. Rural people could appear before urban courts but apparently rarely did so. Local disputes were commonly resolved within local communities by the weight of public opinion, agreed procedures for arbitration, or the informal judgment of a militia captain or parish priest. Throughout the seigneurial lowlands before 1837, most people rarely if ever encountered an agent of the state.

This changed somewhat after the rebellion. The colonial administration replaced justices of the peace with stipendiary (salaried) magistrates, and for a time placed constables in the countryside, less to keep public order than to ferret out subversion. As the countryside was pacified, the constables were removed but not the assumption of a more active social role for the state. The introduction of municipal governments comprising elected officials with some power of taxation and local responsibilities (for roads and schools) was one manifestation of this new order. A confessional public school system (separate Protestant and Catholic schools), financed partly by the state, partly by local communities, and in place, in principle, by 1845, was another. Together with the abolition of the seigneurial system in 1854, these considerable institutional changes were part of an increasingly pervasive social contract being worked out in industrializing societies and intended to create ordered environments for the efficient operation of capital, markets, and governments.

Underneath these changes were still the family farm, the côte or range in which it was inserted, the village nearby, and the local church and parish. They remained the primary settings of most lives. In older settlements there were usually a few dominant surnames, in newer areas the matrix of kin was less developed, but everywhere in this lowland, Canadians lived within ties of kin, neighbourhood, and mutual aid. They were products, now at many generations' remove, of a modest French migration to a considerable tract of usable land that, for some two hundred years, had supported the settlement of farm families. In most of the St. Lawrence lowlands well before 1850, this spatial and environmental opportunity had ended. Potential farmland was taken, and although other employments absorbed some of the young, many would seek livelihoods elsewhere.

The Cities

During the last four decades of the eighteenth century, Quebec and Montreal remained the small administrative, military, and commercial centres they had always been. In 1800 the civilian and military population of Quebec was less than ten thousand, and of Montreal some seven thousand. Only 7 percent of the population of Lower Canada was urban (compared to 20 percent late in the French regime). Quebec, accessible to deep-sea sailing vessels, remained the colony's port, and Montreal the point of contact by canoe with the continental interior. Small wind- or oar-powered riverboats made the connection between the two. Although exports of wheat and flour had increased, the British merchants who now controlled the bulk of external trade had been little more successful than their predecessors before 1760 in diversifying an export economy that still depended primarily on furs. If anything, the military presence in the towns had expanded. In Quebec, the British army repaired and enlarged the fortifications, turned some of the institutional buildings of the French regime (the Jesuit College, the Intendant's Palace) into barracks and military stores, and appropriated 40 percent of the upper town. Most of the town's British immigrants and their descendants lived there, the primary locus of British administrative and military power in Lower Canada. However, Canadians remained the large majority in both Quebec and Montreal.

Almost all of this changed during the early nineteenth century. The towns repositioned themselves in relation to each other and to the continent, they grew rapidly, and their economies shifted from commerce towards industrial manufacturing.

New transportation technologies, and with them changing relations of space and time, reworked the relative location of the towns along the St. Lawrence River and even of the St. Lawrence corridor itself. The river became a different medium. By 1820 river steamboats were common on it, and small canals were built above Montreal in the 1820s. In 1832 the completion of the Rideau Canal, between Kingston at the eastern end of Lake Ontario and Bytown (later Ottawa), and of canals on the Ottawa River, opened a viable, if roundabout, steamboat connection between Montreal and Lake Ontario (Figure 8.4). In the late 1840s, canals were improved on the upper St. Lawrence, and in the early 1850s dredging gave large deep-sea steamships direct access to Montreal. Land transportation also changed. In 1836, only six years after the opening of the first public railway in Britain, twenty kilometres of wooden rails linked the south shore of the St. Lawrence opposite Montreal to the Richelieu River. By the early 1850s, two

FIGURE 8.4 *Locks on the Rideau Canal,* 1838 (artist, W.H. Bartlett). British military expenditure linking Lower Canada to Lake Ontario: the Ottawa River end of the Rideau Canal. | *Canadian Scenery,* vol. 2, following p. 6.

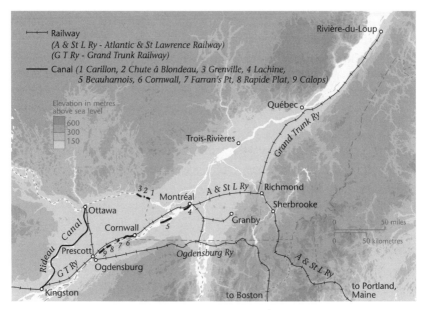

MAP 8.6 St. Lawrence transportation system, 1860 | After D.G.G. Kerr, ed., *A Historical Atlas of Canada* (Toronto: Thomas Nelson and Sons, 1961), 48-49; and Pierre Camu, *Le Saint-Laurent et Les Grands Lacs au temps de la voile, 1608-1950* (Quebec City: Éditions Hurtubise, 1996), 109.

railways ran south from Montreal to the border and to connections with American railways; a third ran east to the small town of Sherbrooke in the Eastern Townships, then southeast to Portland, Maine. Shortly thereafter another railway company, the Grand Trunk, built southwestward to Toronto and northeastward to Lévis on the south shore opposite Quebec and on downriver as far as Rivière-du-Loup. Montreal had gained direct railway access to three ice-free American ports: Portland, Boston, and New York. Quebec was no longer the essential port of entry to the St. Lawrence Valley. Map 8.6 shows this reconfigured system of transportation as it was in 1860.

Behind these developments lay a commercial struggle, waged principally between merchants in New York, Boston, and Montreal, for the trade of the continental interior. The Erie Canal, which connected Albany on the Hudson River to Buffalo on Lake Erie (in 1825) and to Oswego on Lake Ontario (in 1828), had given New York a decisive commercial advantage, to which the response in Boston was to build railways. Directly challenging the St. Lawrence trading system, one of them ran to Ogdensburg on the south bank of the St. Lawrence well above Montreal, and from there north to Bytown (Map 8.6). Merchants in Montreal – the "river barons," business historian Gerald Tulchinsky calls them – sought to improve the navigability of the St. Lawrence and, faced with the British adoption of free trade (1846) and a growing American demand for lumber, to establish rail connections to American markets and ice-free ports. This was a struggle Montreal would neither win nor altogether lose. It did not capture the interior trade and become the metropolis of eastern North America – that was the prize – but did retain an edge of the interior trade. In 1821, with the merger of the North West and Hudson's Bay Companies (Chapter 10), fur exports shifted to Hudson Bay, but by this date Upper Canada was being rapidly settled (Chapter 9), the centre of gravity of the Lower and Upper Canadian population was moving westward, and a good deal of Upper Canadian wheat, flour, and potash entered the St. Lawrence trading system. As it did, a thin transcontinental connection (in the fur trade) gave way to a thicker, more proximate westward trade facilitated by new transportation systems and the increasingly sophisticated financial services of banks and insurance firms, mostly based in Montreal. At the same time, marine shipping moved more easily upriver to Montreal, often bypassing Quebec altogether. In these circumstances the urban system along the St. Lawrence shifted westward. In 1830 Montreal and Quebec were approximately the same size. Twenty years later, Montreal was a third larger than Quebec; in 1861 it was almost twice as large.

During these same years, the sluggish population growth that characterized both Quebec and Montreal in the late eighteenth century was replaced by average annual growth rates well in excess of those in the countryside. In Montreal between 1825 and 1861, the average rate of population growth was 4.4 percent; in Quebec for several decades after 1805, the rate was about 3.5 percent. In these changed demographic circumstances, the urban percentage of the population began to increase, rising to 10 percent by 1825, 13 percent in 1851, and 16 percent in 1861. By the latter date, Montreal, with just over ninety thousand inhabitants, was by far the largest place in British North America. Quebec, the second largest, had just over fifty thousand inhabitants.

Urban growth was fuelled by both British and Canadian migrations. Until the mid-1840s, the former predominated, and the towns became more British. In 1844, 57 percent of the population of Montreal and 40 percent of the population in Quebec were anglophone. At this date, the Irish comprised some 22 percent of Montrealers. Only Trois-Rivières remained overwhelmingly Canadian. By the mid-1840s, however, the tide was turning, and through most of the 1850s, as historian Jean-Claude Robert has shown, people born in Lower Canada accounted for 83 percent of Montreal's population growth. Most of these migrants were Canadians from the nearby countryside (Map 8.7). For the most part, they were young adults; a slight majority were women, many of whom would find employment as domestic servants. Overall, they were part of a much larger exodus from farms and villages in the St. Lawrence lowlands to the fringe of the Canadian Shield, the Eastern Townships, and particularly to industrial towns in the United States – places where young Canadians could hope to find work compatible with their experience and family commitments. As this migration proceeded, the anglicizing of the towns was reversed. Early in the 1860s, Canadians again became the majority in Montreal.

Throughout the first half of the nineteenth century, the towns' economies depended primarily on commerce. Broadly considered, that commerce operated at three interrelated scales, one imperial and tied to the St. Lawrence River, another regional and channelled through St. Lawrence tributaries and networks of local roads, and the third internal to the towns themselves. The colony's grand commerce linked the continental interior

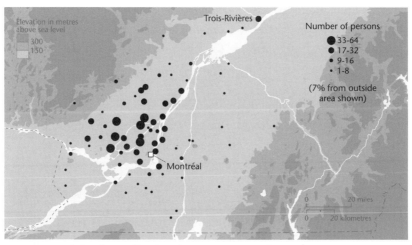

MAP 8.7   Origin of Canadian immigrants to Montreal, 1859 | After S. Olson and P. Thornton, "'Pour Se Créer un Avenir': Stratégies de Couples Montréalais au XIXe siècle," *Revue d'histoire de l'Amérique française* 51, 3 (1998): 365.

via the St. Lawrence to Britain. For all the transportation changes of the early nineteenth century, Quebec remained the primary port of entry for a great variety of British manufactures until well into the 1850s. With the abrupt growth of the timber trade in the first decade of the nineteenth century (Chapter 7), squared timber became Quebec's principal export (Figure 8.5). In a busy day during the shipping season, as many as fifty ships arrived at Quebec; in 1830 the 922 ships that cleared Quebec placed it third (in tonnage) among North American ports. In any given day, some three thousand sailors were likely to be in town. In Montreal, forwarding merchants relayed goods imported at Quebec (or, increasingly, imported directly to Montreal) westward along the St. Lawrence or Ottawa Rivers. The larger of these Montreal firms, many of them in partnerships with firms in Upper Canada, operated steamboats, barges, and sloops along the improving system of rivers and canals that gave access to the Great Lakes (Figure 8.6). Long before the enlargement of the St. Lawrence canals in the late 1840s, this system carried a large two-way import-export trade. In both Quebec and Montreal, it supported a broad spectrum of urban employments: stevedores, artisans and tradespeople associated with a port, inn- and tavernkeepers, prostitutes, ship chandlers, company managers and clerks, insurance brokers, and bankers and their employees, among others. There were also regional trades between the towns and their countrysides. Quebec served all the settlements along the lower St. Lawrence, including those some distance inland, as along the Chaudière River south of the St. Lawrence and along the Saguenay River to the north. Trois-Rivières was the central place for the settlements in the middle of the colony, as was Montreal for the much larger populations on the Montreal plain and eastern Upper Canada. In these regional trades, connections between urban and village merchants depended on a great variety of river shipping and on local roads, often passable only in winter or midsummer, that connected inland farms and villages to navigable water. More locally yet, hundreds of shops, booths, and peddlers served internal urban markets.

While the towns participated in and prospered from these different scales of trade, their production was slowly being industrialized. In the process, work became more specialized and usually less skilled, and was relocated in factories where it was narrowly divided into particular tasks and supervised by foremen. These developments transformed the social

FIGURE 8.5 *Timber Depot near Quebec,* 1838 (artist, W.H. Bartlett). In these vast marshalling yards, squared timber from the Ottawa Valley and elsewhere in the St. Lawrence watershed was collected, sorted, and loaded for shipment to Britain. | *Canadian Scenery,* vol. 2, facing p. 12.

FIGURE 8.6 *View of the Port and of the Rue des Commissaires,* 1843 (artist, James Duncan). Steamboats on the St. Lawrence River shifted commerce towards Montreal and considerably stimulated the bustling waterfront depicted here. | McGill University Library, Rare Books and Special Collections.

relations of production. The close interpersonal relations of master, jour-neyman, and apprentice, all of whom usually lived and worked in the same household, were sundered. Workers were becoming a proletariat, and factory owners members of a bourgeoisie, a momentous reorganization that proceeded in different ways and at different rates in different sectors of the manufacturing economy. In general, the sequence of change may be thought of as follows: The point of departure was an artisanal economy dependent on manual labour, an array of traditional skills, and close, dependent relationships within small groups of producers in the craft household, the fundamental unit of production. At some stage machine tools (often powered initially by their operators), an increasing division of labour, and the employment of less skilled workers penetrated and increasingly displaced these small local units of work. As they did, the size and output of workplaces increased, and products became more standardized. Parts of the productive process that could not yet be mechanized were usually put out to domestic workers, whose employment often increased. Eventually, as machines became more elaborate, divisions of labour became finer, all steps of production were mechanized, and steam power was introduced, the full factory system emerged. Labour had been "freed" from its social context, detached from its place of residence, hired for wages, and made responsible for its own social reproduction. The factory owner, unlike the master of a household, paid a wage but otherwise had no responsibility for the lives of workers. The change was drastic but partial. Artisans and small manufactories remained long after the introduction of factories.

Shoe manufacturing provides a vivid example of these developments in an industry that by 1871 accounted for a quarter of Montreal's manufacturing employment. In 1820, historian Joanne Burgess has shown, shoemaking was still the occupation of a master artisan assisted by an apprentice or two and perhaps a journeyman and a son, all of whom worked in a small shop attached to the master's residence, using tools and methods that had been employed for centuries. Most shoes were custom-made. This system began to change in the 1820s as shoe merchants started to sell ready-made shoes and to divide shoemaking into specialized tasks located either in larger shops or, in the case of the women who increasingly sewed the uppers, at home. Well before the introduction of machines, therefore, shoe manufacture had changed drastically. The first machine, for rolling and preparing leather, was introduced in 1849. Thirty times as efficient as manual labour, it exerted pressure towards mechanization on all subsequent stages of production. Other machines followed, each displacing work previously done by hand but, because volumes were growing, creating much other work (often for women at home) in the remaining unmechanized stages of production. In 1864, with the advent of steam power and a machine for stitching soles to uppers, the full factory system was achieved. Work now took place in a factory. Much of the workforce was deskilled, wages declined in the short run, and employees functioned within the time discipline of industrial capitalism. Although the process of industrialization had been fought at every step of the way, the factory owners had prevailed. Some of them became wealthy, boots and shoes were cheaper than they had been, and the lives of working people were transformed.

Broadly similar changes were occurring in most sectors of manufacturing. With the exception of wooden shipbuilding (which combined traditional craftsmanship with large concentrations of labour), almost all production in Quebec and Montreal was artisanal in 1825, whereas by 1870 most of it took place within the factory system. In detail, however, the economies of the two cities had developed differently.

Through the first half and a little more of the nineteenth century, manufacturing in Quebec focused primarily on shipbuilding. In most years, a dozen or more shipyards operated there and, depending on the market for ships, employed seasonally (shipbuilding was largely winter work) as many as two thousand men. The largest wooden sailing ships built anywhere in the nineteenth century came from these yards. They were products of large workforces, traditional craftsmanship, sharp divisions of labour, and essentially manual power. By 1860, however, the market for wooden ships was declining, and Quebec had lost its position as the port of entry for Lower and Upper Canada. In these circumstances, population decline was averted only by the growth of a diverse array of manufactures. The most important was shoemaking (2,200 workers in 1871), but there were many others: furniture makers (300 workers), foundries (400 workers), a rubber factory (118 workers), printers (376 workers), clothing establishments (567 workers), as well as producers of tools, moulds, brushes, glue, matches, soap, candles, and so on. Although in 1871 there were still many artisans and small partially mechanized workshops, most of this production took place in factories. Quebec's advantages for manufacturing were its ready supply of cheap labour and its central position in a regional economy. Its disadvantage, compared to Montreal, was its lack of a continental hinterland. As Quebec's relative position declined, its British elite tended to relocate in Montreal. Canadians owned most of its new factories.

In Montreal, a broad base of manufacturing appeared much earlier than in Quebec and, in association with a diverse trade and the growth of financial services, was the platform for an earlier and more comprehensive industrialization. Shipbuilding was never as important in Montreal as in Quebec, although many barges, sailing vessels, and steamboats were built there, the great majority intended for use on inland waterways. The engines for steamboats, also built in Montreal, required foundries and machine shops that, in turn, required skilled, specialized labour (usually imported from New England or Britain) and technologies that could be put to many industrial purposes. By the mid-1840s, Montreal had developed a diverse manufacturing base that ranged from the simple processing of raw materials (gristmills, sawmills), to distilling and brewing, to the making of tools, clothing, pharmaceuticals, and many types of machinery. At this date most production still took place in small partly mechanized manufactories scattered through the city. Then, in the late 1840s and early 1850s, a factory district, the first in British North America, emerged to the south of the business area along the eastern end of the recently improved Lachine Canal. Developed by a new group of entrepreneurs (mostly from the United States), it utilized hydraulic power associated with the canal locks as well as steam. This dense concentration of factories – flourmills, sawmills, foundries, metal- and woodworking factories, cotton and woollen mills – employed some two thousand workers by the mid-1850s. The yards of the Grand Trunk Railway, just south of the canal, employed another twelve hundred. Other factories, some very large, lay north of the business district, interspersed with new working-class housing. As early as 1856, a clothing factory built by two English Jews, Edward and David Moss, employed eight hundred people, most of them women and children. Large shoe and tobacco factories, opening in the 1860s, were also heavy employers of female labour. In Old Montreal, new factories coexisted with a great variety of small partially mechanized workshops. Overall, Montreal was industrializing rapidly. Church spires were giving way to factory chimneys, and an economy that had been dependent on commerce was shifting to one dependent on steam, iron, and an industrial proletariat. Map 8.8, which plots the distribution by value of industrial production in the Canadas in 1871, suggests something of the relative importance of Montreal's industrialization.

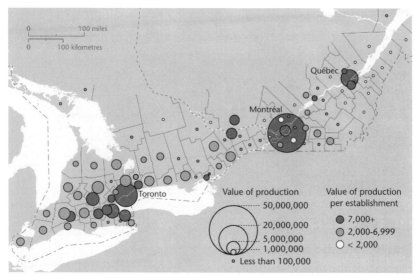

MAP 8.8   Value of industrial production, St. Lawrence corridor, 1871 | After R.H. Walder, in *Historical Atlas of Canada*, vol. 2, *The Land Transformed*, ed. R. Louis Gentilcore, cart. Geoffrey J. Matthews (Toronto: University of Toronto Press, 1993), plate 48.

As industrialization reshaped the social relations of work, the urban geography of class, ethnicity, and occupation changed. Old inner cities lost much of their residential function as place of work was separated from place of residence. As historical geographer Robert Lewis has shown, the elite were moving away from Old Montreal, either to spacious residential suburbs or close to the factories they owned. Anglophones were going to the southern slopes of Mount Royal, and francophones to pockets of expensive housing north of Old Montreal. The businesses that now dominated Old Montreal were increasingly segregated: retailing close to the waterfront along St. Paul Street, a financial district two blocks away along St. James Street, a legal district just north of the financial area. Working-class suburbs, already substantial north and south of the central business district in 1847, expanded as factories were built nearby. Those to the northeast were almost entirely Canadian; those to the southwest were more mixed but predominantly anglophone (Map 8.9). Overall, people were sharply segregated by ethnicity and class. In Quebec the largely British elite concentrated in the upper town and west in the new suburb of Saint-Jean; the working-class suburb of Saint-Roch, below the upper town to the north

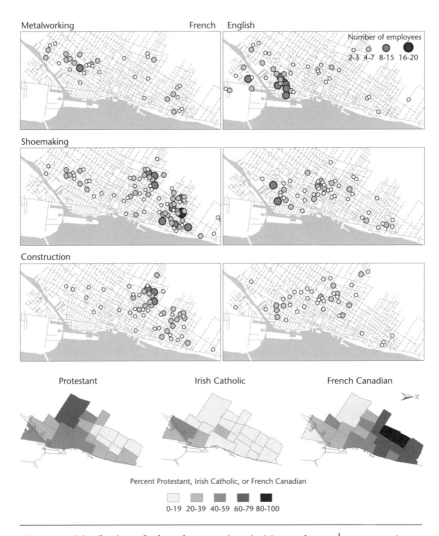

MAP 8.9   Distribution of selected occupations in Montreal, 1861 | Courtesy of
S. Olson, Historical Geography Cartographic Laboratory, McGill University.

and close to the shipyards, was 90 percent Canadian. In either town, the
extremes were great. On the one hand were tiny squared-log houses or,
from the late 1850s, two-storey duplexes and fourplexes crowded along
narrow streets, with privies and perhaps chicken coops and pigpens behind. On the other were villas built in the latest Victorian style, with green-
houses and extensive gardens (Figure 8.7). Historical geographer David
Hanna suggests that the duplex form was largely derived from industrial

a)

b)

FIGURE 8.7   Housing in Montreal: a) fourplex and duplex (artist, Carmen Jensen); b) *St. Antoine Hall,* 1850 (artist, James Duncan). By the 1860s duplexes and four-plexes comprised some 90 percent of Montreal's new housing. The well off lived in altogether more spacious circumstances, such as St. Antoine Hall. | a) Hanna and Olson, *Historical Atlas of Canada,* vol. 2, *The Land Transformed,* ed. R. Louis Gentilcore, cart. Geoffrey J. Matthews (Toronto: University of Toronto Press, 1993), plate 49; b) with permission of the Royal Ontario Museum © ROM, 9057.17.1.

housing in Scotland and that officials of the Grand Trunk Railway en-couraged its diffusion in Montreal. Its flat roof (felt, tar, and gravel) re-duced building costs; its brick facade met fire regulations. Providing cheap housing in a low-wage environment, it quickly became the characteristic residence of working-class families in Montreal. Between these extremes was a great variety of housing, some of it still located where different so-cial classes and building types were jumbled.

Each of the principal ethnicities in the towns – Anglo-Protestants, Irish Catholics, and Canadians – was represented throughout the class hierar-chy, but in very different proportions. Probably the poorest, overall, were the Irish, especially the famine Irish arriving in the late 1840s; the most

FIGURE 8.8   *Canada Marine Works, Augustin Cantin, Montreal, Canada East, 1857.*
In the 1850s, Cantin, a Canadian, owned one of the larger industrial operations in
British North America. It comprised a sawmill (right), shipyards, and engineering
works (left). By 1857 Cantin had built ninety-four steamships. | Lithograph by Sarony,
Major, and Knapp, New York, 1857, in Charles P. DeVolpi, *Montreal, a Pictorial Record, 1535-1885,*
vol. 1 (Montreal: Dev-Sco Publications, 1963), 127.

prosperous, by a good margin, were the Anglo-Protestants, a great many
of them Scots. Although there were some wealthy Canadians – Joseph
Masson, for example, who amassed a fortune in the import-export business, and Augustin Cantin, who became Montreal's pre-eminent steamboat builder (Figure 8.8) – the occupational profile of the Canadians was
closer to that of the Irish than of the Anglo-Protestants. Canadians were
well represented among the professions (notaries, doctors), shopkeepers,
and artisans. They tended to dominate the regional trade between town
and countryside but not the import-export trades. They were weakly represented among Montreal factory owners. Like the Irish, a large portion
of them were labourers, many of whom had recently arrived in the city.
The Anglo-Protestant elite, many of them also recent arrivals, were rarely
self-made men; they had come, rather, with capital, business experience,
and connections.

Life for most people in the towns was a struggle. The poorer districts
were exceedingly unhealthy, particularly in summer. Typhoid, typhus, and
cholera, diseases associated with filth, contaminated water, and malnutrition, were common. At midcentury, more than a quarter of the babies
born to Canadian parents in Montreal died in their first year, a third within

five years. With competition for work from two streams of migrating labour – from Britain and the Canadian countryside – wages were low (one
rarely supported a family) and poverty was at hand. Work by historian
Bettina Bradbury and geographer Sherry Olson has shown how people
survived. The wife was key, not only to cook, sew, patch, and clean, but
also to tend the few livestock the family might own, stretch meagre wages
as far as they could go, and perhaps sell a little sewing. The children, both
girls and boys, worked as soon as they were able, their small earnings critical. As in pioneer countrysides, the nuclear family required the labour of
all its available parts, as well as an extended network of mutual aid provided by relatives and neighbours. There was no state-supported welfare,
nor even, for most families, the security of home ownership. Compared to
those of almost every other North American city of the day, the housing
markets in Montreal and Quebec were dominated by tenants. In 1861, 85
percent of Montreal's working-class population rented. On 1 May, many
of them moved, usually just down the block or around the corner, still
within walking distance of the factory and the sustaining network of kin
and neighbourhood. In dire circumstances, some would return briefly to
the countryside.

Indeed, for most urban Canadians the countryside was not far away.
The grandparents of 40 percent of the Canadian babies baptized in Montreal in 1859 lived in nearby villages or farms. Throughout the early nineteenth century, there had been a growing two-way traffic of people and
goods between town and countryside. In innumerable ways, each bore on
the other. For many other people in the towns, however, the countryside
was almost invisible. The imaginations of these English-speaking people
led elsewhere, as did much of the urban economy. In good part, Montreal
and Quebec owed their size to these external connections. The urban hierarchy in Lower Canada in the mid-nineteenth century suggests as much:
two large towns and a smaller one along the river, then hundreds of villages, only the few largest of which might be considered small towns.

THE SHIELD FRINGE

In the early nineteenth century, capital, labour, pioneer farm families,
and, here and there, Native people converged and variously interacted in
the forested valleys and uplands immediately north and west of the St.
Lawrence lowlands. The capital, which was largely British, arrived suddenly

after 1806, when Napoleon's continental blockade cut off supplies of Baltic timber, and in response the British government sought to protect colonial wood in the imperial market. In 1809 it set the tariff on foreign wood at twenty-seven shillings a load (fifty cubic feet), in 1810 at thirty-four shillings, and in 1821 at fifty-five shillings. At the last rate, and allowing for different shipping costs and a tariff on colonial wood of ten shillings, the colonial preference per load of wood was some thirty shillings, quite enough to attract British capital to the largely coniferous forests of Britain's North American colonies. The labour and the pioneer farm families that accompanied this capital came out of the transatlantic and eastern North American folk migrations that surged around Lower Canada in the early nineteenth century. These various peoples – Canadians, Irish, Scots, Americans, and a few English – sought employment and livelihoods that, had they remained in situ, they could not find. On the whole, the Canadians and Americans were accustomed to chopping and clearing. The others were not, but soon learned. All this activity, driven by the interest of capital in profit, of labour in employment, and of settlers in land, was superimposed on an exceedingly sparsely inhabited land where, for some two hundred years, the fur trade had largely shaped Native–non-Native relations. During this long time, Native ways had been much altered, and probably Native populations had been much reduced, but in Native eyes the land was theirs. No one else had ever tried to use it.

Nor would outsiders use it easily, except perhaps in the Ottawa Valley and, with more delay, in the Saguenay (Map 8.10). The Ottawa River, long a major artery towards the western fur trade and a potential passage along its lower course for settlers and timber rafts, began to draw colonists at the beginning of the nineteenth century. In 1800 a group from Massachusetts took up land near the present city of Hull; a few years later a Scottish merchant in Montreal established a few Gaelic-speaking Highlanders in townships closer to Montreal. Although these people came to farm, the New Englanders sent a timber raft down the Ottawa River in 1806; a year later Joseph Papineau, seigneur of the Ottawa Valley seigneurie of Petite-Nation, did the same, two forays into the timber trade before protective imperial tariffs were in place. By the mid-1820s, when timber rafting was common on the Ottawa River, there were perhaps two thousand settlers in the valley, almost all of them Americans, Scots, or Canadians. For the most part, they spoke different languages and lived apart. At this time the

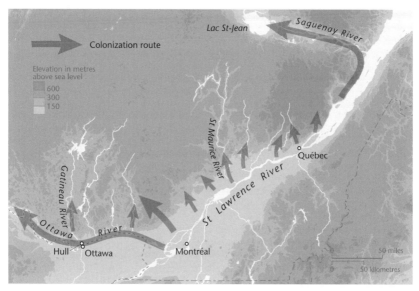

MAP 8.10   Colonizing the fringe of the Canadian Shield

Saguenay Valley, a trading preserve of the Hudson's Bay Company, was closed to colonization, which began there, illegally, only in 1838. The impetus to settle the Saguenay came from timber interests and land-hungry families in Charlevoix (Map 8.10). Apparently with capital from William Price, one of the most successful timber merchants in Lower Canada, settlers built nine sawmills in the Saguenay in four years, an illegal ruse that had its desired effect. In 1842, when the Hudson's Bay Company lease expired, it was not renewed; by 1850 there were more than four thousand settlers in the Saguenay Valley. At this date, as Louise Dechêne has shown, William Price controlled some forty sawmills in Lower Canada, many of them in the Saguenay. His mills at Grande-Baie, far from his largest in the valley, were capitalized, together with their equipment and appurtenances, at more than £16,000. He was, by far, the valley's principal employer.

Elsewhere, settlement expanded northward, then hesitated at the edge of the Canadian Shield. In the Mauricie, the region north of Trois-Rivières centred on the St. Maurice River, settlers occupied the sandy soils and largely coniferous forests immediately south of the Shield in the 1820s and 1830s. There, they created the many small forest-related industries (pot and pearl asheries, tanneries, small sawmills) that often were the principal support of pioneer families. With few exceptions, however, neither settlers nor capital touched the Canadian Shield until the early 1850s, when the government began to build timber slides around the principal waterfalls and rapids on the St. Maurice River. These slides suddenly opened the upper river and its tributaries to timber speculators, timber drives, and – very minimally in this rocky terrain – colonization. In the Laurentides, north of Montreal, where the valleys leading into the Shield had a little more soil and were more accessible than those in the Mauricie, settlers began to push into the Shield a little earlier. Some were Scots or Irish, but more were Canadians. Usually, timber interests had preceded them. Map 8.10 sketches these various movements towards and into the margins of the Canadian Shield.

The land policies that accompanied capital and settlers as they moved into the Canadian Shield evolved over the years and were always much debated. In the early years, capital often took what it wanted and settlers squatted, but in the longer run two different and somewhat contradictory sets of land policies emerged. One was designed to regulate, but also to encourage, large timber operations, the other to promote pioneer family farming. The former, which began to be put in place in the 1820s, was intended to generate revenue for the government, but also to limit the size of timber concessions and to ensure that they were developed. At the same time, the holders of timber concessions, some of the wealthiest men in Lower Canada, wielded political influence, and politicians and government officials heeded their assertions that only large, secure landholdings warranted the cost of exploiting distant and inaccessible forests. The result was a pattern of shifting and, on the whole, ineffective regulation. In the 1820s the Crown began to establish charges based on the volume of timber cut and to limit the size of timber concessions. In 1846 it tried to enforce minimum cuts (a thousand cubic feet per square mile) and to limit timber leases to twenty-five square miles. Occasionally it confiscated timber rafts for the non-payment of fees. But, as long as the holders of timber concessions paid the small charges for the timber they had cut (and often when they did not), they could do pretty much as they pleased with the forests on their concessions. In the Mauricie, fourteen applicants received some six thousand square miles of forested land in 1852, two of them more than half of this huge tract. In the Ottawa Valley, each of the drainage basins of the major northern tributaries (the Gatineau and the Rouge) was characteristically allocated to one operator (individual, group, or company) who assumed the costs of improving the river for the spring drives in return for a monopoly of the timber in its watershed. Basically, the Crown allocated timber land in large tracts at modest cost to a few. It did the opposite with potential farmland, allocating such land in small lots to many. A hundred-acre lot in the townships could be obtained from the Crown for twenty dollars, a fifth paid at the time of purchase. A house was to be built within six months, and ten acres were to be cleared within four years – conditions that were rarely enforced. Often these lots were on land that had already been logged, or on which the merchantable timber had already been allocated. Everywhere, even at midcentury, many settlers squatted and many more cut timber illegally.

British capital had entered the forests of Lower Canada and New Brunswick at much the same time and on broadly similar terms (Chapter 7). In either colony, it sought similar woods for similar markets and exploited the forest with technologies common in northeastern North American forests in the first half of the nineteenth century. The early focus in the forests of Lower Canada, as in those of New Brunswick, was on white and, to a lesser extent, red pine; later, as the pine stands became depleted, the emphasis switched to spruce and fir. The principal early product was squared timber; later it was lumber, but throughout the early nineteenth century squared timber, lumber of various dimensions, and staves were all regular exports. Logging, squaring, and hauling to a watercourse were winter work, dependent on snow cover. Timber drives took place when ice broke up and the squared timbers and logs that were piled on a lakeshore or a riverbank could be discharged into the spring flood. Often watercourses were considerably remade: bushes and trees cleared from their banks, obstructing rocks dynamited from riverbeds, banks cribbed, dams built to raise water levels, sluices built around rapids and waterfalls. The government financed some of this work only at major obstructions on major rivers, as on the St. Maurice in 1852.

The work itself depended on men, horses, and oxen. The large cross-cut saw (*godendard*) had not yet come to these forests. Cutting, limbing, and squaring were all done with axes or adzes. Hauling required horses or oxen. Gangs of men worked in the forest, and some of them, later, followed the spring timber drives. Labour was cheap, and most of it seems to have been hired by subcontractors. They would obtain contracts with the holders of timber concessions to cut and deliver given quantities of timber, and then hire workers. The number of men involved, though certainly large, cannot be precisely known. Historian Chad Gaffield estimates that by the mid-1840s some eight thousand men, most of them young and single, were employed seasonally in the forest economy along the north side of the Ottawa River. From the Ottawa River to the Saguenay, the principal Canadian component of this labour came from adjacent rural parishes to the south; the Scots in the Ottawa Valley came from the enclaves of Scottish settlement there; some of the Irish, as they began to enter this workforce in the 1830s and 1840s, were recent immigrants. By and large, men worked in camps with others of their ethnicity. At the scale of the Ottawa Valley and the Laurentides, the labour force was mixed; in the Mauricie and the Saguenay it was almost entirely Canadian. Bosses were usually British.

This work took men into the forest for most of the winter. There, in groups usually of ten to thirty, they lived in a *cambuse,* a roughly made and often dirt-floored log building with an open fire in the centre, a smokehole in the roof, and low bunks, covered with spruce branches, around the walls. Attached sometimes to the cambuse were a stable for horses and oxen and a shed for provisions (logging camps were much the same throughout the northeastern pine forests; see Figure 7.2). Men slept in the cambuse between days of dawn-to-dusk work and ate their morning and evening meals: beans, salt pork, peas, bread, a little molasses. Space was cramped. There were few opportunities for drying or washing sweat-soaked clothing, or for shedding fleas and lice. The cambuse was an incubator for contagious diseases, and limited diets encouraged ailments associated with malnutrition, such as scurvy. Yet, men worked in these conditions and often competed for jobs. Usually, they were paid by the month, sometimes in cash but commonly in kind, at a rate that varied, depending on individual skill and productivity, between six and fifteen dollars a month (two and a half to six cents an hour) in the 1840s and 1850s. This for exceedingly hard work six days a week as men, vying for wages and esteem, strove to cut or haul more than their peers – or simply to avoid being fired. Among these groups of young and predominantly single men, a male bravado emphasized feats of strength, daring, and courage, a side of life in the woods and on the drives that has long dominated the folklore of the timber trade. As historians René Hardy and Normand Séguin point out, however, the reality was more sombre. An abundant, unorganized labour force with, as yet, no collective means for its self-defence, had encountered a capitalist labour market that had no need to pay for the social reproduction of its workforce.

In some places, pioneer farm families accompanied these seasonal incursions of capital and labour into the forest. In the Ottawa Valley, the first such families were Americans and Scots. Later, there and in the Laurentides, others were Irish or occasionally English, but across the whole front of the Canadian Shield in Lower Canada, the majority were Canadians, most of whom came out of local migration fields that connected adjacent parishes in the St. Lawrence lowlands to new land farther north. These migrations to new land, like others before them in the lowlands, usually comprised groups of related people – a nuclear or an extended family, perhaps several brothers – and resulted in new settlements that were only somewhat less closely intertwined by kinship than those left behind. They also brought an experience with pioneering and farming that was grounded in the St. Lawrence lowlands, but that had been relocated on indifferent soils at the climatic limit of agriculture in a recently commercialized forest.

In these circumstances, rudimentary, slow-growing farms emerged in forest clearings, each a site of family life and labour and a precarious means of family-centred survival. Gérard Bouchard emphasizes their primitiveness in the Saguenay: Tools largely wooden and mostly made on the farm. Grain (saved from the previous year's crop) sown broadcast and harvested with sickles. Minimal crop rotations comprising, characteristically, a couple of years of grains, one of hay, one of pasture, then a single light ploughing, then grain again. Stock left to forage in the forest through as much of the year as possible. Low yields except on newly cleared land. No money for better seed, improved stock, or equipment. A type of farming that, overwhelmingly, produced for domestic consumption, not for sale. Bouchard likens it to agriculture in the lowlands during the French regime, but a closer comparison may be with the uplands of Cape Breton where, when the Saguenay was being settled, another people (immigrant Highland Scots) struggled at another northern continental margin of agriculture.

In the Saguenay, and elsewhere along the margin of the Canadian Shield in Lower Canada, pioneer agriculture was inserted in a forest economy and responded to it in various ways. Some who acquired farm lots had no intention of farming; in spite of regulations forbidding the practice, they came to harvest the commercial timber, then move on. Basing his conclusions on a study of an early parish in the eastern Saguenay, historical geographer Marc St-Hilaire suggests that, by the 1860s, some half of all lots were acquired only for their forests. Many settlers who did farm derived their principal income from the forest, perhaps by selling cordwood, pot or pearl ash (used in textile manufacture and a commercial "crop" in pioneer areas throughout eastern North America), hemlock bark (for tanning), or logs to an accessible sawmill. There was also the possibility that the head of a family or, more likely, his grown sons, might find work in a logging camp and spend the winter in a cambuse. All such activities, plus the relentless work of clearing, took time away from farming, much of which, as in other pioneer areas, fell to the women and children. Here and there, farming developed to the point where at least some hay could be sold to the timber camps, although most of the large timber concerns operated their own sizable farms. Overall, the economy of pioneer settlement along the margin of the Canadian Shield depended as much or more on the forest as on farming. Those who, as in the Maritimes, railed at the nefarious influence of forestry on agriculture did not understand the realities of pioneering in settings where an economy of multiple occupations (pluriactivité) was often the only means of survival.

And yet, from the perspective of many of the Canadian elite, and especially of the clergy, the agricultural colonization of the fringe of the Canadian Shield came to embrace a version of an age-old agrarian myth that associated a particular goodness and felicity with lives attached to the soil. In the early nineteenth century, a form of agrarianism closely associated with the conquest of space was in the air. It was embedded in the rhetoric of American westward expansion and in an array of British promotional literatures intended to direct British emigrants to British colonies and away from the United States. Serge Courville has shown that the Canadian elite drew on this spatialized agrarianism to fashion a program for the preservation of religion, language, and the Canadian race that depended on the colonization of the Shield. When all the agricultural land in the St. Lawrence lowlands was occupied, British immigrants were pouring into the Canadas, and young Canadians were emigrating to the factory towns of New England, the north, a vaguely defined territory that stretched in some minds to the Rockies, was the logical space for Canadian expansion. Its climate was less harsh than feared, its soils generally fertile, its mountains as productive as plains because, as Curé François-Xavier-Antoine Labelle, the most famous of the colonizing priests, wrote in an outburst of natural theology, "the globe is almost entirely covered by mountains." Here was the space, created by God, for the Canadian people. Such clerical thinking, coupled with the interest of the Canadian bourgeoisie in maintaining Canadian markets, led to the creation of many colonization societies and to much dedicated work to recruit and establish colonists, especially in the Laurentides where potential farmland seemed particularly threatened by Protestant settlement. Settlers, however, appraised the land more realistically. Even in the Saguenay, the most favoured valley around the fringe of the Shield, Gérard Bouchard has shown that the colonization societies attracted only a few dozen actual settlers, most of whom quickly left. Overall, the Shield and an agrarian vision were barely compatible. Most of those who attempted to farm there, they or their progeny would eventually give up.

Throughout these years, the forest was assaulted and changed. Accessible white pine – the largest trees more than fifty metres tall and a metre and a half in diameter at the butt – were cut. Stands of mature white pine disappeared, replaced by tangles of broken trees and the large portion of any tree – branches, the top half or more of the trunk, piles of chips from squaring the sides of logs – that logging left behind. All of this was fuel for fires. Because the dense groundcover that followed logging and fires favoured species that germinated in heavy shade, the composition of the forest began to change: more poplar, aspen, white birch, and fir, fewer pine, and eventually fewer spruce. Clearings and homesteads, almost all of them displaying the stump-strewn roughness of pioneering, appeared here and there in this changing forest. Usually, something in the appearance or construction of the log house or the arrangement of farm buildings revealed the ethnicity of their builders. The Canadian pioneer landscape, common in the St. Lawrence lowlands, was transferred to the Shield and largely reproduced on its wider, shorter township lots. Where the terrain was rough, farms were more widely spaced, their location dependent on pockets of arable land rather than on the regularity of the township survey. *The Habitant Farm* (1856), a well-known painting by the German-Dutch genre painter Cornelius Krieghoff, depicts such a

FIGURE 8.9   *The Habitant Farm,* 1856 (artist, Cornelius Krieghoff). A charming
scene disguising a more sombre reality, a family's struggle to survive on land
ill-suited for farming. | © National Gallery of Canada.

homestead. Krieghoff bathed the scene in a romantic glow, but its underlying realities are clear enough: a tiny house, a large family, forest surrounding a meagre clearing, a setting for a losing struggle with an intractable land
(Figure 8.9).

    At the beginning of the modern settlement of the Ottawa Valley, Na-
tive chiefs told American settlers that the land belonged to them. The settlers, they said, were driving away game and threatening the way of life of
their people. Other chiefs probably said as much, but small scattered
populations of hunters and gatherers had no power to stop the advance of
capital and settlers into their territories. For the most part, the Native presence was ignored and virtually invisible. Their land was wanted and taken.
It was assumed to be uninhabited, or inhabited so thinly by wandering
people that their land uses were inconsequential – common, legitimating
tropes worldwide of settler colonialism. But the chiefs were almost certainly right. The newcomers were driving away game, and peoples whose
lives and livelihoods had been buffeted for more than two centuries by
introduced diseases and the ecological changes associated with the fur trade
(Chapter 10), were buffeted again. They usually had no choice but to move
away, in so doing encroaching on the territories and compounding the
problems of other struggling Native peoples.

The Eastern Townships

The Appalachian valleys and uplands between the St. Lawrence lowlands and the American border contained neither large pure stands of white or red pine nor rivers giving easy access to the forests. The region was not, therefore, a focus of the squared-timber trade. Nor, in the early absence of roads from the north or west, was it accessible from the seigneuries. On the other hand, it lay at an edge of American expansion and drew an American population of experienced backwoods settlers. A few were Loyalists, but most were not. They were land seekers, many of whom hardly knew or cared on which side of the border they found themselves. Detached from the St. Lawrence lowlands but open to the south, they created an enclave of the northern American frontier in British North America. With them came, first, the backwoods ways of pioneer New England, then, later, the methods and machinery of early New England industrialization. Circuit-riding preachers crossed the border freely. American newspapers circulated widely and American textbooks served in the schools. Later, as roads were built into the Eastern Townships from the north and west, as British and Canadian settlers percolated into them from the north, and as the government acquired more purchase over the region, this American dominance diminished, but even in the 1860s most of the population in the Eastern Townships was of American origin. In the border townships especially, the stamp of New England on the land was apparent everywhere.

In 1792, the government opened land south and east of the seigneuries to the rights of private property (free and common socage) within a system of townships. Townships ten miles square or nine by twelve miles along navigable rivers would be divided into two-hundred-acre (eighty-hectare) lots, one-seventh of which were reserved for the Crown and another seventh for the Anglican clergy. Unwilling to accept the cost of surveying and administering this land, and of building roads and bridges, the government began to allocate townships to groups comprising a leader and associates. In this system, the leader was to assemble a group of settlers and defray the costs of surveying, administration, and road building, in return for which he would be entitled to up to twelve hundred acres per settler family (two hundred for the family, the rest for himself) – a system that produced lists of bogus settlers, much argument, and only six township grants between 1792 and 1800. Then the government began to grant large tracts to men of substance (most of them merchants or government officials) who it hoped would develop their land, in this way alienating some 400,000 acres (167,000 hectares) between 1800 and 1810. The decision in 1826 to auction off Crown and clergy reserves also favoured the consolidation of large landholdings. And in 1833 the secretary of state for the colonies in London entered into an agreement with the British American Land Company, a creation of British merchants, for the sale, at one-sixth of market value, of 800,000 acres (320,000 hectares) of land in the Eastern Townships. In return the company was to build roads and bridges, establish Protestant schools, and attract British immigrants. For a few years it attempted to do so, but overall, and by various means between 1792 and 1840, much of the Eastern Townships passed into the hands of land speculators who were more inclined to wait for land prices to rise than to develop their holdings. As a result, settlement was retarded, there was much squatting, and many other settlers, fed up with the problems of land access or title, moved away.

Until the War of 1812, virtually all immigrants to the Eastern Townships were part of a stream of backwoods migration that originated in densely populated southern New England in the 1760s and 1770s and moved north through New Hampshire and Vermont to reach and cross an edge of British North America. This migration stopped during the war and, because of a succession of disastrous harvests, hardly resumed until the mid-1820s. Then, as historian Jean-Pierre Kesteman has pointed out, it brought a somewhat different class of immigrant: more skilled artisans, professionals, and entrepreneurs with capital and connections. At the same time, the population of prior American settlers in the townships was growing rapidly by natural increase, and parents, like those in the seigneuries, were finding it difficult to place their progeny. The frontier mobility that had brought them to the Eastern Townships continued; a great many moved on, either, as one immigrant put it, "further into the bush," or beyond the Eastern Townships to Upper Canada, Ohio, Illinois, or Wisconsin. From as early as 1815, there was also a trickle of immigration from the British Isles, particularly from Scotland and Ireland. Canadians came as well, some to take up land, more to work for wages. In 1844, 23 percent of the sixty-three thousand people in the Eastern Townships were French speakers. The townships became a patchwork of settlements, the whole region considerably isolated from the St. Lawrence lowlands by tracts of marsh and forest, and even the settled areas fractured by topography and land speculations.

Pioneering in the Eastern Townships, as throughout the eastern North American forests, was a matter of tiny clearings, rough and minimal buildings, relentless family work, mixed subsistence economies supplemented by sales of potash and (when it could be found) by off-farm employment, and, always, a narrow margin between getting by and not. As the pioneer years passed, an agricultural economy emerged that centred on livestock and depended on family labour supplemented, perhaps, by hired hands during haying and harvest. On most farms about a third of the cleared land was in grains, a third in meadow, and a third in pasture. The marketable surplus was usually cattle or sheep on the hoof, salted and barrelled beef or pork, wool, butter, or cheese, most of it destined either for American markets or, although hard to reach, for markets in Quebec or Montreal. Quite different were a few large specialized operations. Often owned by major land speculators or by gentry farmers, and dependent on hired labour (some one hundred summer workers on the largest of these operations), they imported quality breeding stock and practised complex rotations of grains and fodder crops. Approximate equivalents in the townships of William Evans' farm on the outskirts of Montreal, but in far more isolated circumstances, they tended to consume wealth.

Even more, probably, than in the seigneurial lowlands, there was a profusion of artisanal and manufacturing activities. Grist- and sawmills accompanied virtually every settlement, distilleries were almost as ubiquitous, and there were soon tanneries, asheries, carding- and fulling mills, and, though much less common, breweries, paper mills, and foundries. Almost all of them were small operations, usually a man and son, perhaps a couple of employees. But there were soon innovations and changes of scale. One was to put several different activities – gristmilling, sawmilling, and carding – in one large water-powered mill. Usually, millers rented space in such a building from the entrepreneur who built it. Another was to put all the operations associated with cloth production in one building and to mechanize as many of the operations as possible. Two such woollen manufactories appeared in the townships in the mid-1820s. Carding and spinning (spinning jennies) were mechanized, but weaving was not. The technology was based on American adaptations of British inventions, the machinery was built in New Hampshire – its manufacturer, Stephen

FIGURE 8.10   Mill at Sherbrooke on the Magog River, 1838 (artist W.H. Bartlett). A gothic view of two of the mills identified on Map 8.12. On the left the BALC sawmill, on the right the Goodhue woollen mill. | *Canadian Scenery,* vol. 2 (London, George Virtue, 1842), facing p. 13.

Underwood, came to Sherbrooke to install it – and the capital and entrepreneurship came from Massachusetts and Vermont (Figure 8.10).

The social fabric of the townships, as of other pioneer areas, was relatively egalitarian in the early years, then more differentiated. Even among the family farmers, the gap between the more and less well off widened fairly quickly. Examining several townships that, in 1831, had been settled for four decades, Jean-Pierre Kesteman notes that only 38 percent of farm households had forty or more hectares (a hundred acres) of cultivated land; 19 percent had less than twenty hectares. Apparently, farms were being subdivided as population pressures rose. Below this farming population on the social scale were landless labourers, many of them transient Canadians or Irish en route to the United States. Above it were the most prosperous artisans, innkeepers, and mill owners, professionals, merchants, the major land speculators, and a small group of British gentry drawn to the townships by their beauty, climate, and pastoral economy. In the early years, however, gentry were anomalies in the American culture of the southern townships. Most accents were the same on either side of the border. Institutions beyond the family were weak, and apparently many settlers had no formal religious affiliation. A strong sense of independence and attachment to local democracy, distrust of more distant authority, and suspicion of social refinements were in the air. For some of the gentry, this population seemed a rabble, as it often did to officials in Quebec and Montreal. British colonial administrators had not supported the Loyalists in the townships, fearing they were too American and too close to the border, a perception that lingered in official circles. Overall, the Eastern Townships reproduced the earlier tension in Nova Scotia between American settlers' attachment to local institutions and distrust of external authority, and a managerial and centralizing colonial administration (Chapter 7).

Soon after 1840, American pioneering in the townships declined and ended. The few immigrants from the United States after this date settled in the towns and villages. At the same time, Canadian and British settlers, the latter mostly displaced crofters from the Isle of Lewis in the Outer Hebrides, were moving into the townships. These people were poor, and the high land costs in established townships were beyond their means. On the other hand, land speculation and isolation had left the northern and northeastern townships largely unsettled. As colonization roads were built into these areas, colonization societies bought up land and made it available to settlers, taxes encouraged absentee landowners to sell their holdings, and the government (after 1848) began to make free fifty-acre (twenty-hectare) grants of the remaining Crown land, a good deal of this land was taken up. With these migrations, the ethnicity of the Eastern Township population changed: from 77 percent of American or British origin in 1844, to 53 percent in 1861, to 42 percent in 1871. The populations of the southern townships remained predominantly anglophone and of mixed American-British descent. The northern and northeastern townships became predominantly Canadian with a block of Gaelic-speaking Protestant Scots.

By the 1850s and 1860s, the settlements in the southern townships were three generations old and well established. Agriculture remained the basis of their economy, and stock raising the basis of agriculture. Some four-fifths of cleared land was now in meadow or pasture. Some farms were small subsistent operations, but many others were comfortable family ventures with 80-120 acres of cleared land, sizable herds and flocks, some mechanized equipment, and perhaps a couple of hired hands. Most townships also contained a few large capitalist farms – specialized producers entirely dependent on hired labour. In one or two townships, such farms may have been the majority. The owners of the largest of these farms were usually businessmen with many irons in the fire. They invested heavily in purebred livestock and farm equipment, and incorporated elements of current agronomic practice. Such agriculture produced profits, some of which were invested locally. Much manufacturing remained artisanal, small-scale, and local, but an increasing fraction was factory-based. Fully mechanized woollen factories operated in the Eastern Townships in the 1840s, as did a cotton factory, the first in British North America. In 1852 a mechanized paper mill began producing newsprint. In the mid-1850s, with the coming of railways and the Reciprocity Treaty with the United States, large mechanized sawmilling became feasible. One such mill, built in 1853 on the St. Francis River just below Sherbrooke by lumbermen from Bangor, Maine, employed 150 men, worked round the clock eight months a year, and produced seventy-five thousand board feet a day.

In such ways, a web of manufacturing was superimposed on an essentially prosperous countryside and a population that, even in 1860, was 95 percent rural. Most people lived on isolated farmsteads served by networks of irregular roads. Hamlets and small villages housed millers and other artisans, shop- and tavernkeepers, ministers of various Protestant denominations, teachers, and perhaps some small partly mechanized manufacturing. Such places served their surrounding populations (Map 8.11). At the same time, another, more urban system was coming into being. It required both railway connections and waterpower, and at several such sites towns given as much to manufacturing as to the provision of regional services were emerging. Factory owners lived adjacent to (sometimes within) their factories; their employees lived nearby. They imported skilled workers, often from Britain, and usually recruited unskilled labour, often women and children, from among the Canadians or, less commonly, the Irish. Wages were low for twelve hours of work a day in often unhealthy conditions, but families that placed several daughters in a factory would get by. Industrial towns were coming into being. Sherbrooke, with twenty-five hundred inhabitants in 1852 and forty-four hundred in 1871, was the largest of them, a centre of manufacturing and an emerging regional capital. The most substantial bank in the townships, the Eastern Townships Bank, opened there in 1859. The manufactures established in Sherbrooke along the Magog River between 1827 and 1867 are located and identified on Map 8.12.

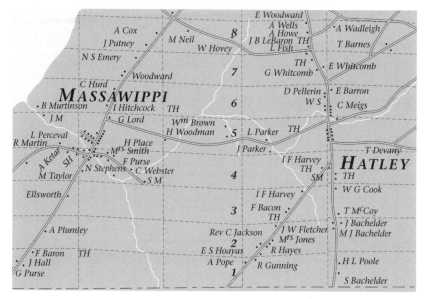

MAP 8.11   District of St. Francis, Canada East (detail), 1863 | From Heather Maddick, *County Maps: Land Ownership Maps of Canada in the 19th Century* (Ottawa: Public Archives of Canada, 1976), p. 79.

Settlement of the northern townships, on the other hand, more closely resembled that in the valleys of the Canadian Shield. The land was barely fit for agriculture; forests were the principal resource, and the state had turned over most of them to large lumber firms. It, and a variety of clerical and private interests, also promoted colonization.

Map 8.13 shows the pattern of land acquisition by ethnic group in a northern township, Winslow, that historian J.I. Little has studied in detail. The Scots were Gaelic-speaking Protestants displaced by the collapse of crofting (Chapter 7) and, in the mid-1840s, by the total failure of the potato crop. Theirs was either an assisted migration of destitute people, many of whom arrived in Winslow with nothing, or a chain migration of kin, many of whom were almost equally destitute. The Canadians came from the south shore of the St. Lawrence near Quebec (Lévis to Lotbinière, page 253), most of them apparently from farming backgrounds. They were little better off than the Scots but had far more forest-related experience. Both groups acquired free fifty-acre lots, all with severe limitations for agriculture, which over time they tended to enlarge by purchases or squatting. Both moved to Winslow within dense networks of kin and

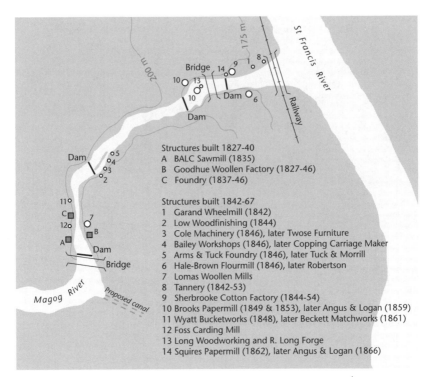

MAP 8.12   Dams and manufacturies along the Magog River, 1827-67 | After Jean-Pierre Kesteman, *Histoire de Sherbrooke Tome 1: de l'âge de l'eau à l'ère de la vapeur (1802-1866)* (Sherbrooke: Collection Patrimoine, G.G.C. éditions, 2000), 164.

maintained them there. They settled apart, but created similar mixed subsistent agricultural economies. The Scots cleared, on average, a little more land than the Canadians, planted somewhat more barley and potatoes and less rye, tobacco, and peas, and collected less maple syrup. The Canadians were more inclined to work in the forests, either for the logging companies or on their own, but the Scots also depended on a combination of farming and off-farm work. Both relied on oats and buckwheat as principal grains, kept much the same livestock, and achieved much the same yields. Both populations included millers, artisans, and shopkeepers; in neither was the economic range very great. There was no wealth, and most farms were much of a size. Almost everyone lived in a small log house, its dimensions rarely more than twenty by twenty-four feet. The money that was made out of Winslow Township went elsewhere. Most of its forests were controlled by the group of Bangor lumbermen who, in

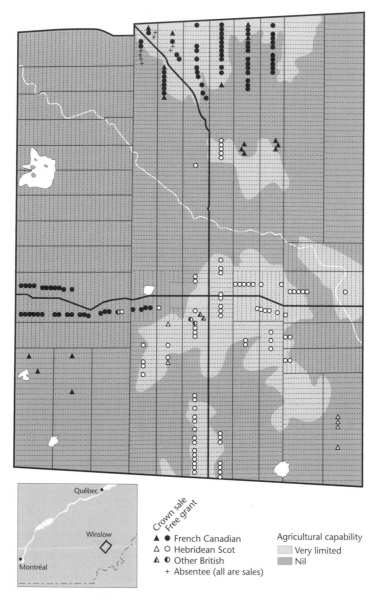

MAP 8.13   Free grants and Crown sales in Winslow Township, 1850-60 | After J.I. Little, *Crofters and Habitants: Settler Society, Economy, and Culture in a Quebec Township, 1848-1881* (Montreal and Kingston: McGill-Queen's University Press, 1991), 6, 65.

1853, built the large sawmill near Sherbrooke where much of the timber cut in Winslow Township and droved down the St. Francis River was made into lumber.

What, then, is to be made of ethnicity and culture in the Eastern Townships in the decades before Confederation? In many ways, they were critical. Different peoples lived apart in communities defined by language, religion, and historical experience. There was not much crossing over; in an age of belief, religion drew sharp boundaries. Language, too, threw up barriers as, somewhat less obtrusively, did the vastly different experiences out of which people had come. This is clear enough. The influence of ethnicity and culture on the strikingly diverse economies that emerged in the townships is another matter. I would make these points: Canadian and Scottish settlers in the northern townships brought almost no capital to a meagre economic opportunity. They found some marginal agricultural land far from markets and some limited access to forests largely controlled by timber companies. In these circumstances, there was little alternative to what emerged: subsistent agriculture supplemented, if possible, by seasonal off-farm work, no local wealth, and weak local economic differentiation. None of these outcomes was affected by religion or ethnicity. On the other hand, had the terms of access to land been different – had, for example, the Crown granted the forests of Winslow Township in sizable lots to settlers rather than to a timber company – the economic and social equation would have changed. A few settlers would have prospered, and more economic differentiation would have developed. In the southern townships, the soil was much better, markets were closer, and some settlers brought a good deal of capital. These circumstances offered far more potential for the local generation of wealth. Moreover, settlers in the south participated in the larger New England economy, and some of them had direct access to lines of credit, recent inventions, and current business practices. These huge contextual advantages underlay the economic achievement of the southern townships. It is likely, of course, that had Canadians or Highland Scots settled the southern townships, they would have had less access, by virtue of language, religion (in the case of the Canadians), and culture, to New England capital and expertise than the New Englanders who did settle there. It is also possible, though hard to prove, that the most successful New Englanders, largely men of evan-gelical faith and practical work experience, brought a particularly aggressive entrepreneurialism to the townships. Much more basically, here as elsewhere, different contexts encouraged varying economic and social outcomes.

FIGURE 8.11   *Stanstead, Lower Canada* (detail), 1842 (artist, W.H. Bartlett). Situated close to the American border and settled from the south, Stanstead reproduced the architecture and landscape of northern New England. | *Canadian Scenery*, vol. 2 (London, George Virtue, 1842), facing p. 93.

Different contexts and different landscapes. The New Englanders brought their landscapes to the townships (Figure 8.11). Most of their farmhouses were frame structures covered with clapboard and painted white. Usually, one gable end faced the road, and a shed at the other end connected with a stable. Occasionally a covered connection, through shed and stable, linked house to barn. Barns were often built into hillsides with entry to the loft by a ramp at the gable end. Commonly this house-barn complex was located well back from the road on higher, well-drained land; depending on the terrain, a farm family could be a kilometre from its nearest neighbour. The hamlets and villages that had formed at crossroads and waterpower sites were sometimes laid out around village greens but more often formed elongated street villages. Similar morphologically to villages in the seigneurial lowlands, they differed in texture and feel (compare Figures 8.3 and 8.11). Almost every hamlet had several churches, usually trim white frame buildings of simplified Gothic or neo-classical line. By the 1850s, main streets in the larger villages and small towns were beginning to be lined with explicitly urban two- and three-storey brick facades. Accompanying the Canadians, on the other hand, were building styles and landscapes derived from the French regime along the lower St. Lawrence.

The townships are inadequately conceptualized, however, as a contact zone between two North American peoples: Canadians and New Englanders. Even many elements of the landscape, particularly the stone Gothic revival Anglican churches, were British. From the early 1840s, the number of British-born in the townships was consistently greater than the number of American-born (although descendants of American settlers outnumbered both). Moreover, the Americans were in a British colony, which meant that they were detached from some of their own institutions and were subject to the conservative, managerial, and centralizing tendencies of British colonial administrations. J.I. Little has also recently shown that American missionary societies put their effort into the American settlement frontier, leaving space in the townships for British missionaries from the Society for the Propagation of the Gospel (high-church Anglican) and the Wesleyan Missionary Society (Methodist). Anglicanism and Wesleyan Methodism were, as a result, the dominant Protestant denominations in the townships. Anglican worship assumed that an ordered, loyal population underlay a Christian society, views probably related to the fact that far less radical sectarianism existed in the political culture of the townships than in adjacent New England. Essentially, Little suggests that a distinctively English Canadian identity representing, in his words, "a still somewhat lumpy synthesis of American and British values" was emerging in the townships. The Canadian identity of French speakers in the townships had been established, of course, long since.

LOWER CANADIAN STORIES

The 1871 population distribution in Lower Canada, or the Province of Quebec as it had recently become, is shown in Map 8.14. Some 1,190,000 people, the great majority of them francophones, lived in the bounded patch of land left by the Treaty of Paris of 1783 and the Constitutional Act of 1791. Settlement was densest on the Montreal plain. Montreal, with more than 107,000 inhabitants, was the largest city in British North America. West of Quebec City and south of the St. Lawrence, a pattern of interrupted settlement extended to the American border. North of the river,

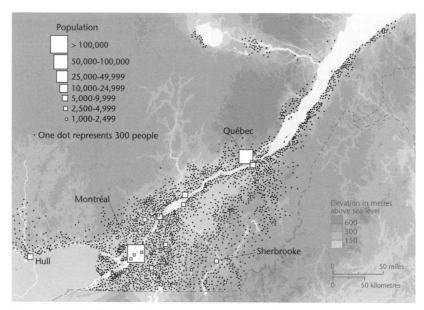

MAP 8.14   Distribution of population, Quebec, 1871 | After D. Measner and
C. Hampson, in Gentilcore and Matthews, *Historical Atlas of Canada,* vol. 2, plate 29.

settlement was more confined but had pushed some distance into the
Shield, particularly along the Ottawa and Saguenay Valleys.

Of the many stories embedded in these patterns, the most dominant
concerned the Canadians, the people who occupied the banks of the lower
St. Lawrence when others began to arrive after 1760. As newcomers took
over most of the command positions in the towns, Canadian settlement
had expanded, generation by generation, throughout the old seigneurial
lowlands. Eventually, almost all land suitable for cultivation was taken up.
Then young Canadians began to move away, often via a local village, to
employment in Montreal or Quebec, to farm lots or timber camps in the
fringe of the Canadian Shield, to farm lots or factory jobs in the Eastern
Townships, or, more commonly, to jobs in the New England factory towns.
Between 1850 and 1870, some 170,000 of them emigrated to the United
States. These migrations usually placed them face to face with harsh physical
environments (where, try as they might, creating more than a bare subsistence agriculture was virtually impossible) and/or with the conditions
of work associated with early industrial capitalism. Probably no people

anywhere were more prepared for the rigours of pioneering in rocky, forested, northern environments, but the Canadians were less prepared for industrial capitalism, to which they often brought a variety of largely irrelevant skills from the countryside. Many of them, therefore, became ill-paid wage labourers in the lower ranks of the industrial hierarchy. Although not the only Canadian story, this was the most common. Many Scots, Irish, Americans, and English in Lower Canada could tell a good deal of it. A version circulated in the Maritimes where, again, people struggled with a limited land and a new industrial order, and where, as in Lower Canada, many of them emigrated to New England. Circumstances along the northern margins of the North American agricultural ecumene, like their causes and effects, were remarkably similar.

There were many other Lower Canadian stories, of course. Some Canadians prospered as substantial farmers, successful artisans, merchants, or professionals. Some Scots – usually well connected, Protestant, and moneyed – became prominent businessmen. Some English brought gentry pretensions and established estates; others, skilled labourers, worked in the machine shops and foundries along the Lachine Canal. Yet others, unskilled, were casual urban labourers. Some New Englanders were pioneers by vocation, some became successful farmers, some others successful entrepreneurs. Irish immigrants created substantial communities in Quebec and Montreal before the famine migrations of the 1840s, for which they provided some cushion. There were even some Jewish stories: a fur trader in the 1770s, a few general merchants, a couple of factory owners, artisans in various trades. Over the years, stories reflected more of Lower Canada, or of the particular patch of it where the storyteller lived, and less of homelands left behind. Immigrants were putting down roots and told stories accordingly. Increasingly, most of those who had arrived as English, Scots, Irish, or Americans began – they or their progeny – to consider themselves Canadian. As they did so, identifications changed. It became necessary to speak of French Canadians and English Canadians, rubrics that disguised far more than they revealed but usually did identify a mother tongue.

For the most part, the tellers of different stories kept to themselves. Religion and ethnicity threw up barriers. Even in Montreal, where a greater variety of peoples lived in closer proximity than elsewhere in Lower Canada, space was sharply divided between a French-speaking Catholic east and a largely Protestant English-speaking west. The Irish in Montreal, English-speaking and Catholic for the most part, were more likely to marry francophone Catholics rather than anglophone Protestants, but usually stayed away from both. Marriages between French-speaking Catholics and English-speaking Protestants were exceedingly rare. People lived within their religion, culture, and prejudices. Different public schools for different religious-ethnic communities maintained and perhaps strengthened boundaries. As almost everywhere else in British North America, the site of most lives was a local ethnically homogeneous community with close horizons. The difference in Lower Canada was that, however isolated from each other, a large majority of the population shared a story about life in the St. Lawrence Valley that led back into the French regime. They did so, of course, with accretions, adding an Irish lilt in their music and applying the brick facades of duplexes and fourplexes in Montreal over the squared-log pièce sur pièce construction that had been common in Canada from the seventeenth century.

BIBLIOGRAPHY

The Lowlands

There are large and contentious literatures on the matters addressed in this section. I have tried to represent something of the range of these debates as well as the variety of empirical work that bears on them, and then to suggest the broader conclusions that seem most consistent with the evidence at hand. To expand my interpretations, or to assess their value, readers will have to get into the literature themselves. Serge Courville and Normand Séguin, *Rural Life in Nineteenth Century Quebec*, Canadian Historical Association Booklet No. 47 (Ottawa: Canadian Historical Association, 1989), is perhaps a place to start. A more complex introduction that provides a great deal of basic information about population growth, settlement patterns, transportation changes, and economic development is Serge Courville, Jean-Claude Robert, and Normand Séguin, *Atlas historique du Québec, Le pays laurentien au XIXe siècle, Les morphologies de base* (Sainte-Foy: Les Presses de l'Université Laval, 1995). Basic demographic information is in Hubert Charbonneau, *La Population du Québec: études rétrospectives* (Montreal: Les editions du boréal express, 1973).

The book that launched much of the debate about early nineteenth-century agriculture in Lower Canada is Fernand Ouellet, *Histoire économique et sociale du Québec, 1760-1850* (Montreal: Fides, 1966). In it Ouellet argued that the rise of Canadian nationalism was tied to a failing agricultural economy that, in turn, was a reflection of the retrospective, unprogressive mentality of Canadian farmers. His most immediate critics were Gilles Paquet and Jean-Pierre Wallot, particularly in "Le Bas-Canada au début du XIXe siècle: une hypothèse," *Revue d'histoire de l'Amérique française* 25, 1 (1971): 39-61; and "Crise agricole et tensions socio-ethniques dans le Bas-Canada, 1802-1812: éléments pour une réinterpretation," *Revue d'histoire de l'Amérique française* 26, 2 (1972): 185-237. On the other hand, in *Québec en Amérique au XIXe Siècle: Essai sur les caractères èconomique de la Laurentie* (Montreal: Fides, 1973), Albert Faucher largely assumed Ouellet's central arguments.

A few years later, John McCallum sought to show that the weakness of Lower Canadian agriculture reflected not mentality so much as disadvantaged competitive circumstances as, at a continental scale, settlement spread to richer western lands: *Unequal Beginnings: Agriculture and Economic Development in Quebec and Ontario until 1870* (Toronto: University of Toronto Press, 1980), chap. 3. In a long two-part article – "La crise agricole du Bas-Canada, éléments d'une réflexion géographique," *Cahiers de Géographie du Québec* 24, 62 (1980): 193-224; 24, 63 (1980): 385-427 – Serge Courville argued that no agricultural crisis occurred in the early nineteenth century. Frank D. Lewis and R. Marvin McInnis brought an econometric analysis to bear in "The Efficiency of the French Canadian Farmer in the Nineteenth Century," *Journal of Economic History* 40, 3 (1980): 497-51. A couple of years later, Marvin McInnis published his influential "Reconsideration of the State of Agriculture in Lower Canada in the First Half of the Nineteenth Century," *Canadian Papers in Rural History* 3 (1982): 9-49. Meanwhile, Fernand Ouellet offered a vigorous defence of his earlier arguments: *Le Bas-Canada, 1791-1840, changements structuraux et crise* (Ottawa: Éditions de l'Université d'Ottawa, 1980).

Since then, the emphasis in studies of rural Lower Canada has tended to become more social. Among the most influential of this work has been Gérard Bouchard's analysis of pioneer societies. See, for example, his articles "La dynamique communautaire et l'evolution des sociétés rurales québecoises aux 19e et 20e siècles. Construction d'un modèle," *Revue d'histoire de l'Amérique française* 40, 2 (1986): 51-71; and "Sur la reproduction familiale en milieu rural: systèmes ouverts et systèmes clos," *Recherches sociographiques* 28, 2-3 (1987): 283-310. Although directed more to the Saguenay than to the St. Lawrence Valley, Bouchard's *Quelques arpents d'Amérique: Population, économie, famille au Saguenay, 1838-1971* (Montreal: Les Éditions du Boréal, 1996) is a major synthesis of his research. Serge Courville has also contributed important studies, particularly perhaps *Entre ville et campagne: L'essor du village dans les seigneuries du Bas-Canada* (Sainte-Foy: Les Presses de l'Université Laval, 1990); and "Tradition et modernité, les significations spatiales," *Recherches sociographiques* 34, 2 (1993): 211-31. Christian Dessureault provides an intriguing analysis of social structure in "Reproduction sociale dans le Québec préindustriel: les 'élus' et les 'exclus,'" in Gérard Bouchard, John A. Dickinson, and Joseph Goy, eds., *Les Exclus de la Terre en France et au Québec, XVIIe–XXe siècles* (Sillery: Éditions du Septentrion, 1998), 51-72. For a much more general comment from the early 1990s on the literature on Canadian rural society, see Ronald Rudin, "Revisionism and the Search for a Normal Society," *Canadian Historical Review* 73, 1 (1992): 30-61; in translation, "La Quête d'une société normale," *Bulletin d'histoire politique* 3, 2 (1995): 9-42.

The regional examples of economic and social change in the countryside are taken from the following. Allan Greer, *Peasant, Lord and Merchant: Rural Society in Three Quebec Parishes, 1740-1840* (Toronto: University of Toronto Press, 1985). Christian Dessureault, "Crise ou modernization? La société rurale maskoutaine durant le premier tiers du XIXe siècle," *Revue d'histoire de l'Amérique française* 42, 3 (1989): 359-87. Serge Laurin, *Histoire des Laurentides* (Quebec City: Institut québécois de recherche sur la culture, 1989). Jean-Claude Robert, "Activités agricoles et urbanisation dans la paroisse de Montréal, 1820-1840," in Francois Lebrun and Normand Séguin, eds., *Sociétés villageoises et rapports villes-campagnes au Québec et dans la France de l'Ouest: actes du colloque franco-québécois de Québec* (Trois-Rivières: Centre de recherche en études québécoises, 1987), 91-100. Serge Courville, "Le marché des subsistances. L'agriculture de la plaine de Montréal au début des années 1830: une perspective géographique," *Revue d'histoire de l'Amérique française* 42, 2 (1988): 193-239. Colin M. Coates, *The Metamorphoses of Landscape and Community in Early Quebec* (Montreal and Kingston: McGill-Queen's University Press, 2000). Roch Samson, André Hérous, Diane Saint-Pierre, and Martine Côté, *Histoire de Lévis-Lotbinière* (Sainte-Foy: Les Presses de l'Université Laval, 1996). Alain Laberge, Martine Côté, Diane Saint-Pierre, and Jacques Saint-Pierre, eds., *Histoire de la Côte du Sud* (Sainte-Foy: Les Presses de l'Université Laval, 1993).

The Towns
For elements of the urban context, see *Historical Atlas of Canada,* vol. 2, *The Land Transformed, 1800-1891,* ed. R. Louis Gentilcore, cart. Geoffrey J. Matthews (Toronto: University of Toronto Press, 1993), plates 20, 45, 47, and 49. For a cartographic introduction to nineteenth-century Montreal, consult Jean-Claude Robert, *Atlas Historique de Montréal* (Montreal: Art Global, Libre Expression, 1994), part 5. For an uneven but informative general history of Quebec, see John Hare, Marc Lafrance, and David-Thiery Ruddel, *Histoire de la Ville de Québec, 1608-1871* (Montreal: Boréal, 1987).

On more specialized topics, the following are particularly useful. Jean-Paul Bernard, Paul-André Linteau, and Jean-Claude Robert, "La Structure Professionnelle de Montréal en 1825," *Revue d'histoire de l'Amérique française* 30, 3 (1976): 383-407. Jean-Claude Robert, "Urbanisation et population: le cas de Montréal en 1861," *Revue d'histoire de l'Amérique française* 35, 4 (1982): 523-35. Gerald J.J. Tulchinsky, *The River Barons: Montreal Businessmen and the Growth of Industry and Transportation, 1837-53* (Toronto: University of Toronto Press, 1977). Joanne Burgess, "L'Industrie de la Chaussureçà Montréal: 1840-1870 – Le Passage de l'Artisanat à la Fabrique," *Revue d'histoire de l'Amérique française* 31, 2 (1977): 187-210. Bettina Bradbury, *Working Families: Age, Gender, and Daily Survival in Industrializing Montreal* (Toronto: McClelland and Stewart, 1993); published in French as *Familles ouvrières à Montréal* (Montreal: Boréal, 1995). Sherry Olson and Patricia Thornton, "'Pour Se Créer un Avenir': Stratégies de Couples Montréalais au XIXe siècle," *Revue d'histoire de l'Amérique française* 51, 3 (1998): 357-89. Sherry Olson, "The Challenge of the Irish Catholic Community in Nineteenth-Century Montreal," *Histoire sociale/Social History* 70 (2002): 331-62. Stephen Hertzog and Robert D. Lewis, "A City of Tenants: Home Ownership and Social Class in Montreal, 1847-1881," *Canadian Geographer* 30, 4 (1986): 316-22. D.B. Hanna and François Dufaux, "Montreal: A Rich Tradition in Medium Density Housing" (research report prepared for Central Mortgage and Housing Corporation, External Research Program, 2002). A substantial collection of essays, maps, and pictures relevant to late eighteenth- and nineteenth-century Quebec is in Serge Courville and Robert Garon, eds., *Québec: ville et capitale* (Sainte-Foy: Les Presses de l'Université Laval, 2001), especially 115-246.

The Shield Fringe
A useful overview and starting point is Serge Courville, *Le Québec, Genèse et mutations du territoire* (Sainte-Foy: Les Presses de l'Université Laval, 2000), chap. 8. Among more regional treatments of parts of the Shield, the following are particularly important. On the Saguenay: Normand Séguin, *La Conquête du Sol au 19e Siècle* (Montreal: Les éditions du boréal express, 1977). Gerard Bouchard, *Quelques arpents d'Amérique: Population, économie, famille au Saguenay, 1838-1971* (Montreal: Les Éditions du Boréal, 1996). In connection with this important and much discussed work, see also Christian Dessureault, Thomas Wien, and Gérard Bouchard, "A Propos de *Quelques arpents d'Amérique* de Gérard Bouchard," *Revue d'histoire de l'Amérique française* 50, 3 (1997): 401-36. Marc St-Hilaire, *Peuplement et dynamique migratoire au Saguenay, 1840-1960* (Sainte-Foy: Les Presses de l'Université Laval, 1996), particularly chap. 3. On the Mauricie: René Hardy and Normand Séguin, *Forêt et société en Mauricie* (Montreal: Boréal Express/Musée National de l'Homme, 1984); and Hardy and Séguin, *Histoire de la Mauricie* (Quebec City: Institut québécois de recherche sur la culture, 2004). On the Laurentides: Serge Laurin, *Histoire des Laurentides* (Quebec City: Institut québécois de recherche sur la culture, 1989). On the Ottawa Valley: Chad Gaffield, *History of the Outaouais* (Quebec City: Institut québécois de recherche sur la culture, Les Presses de l'Université Laval, 1997). On the colonization societies and their rhetoric: Serge Courville, *Immigration, colonisation et Propagande: du rêve américain au rêve colonial* (Sainte-Foy: Éditions MultiMondes, 2002).

The Eastern Townships
The key general work on the Eastern Townships is a regional history by Jean-Pierre Kesteman, Peter Southam, and Diane Saint-Pierre, *Histoire des Cantons de l'Est*

(Quebec City: Institut québécois de recherche sur la culture, Les Presses de l'Université Laval, 1998), chaps. 3-9. Kesteman's book on Sherbrooke, *Histoire de Sherbrooke Tome 1: de l'âge de l'eau à l'ére de la vapeur (1802-1866)* (Sherbrooke: Collection Patrimoine, G.G.C. éditions, 2000), is also helpful. The movement of settlers and capital into the northern townships is well analyzed in two books by J.I. Little: *Nationalism, Capitalism, and Colonization in Nineteenth-Century Quebec: The Upper St. Francis District* (Montreal and Kingston: McGill-Queen's University Press, 1989), especially chaps. 1-5; and *Crofters and Habitants: Settler Society, Economy, and Culture in a Quebec Township, 1848-1881* (Montreal and Kingston: McGill-Queen's University Press, 1991). Also by Little, and on the emergence of an English Canadian identity in the townships, *Borderland Religion: The Emergence of an English-Canadian Identity, 1792-1852* (Toronto: University of Toronto Press, 2004).

9

Upper Canada

In the early 1760s, a few thousand Algonquian-speaking peoples, most of them Ojibwa, occupied the territory that in 1791 became known as Upper Canada and is now called southern Ontario.* They practised mixed economies – fishing, hunting, gathering, some agriculture – and lived amid forests. In the mid-1860s, close to 1.5 million people spread across the same territory and lived for the most part within a rectangular geography of fields and farms. The energy that accomplished this massive transformation had originated elsewhere. Immediately to the south was the expansive momentum of the new United States, while across the Atlantic in the British Isles, pressures on land and livelihoods had become acute. After the American Revolution, Upper Canada attracted political refugees – Loyalists – and then land seekers from the United States. After the Napoleonic Wars, it became for a time the principal overseas destination for hundreds of thousands of Britons displaced by population growth, enclosures, and industrialization – by the long drift away from custom and towards the market. For most of these people, it seemed to offer land and the prospect of a livelihood. Immigrants poured in and the forest yielded.

A British settler colony rapidly took shape in an elongated, irregular, and almost completely forested peninsula some eight hundred kilometres long, bounded on the north by the Canadian Shield or the Ottawa River and on the south and west by the St. Lawrence River or one of the three

---

* In 1841, Upper Canada became Canada West, but here, in the interest of simplicity, Upper Canada is used throughout.

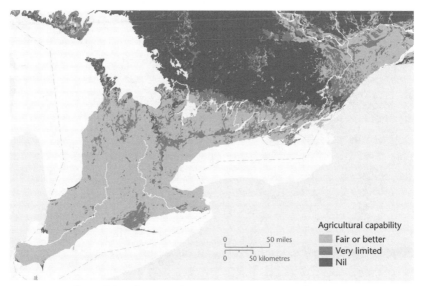

MAP 9.1   Soil capability for agriculture (southern Ontario) | Canada Land Inventory, Lands Directorate, Environment Canada.

most easterly Great Lakes. A northern margin of the vast deciduous forest of eastern North America extended along the Lake Ontario and Lake Erie shores and for some distance inland. Sugar maple, beech, white elm, basswood, and red and white oaks were dominant species. Farther north, in a transitional zone between the deciduous forest to the south and the boreal forest to the north, white and red pine, eastern hemlock, and yellow birch became common. The soils under these forests had formed on moraines or till, sand, or clay plains associated with either the last continental glaciation or post-glacial lakes. Most of them were fertile – according to the Canada land inventory, more than half are soils with "no significant limitations to use for crops." By British North American standards, this bounded peninsula contained a large area of potential farmland (Map 9.1).

It was occupied, of course, by others. Although it was briefly depopulated after the Iroquois wars of the late 1640s (Chapter 4), Iroquois hunted there in the 1650s and 1660s, and in the 1670s established agricultural villages along the north shore of Lake Ontario. Then, in another series of bloody but less-known wars, the Ojibwa, people who had lived between the eastern end of Lake Superior and Georgian Bay, drove the Iroquois out and, as they retreated, occupied most of the future Upper Canada.

The Ojibwa lived in bands, each usually associated with a river basin. They planted corn, beans, and squash, and hunted a variety of animals, but were primarily fishers whose seasonal rounds turned around major fall (salmon, trout, whitefish) and spring (pickerel, muskellunge, suckers, black bass, sturgeon) fisheries. To a large extent, they were river and marsh people. Although bands converged seasonally at major fishing sites, there to socialize and trade, confirm alliances, and, as need arose, organize large war parties, Ojibwa social structure was atomistic, local, and mediated by kin relationships. It depended on communal systems of property rights organized at the scale of band and watershed.

During the French regime, when the Ojibwa were crucial members of the French-Native alliance and well within reach of English traders, they benefited from a trading relationship dependent on presents and low prices for European goods. After the conquest and the end of French-British rivalries, their commercial and geopolitical leverage was much reduced. Although the Royal Proclamation of 1763 (Chapter 5) accorded them a measure of legal protection, from a British perspective they became increasingly dispensable. As colonial administrations needed Ojibwa land for settlers, they took it, and the legal means to do so after the Royal Proclamation was by treaty. The first treaty, in 1764, was for a strip of land along the Niagara River. Three treaties in the 1780s took most of the north shore of Lake Ontario as well as the Niagara Peninsula (between Lakes Ontario and Erie). In 1790, almost 1.5 million acres north of Lake Erie were acquired by treaty and purchase (for £1,200). In the nineteenth century, beginning with the Toronto purchase in 1806, the Crown acquired title to all remaining Native land in Upper Canada in return for presents, paltry cash payments, and a scatter of reserves. Historian Michael Thoms argues that the Ojibwa sought to protect their aquatic ecology – points of land, river mouths, islands – for their exclusive fishing and hunting but were prepared to cede (or, in some Native understandings, rent) upland. If so, the strategy failed. Their demands were rarely recorded, settlers dammed rivers and encroached on fishing sites, and the Ojibwa, weakened by disease, alcohol, and the loss of traditional leadership, were confined to small reserves, which, as settlers pressed around them, often became smaller or were withdrawn altogether. In this situation, the fundamental problem for the Ojibwa, the loss of their land, constituted the opportunity of the settlers and speculators who acquired it. Supporting their acquisitions was the full array of powers embodied in the colonial state.

Upper Canada emerged out of the convergence of this land, suitable for agriculture and available for settlement, with a flood of immigrants whose prior livelihoods had been threatened or lost. In this chapter, I consider the immigrants and the circumstances of their emigration, and then the ways in which land was available to them. I follow this with a brief discussion of the resettlement of Upper Canada and of its emerging rural economies. I then comment on Upper Canada as it was about 1850 and interpret some elements of its social structure, culture, and values just before railways and the beginnings of industrialization. In the final section, I consider Upper Canada during the last twenty years before Confederation, by which time land was becoming scarce and new processes were in train.

IMMIGRANTS

They came almost entirely from the United States or the British Isles. The first of the former were Loyalists, dislocated by war, who arrived in the 1780s. They were soon followed by other Americans – the northern edge of a massive westward migration – drawn by land rather than loyalty. Some 80 percent of the sixty to seventy-five thousand people in Upper Canada in 1811 were immigrants from the United States or their descendants. The principal long-term effect of the War of 1812 (Chapter 5) was to stop this American flow; when it resumed in the 1820s, it was dwarfed by the scale of British immigration. Between 1815 and 1855 perhaps a million British immigrants landed at Quebec. Most of them continued to Upper Canada or passed through it to the United States. By midcentury most of the potential agricultural land in Upper Canada was taken; with little urban employment, the growing volume of emigration from Britain turned to opportunities elsewhere: Australia, New Zealand, and, principally, the United States (Figure 9.1).

Most of the Loyalists who arrived in Upper Canada – some eight thousand people by most estimates – were soldiers from disbanded provincial regiments that had remained loyal to the Crown. About half were Scottish or German peasants who had emigrated to North America in the decade before the revolution and had fetched up as pioneer farmers in Pennsylvania or northwestern New York. About two thousand were Iroquois –

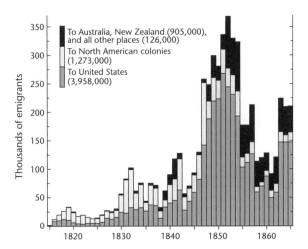

FIGURE 9.1

Emigration from the British Isles, 1815-65 | After J. Weaver, J. De Jonge, and D. Norris, in *Historical Atlas of Canada*, vol. 2, *The Land Transformed*, ed. R. Louis Gentilcore, cart. Geoffrey J. Matthews (Toronto: University of Toronto Press, 1993), plate 9.

Mohawks – who had borne the brunt of some of the heaviest fighting. Only a few, usually the most educated and prosperous, came because they were ideologically committed to a stratified and deferential British society, but even they, as historian George Rawlyk has shown, shared many of the views of American federalists, who also distrusted republican democracy. All these people were political refugees. Later arrivals from the United States were land seekers, most of whom had already been pioneer farmers and who became so again. They were a diverse collection: Mennonites, Quakers, a few blacks, an edge of the religious and ethnic mix of peoples moving westward from New England, New York, and Pennsylvania, and far more focused on land than on political borders. British officials in a colony formed in reaction to the American Revolution welcomed them because in these years there was no ready alternative.

Some half of the British immigrants were Irish, and more of these Irish were Protestant than Catholic. Early Irish emigrants were likely to be relatively prosperous and Protestant; the famine migration of 1847, when more than 100,000 impoverished and predominantly Catholic Irish landed at Quebec, was not typical of Irish migration to British North America in the first half of the nineteenth century. Yet behind all Irish migrations were the rising cost of land, the falling relative cost of labour, and the difficulty for most people of making a bare livelihood. In Ulster, source of most of the Irish emigrants, rural population densities in some parishes reached 750 people per square mile. In county Armagh in 1841, half the farms were from one to five acres. Many families relied on a potato patch, a cow, a loom, and the revenue, such as it was, from homespun cloth contracted to a merchant in a putting-out trade (Chapter 7). In Tipperary in central Ireland, another region of Irish emigration to Upper Canada, landlords responded to population pressures by raising rents, renting for shorter periods, and evicting tenants. They reduced tillage and expanded grazing, either by renting land to sheep farmers or by expanding their own pastoral farms. Displaced tenants became labourers in an overstocked labour market or attempted to work patches of rocky or marshy waste. Lazy beds – ridged potato plots cultivated with spades – spread up rocky hillsides. Almost everywhere in Ireland, the encroachments of landlords, declining returns from domestic crafts in the face of factory production, rising land costs in relation to the value of labour, or all of these together, squeezed families of modest means. Protestants, who on average were considerably more prosperous than Catholics and less rooted in Ireland, were more likely to leave.

The Scots, perhaps a quarter of British immigrants, were both Highlanders and Lowlanders. Probably not more than half of the former were from the west coast and islands, the source of the Cape Breton Scots. Well over half of the Scots were Protestants. Even more than its Irish counterpart, this was a migration of different values and backgrounds. At one extreme were the Gaelic-speaking crofters (Catholic or Protestant) from the Hebrides, people who, after the collapse of kelping (Chapter 7), could no longer live on the three- to five-acre crofts allotted them by their landlords. For the crofters, there was neither wage work nor more than toeholds on some of the most difficult agricultural land in Britain. Deeply attached to their communities, they left because they had to and because, often, their landlords shovelled them out, paying for their passage away – a migration by shipload, by groups of families. At the other extreme were literate Protestant English-speaking emigrants from the Lowlands, people relatively accustomed to relocation, market economies, the rights of private property, and individual choice. In the Lowlands, the hodge-podge of small irregular fields to which many people had some claim, however small, had given way by the 1820s to an improvers' landscape of large farms and rectangular fields, and a rural society largely composed of prosperous farmers and their employees. There was work in the Lowlands, both in the factory towns and on the improvers' farms; workers, artisans, and even shopkeepers moved between Lowland counties and from countryside to town. Emigration was one of their options. Many emigration societies existed, some of them organized by workers, as did some philanthropic assistance, but this was not a migration of the desperate so much as of those who had calculated, often after receiving reports from relatives, that life would be better overseas.

English immigrants to Upper Canada came from all English counties but principally from the north and southwest (Map 9.2), and particularly in the 1840s and 1850s. Overall, they were, perhaps, a little better off than the Irish and Scots. Although most came as unassisted individuals or nuclear families, a good many were supported by parish committees seeking to reduce their financial responsibility for the poor. Although these English emigrated for many reasons, the pressures on them were broadly similar to those faced by many of the Irish and Lowland Scots. The rural population was rising, and some domestic rural industries (particularly spinning and weaving) were giving way to factory production. The type of agriculture favoured by the improvers was steadily gaining ground: larger, more consolidated farms, improved crop rotations, better-quality stock, more mechanization, considerably higher yields overall. In these circumstances, opportunities for small farmers diminished, and the number of landless labourers increased. Agricultural employment declined with farm size, and whenever enclosures converted arable land to pasture, rural underemployment became chronic. The return of an increasingly efficient agriculture accrued principally to landowners and prosperous farmers, while the poor became more numerous. Riots and violence, usually brutally suppressed, became fairly common in the countryside. Again, it was rarely the poorest who left, rather those whose livelihoods were threatened and could assemble the capital to relocate. Often they were encouraged by letters from relatives already established in Upper Canada: "now I am goun to Work on My One frme of 50 Eakers wich I bot at 55£ and I have 5 years to pay it in. I have bot Me a Cow and 5 pigs ... If I had staid at Corsley [Wiltshire, England] I never should had nothing. I like the Contry very Much – I am at librty to shout terky, Quill, Pigons, Phesents, Dear, and all kind of Geam wch I have on My Back Wood."

Overall, ordinary people were moving because accustomed livelihoods were threatened, and this, most immediately, because they were increasingly detached from land. In Ireland in the 1830s and 1840s, ordinary

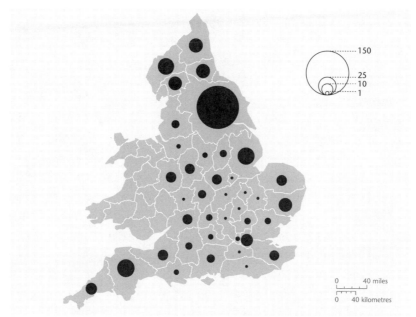

MAP 9.2   English origins by county, as recorded on gravestones in Peel, Halton, and York Counties | After Bruce S. Elliott, "Regional Patterns of English Immigration and Settlement in Upper Canada," in Barbara J. Messamore, ed., *Canadian Migration Patterns from Britain and North America* (Ottawa: University of Ottawa Press, 2004), 79.

labour fetched roughly £10-£12 a year, and the price of a tenant right (the right, particularly in Ulster, to rent land on secure terms from a landlord) was about £10 an acre. In these circumstances, a small farmer with a tenancy to sell might acquire some capital for emigration, but a labourer could not acquire land. In Lowland Scotland in the 1830s and 1840s, wage rates apparently rose overall; in the early 1850s farmers paid some £30 a year (often in kind) for labour. However, landholdings had been consolidated, few farms were less than a hundred acres, and even the stocking of a hundred-acre farm required at least £500 – a sum far beyond the reach of the labouring poor. Throughout rural England, the situation was much the same. Ordinary working people were increasingly separated from land, except as they worked on it for wages. In effect, the pervasive and centuries-long undertaking to open land to the market had largely succeeded. In feudal regimes, land had been situated within a matrix of social rights and obligations. Custom influenced land uses, and custom was local. Land law varied regionally, therefore, and usually favoured the protection of social relationships above the claims of the market. However, by the end of the eighteenth century, the high courts of the land, the custodians and dispensers of the common law, had erased most of these local legal defences of custom. An English common law based, so it was claimed, on universal principles and backed, as historian E.P. Thompson has shown, by a succession of legal judgments, had come to reinforce the absolute rights of property ownership based on free and common socage tenures and fee simple estates. Such rights were what the Highlanders, displaced from their clachans and then their crofts (Chapter 7), dealt with, so too the many English small farmers and labourers whose ancestors had some access, by right of custom, to land in various forms. Although in the early nineteenth century this transformation was incomplete – there were still manorial courts and many enclaves of customary law – the power and reach of the common law were large and growing. This was a body of law that protected individuals and the rights of private property; it protected neither custom nor community. Individuals were increasingly exposed, therefore, and emigration, which was one of their options, only increased the separation, already sanctioned by the common law, between individuals and land.

The same can be said of work. In pre-industrial societies, units of production were small, work was usually embedded in social relations – the family, the workshop, the reciprocal responsibilities of master and servant – and people often engaged in many different types of work (economies of multiple occupation) such that if one pursuit failed another might suffice. As work shifted into a factory, it became a commodity available for a wage and dependent on the social relations of capital. Without other options, labour moved to work, as theorists thought it should in an efficient labour market. Disciples of Adam Smith held that subsidized labour in any form encouraged sloth; Thomas Malthus held that it encouraged procreation and hence more poor. Labour should move to the market and attach itself there. Workhouses would prevent starvation but should be less attractive, claimed the report that led to the New Poor Law of 1834, than "the situation of the independent labourer of the lowest class." Notions of locality and community did not figure into the equation.

Moreover, these were years of rapid time-space compression associated with turnpike roads, canals, and, by the 1830s, railways. The declining costs of distance, coupled with factory production, facilitated the dissemination of standardized goods that undermined many local crafts. An expanding technology of management, coupled with the increasing speed and declining cost of overland transportation, increased the state's capacity to manage populations: a constabulary (state police), regular national censuses, an ordnance survey (detailed, large-scale mapping, begun in 1791), the common law and a hierarchy of courts now well in place, standardized weights and measures, an enlarged bureaucracy. In sociologist Charles Tilly's terms, the state was moving from a system of indirect rule (through local intermediaries) to direct rule (through state officials), and, increasingly, to national standards. Moreover, political power was shifting from the old landed elite towards the new captains of industry. A conservative ideology that emphasized the bonds of interdependence in hierarchical organic societies in which people knew their place and deferred to their betters was slowly giving way to a liberal ideology predicated on the individual and the market. The transformation was never complete, but the balance was changing, and neither liberal philosophy nor laissez-faire economics offered any protection for embedded local cultures.

In the early nineteenth century the British Isles were still a patchwork of regional cultures and identities on which was superimposed, historian Linda Colley points out, a measure of patriotism born of wars (mostly against the French) and Protestantism. Although nominally British after 1707, Scots, Irish, Welsh, and English were different people, each composed of myriad local ways. If, very generally, they identified themselves as British, or Scots, or Irish, more tangibly they were Highlanders from the Isle of Lewis or Yorkshiremen and -women who, at close range, came from a particular vale. English was their predominant but by no means only language, and English dialects were often barely mutually comprehensible. Accents, house types, tools, songs, and stories were, for the most part, vernacular and local. Local worlds were intensely known, horizons close by, and the world beyond somewhat threatening. The elite lived in wider circuits, but most ordinary folk did not, and it was their local ways and the livelihoods on which they depended that were under assault. Among many coping strategies, one was emigration; in the first half of the nineteenth century, the largest tract of land in the British empire suitable for agricultural colonization was in Upper Canada. There, emigrants from Britain would encounter a forest and in some ways would step back in time, but in other ways their experience would embody the new pressures and conflicting values of their day. The farm lots they sought were part of a standardized survey, part of the apparatus of an increasingly managerial form of government. Free and common socage tenures and fee simple estates were aspects of the new legal order of the common law that increasingly overrode custom. Large land grants to favoured individuals were part of a conservative ideology to which many in the Colonial Office and most of the Upper Canadian elite still adhered. If most ordinary settlers shared neither this ideology nor, had they heard of them, the views of the liberal philosophers, they were detached in space and time from the more comfortable, less articulate, and deeply conservative social formation situated in the local places and peoples in which ordinary lives had once been embedded.

THE AVAILABILITY OF LAND

After the treaties with and purchases from Native people, the Colonial Office in London became responsible for the disposition of land. For the most part, British officials in both London and Upper Canada believed in ordered, stable, hierarchical societies in which privilege conferred responsibility towards social inferiors who knew their place and deferred to their betters within established social orders. They were not democrats. Most of them held that the British state and monarchy, the Anglican Church, and the rights of private property were cornerstones of society, rightly conceived. As they translated these beliefs into land policy, they sought to create an ordered system of land allocation based on the common law, prior survey and careful record keeping, grants of different size to applicants of different social standing, and reserves of land for the Crown (to defray government expenses or reward deserving later applicants) and the Anglican Church.

Prior to settlement, land was to be surveyed into townships; within townships, road allowances and lot lines were to be laid out geometrically. In 1789 the dimensions of townships along navigable waterways were set at nine by twelve miles, those in the interior at ten miles square, dimensions that would be approximately followed. The first township surveys (Map 9.3a) envisaged market towns set amid suburban lots ("town parks") and two-hundred-acre farms. Later, surveys were simplified; Map 9.3b shows the model, approved in 1794, which surveyors were intended

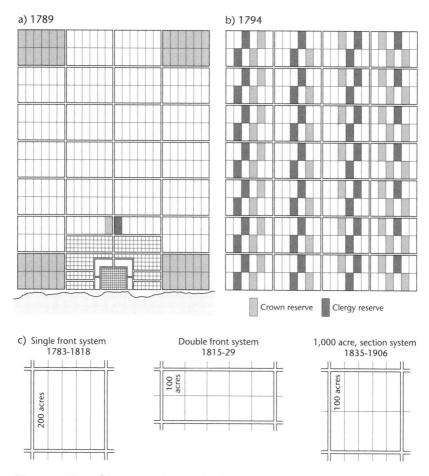

MAP 9.3   Township surveys: a) 1780s; b) plan approved in 1794; c) common road and lot surveys | From George C. Patterson, *Land Settlement in Upper Canada, 1783-1840,* 16th report, Department of Archives (Toronto: Province of Ontario, 1920), 34, 47; and C. Harris and J. Warkentin, *Canada before Confederation: A Historical Geography* (New York and Toronto: Oxford University Press, 1974), 124.

to follow. In fact, Crown and clergy reserves (each a seventh of a township) would sometimes be surveyed in blocks, and there would be many road and lot patterns, although at least 90 percent of the townships in Upper Canada would be surveyed in one of the three methods shown in Map 9.3c.

Initially, Crown land grants in Upper Canada were free, although subject to fees (varying over the years between £3 and £30 for a farm lot of two hundred acres) and settlement duties. Fees and, usually, the settlement duties were waived for disbanded soldiers and Loyalists, and for most large grant holders. Ordinary grants included the requirements to build a house (sixteen by twenty feet), clear and fence five acres, and clear half the adjacent road allowance, all within a year. These stipulations were indifferently enforced, partly because of the problem, when officials were few, of inspecting distant lots, partly because officials feared that, if pressed too far, settlers would leave for the United States. The size of land grants varied over the years and with the status of the grantee. Common people received a hundred or two hundred acres, with opportunity in the early years for additional grants for sons. In the 1790s, retired field officers received five thousand acres, captains three thousand, members of the legislative council six thousand, and well-connected applicants as much or more – plus twelve hundred acres for a wife and for each child. As in the Eastern Townships of Lower Canada (Chapter 8), there were various schemes of leaders and associates, various ways in which land passed not to the principled and worthy, but to speculators. By 1825, 13 million acres had been granted, almost 90 acres for each of the some 150,000 people in the colony. Another 3 million acres was held in Crown or clergy reserves. Most granted land was unsettled, land issues dominated colonial politics, and free land grants were increasingly criticized. In 1817, the departing lieutenant-governor, Francis Gore, asserted that "all gratuitous grants of land" should end; they had "introduced a dangerous population and afforded no revenue."

By this time, political economists in Britain were advancing similar arguments. The reproduction of British society in overseas colonies depended, they claimed, on low labour costs achieved by limiting access to land and controlling the rate of immigration. Access to land could be managed by the rate at which it was made available and the price at which it was sold; the rate of immigration (the supply of labour) could be controlled by British emigration policy. By fitting the price of land to the rate of immigration, a desired social effect – in this case, a stratified, hierarchical society – could be achieved. Such ideas convinced officials in the Colonial Office to sell colonial land and to create a central Land Board in London to distribute immigrants around the empire in proportion to the rate of land sales. This exercise in imperial social engineering did not work – the Colonial Office could control neither rates of immigration nor colonial land markets – but the period of free land grants to ordinary settlers was over. Late in 1824, the British government sold (for an average price of two shillings and tenpence per acre) most of the Crown reserves plus a block of over a million acres to the Canada Company, a private land venture financed in London. In 1827 it authorized the sale of clergy reserves, some of them by public auction. Upset prices were established in the different districts, and unsold land was either held over for subsequent auctions or sold in the meantime to buyers who offered the upset price. Sales, the Colonial Office intended, would force more immigrants into the labour market, depress the price of labour, and increase colonial revenue. "Without some division of labour, without a class of persons willing to work for wages," wrote the colonial secretary, "how can a society be prevented from falling into a state of almost primitive rudeness, and how are the comforts and refinements of civilized life to be procured?"

In fact, a market for land already alienated by the Crown had existed in Upper Canada from the late 1780s, and over time purchasing or renting land became the principal means of acquiring it. The most detailed analysis of the purchase price of land in Upper Canada, by historical geographer John Clarke, is based on the land records in Essex County, in the colony's southwestern corner. Figure 9.2 is his graph of land prices in Essex between 1800 and 1850. For the most part, these are prices per acre for farm lots on which there were farm buildings and cleared land. The price of uncleared land was considerably lower, some eight to ten shillings an acre in the 1830s; occasionally, cleared land appropriated for indebtedness could

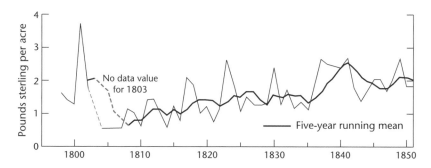

FIGURE 9.2   Land prices in Essex County, 1800-50 | After John Clarke, *Land, Power, and Economics on the Frontier of Upper Canada* (Montreal and Kingston: McGill-Queen's University Press, 2001), 231.

be had for even less. Clarke calculates that, at midcentury, an average farm in Essex (eighty-three acres, partly cleared, plus farm buildings) cost between £107 and £234, and that an uncleared farm lot of the same size cost about £33, prices that seem to have been fairly representative for outlying areas. Data gathered by historian David Gagan and historical geographer Peter Ennals for land close to the towns along the Lake Ontario shore suggest that uncleared land there was almost four times and cleared land more than twice as expensive as equivalent land in Essex.

In Upper Canada in the 1830s and much of the 1840s, agricultural labour commanded an average yearly price of about £30 (more in outlying areas) including room and board, and skilled labour two to four times as much. At these rates in outlying districts, the value of a year of farm work and of an uncleared farm lot of about a hundred acres were similar. There were start-up costs: some £20 for a yoke of oxen, a logging chain, and a harrow, £8 for a cow and a few pigs, £22 for a year's provisions, and perhaps another £50 for hired labour. Some £100 was necessary to start a bush farm that would have some prospect of success. Average clearing rates have sometimes been estimated to have been as high as 10 to 12 acres a year, but historian Peter Russell's statistical analysis of townships along the St. Lawrence River and the Lake Ontario shore shows that, at least in these townships, the average annual rate was about 1.5 acres. On the other hand, historical geographer Darrell Norris finds an average rate of land clearance of 4 to 5 acres a year in a township south of Georgian Bay in the late 1840s. At either of these latter rates, a farm would probably not support a family for several years unless labour were hired. According to Russell, about a quarter of the immigrants he studied had the capital (at least £100) either to purchase labour for clearing or to buy or rent a partly cleared farm. Unskilled immigrants with little or no capital usually faced several years of wage work before land in Upper Canada began to be accessible to them.

In short, in the early nineteenth century there was a huge difference between the relative cost of land and labour in Upper Canada and their relative costs anywhere in the British Isles. Upper Canada held out the prospect that a poor immigrant could acquire a farm and, thereby, a livelihood for a family, a prospect that was fast becoming no more than a memory for the British poor. In this difference lay most of the momentum to emigrate to and settle in Upper Canada.

THE SPREAD OF SETTLEMENT

When the first lieutenant-governor of Upper Canada, John Graves Simcoe, arrived in 1792, a scatter of discontinuous Loyalist settlements lay along the St. Lawrence River to the eastern end of Lake Ontario, in the Niagara Peninsula, across the St. Clair River from Detroit, and at several spots along or north of the Lake Erie shore (Map 9.4). With defence against the Americans in mind, Simcoe laid plans to create a series of garrisons along the lakes (each also to serve as a focus of agricultural settlement), as well as for a string of towns in the interior. He intended that London, at the forks of the Thames River, would become the colonial capital, and proposed two trunk roads: the first, Yonge Street, would run north from York (renamed Toronto in 1834) to Georgian Bay and connections with the upper Great Lakes; the second, Dundas Street, would strike west from York to the head of Lake Ontario and then westward along the route of the principal east-west Indian trail to London and Detroit. Most of Simcoe's proposed townsites were surveyed, but the governor-in-chief in the Canadas, Lord Dorchester, insisted that the capital be moved from London to York.

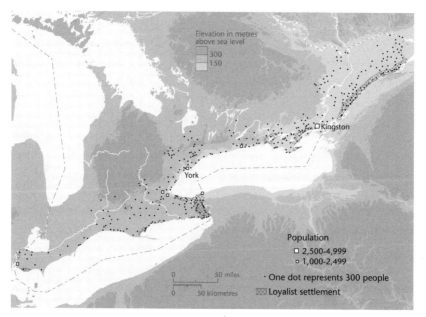

MAP 9.4   Distribution of population, 1825 | After B. Osborne, J-C Robert, and D. Sutherland, in *Historical Atlas of Canada*, vol. 2, *The Land Transformed*, ed. R. Louis Gentilcore, cart. Geoffrey J. Matthews (Toronto: University of Toronto Press, 1993), plate 10.

London, he judged, was too remote, whereas York, on Lake Ontario, had a fine harbour well away from the American border and lay at the southern terminus of the overland fur trade route from Georgian Bay, the importance of which colonial officials had much exaggerated.

As the population grew beyond its early Loyalist enclaves, settlement expanded north or west from Lake Ontario and Lake Erie, and westward in the Ottawa Valley. As political refugees, the Loyalists had received government assistance; for some ten years after 1815, the British government subsidized several group migrations, as when it relocated approximately two thousand Irish paupers from adjacent southern Irish villages in several previously unsettled townships near what is now Peterborough. However, most immigrants came unassisted. In 1825 a patchy, irregular band of settlement stretched some eight hundred kilometres along the St. Lawrence River and the two lower Great Lakes (Map 9.4). Most of Simcoe's townsites were now villages. Along Lake Ontario and Lake Erie was a scatter of small ports, and west from the head of Lake Ontario a line of central places was beginning to develop. An incipient urban system was emerging along the corridors by which Upper Canada was being penetrated and settled: the lakefronts, the principal routes inland. At this date Kingston, with some twenty-five hundred inhabitants, was twice as large as York. Once primarily a fort and garrison, Kingston had tied its fortunes to the St. Lawrence trading system in which it had become an inland entrepôt, the point of transshipment between boats on the upper St. Lawrence and sailing ships serving both shores of Lake Ontario. York controlled little trade, but it was the capital and its principal citizens were influential. These small towns were the primary loci of government administration, military spending, financial management, and import-export trades. In these senses they were, to use sociologist Anthony Giddens' phrase, the power containers of Upper Canadian society. Yet in 1825 only 3 percent of an Upper Canadian population of about 150,000 lived in them. The colony was overwhelmingly rural, and the spread of settlement was accomplished, in effect, by the spread of family farms.

Why people settled where they did is not always clear. Accessibility to the lakefront, a trunk road, or a gristmill and store in a village was obviously important; no families intended to become completely self-sufficient. But how much accessibility did pioneer families need? Yonge and Dundas Streets and many other early trunk roads, originally log- and

FIGURE 9.3 *Road between Kingston and York [Toronto], Upper Canada* (detail), c. 1830 (artist, J.P. Pattison). By the early 1830s, the trunk road along the north shore of Lake Ontario, a section of which is shown here, was clear of stumps and passable for wagons, carriages, or sleds during most of the year. | Library and Archives Canada, 1934-402.

stump-strewn swaths through the forest, were bone-jarring experiences for English visitors. For settlers, however, they were useful roads, axes of travel by sled in winter and wagon in summer (Figure 9.3). Most of the smaller roads seem to have been built by the settlers themselves: as historical geographer Tom McIlwraith has shown, settlers would take up land a good twenty kilometres from an existing road and settlement, quickly building the minimal roads – essentially sled tracks – that pioneer farms required. There are accounts of settlers cutting a road into a new area literally as they went; certainly, roads and land clearing appeared simultaneously. Occupancy appears to have created roads, and roads permitted settlers to develop lots and settle new ones. In general, then, the principal access routes – the St. Lawrence River, the lakefronts, the trunk roads – shaped the broad pattern of settlement expansion, whereas the infilling reflected the settlers' ability, up to a point, to build a sufficient minimal network of roads themselves.

Nor is it clear that settlers discriminated much between sites of varying quality. Settlers' guidebooks warned immigrants away from swamp and marsh, and from land covered by birch, tamarack, pine, cedar, and hemlock; they usually favoured land under beech, maple, basswood, elm, hickory, and several other hardwoods. How much the guidebooks influenced settlers is another matter. With the exception of swamps and, for the most part, sandy morainic ridges, very diverse soils (some ill-suited for agriculture) under different forests were all settled. Historical geographer Alan Brunger, finding no significant variation between the settlement dates of land of dissimilar quality in the London district, holds that settlers did not distinguish land quality on the basis of forest cover. John Clarke, finding that early settlers in Essex County established themselves on well-drained, lightly textured loams and avoided poorly drained soils, suggests that they may have identified the former on the basis of the oak-hickory-chestnut forests that covered them. There is some evidence that poorer settlers tended to seek land that was easily cleared, such as the oak-opening parkland along the Lake Erie shore (although some considered parkland sterile), and that some more prosperous settlers accepted high initial costs of clearing and drainage in return, later, for high yields on rich soils. Although one might expect that American settlers with previous pioneer experience would be particularly discerning, there is no evidence that different ethnic or national groups selected different soil or vegetation types.

What, then, drew some settlers as much as twenty kilometres from existing roads? Probably such settlers sought out land in the interstices, as it were, of large undeveloped landholdings. Some large landowners were active developers, but many were speculators waiting for land prices to rise. Edward Gibbon Wakefield, author of the land policy sections in Lord Durham's *Report on the Affairs of British North America* (1839), and as much a critic of large as of free land grants, held that large undeveloped landholdings created "deserts ... interposed between the industrious settlers" and that they "scattered [inhabitants] over a wide space of country." Settlers, he wrote, were "separated from each other by impassable wastes" (his English eye did not see sled roads) that posed great obstacles "to co-operation in labour, to exchange, to the division of employment, [and] to combination of municipal or other public purposes." He calculated that over half of the surveyed lands at the disposal of the Crown in Upper

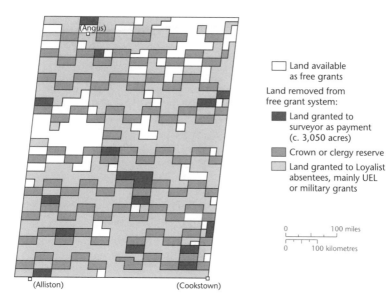

MAP 9.5   Initial allocation of land in Essa Township, Northern Home District, c. 1821 | After J. David Wood, *Making Ontario: Agricultural Colonization and Landscape Re-creation before the Railway* (Montreal and Kingston: McGill-Queen's University Press, 2000), 95.

Canada had been alienated in large grants, and that, of these, only a small proportion ("perhaps less than a tenth") had been occupied by settlers. Many in the Upper Canada of his day agreed with him, as do the findings of contemporary research. Map 9.5 shows the initial allocation of land, as of 1821, in a township (Essa) some seventy kilometres north of Toronto. Only 12 percent of the land in this township was available as free grants to settlers, and most of this land was sandy or ill-drained. The immediate effects of absentee landholdings were to exclude much potential farmland from the land market, to "fill" many townships with only a few settlers, and to shift the criteria of land selection from soil quality or accessibility and towards availability.

There is abundant evidence that immigrants tended to settle near others of their kind. In some cases, as with the Peterborough Irish, they emigrated in groups of families and were settled accordingly. More commonly, immigrants travelling as individuals or in nuclear families went to relatives already established. They had received encouraging word or letters, set out to join relatives, and (the availability of land permitting) would settle as close to them as possible. Probably, more immigrants settled near

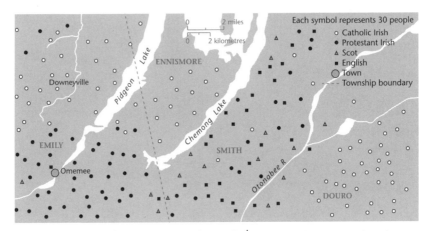

MAP 9.6   Rural settlement near Peterborough | After John Mannion, *Irish Settlements in Eastern Canada: A Study of Cultural Transfer and Adaptation* (Toronto: University of Toronto Press, 1974), 26.

people who, though not relatives, were of their own ethnicity. This occurred partly because the circumstances of their coming made it convenient to do so – they had sailed from a regional port with others from the same corner of Britain, arriving when land was relatively available in particular places – and partly because, as for most immigrants everywhere, common ethnicity provided a measure of cultural and economic security in strange places. As Map 9.6 suggests, Protestant and Catholic Irish settled apart as much as possible. In Essex County, as John Clarke has shown, Canadians (whose ancestors had settled there before 1760), Irish, English, and even, to a lesser degree, Scots and Americans, all tended to live apart. Even their land transactions largely took place within ethnic groups; Canadians in Essex bought and sold from each other, as did the Irish. Within the parameters set by the accessibility and availability of land, it is likely that ethnicity and family were the most common determinants of settler location in Upper Canada.

However families reached a forested lot, its settlement began with simple manual tools, probably a pair of oxen, and usually not much capital or relevant experience. As elsewhere, pioneering was a struggle, with no certainties except work (Figure 9.4). It required a family and such help from neighbours as could be had. A single man could hardly establish a farm; he required a wife and, preferably, children old enough to work. Everything had to be made: a clearing, fencing, fields, a garden, sheds, a barn, a dwelling of sorts, and as much of its contents as possible. Crops had to be planted and harvested, and infants tended. Everywhere there was work; every able member of the family worked. For some, pioneering became overwhelming. The rate of insanity in pioneer societies was high, and there are instances in the records of people who gave up and walked away – a man, for example, who set off for the local gristmill with a little grain, sold it, and carried on. The woman and children left behind would find another man or would soon leave. Similarly, if a wife died in childbirth or, as also was often the case, from swamp fever (malaria), her husband would not cope on his own for long. There was usually too little margin. Often there was some sharing of labour among neighbours for specialized tasks – a bee for raising the frame of a barn, for example – and some pioneer families were able to hire labour, but essentially the assault on the forest proceeded family by family (Figure 9.5). It created holes in the forest, rough patches of open land littered with stumps or perhaps supporting the skeletons of trees killed by girdling (removing a band of bark from around the trunk). Eventually these patches became farms, and the forest between adjacent farms was cleared. A countryside began to emerge (Figure 9.6), but often not one that those who had begun to make it would either have lived or remained to see.

FIGURE 9.4 *A Clearing, Upper Canada* (detail), 1839 (artist, Philip J. Bainbrigge). The simplest pioneer beginning: few assets and fragile prospects. | Library and Archives Canada, 1934-402.

FIGURE 9.5   *First Home in Canada,* n.d. (artist, William Armstrong). This rough pioneer scene, reminiscent of countless others in Upper Canada, was the product of an intense family-centred struggle to rework a forest into a farm and, in so doing, create an independent livelihood. | With permission of the Royal Ontario Museum © ROM, 955.102.1.

FIGURE 9.6   *Adolphustown, Upper Canada,* c. 1830 (artist, John Burrows). After years of unremitting work, clearings coalesced and forest became countryside. Roads were improved and although stumps remained in some fields, farms and some community institutions (in this case a church) were established. | Archives of Ontario, C 1-0-0-0-97, Thomas Burrowes fonds.

In the quarter century after 1825, the population grew almost six times and Upper Canada was largely settled. By 1850, almost all potential farmland was claimed. Population densities and the proportion of cleared land per township were, however, exceedingly variable (Map 9.7). Around Lake Ontario and for some distance inland, more than a third of the land was cleared and under some form of cultivation. Elsewhere, the proportion was much lower. There was a sharp age gradient: the population was older around the lakes and younger farther north. Ethnic distributions varied considerably. The Irish, almost ubiquitous, were most heavily represented in the east (particularly in the Ottawa Valley) and in a tier of townships well north of the lakes. The largest percentages of English lived in the southwest and along much of the Lake Ontario shore. The Scots tended to be in the southwest as well, and in settlements east of Lake Huron, although Lowland Scots and Americans mixed more than others with people of different backgrounds. Within these general patterns lay pockets of sharp difference: Gaelic-speaking Highlanders, German-speaking Mennonites, French-speaking Canadians, a few blacks, a few Ojibwa and Mohawk on reserves.

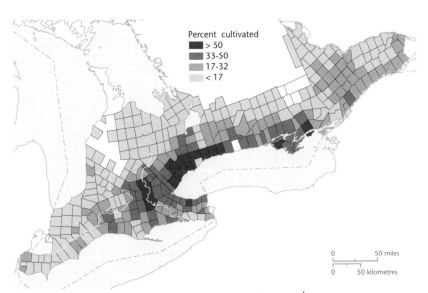

MAP 9.7 Percentage of cultivated land per township, 1851 | After Wood, *Making Ontario*, 160.

However, little of this was static. It is now clear that there was a large and rapid turnover of many settler populations. Immigrants did not, as a rule, settle firmly on a farm lot, there to raise a family and live out their lives. A great many of them were moving through the land, clearing a few acres or picking up work as they could and moving on when prospects elsewhere seemed brighter. The most thorough analysis of this internal mobility, by historian David Gagan, focuses on Peel County, a tract of productive soils and predominantly Irish and English settlement just west of Toronto. Gagan finds that at midcentury more than half of all Peel County households left each decade, and that their places were usually taken by young, recent immigrants for most of whom Peel provided work rather than land. In this way, the population remained largely foreign-born; in 1852 only some 12 percent of household heads in a county settled for several decades were born in Upper Canada (in Upper Canada as a whole, the figure was over 50 percent). Farmers were only somewhat more rooted than others. Gagan suggests that people appear to have been moving to work rather than to land.

With farm lots characteristically about a hundred acres, and a good deal of undeveloped land held by absentee owners, population densities were low. In such circumstances, a small population could quickly take up all available land in a given township. Land prices would rise, and both new immigrants and the progeny of settled families would find it difficult to establish a farm. The problems of access to land and of family succession being encountered at the time in Lower Canada (Chapter 8) soon became pressing in Upper Canada. After the very early period, most immigrants seem to have worked for a number of years, partly to raise the necessary funds, partly in many cases until their children were old enough to assist in the work of farm making, before attempting to establish a farm. The problem for the progeny of established families was tied to inheritance coupled with the shortage of locally available land. David Gagan has shown that, as in Lower Canada, most hundred-acre farms were not subdivided, and that most inheritances were neither partible (equal division among all offspring) nor impartible (the entire inheritance to one offspring). Rather, as in Lower Canada, one son usually took over the farm together with an obligation to make payments to some or all of his siblings – a system, Gagan claims, that produced farmers who were land rich and cash poor. It did mean that some young sons of farm families inherited a little money that could be put towards the establishment of a farm elsewhere, and that some who inherited farms may have found them so burdened by obligations that it was prudent to sell and move. Daughters, as historical sociologist Marjorie Griffin Cohen has shown, inherited relatively little. There is also evidence, again as in Lower Canada, that some farm families – parents and children together – moved to new, cheaper land where parents and at least some of their sons could expect to live close by. All of this would seem to bear on the high rates of mobility that Gagan finds in Peel County.

It is now clear that a good many of the immigrants who worked for a time in Peel County moved on to cheap and still accessible land southwest of Georgian Bay (the Queen's Bush). There they took up land and usually settled down. On the basis of a study of immigrant family life cycles in a Queen's Bush township, Darrell Norris has found that the heads of most of these families were born and raised in Ireland, emigrated well before the famine, worked for a number of years in Upper Canada, usually in Peel County, and tended to move north to the Queen's Bush only when their children were of working age. The attraction of the Queen's Bush was cheap land, not only for themselves but also for their sons, most of whom also settled there. One lifetime, therefore, included periods of mobility and others of stability, just as, at different times, different parts of Upper Canada were conducive to one or the other. Yet, the acquisition of land was a common goal, and for some its primary value may well have been, as Norris suggests, the luxury of family immobility.

The different peoples who came to Upper Canada, the considerable reach of land available for settlement, and the internal mobility of settlers created a texture of kin, religion, and ethnicity quite unlike that in the seigneurial lowlands of Lower Canada or in the patches of discontinuous settlement in the Maritimes. Although clusters of kin were common in Upper Canada, given the pace of settlement and the mobility of settlers, their development was relatively circumscribed. Ethnicity and religion separated Upper Canadians, as they did people elsewhere. Yet, overall, there could be nothing like the religious and ethnic homogeneity of the seigneurial lowlands in Lower Canada, where the great majority of the population were the French-speaking Catholic descendants of a small number of

French immigrants, or of the rock-bound patches of settlement in the Maritimes that usually had filled up quickly with people of one ethnicity. Along many concession line roads in Upper Canada, religious and ethnic affiliations were mixed (a Scottish Presbyterian next to an American Baptist next to an English Methodist), along others quite homogeneous, but in any area of township size both types of settlement were likely. Although largely English-speaking and Protestant, the settlement of Upper Canada had shaken people up, exposing them to peoples and ways of life that most of them had not encountered before.

THE RURAL ECONOMY

The farm household, characteristically on a farm lot of about a hundred acres, was the basic unit of production throughout most of Upper Canada. It was situated amid many other small independent producers, most of whom dealt with broadly similar physical circumstances and markets. Moreover, most households shared similar goals – a family's livelihood and a measure of family-centred security. As commonly throughout northeastern North America, the farm household usually aimed to produce as many as possible of the goods and services that it required, plus a marketable surplus to pay down debts and provide needed goods and services that its own economy could not provide. If the marketable surplus were for export, it had to be durable and valuable enough to withstand shipping costs and lengthy travel times. If for internal consumption, it had to find a market among a dispersed, low-density population connected by poor roads. Yet, from the early days of Upper Canadian colonial settlement, when most Loyalists received direct subsidies and/or compensation from the British government, retired military officers received half pay, and British troops had to be fed, there was an internal market for farm produce. Later, as immigrants poured into Upper Canada, and as both the urban and rural non-farm populations slowly increased – in Peel County in 1851 fewer than two-thirds of household heads were farmers or farm workers – the internal market expanded. In effect, the farm household negotiated a complex set of variables: some were ecological, some concerned the allocation of labour and the balance of domestic and market production, and some bore on choices between different possible markets. In such decision making, equity was not a characteristic of households in which the head was almost always a man whose power was reinforced by the law and his status as a landowner.

The forest itself constituted both barrier and opportunity. Settlers attacked it and many feared it. It stood between them and a farm. People were lost in the forest; sometimes children disappeared there, perhaps eaten, their parents feared, by wolves or bears (animals that had not been seen in the British Isles for hundreds of years), perhaps stolen by Indians. Yet, in many cases the forest also provided the pioneer farm's first economic opportunity. Ashes from clearing fires could be collected, washed, and dried to make potash (impure potassium carbonate), an export commodity that fetched four times as much per barrel as flour. The making of oaken barrel staves, also primarily for export, became winter work on many farms. Often there were sales of logs to local sawmills, by far the most ubiquitous manufactories in Upper Canada. Moreover, the forest provided fuel wood and game, both indispensable on pioneer farms. Where there were logging camps in the vicinity, as in some of the river basins draining into Lake Ontario and Lake Erie (as well as in the Ottawa Valley), it might provide off-farm winter work. In such ways, the forest was variously integrated into the economy of the farm household at the scales of the farm, the local region, or the St. Lawrence trading system.

However, most households depended primarily on agriculture, and the common model not only of pioneer agriculture but of most agriculture in Upper Canada until at least the mid-nineteenth century is the wheat-fallow-wheat farm. In their first small clearing, settlers planted potatoes, vegetables, and wheat around the stumps. A three-acre clearing supplemented by game provided most of the food for a small family. Cattle and hogs browsed in the woods most of the year and survived the dead of winter on branches piled in the yard. Later, when three small fields had been fenced, usually in these early years with piles of tree trunks and branches, the wheat-fallow-wheat farm was established in its essentials. The smallest field was planted in vegetables for domestic consumption, another was in wheat, and the third in fallow. As clearing proceeded, the wheat and fallow fields were enlarged, but the agricultural system did not change. In this model of Upper Canadian agriculture, animals still browsed in the woods, manure went uncollected, the fallow was ploughed at least twice a year, and wheat was grown in a two-course rotation of wheat and fallow.

Kenneth Kelly, a historical geographer who has provided the most careful analysis of wheat-fallow-wheat farming, suggests that it allowed settlers with little capital to emphasize the raising of produce for sale or barter within a few years of initial settlement, devote much of their time to clearing, combat with some success the recolonization of fields by forest species, and produce the one crop for which there was a substantial market. Although most farmers depended on wheat as their principal cash crop, some held that growing wheat in the same field in successive years exhausted the soil, and almost all found that successive wheat crops made it impossible to check the regrowth of forest species. Clearings in hardwood forests could quickly become patches of fireweed, chokecherry, and hardwood suckers; those in coniferous forests sprouted in wild raspberries and poplar. In most farmers' eyes, alternating wheat and fallow was sufficient to prevent soil exhaustion; a bare fallow ploughed at least twice was a sufficient check on weeds. Such a farm required relatively little attention. Women and children tended the garden; stock lived primarily in the woods and were rarely housed even in winter. Fields were ploughed and planted, and grain harvested and threshed, but much of the farmer's year was free for clearing. The capital investment was low: wheat seed, a few simple tools, a pair of oxen, and the family labour of pioneering were sufficient to bring a farm into production. This was sedentary agriculture pared to the bare essentials, producing one marketable commodity with little capital or labour. Most settlers saw no point in a more complex rotation of unmarketable crops or in carefully tending livestock when there was little demand for livestock products. In alternating wheat and fallow, they made extensive use of land, but land was more abundant than any of the other essentials of this agricultural system.

However clear and persuasive the model of wheat-fallow-wheat farming, it is less clear how common this agricultural system actually was. Certainly there were always gentlemen farmers, people of means, who were acquainted with the writings of contemporary British agronomists and who assumed that a regular rotation of wheat and fallow exhausted the soil. They established mixed farms, hired labour, practised elaborate rotations, and introduced new crops and purebred stock. As a rule, their farms fit more closely with the ideals of British agricultural improvers than with Upper Canadian markets, although they may have been points from which, eventually, new agricultural methods diffused. Yet, these farms were few and unrepresentative. The question, really, is to what extent wheat-fallow-wheat farming describes standard agricultural practice on ordinary Upper Canadian farms.

The most convincing qualification of the wheat-fallow-wheat model comes indirectly from economic historian Douglas McCalla and is part of his argument that analyses of the Upper Canadian economy have exaggerated the importance of staples (lightly processed raw materials for export) while underplaying the internal economy. McCalla estimates that wheat production in Upper Canada throughout most of the first half of the nineteenth century required only about a fifth of the land under cultivation. It was difficult, he suggests, for a farm family to plant and harvest more than about ten acres of wheat; consequently, as farms grew larger, wheat acreage did not expand in proportion. In most years wheat exports were half or less of wheat consumption in the region of production, and the average value of wheat exports per farm was low: about £6 per household in the 1830s. After analyzing the ledgers of local shopkeepers, McCalla finds that in the 1830s only a sixth to a third of farmers' payments in kind were characteristically in wheat. Surviving farm accounts suggest that wheat, though always important and usually the largest single source of revenue, comprised only some 20-50 percent of farm income. Oats, peas, potatoes, hay, butter, pork, and wool were commonly marketed, and also, probably, vegetables, fruit, and poultry – which, the products of women's work, were less recorded. He thinks that farmers recognized that specialization was inherently risky, partly because crop failures were always possible, partly because of the uncertainty of the British market (which British Corn Laws closed when the British price of wheat was low). With purchases that had to be made and debts that had to be serviced, a retreat into self-sufficiency was not an option; farms needed, therefore, a commercial alternative to wheat. McCalla pictures a modest mixed agriculture producing mainly for household consumption and local markets. Surpluses were small, commonly not more than enough to feed one other household. If he is right, as he probably is, this was not the mixed farming of the agricultural improvers. There were no intricate crop rotations, no complex cycling of fodder and nitrogen-fixing crops, grains, and manuring. It was the extensive agricultural system that Kelly describes, but with, characteristically, a more varied production than the wheat-fallow-wheat model suggests. Of course, the capacity to diversify sales of farm produce increased as rural roads improved and accessible non-farm populations grew. For a time in isolated pioneer circumstances, wheat-fallow-wheat farming may well have been common.

Over the years on any given farm, as land was cleared and roads improved, the amount of work oriented to the market usually expanded. At the beginning of clearing, the pioneer family threw itself into the challenge of securing its subsistence. Its work was gendered. Clearing, field making, and building were for men; tending children, cooking, maintaining the household, and looking after garden, poultry, and cow, for women and children. As need arose, which it frequently did, women did men's work; in dire emergencies men might do women's work. As soon as possible, some of this work was oriented towards the market, but in isolated farmsteads connected by minimal roads, market opportunities were few and particularly constrained, Marjorie Griffin Cohen argues, for women. Although women were indispensable to the farm economy, it was the men, as household heads, landowners, and principal field workers, who made market connections and controlled farm income, such as it was. They took wheat to the gristmill or logs to the sawmill, whereas women remained on the farm with children. Later, as roads improved and the local market expanded and diversified, farm production became more varied, and women connected with the market more directly, often selling eggs, butter, vegetables, fruit, and, in some cases, homespun cloth. The nearer farms were to towns or villages, the more feasible such sales were.

Whatever the strategies to enable a pioneer farm to secure a family's livelihood, they were often inadequate. Some pioneer families were defeated by the forest; for them pioneering was simply too hard. Some, pioneers by vocation, sold and moved. Another option was to find off-farm work, which many men and some young women did. There were more such opportunities for men: in logging camps (especially in the Ottawa Valley but also at various times throughout much of Upper Canada), in road work associated with trunk roads, on the canals and on river and lake shipping, in small manufactories, and as workers on farms nearby. When the man was away, his wife and children ran the farm. Off-farm employments for women were limited, essentially, to early teenaged girls working as domestic servants for very low wages. The frequency of off-farm work cannot be established precisely, but it was undoubtedly common;

FIGURE 9.7 *Grist Mill, Saw Mills, Etc. on the Nappanee River, at Nappanee Village* (detail), c. 1830 (artist, John Burrows). The large building at the right is a gristmill, the small building at the left, a sawmill, and at the extreme left, a village. | Archives of Ontario, C 1-0-0-0-105, Thomas Burrowes fonds.

on a pioneer farm, its earnings may often have made the difference between establishment and failure.

From the earliest years of colonial settlement in Upper Canada, there were always artisans, mill workers, merchants, and professionals in rural areas, people who depended for their livelihoods on the surrounding agricultural population but were not themselves farmers or farm workers. By midcentury such people constituted at least 15 percent of the rural population in almost all areas and considerably more in the counties around the head of Lake Ontario. Most of them were involved in manufacturing and worked in a great variety of small scattered establishments producing for local markets and in some cases for export. The most common and ephemeral of these were sawmills – approximately a thousand in Upper Canada in 1840, about sixteen hundred in 1848 – the great majority of them seasonal operations employing perhaps two or three men. There were over a thousand potash works in 1842, and more than 350 gristmills in 1836 (Figure 9.7). There were 186 cardingmills (for combing wool prior to spinning) and 144 fulling mills (for cleaning, beating, and fluffing cloth) in 1842. Distilleries, many of them attached to gristmills, were common, as were tanneries and, to a lesser extent, breweries, wagon works, and furniture plants. Outside the principal towns, few if any of these manufactories had as many as ten full-time, year-round employees. The most common artisans in rural areas, besides those in these establishments, were carpenters, blacksmiths, and shoemakers, most of whom were adept at a considerable variety of loosely related tasks. In sum, these small manufacturing establishments, workshops, and artisans provided an array of consumer goods and services required by an emerging countryside. They were geographically dispersed. They depended overwhelmingly on water- or human power and on craft skills. Work was neither much mechanized nor, a few urban exceptions apart, situated in factories.

The market for such work was a low-density farming population connected by poor roads. The concentration of manufacturing in a few urban centres was hardly feasible when the cost of overland transportation was high, most raw materials used in manufacturing – wheat, wool, wood, barley, bark, hides – were widely and locally available, the location of energy was still tied to dam sites and waterwheels on rivers and streams, and the value added by manufacturing was often low. Nor, for the most part, were factories competitive, not only because of the difficulty of reaching a dispersed market, but also because the relatively high cost of labour (compared to that of Britain) and the economies of scale in large well-established British, and increasingly American, factories meant that many goods – cloth, thread, glass, some farm tools, hardware – could be imported more cheaply than they could be manufactured in Upper Canada. By the 1840s this seems to have been particularly the case with cotton and woollen cloth, Upper Canada's two principal imports, although the first small Upper Canadian woollen factories had appeared and many farm wives and daughters still spun and wove. Small high-value imports such as china, silverware, and silk cloth easily withstood shipping costs, but their market was primarily urban. Essentially, the artisans and small industries in the countryside provided many of the basic goods and virtually all the services required by a population of small farmers who supplied their own needs as much as possible.

Linking the rural economy were trading relationships that, as in the Maritimes (Chapter 7), depended on barter and credit and connected the backcountry to lakefront ports. Merchants in the ports relied, on the one hand, on commercial intelligence, import-export agencies, and firms in Lower Canada, New York, and Britain, and, on the other, on a hinterland of local merchants, shopkeepers, and millers who were their links to a dispersed population of independent producers. Imported goods moved inland from the ports, and some of the produce of the interior moved to the ports, to be consumed or exported. By means of these connections, a hierarchy of credit relations could extend from an export firm in London to a farm household anywhere in Upper Canada. From the perspective of the farmer, the key component of the hierarchy was usually a local shop-keeper who received merchandise and credit from a wholesaler in one of the ports, bartered this merchandise for such goods as the farmer had to offer, and, when the latter would not cover the former, extended credit. In rural economies tied to uncertain yields and fluctuating prices, only a few relatively well-capitalized farmers would escape debt; for the rest the local availability of credit was essential. Some farmers, their debts heavy and their credit exhausted, would give up and move on, but for others the opportunity to borrow provided the means to establish themselves. Bartering and borrowing ran through the rural economy, and a good many farmers, as Douglas McCalla has pointed out, were both creditors and debtors.

All of these developments were tied principally to the farm household. Capital – invested principally in the pine forests of the Ottawa Valley and in pine, oak, and other hardwoods elsewhere – created an altogether different spatial economy. Although involved in the stave and potash trades, it focused on squared timber, deals (large, thick planks), and lumber. Most of the squared timber and deals came from vast and relatively accessible pine forests of the Ottawa Valley (Map 9.8a) where, particularly above Bytown (Ottawa), the Upper Canadian side of the river furnished the larger part of the timber harvest. There, as in Lower Canada (Chapter 8) and New Brunswick (Chapter 7), were work camps in the winter woods (shanties), hauling tracks to stream and riverbanks, and, as the ice broke up, timber drives to a port or deal mill – the common spatial organization of the early nineteenth-century timber trade in northeastern North America. For a time in the 1840s a dozen large industrial deal mills operated downriver towards Montreal, the largest with a reported capacity of 600,000 deals a year. In the male world of the Ottawa Valley logging camps, much of the labour force was Canadian, as it was in the deal mills. Indeed, the whole Ottawa Valley was largely tributary to Montreal and Quebec, where most of the timber barons lived and through which its squared timber and deals were exported to Britain. Because of rapids on the river and the distribution of pine, capital was less interested in the forests reached by the St. Lawrence, although it exploited portions of the Canadian Shield accessible from the eastern corner of Lake Ontario, and also, to a much lesser extent, oak forests north of Lake Erie. Sawmilling in the main areas of settlement was widely distributed in small mills dependent on local supplies and markets (Map 9.8b). Nevertheless, as lumber exports to American markets grew rapidly in the 1840s, they generated shanties and timber drives in some of the drainage basins and along some of the rivers leading to lakefront ports. Overall, however, wage work in the forests and farm households (many of which produced sawlogs, fenceposts and rails, staves, potash, and cordwood) were relatively separate in Upper Canada before 1850, partly because wage work was concentrated in the Ottawa Valley, partly because much of the rest of Upper Canada was settled when there was little accessible external market for wood products other than potash and staves. Although wood accounted for at least half the value of Upper Canadian exports between 1815 and 1840, and for almost half during the 1840s, from the perspective of most farm families, shanties and timber drives were another world.

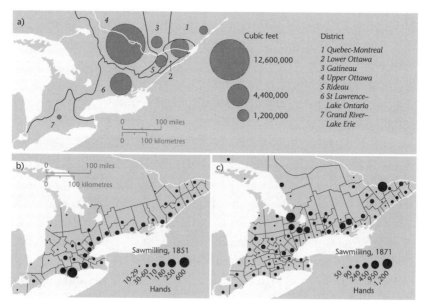

MAP 9.8   Wood production: a) squared timber, 1845; b) sawmill workers, 1851; c) sawmill workers, 1871 | After C. Grant Head, "An Introduction to Forest Exploitation in Nineteenth Century Ontario," in J. David Wood, ed., *Perspectives on Landscape and Settlement in Nineteenth Century Ontario*, Carleton Library No. 91 (Toronto: McClelland and Stewart, 1975), 84, 92.

The Changing Land

As the forest was cleared in Upper Canada, the underlying geometry of the survey gradually asserted itself. What had begun as patches of cleared land linked by irregular trails and sled roads increasingly became a landscape of straight lines. Snake or post-and-rail fences came to mark property boundaries, and fields on either side of these boundaries came to be laid out in rectangular order. Straight concession line roads replaced earlier, more wandering, sled roads. In areas of new settlement, the geometry of the survey was invisible, but as the years passed and the forest gave way to fields, it invariably appeared, a geometry that could be deflected here and there by rivers, lakes, or abrupt slopes but not halted. The order of the survey reflected a new, circumscribed ecological order on the land.

This new order was, for the most part, a product of the requirements of farming, for which much else had been pushed aside. Most forest animals lost habitat; many became pests. Bears, wolves, foxes, cougar, lynx, wildcat, and marten, all in this category, were trapped, poisoned, or shot. The government paid a bounty on wolf scalps. Beaver were hunted for their pelts and to remove their dams and ponds. Well before midcentury, all these animals were essentially gone from the older areas of settlement, their places taken by the livestock farmers introduced and defended. Although plants, many of them weeds (Scotch thistles, spurge, burdock, wild mustard), were also introduced, ecologies were greatly simplified as cropped fields – intended to be small monocultures – replaced forests. The changed vegetative surface created by farming held water and distributed heat less effectively than forests. Rates of runoff increased as the forest was cleared, groundwater tables fell, and the land dried out more rapidly. Surface land temperatures were higher in midsummer days and lower in winter nights. Wherever cleared land sloped, heavy rains caused sheet erosion, and the A and even B soil horizons began to move downhill, accumulating in hollows and flatlands or being transported away by running water. In this way, watercourses carried heavier silt loads, and their patterns of erosion and deposition changed. In a few cases, where clearing exposed former beach ridges and sand dunes, sand began to blow again, as it had not for many thousands of years. Here and there, ditching and (very rarely before 1850) underground drains were beginning to diminish wetlands. Behind all these ecological changes lay the pinched conditions that immigrants had known at home, the land-hunger they generated, and, for all the difficulties of pioneering, the opportunity that land in Upper Canada provided, but on the condition of its remaking.

Farms were not the only agents of ecological change. The many hundreds of gristmills and sawmills in Upper Canada depended on waterpower and hence on dams that blocked watercourses. Sawmill waste was dumped into rivers and streams, frequently clogging channels and spawning beds. Such developments, coupled with increased silt loads and, in association with timber drives, the regularization of stream and river channels, considerably damaged the abundant aquatic environments that had once sustained the Ojibwa. Populations of Atlantic salmon dwindled; by mid-century salmon had disappeared from many streams. The logging operations associated with capital resulted either, as in the timber trade, in the culling of mature pine, or, as in the lumber trade, in the cutting of many species in mixed-age or mature forests. In either case, a large portion of the wood was left behind to become tinder for fires as it dried. As in New Brunswick and Lower Canada, the incidence and size of forest fires increased. When trees grew back through the dense new groundcover on logged and burned-over land, the frequency of tree species had changed – in the upper Ottawa Valley, for example, away from pine and towards shade-tolerant deciduous trees.

In sum, all these ecological changes supported livelihoods or profits, at least for a time. Among the accepted corollaries of the coming of settlers and capital, they fit and enhanced the rhetoric of progress in the nineteenth-century air. There were few contrary voices and little controlling legislation, none of it effective: restrictions in the 1820s on the taking of salmon and in the 1840s some legislated limitations on hunting and the destruction of riverbanks.

Upper Canada about 1850

Map 9.9 suggests the distribution of the some 950,000 people in Upper Canada in 1851. Population densities were highest in a broad band around the head of Lake Ontario and west to the Grand River Valley; they were considerably lower elsewhere, particularly to the north. In a few places, settlement had pushed a short distance into the Canadian Shield. Where population densities were highest, the land was becoming a settled countryside. Where densities were low, scattered pioneer clearings were inserted in forests. There was no single dominating centre. Toronto (called York

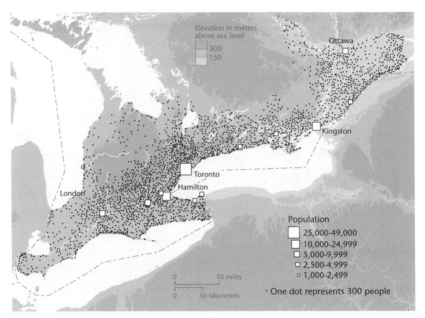

MAP 9.9 Population distribution, 1851 | After B. Osborne, J-C Robert, and
D. Sutherland, in Gentilcore and Matthews, *Historical Atlas of Canada*, vol. 2, plate 10.

until 1834), with just over thirty thousand inhabitants, was now the largest
city in Upper Canada, but accounted for only 20 percent of the urban
population (only 3 percent of the total population), whereas thirty-three
small towns, each with one to five thousand inhabitants, accounted for
almost half of it. A well-defined urban axis ran along the St. Lawrence
River, the north shore of Lake Ontario to Hamilton, and on, through the
Grand River Valley to London. From it, roads extended inland; along these
roads, in sum, were dozens of villages and hamlets.

As in 1825, the urban pattern in 1851 reflected the colony's principal
corridor of access to the larger world, although in the intervening years
the relative importance of the St. Lawrence entry had declined. The completion of the Erie Canal from Albany to Buffalo in 1825, and of a feeder
canal to Oswego on Lake Ontario in 1828, had opened Upper Canada to
the Hudson-Mohawk route to New York. The St. Lawrence trading system
responded rapidly, building the Welland Canal in 1829 to bypass Niagara
Falls and connect Lake Erie shipping to Lake Ontario. But the St. Lawrence itself was inadequately canalized, and for several years in the 1830s,
Upper Canadian merchants shipped several times as much wheat across

the lakes as to Montreal. In the 1840s, the American demand for Upper Canadian lumber grew rapidly, and the American Drawback Acts of 1845-46 permitted Canadian goods bound for overseas markets to pass duty-free through New York. In these circumstances, Upper Canada acquired two broad routes of access and many specific points of connection to the outside world. Kingston declined relatively, while the importance of centres farther west that were less dependent on one trade route tended to grow. Compared to that of Lower Canada, the urban pattern in Upper Canada, as historian John McCallum has pointed out, was notably decentred. Whereas Montreal and Quebec alone accounted for three-quarters of the urban population of Lower Canada in 1851, the fifteen largest centres in Upper Canada accounted for a similar percentage. McCallum attributes this difference to the commercial vigour of an Upper Canadian rural economy based on wheat, an interpretation that may warrant review. Wheat was not as dominant during the years when the Upper Canadian urban system was forming as McCallum has postulated. Moreover, the levels of urbanization in Upper and Lower Canada in 1851 were virtually the same (just under 15 percent). It is possible that different patterns of population distribution and different spatial patterns of trade – the one tied to the St. Lawrence, the other much more diffuse – entailed different geographical patterns of urban growth.

However, McCallum is clearly right that in 1851 the towns were still commercial centres dependent on the countryside. At issue is whether their trade focused on exports of wheat and flour or was both more diversified and more internal. McCallum himself suggests that immigrant demand for goods and services provided the early momentum of urban development and that it was in the 1840s, as wheat exports expanded and established farmers prospered, that wheat propelled urban growth. By the early 1840s, however, the urban pattern was largely established, and McCallum's argument would seem to bear, rather, on the rate of urban growth. The whole matter warrants more investigation. It is clear that town and countryside were interdependent, and that there were many points of access to the latter. Each principal port along the north shore of Lake Ontario dominated its own hinterland and shipped goods away (Figure 9.8). Each was a relay point from which imports moved inland and some of the hinterland's surplus moved out. Wholesalers in these ports dealt, on the one hand, with import-export firms beyond Upper Canada, and, on the other,

FIGURE 9.8   *Cobourg,* 1838 (artist, W.H. Bartlett). One of the many small towns vying for commercial eminence along the north shore of Lake Ontario, each of them connected inland to its own hinterland and within the far larger hinterlands of New York and Montreal. Note the government building (centre) and the American architecture of the church. | *Canadian Scenery,* vol. 1 (London: Nathaniel Parker, 1842), facing p. x.

with retailers in their backcountry. Some were both wholesalers and retailers. This trade and the urbanization associated with it were most concentrated where rural population densities and the percentage of cleared land were highest, that is, in a broad crescent around the western end of Lake Ontario and extending to the Grand River Valley.

Within the urban belt, Toronto, which had grown almost twenty times since 1825 to become a thriving commercial city, was beginning to establish a measure of urban dominance (Figure 9.9). The city had several geographical advantages: an excellent port at the junction of Upper Canada's main east-west and north-south roads, a location near the centre of gravity of the Upper Canadian population (excluding the Ottawa Valley) and at the front of a large backcountry of cleared and productive agricultural land. It had also been the colonial capital, and long before 1841, when the capital was moved to Kingston, had acquired an array of financial institutions (for example, the colony's first bank, the Bank of Upper Canada, established in 1821) and professional services that no other centre could match. So advantaged, by midcentury Toronto was slowly capturing the import trade as importers found it efficient to ship goods to one port. The

FIGURE 9.9   *Toronto, Canada West. From the Top of the Jail* (detail), 1854 (artist, Edwin Whitefield). Note the essentially Georgian architecture, the virtual absence of smokestacks in this still largely pre-industrial city, and the exaggerated activity in the harbour, intended to suggest economic vitality. | Library and Archives Canada, 1970-188-1478.

process of capture was far from complete – in 1851 the value of imports to Hamilton ($2.2 million) almost equalled those to Toronto ($2.6 million) – but Toronto was becoming the distribution point for ports nearby, particularly for American goods. Wholesale merchants comprised the city's new elite.

The most thorough study of the social structure of the small mid-nineteenth century commercial cities in Upper Canada remains historian Michael Katz's exemplary analysis of Hamilton, published thirty years ago. He found a city composed in 1851 of foreign-born (only 9 percent of Hamilton's fourteen thousand inhabitants were born in Upper Canada) and of transients (only a third of those in Hamilton in 1851 were there a decade later). The Irish, the largest ethnic group in the city, were also the poorest. Overall, the most prosperous were the Americans or those born in Upper Canada, and the Wesleyan Methodists. The social hierarchy was steep. The most affluent 10 percent of the population owned almost 90 percent of the city's property and commanded considerably more than half its income, whereas the poorest 40 percent owned no property and received 1 percent of the income. Different spheres of power reinforced each other; the wealthy also formed the political and social elite. In the inner city, rich and poor might live in close proximity, the one in large households (including servants and extended family) in three-storey brick or stone houses surrounded by ample grounds, the other in cramped and squalid rooms. In a more segregated periphery were both stately homes on higher ground south of the city and ethnically somewhat sorted working-class suburbs. The poor did not vote and had no voice. Many families lived on the edge of absolute destitution; some immigrant Catholic Irish were transported in wagonloads to country towns and dumped there. In this still pre-industrial city, small home-scale activities were typical. Of 282 industrial establishments in Hamilton in 1851, half had no employees, only 7 percent had ten or more, and only 3 percent had at least twenty. None of the largest employers – foundries and coach and carriage works – had as many as a hundred employees. Manufacturing, wholesaling and retailing, professional and financial services, and residences mixed in the inner city, although, as historical geographers Ian Davey and Michael Doucette have shown, there was some block-by-block segregation.

Beyond these commercial cities were the farms, hamlets, and villages on which they relied and where 85 percent of the Upper Canadian population lived. Almost everywhere, clearing was still going on, and farms and countryside were still being made. On average, some 37 percent of occupied land had been cleared, less in newer areas, more in older, but never, at the township scale, reaching the levels of clearing (75-80 percent) that became common towards the end of the century. The basic unit of settlement and economy remained the family farm, usually on a lot of about a hundred acres. These farms are best thought of, as economic historian Marvin McInnis has most recently shown, as mixed operations that combined livestock, cereals, and vegetables to meet the subsistence needs of a family and, as far as possible, produce a surplus for sale. On many farms, especially in areas of recent settlement, there was virtually no surplus, on others the value of the surplus considerably exceeded the value of on-farm consumption. Somewhat specialized agricultural regions were beginning to appear, although almost always overlain on a base of mixed farming. Wheat, the major farm export and principal agricultural specialization, was grown primarily on fertile and relatively densely settled land around the head of Lake Ontario and west to the Grand River Valley. Here as much as a quarter of improved land was in wheat, which, allowing for a bare fallow (wheat-fallow-wheat), may have been close to the limit of possible specialization on a mixed farm that carried considerable numbers of livestock. Upper

Canadian wheat exports, which had found a secure British market only after the 1846 repeal of the Corn Laws, came from this region. Elsewhere, except on small pioneer farms, the percentage of land in wheat was much lower, and other specializations were emerging: oats and livestock in the Ottawa Valley, dairying along the upper St. Lawrence River, oats and rye in the backcountry north of Kingston, market gardening near the principal towns, sheep (raised for wool) in parts of southwestern Upper Canada, and tobacco in the extreme southwest. In sum, this agriculture achieved what was intended: it provided for the subsistence needs of families and for some of them a modest but comfortable prosperity. The extent to which, at midcentury, exports of wheat and flour contributed to this prosperity and to the larger Upper Canadian economy, remains a matter of debate among economic historians. At midcentury wheat was not a dominant crop in many areas; where it was, it is not clear that wheat exports contributed more to the economy than the variety of crops (including wheat) and livestock raised for domestic consumption and internal markets. Moreover, mixed agriculture provided alternatives; the farm economy was not dependent on a single export staple.

Even where the land was well settled and substantially cleared, the population density was lower than in the places from which most immigrants had come, commonly not more than twenty or thirty people per square mile, often far less (Map 9.10a). Farmhouses were characteristically some distance back from the concession line road and, depending on the survey and the length of settlement, roughly a third of a kilometre from their nearest neighbour. In pioneer areas, and occasionally even where settlement was well established, the dwelling was no more than a shanty (Figure 9.10a). More commonly by midcentury, it had been replaced by a small squared-log house with dovetailed corners, a central door with windows on either side, a plank floor with a root cellar underneath, a half-attic above, and a stone or brick fireplace and chimney (Figure 9.10b). At midcentury, this simple building, introduced into Upper Canada from the south and embodying rudimentary Georgian principles of order and symmetry, was the common Upper Canadian farmhouse. Some more prosperous farmers covered their log house with boards or brick; others built similar, if usually slightly larger, houses in these materials or stone (Figure 9.10c). Full two-storey houses, often with five evenly spaced windows along the front of the second floor and two on either side of the front door

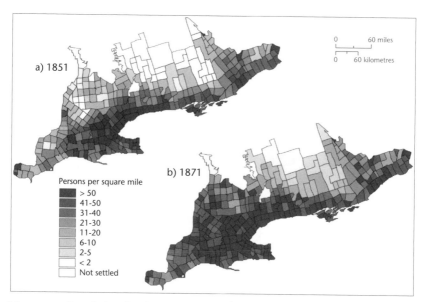

MAP 9.10   Population density, 1851 and 1871 | After J. Clarke, H. Taylor, and R. Wightman, "Area Patterns of Population Change in Southern Ontario, 1831-1891: Core, Frontier and Intervening Space," *Ontario Geography* 12 (1978): 30.

(Figure 9.10d), were usually located in villages and built by immigrants of means or by rural merchants.

Behind or to the side of the farmhouse on most established farms was a small log or timber-frame barn with a large central door in each long side (Figure 9.11a). Between the two doors was a drive floor and on either side a bay, or storage area, suitable for grain, hay, or livestock. This two-bay barn, probably introduced from Pennsylvania or upstate New York, served Upper Canadian farmers well until, in the 1860s and later, dairying became common. Small and with a narrow span, it was easily built and roofed. Were more space required, a farmer usually built another barn, sometimes adding it to one end of the older building, sometimes creating L-shaped, U-shaped, or even square arrangements around a barnyard. Usually, one small barn sufficed. One bay served as a granary, the other to store a few implements and house a few stock. With both doors open on a windy day, the drive floor could become a threshing floor.

Surrounding house and barn were the fields of a farm. Bounding them at the back was forest, at the front a concession line road. Along the road were similar farms – sometimes occupied by kin or others of the same

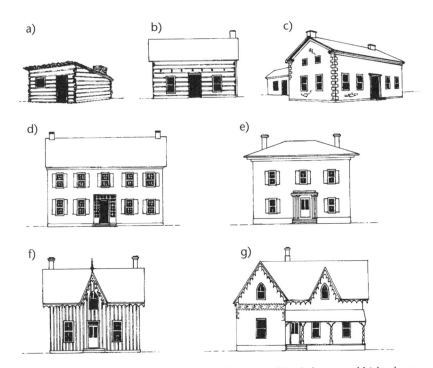

FIGURE 9.10   Ontario house types (artist, Peter Ennals): a) shanty and b) log house were both common in pioneer areas before Confederation; c) Georgian stone house (also frame or brick), built until midcentury or even later; d) a larger Georgian or "Loyalist" house built, with changes in detail, until the 1850s; e) a substantial house (c. 1825-60), showing Regency and classical influences; f) small board-and-batten house with Gothic window and fretwork trip. Whether of frame, brick, or stone construction, this was the most common Ontario house from approximately 1855 to the end of the century; g) a substantial brick farmhouse of a type that was becoming common by Confederation. | C. Harris and J. Warkentin, *Canada before Confederation: A Historical Geography* (New York and Toronto: Oxford University Press, 1974), 131.

ethnicity and religion, sometimes not – and somewhat farther away, a hamlet or village probably including a sawmill, a gristmill, a smithy, a general store, a post office, perhaps a school, and perhaps even a church of an appropriate denomination. Usually considerably farther off and rarely visited was a regional town, perhaps a lake port. Such, in outline, was the physical context of most lives, a context that was shaped by, but that also shaped, the lives it contained.

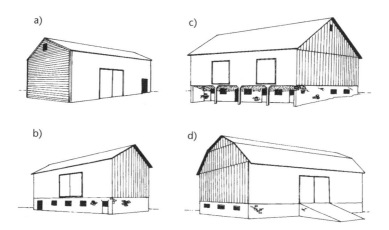

FIGURE 9.11   Ontario barns (artist, Peter Ennals): a) two-bay barn; b) raised two-bay barn; c) Pennsylvania barn; d) central Ontario barn | Harris and Warkentin, *Canada before Confederation*, 133.

Upper Canada had provided land for the creation of many thousands of small yeoman farms, a type of farm that immigrants knew in their home-lands but could rarely acquire. The basis, however, for small freehold farms had been laid. Well before the emigration to Upper Canada, older regimes of customary law had been weakened or broken, and the common law had established the legal dominance of private property rights embodied in free and common socage tenures and fee simple estates. Moreover, the memory of family life on the land remained, if, increasingly, the possibil-ity did not. In these circumstances, one option for the landless was wage work, if it could be had, in the countryside; another was work in a factory, under a boss, and within the time discipline of industrial capitalism; yet another was emigration. Those who emigrated to Upper Canada found themselves in a situation where, relative to what they had known, the value of land had plummeted and that of labour had risen. In these changed circumstances, a good many of them were able to create or acquire a fam-ily farm of a type for which their backgrounds offered general precedent but no opportunity. These farms were transplants. Exotic crops and live-stock were in their fields. Even the small Georgian farmhouse surrounded by its fields could be found, with regional variations in style and materi-als, in all the immigrants' homelands. A model of the small independent farm, well known but out of reach for most in the British Isles, had encountered enough space in Upper Canada to become a common reality.

At the same time, the social and cultural context of the family farm had changed. The social range in the British countryside, measured on the one hand by the great walled estates with their parks and mansions, on the other by the most dire poverty, and between by finely calibrated social structures in which people knew their fit, their betters, and their inferiors, had given way to a much flatter social structure in which there were still pockets of grinding poverty but neither the social range nor the precision of social identifications that characterized British rural society. For this, the relative availability of land, coupled with the scarcity of labour, the lack of time for the generational accumulation of wealth, and an economy focused on farm families producing first and foremost for their own consumption, were largely responsible. Moreover, the cultural context of the family farm had been rearranged. Many former ways had been discarded because they did not fit the circumstances of farming in a forested realm dominated by a northern continental climate; others had faded because there was no longer a critical mass of people who shared them. Settlers had come from places where those around them spoke with similar accents, told familiar stories, and laughed at similar jokes, whereas in Upper Canada they encountered, and commonly lived among, people who did not share an imported local culture. If similar people usually clustered as much as they could, the land system, the pace of settlement, and the mobility of settler society all worked against such concentration. In these circumstances, only fragments of the local regional cultures within which people had lived in Britain could be reproduced. Migration transplanted families much more successfully than it did particular local cultures. Already under assault in the British Isles, such ways could hardly be reassembled out of a migration that detached individuals and nuclear families from communities, and out of settlements composed of people who, even if predominantly Irish, came from different local Irish cultures.

In effect, the farm household had been recontextualized in Upper Canada. The dispossession of the Ojibwa had created a relatively clean slate, the traces of customary law that had survived in England were not reproduced, and the common law, with its emphasis on individual rights and private property, took over. If, as legal historian Philip Girard has shown,

Upper Canadian law evolved some limited protection for members of families, an essentially liberal system of property law bent no farther towards community. Moreover, the farm household was situated in a different landscape, in a different arrangement of people on the land. Families lived in more isolation from each other, not only because they lived farther apart, but also because the cultural distance between neighbours had increased. In these circumstances, the patriarchal nuclear family became more salient. Ethnic affiliations also changed as they shifted in scale and were generalized. Distinctions between immigrants from Yorkshire, Devon, or Wiltshire faded; they all became English. Ethnicity was losing its local vernacular content and gaining a different and more symbolic register in which signs and badges (wedding ceremonies, national days, national flags, and the like) marked ethnic belonging. In an age of belief, religion undoubtedly filled much of the relative social vacuum that emigration and settlement on a farm lot in Upper Canada had created. Most settlers sought to build a church and attract a minister of their denomination. However understood, God was at hand, and for many, the rituals of particular churches became part of the precious symbolic vocabulary of home.

In mid-nineteenth century Upper Canada, the Loyal Orange Lodge, a product of Protestant-Catholic feuding in Ulster, flourished in the weakened social and institutional space beyond the farm household. The lodge was a semi-secret society based on rituals, passwords, and secret signs (modelled on Freemasonry), and on an ideology of militant Protestantism and loyalty to the British Crown. In Upper Canada, the small meeting house of the Loyal Orange Lodge was probably more ubiquitous and certainly more accessible to men of differing Protestant denominations than any particular Protestant church. Lodge membership expanded well beyond the Protestant Irish to include all Protestants who would swear the Orangeman's oath and pay a small fee. Socially, the lodge compensated for the weakness of neighbourhood, serving, as historical geographers William Smyth and Cecil Houston have shown, as a loosely religious setting where men could escape the burdens of work, socialize, and "return momentarily to a realm of certain myth and familiar tradition." Politically and ideologically, the lodge reproduced elements of the mind and garrison mentality of Protestant Ulster in an Upper Canada that, in the eyes of many Orangemen, was hemmed in by the American republic to the south and the predominantly French-speaking and Roman Catholic population to the east. It serves as an example of how, in the socially disruptive circumstances of emigration and resettlement, identity and allegiance tended to shift from the local and familiar to the general and symbolic – in the case of the Orangemen, to Protestantism and the British Crown and empire.

In all of this were the ingredients for the making of a peculiar form of a predominantly liberal society, that is, a society predicated on individual rights and a competitive market economy. Historian Ian McKay has recently argued – and few would disagree with him – that the creation of such a society, effacing as it did centuries of tradition and divorcing people from their surroundings, marked a huge transformation in the conception of society and the realities of social life. However, when he attributes this transformation in Upper Canada (among other British North American locations) to the influence of "a small vanguard of true believers" – the leaders of the Rebellion of 1837, Lord Durham, and other political figures – he is on less secure ground. The basis of Upper Canadian liberalism, if that is the right word, lay not in the persuasions of a segment of the political elite, but in a range of social, economic, and legal changes that had been developing in Britain over several centuries and were accelerated by emigration and resettlement in Upper Canada. This relocation abruptly detached people from the remaining matrix of local relationships within which, even in the early nineteenth century, most rural British lives were situated. At a vernacular level, a venerable axis of peasant tradition was lost. Nor did a more philosophical conservatism, based on a conception of society as an organic whole in which people had their proper places and responsibilities, fit a society composed primarily of small farmers assembled, even along many a concession line road, from different places and adhering to different Christian denominations. The hierarchical, deferential, and culturally fairly uniform society of an Anglican parish in rural England was not at hand. In short, as the vernacular and philosophical bases of conservatism receded, ideological space opened for a qualified liberalism. However, very considerably moderating the idea of the autonomous liberal individual in Upper Canada was a deep sense of family, some measure of local community (more here, less there), a general though certainly not unanimous appreciation of the rightness of the British empire and its institutions, and a distaste for republican democracy – a liberalism that was conservatively embedded in family and empire.

Of course, at midcentury some Upper Canadians did not share this qualified liberal consensus. The urban Tory elite did not; nor did the communitarian, inward-looking Mennonites in the Grand River Valley. Nor did the Ojibwa, or the Mohawk on whose lands the Mennonites had settled. The Ojibwa had lost their land and with it their former economy. As one of their chiefs, Kahkewaquonaby (Peter Jones as he was known in English), put it: "We are surrounded on all sides by white settlers, still encroaching on us; and I am afraid that in a few years we will hardly have space enough left to lay down our bones upon." Kahkewaquonaby, a well-educated Methodist, thought that the only solution was to adopt a sedentary, agricultural way of life; indeed, at midcentury agriculture provided the basic livelihood on all the Ojibwa reserves in Upper Canada. Commonly adopted as an alternative to extinction, it was, for the most part, a minimal agriculture practised on inadequate reserves by people who, recently, had been fishers and hunters. Although most of the Ojibwa were Methodists, they had neither assimilated into white society nor wished to. The Mohawk in the Grand River Valley also considered themselves a people apart, one subject to their own laws, a status that, well before midcentury, Upper Canadian law was unwilling to recognize. It did not defend the Mohawk from squatter encroachments on their lands, although by the terms of the Royal Proclamation (1763) only the British Crown could acquire Native land. The most prominent jurist in Upper Canada, John Beverley Robinson, went so far as to argue that the large Mohawk reserve along the Grand River had been acquired illegally; the Mohawk, therefore, were not its fee simple owners and could not prevent others from occupying it. As commonly elsewhere in settler colonies, the law was put to the service not of principle or vested rights but, in various combinations, of privilege and settlers.

1850-70

Immigration declined during these years until, by the 1860s, more people were leaving than entering Upper Canada. Moreover, women were beginning to marry a year or two later on average, and as they did the number of children they bore declined slightly. In these circumstances, the rate of population growth slowed: in the 1850s it was about 4 percent a year, in the 1860s just 1.5 percent. Whereas the Upper Canadian population had increased more than six times between 1825 and 1851, it increased by only two-thirds between 1851 and 1871, growing from 950,000 to just over 1,600,000. Over the same years, it became more urbanized – in 1871 21 percent lived in eighty-four towns and cities with a thousand or more inhabitants – but not much more focused. Only 3.5 percent of the provincial population lived in Toronto in 1871. Half of those whose occupations were listed in the census were farmers. Upper Canada – or, as it had now become, the Province of Ontario – was still overwhelmingly rural, its population still spread across the land.

In a largely rural economy, increasing emigration and lower fertility rates reflected the decreasing availability of land. The opportunity was diminishing for both poor immigrants and many of the progeny of established families to secure farms of their own. Young adults were inclined to stay somewhat longer on their parents' farms and to marry later. With less land available nearby or, by these years, elsewhere in Upper Canada, more of them moved south or west, into the United States. For many others, however, rural Upper Canada still provided opportunity, less now by territorial expansion than by infilling. Patented stumping machines, introduced from the United States in the 1850s, greatly reduced clearing costs, the process of farm making continued (the number of farms in Upper Canada increased by 80 percent in the twenty years after 1850), and the population density increased. A comparison of population density in 1851 and 1871 (Map 9.10) indicates the extent of change. The southwest, the Lake Huron shore, and the Queen's Bush south of Georgian Bay had filled in, and the limits of settled land were usually defined by water or rock.

Railways, which had been promoted in Upper Canada for years, began to be built in the 1850s, always with an eye to American trade; by the end of the decade over two thousand kilometres of railway track had been laid (Map 9.11). The Grand Trunk, built west from Montreal to Sarnia at the foot of Lake Huron, was yet another attempt (following canals) by Montreal merchants with British financing to capture the American trade of the upper Great Lakes. Both the Great Western and the Buffalo and Lake Huron were promoted as through lines for American carriers; the shorter lines built at right angles to the lakes or the St. Lawrence were intended to connect with American railways and move Upper Canadian exports to American markets. The most important of these shorter railways, the Northern, completed from Toronto to Collingwood on Georgian Bay in 1855, suddenly opened the vast pineries around Georgian Bay to the timber

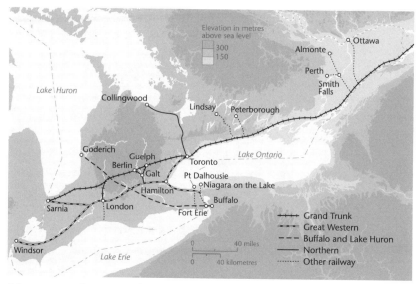

MAP 9.11 Railways, 1860 | After Harris and Warkentin, *Canada before Confederation*, 155.

companies (Map 9.8c). Overall, the effect of the railways was suddenly to decrease the cost and improve the reliability and speed of overland transportation, thus increasing the capacity for the spatial integration of the economy. Coupled with the Reciprocity Treaty of 1854 – an agreement for free trade with the United States in agricultural and forest products, minerals, and fish – they intensified the American orientation of Upper Canadian trade. In 1856 exports to the United States were ten times the shipments along the St. Lawrence. In 1859 only 2 percent of the large tonnage of wheat and flour shipped from Toronto went to Montreal. Toronto, and with it much of Upper Canada, moved firmly into the hinterland of New York. Within Upper Canada, as Douglas McCalla has noted, railways tended to strengthen the position of established cities and to diminish economic isolation by increasing both the range and complexity of markets and the integration of town and countryside.

At the same time, industrial, factory-based production, much of it now steam powered, was gaining a secure foothold. Economies of scale favoured larger units of production, and agglomeration economies (advantages associated with proximity to other producers, services, labour pools, and markets) favoured the location of manufacturing in larger centres. The long-run effect of declining transfer costs, coupled with economies of scale and agglomeration, was to reduce the number of small widely distributed manufactories, concentrate manufacturing in a few large centrally located plants, and shift the focus of economic growth to the largest cities. In the 1850s and 1860s these processes, which would reshape the economic geography of southern Ontario, were just beginning.

In most cases, craft production tended to shift into larger establishments that were still mainly dependent on manual labour, and then into more mechanized factories, although industry by industry the timing of this transformation was uneven, and in 1870 craft production in small workshops remained common. Tanning, for example, was still small-scale and local; the 420 tanneries in the province each employed an average of four people. Brewing was only a little more concentrated; some 550 people worked in just over one hundred breweries, all of which had fewer than 50 employees. On the other hand, there were some one hundred licensed distillers in Upper Canada in 1851, and only seventeen two decades later, two of which, in Toronto, employed 37 percent of the industry's workers. In the same years, the manufacture of agricultural implements shifted from many small operations – often little more than blacksmiths' shops – to small factories. In 1871 half of the output in this industry came from forty-one firms with an average of twenty-four employees. The concentration in new industries associated with the railways was more striking: in 1861 one Toronto foundry employed over four hundred men.

By 1870 what may be loosely described as a manufacturing belt had emerged around the western end of Lake Ontario and westward to the Grand River Valley. Within this belt, Toronto and Hamilton were particular foci of industrial employment. However, more remarkable in the 1850s and 1860s than concentration was the continuing dispersal of industry throughout the cities and towns of Upper Canada. In 1870, as Douglas McCalla points out, the thirty-three largest urban flourmills were located in twenty-four different urban centres. The thirty-four leading furniture and cabinet-making establishments were in twenty-five different centres, as were the leading makers of agricultural implements. Some industries – lithography or foundries, for example – were concentrated in a few places, but most were not. Although services were most available in the principal cities, many were widely distributed. In 1871, Toronto had nine banks, Ottawa, Hamilton, and London each had five, Kingston had three, and some forty other towns had at least one. Seventeen of the twenty-four daily newspapers were published in one of the five principal cities, but

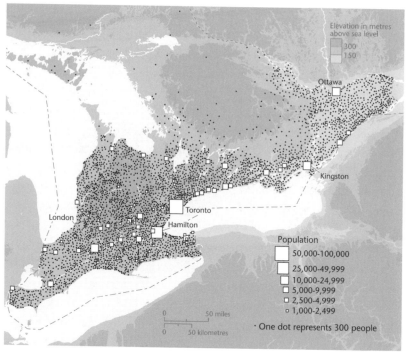

MAP 9.12   Population distribution, 1871 | After D. Measner and C. Hampson, in *Gentilcore and Matthews, Historical Atlas of Canada*, vol. 2, plate 29.

there were weeklies in more than two hundred places. In short, though the relative importance of the principal cities was growing, the dispersed urban system that had been established by 1851 remained essentially intact (Map 9.12). The percentage of the Upper Canadian population in Toronto, Hamilton, Ottawa, and London increased only fractionally (from 6.3 percent to 7.4 percent), and Toronto's share from 3.2 percent to only 3.5 percent. In the 1850s, Toronto's growth rate did not exceed the Upper Canadian average; in the 1860s, it slightly outpaced it (2.3 percent against 1.5 percent).

Nevertheless, labour historian Greg Kealey maintains that Toronto underwent an "industrial revolution" in these years, and that major sectors of its economy were highly industrialized by 1871. By that year, forty-six Toronto factories each employed more than fifty workers, and most of the some ten thousand industrial workers in the city laboured in factories for wages. The clothing industry, with 2,160 workers (three-quarters of them women and children), was the largest employer. In these circumstances, the fine grain of the pre-industrial city, in which different urban functions and people of different station were interdigitated, gave way to a coarser urban grid that was increasingly segregated by function and class. Relatively homogeneous commercial and manufacturing districts began to emerge, the well-to-do moved increasingly to the suburbs, and the poor took over deteriorating housing close to the warehouses and factories where many of them worked. The changing Toronto waterfront illustrates this process. In 1850 it consisted of a jumble of transshipment, storage, wholesale, retail, and residential functions, some manufacturing around the mouth of the Don River, and some fine swimming beaches lined by distinguished residences. With the coming of the railway in the 1850s, the volume of trade increased; Toronto merchants became more specialized as they drew larger numbers of customers to their premises and employed travelling salesmen to take their wares to every railway stop. Warehouses became larger, and the largest firms separated storage and showrooms in different buildings. By the late 1860s, a warehouse district comprising three- to five-storey brick and stone buildings had emerged at the waterfront, and different types of wholesaling were becoming sharply segregated within it. The swimming beaches and the homes of the well-to-do were gone; the railway and commercial land uses had taken over the Toronto waterfront. Those who had argued for parks and other civic improvements there – usually members of the city's older Tory elite – were a small minority in a city dominated by businessmen and an ethic of progress in which the railway was a pre-eminent symbol.

In Hamilton in 1851, as noted above, almost all manufacturing took place in small establishments located in the inner city. A decade later, some three-quarters of them were still well within a kilometre of the busiest downtown intersection. By this date, however, the Great Western Railway ran through the city, and a few larger plants – a felt-hat factory employing 150 men, an agricultural implements factory, a steam engine and boiler works, a locomotive construction and repair shop – had been established along it (Map 9.13). In 1861 they accounted for only 10 percent of Hamilton's manufacturing establishments, but for 21 percent of its manufacturing employment. They depended on steam power, on direct rail connections, and in some cases on space for the assembly of bulky raw materials and the storage of finished product. Hamilton's business class was investing

MAP 9.13
Manufacturing
establishments in
Hamilton, 1860 |
After Harris and
Warkentin, *Canada
before Confederation,*
161.

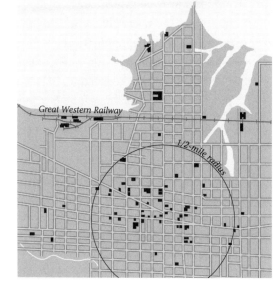

■ Manufacturing
establishment

0   1,000 feet

0   300 metres

in heavy industry; in so doing, it was rapidly creating a separate manufacturing district that met these requirements and was well removed from the inner city. Hamilton was becoming an industrial city, one that, with neither clothing nor boot and shoe factories, employed very few women and children.

Hamilton's transition from commercial to industrial capital was achieved, Michael Katz argues, without a basic change in its power structure or in the hierarchy of inequality that had existed in the earlier city. Capitalists still organized work and accumulated capital; workers still took the jobs they offered. This workforce was particularly transient. Even allowing for mortality, only a third of the people in Hamilton in 1851 or 1861 remained in the city a decade later. Among the least skilled, the rate of transiency was much higher. The large majority of household heads were immigrants who stopped in Hamilton for a time, then moved on, looking for employment elsewhere. The city was a funnel through which people passed, some to farmland in Upper Canada but probably more to work in other (commonly American) cities. The relatively stable community in Hamilton was the city's elite, people who owned a good deal of property and controlled the city's business, political, and philanthropic life. Stability, Katz suggests, was one of the privileges of power, and also, given the opportunities it provided to enhance economic, social, and political relationships, one of the means by which power consolidated itself. For the working class, on the other hand, transience was a manifestation of powerlessness. Neither a sense of community nor institutions of class defence were easily put in place when people were on the move and there were always newcomers looking for work. Neighbours were commonly strangers, and if people participated in events such as parades, festivals, or riots, they did so, Katz maintains, less out of ties of friendship or culture than because they shared objective characteristics such as nation of birth, religion, or occupation. In these circumstances, as in the countryside, the identity of immigrants lost most of its former vernacular content while becoming increasingly symbolic. At the same time, the patriarchal nuclear family assumed a particular salience. With remunerated work now male and almost entirely separated from the home, the gendered separation of work and residence made domestic space more female. Men were separated from child-rearing, which became the primary responsibility of women and, with the spread of public schooling, of the state.

Being re-created in Hamilton, and increasingly in towns and cities throughout Upper Canada, were many of the conditions that early nineteenth-century emigrants from Britain had fled. Labour was detached from land, obtained for a wage, and subject to the time and work discipline of industrial capitalism. It was exposed to the uncertainties of the market, increasing competition from other workers, and long hours in unhealthy and often dangerous work environments. For young people growing up on Upper Canadian farms, these conditions appear to have been as unattractive as they had been for their parents or grandparents when they chose to emigrate rather than move to an industrializing British city. Although more work is needed on the topic, it appears that urban population growth was generated by overseas immigrants, a minority of whom, in the 1850s and 1860s, eventually became Upper Canadian farmers. Apparently, the surplus young from the countryside were not moving in number to Hamilton or the other principal Upper Canadian cities, perhaps because they would have to compete there with cheap immigrant labour, but also, one suspects, because they sought to reproduce the way of life of the small independent farm family in which they had grown up. Some would still do so in Upper Canada, although this had become increasingly difficult by the 1850s and 1860s. In a study of a large area of central Upper Canada, sociologist Gordon Darroch shows that between 1861 and 1871 only 16 percent of the sons of farmers stayed there and became farmers. Some remained nearby and took up a trade; others sought land elsewhere in Upper Canada or moved to the United States. Eventually, urban wage labour would absorb many of them or, more likely, their progeny, a prospect that second- or third-generation Upper Canadians seem to have fended off as long as possible.

The Upper Canadian countryside still supported a great many family farms that, as Gordon Darroch and Lee Soltow have shown, remained relatively accessible, compared to anywhere in the British Isles, to people of modest means. Land costs were highest in older areas of settlement near the cities (as in Peel County), but declined sharply to the north where population densities were lower. It was still possible – a result of inheritance, mobility, or a combination of the two – for a fair portion of the rural young to establish themselves on their own farms somewhere in Upper Canada. The frequency of landownership and the average size of farms changed very little during the twenty years after 1851. In 1871 over 60 percent of the province's farmers were landowners; of those who were not, many were adult sons still living with their parents. At age fifty, some 85 percent of farm men owned their own land. The largest landowners, with more than five hundred acres (less than 1 percent of all farmers), held 6.4 percent of all farmland; those with over two hundred acres (9.8 percent of all farmers) held 37.6 percent, but most farmers held about a hundred acres. More striking in this countryside than inequality, Darroch and Soltow argue, were the breadth of access to modest farms and the relative social equality, compared to that of rural Britain and urban Upper Canada, entailed by such access. Upper Canadian towns and cities, they write, "were islands of wealth accumulation and inequality in a wider sea of relative rural equality." Overall, Upper Canada had only selectively industrialized, small independent producers were still the basis of its economy, and the common understanding of the day that land was a source of opportunity for the working poor was not yet an illusion.

The 1850s and 1860s were generally prosperous years in rural Upper Canada; internal and external markets for agricultural produce, agricultural prices, and rural living standards were all increasing. The average price of Upper Canadian wheat, regularly exported to Britain from the late 1840s, was half again as high in the 1850s as in the 1840s, and at times during the Crimean War (1854-56) more than twice as high. A Reciprocity Treaty (free trade in natural products) with the United States (1854-66), coupled with demand generated by the American Civil War (1861-65), expanded access to American markets that did not close when the Reciprocity Treaty ended. During most of the 1850s and 1860s, Upper Canada exported more than 8 million bushels of wheat a year, as well as growing quantities of flour, barley, peas, pork, beef (or swine and cattle on the hoof), and dairy products (butter and cheese). Moreover, with railway construction and an expanding urban population, the local market for agricultural produce was diversifying and growing. For most of these years, wheat and flour were Upper Canada's dominant agricultural exports (by value): in 1856 they accounted for almost two-thirds of the value of all Upper Canadian exports. However, most farms remained mixed operations that produced a variety of goods for domestic consumption and a surplus – about half the production of an average hundred-acre farm in 1860 – for sale. In 1870 wheat accounted for some 22 percent of land under crops, but, John McCallum estimates, for only 15 percent of the gross value of Upper Canadian agricultural production. These generalizations disguise sharp regional variations – in 1870 wheat production was highest where it had been highest in 1850 and still very low in the Ottawa Valley and along the lower St. Lawrence – yet suggest that, even during the years when wheat exports were at their peak, it is misleading to associate an expanding and increasingly prosperous Upper Canadian rural economy with an export staple.

Rather, a variety of marketed goods supported a growing, but still very moderate, rural prosperity. In an analysis of eleven hundred farms randomly sampled from the 1861 census, Marvin McInnis calculates that the average farm produced a marketable surplus worth $210, that half of all farms produced marketable surpluses under $150, that a sixth produced no surplus, and that only 5 percent generated surpluses over $830. Most farms were producing well beyond domestic requirements but rarely more than enough to feed one or two other families. Their market, for the most part, was the local non-agricultural population. Only a few farms were specialized producers for the market, and although they tended to create an impression of specialization and exchange, McInnis holds that "the majority of farmers ... produced a variety of products that were essentially an extension of the self-sufficient production of the farm. They required, and mainly catered to, a local market provided by the non-agricultural population of nearby farms, villages, rural craftsmen, and functionaries." This essential, but limited, market dependency is consistent, he points out, with our understanding of an economy in which "farm productivity was still relatively low, and the farm population made up half or more of the total."

In the longer run, wheat cultivation would shift out of Upper Canada to cheaper western land, and regional agricultural specializations within Upper Canada would become more pronounced. As shipping costs declined, the nature of agricultural production would become more sensitive to local environments and to the relative cost of land. More intensive land uses (such as market gardening) would emerge near the towns, and specialized agricultural regions (such as tobacco cultivation on sandy soils north of Lake Erie) would emerge in particular environments. Even before 1850, and increasingly by 1870, these adaptations to particular environmental and economic conditions were slowly being expressed. The more pervasive change, towards dairying, came slightly later. Only 8 percent of the farms in McInnis' 1861 sample had enough milk cows to begin to engage in commercial dairying. The first cheese factory opened only in 1864; in 1870, butter and cheese accounted for only about 4 percent of the value of exports. That figure would soon rise, but at Confederation, agriculture in what then became the Province of Ontario was still dominated, as it had been in 1850, by a great many unspecialized family farms.

In the older areas of settlement, the rural landscape had become comfortable. The rawness of pioneering was a generation or two behind, forests had become woodlots, and a modest rural prosperity was apparent in the landscape. A countryside had been made, and marked out by improved concession line roads, well-established farms, and networks of villages and hamlets. A general store, a post office, a school, a relevant church, and artisans of various types lay within range of most farms. Many farms themselves looked complete and substantial. Machinery was in many fields, particularly mowers and reapers, of which there were some thirty-seven thousand in Upper Canada by 1871 (purchased at, for the day, the considerable average cost of $125-$130 each). Barns became larger, partly in response to the capacity of reapers and mowers, but principally to the growing importance of livestock in the farm economy. Increasingly, two-bay barns were constructed above a stone foundation storey where livestock were housed (Figure 9.11b). Hay was kept above. Here and there by the 1860s, there were large dairy barns with a ramp to a central door on the long side (Figure 9.11d). Farmhouses, too, were getting bigger and were slipping from Georgian into early Victorian styles. Log farmhouses were being covered or replaced; Figure 9.10f depicts what was probably the most common Ontario farmhouse by the 1850s. Compared to its predecessors, the roof has been raised a little, a small gable inserted above the central door, and elements of Gothic revival style (picked up from pattern books) introduced. By the 1860s, a few prosperous farmers were building more elaborate and asymmetrical Gothic revival houses (Figure 9.10g). By British standards, there was no wealth in this countryside; on the other hand, most of the capital in Upper Canada at Confederation was located there, as were the most common settings in which immigrants and their descendants had created Upper Canadian livelihoods.

But for how long? By the 1850s and 1860s, Upper Canada was rapidly filling in, and many Upper Canadians were leaving for the United States. Their number cannot be established precisely but was high enough to trouble many of the elite. Upper Canadian prosperity had been built, they held, on trade and the expansion of farming; if that expansion ended, the economy would stagnate. The comparison with the United States was particularly galling. Whereas American business benefited from the vast momentum of American westward expansion, its Upper Canadian counterpart risked being confined, as one retired fur trader put it, to a "comparatively small fragment of the continent" that "would soon be both too narrow and too short for them, too small a field on which to exercise and develop their new born energies." In 1856 the commissioner of Crown lands reported that many of the province's young men as well as some of its older settlers found easier livelihoods on the open western prairies "where the plough can be immediately used, and great crops obtained with comparatively little labour." Hence, he argued, the attraction of the United States. In Upper Canada, which had no open prairies, this analysis embodied a challenge to find competitive agricultural land elsewhere in British North America.

The most accessible land lay to the north in what is now known as the Canadian Shield, but was then a vast tract of little-known land. The commissioner of Crown lands reported in 1856 that almost 57 million acres of

Crown land lay north of Lakes Superior and Huron, and eastward from Lake Huron to the Ottawa Valley, but it was an open question as to how much, if any, of this huge territory was suitable for farming. In official eyes it came down, as historian A.R.M. Lower suggested years ago, to a question of land classification. Timber interests held that the land was rough, often nothing but pine and rock, and that settlers on isolated patches of cultivable land would "spread fire and havoc through the pine forests." This land, they argued, should be classified for lumbering, not agriculture. A clear territorial separation – "as nature has laid it down" – should be established between the two economies. The government was not so sure. The image of the yeoman farmer and a great deal of agrarian rhetoric were in the air, many of the business elite strongly favoured agricultural colonization, and tantalizing accounts, which the government wanted to believe, told of good potential farmland to the north. The commissioner of Crown lands reported that excellent land near Lake Nipissing (northeast of Georgian Bay) had been found "to extend far into the interior." The provincial geologist reported that "extensive valleys of fertile lands lie behind the rocky hills which skirt the northerly shore of Lake Huron." According to several reports, the best unoccupied wheat country in Upper Canada was in the Ottawa-Huron Tract east of Lake Huron. This tract, wrote the minister of agriculture in 1856, was "capable both as to Soil and Climate, of producing abundant crops of winter wheat of excellent quality and full weight, and also crops of every other description of farm produce grown in the best and longest cultivated districts of the Province, and fully as good." He thought the Ottawa-Huron Tract capable of supporting 8 million people. Enticed by such assessments, the government began to lay out townships there, offer settlers free fifty-acre land grants, and build colonization roads, some eight hundred miles of which were completed by 1868 (Map 9.14).

Settlement of the free grant lots began in 1855 along the Ottawa and Opeongo Road (Map 9.14) where four years later more than two hundred lots were occupied. A local road agent thought the land "as good as any to be found in Canada," and the commissioner of Crown lands reported that the settlement of the Ottawa-Huron Tract had succeeded beyond all expectations. However, by the early 1860s settlers were leaving. There were no newcomers along some roads, and bare handfuls along others. Clearing

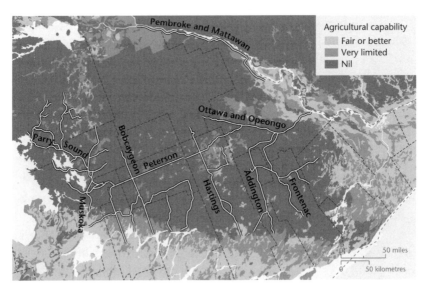

MAP 9.14   Colonization roads in the Ottawa-Huron Tract | After F.B. Murray, *Muskoka and Haliburton, 1615-1875* (Toronto: Champlain Society, 1963), 185.

had stalled. The few settlers were usually recent immigrants from the British Isles (principally Irish), or Germans. Upper Canadians, it was claimed, sought land along the colonization roads only for the timber. Immigrants complained that they had been misled by deceptive government publicity. Some who took up snow-covered land in winter found mostly rock in the spring. In some years, early frosts ruined grain and potato crops. From a comfortable urban vantage point, the Ottawa-Huron Tract was a potential agrarian landscape, the possible home of 8 million people; from closer at hand it had more to do with rock, acidic soils, blackflies, and frost. By 1865, the commissioner of Crown lands almost acknowledged as much. "From their remoteness and their character," he wrote, the remaining public lands of Upper Canada were "much less desirable for settlement" than the land already taken up to their south. Yet he thought they were as good as land in northern Europe, and that, if they were adapted for settlement, "human life can be permanently maintained." Faced with the prospect that "Canada would remain a mere frontier strip bordering the margin of the St. Lawrence and the Great Lakes," he continued to advocate the rapid colonization of northern land. In effect, his vision of Canada required settlers, however wracked their lives. Potential settlers themselves, in search of reasonable livelihoods rather than eked-out existences, judged the agricultural potential of these lands as harshly as had the lumber interests. Although agrarian visions lingered at official levels, in 1871 the government began to auction unclaimed free grant lands to lumbermen.

In these circumstances, Upper Canadian expansionism turned increasingly to the northern plains, the North West of the old Montreal fur trade that after 1821 had become a trading preserve of the Hudson's Bay Company (Chapter 10). Here, in this rightful hinterland of Canada, was the space for a commercial and agricultural empire that would eventually rival the power of Britain herself and make Canada "one of the Great Powers of the earth." The very fact that the North West was available for settlement was providential; had it not been kept from the world until Canada – Upper Canada for the most part – was able to occupy it? Needed was a railway. With it, the commercial empire of the St. Lawrence would expand across a continent, and the northern plains would be settled by an industrious farming population whose agricultural exports would pay for eastern manufactures. When this vision of transcontinental empire emerged in the late 1840s, it was held by only a few influential men, most of them in Toronto or Ottawa. A decade later, however, as historian Doug Owram has shown, it was incorporated in a pervasive political discourse that assumed an English Canadian trusteeship of the North West in the name of civilization and the British empire.

The British empire. Most Upper Canadians were proudly attached to it, if in differing and often incompatible ways. When eighteen-year-old Albert Edward, Prince of Wales (the future King Edward VII), visited Upper Canada in 1860, these differences were suddenly revealed. Whereas in Lower Canada, said Le Courier du Canada, he had been "welcomed with the most respectful loyalty," the royal party was unable to land at Kingston and Belleville, its first intended Upper Canadian stops. The Orange Order, in full flight of Protestant loyalty and with all its regalia on display, had taken charge of the streets. The prince was to pass under the Orangemen's arches, thus endorsing the order and its brand of militant Protestantism. Moreover, after the visit to Lower Canada, whose politicians, Orangemen held, dominated Upper Canada (Canada West) and where, in a British colony, the mayor of Quebec had addressed the prince in French, there was a balance to redress. All of this insulted Upper Canadian Catholics,

FIGURE 9.12   *Reception of His Royal Highness the Prince of Wales by the Inhabitants of Toronto, Canada West, 27 Oct. 1860* (detail) (artist, G.H. Andrews). Note the size of the crowd and the imperial pomp and circumstance. | Library and Archives Canada, C-010912.

who professed their loyalty but would not march under an Orange arch or turn over the streets to Orangemen. Nor would the duke of Newcastle, the colonial secretary and the prince's political advisor and travelling companion. The British monarchy, he said, ruled over Christians of every form and could not defer to the symbols of one when they gave grave offence to another. Newcastle was also aware that the government of which he was a part had introduced legislation to ban Orange parades in Ireland. The prince, therefore, would neither march under an Orange arch nor visit a city where Orangemen demonstrated in their regalia. Newcastle meant what he said, and the young prince, who was fond of dancing, could indulge himself only when the royal party reached Cobourg and Toronto (Figure 9.12). The whole incident, as historian Ian Radforth has shown, reveals something of the complexity of Britishness in an Upper Canada impregnated with Irish rivalries, situated in close proximity to French-speaking Catholics to the east and republican Americans to the south, and still managed, at the highest levels, by politicians in London.

BIBLIOGRAPHY

As historian J.K. Johnson notes in "Gerald Craig's Upper Canada: The Formative Years and the Writing of Upper Canadian History," *Ontario History* 90, 2 (1998): 117-33, the focus of scholarly interest in early Ontario has shifted to the late nineteenth and twentieth centuries. A proliferation of good work has focused on Quebec in the century after 1760, but relatively few comparable studies, especially over the last two decades, have examined Ontario in the same period. Nevertheless, the literature is substantial, and this bibliography identifies the parts of it that I have found most useful.

Aboriginal Peoples

For a good, if substantially political, history of the Ojibwa, see Peter S. Schmalz, *The Ojibwa of Southern Ontario* (Toronto: University of Toronto Press, 1991), particularly chaps. 2-7. The Ojibwa economy and Ojibwa objectives and understandings in the treaty process receive a fuller analysis in J. Michael Thoms, "Ojibwa Fishing Grounds: A History of Ontario Fisheries Law, Science, and the Sportsmen's Challenge to Ojibwa Treaty Rights, 1650-1900" (PhD diss., University of British Columbia, 2004). There are helpful essays by E. Reginald Good on Mennonite-Ojibwa, and by Sidney L. Harring on issues of sovereignty and law in the Grand River Valley Mohawk reserve, in David T. McNab, ed., *Earth, Water, Air and Fire: Studies in Canadian Ethnohistory* (Waterloo: Wilfrid Laurier University Press, 1998), 145-80, 181-229. On law and Native rights, see also Sidney L. Harring, *White Man's Law: Native People in Nineteenth-Century Canadian Jurisprudence* (Toronto: University of Toronto Press, 1998), chaps. 2 and 3.

Immigrants

The diffuse literature on the Loyalists is not easily penetrated. Among recent scholarly works, I have found the following particularly helpful. For a short, informed introduction, see George A. Rawlyk, "Loyalist Military Settlement in Upper Canada," in R.S. Allen and B. Pothier, eds., *The Loyal Americans* (Ottawa: National Museums of Canada, 1983), 99-103. On Loyalist ideology, consult Jane Errington and George A. Rawlyk, "Creating a British-American Political Community in Upper Canada," in Robert Calhoon, Timothy Barnes, and George Rawlyk, eds., *Loyalists and Community in North America* (Westport: Greenwood Press, 1994), 187-200. For the distinction between "Loyalists" and "Late Loyalists," refer to Peter Marshall, "Americans in Upper Canada, 1791-1812: 'Late-Loyalists' or Early Immigrants?" in Barbara J. Messamore, ed., *Canadian Migration Patterns from Britain and North America* (Ottawa: University of Ottawa Press, 2004), 33-44.

As well as the sources on Irish and Scottish emigration listed in Chapter 7, see Cecil J. Houston and William J. Smyth, *Irish Emigration and Canadian Settlement: Patterns, Links, and Letters* (Toronto: University of Toronto Press, 1990), chap. 3; Bruce S. Elliott, *Irish Migrants in the Canadas: A New Approach,* 2nd ed. (Montreal and Kingston: McGill-Queen's University Press, 2004), chap. 3; and Malcolm Gray, "Scottish Emigration: The Social Impact of Agrarian Change in the Rural Lowlands, 1775-1875," in Donald Fleming and Bernard Bailyn, eds., *Perspectives in American History,* vol. 7 (Cambridge, MA: Charles Warren Center for American History, 1973), 95-174.

On English immigrants, see Bruce S. Elliott, "Regional Patterns of English Immigration and Settlement in Upper Canada"; Wendy Cameron, "English Immigrants in 1830s Upper Canada: The Petworth Emigration Scheme"; and Terry McDonald, "A Door of Escape: Letters Home from Wiltshire and Somerset Emigrants to Upper Canada, 1830-1832," all in Messamore, *Canadian Migration Patterns from Britain and North America,* 51-90, 91-100, 101-20. There is an abundance of excellent material on the background of these migrations in G.E. Mingay, ed., *The Agrarian History of England and Wales,* vol. 6, *1750-1850* (Cambridge: Cambridge University Press, 1989), especially chaps. 8 and 10. On British patriotism and local regionalism, see Linda Colley, *Britons: Forging the Nation 1707-1837* (New Haven and London: Yale University Press, 1992), particularly chap. 1 and the Conclusion. On changing relationships with space in the British Isles, refer to R.A. Dodgshon, "The Changing Evaluation of Space, 1500-1914," in R.A. Dodgshon and R.A. Butlin, eds., *An Historical Geography of England and Wales,* 2nd ed. (London: Academic Press, 1990), 255-83. For Charles Tilly on indirect and direct rule, see his *Coercion, Capital, and European States, AD 990-1990* (Oxford: Blackwell, 1990), chap. 4. For E.P. Thompson on the expanding range and power of the common law, see *Whigs and Hunters: The Origin of the Black Act* (New York: Pantheon, 1975).

Land Access

On colonial land policy and cost, see particularly John Clarke, *Land, Power, and Economics on the Frontier of Upper Canada* (Montreal and Kingston: McGill-Queen's University Press, 2001), especially chaps. 3-5; David Gagan, *Hopeful Travellers: Families, Land, and Social Change in Mid-Victorian Peel County, Canada West* (Toronto: University of Toronto Press, 1981); Peter A. Russell, "Upper Canada: A Poor Man's Country? Some Statistical Evidence," in Donald H. Akenson, ed., *Canadian Papers in Rural History,* vol. 3 (Gananoque, ON: Langdale Press, 1982), 129-47; and Robert E. Ankli and Kenneth J. Duncan, "Farm Making Costs in Early Ontario," in Akenson, *Canadian Papers in Rural History,* vol. 4 (1984), 33-49. Also, for much important information within a type of narrative history that is no longer written, see George C. Patterson, *Land Settlement in Upper Canada, 1783-1840,* 16th report, Department of Archives (Toronto: Province of Ontario, 1920).

The Spread of Settlement

Most of the literature on settlement is not new. For introductions to the topic, see R. Louis Gentilcore and David Wood, "A Military Colony in a Wilderness: The Upper Canada Frontier," in J. David Wood, ed., *Perspectives on Landscape and Settlement in Nineteenth Century Ontario*, Carleton Library No. 91 (Toronto: McClelland and Stewart, 1975), 32-50; and Leo A. Johnson, "Land Policy, Population Growth and Social Structure in the Home District, 1793-1851," *Ontario History* 63 (1971): 41-60. Among the literature bearing on ethnicity and settlement, see particularly John Mannion, *Irish Settlements in Eastern Canada: A Study of Cultural Transfer and Adaptation* (Toronto: University of Toronto Press, 1974); Alan G. Brunger, "Geographical Propinquity among Pre-famine Catholic Irish Settlers in Upper Canada," *Journal of Historical Geography* 8, 3 (1982): 265-82; and John Clarke, "Social Integration in the Upper Canadian Frontier: Elements of Community in Essex County, 1790-1850," *Journal of Historical Geography* 17, 4 (1991): 390-412. On settler mobility, the key work is David Gagan's *Hopeful Travellers*. In conjunction with this study, see his (with Hubert Mays) "Historical Demography and Canadian Social History: Families and Land in Peel County, Ontario," *Canadian Historical Review* 54, 1 (1973): 27-47; "Geographical and Social Mobility in Nineteenth-Century Ontario: A Microstudy," *Canadian Review of Sociology and Anthropology* 13, 2 (1976): 152-64; and "The Indivisibility of Land: A Microanalysis of the System of Inheritance in Nineteenth Century Ontario," *Journal of Economic History* 36 (1976): 126-41 (also, in the same issue, see the commentary by Marvin McInnis, 142-46). An essay that usefully locates some of the migrants from Gagan's Peel County study area is Darrell A. Norris, "Migration, Pioneer Settlement, and the Life Course: The First Families of an Ontario Township," in Akenson, *Canadian Papers in Rural History*, vol. 4, 130-52. On persistence as well as mobility, see Herbert J. Mays, "A Place to Stand: Families, Land, and Permanence in Toronto Gore Township, 1820-1890," *Canadian Historical Association Historical Papers* (1980): 185-215.

The Rural Economy

For an orienting overview, see J. David Wood, *Making Ontario: Agricultural Colonization and Landscape Re-creation before the Railway* (Montreal and Kingston: McGill-Queen's University Press, 2000), chap. 5. On wheat-fallow-wheat farming, see Kenneth Kelly, "Wheat Farming in Simcoe County in the Mid-nineteenth Century," *Canadian Geographer* 15 (1971): 95-112. A vigorous argument for the importance of wheat as export staple and motor of economic development is made by John McCallum in *Unequal Beginnings: Agriculture and Economic Development in Quebec and Ontario until 1870* (Toronto: University of Toronto Press, 1980), chap. 2. Douglas McCalla offers much the most thorough and comprehensive analysis of the Upper Canadian economy, and also a critique of McCallum's emphasis on the wheat staple, in *Planting the Province: The Economic History of Upper Canada, 1784-1870* (Toronto: University of Toronto Press, 1993). Marvin McInnis considers the wheat staple and provides an analysis of Upper Canadian agriculture at midcentury in "Perspectives on Ontario Agriculture, 1815-1930," in Akenson, *Canadian Papers in Rural History,* vol. 8 (1992), 17-83. The role of women in a rural staples economy is analyzed by Marjorie Griffin Cohen in *Women's Work, Markets, and Economic Development in Nineteenth-Century Ontario* (Toronto: University of Toronto Press, 1988), chap. 4. On the forest industry, see C. Grant Head, "An Introduction to Forest Exploitation in Nineteenth Century Ontario," in Wood, *Perspectives on Landscape and Settlement,* 78-112.

The Changing Land
For a useful general survey, see Wood, *Making Ontario,* chap. 2. On environmental change associated with logging, see Head, "An Introduction to Forest Exploitation," in Wood, *Perspectives on Landscape and Settlement,* 78-112. A relevant article on a slightly later period is Kenneth Kelly, "Damaged and Efficient Landscapes in Rural Southern Ontario, 1880-1900," *Ontario History* 66 (1974): 1-14; reprinted in Graeme Wynn, ed., *People Places Patterns Process: Geographical Perspectives on the Canadian Past* (Toronto: Copp Clark Pitman, 1990), 213-27. For an influential treatment of the topic in a region similar to Upper Canada, consult William Cronon, *Changes in the Land: Indians, Colonists, and the Ecology of New England* (New York: Hill and Wang, 1983).

Upper Canada about 1850
On the urban system, Jacob Spelt, *The Urban Development of South Central Ontario* (Assen, Netherlands: Van Gorcum, 1955), and reprinted by Carleton Library No. 57 (Ottawa: Carleton University Press, 1983), is still useful. On the same topic, see Wood, *Making Ontario,* chap. 9. The best analysis of urban social structure at midcentury remains Michael B. Katz, *The People of Hamilton, Canada West: Family and Class in a Mid-nineteenth Century City* (Cambridge, MA: Harvard University Press, 1975), especially chap. 1 and Appendix 1 ("The Social Geography of a Commercial City ca. 1853," by Ian Davey and Michael Doucet). On the countryside, the principal works are cited above, but see also John Clarke and John Buffone, "Social Regions in Mid-nineteenth Century Ontario," *Histoire sociale/Social History* 28, 55 (1995): 193-218. On a more ideological track, the following are suggestive in various ways: Cecil J. Houston and William J. Smyth, *The Sash Canada Wore: A Historical Geography of the Orange Order in Canada* (Toronto: University of Toronto Press, 1980), especially chaps. 2, 3, 6, and 7; S.F. Wise, *God's Peculiar Peoples: Essays on the Political Culture in Nineteenth-Century Canada* (Ottawa: Carleton University Press, 1993), especially chap. 9; Phillip Girard, "Land Law, Liberalism, and the Agrarian Ideal: British North America, 1750-1920," in John McLaren, A.R. Buck, and Nancy E. Wright, eds., *Despotic Dominions: Property Rights in British Settler Societies* (Vancouver: UBC Press, 2005), chap. 6;

and Ian McKay, "The Liberal Order Framework: A Prospectus for a Reconnaissance of Canadian History," *Canadian Historical Review* 81, 4 (2000): 617-45.

1850-70

Much of the literature cited above is also relevant here. On Hamilton and Toronto, see also Michael B. Katz, Michael J. Doucet, and Mark J. Stern, *The Social Organization of Early Industrial Capitalism* (Cambridge, MA: Harvard University Press, 1982), chaps. 2-4; and Gregory S. Kealey, *Toronto Workers Respond to Industrial Capitalism, 1867-1892* (Toronto: University of Toronto Press, 1980), especially chap. 2. The transformation of the Toronto waterfront with the coming of railways is described by Donald Kerr and Jacob Spelt in *The Changing Face of Toronto: A Study in Urban Geography*, Memoir 11, Geographical Branch, Mines and Technical Surveys (Ottawa: Queen's Printer, 1965), 69-72.

Gagan's *Hopeful Travellers* and McCalla's *Planting the Province*, cited above, should also be consulted for this later period. See also the following: Marvin McInnis, "Marketable Surpluses in Ontario Farming, 1860," *Social Science History* 8, 4 (1984): 395-424; Richard Pomfret, "The Mechanization of Reaping in Nineteenth-Century Ontario: A Case Study of the Pace and Causes of the Diffusion of Embodied Technological Change," *Journal of Economic History* 36, 2 (1976): 339-415; William L. Marr, "Tenant vs. Owner Occupied Farms in York County, Ontario, 1871," in Akenson, *Canadian Papers in Rural History*, vol. 4 (1984), 50-71. Gordon Darroch and Lee Soltow offer an important analysis of the rural social structure in *Property and Inequality in Victorian Ontario: Structural Patterns and Cultural Communities in the 1871 Census* (Toronto: University of Toronto Press, 1994). For a readable introduction to some components of Ontario's mid-nineteenth-century rural landscape, see Thomas F. McIlwraith, *Looking for Old Ontario: Two Centuries of Landscape Change* (Toronto: University of Toronto Press, 1997).

On the settlement of the Shield fringe, A.R.M. Lower, *Settlement and the Forest Frontier in Eastern Canada* (Toronto: Macmillan, 1936), chap. 5, remains an intelligent and useful account. The quotations from government officials in the 1850s and 1860s are taken from the following: "Report of the Commissioner of Crown Lands of Canada for the Year 1856," *Journals of the Legislative Assembly of the Province of Canada* 15 (1857): Appendix 25; "Annual Report of the Minister of Agriculture for 1856," ibid. 15 (1857): Appendix 54; "Report of the Commissioner of Crown Lands of Canada, 1858," ibid. 17 (1859): Appendix 17; and "Report of the Commissioner of Crown Lands of Canada for the Year Ending 30th June, 1865," *Sessional Papers, Fifth Session of Eighth Parliament of the Province of Canada* 1 (1865). See also a substantial paper by Susan L. Laskin, "The Myth of a Northern Agricultural Frontier in Nineteenth Century Ontario" (MA research paper, Department of Geography, University of Toronto, 1979). On Upper Canadian interest in the western interior, see Doug

Owram, *Promise of Eden: The Canadian Expansionist Movement and the Idea of the West, 1856-1900* (Toronto: University of Toronto Press, 1980), chaps. 2-3.

My remarks about the 1860 visit of the Prince of Wales are drawn from Ian Radforth, *Royal Spectacle: The 1860 Visit of the Prince of Wales to Canada and the United States* (Toronto: University of Toronto Press, 2004), especially chap. 5.

10

The Northwestern Interior, 1760-1870

The vast northern territory bounded by Hudson Bay, the Cordillera, the forest-tundra margin, and approximately the height of land between the Gulf of Mexico and Hudson Bay was exposed to European influences long before it attracted much European settlement. Carried by Native middlemen, European trade goods had reached the Assiniboine and Western Cree around Lake Winnipeg before 1650, all the peoples of the northern plains before 1700, and the Athapascan speakers in the Mackenzie Valley before 1750. Horses diffusing northward from Spanish settlements near Santa Fe arrived on the northern plains in the 1730s. Smallpox, coming from the east in 1737-38 and from the south in the early 1780s, devastated the peoples of the northern plains and boreal forest. But Europeans themselves came sparingly to land they found inaccessible and forbidding. As late as 1870, some two hundred years after the first European trading posts were established on Hudson Bay and around the western Great Lakes, hardly forty thousand people lived in this huge territory. No more than 5 percent of them were white, between one-quarter and one-third were of mixed European-Native descent (Métis), and the rest were Native. Although external influences had transformed Native lives, European settlement had hardly begun. Even at Red River, where most of the whites lived, more than 80 percent of the population was Métis.

The problems for Europeans were the remoteness of the northwestern interior, its perceived harshness, and the difficulty of establishing viable economies other than fur trading. The region was deep in the continent and only high value–low bulk goods withstood shipping costs. The most

FIGURE 10.1   *Indians Completing a Portage, 1873* (detail) (artist, William Armstrong).
This transportation technology carried the fur trade westward from Lake Superior
to the plains and well beyond. In various combinations, the labour force was Native,
Métis, and Canadian. | Library and Archives Canada, 1970-188-2244.

direct transatlantic route inbound led to the trading posts on Hudson
Bay, an eight-week voyage from London during a short ice-free season.
From York Factory on Hudson Bay, the trip inland by riverboat and canoe
to Lake Winnipeg took almost four weeks, yet Lake Winnipeg itself was
no more than a platform from which trade routes headed far to the west
or into the maze of rivers, lakes, and rock to the east. The approach from
Montreal was even more arduous: by canoe for well over a month to a
post on the northwest shore of Lake Superior, then on in smaller canoes
for three more weeks to Lake Winnipeg (Figure 10.1). After this route was
virtually abandoned in 1821, Hudson Bay dominated external connections
until the 1840s, when cart brigades began to link the northern plains to
steamboats at St. Paul on the Mississippi and at Fort Benton on the Missouri. After 1859, when a steamboat first reached the Red River settlements,
the economy oriented itself more firmly southward to connect with American railways and steamboats. Yet even in 1870 the settlements at Red River
were two full weeks from Montreal or New York. Beyond them, the older
regime of river- or lake boat, canoe, and cart remained in place. Cartage
from Fort Garry on the Red River to Fort Edmonton on the North Saskatchewan still took more than fifty days.

Over more than two centuries, isolation and a perception of daunting land held the outside world somewhat at bay. It arrived selectively –

infectious diseases, horses, traders and trade goods associated with commercial capital, Protestant and Catholic missionaries, a few settlers, a few schemes for economic diversification – but not in these years in the form of many immigrants or of successful commercial economies unrelated to the fur trade. The peoples of the region dealt with external influences but not yet with the weight of immigrant numbers or, except at Red River, with settler claims to land. In these circumstances, there was space and time for local adaptations to external influences.

On the eve of the Seven Years' War, the British and French trading systems that had disputed the fur trade of the northwestern interior for most of the previous hundred years and had deeply affected the lives and livelihoods of all Native people there (Chapter 4), were arranged approximately as shown in Map 10.1. Many Native economies revolved around the fur trade. The Cree who had settled near the Hudson's Bay Company (HBC) posts on the Bay (the Homeguard Cree) lived off the provisioning trade and depended on firearms, cloth, and leather obtained at the posts. Other Cree, and some Assiniboine, had become specialized traders. The seasonal rounds of most of those who hunted and trapped had been adjusted to allow more time to take beaver and marten, the principal trade furs. European goods were widely used and appreciated. Some Native populations had plummeted, a result of the increasing frequency and intensity of warfare associated with the differential introduction of firearms, and also of introduced infectious diseases. Together, warfare and disease shifted the location of many Native groups and also the boundaries between them. Between 1720 and 1760 the Assiniboine and Cree had expanded slightly westward, while losing territory southeast of Lake Winnipeg to the Ojibwa, a more easterly Algonquian-speaking people who occupied the relative vacuum created by the Sioux wars and disease. In the north, the Chipewyan, now well armed, advanced some way into Cree territory. South of the Missouri, the Shoshone, better supplied with horses than the peoples north of them, expanded their influence northward. For all of these displacements and cultural changes, the northern continental interior remained Native space within which British and French trading posts were pinpoints of European control. Except along the principal transportation corridors, the animal populations on which the trade relied were still robust.

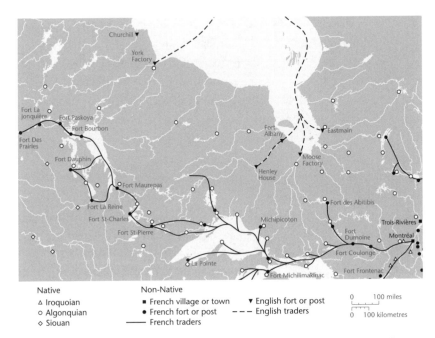

MAP 10.1   French and British trade routes in the northwestern interior, 1755 |
After C. Heidenreich, in *Historical Atlas of Canada*, vol. 1, *From the Beginning to 1800*, ed. R. Cole
Harris, cart. Geoffrey J. Matthews (Toronto: University of Toronto Press, 1987), plate 40.

Changing Patterns of Trade and Settlement, 1760-1821

The Seven Years' War and the fall of New France gave the HBC a brief
monopoly of the northern fur trade, but Montreal traders were back on
the Saskatchewan River by 1765. Increasingly, these Montrealers were Scots
or New Englanders, but the logistics of the Montreal trade, the labour on
which it relied, and even the organization of trading companies remained
much as they had been under the French. As before, the system was inherently expansionistic as it competed with, and sought to encircle, the HBC
position on the Bay. In 1778-79 Peter Pond, a Connecticut Yankee who had
traded west of Lake Michigan before being drawn into the competitive
Montreal trade, crossed the Methy portage between the Saskatchewan and
Mackenzie River systems and established a post on Lake Athabasca, opening up the fur-rich watershed of the Mackenzie River. A decade later the
Scot Alexander Mackenzie descended the Mackenzie to the Arctic Ocean,
in so doing establishing the outer limit of the fur trade east of the Cordillera
and outflanking the HBC around a vast crescent. Having little choice but

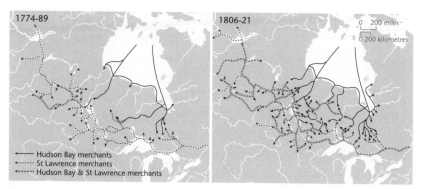

MAP 10.2   Trade routes in the northwestern interior, 1774-89 and 1806-21 | After D.W. Moodie, V.P. Lytwyn, B. Kaye, and A.J. Ray, in Harris and Matthews, *Historical Atlas of Canada*, vol. 1, plate 61.

to respond to such advances, the HBC established its first major inland post in 1774, Fort Cumberland on the Saskatchewan River, eight hundred kilometres southwest of York Factory; thereafter, it struggled to catch up to the Montreal traders in the interior. Map 10.2a shows the evolving geographical positions of the two trading systems before 1789.

In the years between the mid-1760s, when the Montreal trade resumed, and the 1821 merger of the North West and Hudson's Bay Companies, intense commercial competition dominated the fur trade of the northern interior and, in many ways, the livelihoods of all the peoples living there. Even the natural environment was profoundly affected. Competition took place, both between the HBC and the Montrealers, and within the Montreal trade itself. As it resumed in the 1760s, the latter was a miscellany of partnerships and small firms that quickly consolidated into a few more powerful ventures, most conspicuously the North West Company (NWC), which became a general co-partnership in 1779 and a loosely organized company eight years later. As the logistics of trade became more elaborate and costly, they tended to weed out the weaker companies and partnerships. By 1804 the NWC had absorbed all its Montreal-based competitors. Thereafter, a monopoly based on Hudson Bay and another based on the lower St. Lawrence engaged in a bitter, frequently ruthless competition for the fur trade of the northern interior.

These were years when the trade was managed with increasing precision as companies built supply depots and coordinated the timing of brigades and the distribution of trade goods and provisions over vast distances and among an escalating number of trading posts. The North West Company put schooners and sloops on Lake Superior, and developed a large lake canoe, the *canot du maître,* which held up to three tons of freight and crews of six to fourteen. Less experienced with canoes and lacking accessible supplies of birchbark, the HBC put wooden *bâteau* and boats on the major rivers, craft that carried more freight than the canoes but were more difficult to portage. Increasingly, as it moved farther inland, it purchased Native-built canoes and hired experienced voyageurs, usually Métis or French Canadians. Both trading systems competed by building trading posts. In 1774 there had been 17 posts in the northern interior; in 1821 there were 109 (Map 10.3a). In the intervening years, some 600 were built, almost all of them in the boreal forest or parkland and most operated for only a few years. Sometimes rival posts stood side by side. By 1800 the HBC was building almost as many as the NWC; in 1815 it was able to penetrate the Athabasca district (Mackenzie watershed), the richest corner of the northern fur trade, there to establish several posts that, although unprofitable, broke the NWC monopoly. With extended and overlapping trade routes and many duplicated posts, competition between the two companies became fierce to the point of violence. In 1818 the HBC sent an expeditionary force of almost two hundred men to protect its newly acquired position in the Athabasca district, and on the Grand Rapids of the Saskatchewan River it deployed a cannon and two swivel guns to arrest seven wintering partners of the NWC and confiscate their furs. Map 10.2b, which shows the HBC and NWC trade routes in the northwestern interior between 1806 and 1821, suggests something of the intensity of the competition between them.

This bitter commercial struggle was played out among Native populations decimated by increasingly frequent epidemics. The most severe of them was a smallpox epidemic that broke out in Mexico City in 1779 and reached Santa Fe early in 1781. From there it moved rapidly northward as it entered the equestrian trading system of the plains and the associated raiding and fighting (horses moving north, guns south). As it left the grassland for the boreal forest and the horse for the canoe, it moved more slowly. Smallpox arrived on the northern plains in the summer of 1781 when a war party of Cree, Assiniboine, Blood, Piegan, and others contracted the disease from dying Shoshone warriors in what is now southern Alberta. At about the same time, it entered the Red River area when a war party of Cree, Assiniboine, and Ojibwa attacked infected Hidatsa and Mandan

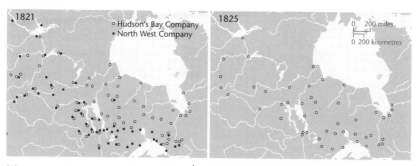

MAP 10.3   Fur posts in 1821 and 1825 | After D.W. Moodie, V.P. Lytwyn, and B. Kaye, in Harris and Matthews, *Historical Atlas of Canada,* vol. 1, plate 62.

settlements on the Missouri. Two years later it had reached the forest-tundra margin, and eastward well along the north shore of Lake Superior. The disease missed only a few bands; some were entirely wiped out. The historical geographer Paul Hackett, the most thorough analyst of the early epidemics in the northwestern interior, estimates that it killed half to three-quarters of the Ojibwa living west of Lake Superior and three-quarters of the Woodland Cree. The HBC trader Samuel Hearne estimated that it had killed 90 percent of the Chipewyan living near Fort Churchill. Precise mortality rates will never be known, but the smallpox epidemic of the early 1780s was, undoubtedly, a human catastrophe of unimaginable proportions, the background event that, more than any other, underlies the modern history of western Canada.

The common effects of such depopulations are known – the loss of cultural memory and confidence, the amalgamation of remnants of different groups, the relocation of people in depopulated space, new geopolitical balances of power – but the effects among particular groups in the northern continental interior of the smallpox epidemic of the early 1780s are exceedingly difficult to work out. Some Native populations rebounded quickly; others did not. It is likely that depopulation accelerated the rate at which European traders advanced inland (as it had, for example, after the collapse of Huronia) because there were suddenly fewer Native middlemen. This, in turn, probably eliminated weaker traders who could not sustain the costs of expansion. The extraordinary proliferation of posts was an effect of competition, but also, it would seem, of an epidemic that had undermined Native populations and trading systems and had affected the nature of competition itself.

The expansion of posts placed traders from Montreal or Hudson Bay close to the source of furs. Native hunters and trappers could now reach fur posts themselves and could usually trade with either company. They no longer dealt with Cree or Assiniboine middlemen. In these circumstances, white traders gave more presents, extended credit more liberally, and offered more for furs. The northwestern interior was flooded with European trade goods, and as European traders competed for furs, they relied, more than ever, on present-giving and addictive non-durables. Native demand for consumer durables remained relatively inelastic, but the trade in alcohol and tobacco increased dramatically. Travelling shorter distances to the posts, Native traders had more time to linger there to drink and smoke, and could take more away with them. Often, on hearing that they were in the vicinity, traders would leave their post to intercept Native bands and lure them to trade with tobacco and liquor. Casks of alcohol returned to Native settlements; as alcohol abuse became common, the authority of elders probably diminished while that of the Native traders who brought alcohol and tobacco increased. In such conditions, trade was often turbulent. In the Mackenzie Valley, NWC traders, frustrated at their inability to collect debts incurred by Chipewyan hunters, captured and sold Chipewyan women. In 1807 one NWC trader on the Mackenzie wrote in despair: "Indolence, robbery and murder are the consequences of an opposition in trade: people would suppose it would rouse their attention to industry, having goods at a lower price, but far to the contrary; drunkenness, idleness and vice are preferred ... no good can be derived from the turbulent struggles of opposition in this country; it destroys trade, creates vice, and renders people crafty, ruins good morals, and almost totally abolishes every humane sentiment in both Christian and Indian breast."

The proliferation of posts and the growing number of fur trade employees increased the demand for provisions, principally for meat and fish. Employees worked long hours and ate heavily: the ration for a man was seven to nine pounds of fresh meat or fish a day, or one and a half pounds of pemmican (dried bison meat flavoured with berries). With an average of some fifteen hundred men employed annually in the northern interior fur trade between 1790 and 1820, the demand for provisions was met by fishing, fowling, and hunting deer, moose, and caribou but principally by taking bison in the grassland. To this end the traders built provisioning posts in the parkland, and many Cree and Assiniboine, no longer accustomed to trapping or required as middlemen, became bison hunters and provision traders. To maintain control of this new trade, they often burned the grassland around the posts in the parkland, intending thereby to keep the bison out of reach of post employees.

This commercial reorientation, combined with the epidemics, shifted the locations of the Native peoples of the parkland and adjacent boreal forest. The Assiniboine abandoned the Red River Valley and the boreal forest to the east, becoming, essentially, people of the grassland and parkland, competing for bison with others to their south and west. The Cree left the large territory between Lake Superior and Lake Winnipeg, the interlake region of Manitoba, and the Assiniboine Valley; many of them moved southwestward into the parkland and slightly into the grassland. In the north, the Chipewyan occupied territory abandoned by the Cree. The Ojibwa moved massively westward, into land depopulated by the epidemics and by the Cree and Assiniboine displacements. Theodore Binnema has shown that on the northwestern grassland, where both guns and horses had become widely available after 1780, the balance of power shifted away from a southern alliance dominated by the Shoshone to a northern alliance dominated by the Blackfoot, who had direct access to firearms, a huge military advantage that they were able to protect for several decades. The Kutenai, a foothills people whom the Blackfoot kept from the trading posts, were killed or forced across the mountains.

While these broad movements were taking place, beaver and big-game animals such as caribou and moose were becoming scarce throughout most of the vast forested lands south of the Churchill River and west of James Bay. The progressive elimination of beaver in the southeastern corner of this huge territory, the Petit Nord as the traders called it, is shown in Map 10.4. Beginning in the 1780s, the NWC and its Montreal-based rivals imported Iroquois hunters from the lower St. Lawrence and equipped them with steel traps and castorium (bait made from peri-renal beaver glands) to forestall competition by stripping a region of its beaver. Increasingly specialized Native economies probably exerted a more pervasive ecological influence. When Native people could no longer supply their own needs for foodstuffs, clothing, and tools, they had no recourse but to their trading posts. Their livelihoods became doubly dependent: on goods the supply of which depended on access to tradable quantities of furs or provisions. In these circumstances, the diversified, mobile, sharing economies

MAP 10.4 Depletion of beaver in the Petit Nord |
After V. Lytwyn, in Harris and Matthews, *Historical Atlas of Canada,* vol. 1, plate 63.

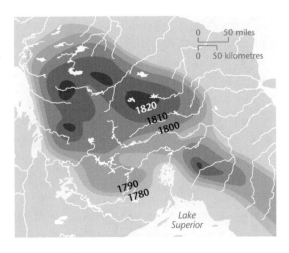

that had long sustained the peoples of the region weakened, while Native peoples' growing dependence on specialized commercial economies focused the ecological relationships that still underpinned their livelihoods. As economies came to depend on particular animals, they were over-hunted. Scarcity became chronic rather than occasional. Nor, Arthur Ray points out, had Native societies the institutional means to deal with such scarcity. If one band reduced hunting or trapping to conserve beaver or deer, another would exploit them – an accepted sharing when economies were varied and scarcity was localized and intermittent, but potentially devastating when economies depended on a particular resource. A result, Ray suggests, was the decline of intergroup sharing, less mobility, and more local territorial defensiveness. Within their more defined territories, people often came to rely on small animals such as hare that were subject to extreme population cycles. In short, throughout most of the woodland and parkland, the ecological basis of Native life was being undermined. On the grassland, however, the availability of bison, and the many uses to which the animal could be put, probably allowed groups that had recently moved there to reduce for a time their dependence on European traders and their goods.

It was amid these increasingly tumultuous circumstances that a Scottish aristocrat, Lord Selkirk, dropped a settlement of Highland Scots at Red River in 1812. His plan for a settlement at Red River was partly philanthropic – to alleviate the plight of Highlanders dispossessed by the clearances – and partly to provision HBC posts while creating a place to which company servants and their Native or Métis wives might retire. He and two partners had recently purchased a controlling interest in the HBC, and the shareholders had awarded him a huge fee simple land grant – 116,000 square miles – and even agreed that the company would transport colonists. The first contingent, mainly from the Hebrides and Ireland, arrived at Red River in 1812; Presbyterian Highlanders from Kildonan (near the northeastern tip of mainland Scotland) arrived two years later. In three years, some three hundred people, among them women and children, were relocated in the middle of a continent. Landscapes never previously seen in the northern interior began to appear along the banks of the Red River: tiny log cabins on the levees along the river, patches of cultivated land, and the beginnings of long-lot farms (Map 10.5), a cadastral system introduced from Lower Canada by the governor of the colony, Miles Macdonnell.

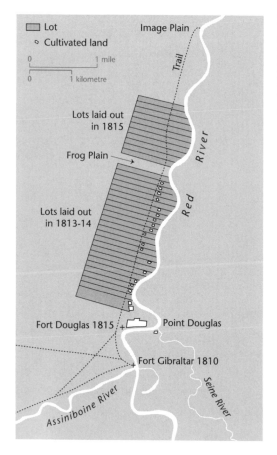

MAP 10.5   Red River settlement, 1816 | After B. Kaye, "Some Aspects of the Historical Geography of the Red River Settlement from 1812 to 1870" (MA thesis, University of Manitoba, 1967), 33.

From the perspective of the NWC, the Red River colony threatened its transportation and provisioning systems – therefore its existence; for the Métis it seemed to threaten their way of life. In 1814 Macdonnell had forbidden the running of buffalo from horseback, the basis of the Métis hunt. For both the Nor'Westers and the Métis, the settlement was better eradicated, and NWC traders pressed willing young Métis to harass it. The events that followed are part of the lore of western Canada. The burning of cabins and fields; the 1815 conveyance by the NWC of some 140 intimidated settlers to Canada; the 1816 battle at Seven Oaks between settlers and Métis in which twenty-one men under the new governor, Robert Semple, were killed; the expeditionary force of some eighty mercenary soldiers (mainly German and Swiss), commanded by Selkirk, that set out from Canada, captured Fort William, the NWC entrepôt on Lake Superior, and reached Red River in 1817, where Selkirk reasserted his authority. He signed a treaty with representatives of the local Cree, Assiniboine, and Ojibwa for, as he understood it, the extinguishments of their land titles, the first of many such treaties and their associated misunderstandings in western Canada. He induced most of the mercenaries (known as the de Meurons) to stay. Selkirk had stabilized his colony. It would continue to exist, though in these years the Red River settlers depended as much on bison hunting and fishing as on farming. Confronted with an environment radically different from any they had known, none of them knew quite what to grow or how to grow it, many lacked agricultural experience, and supplies of tools and seed were inadequate.

These events at Red River served to focus attention on the Métis as a distinct people. Liaisons between Native women and European men had always been part of the fur trade, but for years the offspring of these matches were raised in Native societies and became, effectively, Native people. By the mid-eighteenth century, many of the Homeguard Cree near HBC posts on the Bay were of mixed descent, although, as historian Sylvia Van Kirk has pointed out, the HBC (and presumably also the Cree) did not yet distinguish between degrees of Indianness. The Montrealers sent men to trade in Native settlements, even to over-winter there, and their security usually depended on marriages to the daughters of prominent Native men. Some of them stayed in the west, living with Native people when their terms of service expired and becoming known as *hommes libres* (freemen).

With attachments to both trading posts and Native society, they were useful intermediaries in the Montreal fur trade during its most competitive years. When freemen families began to live apart from Native bands and together, for at least part of the year, with other such families, and when their progeny tended to intermarry, the conditions for the emergence of a distinct people were at hand. By the 1790s, proto-Métis groups (descended from Assiniboine or Cree mothers and Canadian fathers) lived along the forested edge of the parkland. Other children of mixed marriages were raised at the fur posts, there to receive primarily European upbringings; a few lads were sent east for more formal educations. Yet another source of people of mixed descent lay west of Lake Michigan where, in the aftermath of the wars and dispersions of the 1640s and '50s (Chapter 4), refugee Native women and French traders had created much the same cultural and economic hybridity that was emerging in the parkland a century later. As the pressures of American settlement mounted early in the nineteenth century, some of these people migrated to Red River.

By the beginning of the nineteenth century, both HBC and Montreal traders increasingly distinguished people of mixed descent from Natives. They employed them in positions in which they would not employ Natives, and married them in preference to Native women. In 1806, in an attempt to economize by reducing the population at its posts, the NWC forbade its servants to marry Native women but accepted Métis women. Recognizing their own separateness, the Métis marked it in various ways, as, for example, in their dress. And so, when NWC traders determined to harass the Selkirk settlers (and perhaps to drive them away), there was an identifiable group to turn to. The Métis leader, Cuthbert Grant, was an articulate, educated man, and his success at Seven Oaks only strengthened an emerging Métis identity.

Yet, in 1821, on the eve of the HBC-NWC merger, the northern continental interior remained overwhelmingly Native space. Some six hundred settlers lived at Red River, and well over two thousand employees worked in 109 active fur posts east of the Rockies (Map 10.3a). Even in these most European spaces, however, there were many Native influences. Many of the employees at the posts were Métis; almost all the traders and many of the men had a country wife – a Métis or Native woman. These women, as Jennifer Brown and Sylvia Van Kirk have shown, provided essential domestic labour and links between European and Native traders; they were also partners for lonely men and mothers for their children. Some of these relationships were casual and fleeting, others deep and enduring. Although outliers of commercial capital, the posts contained internal spaces of cultural hybridity. Beyond the posts, the HBC claimed the vast territory draining into Hudson Bay by right of its royal charter of 1670, and Lord Selkirk's heirs (Selkirk had died in southern France in 1820) claimed his 116,000-square-mile land grant from the company, but these were paper rights with little reality on the ground. Various Native peoples and a small but growing number of Métis still occupied the land and used it in many traditional ways.

Their lives, however, had been profoundly unsettled by disease, heightened warfare associated with the differential introduction of firearms and horses, and alcohol. Many of the territorial dislocations apparent before 1760 had been intensified. The Cree and Assiniboine had left the Red River Valley, which, together with territory to the Saskatchewan River and beyond, the Ojibwa had reoccupied. The Ojibwa were forest people who lived in small bands, depended on the fur trade and a little horticulture, and made almost no use of the grassland. The Assiniboine had moved westward, occupying most of what is now southern Saskatchewan, there continuing the age-old seasonal movement between parkland and grassland. The Western Cree had lost territory in the north to the Chipewyan but had expanded southward, and some bands along their southern margin lived at the parkland-grassland interface, much like the Assiniboine (Map 10.6a). Game animals had become scarce throughout much of the boreal forest, and many groups there depended on the fur posts for seasonal employment and provisions. The eastern range of the bison had contracted, but on the grassland farther west, where bison were still abundant, people were more autonomous. The Blackfoot, well equipped with guns and horses, were formidable warriors. Yet, little stability existed anywhere. In 1821 most of the peoples in the northwestern continental interior were reeling from the almost simultaneous arrival, during the two previous years, of measles and whooping cough, the combined effects of which had been almost as severe as of the smallpox epidemic forty years before. In the whole northwestern continental interior, the population cannot have been more than about twenty thousand. There were far fewer people

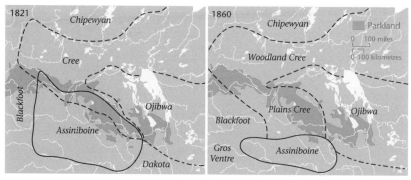

MAP 10.6   Distribution of Native peoples in 1821 and 1860 | After A.J. Ray, *Indians in the Fur Trade*, 2nd ed. (Toronto: University of Toronto Press, 1998), 101, 184.

in most places – particularly in the boreal forest – than two hundred years before.

MANAGING LAND AND LIFE AFTER 1821

Pressured by the British government and by the ruinous costs of competition, the HBC and NWC merged in 1821. It was a balanced merger – the proprietors of the HBC and NWC each received the same number of shares – but the name of the Hudson's Bay Company was retained, as were its headquarters in London. Essentially, as historian Gerald Friesen and others have pointed out, the arrangement combined the administrative and financial stability of the HBC with the Nor'Westers' field experience. It replaced competition with monopoly, and placed a young North American governor, George Simpson, in charge of a huge trading empire.

Simpson was a relentless manager who was determined to rationalize and stabilize what he considered an extravagant, wasteful trade. To do so, he set out to reorganize not only the company's internal procedures but also its relations with Native people and theirs with the environment. In the interest of efficiency, he closed the long and costly route west from Montreal, which for almost two hundred years had linked Canada with the upper Great Lakes and beyond. Henceforth, the northwestern interior was to be connected to London via Hudson Bay. By 1825 he had closed more than half the posts in the northern interior (Map 10.3b), in the process cutting the fur trade labour force by as much as two-thirds and creating the trading post geography that would approximately survive for the next fifty years and more. He sought to reduce, or even eliminate, present-giving, and considered that traders had extended credit too liberally. They were instructed to curtail both. He thought that the company should offer cheaper, lower-quality goods, and that, following the term of the company's charter of 1821, it should curtail the trade in alcohol. Knowing that much of this agenda depended on monopoly, he relaxed it wherever trade was competitive. Such was the case in the parkland and northern grassland, where the company required supplies of pemmican obtained from Native traders and felt the competition of American traders on the Missouri. It also obtained in the boundary country between Red River and Lake Superior, where American traders were also operating. Farther north, where the HBC monopoly was secure and Native people had little choice but to trade on company terms, more of Simpson's reforms were put into effect. Yet, by the 1860s, even groups living on the grassland could not obtain alcohol from the HBC – a failure greatly to the encouragement of American whisky traders who established posts in what is now southern Alberta. Overall, monopoly reduced the price of Native furs while increasing the stability of trade. As the years went by and competition increased in the south, the company's monopoly became more porous without dissolving into the competitive fury of the years before 1821.

Simpson also undertook to stabilize the fur trade's ecological foundations. He tried to discourage the summer hunting of beaver and to encourage the trapping of other species. He banned steel traps and castorium, except in competitive border areas, and shut some posts to discourage trapping nearby. In 1826 he established a quota system based on an average of a post's fur returns over the previous three years. Except in competitive areas, he allowed traders to take only a fifth to a half of the previous average. And, recognizing the difficulty of managing the resource use of mobile trappers, he sought to establish Native people in defined, bounded territories, a project that envisaged a drastic reorganization of Native lifeworlds and land uses. Taken together, these measures were an early attempt – perhaps the first of its kind in North America – to manage a primary resource on a sustained yield basis.

Bold and comprehensive as it was, Simpson's conservation program faced daunting challenges in the dispersed cross-cultural world of the fur trade. First was the problem of competition. Simpson's measures could work only in monopoly conditions: where they did not prevail, competitors would reap the short-term benefits from, and in so doing quickly annul, any ecological gains. Yet, even where the HBC monopoly prevailed, his conservation measures usually failed. Company traders themselves, knowing that promotion depended on successful trade and fearing the loss of trade to other company posts, tended to relax the rules. Native hunters shot beaver in summer because food was scarce, and would do so whether or not company traders accepted such furs. They were often fatalistic about conservation, assuming that animal populations depended on Manitou and propitiatory rites, not human actions. Moreover, in the conditions of scarcity that prevailed in much of the northwestern interior, if one group did not take available animals, another would. When game was relatively plentiful and people ranged across considerable territories within economies of multiple occupations, such actions were accepted and reciprocated. No coercive Native institutions existed to prevent them. Later, when food was scarce and European trade goods were required, people took what they could, and local ecological monopolies could not be enforced. Simpson's model of bounded Native territories fit best where people relied on local populations of fish and hare, but even there bounded lives dependent on animal populations subject to cyclical downturns faced periodic starvation. The boreal forest no longer supported the human population it once had, and in these circumstances longer-term plans for conservation faltered on the immediate needs of survival as, in much of the contemporary world, they still do.

As Arthur Ray has pointed out, a new ecological system was emerging in the boreal forest. Once, small Aboriginal bands had depended on a variety of resources obtained by seasonal migrations within well-known territories; now, Native people increasingly relied on imported goods obtained at the fur posts. Elements of older ways remained but were pressured by ecological scarcity and by company traders who considered Native labour better deployed in pursuit of furs rather than food. In the earlier years of the fur trade, the social costs of reproducing Native labour had been largely borne by Native society, but as the ecological basis of Native life faltered, the company increasingly assumed them. In this way, Native labour became ever more enmeshed in the nodes, circuits, and long-distance ecological relationships of the world economy. The connection, however, was frail and uncertain. The company often had difficulty securing enough labour, and Native people enough provisions to live by. As the isolation of the peoples of the boreal forest diminished, infectious diseases arrived in increasing variety and frequency, and with particularly harsh consequences among malnourished people. Moreover, many peoples of the boreal forest moved south towards the parkland and grassland, where more food was available, or, especially the Métis among them, to the Red River settlements. To hold its labour force, the company had little alternative but to be generous with credit (even to the point of forgiving debts), provide summer employment for reliable hunters, and practise, in effect, an early form of social welfare. Company traders, many of whom had relatives and friends in Native society, dispensed medicines, vaccinated against smallpox, and provided relief in times of starvation. Many did what they could, but when an age-old ecological system had largely broken down, and another, of which the traders were a part, had provided a precarious alternative, there was only so much they could do.

Even on the grassland, the ecological basis of Native livelihoods was increasingly threatened. Simpson's closure of posts and release of employees (mostly Métis) after 1821 diminished the HBC demand for provisions and increased the competition for bison and the contracted provisioning market, as former employees of the fur trade moved southward. During the 1820s and 1830s, the annual Métis bison hunt ranged ever farther to the southwest, a caravan of people, horses, oxen, and Red River carts (Figure 10.2). Responding partly to this pressure, the Assiniboine moved farther out onto the plains, becoming essentially a grassland people straddling the international border and trading more at American posts on the Missouri than at HBC posts in the parkland. With cheap water access to St. Louis and the Mississippi, American traders had developed a lucrative business in bison robes, trading in some years as many as 200,000 of them – a venture in which the Red River Métis began to participate when they opened a cart trail to St. Paul in 1844. In the face of these hunting pressures, the bison herds contracted steadily westward. By the late 1820s they were uncommon in southwestern Manitoba; by the 1850s bison were rarely seen along the Saskatchewan River. The staple that, for thousands of years, had sustained the peoples of the grassland and parkland was disappearing.

Almost everywhere in the northwestern interior, epidemic diseases had increased in frequency and variety as isolation from the eastern North

FIGURE 10.2 *Half Breeds Travelling* (detail), sketched in 1846, painted 1848-56 (artist, Paul Kane). An amazing picture of one of the largest bison hunts and of the mobile, in-between world of the Métis. | With permission of the Royal Ontario Museum © ROM, 912.1.24.

American disease pool diminished. In the 1820s and 1830s in one of the remotest corners of the continent, the Kutchin, an Athapascan people whose territory extended from the lower Mackenzie River across much of what is now the northern Yukon and well into northeastern Alaska, were ravaged by repeated epidemics of largely unidentifiable diseases. Smallpox, however, was partly contained. The HBC supplied traders with vaccines, and the diffusion of the disease reflected the pattern of their work. Late in 1837 smallpox entered the northern plains from Fort Union on the Missouri but was checked in most of the parkland and boreal forest by vaccination. On the grassland, where people were more isolated from company posts, the mortality rate reached virgin-soil proportions. Company traders estimated that up to three-quarters of the Assiniboine died; in what is now southern Alberta, similar rates of mortality were reported among the Blackfoot, Blood, Sarsi, and Piegan. Such depopulations opened space for the Cree. By 1860 the Plains Cree occupied virtually all the central parkland and adjacent grassland (Map 10.6b). Warfare accompanied all such relocations.

Until the early nineteenth century, profit-seeking commercial capital and disease provided the principal momentum to change livelihoods and ecologies in the northwestern interior. Beginning in 1818, when two Roman Catholic priests reached Red River, another vector of European

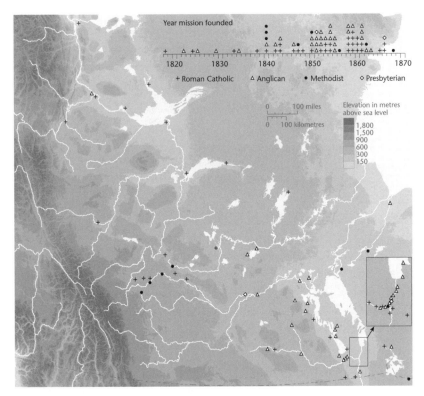

MAP 10.7   The establishment of missions | After D.W. Moodie, B. Kaye, and V.P. Lytwyn, in *Historical Atlas of Canada*, vol. 2, *The Land Transformed*, ed. R. Louis Gentilcore, cart. Geoffrey J. Matthews (Toronto: University of Toronto Press, 1993), plate 17.

influence arrived, this one interested in the conduct of human bodies and the fate of their souls. Protestant missionaries, most of them Anglican, soon followed. The first missions were among the Red River settlements, but well before 1870 others had opened throughout the parkland and even along the Mackenzie River. The graph accompanying Map 10.7 shows when different churches established missions, and the map show where. Many, of course, were short-lived.

Although missionaries of different faiths competed vigorously with each other, they held much in common. All thought that their church possessed the truth, and that other beliefs were in error. Possessed of the truth, they had, as it were, a particular access to God and His kingdom. This was an incalculable blessing that not only gave them confidence to go to the corners of the earth but imparted urgency to their going. The fate of souls – the glories of heaven or the fires of hell – hung in the balance. Most of them thought that the people they had gone to save were God's children and in this sense were the same as anyone else. Departing from prevailing currents of mid-nineteenth-century European thought, they did not hold that there were immutable racial differences (of intelligence or sensitivity, for example) that would prevent their converts from becoming full beneficiaries of the joys and rewards of Christianity. In this sense, they were not racists. But they did think that alongside the tenets of Christian theology was the civilized Christian life to which, as they did their work, savagery would yield. Moreover, the Christian life could be observed, as Christian belief could not, which is why in the cross-cultural world of the missionary, where thoughts were always somewhat inscrutable, the former readily became a marker for the latter. And so, to the extent that they could, the missionaries watched. They were moralists on the lookout for sin, particularly for sins of the flesh. In the missionary world of truth and error, there was not much room for compromise. Native beliefs were pagan idolatry with which there could be no accommodation, and Native lives were to be remade into Christian ones that, with denominational shades of emphasis, derived from European ideals and models.

The preferred missionary space was the Christian village, a sedentary residential space where lives were anchored in the routines of farming and where people could be taught and watched. In the view of the missionaries, and of most other Europeans of their day, nomadic ways were savage. They were conducive to laziness and sin, for which the spatial remedy was the sedentary life. Most of the Catholic priests in the northern interior were Oblates, an order founded in southern France in 1818 and bitterly opposed to the urban, secular materialism of nineteenth-century France. The Oblate vision was retrospective – a priest surrounded by a faithful peasantry – a vision that shaped the order's mission work in France and accompanied Oblate priests to North America. Moreover, the Oblates had been trained in seminaries where all group activities were monitored, and this too, this discipline of watching, accompanied them. Where they could, they established agricultural villages; where they could, they watched. If they could not be present (most of them served several missions) they appointed watchmen, and sometimes watchmen of the watchmen. In these regards the Anglicans were little different.

Mission villages were difficult creations. Many Native people had nothing to do with the missionaries; many others associated with them only to benefit from playing one denomination against another. Missionaries often found that the only way to reach Native people was to travel with them; in such cases the model of the mission village had completely broken down. Even the HBC became suspicious of missions, considering them (with some justification) to be sites from which free traders operated to the company's detriment. Yet the missionaries persisted, and over the years more of their missions stuck. They were sites where Native people learned the rudiments of farming and (as the missionaries understood it) the basis of a civilized Christian life. Children learned some English or French. The Christian calendar was observed and biblical stories learned and interpreted in the light of denominational theologies. As far as possible, shamanism and the Native spirit world were banished. New disciplines and moral codes were imposed. In some missions, the church bell marked out the day. In all of them, polygamy became a mortal sin. The small log houses on the missions – homes for families – reflected a sexual politics focused on the patriarchal nuclear family sanctioned by Christian marriage.

As they created and served their missions and struggled with innumerable hardships, many missionaries gave most of their lives to Native people, a giving intended to reconfigure Native minds and civilize Native bodies by sharing Christian truths. The extent to which minds and bodies were remade is another matter. For an increasing number of Native people, there were good reasons to pay some attention to the missionaries. When other subsistence systems were failing, the missionaries taught agriculture. They provided medicines that tended to work. In a world that Native people understood to be infused with spirit-beings, they offered a bridge to white spirit power. But had Native people become Christian, and what in the northern interior of North America in the mid-nineteenth century could conversion mean? After years in their mission fields, some missionaries concluded, ruefully, that they had not made one true convert. Recent scholarship usually suggests that their work resulted in syncretic beliefs that blended Christian and Native understandings, or that grafted the former on the latter. However this is understood, it is clear that during a time when Native economies were collapsing, the missionaries introduced a comprehensive, sustained assault on Native cultures together with retrospective and somewhat utopian European alternatives to them.

RED RIVER AFTER 1821

After the arrival of some forty French-speaking Canadians in 1818 (recruited by the first Catholic missionaries) and of some 170 Swiss in 1821 (recruited by Selkirk's agents), the population at Red River grew almost entirely by natural increase or from the resettlement of people already in the northern interior. Of the latter, there were two groups: the first were former HBC servants, usually Orkneymen, and their Native or mixed-blood wives and children; the second were mixed-bloods of primarily French paternity moving to Red River from the grassland or parkland or, in 1824, upriver from Pembina when it became clear that the Métis settlement there was south of the border. On the other hand, the de Meurons and Swiss soon drifted away to the United States, the last of them driven out by flooding in 1826. In the 1840s some of the original Scottish settlers or their descendants left as well. In these circumstances, Red River became predominantly a Métis colony. An 1856 census recorded some sixty-five hundred people distributed as shown on Map 10.8. Scots or English Métis lived in the parishes along the Red River north of the Assiniboine, and French Métis, with whom the few Canadian settlers had blended, in St-Boniface, St-Norbert, and the three parishes along the Assiniboine.

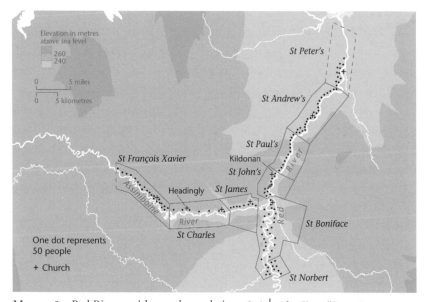

MAP 10.8   Red River parishes and population, 1856 | After Kaye, "Some Aspects of the Historical Geography," 134, 151.

Some of the Red River settlers squatted on unsurveyed land, but more of them obtained land grants of approximately a hundred acres in return for an annual rent of five bushels of wheat and a few days of work on the public roads. They could also purchase land outright for five shillings an acre. When the Hudson's Bay Company took over the colony's administration in 1835, such purchases became standard. Map 10.5 shows the earliest surveys, a cadastral system derived from the lower St. Lawrence that would dominate the colony until 1870. When allocated, the lots were usually two miles deep (the width of the band of land that Selkirk had obtained by treaty from the Cree and Saulteaux) and less than a hundred yards wide. Settlers supplemented the narrowest lots by purchasing additional strips to make potentially viable farms. When the river was the principal artery of communication and the prairie was judged unfit for agricultural settlement (tough sod and little water and wood), the long-lot system had many advantages. As in Canada during the French regime, it allowed people to live on their own land yet close to neighbours. It shared access to the river and to the timber that grew along it, to building sites and well-drained soils along the levee, and to hay in the grassland behind. As in early Canada, it led to continuous ribbons of settlement, to "a long serpentine village" as one visitor put it. Nowhere was this new countryside more than one farm deep.

The Red River settlement developed where the market for agricultural produce was weak; where hunting and, to a more limited extent, fishing, yielded large quantities of food, some of which could be processed and sold; and where some men could obtain seasonal employment from the HBC as boatmen (tripmen). During the earliest years, when farming was hardly established, everyone depended heavily on hunting and fishing, but by the early 1830s a mixed and largely subsistence economy prevailed in which the household was the basic unit of production and the maintenance and replication of the household the basic aim. As in peasant economies elsewhere, the household depended on the sale or barter of some surplus, which, at Red River, was obtained by modest sales to the HBC of agricultural produce, processed bison meat, or labour.

In these circumstances, farms were small and diversified with, on average, not much more than an acre of cultivated land per person. A good-sized field was five acres. Wheat was the principal crop, and yields were high for many years on the fine-grained riverine loams where most farming took place, but demand was small. Barley was also a field crop, and most of the hardy European vegetables were grown in kitchen gardens. Most farmers had a few cattle, perhaps a couple of oxen, perhaps a horse, perhaps a few sheep, perhaps some pigs and chickens. This was mixed farming of, broadly, a northwest European type, but with rudimentary tools, scrawny, unbred stock, and little or no crop rotation. As elsewhere in pioneer settings, land was substituted for labour. In June and July most people left these farms – leaving behind the elderly, a few women, a few children, and the Kildonan Scots – to hunt bison on the plains. In the earliest years, bison could be taken close to Red River, but by the 1820s the herds were farther away, and expeditions were mounted to hunt them. By 1840 the expedition had become a caravan of twelve hundred Red River carts and more than fifteen hundred men, women, and children (Figure 10.2). The organization and technologies of these hunts, which reached ever farther onto the plains and often provoked fighting with the Sioux, combined Cree, Assiniboine, and European ways. Their products, dried and pounded bison meat (pemmican) and bison robes, were either consumed by the Métis domestic economy or traded to the HBC. A second, usually smaller hunt took place from late September to early November and returned with large quantities of frozen meat. Later in November some Métis took whitefish in Lake Winnipeg or Lake Manitoba, where in April and May some hunted duck and geese. In the 1830s, the HBC employed some two hundred to three hundred Métis each summer as boatmen.

It has long been held that the French Métis were particularly given to hunting and fishing, and the British Métis to agriculture, but historian Gerhard Ens has recently shown that in the 1830s and early 1840s the economies of both groups were similar. British Métis participated in the bison hunts as much as the French, and the farms of both French and British Métis were much the same. For both groups, a mixed, mobile economy of multiple occupations worked approximately as intended. It provided livings for families (Figure 10.3). In any given year, one element of the economy might fail, but overall there was usually enough to eat and enough firewood for winter (if, after a time, more difficult to gather). Much as in Acadia a century and more before, Red River in the 1830s and early 1840s was a place where livings could be found, but markets were weak. Given the surviving data, the birth rate in Red River in the 1830s cannot be reliably calculated, but the mortality rate, particularly the infant mortality rate, was slightly lower than in rural Quebec and much lower than in most of peasant Europe. As Ens puts it, "dearth, extreme poverty and dire necessity, which characterized peasant life in Europe, were not nearly as prevalent in Red River." Compared, for example, to what the Kildonan settlers had known in Scotland, there was relative opportunity for the poor, and the social hierarchy was much compressed. The colony's elite were retired HBC officers and the clergy, but the poor had gained livelihoods, and there was little to attract or create wealth. The expansion of settlement was driven by demographic rather than commercial pressures. In 1857 an officer at Red River put it this way: "the demand [for land] arises from the increase of families; the families increase very largely, and the original allotments are too small, and they go further up the Assiniboine as squatters ... because when the family is too large for the estate they go off and take land, and squat themselves in some instances." As well as space for farming, the landed (resource based) opportunity at Red River included bison hunts on the plains, fishing and fowling at Lake Winnipeg and Lake Manitoba, even tripping for the HBC.

In 1844 six ox carts from Red River reached St. Paul on the Mississippi, the beginning of a southward trade in bison robes that broke the HBC monopoly on the northern plains and created new commercial opportunities there. In 1865 fourteen hundred Red River carts made this trip, carrying merchandise (mainly bison robes) worth $300,000. Independent

FIGURE 10.3   *Manitoba Settler's House and Red River Cart,* c. 1870 (artist, William Hind). The house at the right (and probably the one on the left) is of Red River frame construction, that is, pièce sur pièce en coulisse, introduced from the lower St. Lawrence. The Red River cart, shown here, also served on the bison hunts. |
Library and Archives Canada, 1937-283-1.

traders established themselves at Red River, and the HBC itself became a major buyer of robes. Bison robes, the focus of this trade, were tanned on one side and retained the thick winter hair of the bison on the other. Hides, at their best from late November to February, when the bison's coat was thickest, required a great deal of work to create a tanned and supple robe. The result was a valuable commodity that could be obtained by family labour. It was immediately attractive to the Red River Métis, particularly to the French Métis, many of whose families had long histories as middle-men in the fur trade.

As some Red River Métis families became involved in this trade, they began to over-winter on the plains *(hivernants)* close to the bison. Their economies became more specialized as hunters, artisans, or in some cases highly successful traders. Their social hierarchies became more complex and longer. Because it was easy for young men to become bison hunters and because a great deal of family labour was required to dress bison hides, the marriage age dropped and family size increased. Women associated with the bison trade and who survived their reproductive years, had, on average, ten to twelve children, two or three more than women situated in predominantly agricultural economies at Red River. They were also more likely to speak Cree, Assiniboine, or Michif, a Métis language that combined French, Cree, and Assiniboine. And, as the trade in bison robes became a successful (and for some a highly profitable) means of social reproduction, it entailed a disengagement from sedentary agriculture at Red River. In the parish most involved with this trade, the amount of cleared land per person dropped by half from the mid-1830s to the mid-1850s. Indian corn ("horse teeth" corn), squashes, melons, and tobacco introduced from the Mandan and Hidatsa villages on the Missouri were planted in hills on some of the remaining patches of cultivated land, then usually left untended. Eventually, the bison were so far west that a choice had to be made: either to farm at Red River or to relocate closer to the bison. In 1866 only 150 carts left Red River on the summer buffalo hunt. The bison were five hundred miles away. In these circumstances about six hundred Red River Métis, the majority French Métis, emigrated westward in the 1850s and 1860s.

In spite of their departure, between 1856 and 1870 the population in the older parishes along the Red and Assiniboine Rivers almost doubled, and settlement expanded as shown on Map 10.9. In these years a few

English Canadians arrived, most of them settling well up the Assiniboine River near Portage La Prairie. A few farmers began using new farm equipment imported from St. Paul, Minnesota, and experimenting with improved rotations and new seeds. A few American merchants arrived and some American soldiers, deserters from frontier posts. But, essentially, the older economies and ways of life at Red River remained in place. There were still bison hunts far out onto the plains, if far less productive than formerly because the bison herds were disappearing; fishing and fowling still took place at Lakes Winnipeg and Manitoba. Agriculture remained small-scale, mixed, and largely subsistent. If anything, the HBC market had contracted. Until almost 1870 there was no village anywhere in the Red River settlements, a measure of the weakness of the commercial economy. Trade in plains provisions and agricultural produce still took place

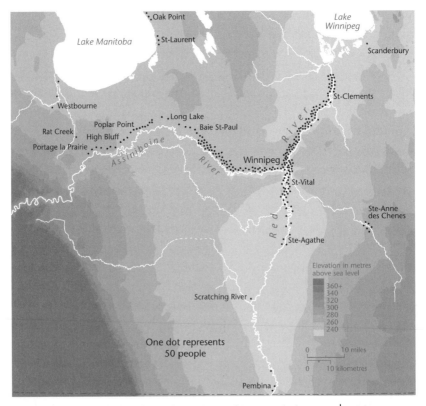

MAP 10.9   Distribution of population in southern Manitoba, 1870 | After maps by Kaye, "Some Aspects of the Historical Geography," 228-29.

at the HBC posts. But, as the population in the Red River settlements grew and the bison disappeared, the balance of the older economies had shifted towards agriculture, which, in the changing ecological and demographic circumstances of the 1860s, was becoming the only viable longer-term option for most people in the Red River settlements. In the Métis parish of St-Laurent at the foot of Lake Manitoba, where there was little agriculture, the balance shifted towards fishing.

NEW VISIONS IN THE 1850S AND 1860S

The evolving worlds of fur traders, Native people, and Métis in the northwestern interior had been sheltered somewhat by distance and also by the perception that the whole enormous region was bleak and largely worthless. If British critics of the HBC's monopoly had long argued that a secretive company fearful of competition had hidden the region's resources, particularly its agricultural potential, from outside eyes, their rhetoric almost always outran their evidence. In fact, the environment of the northwestern interior was very little known. As late as the mid-1840s, the prevailing view was that the region was a vast inhospitable wilderness suitable for a few Native people and fur traders but not much else. Its north was too cold for settlement, its south too dry. Treeless grasslands were thought to reflect a level of aridity that made agriculture impossible. Such a region could not be a settlement frontier. The settlement at Red River was seen as an oasis in what an early Anglican missionary called "dreary wilds," and a later one "an immense region of barbarism." In such imagery, moral and physical wildernesses compounded each other.

By the late 1840s, as historian Doug Owram has shown, this perception began to change, especially in the view of a small but influential group of Canadians, most notable among them George Brown, editor of the *Toronto Globe*. The northwestern interior began to be seen as an extension of Canada with a future beyond the fur trade, and there was the first talk, albeit visionary at this stage, of a railway through British North America to the Pacific. It began to be said that by channelling trade through Hudson Bay, the HBC had broken Canada's historic connection with the northwest, a connection pioneered by the French and maintained by the NWC. After 1821 the wealth to be derived from the continental interior had not reached Canada, whereas eastern American towns had benefited from rapidly expanding continental hinterlands. As settlement in what is now southern Ontario pushed to the margin of the Canadian Shield in the late 1840s and 1850s (earlier in Quebec), it became increasingly apparent that, by continental standards, Canada was a narrow, confined space bounded by an international border, rock, and cold. The prosperity that had accompanied the rapid immigration to and settlement of the southern Ontario peninsula seemed about to stall. Such a prospect anticipated an increasingly pinched British imperial position in North America, even the annexation of the British colonies by the United States. It suggested that commercial opportunities would stagnate. Towns would not grow, because their hinterlands were fixed; immigrants would turn elsewhere; and many of the rural young would leave. Expansion into the North West, the common term in the Canadas for the northern plains, was increasingly seen as the remedy for such ills. The vision of a few in the late 1840s, it became commonplace in Canadian commercial and political circles by the mid-1850s. In 1857 when a Select Committee of the British House of Commons accepted the principle that Canada annex the northern interior, the debate was largely over. Even HBC officials knew that the company's charter monopoly of trade would soon end.

There was still, however, much uncertainty about the nature of this vast region, and specifically about its suitability for agriculture. Its southern parts, where agriculture seemed most feasible, were situated between land that was either too cold or too dry to farm. In such circumstances, and with limited climatological data, the margins of potential agriculture were subject to widely differing calculations. More information was needed; to get it both the British and colonial Canadian governments sent scientific expeditions into the region in 1857, the one headed by Captain John Palliser, a member of the Irish gentry, the other by Simon J. Dawson, a civil engineer, and Henry Youle Hind, a professor of geology and chemistry at Trinity College, Toronto. Both expeditions were to assess the potential of the grassland and parkland beyond Red River for agricultural settlement. The British expedition was in the field for three years, the Canadian for two. Their reports replaced broad, prior generalizations with much more nuanced descriptions of the physical geography of these areas while establishing a stark but accessible and essentially attractive land classification. Following them, the terms "Palliser's Triangle" and the "Fertile Belt" were incorporated in expansionist rhetoric. The former was, essentially, the shortgrass prairie region in what is now southwestern

Saskatchewan and southeastern Alberta, which both expeditions identified as an extension of the Great American Desert and considered unfit for agricultural settlement. The latter, an arc of land between the full boreal forest and the shortgrass prairie, stretched from Red River to the Rocky Mountains (Map 10.10). Hind described it as, potentially, both a continuous corridor for agricultural settlement and a unique opportunity, given that westward advance in the United States was everywhere checked by desert. Therefore, he remarked, a railway along the Fertile Belt "will eventually enjoy the great advantage of being fed by an agricultural population from one extremity to the other." More than 11 million acres of prime agricultural land awaited cultivation. Both he and Dawson described them rhapsodically:

> Such a country as we have passed through to-day I have never before
> seen in a state of nature. The beautiful green of the rolling prairie, the
> trees rising in isolated groves, looking at a distance as if laid out by
> the hand of art, and the blue hills bounding the prospect, presented a
> picture pleasing in itself and highly interesting when considered in
> relation to the future. It required no great effort of the imagination in
> weary travelers to see civilization advancing in a region so admirably
> prepared by nature for its development, to picture herds of domestic
> cattle roaming over plains still deeply furrowed with the tracks of the
> buffalo, which with the hunters who pursued them have disappeared

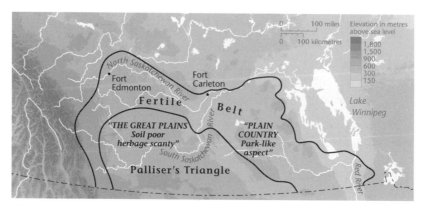

MAP 10.10   Palliser's Triangle and the Fertile Belt | Modified from Doug Owram, *Promise of Eden: The Canadian Expansionist Movement and the Idea of the West, 1856-1900* (Toronto: University of Toronto Press, 1980), xi.

forever; or to plant cottages among groves which seemed but to want them, with the stir of existence, to give the whole the appearance of a highly cultivated country.

Statements like this, which coupled ebullient environmental description with a picture of the northwestern continental interior as a tabula rasa – a clean slate to be written on by settler society – only fuelled expansionist enthusiasm. They began to draw a few Upper Canadian settlers to Red River, all of them committed to the view that the region was a rightful and inevitable theatre for Upper Canadian expansion. Behind them was the increasingly widespread understanding that the progress and destiny of British North America, and the future greatness of Canada, were tied to these lands. The case had been made and accepted in principle in Britain, and now was borne out by scientific analysis. The only remaining questions, apparently, were when and precisely how these lands would be transferred to Canada. Of course, the hunters who pursued buffalo had not disappeared forever (Figure 10.4). Their erasure was textual. Native people

FIGURE 10.4   *Blackfoot Indian Encampment, Foothills of the Rocky Mountains,* c. 1870 (artist, William Armstrong). The Blackfoot, living in what is now southwestern Alberta, were less affected by the fur trade than other Native peoples in the northwestern interior. In this picture, the Blackfoot are shown to have incorporated horses, Red River carts, guns, and iron cauldrons – all introductions – in their own lifeworld. |
With permission of the Royal Ontario Museum © ROM, 952.169.1.

FIGURE 10.5   *Main Street, Winnipeg,* 1871 (artist, E.J. Hutchins). The marks of a new order, neither Native, nor Métis, nor associated with the fur trade. | Library and Archives Canada, 1997-125-2.

remained throughout the northern interior, the Métis were well established in several settlements, and the largely Métis settlement at Red River was growing rapidly. From the vantage point of Toronto, Red River now seemed a staging point from which British North American settlement would expand westward through the Fertile Belt (Figure 10.5), a vision that contradicted the human geography that had emerged on the ground.

THE NORTHWESTERN INTERIOR ON THE EVE OF CONFEDERATION

By the late 1860s, and long before in many areas, the northwestern interior had become primarily fur trade territory. Native people remained the principal population and still possessed almost all the land, but their livelihoods had become enmeshed in the particular system of commercial capital that over the previous two hundred years had increasingly dominated this huge region. Many of them still hunted, fished, and gathered, and often relied on knowledge and technologies that were centuries old, but these activities now sustained what had become, in effect, the dispersed labour force of the fur trade. Hunting, fishing, and gathering both contributed to the subsistence and reproduction of this labour force and generated products that Native people traded for the European goods that had become essential for their survival. Commercial and subsistence economies were integrated with each other within a fur trade economy that, as historical geographer Frank Tough has shown, allocated labour time and sustained local populations while generating income for a trading company.

The fur trade economy was both local and global. Locally, economies were dominated by particular fur posts and their requirements of labour, provisions, and furs. Local posts employed some Native people seasonally.

Others traded there, negotiating credit and bringing provisions or furs to exchange for foodstuffs and European manufactures. Because these post-oriented economies were situated in different environments and in different positions in the transportation hierarchy of the HBC, they involved different patterns of seasonal activities – but activities always oriented around the production or transportation of furs. Map 10.11, which shows the activities that circled around Norway House about 1870, suggests how complex and interrelated they had become. Located at the northeastern corner of Lake Winnipeg on the route from York Factory, Norway House was a district headquarters, a relay point in the HBC transportation system, a centre of York boat construction, and a trading post in its own right. An integrated local economy revolved around it. With large demands for green wood (for boat building) and firewood, hay (for the oxen used to haul wood), food, and labour, it depended on local gardens and a large regional supply of labour, materials, and provisions, as well as on furs, most of which were supplied by Native people from the Methodist mission village nearby and by others living in the bush. At York Factory, twice as large an establishment as Norway House, twenty to thirty men were employed just to cut the three thousand cords of firewood required each winter and to transport them from as much as 120 miles away.

Like other posts, Norway House was also integrated in a trading system that linked it to London, England, on the one hand, and far into the northern interior on the other. Its position in these larger circuits is shown schematically in Map 10.11. The fur trade drew on the products of boreal forest, parkland, and grassland, and in the late 1860s still did so within a pre-industrial transportation technology dependent on manual labour. The HBC operated some eighty York boats on routes inland from York Factory, and the rhythm of life at many posts was marked by the coming and going of brigades of these boats. With seven or eight men to a boat, the brigades were large employers of Natives and Métis – who pulled at heavy oars for hours on end or, at portages, hauled cumbersome boats and carried two-hundred-pound loads. This was impossibly gruelling work for as much as sixteen or eighteen hours a day (few tripmen lived to fifty), but when other options were closing down it provided a livelihood of sorts. Together with canoe or horse brigades where York boats could not reach, such labour bound the HBC trading system from the Bay to the Rockies.

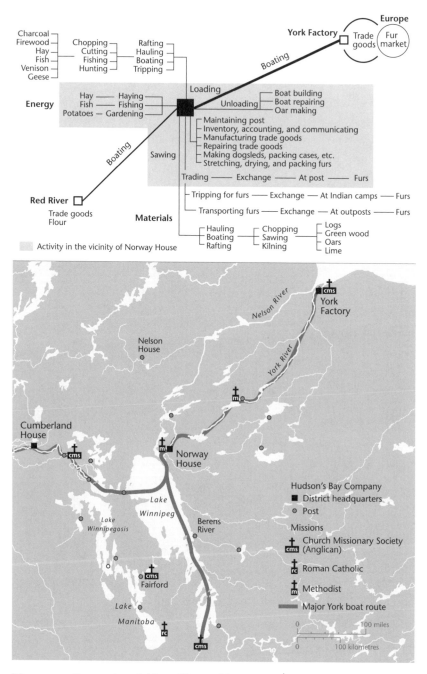

MAP 10.11 Economic activities at Norway House, 1870 | After Frank Tough, "*As Their Natural Resources Fail*": *Native Peoples and the Economic History of Northern Manitoba, 1870-1930* (Vancouver: UBC Press, 1996), 2, 22.

Although the system was still profitable, by the late 1860s neither it nor the old hunting, fishing, and gathering economies that it had replaced were able to sustain the Native peoples of the northern interior. As a Cree chief put it starkly a few years later, "our country is no longer able to support us." Bison, which had become scarce in southwestern Manitoba in the 1830s, were scarce in much of the parkland by the 1860s. The HBC began carting in food for Native people at places where, not long before, it had obtained its principal supplies of pemmican. In effect, environmental depletions had spread from the boreal forest through the parkland and onto the grassland; dependency followed in their train. The chief was right. His people could no longer live as they had; nor could most other Native people in the northwestern interior. Pre-fur-trade economies could not be retrieved, in some cases because requisite skills had been lost but principally because their ecological bases had been undermined. The fur trade provided diverse employments, credit, and welfare, but not enough year in and year out to sustain even the reduced Native populations that still inhabited the boreal forest. In some years people got by, in some years not, and when they did not they starved.

An alternative, however, had emerged in the many Métis settlements in the northwestern interior, and particularly along the Red and Assiniboine Rivers where, by the late 1860s, there were almost ten thousand Métis, about a thousand whites, and a few hundred Native people. Virtually all the Métis and Natives at Red River, and a good many of the whites, had been born in the northwestern interior. They were a rapidly expanding population, most of whom had grown out of the fur trade but were increasingly detached from it. These settlements shipped a large variety of provisions to Norway House, but in any given year many of the growing number of small farms in the Red River settlements sold nothing, and the others very modest quantities. The rationale for these farms, and for the hunting and fishing that were often associated with them, was less their commercial connection with the fur trade than the subsistence they provided for the families they fed and housed. For all the problems of early frosts, drought, grasshoppers, fires, and floods, they were successful in this respect, as the rapid growth of the Red River population suggests – from six hundred families in 1835 to more than twenty-five hundred in 1870. Amid the difficult conditions of the late fur trade years, a niche had emerged for the social reproduction of families. There were more limited steps in the same direction at some of the missions. These were agricultural econo-mies of a sort, more so as the bison disappeared. Judged from the east, however, they were not the right type of agriculture; nor were most of its practitioners the right type of people. These deeply racialized judgments, situated in another culture and place, had every potential to override what by the late 1860s had become the most vibrant creation of the evolving and often calamitous circumstances of land and life in the northwestern interior over the previous century.

BIBLIOGRAPHY

For the purposes of this chapter, the points of departure are *Historical Atlas of Can-ada*, vol. 1, *From the Beginning to 1800*, ed. R. Cole Harris, cart. Geoffrey J. Matthews (Toronto: University of Toronto Press, 1987), plates 57-65; *Historical Atlas of Canada*, vol. 2, *The Land Transformed*, 1800-1891, ed. R. Louis Gentilcore, cart. Geoffrey J. Matthews (Toronto: University of Toronto Press, 1993), plates 17-18; and Gerald Friesen's fine regional history *The Canadian Prairies: A History* (Toronto: University of Toronto Press, 1984), chaps. 1-7.

The analysis of the fur trade presented above, and of Native-European relations associated with it, has been substantially influenced by Arthur Ray's research and writing, more particularly by his *Indians in the Fur Trade: Their Role as Trappers, Hunters, and Middlemen in the Lands Southwest of Hudson Bay, 1660-1870* (1974; repr. with a new introduction, Toronto: University of Toronto Press, 1998); "Periodic Short-ages, Native Welfare, and the Hudson's Bay Company, 1670-1930," in Shepard Krech III, ed., *The Subarctic Fur Trade: Native Social and Economic Adaptations* (Vancou-ver: UBC Press, 1984), 1-20; and "Some Conservation Schemes of the Hudson's Bay Company, 1821-1850: An Examination of the Problems of Resource Management in the Fur Trade," *Journal of Historical Geography* 1, 1 (1975): 49-68. Whereas Ray writes from the perspective of Hudson Bay, a useful analysis of the geopolitical ramifica-tions of the trade from the perspective of the northwestern grassland is Theodore Binnema, *Common and Contested Ground: A Human and Environmental History of the Northwestern Plains* (Norman: University of Oklahoma Press, 2001). The distri-bution of trading posts as the HBC expanded inland is described by D. Wayne Moodie, "The Trading Post Settlement of the Canadian Northwest, 1774-1821," *Journal of His-torical Geography* 13, 4 (1987): 360-74. Issues of family and gender, briefly treated above, are explored in two works that have become Canadian classics: Jennifer S.H. Brown, *Strangers in Blood: Fur Trade Company Families in Indian Country* (Vancou-ver: UBC Press, 1980); and Sylvia Van Kirk, *"Many Tender Ties": Women in Fur Trade Society, 1670-1870* (Winnipeg: Watson and Dwyer, 1980). An argument that HBC servants considerably shaped the terms of their employment is in Edith I. Burley, *Servants of the Honourable Company: Work, Discipline, and Conflict in the Hudson's Bay Company, 1770-1879* (Toronto, New York, and Oxford: Oxford University Press, 1997). Frank Tough's powerful description, from a political economy perspective, of conditions in northern Manitoba about 1870 underlies the above analysis of the late fur trade economy: *"As Their Natural Resources Fail": Native Peoples and the Economic History of Northern Manitoba, 1870-1930* (Vancouver: UBC Press, 1996), chaps. 1 and 2.

The most comprehensive study of the arrival of infectious epidemic diseases in the northern interior is Paul Hackett, *A Very Remarkable Sickness: Epidemics in the Petit Nord, 1670 to 1846* (Winnipeg: University of Manitoba Press, 2002). See also Shepard Krech III, "On the Aboriginal Population of the Kutchin," *Arctic Anthropology* 15, 1 (1978): 89-104; reprinted in Kenneth S. Coates and William R. Morrison, eds., *Interpreting Canada's North: Selected Readings* (Toronto: Copp Clark Pitman, 1989), 53-76.

Much useful information about the establishment of missions is in works such as Father Gaston Carrière, O.M.I., "The Early Efforts of the Oblate Missionaries in Western Canada," *Prairie Forum* 4, 1 (1979): 1-25; Robert Choquette, *The Oblate Assault on Canada's Northwest* (Ottawa: University of Ottawa Press, 1995); or J.F. Klaus, "The Early Missions of the Swan River District," *Saskatchewan History* 17, 1 (1964): 60-76. The short account in this chapter is also influenced by the more theorized analyses in Brett Christophers, *Positioning the Missionary: John Booth Good and the Confluence of Cultures in Nineteenth-Century British Columbia* (Vancouver: UBC Press, 1998); and Lynn A. Blake, "Let the Cross Take Possession of the Earth: Missionary Geographies of Power in Nineteenth Century British Columbia" (PhD diss., Geography, University of British Columbia, 1997). Carolyn Podruchny's essay "'I Have Embraced the White Man's Religion': The Relations between the Peguis Band and the Church Missionary Society, 1820-1838," in D.H. Pentland, ed., *Papers of the 26th Algonquian Conference* (Winnipeg: Algonquian Conference, 1996), 350-78, is an excellent case study of missionary activity at Red River. A fine survey of the context of mid-nineteenth-century missionary thought is Julie Evans, Patricia Grimshaw, David Philips, and Shurlee Swain, *Equal Subjects, Unequal Rights: Indigenous Peoples in British Settler Colonies, 1830-1910* (Manchester and New York: Manchester University Press, 2003), especially chap. 1.

The classic, and now highly controversial, work on the Métis is Marcel Giraud, *Le Métis Canadien: son Rôle dans l'Histoire des Provinces de l'Est* (Paris: Institut d'Ethnologie, 1945), but the most comprehensive recent account of Métis economy and society is Gerhard J. Ens, *Homeland to Hinterland: The Changing Worlds of the Red River Metis in the Nineteenth Century* (Toronto: University of Toronto Press, 1996). On the genesis of the Métis, see Heather Devine, "Les Desjarlais: The Development and Dispersion of a Proto-Métis Hunting Band, 1785-1870," in Theodore

Binnema, Gerhard J. Ens, and R.C. MacLeod, eds., *From Rupert's Land to Canada: Essays in Honour of John E. Foster* (Edmonton: University of Alberta Press, 2001), 129-58; and John E. Foster, "Wintering, the Outsider Adult Male and the Ethnogenesis of the Western Plains Métis," *Prairie Forum* 19, 1 (1994): 1-13; reprinted in Binnema, Ens, and MacLeod, *From Rupert's Land to Canada*, 179-92. On Métis agriculture, see W.L. Morton, "Agriculture in the Red River Colony," *Canadian Historical Review* 30 (December 1949): 305-21; Barry Kaye, "Some Aspects of the Historical Geography of the Red River Settlement from 1812 to 1870" (MA thesis, University of Manitoba, 1967); and, particularly on the British Métis, Robert Coutts, *The Road to the Rapids: Nineteenth Century Church and Society at St. Andrew's Parish, Red River* (Calgary: University of Calgary Press, 2000). An article by Nicole St-Onge, "Variations in Red River: The Traders and Free Métis of Saint-Laurent, Manitoba," *Canadian Ethnic Studies* 24, 2 (1992): 1-21, is a reminder of the variety of Métis experience. Her more recent book *Saint-Laurent Manitoba: Evolving Métis Identities, 1850-1914* (Regina: Canadian Plains Research Centre, 2004) provides a fuller picture. Irene Spry, "The Great Transformation: The Disappearance of the Commons in Western Canada," in Richard A. Allen, ed., *Man and Nature on the Prairies*, Canadian Plains Studies 6 (Regina: University of Regina, Canadian Plains Research Centre, 1976), 21-45, is an overview by a wise economic historian.

Eric Ross' charming book *Beyond the River and the Bay: Some Observations on the State of the Canadian Northwest in 1811 with a View to Providing the Intending Settler with an Intimate Knowledge of That Country* (Toronto: University of Toronto Press, 1970) is both a regional description and a study of perception. D. Wayne Moodie examines eighteenth-century perceptions of agricultural potential in "Early British Images of Rupert's Land," in Allen, *Man and Nature on the Prairies*, 1-20. Doug Owram provides a fundamental analysis of changing eastern Canadian views of the west on the eve of Confederation in *Promise of Eden: The Canadian Expansionist Movement and the Idea of the West, 1856-1900* (Toronto: University of Toronto Press, 1980), chaps. 1-3. John Warkentin has gathered texts of explorers, travellers, and surveyors, including the essential Palliser and Hind texts, in *The Western Interior of Canada: A Record of Geographical Discovery, 1612-1917*, Carleton Library No. 15 (Toronto: McClelland and Stewart, 1964).

11

British Columbia

Europeans reached the coast of what is now British Columbia late in the
eighteenth century, almost three hundred years after the eastern landfalls
of Columbus and Cabot and well after the first industrial factories were
operating in Britain. Their coming ended the long isolation of this coast
from an expanding European civilization and altered age-old lifeworlds.
During the hundred years between 1770 and 1870, the Native population
declined by perhaps 90 percent, commercial and industrial capital arrived,
and two settler colonies were established. Native people began to be allocated small reserves, while their former lands were opened for development. Even the face of the land began to change, but slowly because neither
settlers nor capital could reach most of this huge Cordilleran territory. In
1870, they were largely arranged along a single corridor from the coast to
the interior, beyond which was drastically depopulated Native land.

This changing human geography was the product of the introduction
of diseases, capital, settlers, and the values, technologies, and institutions
that accompanied them, to an altogether un-European space (Chapter 1).
It had no single trajectory. Outside influences reached different parts of
the Cordillera at different times and in different ways, and with different
consequences. Yet there were patterns in the way that power was exercised
in early modern British Columbia, and they are the subject of this chapter.

THE PRECOLONIAL YEARS

In the mid-1770s, the Spanish-Mexican explorers Juan Pérez and Bodega
y Quadra sailed cautiously along the outer coast of British Columbia,
looking for, but not finding, the Russians whom Spanish diplomacy had

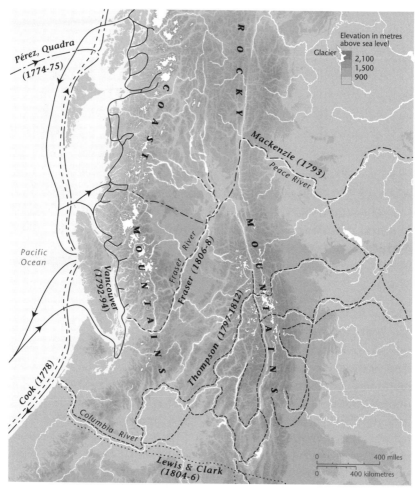

MAP 11.1 Principal European explorations in the Cordillera, 1774-1811 | After R. Ruggles, in *Historical Atlas of Canada*, vol. 1, *From the Beginning to 1800*, ed. R. Cole Harris, cart. Geoffrey J. Matthews (Toronto: University of Toronto Press, 1987), plate 67.

reported there (Map 11.1). In 1778 Captain Cook, the commander of an expedition authorized by the British Admiralty, put in at Nootka Sound on the west coast of Vancouver Island to repair his ships before heading north in search of a passage to the Atlantic thought to lie at about 60°N (Figure 11.1). These expeditions established the general configuration of the coast, and in the early 1790s Captain Vancouver's meticulous surveys, also for the British Admiralty, filled in many of the details. A remote, convoluted coastline came into European focus and drew subsequent investigations. The Montreal fur trade entered the northern Cordillera from the east in 1793 when Alexander Mackenzie ascended the Peace River (arctic drainage), portaged to the Fraser River (Pacific drainage), and turned west on Native trails to touch the Pacific Ocean at the end of a long fjord. Convinced he had found a viable trade route, Mackenzie returned to Montreal and London to lobby for a Pacific depot for trans-Pacific trade with China – an early nineteenth-century vision of a northwest passage. A dozen years later Simon Fraser, another Montreal-based trader/explorer, established four posts on or near the upper Fraser River; in 1808 he descended this river to its mouth, in so doing realizing that it was not the Columbia as he had thought, and that it was too turbulent to serve as a trade route. In 1811, David Thompson, more geographer than fur trader, did reach the mouth of the Columbia after reconnoitering a southern pass through the Rockies and the river's complex upper watershed. Several years before, the Americans Lewis and Clark had come by a more southerly route (Map 11.1).

In these ways outsiders entered lands previously unknown to them, recorded something of what they saw, and transmitted reports and maps back to distant "centres of calculation" where they began to affect economic and geopolitical decisions (Chapter 2). Other introductions, with immediately devastating local effects, were invisible from afar. Around the large inlet he named Puget Sound (site of modern Seattle), Vancouver found a depopulated land and saw pockmarks on the faces of some of the few people he encountered. Fraser saw similar faces in a Fraser Canyon village. Thompson understood that the Kootenai, the people he met after crossing the Rockies, had once been numerous and had been decimated by smallpox. Apparently, there were two late eighteenth-century smallpox epidemics (Map 11.2). In the 1770s, an epidemic probably associated with Russian traders in Alaska spread south as far as the Queen Charlotte Islands. In 1781 or 1782 a pandemic that originated in Mexico City in 1779 and decimated most peoples in the northern continental interior (Chapter 10) crossed the Rockies and infected populations throughout the Columbia drainage, along the coast north to the Strait of Georgia (between Vancouver Island and the mainland), and some distance up the Fraser River. These epidemics reached populations with no previous history of smallpox (what epidemiologists call virgin-soil epidemics). Years later an elderly Native man on the lower Fraser told the ethnographer Diamond

FIGURE 11.1   *View of the Habitations in Nootka Sound* (detail) (engraving by Samuel Smith from drawing by John Webber, 1778). With Cook's arrival in Nootka Sound, the British Admiralty and Enlightenment science dropped into a Native world. Here a British longboat and crew are depicted with Native people on a beach below a sizable plank-house village. | Captain James Cook and Captain James King, *A Voyage to the Pacific Ocean*, vol. 2 (London: Lords Commissioners of the Admiralty, 1784), 313.

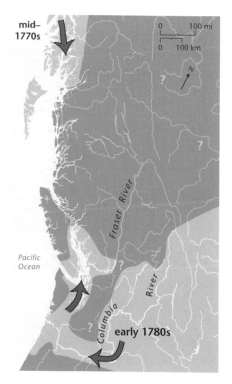

MAP 11.2   Smallpox epidemics, eighteenth century | After C. Harris, "Social Power and Cultural Change in Pre-colonial British Columbia," *BC Studies* 115-16 (1997-98): 52.

Jenness of houses and villages where everyone died and claimed that, over-all, three-quarters of his people had perished. Possibly he was right.

Commercial capital, another powerful agent of change, accompanied or shortly followed these depopulations. Some of Cook's men obtained a few sea otter pelts in Nootka Sound, and then were astonished by the prices they fetched in China. When this news was published in England, a trade that the Russians in Alaska had quietly conducted for years became public knowledge. James Hanna, the first English sea otter trader, reached the northwest coast in 1785, the beginning of the maritime fur trade along the coast of British Columbia. Commercial capital arrived a little later in the interior. Mackenzie's plans for a Pacific base and trans-Pacific trade were beyond both the daring of North West Company officials in Montreal and the capacity of the rival company Mackenzie formed to challenge them. Only in 1804, when the North West Company absorbed its rival (the XY Company) and the North West Company directorship changed, did it become possible to extend the Montreal fur trade into northcentral British Columbia. Simon Fraser's posts there were like hundreds of others farther east, part of an experienced trade that had originated along the St. Lawrence River some two hundred years before (Chapters 2 and 4).

The maritime fur trade had none of this experience behind it. During its short life – the sea otter were seriously depleted by 1820 – there were some 650 sailings to the northwest coast, most by captains who made the trip only once or twice. For the English who arrived first, or the New Englanders who dominated the trade by 1800, the northwest coast was forbidding, alien territory that was the better part of a year away. They sailed, therefore, with commercial intelligence that was some two years old, and dealt with Native people they hardly knew – although trading pidgins and mixed-blood children soon appeared. They established no forts, and in the early years ships often travelled in pairs, one the well-armed protector of the other. Their object was to acquire sea otter pelts and to sell them in China; a successful voyage could yield a profit of several hundred percent. From a Native perspective, these traders and their goods appeared to have dropped from the blue. They disrupted former alliances and trading patterns as people scrambled to reposition themselves to take advantage of new sources of wealth. Overall, the trade had a frenetic quality as greed drew together people who misunderstood and deeply distrusted each other.

It moved quickly through the spaces of the coast, first depleting the sea otters on the outer coast and then entering the more difficult fjorded waters of the inner coast. It rapidly bid up the price of trade goods: a sea otter pelt worth about a seventh of a musket in the late 1780s was worth three muskets in 1802. It injected an enormous quantity of new goods into Native economies, principally blankets, iron goods of various sorts, copper, firearms, cloth, liquor, and foodstuffs. In 1802 American traders obtained some fifteen thousand sea otter pelts, which at the prices then current on what the traders called the Queen Charlotte Islands (Haida Gwaii) was equivalent to forty-five thousand muskets or seventy-five thousand blankets.

Recent studies of the maritime fur trade emphasize its violence. Here and there, Natives attacked ships and, by relying on surprise, occasionally took poorly equipped or carelessly defended vessels. Ship captains were not above flogging Native people, clapping them in irons, or holding them for a ransom to be paid in sea otter pelts. A few of them turned cannon, loaded with grapeshot, on flotillas of Native canoes, or bombarded and burned Native villages. Such violence may be understood as a byproduct of the precarious economics of a trade that could yield spectacular profits, or yield nothing because traders had brought goods that were no longer in demand. In such circumstances, a political economy of violence made some sense. If trade could not squeeze pelts out of coastal peoples, violence might, especially as most traders would never return to the northwest coast and would not have to deal with the consequences of their actions. A captured chief brought a ransom. Floggings or killings reminded people of what might happen if they did not trade. A bombardment that drove people from a village gave traders its contents. Historian Mary Malloy and historical geographer Daniel Clayton also suggest that the maritime fur trade operated within what might be called a culture of terror. Shipboard society itself, Malloy notes, was violent. Clayton suggests that the northwest coast begins to look like the jungles along the Putumayo, an Amazon tributary, during the rubber boom where, anthropologist Michael Tausig has shown, traders and Natives interacted in violent incomprehension, terror acquired a life of its own, and torture and killing ceased to be rational acts. Northwest coast violence never matched that along the Putumayo, but violence and terror probably did acquire their own momentum there. The ingredients were at hand: a shipload of tough men, accustomed to violence and dropped on an unsuspecting Native village, a frightened captain firing on apparently threatening canoes, Native revenge meted out on the next whites to come along (more evidence of blood-thirsty savages), more killings in response. Terror and violence, intertwined and ongoing.

Native economies and polities responded immediately to the maritime fur traders, as individuals and groups sought to reposition themselves to take advantage of new opportunities and to secure the best prices for the goods offered. In the process, the spatial economies and geopolitics of coastal life were substantially reworked. Those who lived near the places where traders converged usually did well, at least initially. Larger geopolitical alignments fared better than small ones. Some chiefs who were particularly shrewd and well positioned amassed great wealth and prestige, and redistributed unprecedented quantities of goods at feasts. Others lost status. Some groups were absorbed into new geopolitical alignments or were wiped out in wars. Responses were exceedingly uneven. But it seems clear that the maritime fur trade introduced and concentrated new wealth, emphasized the power of some chiefs, houses, and tribes, and provoked some bloody inter-Native wars and slaving raids in which, as elsewhere across North America, the uneven possession of firearms conferred advantage. Over all this activity hung the uncertainties of capital moving quickly through the spaces of the northwest coast, exhausting the resource that drew it in the first place and responding to an outside calculus of profit and loss.

With the increased concentration of wealth, Native feasts became much larger, though there is no evidence for the suggestion that the inter-village feast (potlatch in the Chinook trading pidgin) was invented at this time. Many thousands of blankets, increasingly the standard gift, might be given away at a single feast – just as, as anthropologist Lisette Josephides has shown, pig feasts in the New Guinea Highlands became more extravagant after contact than anyone could remember. The long-held view that totemic carving increased seems to be correct. Iron tools may have made carving easier, and chiefs with new wealth on their hands were in a position to commission new poles. Disease, which opened up places in social hierarchies, and the pressures of trade, which destabilized alliances and status positions, required new affirmations of status that were reflected in a competition of poles in front of villages.

In the interior, traders struggled with distance and, in the south, with a radically unfamiliar environment. Fraser's posts in the north were still within the boreal forest and could just be reached by canoe from Montreal, but to the south in the Columbia basin, where John Jacob Astor, a New York businessman, established his Pacific Fur Company in 1811-12, the fur trade encountered semi-desert that was out of transcontinental range. Astor intended that his main depot at the mouth of the Columbia would be supplied by sea and, following Mackenzie's vision, would enter the China trade – a scheme that, perched in hostile Native territory and mismanaged from afar, quickly ran out of time. With news of the War of 1812, disaffected senior partners on the Columbia sold the company's goods and furs for $80,000 to the North West Company, which then found itself with posts and personnel in a trading territory like no other in its experience. Long stretches of its rivers were impassable, even after the first epidemics Native people along the lower Columbia were numerous and little given to hunting, and the difficulties of mountain passes coupled with distance made it almost impossible to supply the region overland from Montreal. Over the next several years, the company struggled to adjust to these conditions, often continuing practices the Astorians had introduced. It experimented with packhorses and riverboats. It brought in supplies by sea, in so doing establishing trading connections with Monterey (Mexico), Sitka (Alaska), and the Sandwich Islands (Hawaii). It brought in Hawaiian workers (Kanakas), and in 1815 a contingent of Canadian Iroquois whom it began to organize into trapping brigades, intending thereby to bypass local fishing peoples little interested in hunting. By 1820 it was supplying the northern posts, a region traders had come to call New Caledonia, from the south via the Columbia. The distribution of trading posts established before 1821 (Map 11.3) suggests something of the magnitude of this commercial effort as a Montreal-based company attempted to manage trade in an unfamiliar environment on the other side of a continent. As it turned out, the China trade was the company's Achilles heel. The East India Company, which held a monopoly of British trade with China, allowed the NWC to ship furs to China but not to take goods away; in a few years the company lost about £40,000 on its China ventures, a loss, historian Richard Mackie notes, that contributed to its merger with the Hudson's Bay Company in 1821.

When the HBC took over the land-based fur trade in the northern Cordillera, the whole region – the Oregon Territory – had recently become a free trade area open to British and American traders (Chapter 5). Americans controlled the coastal trade south of the Russians in Alaska and, as sea otter became scarce, increasingly traded for land furs, thus competing with the company's posts in New Caledonia. For the Hudson's Bay Company, and particularly for George Simpson, governor of its Northern Department, commercial and imperial interests converged as he sought to create a profitable trade and to eliminate Americans from a region intended to become a secure theatre of British trade. Simpson's plans were elaborate and, as Richard Mackie has shown, most of them worked. Posts were expected to raise most of their own food. American competition was largely eliminated by hunting out beaver south and east of the Columbia, engaging in severe price competition there and along the coast, building coastal forts and, in the 1830s, placing a steamer (the *Beaver*) on the coast. New Caledonia and the Columbia District were combined into the Columbia Department, and supplied by sea. New objects of trade – principally lumber, salmon, and flour – were aggressively developed, mostly with Native or Hawaiian labour. On the other hand, Simpson's plan to make the Fraser the principal artery of trade, and Fort Langley, the fort established near its mouth in 1827, the company's main Pacific depot, was abandoned when, after descending the river himself in 1828, he accepted Fraser's judgment that the river was unnavigable. Fort Vancouver, located on the north bank of the Columbia some 150 kilometres from its mouth, remained the main supply depot. Nor did Simpson succeed in gaining direct, profitable access to the Chinese market, but he did establish a Hudson's Bay Company agency in Hawaii and another, briefly, at Yerba Buena (San Francisco). The Hawaiian agency became the hub of the company's Pacific operations, the clearing house for imports to and exports from the Columbia, and the point of contact with whaling fleets as well as suppliers and markets around the Pacific rim.

By the early 1830s these measures had driven most American traders off the coast, blocked the westward expansion of American traders on the upper Missouri, and imposed a trading monopoly over a huge area. The posts and trade routes shown on Map 11.3 suggest something of the extent and scope of the company's operations in the early 1840s. By this date the economy of the Columbia Department had diversified considerably. Along

FIGURE 11.2 *View from Fort Langley,* c. 1858 (artist, J.M. Alden). A corner of Fort Langley (right), sheds for barrelling salmon (left), and across the Fraser River a Coast Salish village relocated close to the fort to control, as much as possible, the access of other Native traders to the fort and fur trade. | UBC Library, Special Collections.

the lower Columbia, water-powered mills cut lumber for export; at Fort Langley on the lower Fraser, salted and barrelled salmon were a more important export than furs (Figure 11.2). Agriculture at Fort Vancouver and elsewhere had expanded to the point that, in 1839, the Hudson's Bay Company entered into a contract with the Russians in Alaska to supply annually three hundred tons of wheat and almost fifty tons of salted beef, flour, butter, peas, and barley. In effect, a trading company on the lookout for profit had encountered an environment, and a set of Pacific connections, that made diversification possible. In various ways, as Map 11.3 suggests, the company had done what it had set out to do, forestalling the Americans and establishing a British trading empire through much of the northern Cordillera.

However, it had not brought settlers, and in the early 1840s when American settlers ("worthless and lawless characters of every description," according to Simpson) began to arrive over the Oregon Trail, the Hudson's Bay Company was suddenly on the defensive. The border had not been established, and although company traders hoped it would be drawn along the Columbia, they feared that the British government would accept a

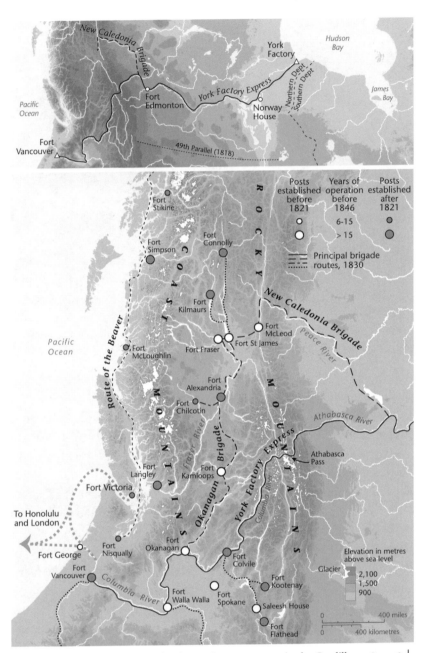

MAP 11.3   North West and Hudson's Bay Company posts in the Cordillera, 1805-46
Adapted from R. Galois, in Harris and Matthews, *Historical Atlas of Canada*, vol. 1, plate 66;
and Richard Mackie, *Trading beyond the Mountains: The British Fur Trade on the Pacific, 1793-1843* (Vancouver: UBC Press, 1997), 97.

more northerly solution. Partly with this in mind, Simpson established Fort Victoria at the southern tip of Vancouver Island in 1843, a central deep-sea port for Pacific trade in territory that almost certainly would remain British. When the border settlement came in 1846 (Chapter 5), a disgusted Simpson retained his Pacific port but had to deal with a bifurcated trading network. The Columbia route inland was in American hands. The only recourse was to the Fraser where, near the head of navigation, the HBC established two small forts and cut packhorse trails inland from them across mountain passes that were snowbound until late June.

All these developments were superimposed on Native people and their land. As elsewhere, Native people sought European goods, particularly firearms and blankets, but reacted when traders broke the protocols of Native life: using a portage without permission or paying tolls, sending trapping parties onto Native land. In the early years along the lower Columbia, levels of violence approached those of the maritime trade. Posts there were defensive sites; on dangerous stretches away from the posts, traders and their men moved in military formation. They had the advantage of firepower, of organization built around an overriding objective (profit), and of clear cultural stereotypes (the civilized, the savage) that enabled them to identify their enemies and coordinate their strategies. They exploited divisions in Native societies, almost always finding some people who welcomed an opportunity to settle old scores with traditional enemies. They operated within an ongoing theatre of power: a confident bravado, dress, salutes fired by fort guns, demonstrations of superior marksmanship, beatings. They always assumed that any assault on company personnel or property should be met with quick, violent retaliation, preferably in public displays of power (hangings, shootings, whippings) intended to convince viewers that they too could become victims – a discipline of fear ("respect" or "terror" were the traders' common words) employed where more elaborate machineries of surveillance and social management were absent.

North of the lower Columbia, these measures were less in evidence, and as the years went by the trade settled down everywhere. Fort life revolved around daily and seasonal routines; brigade departures and arrivals were the main events of the year. The men at the forts spoke Chinook and usually something of a Native language; most of them lived with

Native women. Some Native groups relocated themselves close to the fur posts (Figure 11.2), and Native economies shifted towards pursuits connected with the fur trade. Native labour – particularly female labour – was increasingly employed at the posts. Native men engaged in commodity production, and some were employed in transportation. Overall, the fur trade had become part of the fabric of regional life.

Although at midcentury the Native population in what is now British Columbia was far smaller than it had been eighty years before, Native people still outnumbered non-Natives by approximately a hundred to one. In the 1830s there had been another smallpox epidemic, this one along the coast north of Vancouver Island; in 1848-49 a much more widespread epidemic of measles was followed by influenza, the two together, historical geographer Robert Galois has suggested, as lethal as smallpox. Dysentery, whooping cough, typhus, typhoid fever, syphilis, gonorrhea, and tuberculosis were all present. Even where there had been no major epidemic, Native populations were declining. Depopulation reshuffled people as survivors gathered in some settlements and abandoned others; it opened social hierarchies, destroyed much local knowledge, and weakened cultural confidence. Compounding these changes were the influences of the fur trades. Many new goods circulated, their meanings undoubtedly recontextualized in Native societies. Much trade was reconfigured around the forts and harbours that were the foci of European-Native interaction. Native geopolities were rearranged as some groups became more powerful while others were weakened or eliminated. Ecologies were considerably altered as human population densities changed, as beaver were trapped out in many areas, and as sea otter were eliminated from the coast. (Sea urchins, a staple of the otter diet, proliferated as the otter disappeared. As the urchins fed on kelp, their exploding population diminished the kelp beds that sheltered inshore fishes, in so doing changing the coastal ecology – with effects on Native livelihoods that are not well understood.) The presence of previously unimagined newcomers, as well as the stories and the traces of Christianity that accompanied them, must have affected the way Native people imagined themselves. From this distance, the impression is of lifeworlds in flux, of Native people adjusting as they could to new circumstances. They were not passive victims. They bargained hard and some were skilled geopoliticians, but they were coping with a sequence of extraordinary developments, many of them strange and most beyond their control. Yet, they were still on the land, which, with the exception of the few hectares taken by fur posts and farms, they largely controlled and considered theirs. The border settlement of 1846, which divided much of the Cordillera between Britain and the United States without mentioning Native people (Chapter 5), lay outside their field of vision.

THE ESTABLISHMENT OF SETTLER COLONIES

The Oregon Treaty of 1846 was a legal understanding between the British and American governments "respecting the sovereignty and government of the territory on the northwest coast of America." This treaty, coupled with British fears of American settlement in and eventual annexation of land north of the new border, led the British government in 1849 to convert Vancouver Island into a colony under the proprietorship of the Hudson's Bay Company. The company was to establish British colonists within five years, make land available at a reasonable price, and forego its trading monopoly.

The creation of a settler colony shifted a European-Native relationship based on trade towards one based on land. It entailed dispossessing Native people of most of their land and reallocating it to settlers and capital. There was a practical issue of dispossession, about which officials in the Colonial Office and the HBC were of fairly clear mind: Native people should be placed on reserves. There was also a legal issue – whether Native title to land burdened the sovereignty of the Crown – about which there was no consensus in London in 1849. Although offering differing opinions on Native title from time to time, the Colonial Office preferred to leave the matter to the HBC. In this climate of legal uncertainty, James Douglas, chief factor on Vancouver Island in 1849 and soon the colony's governor, entered into "agreements," as he called them, with Native people for the purchase of their land. Between 1850 and 1854 he made fourteen purchases, all but three of land near Victoria. In the written form of these agreements (what passed orally between parties in no position to understand each other is another matter), Native groups surrendered their land "entirely and for ever" with the understanding that their "village sites" and "enclosed fields" would be kept for their uses and that they were free to hunt over unoccupied lands and to fish as formerly. Years later, the courts confirmed that these agreements were treaties – the Douglas Treaties. The meanings of their short, vague phrases have been much debated, but on

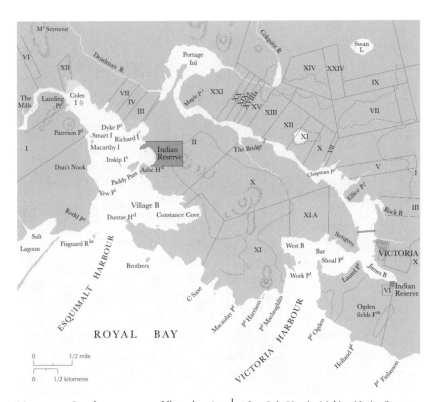

MAP 11.4   Land surveys near Victoria, 1855 | After Cole Harris, *Making Native Space: Colonialism, Resistance, and Reserves in British Columbia* (Vancouver: UBC Press, 2002), 29.

southern Vancouver Island in the 1850s their terms were translated un-ambiguously into surveyed realities. Map 11.4 shows what was taking place near Victoria as Native people were allotted small reserves and the land was renamed and surveyed for others. At Nanaimo, site of a company col-liery and of the last of Douglas' purchases, "village sites" and "enclosed fields" became 250 acres in three reserves – a quarter of an acre for each of the Nanaimo people. There, as elsewhere within the field of the Douglas Treaties, the rest of the land was opened to settlers and capital.

The terms by which former Native land was made available to others were dictated in London and reflected the views of the English political economist Edward Gibbon Wakefield. Wakefield held that social struc-tures were products of the relative cost of land, labour, and capital, and that in colonial settings it was possible to manipulate these costs to achieve desired social effects. A common mistake, he thought, was to set the price of land too low, which had the effect of driving up the cost of labour and, therefore, of discouraging capital. The result was a rabble rather than the ordered, hierarchical society that he, as well as officials in the Colonial Office and at Beaver House, the London headquarters of the HBC, much preferred. Translated into land policy on Vancouver Island in the 1850s, the ideas created a basic price of £1 per acre for country land with a minimum purchase of twenty acres, and £10 for town lots. Men owning twenty or more acres could vote; those owning over three hundred acres could run for public office. Like most other colonists on Vancouver Island, Douglas considered these charges excessive (land was virtually free in American territory nearby); he attempted to soften them by not charging for rock and swampland. Otherwise in the 1850s, London's terms held on the land Douglas had purchased from Native people. Beyond these "settlements," as he called them, lay "Indian country," where he had made no purchases, fearing that if he did so, and if settlement followed, he would not be able to protect the settlers. Without the check of quick retaliation, Native warriors would be emboldened, an assumption from Douglas' years as a fur trader.

These terms of access to land, combined with Vancouver Island's meagre agricultural potential, the allure of low land costs and high wages in Washington and Oregon, and the draw of gold in California, were not conducive to rapid settlement. Five years after the founding of the colony, the non-Native population of Vancouver Island was 774; in the early spring of 1858, it was barely 1,000. Overwhelmingly, these people were either retired HBC employees or indentured workers and their families sent from Britain. The latter entered a society in which former HBC officers owned most of the agricultural land, dominated a steep social hierarchy, and largely controlled the political culture. A conservative Wakefieldian society had been approximately created, with its colonial schools, Anglican clergy, English laws, and large landowners. The limited extent of agricultural land and the threat of Native attack had prevented squatting on an unmanageable frontier – the undoing of many Wakefieldian schemes elsewhere – while the presence of retired and financially secure HBC officers who deeply suspected American republican culture had created a pool of buyers for relatively expensive land. Supporting these settlers was a mixed economy, an extension, Richard Mackie has shown, of the mixed Pacific economy of the HBC, and stimulated by the California gold rush (1849) and its aftermath. The company operated a modern colliery at Nanaimo, north of Victoria, the colony's first experience with industrial capital. Independent merchants, many of them bitter critics of Governor Douglas and of the legacy of the hierarchical ways of the HBC, sold masts, lumber, squared timber, shingles, and dogfish and whale oil, all partly or entirely produced by Native labour, in San Francisco and Hawaii. Farms near Victoria, the largest of them owned by an HBC subsidiary, supplied foodstuffs to the Russians in Alaska and, in good years, almost fed the settlements. On Vancouver Island by the mid-1850s, the HBC had approximately reproduced itself in settler colonial form. At a corner of what is now British Columbia, a sharply stratified British society and a mixed economy dependent on Native labour and the varied natural resources of the Pacific coast had come into being.

On the mainland in the mid-1850s, the older regime of the fur trade still held. Not more than two hundred whites, virtually all of them living at the fur posts, were reliant on the Native world that surrounded them.

Then suddenly, in the spring and summer of 1858, a gold rush converged on the Fraser River. An offshoot of the Californian rush of 1849, it was fuelled by underemployed miners and brought the technologies, institutions, and values that had dominated the Californian gold fields. Some thirty thousand miners arrived, some coming overland through the Okanagan Valley (the axis of the fur trade before 1846), more ascending the Fraser River from the coast. The population of Victoria rose in a matter of days to more than three thousand; Fort Yale, at the head of steamboat navigation on the lower Fraser (Figure 11.3), became an instant tent town. As the spring floodwaters of the Fraser subsided, gravel bars below and above Yale began to be worked; elected committees of miners administered versions of Californian mining laws. Other miners pushed farther up a river that drew huge salmon runs and supported thousands of Native people. As they advanced, they pilfered gardens (potato cultivation had diffused from the fur posts), abused Native women, and began to wash away terraces on which Native people passed the winter in semi-subterranean pit houses. When fighting broke out, the miners fell back on techniques of Indian fighting developed in the American southwest. Armed with six-shooters and spiral-bored rifles, they organized themselves into companies, elected captains and other officers, and proceeded in paramilitary order. For many miners, good Indians were dead ones. Native people could

FIGURE 11.3   *Fort Yale, British Columbia* (detail), 1864 (artist, Frederick Whymper). Formerly a Hudson's Bay Company fort at the southern end of the Fraser Canyon, Yale became an instant gold rush town, the terminus of steamboat navigation on the lower Fraser River and the beginning of an overland route to the Cariboo. | Library and Archives Canada, 1935-124.

not handle these organized parties of men bristling with firepower and racial venom. In some cases they entered into treaties with them – which the miners had no authority to make and considered no more than ruses to gain access to land.

The rush had its own energy – the prospect of instant wealth and upward social mobility – and operated in space over which, initially, the British government had little control. Douglas, governor of Vancouver Island and chief factor of the HBC on the mainland, attempted to license miners in Victoria and placed three officials in the Fraser Canyon in the summer of 1858 – two revenue collectors and a justice of the peace – whom, as historian Tina Loo has shown, the miners hardly took seriously. In Britain, parliament voted to create a new Crown colony, British Columbia, and at Fort Langley in November, after most of the miners had left the Fraser for the winter, the HBC's trading monopoly on the mainland was rescinded, the new colony proclaimed, and Douglas appointed its governor.

The next decade on the mainland was dominated by the unpredictable momentum of recurrent gold rushes and by the attempts of a colonial administration to manage them while laying the basis for a settler colony. The Fraser rush moved upriver; by 1862 it focused on the Cariboo, a region east of the Fraser River and some four hundred kilometres north of Yale. There were other widely separated finds and, with each of them, a flurry of mining excitement – this in a vast, largely mountainous space where overland transportation was exceedingly difficult and Native people claimed the land. Their hold on it, however, was tenuous, as increasingly they knew. They had not been able to contain the gold rushes and had been devastated by yet another smallpox epidemic, this one accompanying miners in 1862. They knew only too well the results south of the border of fighting between Native warriors and American soldiers.

Like other rushes around the Pacific rim, these gold rushes brought few people who had any intention of staying in the out-of-the-way places to which the lure of gold had brought them. Largely male and poor, gold seekers were drawn rather by the prospect of getting there first, staking a claim, making a fortune, and leaving. Placer gold mining (for loose gold in gravel) encouraged this common illusion. Many people died, however, en route to the gold fields, others when shafts or adits collapsed. Moreover, placer mining quickly moved beyond the simple technology of gold pans and rockers to dams on small tributary streams, wooden flumes and ditches (some many kilometres long), and, in some cases, hoses and water under pressure. Such operations required capital and men who worked for wages. Most men did not stay long; they responded to rumours of finds elsewhere or left the colony. In these circumstances, settlements near the gold fields were hasty, ramshackle places built with no eye to the future. Freshly eroded gullies, flumes, shaft heads, gravel heaps, and miners' shacks were jumbled for miles along the richest creeks (Figure 11.4). The ecological impact was focused and massive. As they attacked the fluvial deposits that contained minute quantities of gold, miners washed hundreds of thousands of tons of sands and gravels into creeks or rivers. The coarser materials settled out quickly, some of the fines travelled as far as the Fraser Delta, where today geomorphologists find traces of the mercury that miners had used to separate out gold. Left behind were churned-over boulder fields and logged or burned hillsides, products, like the mining settlements, of the largely unregulated energy of a gold rush. Considered

FIGURE 11.4   "Gold Mining, Cariboo" (detail), n.d. (photographer unknown). Barkerville in the late 1860s. Note the denuded hillsides, the miners' shacks, the trestles, waterwheel, and flumes for moving water and gold-bearing gravels, the reworked valley floor, and the huddle of commercial building that comprised Barkerville. | Library and Archives Canada, C-024479.

most broadly, the gold rushes were particular effects of the laissez-faire values of the mid- to late nineteenth century and of the drastic nineteenth-century improvements in transportation and communication that had made places like British Columbia accessible to emigrants from the outside world before an apparatus of civil administration was well in place.

Early in the Fraser River rush, the Colonial Office sent a regiment of Royal Engineers to British Columbia, intending that it serve as a reminder of British military strength in an infant colony that was vulnerable to American expansion, and that it establish a framework of land surveys and roads for a settler colony. At the mouth of the Fraser River, the engineers laid out a prime meridian and began to survey farm and town lots. In the interior they guessed at the sites of future towns; by the summer of 1860 they were supervising the construction of a wagon road through the Fraser Canyon above the head of steamboat navigation at Yale. By 1865 this road – the Cariboo Wagon Road – reached Barkerville in the heart of the Cariboo mining district. Essentially a turnpike road in a railway age, it did make a transportation corridor of the route that Simon Fraser had rejected and, in so doing, made a British mainland colony just workable. The Cariboo Wagon Road became the principal axis of a minimal trans-

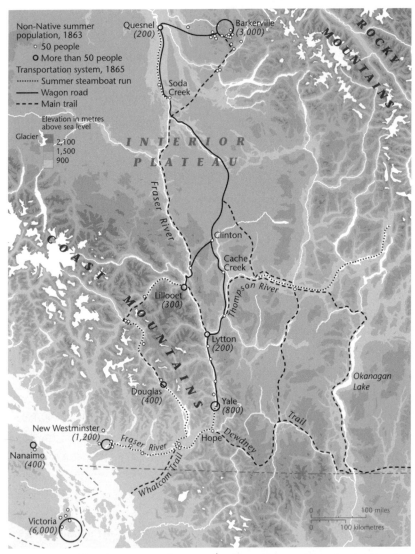

MAP 11.5   Gold rush transportation, 1865 | After C. Harris and J. Warkentin, *Canada before Confederation: A Historical Geography* (New York and Toronto: Oxford University Press, 1974), 301.

portation system (Map 11.5) composed of river steamers on navigable waters, horse trails (some of them old HBC brigade trails), the wagon road itself, and settlements at break-of-bulk points. East of this road, and in spite of a trail (the Dewdney Trail) built eastward close to the border and across the grain of the topography, all new activities drained southward into the United States.

As earlier on Vancouver Island, the creation of a settler colony immediately raised the question of what to do with its Native inhabitants. Immigrants in British Columbia in the early 1860s took for granted that Native people were savages who did not know how to use land properly and would probably die out. They asserted, therefore, that in the interests of progress, development, and the spread of civilization, Natives should be quickly dispossessed. The advance of civilization was held to be a moral imperative – one that legitimized the interest of capital in resources, of settlers in land, and of both in the dispossession of Native people. However, Governor Douglas, a product of the fur trade and to some degree of the liberal humanitarian values of the late eighteenth century, assumed that Native people would participate in both traditional and new economies during a period of transition to new ways. Thus, he instructed surveyors at the beginning of non-Native settlement to determine what chiefs wanted and to allocate reserves accordingly. Some did so (Map 11.6). However, Douglas retired in the spring of 1864, and, as the Colonial Office now favoured responsible government over the protection of Native people, the values of settler society took over when he left. Joseph Trutch, an English engineer and businessman who became the chief commissioner of lands and works, only reflected those values when he reduced the large Douglas reserves to small fractions of their former size (Map 11.6) and discounted the premise that Native title to land was a burden on the sovereignty of the Crown. The colony had established a Native land policy – to grant minuscule reserves and ignore title – that would not change substantially for more than a hundred years. Over and over again, Native leaders protested that their children faced starvation.

As the land was opened for non-Natives, an English regime of property rights began to be put in place. Land would be held in fee simple, an estate that embodied an indestructible right to land, potentially forever. William Blackstone's *Commentaries on the Laws of England*, the reference on English law most commonly cited in the mid-nineteenth century, held

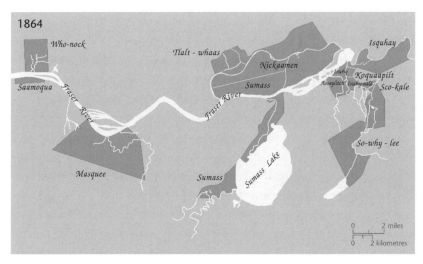

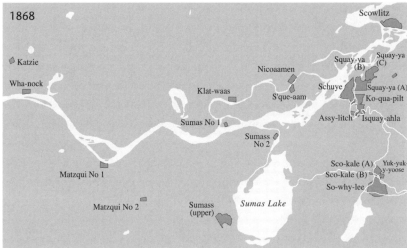

MAP 11.6   Douglas reserves (1864) and reductions (1868) in the lower Fraser Valley |
After Harris, *Making Native Space*, 41, 61.

that the right to private property was an immutable law of nature, a right
that, Blackstone claimed (ethnocentrically and patriarchally), was inherent in every Englishman. Furthermore, the protection of such private rights
was the basis of the public good. These assumptions, and the laws and
other powers that surrounded them, accompanied the settlers and capitalists who started to acquire land in colonial British Columbia. Property
lines began to appear on maps; some of them were marked on the land

by fences or survey posts. For settlers and capital, a regime of private property was their taken-for-granted right, whereas for Native people it increasingly made them trespassers in the local places to which their livelihoods and affections had always been attached.

The proclamation that created the Crown colony of British Columbia specified that English common law would apply there in so far as local circumstances permitted. English common law was laden with social memory; like any complex body of law, it tended to hold onto time and, when shifted in space, to transfer complex ideas, values, and social relationships from one location to another. As its grip on colonial British Columbia tightened, as it did between 1858 and the colony's 1871 entry into Confederation, it provided a framework within which settlers from an English common law tradition could replicate familiar ways. But England was no longer at hand, nor an English relationship with the land, a change reflected most fundamentally, in British Columbia as elsewhere, in the relative cost of land and labour. Over time the altered relationship of these factors of production would modify Old World social structures, but largely within the framework of a transferred body of common law. In some cases, however, English law simply did not fit new conditions; it was then replaced, usually by elements of American law – by water law suited to dry environments or pre-emption law suited to circumstances where settlement preceded surveying. In such ways, English common law adjusted itself in British Columbia while remaining essentially intact. After the first turbulent year of the Fraser gold rush, settler society moved increasingly within the rule of law backed by the colonial state and, at some remove, by the managerial habits of former HBC officers, with the result that violence and vigilante justice were far less common in the gold camps of British Columbia than in those across the border.

BRITISH COLUMBIA CIRCA 1870

In 1870 the colony of British Columbia (with which Vancouver Island was combined in 1866) was in a post-gold-rush slump. Many diggings and gold rush settlements had been abandoned; Victoria, the largest city in the colony, had about three thousand people, half the number there during the heydays of the Cariboo rush. The non-Native population on both Vancouver Island and the mainland was only some twelve to fifteen thousand, somewhat less than half the Native population. (The numbers are approximate because the first British Columbia census was not taken until 1881; it enumerated some fifty thousand people, more than half of them Native.) In the eleven years after 1870, the Native population had declined, whereas the non-Native had grown slowly, the one approximately balancing the other, so that the total population in 1870 and in 1881 was probably much the same. Over the longer term, the rate of immigration had not balanced the rate of Native population decline. In 1870 British Columbia had far fewer inhabitants than in 1770, almost certainly far fewer than at any time for several hundred years.

In 1881, after a decade of economic stagnation between the waning of gold rushes and the coming of the Canadian Pacific Railway, the some fifty thousand people in British Columbia were distributed much as shown on Map 11.7. Native people lived approximately where they always had, but in far smaller numbers. Some parts of the colony – the Kootenays (the southeast), the coasts of the Strait of Georgia north of Nanaimo – were almost completely depopulated. Almost all the whites and Chinese lived along the transportation corridor extending from Victoria, the deep-sea port at the southern tip of Vancouver Island, through New Westminster, the steamboat port just above the mouth of the Fraser River, through Yale, the head of steamboat navigation on the lower Fraser, and thence along the wagon road to the Cariboo. There were a few whites and Chinese at other diggings, and a few white ranchers in valleys in the dry belt, but otherwise British Columbia was still Native space thinly inhabited by the descendants of much more sizable Native populations. In 1881 it was easy to assume, as settlers did, that the land was wilderness, that no one had ever used most of it, and that it awaited development.

Ten years earlier, the total population must have been much the same, and the distribution of non-Natives only slightly less extensive. Americans probably comprised less than 20 percent of the whites. White British Columbia had become predominantly British (English much more than Scottish or Irish) or eastern Canadian (principally Ontarians). Most of these whites were Protestants (principally Anglicans, Presbyterians, or Methodists). Only a few immigrants came from continental Europe, Africa, or South America. The Chinese, who comprised about a quarter of the non-Native population, were easily the largest group of non-Caucasian immigrants. Chinese miners, most of them originally from Guangdong Province in south China, had arrived in numbers from California in 1858 and were

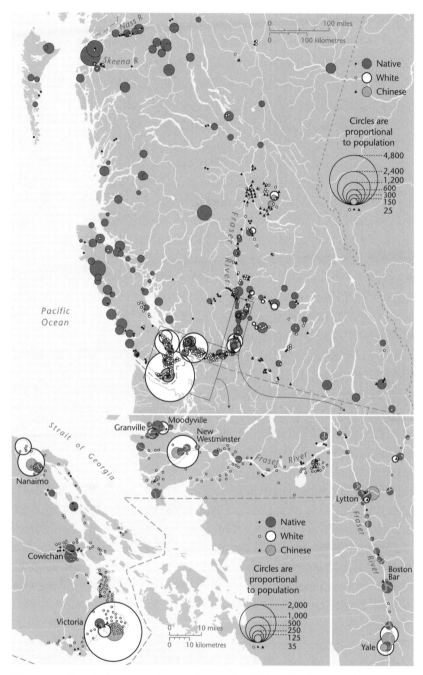

Map 11.7 Population in southern and central British Columbia, 1881 | Adapted from R. Galois and C. Harris, "A Population Geography of British Columbia in 1881," in R. Cole Harris, *The Resettlement of British Columbia* (Vancouver: UBC Press, 1997), 139, 141, and 144.

more inclined to remain at the diggings than whites. Chinese labour brokers supplied crews of unskilled Chinese labourers as needed. All of these non-Native populations were predominantly male. Among the Chinese, the male to female ratio was in the order of thirty or forty to one; among whites it was approximately three to one. Although Native populations were gender balanced, some Native men complained that there were not enough women; too many of their women, they said, were living with white men.

The economy was mixed and spatially disaggregated. Although the excitement of the early years had passed, a good deal of placer mining continued along the middle Fraser and its tributaries, much of it by Chinese. They worked methodically, applying water management skills acquired in the paddy fields of south China and modified in California to the building of flumes and ditches, the washing away of overburden (often to a depth of several metres), and the sluicing of gold-bearing gravels. Left behind were rows of boulders, in the largest operations dozens of hectares of them. New primary resource industries were being established where capitalists and commission merchants, most of them based in Victoria, bet that virtually free access to abundant resources would counteract the problems of isolation and high labour costs. In Burrard Inlet, the future harbour of the city of Vancouver, there were two industrial, steam-powered sawmills, factories for processing huge Douglas fir and western red cedar logs. The long crosscut saws (up to eighteen feet), double-bitted axes, and springboards (planks notched into the tree and on which the loggers stood) required to fell these huge trees had been developed in the redwood forests of northern California. The skilled loggers who cut them and the skilled mill hands who sawed them into lumber were whites (most of British background). In this split and racialized labour force, much of the unskilled manual labour was Native, Hawaiian, or Chinese, many of whom loaded lumber on sailing ships bound for markets around the Pacific rim. The colliery at Nanaimo, its workforce composed of skilled white miners and Natives or Chinese employed as ordinary labourers, exported some coal, much of it to ships of the Royal Navy. In 1870 the first salmon cannery in British Columbia had just been built at New Westminster, its operation largely manual, its output small. Agriculture was practised near Victoria and at other locations on southeastern Vancouver Island, in the lower Fraser Valley (though much hindered by the size of the forest), at points along the wagon road to the Cariboo, and in some of the interior valleys in the dry belt, mostly on small, mixed, and largely subsistent family farms. Immigrant British Columbia did not feed itself. The only signs of agricultural specialization were in the interior dry belt, where a cattle complex of Hispanic origin had arrived from the south in the early 1860s, and near Victoria and New Westminster, where there was some emerging emphasis on dairying and market gardening. Throughout the northern half of the colony, the fur trade economy still held. Overall, however, the fur trade was much reduced, the gold rushes had come and largely gone, and other economies were just beginning to emerge. The colony was still exceedingly remote; even from within it, most potential resources were inaccessible.

What sort of society lived in this colony composed of peoples of diverse historical backgrounds who were caught up in different economies in isolated places, who spoke many languages, and who had no means of knowing much, if anything, about each other? Victoria was the most English place in the British Columbia of 1870, but no English city contained Victoria's mix of English, Scots, Irish, and Americans, or its Chinatown, or its largely transient Native people who, in sum, spoke every language of the coast. In some ways, Nanaimo was a Nonconformist colliery town of northern English background, but whites, Chinese, and Natives worked in the mines, and a Native reserve lay on the edge of town. Although the industrial work around Burrard Inlet was polyglot and multiracial, Chinese and white workers lived apart, and Native workers lived on reserves. Some of the Chinese at placer sites along the Fraser worked for months or years in a closed, male, Cantonese-speaking society. An English rancher in the dry belt, who claimed to be descended from King John, imported English foxhounds and hunted coyotes, the best he could manage in the circumstances.

It was, in many ways, a society of exclusions. Racial categories labelled the "otherness" that permeated British Columbia, providing simple identifications and imposing closures that sealed off people, already different enough, from each other. In the white view, Native people were inferior savages. Many whites were biological racists; even the missionaries, most of whom thought Native people were God's children and capable of instruction, assumed a deep divide between civilization and savagery. Reserves were places apart for people whom self-interest and racism defined apart. The Chinese, too, were clearly "other." With a bottomless pool of potential Chinese immigrants across the Pacific, they, obviously, were not going to die out, and were more threatening in the long run to the success of a British settler colony than were Native people. Anti-Orientalism was much in the late nineteenth-century air, and in a place such as British Columbia, where the "Orient" was only an ocean away and the cultural security of an immigrant British society hardly established, it was only intensified. Chinatowns were places apart for the Chinese. Race was a handy disparaging yardstick of difference; in the scramble for resources, position, and cultural security in a new society, white legislative and coercive power, combined with sharp racial categories, eliminated much of the competition. When races mixed, as when white men and Native women married, the categories were transgressed and, as historian Adele Perry has shown, a society that relied on them was troubled.

Class and gender created other exclusions. Given the differences of language and culture, the varieties of work, and the isolation of work sites, a common sense of the working class could not exist in the British Columbia of 1870. Locally it could, as among coal miners in Nanaimo although diluted even there by cultural differences and racism. Class identity was most marked among the elite, the small group of white, Protestant men who dominated the government, the courts, the churches, and the commercial economy. Having access to the levers of power in a new colony, living atop the pyramid of race, class, and gender, and facing a scattered, disaggregated opposition, the elite found British Columbia exceedingly agreeable. Most of them lived in ample homes in and around Victoria, socialized together, and expected their children to intermarry. The maleness of the elite was a measure of the extent to which patriarchy had been transferred to British Columbia. If anything, because of the preponderance of men and the overwhelming maleness of wage work, the colony was even more gendered than the societies from which its immigrants had come. In a sense, it had intensified the growing gendered dichotomy in industrializing societies between home and work. For the men who worked in them, the largely male work camps in British Columbia evoked images, associated with women, of home and civility hundreds or thousands of kilometres away.

More generally, what had been created was a British settler colony in a Native space, in many ways a Pacific colony that resembled Australia and

New Zealand at least as much as it did other parts of British North America. Behind it lay the British Colonial Office and the British military; otherwise, this part of the northern Cordillera would have become American. Inside it was a mix of disparate peoples who hardly knew each other and who readily substituted social categories for understanding. Although Native people were still the majority, power was in the hands of a small group of white men; it was they who, in 1871, would negotiate the terms of British Columbia's entry into Confederation.

BIBLIOGRAPHY

Research on early British Columbia over the last twenty years has brought new areas of enquiry into focus and reworked many older understandings. The new literature is large and is selectively represented here.

On the introduction of epidemic diseases, the principal work is Robert Boyd, *The Coming of the Spirit of Pestilence: Introduced Infectious Diseases and Population Decline among Northwest Coast Indians, 1774-1874* (Vancouver/Seattle: UBC Press/ University of Washington Press, 1999); and, more succinctly and accessibly, Boyd, "The Introduction of Infectious Diseases," in *Handbook of North American Indians*, vol. 7, *Northwest Coast*, ed. Wayne Suttles (Washington DC: Smithsonian Institution, 1990), 71-111. I offer a different argument (which is followed above) about the timing and provenance of the earliest epidemics in "Voices of Disaster: Smallpox around the Strait of Georgia in 1782," *Ethnohistory* 41, 4 (1994): 591-626; reprinted with minor changes in Cole Harris, *The Resettlement of British Columbia: Essays on Colonialism and Geographical Change* (Vancouver: UBC Press, 1997), chap. 1. Measles and influenza in the late 1840s are discussed by Robert Galois, "Measles, 1847-50: The First Modern Epidemic in British Columbia," *BC Studies* 109 (1996): 31-43.

The introductory modern enquiry into the maritime fur trade is Robin Fisher, *Contact and Conflict: Indian-European Relations in British Columbia, 1774-1890* (Vancouver: UBC Press, 1977), chap. 1. More recent studies are James R. Gibson, *Otter Skins, Boston Ships, and China Goods: The Maritime Fur Trade of the Northwest Coast, 1785-1841* (Montreal and Kingston: McGill-Queen's University Press, 1992); Mary Malloy, *"Boston Men" on the Northwest Coast: The American Maritime Fur Trade 1788-1844* (Kingston and Fairbanks: Limestone Press, 1998); and Daniel Clayton, *Islands of Truth: The Imperial Fashioning of Vancouver Island* (Vancouver: UBC Press, 2000), chaps. 6-9. A meticulous examination of contact processes at the beginning of the maritime fur trade is in Robert Galois, ed., *A Voyage to the North West Side of America: The Journals of James Colnett, 1786-89* (Vancouver: UBC Press, 2004), Introduction (particularly 19-66). A few years ago I tried to summarize current understandings of the effects of the maritime fur trade in "Social Power and Cultural Change in Pre-colonial British Columbia," *BC Studies* 115-16 (1997-98): 45-82.

On the spatial strategies and logistics of the land-based fur trade, see Richard Mackie, *Trading beyond the Mountains: The British Fur Trade on the Pacific, 1793-1843* (Vancouver: UBC Press, 1997). For traders' perceptions of Native people, consult Elizabeth Vibert, *Traders' Tales: Narratives of Cultural Encounters in the Columbia Plateau, 1807-1846* (Norman and London: University of Oklahoma Press, 1996). On the traders' deployment of power, refer to my essay "Strategies of Power in the Cordilleran Fur Trade," in Harris, *The Resettlement of British Columbia*, chap. 2. For a critique of this essay, see Duane Thompson and Marianne Ignace, "'They Made Themselves Our Guests': Power Relationships in the Interior Plateau Region of the Cordillera in the Fur Trade Era," *BC Studies* 146 (2005): 3-35.

Fairly recent general accounts of colonial British Columbia are Jean Barman, *The West beyond the West: A History of British Columbia* (Toronto: University of Toronto Press, 1991), chaps. 4 and 5; and Sharon Meen, "Colonial Society and Economy," in Hugh Johnston, ed., *The Pacific Province: A History of British Columbia* (Vancouver and Toronto: Douglas and McIntyre, 1996), chap. 4.

On the British navy and colonialism in British Columbia, see Barry M. Gough, *Gunboat Frontier: British Maritime Authority and Northwest Coast Indians, 1846-1890* (Vancouver: UBC Press, 1984). On Native land policy in colonial British Columbia, consult Paul Tennant, *Aboriginal Peoples and Politics: The Indian Land Question in British Columbia, 1849-1989* (Vancouver: UBC Press, 1990), chaps. 2-4; and Cole Harris, *Making Native Space: Colonialism, Resistance, and Reserves in British Columbia* (Vancouver: UBC Press, 2002), chaps. 1-3. On Native labour in the colonial economy, refer to John Lutz, "After the Fur Trade: The Aboriginal Labouring Class of British Columbia, 1849-90," *Journal of the Canadian Historical Association* 3 (1992): 69-93. For early colonial settlement on Vancouver Island, see Richard Mackie, "The Colonization of Vancouver Island, 1849-58," *BC Studies* 96 (1992-93): 3-40. The gold rushes are described cartographically by Robert Galois, "The Gold Rushes in British Columbia, 1858-1881," in *Historical Atlas of Canada*, vol. 2, *The Land Transformed, 1800-1891*, ed. R. Louis Gentilcore, cart. Geoffrey J. Matthews (Toronto: University of Toronto Press, 1993), plate 36. My essay "The Fraser Canyon Encountered," in Harris, *The Resettlement of British Columbia*, chap. 4, describes a local impact of the rush of 1858. On the canyon war of 1858, see Daniel P. Marshall, "No Parallel: American Miner-Soldiers at War with the Nlaka'pamux of the Canadian West," in John M. Findlay and Ken S. Coates, eds., *Parallel Destinies: Canadian-American Relations West of the Rockies* (Seattle/Montreal and Kingston: University of Washington Press/ McGill-Queen's University Press, 2002), 31-79. On law and social power during the gold rushes, consult Tina Loo, *Making Law, Order, and Authority in British Columbia, 1821-1871* (Toronto: University of Toronto Press, 1994), chaps. 3-7. On race and gender in colonial society, see Adele Perry, *On the Edge of Empire: Gender, Race, and the Making of British Columbia, 1849-1871* (Toronto: University of Toronto Press, 2001). On the population geography and social structure of British Columbia just after the colonial period, see R.M. Galois and R.C. Harris, "Recalibrating Society: The Population Geography of British Columbia in 1881," *Canadian Geographer* 39, 2 (1994): 43-60; reprinted in Harris, *The Resettlement of British Columbia,* chap. 5. A sustained analysis of the colonial economy is not yet in the literature.

12

Confederation and the Pattern of Canada

The roots of the Dominion of Canada created by the Confederation agreements of the late 1860s and early 1870s reached back through a long, slowly-worked-out North American past that established the parameters of what this country is, and of what it is not. That fractured, discontinuous past has been the subject of this book, and for the most part, chapter by chapter, I have dealt with it regionally. In this final chapter I turn to a much more generalized discussion that seeks to identify some of the essential characteristics of pre-Confederation Canada and to suggest their current implications. First, however, just a little about the making of Confederation itself.

Making Confederation

The idea of union circulated in British North America long before Confederation was achieved. For its advocates in the 1840s and 1850s, some form of union of the British North American colonies would strengthen their defensive position against the United States and prevent small, individual British colonies from slipping, one by one, into the American republic. It would create a larger theatre for commerce and enterprise, one that superseded the rock-bound limits of particular colonies and was commensurate with the scale and opportunities of the steam age and the capacity of science to digest and order the land. It would break the political stalemate in the union of the Canadas by giving the French (as Lord Durham and others tended to call French Canadians) their own province and local powers while giving the British the other provinces and a central government in which they would constitute the majority. For some others, it would create a British North American identity and nationality at a scale to be proud of. In a few thoughtful minds, notably that of Sir Edmund Walker Head, governor general of British North America in the late 1850s, it would provide a political framework within which Hudson's Bay Company territory might be acquired and to which new western colonies might be added.

Some argued that a new, enlarged Canada should be a legislative union in which most powers would reside with the central government and that the rest should be allocated to more than one hundred municipal corporations with local powers. In their view, the provinces (former colonies) would disappear. Others held that power in the prospective union should lie with the provinces, except for matters such as currency, customs, postal services, interprovincial trade, and external relations, all of which would be assigned to the central government. By the late 1850s, some variant of the latter view prevailed. Joseph-Charles Taché, a French Canadian physician and intellectual who wrote a book on the matter in 1858, thought that the present union of Canada East and Canada West was indefensible ("on parle beaucoup ... mais on ne gouverne pas") and that union with the Americans ("un peuple qui assassine les nationalités") would be disastrous. He thought the solution was a central government responsible for material things and provincial governments responsible for the moral order, in effect for family life (civil law, education, public welfare, the police, agriculture, roads). For Taché, Confederation was a means of protecting nationality, but he was not far out of line with the prevailing opinion among those promoting union in the late 1850s that power should be vested in the provinces, which then would turn over specified responsibilities (bearing largely on economic management) to a central government. As historian W.L. Morton has shown, there was a growing consensus that a new country would have to divide politically as it expanded economically, and that this could be accomplished only in a union of all British North America. In 1858, the Canadian government went so far as to endorse a federal union, the implementation of which would require agreement in London and the Atlantic colonies.

The convoluted route to that agreement, the subject of a large literature, is less important for this discussion than the convergence of circumstances that by the 1860s made a transcontinental British North American union seem increasingly feasible and desirable. With the Fraser gold rush and the creation of the colony of British Columbia (Chapter 11), and the descriptions of the prairies in the reports of the Palliser and Hind expeditions (Chapter 10), the transcontinental west seemed ever more attractive to interests (particularly in Toronto and the Ottawa Valley) in increasingly land-hungry Canada. A Pacific anchor for a transcontinental union had emerged with, apparently, an abundance of fertile land along the way. Rupert's Land, the vast area surrounding Hudson Bay, would have to be acquired from the Hudson's Bay Company, and an overland transportation route – a road or railway – would have to be built. To accomplish both, a larger government – one that was not controlled by any single province and had some capacity to manage a transcontinental territory and negotiate financial guarantees from Britain – was imperative. Canada's interest lay primarily in access to the west, that of the Maritime colonies in a railway (the Intercolonial) to the trade of the St. Lawrence and lower Great Lakes, but in the bargaining over Confederation the interest of the one tended to support the other as long as its own were satisfied. Two pressing westward interests came to hinge on some form of confederation. It also became clear in the conferences leading up to Confederation that the commitment of French Canadian politicians to the protection of nationality, and therefore to strong provincial governments, found ready support among Maritime politicians committed, in any scheme for union, to a high level of local autonomy. Whatever its merits, a legislative union had become a practical impossibility. In such ways, the territorial opportunities and implications of Confederation, its potentially acceptable terms, and even the negotiations required to achieve them, were all coming into focus.

Moreover, by the mid-1860s the British government had decided to throw its full support behind these initiatives. In the aftermath of the American Civil War, with the consolidation of the United States as *the* continental power, and in the face of strong anti-British sentiment throughout the northern States (a consequence of British neutrality throughout the war and of many Americans' conviction that it had prolonged, even caused, the hostilities), Britain sought to withdraw as much as possible from North America. She had little stomach either for a war with the United States or for the expense of defending a string of British North American colonies. Large numbers of British troops along their border would only provoke the Americans. On the other hand, Britain could withdraw honourably and relatively cheaply from North America were she to leave behind an enlarged, self-governing British colony – matching the transcontinental scale of the United States but posing it no military threat – with responsibility for its own defence. By the mid-1860s, therefore, the British government instructed the governors general in its North American colonies to advance the cause of union in every way possible. When some Maritime politicians balked at the scheme, asserting instead their loyalty to Britain and to their former imperial connection, they were informed that Britain supported union and that loyalty entailed, therefore, their support as well.

The first stage of Confederation, achieved with the British North America Act in 1867, divided the former colony of Canada into the provinces of Quebec and Ontario and united them with the former colonies of New Brunswick and Nova Scotia in what was to be known as the Dominion of Canada. Territorially, it was a modest and incomplete achievement that embodied a small fraction of British North America (Map 12.1). Politically, it was a frail consensus, about which Nova Scotians particularly, suspicious of Canadian imperialism, had severe second thoughts. Yet, with support in London, the agreement held and was expanded. In 1868, British legislation authorized the acquisition of Rupert's Land and other Hudson's Bay Company lands. A year later, negotiations between the HBC and representatives of the British and Canadian governments established the terms of land transfer: £300,000, one-twentieth of the fertile prairie, and specified lands around the trading posts. In 1870 the former Hudson's Bay Company lands were transferred to the new Dominion of Canada, which suddenly became a subcontinental political space, most of it unknown to outsiders, identified simply as the "North-West Territories." Within this vastness, the focus in 1869-70 was on Red River, the principal home of the Métis (Chapter 10). There, in the fall of 1869, the Métis, led by a young, well-educated Louis Riel, stopped a party of Canadian surveyors at the international border and, in the vacuum between the assertion of HBC and Canadian authority, established their own provisional government. This, in traditional Canadian historiography, was the first Riel Rebellion, during the course of which the Métis executed one abusive young Protestant, and, in response, the new Canadian government sent out some British troops and Ontario militiamen. Minor in themselves, these events inflamed opposite religious prejudices in Ontario and Quebec, and raised basic issues about the types of western settlement Confederation would permit. Out of them too, in 1870, came a fifth province, Manitoba, a political space that embodied most Métis demands (provincial status, responsible government, bilingual institutions, denominational schools, guaranteed land titles, federal respect for Indian title) but was only a small rectangle of approximately a hundred miles per side within which the federal government controlled Crown lands. Bounding it on three sides were lands and societies that, in principle, were to be administered from Ottawa.

Shortly after the creation of the small province of Manitoba, three British Columbians arrived in Ottawa to discuss the terms of union. Central to their demands was a wagon road across the continent. Instead, they were offered a railway, which the federal government agreed to begin in two years and complete in ten. The British Columbians had stumbled into a political context they did not understand but were more than prepared to take advantage of – the need, if Confederation were to work, to balance a western railway with the Intercolonial and the further need, given the unrest in Red River, to build the eastern portion of this railway quickly. The terms they took back to British Columbia were ratified there early in

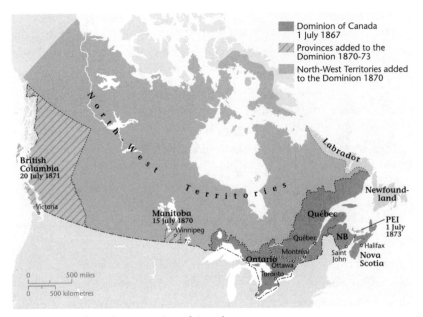

MAP 12.1   Making the Dominion of Canada, 1867-73

1871; later that year it became the sixth Canadian province. In 1873, Prince Edward Island, which had spurned Confederation in 1867, joined the union, drawn there by railway debts and an agreement that allowed the island's legislature to rule against the proprietors' property rights and concentrations of landownership (Chapter 7). By this time the Dominion of Canada had become a transcontinental political territory (Map 12.1) comprising seven provinces, most of them with minimal overland interconnections, a federal government located in a capital recently built on the Ottawa River, a vast territory anchored on the Canadian Shield but extending well beyond it (the North-West Territories), and a scatter of different peoples, most of them living in pockets of settlement near the eastern border with the United States, who harboured their prejudices and knew little or nothing about each other. Newfoundland and, to all intents and purposes, Hudson Bay remained part of the British Atlantic world.

Behind this union lay nothing like the stirring nation-building events of the American Revolution and the liberal philosophical idealism of a John Locke. The creation of the Dominion of Canada was grounded, rather, in pragmatism, compromise, and, as historian Suzanne Zeller has shown, utilitarian natural science. Confederation was a means by which a number of different objectives, held by different people in different places, all appeared to have a reasonable chance of being met. John A. Macdonald, the most central of the Fathers of Confederation and the new country's first prime minister, favoured a legislative union with a dominating central government but knew that, given opinion in Quebec and the Maritimes, such a union was unachievable. His most basic contribution to the Confederation debates was a demonstration of the pragmatic value of compromise. The strand, such as it was, of theoretical originality in the debates emerged most articulately and elaborately from George-Étienne Cartier, French Canadian politician and Macdonald's close colleague. For Cartier, the challenge of Confederation was to protect cultural difference while also creating what he called an overarching political nationality. As Taché had argued before him, Cartier held that the protection of cultural difference depended on strong provincial governments with full powers over cultural matters. Minorities within the provinces would be protected by a sense of fairness and, in some cases, by constitutional rights. The federal government would become an "agglomeration of communities" with, in time, "kindred interests and sympathies," and would become the focus of an emerging political rather than cultural nationality. For Cartier, diverse identities could coexist at different scales within a country of multiple identities. Here, then, as political scientist Samuel LaSelva points out, was the theoretical crux – which also in the British North America of the day was a pressing practical problem – of the Confederation debates: how and to what extent to protect different identities in different scales of government. The American constitution, LaSelva suggests, grew out of a debate over the means of protecting republican liberty, the Canadian over the means of protecting identity. The latter issues were not trivial. They continue to occupy Canadian politicians and the country's moral philosophers.

PATTERNS OF EARLY CANADA

Although there was endless complexity across the lands and peoples on which, eventually, Confederation was superimposed, there was also pattern and a measure of repetitive order. Europeans had not come to northern North America in an infinite variety of ways, but rather within systems of organization that tended to arrange themselves in characteristic patterns. Of these, there were principally three, one associated with imperialism, another with commercial capital, and the third with agricultural settlements composed of family farms. Although the three patterns variously overlapped, their characteristic imprints were distinctive and recurrent.

The Imperial System

Whether during the French regime or the British administrations that followed it, imperial power was primarily arterial and nodal. It derived from governments based in Versailles or London, depended on transatlantic connections, focused on the towns, and reached well inland along known transportation routes. It had the capacity to anchor colonies and territorial claims, and to create expatriate urban cultures with strong metropolitan connections, sophisticated metropolitan manners, and elites that lived comfortably within metropolitan expectations. Its capacity to reach beyond the towns to shape the lives of ordinary people was much more circumscribed.

Much of this power was military. A French military presence, based principally in Quebec and Montreal but capable of sending troops far into the interior, coupled with the alliances made by a succession of governors with Native groups around the Great Lakes, enabled New France to survive in North America for some 150 years. Later, a British military presence, distributed among the British North American towns, enabled scattered British colonies to exist along the northern margin of the United States. Even in the 1860s, when Britain was inclined to withdraw from North America, she poured thousands of troops into her North American colonies (in response to the American Civil War), sent four battalions after the Civil War to counter an invasion of Fenians (militantly anti-monarchist Irish Catholics), and maintained a large naval base at Halifax and a much smaller one near Victoria. As British colonial secretaries were wont to say, such forces were there to deter external aggression but also to keep internal peace, as in Lower Canada during the Rebellion of 1837. Military power could also reach into the countryside to requisition food, billet troops, train militias, and extract soldiers, as with particular energy it did in Canada during the period leading up to the Seven Years' War.

The principal towns were centres of colonial administration and provided its basic apparatus: a governor and other officials, executive councils, courts and systems of law, eventually legislative assemblies. The British imperial system, like the French before it, favoured the centralization of administrative power in a strong executive, as Loyalists and others entering British North America in the late eighteenth century from New England, where local democracy was well established, found to their dismay. From the principal towns, administrative power reached into the countryside, largely by means of the systems of civil and criminal law that accompanied the imperial state, but hardly dominated it. In pre-modern Europe, the state entered the countryside to tax, recruit, and, as need be, quell disturbances, but had neither interest in nor means of regulating the details of local life. Nor did it in northern North America during these years, although some of the preconditions of regulation were emerging. The state standardized civil law, during the French regime replacing many local French coutumes with one of them, the Coutume de Paris, and in the British years replacing what in England was still a welter of local manorial law with English common law. Although there were always irregularities, it also tended to normalize the allocation and surveying of land.

By the mid- to late nineteenth century, European states were acquiring more capacity to oversee and manage their populations, what the French cultural philosopher Michel Foucault called bio-power, the control of bodies. Foucault thought that a whole new paraphernalia of social control

– enlarged bureaucracies, improved means of surveillance, academic disciplines that invented normalcy and deviance, and a host of micro-technologies for the management of populations – was coming into existence. But how much, if any, of this paraphernalia of social management was in place in Canada as the older imperial system withdrew? Public schools with standardized curricula would seem an example, if one somewhat qualified by the curricular variety associated with denominational schools. The nominal census of 1871 would seem another. Foucault would have had much to say about the ordered standardization of life in the asylums for those judged insane. Overall it seems clear, however, that the state was hardly yet in a position to manage populations in the Foucauldian sense, and that social control, which was usually substantial, was exercised far more locally – at the scale of families, local communities, the local church, even of the rough male world of the timber camps. This would change, but as late as 1870, the state still had little interest in or ability to reach into and manage lives in these local societies, especially as distances were great, populations were often scattered, and many settlements were extremely isolated.

Commercial Capital

Through most of the years considered by this book, commercial capital dominated export economies. It organized the early sixteenth-century fisheries along the Atlantic coast and remained active there over the next three and a half centuries. It inaugurated and was always involved in the fur and timber trades. Eventually, it participated – more hesitantly and with far less economic domination – in export trades in various agricultural products. These were Harold Innis' staple trades, the motors, he argued, of the early Canadian economy. Like the imperial system, they depended on connections across vast spaces, connections that linked capital and distant markets to North American raw materials. These trades could operate in closed systems that brought European capital and labour to isolated, seasonal North American work sites where European wage rates and conditions of employment prevailed, as they did throughout the early cod and whale fisheries. At the end of a season's work, ships, men, and a lightly processed resource returned to Europe. They could also operate with North American capital and labour, and within more open systems. In either case they depended on lines of transportation and communication that linked Europe and a North American site of resource procurement, usually as time went on through a North American port. The economic geography of a particular staple trade depended, therefore, on the location and character of the resource, the technologies and sources of labour used to acquire and process it, and the various means of transportation that moved labour to the resource and the resource to market.

The source of commercial capital was urban, and profits from the staple trades accrued to urban merchants and investors. The Newfoundland fishery built mansions in French and English ports and, later, in St. John's. The fur trade out of Hudson Bay enriched investors in London. In its early years the St. Lawrence fur trade profited the French holders of royal monopolies; later, it benefited merchants in the St. Lawrence towns. The timber trade created much of the early nineteenth-century wealth of Saint John, Montreal, and Quebec. Commercial capital and the imperial system converged in the towns, the one reinforcing the other and both drawing in their train the shopkeepers, professionals, artisans, port workers, and others who created the intricate hierarchical societies characteristic of all the principal towns of pre-Confederation Canada.

In many cases, the site of resource extraction – the North American end of the spatial economy of a staple trade – was a work camp situated where the resource, the labour to process it, and the means of transporting it to market all lay at hand. The first work camps were sixteenth-century fishing stations and the last of them in the years considered in this book were the winter cambuses and shanties of the timber trade (Chapters 7 and 8). Wherever they were and whatever they processed, work camps were dominated by particular technologies of resource extraction and by rank in the hierarchy of employment. Men worked for wages or, in the early fisheries, on shares, and under a boss. Women were absent; in effect, work had been detached for a time from its larger social context and surrounded by forest and rock. In the fur trade, on the other hand, the commercial system led to a dispersed labour force of indigenous hunters. It drew Native people and Europeans together, whether at the posts, where goods were traded and Native women often lived with European men, or beyond them, where European traders, operating on their own, lived with Native people and adopted many of their ways. Such, as early as the 1670s, were the coureurs de bois, or farther west after 1821, the freemen who troubled the trading monopoly of the Hudson's Bay Company (Chapters 4 and 10). In these ways, commercial capital could draw Natives and Europeans into an intermediate space, neither Native nor European. It could also make use of immigrant families, as it did in the fishery when the site of resource production shifted from seasonal fishing stations to immigrant fishing families scattered in small harbours along rocky shores. They sold their catches to agents of the fishing firms to whom, characteristically, they were in debt (Chapter 6). In short, commercial capital employed a variety of spatial strategies and labour forces, but always with the ends of overcoming distance, commodifying nature, and connecting lightly processed products to distant markets.

In the last two or three decades before Confederation, industrial capital was beginning to supplant commercial capital. The large sawmills at the mouth of the Saint John River, on the lower Ottawa River, or on Burrard Inlet were factories. So were the woollen mills in the Eastern Townships or the foundries, machine works, and flourmills along the Lachine Canal in Montreal. By 1870, most manufacturing employment in Toronto was located in factories. Hamilton was a centre of heavy industry. The industrial age was finally overtaking the larger British North American cities, reshaping them in the process. Yet, in 1870 only a small fraction of the population of the Dominion of Canada lived in these cities, and many who did so were little affected by the new industrial order. Overall, Canada at Confederation was an amalgam of pre-industrial societies punctuated by a few industrializing cities. Nor was it as dominated by commercial capital as Innis claimed. Innis was often right about staple trades; they existed much as he described them. However, they did not extend nearly as far or as comprehensively into the countryside as he implied, and because they did not he exaggerated their overall importance. If parts of the territory that eventually became Canada – Newfoundland, for example, or the western interior – cannot be understood apart from the influence of staple trades, the essential dynamic of land and life in the agricultural countrysides, where long before Confederation the great majority of British North Americans lived, was not established by commercial capital.

Agricultural Settlement
Agricultural settlement took place in patches aligned between the northern ecological limit of agriculture and, after 1783, the border with the United States. Although no subtropical crops were possible in these locations,

much of the plant-livestock combination of northwestern European agriculture could be approximately reproduced once forests were cleared or marshes drained. As agricultural settlement developed, it usually faced chronic problems created by distance to external markets and fairly limited internal demand. On the other hand, compared to that anywhere in Europe, land was relatively accessible to the poor through, to be sure, the often overwhelming work of pioneering. In these circumstances, small family farms prevailed.

Those who, generation by generation, made these farms, found themselves in settings that reshaped the social structure and cultural fabric of whatever fragment of France or Britain they or their ancestors had left behind. The relative availability of land tended to drive up the price of labour (relative to its European value), and both the low cost of land and the high cost of labour were to the advantage of the poor. On the other hand, these same costs restrained the wealthy when, as throughout pre-industrial rural Europe, most wealth rested on the control of valuable land and the availability of cheap labour. The patches of agricultural settlement in early Canada tended, therefore, to compress European social structures, allowing relatively more opportunity for the poor and less for the rich. These societies were not egalitarian. The desperately poor and the comfortably prosperous often existed within them, but, compared to the societies immigrants left behind, the social range was shifted and reduced. On the other hand, the cultural range, at least in the first instance, usually increased. Immigration assembled people out of different local cultures, and often out of different religious and linguistic backgrounds, in so doing mixing and exposing them to previously unencountered difference. Many French regional backgrounds met and mixed along the lower St. Lawrence during the French regime; even Irish neighbours along a concession line road in Upper Canada usually brought somewhat diverse local cultures from different parts of Ireland. In such circumstances, no particular French or Irish peasant culture could be reproduced. Emerging instead, time allowing, were considerably recalibrated rural cultures that reflected an amalgam of memories drawn from various European backgrounds coupled with the influences of new settings.

Almost everywhere, the principal aim of the farm economy was the sustenance of the farm family and its generational reproduction. The immediate means to these ends was mixed farming with a high subsistence component plus as much market connection as possible. Farms were sites of family work that regularly produced most, but never all, of the family's needs. There were always goods that had to be purchased and often rents or debts to be paid. Farmers tried to sell, therefore, a portion of their production. Some of it, at some times, reached export markets: most commonly pot and pearl ash (made from the ash of clearing fires), horses, wheat, and flour. However, export markets, which always depended on fluctuating, distant prices, were erratic. Overall, farmers usually relied on connections variously made with local markets provided by urban and village populations, garrisons, recent immigrants with some capital, the staple trades (in particular locations, canoe brigades, timber camps, fishing ships), and eventually many small rural industries that processed agricultural products. These outlets were finite – most people lived on farms and were producers rather than consumers of agricultural products – but then, when farm technologies were manual and seed/yield ratios were commonly low, farm surpluses were small. Almost everywhere in the territory that became Canada, it was the exceptional family farm that produced enough surplus to feed one other family. At a quite different scale from these family operations were a few large farms established by seigneurs, timber firms, businessmen, or gentlemen farmers. Worked by wage labourers or (less commonly) by sharecroppers, they were rarely very profitable (especially if managed by gentlemen farmers) and never involved more than a tiny percentage of the rural population.

In these ways, a type of mixed farming that was at once subsistent and commercial sustained most rural families. As the trials – and in many particular instances the failures – of pioneering gave way to established countrysides, mixed farming underlay the farms and farmsteads that were the basic building blocks of rural settlement. They were the primary loci of family life, and families were large. Although comparative data are sparse, high birth rates probably typified all rural societies in early Canada. When local population densities were low, as they were during the early years along the lower St. Lawrence, children could usually be established near the parental farm. However, as population pressures rose and local land was claimed, the establishment of children became much more difficult. Usually, the family farm could not be subdivided into viable holdings. During the French regime and within a system of partible (divided) inheritance, one son characteristically took over the family farm and assumed debts to his brothers and sisters for their equal shares in the inheritance. Later, as land values rose and the debts one son would assume in such a system became insurmountable, patterns of inheritance changed. Then, in a system that commonly was neither partible nor impartible, one son again took over the family farm while usually making some payments, more or less, to some of his siblings. This was also the common system in Upper Canada. Whatever they inherited, as local land prices rose, most siblings could not remain in the vicinity of the family farm. For most, the generational reproduction of the family farm, or the adoption of a non-agricultural vocation, would have to occur elsewhere, and for this reason both mobility and stability were built into the fabric of rural life.

There were many tactics of relocation. The young might leave one by one, or parents might decide to sell the family farm and move *en famille* to a new location where their children could be settled around them. But where? During and well after the French regime, the common destination along the lower St. Lawrence was the Montreal plain, where there was more potential agricultural land than anywhere else in the colony. In Upper Canada, settlement moved north, away from the lakes, often towards the Queen's Bush (southwest of Georgian Bay). Suitable land, however, was quickly filled. Then where? In British North America in these years there was no ongoing agricultural west. For an increasing number, the options were to move farther north (towards rock, the timber camps, and a shorter growing season), into the towns (although they were still small and offered limited employment), or to the United States. From Newfoundland through Lower Canada, the last was often the inescapable resort. Rural British North America came to drain southward. Left behind were rural societies and cultures that were no longer quite European, had little space for newcomers, became increasingly consanguineous, and mixed very little with each other. In short, the patterns of rural settlement and subsequent migration in British North America became, in effect, a mechanism for the creation and maintenance of cultural and ethnic difference. Mixing took place outside British North America in the United States.

Such, in stark outline, were three basic patterns of European encroachment into northern North America, each distinctive but none autonomous. Only a handful of people of European descent – missionaries perhaps, and a few others – were not situated in at least one of them. They intersected, overlapped, and variously supported each other, different components of a common colonialism superimposed on lands that Native people had once considered theirs and continued to do so in most of the vast territory that, at Confederation, had suddenly become the Dominion of Canada.

The Intersection of the Native and the European

The European coming to northern North America introduced a complex of powers that, overall, Native people were unable to resist. As a result, they were progressively dispossessed of their lands, which were then repossessed by newcomers. This, however, was a lengthy, uneven process that began centuries before and continued long after the achievement of Confederation. It was not inexorable. Advantage was not always with the Europeans. Almost everywhere, however, it was facilitated by the prior diffusion of European diseases, particularly smallpox, that decimated populations and undermined survivors' confidence. Often, newcomers did not recognize that they were dealing with the aftermath of this carnage, still less that it was but the northern edge of the overwhelming demographic catastrophe that ensued when the coming of Europeans and Africans broke the western hemisphere's biological isolation.

Where the three patterns of European expansion described above converged, as they did, approximately, in the settler colonies, the complex of European power was strongest and the dispossession of Native people was most rapid and nearly total. Their lands were wanted and taken. The ability to do so rested ultimately on firepower (whether or not used), backed by the state and its military apparatus. Behind this military complex lay a large array of subtler powers that could be put to the management of colonial dispossession: literacy, maps, and numbers, for example, all of which may be thought of as technologies of distance, that is, as means of managing land and people from afar. Property law, which defined who owned and who trespassed, and backed its decisions with the authority of the state, was another crucial tool of colonial dispossession. Settlers themselves became, in a sense, the eyes and local agents of colonial land law when they ordered Native people, who had always hunted or fished in their own familiar places, off what, for settlers, law, and state, had become settler property. Ultimately, a new human geography, backed by an array of diverse powers culminating in the state, had dispossessed Native people. Legitimating such dispossession in the eyes of the dispossessors was a cultural discourse about the location of civilization and savagery and the proper use of land. In its terms, Europeans were civilized, and Native people were savages steeped in pagan superstition. Europeans knew how to use land effectively, Native people did not. Therefore, it was appropriate, even a moral imperative, to replace the latter with the former – or, in the eyes of missionaries, to bring them to God and the Christian life. Some variant of this discourse always accompanied settler colonialism, the legitimating capstone of an edifice of colonial power that, when concentrated in particular settings, had the capacity to overwhelm any Native resistance.

However, the farther one moved from the heartlands of settler colonies, the more the balance of power was likely to change. Settlers were no longer at hand; their appropriations of Native land were no longer part of the equation. Imperial power became more episodic, usually in the form of a few troops or small armies dispatched for particular purposes, or of alliances that held for a time. Eventually, it disappeared altogether. Then, commercial capital in the form of the fur trade found itself alone in a Native world. Moreover, because Europeans traded for the furs of animals that Native people had hunted, skinned, and dressed, the fur trade operated with relatively few Europeans among far greater numbers of Native people in large expanses of Native territory. Because traders and Native people required each other, their relations were commonly peaceful, but could quickly degenerate, particularly where and when the trade was most competitive. In such circumstances, commercial capital protected itself as it could: behind stockades in well-armed forts, by the quasi-military discipline of employees, by an ongoing theatre of power, by quick, violent retaliation for assaults on its personnel or property, by, Foucault would have said, a politics of fear. Usually, these measures were effective, but sometimes not. Posts were occasionally overrun and traders killed. In Native eyes, the land was theirs; nor, except at the fur posts, did capital claim it.

Commercial capital and Native people spent a long time together in the northern continental interior (Chapter 10). As the years passed, land and life there became increasingly hybrid, and Native people increasingly dependent on goods obtained from the fur posts. Hybridity, which took many forms, was most strikingly expressed in the emergence of the Métis, a people between. The roots of dependency were deeply ecological. With its demands for pelts and provisions, the fur trade so changed the ecologies of the boreal forest, parkland, and northern plains that, eventually, Native people could no longer count on obtaining their own sufficient supply of food. When they could not, they starved or depended on the traders' credit. Enmeshed in a fur trade for which they had become a dispersed and dependent labour force, their lives bore little resemblance to those of their pre-fur-trade ancestors. Yet, at Confederation they were still the principal population throughout most of the territory that had become the Dominion of Canada, they still spoke their languages, and they had no doubt about who they were.

THE CONSTRUCTION OF DIFFERENCE

The three basic patterns of early Canada and their various interactions with Native peoples were superimposed on a vast land, much of it dominated by the Canadian Shield, most of it unsuitable for agriculture (Chapter 5). European settlement was peripheral and patchy. These patches, settled by different peoples over more than two centuries, tended to be separated by rock, distance, and poor overland communications. Within them, class, ethnicity, and, particularly in an age of belief, religion, erected barriers. As much as possible, most people lived locally with others of their kind. For most of them, British North America as a whole or, later, the new Dominion of Canada were hardly visible; even the colony-turned-province in which they lived was scarcely in focus. In a sense, the British North America that turned towards Confederation can be thought of as a sprawling, irregular mechanism for the construction of social and cultural difference.

In the background, even allowing for the disruptions and eliminations of colonization, lay the deep differences, rooted in customs, values, and prejudice, that separated European and Native people. Northern North America, once entirely Native, had been Europeanized along some edges. There, small marginalized reserves were the principal remaining containers of Native life. But as one moved inward from these edges, the European began to recede and the Native to come to the fore. Not Native as it had been, but still Native. From the vantage point of the towns – indeed, of the majority of settlers – this Native presence was usually overlooked or denigrated with simple racial stereotypes, but it was there, a basic, underlying constituent of British North America.

Among peoples of European background, difference was variously constructed, not least by the different modes of organization and power within which they were situated. Broadly, the imperial system created an urban elite with metropolitan pretensions, garrisons, and an array of supporting professions and trades. Commercial capital placed merchants, tradespeople, and labourers in the towns, and created a variety of distinctive primary-resource-related employments away from them: on fishing ships and at fishing stations, on canoe brigades and at fur posts, on timber drives, at lumber camps. Agricultural settlement created family farms, hamlets, and villages in newly made countrysides. Lives were lived very differently in these different settings. Basic dichotomies stretched from the middle years of the French regime to Confederation and well beyond: between urban polish and homespun countrysides, between work at home and work in a camp, between immigrant settlements and bush or "wilderness" nearby, and, perhaps most basically, between the prosperous and comfortable and the far more numerous poor.

Difference was also constructed by ethnicity and religion compounded by the limits of economic opportunity in closely bounded spaces, and by the migrations they entailed. It was quite possible, for example, for Catholic Irish and Protestant English communities to survive for generations in adjacent Newfoundland outports. The progeny of first settlers filled the space; there was no room for outsiders, and when some of the young left to find employment elsewhere, they would not go to the adjacent outport, which offered neither room nor welcome, but much farther afield and usually south, probably to Boston. The resulting mixture of peoples took place in the United States, not in British North America. This process operated at many scales, and at the point of departure always tended to protect, and anchor in space, ethnic and religious difference. It was the basic reason, for example, why a largely Catholic, French-speaking Lower Canada and a largely Protestant, English-speaking Upper Canada remained as distinct from each other as they did. British North America was a mosaic of diverse peoples not only because it was composed of immigrants from varying backgrounds, but also because there was little means of mixing them up.

Ethnic and religious differences cropped up almost everywhere, but some of them involved small groups of very distinct people – the Mennonites in the Grand River Valley in Upper Canada, the blacks near Halifax – and many more involved various peoples from the British Isles, most of whom spoke English and had at least some prior exposure to British institutions. These were not the differences that engaged the Fathers of Confederation. Their concerns were broader and turned around the two axes of difference that the settlement of northern North America had thrown up most insistently: one between Protestants and Catholics, the other between speakers of English and speakers of French. Both emphasized the difference between the largely Protestant, English-speaking immigrants (and their descendants) who had arrived after the conquest and the almost entirely Catholic, French-speaking people whose ancestors had settled in North America long before it. The British and the French. There was no getting around this difference. The "French" were numerous and were principally situated along the St. Lawrence entrance to the continental interior, virtually in the middle of the country the Fathers of Confederation sought to create. Given their past, they had a clearer sense of themselves as a distinct regional people than, probably, any other sizable population north of the Rio Grande. Some differences could be put aside, but not this one; if there were to be a northern transcontinental country, it would have to be accommodated.

The accommodation worked out at Confederation depended on the division of power between one central government and seven provincial governments conceived as the principal political repositories of difference. In one of them, Quebec, the French language and French Canadian culture would be predominant. However, within each province – each of the others as much as Quebec – were many different peoples (including both anglophones and francophones), usually living in considerable isolation. A legislative union (well over a hundred municipality-like local governments and a central government) would have been a closer fit with this localness but, particularly in the view of Quebec politicians, would not have provided a sufficient political shield for the defence of the French language and French Canadian culture. A federation in which power over matters of obvious cultural importance, such as education, rested with the provinces came closer to meeting this requirement. Although, given the distribution of French and English speakers within and outside Quebec and the still limited power of governments to manage local affairs, no one government, provincial or federal, could provide a comprehensive cultural shield for French Canadians in British North America. The state had not yet acquired its subsequent salience, either as a source of administrative power or as a focus of identity. Most lives were organized locally, and their larger allegiances – to religion, for example – tended to transcend political boundaries that were hardly yet in focus. In effect, Confederation sought to impose a clear division of political and administrative authority on a thoroughly untidy reality. It was the acceptable geopolitical generalization that, in the late 1860s and early 1870s, could be overlaid on the diversity of British North America. It created the constitutional illusion of an order that, on the ground, British North America did not express. At the same time, it established federal and provincial poles of political power and identification, the one in some tension with the other and both subject to judicial interpretation. To each, over the years, power might accrue and identities attach themselves in ways that could not be foreseen at Confederation.

THE CONSTRUCTION OF SIMILARITY

The construction of difference in British North America grew out of the ways in which, over the years, Europeans of various stripes and prejudices came to northern North America, took over tracts of a Native land, and lived there. It was not premeditated so much as a consequence of the circumstances in which they found themselves and the values they took for granted. In much the same way, the construction of similarity was less a matter of explicit recognition than of a certain sharing, of which most people were largely unaware, of values and experiences.

Confederation amalgamated several British colonies into one large colony that remained securely located within the British empire. During the Confederation debates, virtually no one had argued that this imperial connection be broken. In terms of their ultimate political allegiance, the colonies were, and the Dominion would remain, British. Of course, Britishness meant different things to different people. Some thought of themselves as expatriates whose lives reproduced, as much as possible, British ways and values. Such people tended to approve of ordered, hierarchical, and deferential societies, and to decry what they perceived as the turbulent excesses of republican America. For others, particularly among the Protestant Irish, the imperial connection was a defence against the wiles of the pope and the spread of Roman Catholicism. Yet others stressed the value of British parliamentary institutions and the common law, neither of which, in some minds, could be much improved. For a good many more, Britishness was, simply, a taken-for-granted birthright. Although few French Canadians thought of their Britishness in cultural terms, many found some satisfaction in their position in the British empire. It had saved them, after all, from the anti-clerical horrors of the French Revolution and its aftermath. Moreover, because the British empire had accommodated different peoples and cultures around the world, it could well provide, many thought, a framework for the defence of cultural difference within British North America. Overall, Britishness was an umbrella under which most British North Americans sat fairly comfortably, perhaps because they tended to construct Britishness differently and to face in different directions.

And yet, however they constructed Britishness, they all lived in colonies in which, compared to that of the United States, the authority of the state was relatively salient. In New England and the Middle Colonies, as historian Elizabeth Mancke has pointed out, local autonomy was vigorously defended, so much so that in many minds the function of colonial (provincial) governments was to act as barriers protecting the rights of local self-government. If, as many in Britain theorized, the Thirteen Colonies had been lost because local government had been allowed to progress too far, the mistake was not to be repeated in the colonies Britain acquired in North America in the eighteenth century, and then held. There, where the British Crown had a relatively clean slate, it emphasized the executive, granted few and weak local powers, and situated colonial governments with a vertical hierarchy of power tied to a parliament in London and the authority of the Crown. American immigrants to these colonies almost always felt, on the one hand, the relative weakness of local government and, on the other, the increased weight of the executive and, through it, of centralized state power – an inadvertent perpetuation in a different empire of the centralization of power in Canada during the French regime.

There was also a widespread ambivalence and unease about the United States. There was much to admire in the republic to the south: its energy, its practical inventions (many quickly copied), and the opportunities it provided to get ahead. Many young British North Americans emigrated there, and their accounts tended to draw others. But the United States was also feared, a consequence partly of invasions during the American Revolution and the War of 1812, and also, well into the 1860s, of the perceived risk of invasion, which the large number of British troops and military fortifications in the British colonies were intended to forestall. Apprehensions were particularly great during the American Civil War when, by and large, British North American opinion favoured the South (in good part because a Southern victory would weaken the continental political power of the North) and some politicians in northern states, fed up with British neutrality during the war, talked of annexation. Moreover, many British North Americans were uneasy about the institutions of American republicanism, and a few of them about the construction of a society around a commitment to individual liberty. Such a society, they held, could only become a rabble destructive of community and the social order. Among those of British background, apprehension about the United States was the other side of the Britishness of British North America. Among those of French background, it had more to do with fears about the loss of population and about the religious and cultural vulnerability of French Canadians in the United States. The elites were particularly apprehensive; many of the young and poor, less articulate and established, emigrated.

And there was a widespread agricultural experience with a northern land, an experience to which historian W.L. Morton alluded years ago in an essay on Victorian Canada. He thought that the main task in early Canada was the creation of a habitat, a livable land, and that clearing and cultivating land were the principal means to this end. In so doing, he argued, settlers across the span of British North America were exposed to similar challenges, particularly, in his words, to "a severe climate and often gruelling terrain." They shared, therefore, a common experience. Although I would not frame the case quite so environmentally, I do think that, broadly, Morton was right. This book has dealt with many of the recurrent experiences. Pioneering in northern, forested settings, wherever it took place, was a similarly back-breaking, family-centred activity. The eventual result was a family farm, a vehicle for the maintenance and reproduction of families through long winters and shortish summers in settings where, compared to rural Europe, the value of land was relatively low and the social range was constricted. Farm economies were mixed, usually in good part self-sufficient, and often supplemented by non-agricultural work. Local agricultural land soon ran out, and the generational challenge of family reproduction had to be faced. There was difference, of course, but across the rural span of what became Canada, the similarity of lives and livelihoods is far more striking. People struggled with similar circumstances to similar ends. At the edge of cultivation, whether on Cape Breton Island, along the fringe of the Canadian Shield north of the St. Lawrence lowlands, or along the colonization roads built into the Shield north of Lake Ontario, the challenges and meagre achievements of pioneering were virtually identical. Away from the edge, difference became a little more pronounced, but most recent analyses of early Canadian agriculture have shown that, underneath differences in ethnicity and religion, the values, strategies, and achievements of farm families were far more similar than had been thought.

A Confederation of Multiple Identities

At Confederation many patterns of land and life in the new Dominion of Canada were old and well established, but the idea of Canada as a transcontinental country was relatively new. A sense of identity with a country constructed at this scale did not yet exist, and provincial identities were weak. Even those living in Ontario and Quebec who called themselves Canadians (or French Canadians or English Canadians) did not yet include, for example, Nova Scotians, or the Métis at Red River, or the gold rush society of British Columbia in that identification. In locations such as these, Canadians were known as different people and were often suspected (particularly those from Ontario) of imperial tendencies. Rather, the Dominion was a complex matrix of more local identities organized at various scales. The country George-Étienne Cartier envisaged – a place in which cultural identity was associated with the provinces and an overarching political identity with the federal government – remained, as he well knew, to be created.

Over the years since Confederation, both federal and provincial governments have become more salient, and something approximately like the Canada Cartier envisaged has come into being. Identities are still multiple and variously constructed, but for some, political identities have come to focus on a province, for others on Canada as a whole, and for many more, as Cartier anticipated, on both. As the country filled in somewhat, a pragmatic, fortunate, and, some might even say, tolerably sensible entity has come into being, one that most – though clearly not all – of its citizens appreciate. A rather unlikely creation has endured and, in its fashion, has worked. For many newcomers, it is a haven in a troubled world; for many others whose people have been here much longer, there is satisfaction, even much somewhat inarticulate pride, in being Canadian. Yet Canada, as noted in the preface to this book, is a difficult country to know. It does not readily conform to simple descriptions of itself, has developed a weak symbolic vocabulary, and is allergic to precise definition. In a world of strident nationalisms these may be among its most attractive qualities. That said, Canadians would do well to remember the following four simple understandings drawn from the country's long pre-Confederation past.

Although Native societies were enormously rearranged during the more than 350 years of European advance into northern North America before Confederation, most of them survived in some form. They variously adopted European ways while continuing to think of themselves as people apart. This they achieved both on meagre reserves within settler colonies and throughout the vast territories extending beyond them. Discourses of assimilation, some of them consistently pursued through several generations, were usually unsuccessful. In many particular instances they made Christian converts, but even then did not erase the boundary between newcomer and Native. Although the implication of this long survival was that, in all probability, it would continue, Confederation embodied no understanding – no accommodation – across a boundary that, here as elsewhere around the world, was a basic corollary of aggressive settler colonialism. Rather, it allocated responsibility for the management of Native peoples who, it was widely assumed, would die off or be assimilated. The issues presented by a continuing Native presence were not addressed. Nor would they go away, embedded as they were in British North America before Confederation and, later, in an evolving Canada. This, perhaps, is Confederation's most serious unfinished business. After many years of successful colonialism, it has no simple resolution. Nonetheless, it has to be faced with respect for Native people and a willingness on the part of those who have so largely benefited from their dispossession to return some fraction of the land – the resources – that settler colonial societies took away. Fortunately, in recent years this has begun to happen.

The deepest European presence in Canada is French, and it is the one around which the country has been built. For 150 years, Canada was a French colony. When it became British, and when, shortly thereafter, Britain lost the most populous parts of her North American empire, this formerly French and still overwhelmingly French-speaking colony became the principal refuge of an imperial British presence in North America. Without this anchor, British North America would have been lost to an enlarged United States. Canada would not exist. Even its name, which goes back to the 1530s and Jacques Cartier's interactions with Native people along the St. Lawrence River, suggests this dependence. Moreover, the continuing, substantial, and central presence of a French-speaking, Catholic people presented difference as fact and forced an emerging country to conceive of itself not as a unitary creation, which obviously it was not, but as a place that, however imperfectly, had to come to terms with difference. This, the British North America Act tried to do, as, in various ways and with varying degrees of success, has Canada ever since. A country rooted in difference has structured itself accordingly. In these ways, the Frenchness of Canada lies at its core: at its beginning, near its geographical centre, and embedded in the structure of its constitution. Take away this Frenchness and the country would no longer make much historical, geographical, or constitutional sense. In all likelihood, it would soon experience what, indirectly and ironically, the French presence along the lower St. Lawrence prevented more than two hundred years ago.

A fundamental condition, therefore, of the existence of Canada is the long-term viability of vital, healthy, French-speaking societies. In a largely English-speaking North America, such societies require considerably more protection than their English-speaking counterparts. It needs to be provided, a responsibility not only of the government of Quebec but of the whole country. This is not a price to be paid so much as an opportunity cost of a diverse country that appreciates its differences – especially the difference around which, in so many ways, it has been constructed.

Immigration over some 250 years before Confederation brought diverse peoples to northern North America, and their patterns of settlement and subsequent migrations tended to fossilize this diversity. For all the preferences and exclusions that, later, were built into immigration policy, Canadian multiculturalism is not new. The diversity in the background of Canadian life affects the country's recent multicultural diversity in various ways. On the one hand, it can make it difficult for newcomers to fit into local, ethnically homogeneous societies composed of people who have lived with each other for generations. On the other, it probably has made it easier for them to fit into a country – and to be appreciated by a country – in which diversity is inherent. Different Canadian and European attitudes to recent immigrants stem, essentially, from the fact that, Native people apart, Canada is an immigrant society composed of different peoples that have not been assimilated, either culturally or symbolically, in a particular mould. The conditions that counteracted such assimilation were established long before Confederation.

The sense of being Canadian has been constructed within these circumstances. It cannot take its impetus from a heroic beginning or from first principles, because Confederation, an apparently workable accommodation of different objectives and societies, was itself an unheroic and essentially pragmatic achievement. Even Cartier's theory of federalism, the closest the Confederation debates came to theoretical originality, was an inductive response to the realities at hand. It cannot be a single cultural identity because British North America before Confederation and Canada since have been culturally plural. For this reason, the country's national symbols – maple leaves, beavers, geese – are as culturally neutral as possible. Rather, a sense of being Canadian, a sense of common Canadian citizenship, is a product of different people living for a considerable time with each other, with a huge northern land, with the institutions and iconography of Canadian government, with the same federal politicians, with the wars in which Canada has participated, and with the artists, writers, and musicians who have variously interpreted their circumstances. It did not exist at Confederation and has been an ongoing creation ever since.

Any national society is an imagined community. The Canadian imagination has had to make some collective sense of a vast space, the differences on which Confederation was built, the many diverse peoples who subsequently came to this country, the looming cultural presence of the United States, and an increasingly globalized world in which, in many minds, national identities are superseded. No wonder, then, that it expresses itself hesitantly, that it has not worked out a compelling symbolic vocabulary, or that some reject the very idea of Canada. It could hardly be otherwise. The question, however, is whether this lack of definition and consensus is a problem to be overcome. I much doubt it. An unambiguous nationalism, hardly needed on the world's stage, fits neither what Canada is nor the pre-Confederation background on which it has been superimposed. It does not fit the varied ways in which people have lived here, or the experiences they have shared, usually without quite realizing that they have. It does not fit what is most precious in this country, and what, at its best, Canada is, a society that respects and appreciates the differences of which it is composed, and, ironically, in so doing establishes its own identity more clearly.

BIBLIOGRAPHY

Among the large literature on the politics and debates leading up to Confederation, I have relied particularly on the following: L.F.S. Upton, "The Idea of Confederation: 1754-1858," in W.L. Morton, ed., *The Shield of Achilles* (Toronto: McClelland and Stewart, 1968), 184-207; Peter Waite, *Confederation, 1854-1867* (Toronto: Holt, Rinehart and Winston, 1972); W.L. Morton, *Critical Years: The Union of British North America* (Toronto: McClelland and Stewart, 1964); Ged Martin, *Britain and the Origins of Canadian Confederation, 1837-67* (Vancouver: UBC Press, 1995); Garth Stevenson, *Ex uno plures: Federal Provincial Relations in Canada, 1867-1896* (Montreal and Kingston: McGill-Queen's University Press, 1993), chap. 1; and Samuel V. LaSelva, *The Moral Foundations of Canadian Federalism: Paradoxes, Achievements, and Tragedies of Nationhood* (Montreal and Kingston: McGill-Queen's University Press, 1996), particularly chap. 1. Also, Suzanne Zeller, *Inventing Canada: Early Victorian Science and the Idea of a Transcontinental Nation* (Toronto: University of Toronto Press, 1987), particularly the Introduction and Conclusion; and Rusty Bittermann and Margaret McCallum, "Upholding the Land Legislation of a 'Communistic and Socialist' Assembly: The Benefits of Confederation for Prince Edward Island," *Canadian Historical Review* 87, 1 (2006): 1-28.

For the rest, I have drawn principally on the earlier chapters of this book, essays by two historians of different stripes and generations – W.L. Morton, "Victorian Canada," in Morton, *The Shield of Achilles*, 311-34; and Elizabeth Mancke, "Another British America: A Canadian Model for the Early Modern British Empire," *Journal of Imperial and Commonwealth History* 25, 1 (1997): 1-36 – and on my own more conceptual essays on patterns and power relations in early Canada: "The Simplification of Europe Overseas," *Annals, Association of American Geographers* 67, 4 (1977): 469-83; "The Pattern of Early Canada," *Canadian Geographer* 31, 4 (1987): 290-98; reprinted with considerable revisions in Graeme Wynn, ed., *People, Places, Patterns, Processes: Geographical Perspectives on the Canadian Past* (Toronto: Copp Clark Pitman, 1990), 358-73; "Making an Immigrant Society," in Cole Harris, *The Resettlement of British Columbia* (Vancouver: UBC Press, 1997), chap. 9; "Postmodern Patriotism: Canadian Reflections," *Canadian Geographer* 45, 1 (2001): 193-207; and "How Did Colonialism Dispossess? Comments from an Edge of Empire," *Annals, Association of American Geographers* 94, 1 (2004): 165-82.

Two well-known essays that treat some of the patterns and relationships examined in this chapter are J.M.S. Careless, "Limited Identities in Canada," *Canadian Historical Review* 50 (1969): 1-10; and J.M. Bumsted, "The Cultural Landscape of Early Canada," in Bernard Bailyn and Philip D. Morgan, eds., *Strangers within the Realm: Cultural Margins of the First British Empire* (Chapel Hill: University of North Carolina Press, 1991), 363-92.

Index

Aboîteaux, 55
Acadia, 55-64
Acadians: deportation of, 120-21, 162; in New Brunswick, 190-91; in Nova Scotia, 217; return of, 171
Acheson, T.W., 188, 191
Agricultural capability: British North America, 133-34; Lower Canada, 234-35; Maritimes, 165; Upper Canada, 307, 324
Agricultural land policy: Cape Breton, 203; early Canada, 73-74; Lower Canada, 280-81, 293-94; New Brunswick, 189; PEI, 197; Upper Canada, 316-19; Vancouver Island, 430-31
Agriculture: before 1500, 12-14; Acadia, 55, 57-58; British Columbia, 442-43; early Canada, 74-76, 79; Lower Canada, 242, 244, 247-55, 283, 289, 291-92; Maritimes in 1800, 176; New Brunswick, 190-91; Newfoundland, 145; Nova Scotia, 211-13; Red River, 400-1, 403-4; Upper Canada, 333-36, 363-65. *See also* Family farms
Agricultural settlement (general configuration of), 458-62
Algonquians, 8, 65, 94
Algonquin (peoples), 40, 47, 92-95

Alliance. *See* French-Native alliance
American Revolution, 125
Anglicans, 298, 396-97, 431
Annapolis Royal, 56-57
Annapolis Valley, 167, 211, 217
Annexation of northwestern interior, 405-6, 408
Architecture: church, 84, 192, 260; urban, 69-70, 173-74, 274-75. *See also* Farmhouses
Arichat (Cape Breton Island), 175
Assiniboine (peoples), 100, 109, 112-13, 379, 385, 390, 394-95
Avalon Peninsula (Newfoundland), 24-25, 138, 154

Baffin, William, 27
Banks fishery, 32, 145, 154
Bannister, Gerry, 149
Barkerville (British Columbia), 435-36
Barns: in Lower Canada, 259-60, 297; in Upper Canada, 349, 351, 365-66
Batiscan (Québec), 252
Beothuk, 34, 46, 140, 158
Biard, Father, 47, 48
Binnema, Theodore, 385
Bison, 9, 388, 390, 394, 401-3, 412

Bittermann, Rusty, 200, 204-5

Blackfoot (peoples), 112, 385, 390, 395, 408

Blacks, 168-69, 218, 329, 465

Bouchard, Gérard, 246, 258-59, 283, 285

Bradbury, Bettina, 277

Brandão, José, 96-97

Brisay de Denonville, 102

British American Land Company, 288

British Columbia, 433-45, 452-53

Britishness, 354, 369-70, 467-68

Brown, Jennifer, 107, 389

Brulé, Étienne, 43

Brunger, Alan, 324

Bumsted, Jack, 165-66, 170

Burgess, Joan, 270-71

Button, William, 27

Bylot, Robert, 27

Cabot, John, 21-22, 31

Cadigan, Sean, 157

Calvert, George (Lord Baltimore), 138

Cambuse, 282

Camps. *See* Work camps

Canada Company, 319

Canals, 264-65, 268, 272, 343

Cantin, Augustin, 276

Cape Breton, 203-9

Cariboo (British Columbia), 434-36

Cartier, George-Étienne, 237, 453-54, 470, 473

Cartier, Jacques, 23-24, 26, 41

Cartographic erasure, 21, 26, 29

Champlain, Samuel de, 29-30, 39-44, 92-93

Charlottetown (PEI), 173, 202

Chaste, Aymar de, 39

Chatham (New Brunswick), 188, 194

Chauvin de Tonnetuit, Pierre de, 39

Chéticamp (Cape Breton Island), 175

Chinese, 440-43

Chipewyan (peoples), 10, 112-13, 379, 383-85, 390

Chouart des Groseilliers, 97-98, 100

Church power: Acadia, 60; early Canada, 82-83, 85

Clark, Andrew H., xxi, 55, 201

Clarke, John, 319-20, 324, 326

Class, 157-59, 178, 275, 360-61, 444. *See also* Social hierarchy

Clayton, Daniel, 129, 421

Coal mining: Cape Breton, 207-8; mainland Nova Scotia, 215; Vancouver Island, 432, 442

Coates, Colin, 78, 252-53

Cod fishery: in 16th century, 31-36; in Cape Breton, 206-7; environmental impact of, 48; in Maritimes in 1800, 175; in Newfoundland in 17th century, 137-42; in Newfoundland in 18th century, 142-50; in Newfoundland in 19th century, 150-51, 154-55; spatial economy of, 45-46

Cohen, Marjorie Griffin, 331, 336

Colley, Linda, 315

Colonial cultural discourse, 226, 465

Colonization of Canadian Shield: Lower Canada, 277-86; Upper Canada, 366-69

Colonization societies, 285, 291

Commercial capital (spatial configuration of), 456-58, 465

Common law: in Britain, 314; in British Columbia, 439, 455; in Upper Canada, 316, 351-53

Company of One Hundred Associates (of New France), 43, 52, 73, 93

Confederation: background of, 448-51; and the Canadian imagination, 473-74; creation of, 451-53; and difference, 466-67, 472-73; and French-speaking Canada, 471-72; and multiple identities, 470-76; and Native Canada, 471; originality of 453-54; pragmatism of, 453

Congés, 101

Conservation of beaver, 392-93

Constitutional Act, 1791, 232, 262

Cook, Captain, 17, 131, 417, 419

Corte-Real, Gaspar, 21-22

Côte, 77

Côte du Sud, 253-54

Countryside: Acadia, 58-59; early Canada, 72-85; Lower Canada, 259-60, 277; PEI, 202-3; Upper Canada, 327-28, 365

Coureurs de bois, 98, 100, 104, 109

Courville, Serge, 87, 241, 244, 251-52, 284

Coutume de Paris: Acadia, 61; early Canada, 74, 455; Lower Canada, 237, 243-44

Coyote (trickster/transformer), 15, 17

Cree (peoples), 100, 109, 112-13, 379, 383, 385, 390, 395

Crofts, 170, 181-82, 314

Cultural landscape: Acadia, 58-59; early Canada, 83-84; Lower Canada, 259-61, 297-98; outport Newfoundland, 159; PEI, 202

Cultural transfer and change: Acadia, 62-63; agricultural settlements, 459; British Columbia, 439; early Canada, 80, 82, 87; Newfoundland, 155; Nova Scotia, 219; rural Upper Canada, 352-53

Cunard, Joseph, 188-89

Dakota Sioux, 97, 100, 113

Davey, Ian, 347

Davis, John, 27

Dawson, Simon J., 408

De Meurons, 388, 399

Dechêne, Louise, xx, 71-72, 78, 83, 279

Dependency. *See* Native dependence

Desceliers, Pierre, 24-25

Dessureault, Christian, 249-50

Dickinson, John, 74

Difference (construction of), 461, 464-67

Dikes, 55, 58-60

Disease: 16th century, 46-48; early 17th century, 93; in Cordillera, 428; effects of, c. 1850, 134; in logging camps, 282; among Mi'kmaq, 179; in refugee settlements west of Lake Michigan, 97, 111; in towns, 278. *See also* Smallpox

Dispossession of Native peoples: regional instances of, 178-80, 286, 225-26; powers behind, 462-63

Doucette, Michael, 347

Douglas, James, 429-33, 437

Draper Site, 13

Du Gua de Monts, Pierre, 41-42

Durham, Lord, 245, 354, 448

Durroch, Gordon, 365

Eastern Townships, 287-98

Ecological footprint, 48

Emigration to US: from Cape Breton, 208-9; general, 461; from Lower Canada, 245, 267, 284, 299; from Maritimes, 222; from Upper Canada, 356, 361, 365-66

Ennals, Peter, 320

Ens, Gerhard, 401-2

Environmental impact: of cod fishery, 48-49; of fur trade, 49, 385-86, 412, 428; of gold rush, 434; of logging, 225, 285; of settlement in Newfoundland, 159; of settlement in Upper Canada, 341-42

Erie Canal, 265, 343

Essex County, 319-20, 326

Ethnicity: British Columbia, 440-43; British North America, 465-66; Eastern Townships, 294-96; mainland Nova Scotia (1851), 218; Maritimes (1800), 177-78; Montreal and Quebec, 273-76, 300-1; New Brunswick, 198; PEI, 201; Newfoundland, 144, 152-53, 155; planter Nova Scotia, 165-66; Upper Canada, 25-26, 329, 231-32, 353

Export trades: from Acadia, 55-56; from early Canada, 68, 79; from Lower Canada, 244; from Maritimes in 1800, 175-76; from Maritimes after 1850, 221; from Nova Scotia, 210-11, 217-18; from Upper Canada, 243-45, 248, 357, 363-68. *See also* Cod fishery; Fur trade; Timber trade

Factory production: Britain, 180, 311-14; Eastern townships, 292; Maritimes, 220-21; Montreal and Quebec, 269-72; Upper Canada, 338, 357-62

Family farms: Acadia, 57-60; early Canada, 74-79; Cape Breton, 205-6; common experience with, 459-60, 469-70; Lower Canada, 246-47, 283-86, 289, 294; New Brunswick, 190-91; Newfoundland, 155; Nova Scotia, 212-13, 217; PEI, 197-200; Red River, 400-2; Upper Canada, 326-27, 332-33, 336, 347-48, 352-53, 364-65

Farmer-loggers: Lower Canada, 284; New Brunswick, 190-91; PEI, 200; Upper Canada, 336, 340

Farmhouses: Acadian, 58-59, 193; in early Canada, 80-81; on Cape Breton, 177, 205; in Horton, NS, in 1800, 176; in Lower Canada, 260, 297; at Red River, 402, in Upper Canada, 348-50, 366

Farming. *See* Agriculture

Fernandes, João, 21

Ferryland (Newfoundland), 139, 141-42

Fertile Belt, 408-10

Forest land policy: in Lower Canada, 280-81; in New Brunswick, 184-85; in Upper Canada, 367

Forest regeneration: New Brunswick, 225; Shield fringe, 285; Upper Canada, 342

Foucault, Michel, 85-86, 223, 455-56, 463

Foucher, Albert, 245

Fournier, Martin, 98

Fox, Luke, 28

Franklin, John, 17

Fraser, Simon, 17, 418, 420

Fredericton (New Brunswick), 173, 188, 192

Freemen, 388

French-Native alliance, 40, 102, 104, 108-9, 119-20, 125, 129

Friesen, Gerald, 391

Frobisher, Martin, 27

Frontenac, Louis de Buade, comte de, 101

Fur posts: character of, 44, 107-8; closure of under Simpson, 391-92; in Cordillera, 423-28; Native women at, 108; Norway House, 410-11; proliferation of, 101, 383-85

Fur trade: 16th century, 38-39; early 17th century, 43-44; competition between St. Lawrence and Bay, 100-1, 110, 380-82; in Cordillera, 423-28; coureurs de bois, 98, 100, 104, 109; disciplinary power in, 427, 465; economic specialization in, 113-14, 379; environmental impact of, 49, 385-86, 412, 428; expansion of, 44, 97-98, 106, 380-82, 384-85, 424-26; French policies regarding, 103-6; impact on Native livelihoods, 46, 384-86, 393-94, 412;

Native middlemen in, 43, 93, 109-10, 379, 383-84; in northwest in 1870, 409-11; provisioning of, 384-85; Simpson's policies regarding, 391-93, 424-25, 427; spatial economy of, 45-46

Gaffield, Chad, 282
Gagan, David, 320, 330-31
Galois, Robert, 428
Garrisons: in 1750, 118; Lower Canada, 262, 263; Maritimes, 162, 173, 175, 188; Newfoundland, 142; Quebec and Montreal, 67-68
Gender, 7, 12, 140, 143-44, 154, 198, 336, 362, 444
Giddens, Anthony, 322
Girard, Philip, 352
Gold rush, 432-35
Grand Trunk Railway, 265, 272, 356
Gravé du Pont, François, 40
Greer, Allan, 82, 246-49, 257, 262
Griffiths, Naomi, 55
Gros Ventre (peoples), 112
Gwyn, Julian, 172, 210-11, 222

Habermas, Jürgen, 16, 18
Habitants-pêcheurs, 139-41
Hackett, Paul, 111, 383
Halifax (Nova Scotia): in 1800, 173, 178; in early 19th century, 209-10; mid-19th century, 216-17; establishment of, 120; early industrialization in, 220-21; Loyalists in, 167; population of in 1759, 162; reach of, 223
Hamilton (Ontario), 346-47, 360-62
Handcock, Gordon, 141-42
Hanna, David, 274-76
Harbour Grace (Newfoundland), 147, 158, 159
Hardwood Hill, 211-12
Hardy, René, 282

Hartz, Louis, 54, 62
Hawaiians, 423, 442
Head, Grant, 48, 145
Heidenreich, Conrad, 12, 40, 96-97
Highland immigrants, 169-71, 181-82, 291, 293
Hind, Henry Youle, 408-9
Hochelaga, 23
Hoffmann, Richard, 48
Hornsby, Stephen, 36, 177
Horses, 92, 112, 384
Horton (Nova Scotia), 166, 176-77
Houston, Cecil, 353
Hudson, Henry, 27
Hudson's Bay Company: administration at Red River, 400; charter of, 100; forts, 106, 381-83, 391; merger with NWC, 389, 391; on Pacific slope, 424-27; sale of Rupert's Land, 451; Simpson's policies, 391-93, 424-25, 427; spatial patterns of trade, 109-10, 380-82; transportation system, 410-11; on Vancouver Island, 429-32
Hunt, George T., 96
Hunting, fishing, and gathering, 5-11, 409
Huron (peoples), 15, 43, 46, 47, 92-96
Hybridity, 108, 390, 465

Île St-Jean (Island of St. John), 57, 163, 166-67, 170
Immigration: to Acadia, 53; to early Canada, 52-53, 65-66; to Cape Breton, 205; to Maritimes, 1760-1800, 164-71, 183; to Newfoundland, 143-44, 152-54; to Lower Canada, 183, 233, 288; to Quebec and Montreal, 71, 266-67; to Red River, 386-87; to Upper Canada, 183, 309-12, 358-61
Imperial system (general configuration of), 454-56, 465

Industrialization: British Isles, 180, 182-83, 314; British North America at Confederation, 458; Cape Breton, 207-8; Eastern Townships, 292, 294; mainland Nova Scotia, 215; Montreal and Quebec, 268-72; Saint John and Halifax, 220; Upper Canada, 338, 357-62

Inheritance of family farms: early Canada, 76, 79, 83; general, 460-61; Lower Canada, 240, 243-44, 257, 259; Upper Canada, 330-31

Innis, Harold, xvii, 31, 132, 456, 458

Innu (Montagnais), 40, 46, 47

Inport-outport system, Newfoundland, 147-49

Intervale, 203-5

Irish immigrants: to Maritimes, 182-83; to Upper Canada, 310

Irish: on mainland Nova Scotia, 217; in Montreal, 274-76, 301; in New Brunswick, 193-95; in Newfoundland, 143-44, 153, 155; in Upper Canada, 325-26, 329, 347

Iroquoian social structure, 12-13

Iroquois League, 43, 49, 93-94

Iroquois, wars, 94-97, 102

Jay's Treaty (1794), 128, 232

Jesuits, 17, 93-95, 98-99

Josephides, Lisette, 422

Kaskaskia (upper Mississippi), 106

Katz, Michael, 346, 361-62

Kealey, Greg, 359

Kelly, Kenneth, 334, 336

Kesteman, Jean-Pierre, 288, 294

Kingston (Ontario), 264, 292, 265, 322, 344-45, 358

Kirke, David, 138-39, 141

Krieghoff, Cornelius, 285

La Barre, 102

La Cosa, Jean de, 22

La Salle, 101

Labelle, François-Xavier Antoine, 285

Laberge, Alain, 80, 253-54

Labrador floater fishery, 151, 154

Lac-des-Deux-Montagnes (Québec), 251

Land grants: early Canada, 73; Eastern Townships, 287-88; 291; to planters in Nova Scotia, 165; to proprietors on PEI, 196; to Selkirk at Red River, 387; Upper Canada, 316-19, 367

Land speculators: Eastern Townships, 288; early Nova Scotia, 166; Upper Canada, 324-25

Land value: Britain, 313; Lower Canada, 244; Upper Canada, 319-20, 330

LaSelva, Samuel, 454

Lasserre, Jean-Claude, 248

Latour, Bruno, 26, 408

Laurin, Serge, 251

Le Jeune, Father, 44

Lévis (Québec), 253

Lewis, Robert, 273

Liberalism, 354

Lifeworlds, 14-19, 110, 156

Little, J.I., 293, 298

Local knowledge, 16, 156, 315, 352

Long-lot farms: early Canada, 74-75, 83; Lower Canada, 239-40, 259; Prince Edward Island, 197; Red River, 387, 400

Loo, Tina, 433

Lotbinière (Québec), 253

Louisbourg, 55, 88, 62-63, 119, 122, 129

Louisiana (Québec), 105

Lower, A.R.M., 367

Loyalists: Maritimes, 167-69, 172; Lower Canada, 233; Upper Canada, 309-10, 321

Lunenburg (Nova Scotia), 162, 218

Macdonald, John A., 453
Macdonnell, Miles, 387-88
MacKenzie, Alexander, 380, 418, 420, 423
Mackie, Richard, 423, 431
MacKinnon, Neil, 168
Madawaska (New Brunswick), 171, 194
    Maliseet (peoples), 162, 196, 225-26
Malloy, Mary, 421
Mancke, Elizabeth, 65, 176, 468
Manitoba, 452
Mannion, John, 155
Maritime fur trade, 420-22
Marsden, Susan, 15
Marx, Karl, xvii, 54, 63, 180
Mathieu, Jacques, 80
Mauricie (Québec), 279-80
McCalla, Douglas, 335, 357
McCallum, John, 244, 255, 344
McCann, Larry, 214
McInnis, Marvin, 347, 364
McKay, Ian, 354
Measles, 46
Meinig, Donald, xxi
Mennonites, 329, 355, 465
Mentality debate, Lower Canada, 245-
    47, 258-59
Merchants: Acadia, 62; early Canadian
    countryside, 83; Halifax, 209-11; Lower
    Canada, seigneurial lowlands, 256;
    Maritimes after 1850, 221-22; New
    Brunswick, 186-88; Newfoundland,
    139-40, 144, 150, 154-55; PEI, 200;
    Quebec and Montreal, 65, 98, 263,
    266; Upper Canada, 238-39, 243-44
Merivale, Herman, 181
Métis, 387-89, 394, 399-405, 409, 412-13,
    451, 463
Mi'kmaq (peoples), 14, 15, 25, 34, 47, 63,
    162, 178-80, 196, 217, 225-26

Miami (peoples), 102
Middle River (Cape Breton Island),
    204
Miltary power (generalized deploy-
    ment of), 454-55
Militia: early Canada, 53, 78, 83, 102;
    Lower Canada, 262
Minas Basin (Nova Scotia), 165, 211-12,
    217
Miramichi (New Brunswick), 188-89,
    191-92, 193-94, 209
Missionaries, 17, 93-95, 98-99, 298,
    395-98
Mississauga (peoples), 98
Mohawk (peoples), 94-95, 98, 102, 355
Montreal: before 1760, 67-72; after 1760,
    232, 263-77; surrender of, 122
Montreal Plain, 251-52, 255
Morton, W.L., 449, 469
Multiple identities, 470-74
Munk, Jens, 27-28
Murray, James, 231, 235

Nanaimo (BC), 430, 443-44
Native dependence, 385-86, 393-94, 412,
    465-66
Neutral (peoples), 94-95
New Brunswick, 167, 184-96, 453
New Caledonia, 423-24
Nipissing (peoples), 43,
Norris, Darrell, 320, 331
North West Company, 381-82, 384, 389,
    391, 420, 423
Norway House, 410-12
Nova Scotia: 1760-1800, 164-80; 1800-
    50, 209-19; and Confederation, 453

Oblates, 397-98
Ojibwa (peoples), 94, 98-99, 113, 307-8,
    355, 379, 383, 390
Olson, Sherry, 277

Orange Lodge: in New Brunswick, 195; in Upper Canada, 353-54, 369-70

Oregon Territory, 130-31, 424

Oregon Treaty, 131, 427, 429

Ottawa Valley, 278, 283, 339-40, 367

Ottawa-Huron Tract, 367-68

Ouellet, Fernand, 245

Outports: in Newfoundland, 147-49, 155-56, 158-59; in Maritimes, 175

Owram, Doug, 369, 405

Pacific Fur Company, 423

Palliser, John, 408

Palliser's Triangle, 408-9

Paquet, Gilles, 246

Peel County (Ontario), 330-32

Perry, Adele, 444

Petit Nord, 385

Petun (peoples), 43, 94

Physiographic regions, 4, 132-35

Pictou (Nova Scotia), 212, 217, 219

Placer mining, 434, 442

Plaisance (Placentia), 140, 142-43, 154

Planters: in Newfoundland, 139-41, 154; in Nova Scotia, 164-65, 172

Planting, Gerard, 222

Pond, Peter, 380

Pontiac's "rebellion," 123-24

Pope, Peter, 141-42

Population distribution: Acadia, 57-58; British Columbia, 439-41; British North America in 1851, 134; early Canada, 66-67; France in North America, 1750, 117-18; Lower Canada, 234, 298; Maritimes in 1800, 173-74; New Brunswick in 1850, 184-85; northern North America in 1500, 2, 12; Nova Scotia, 1851; Northwestern Interior in 1821, 389-90; PEI, 1833; Red River, 399; 405-6; Upper Canada, 322, 342-43, 359

Population growth: Acadia, 57; early Canada, 72-73; Cape Breton, 203; New Brunswick, 184; Lower Canada, 233-34; Newfoundland, 143-44, 152-54; PEI, 196; Upper Canada, 329, 355-56

Population pressure, British Isles: England, 312; Ireland, 310-11; Scotland, 181-82, 311-12

Port Royal (Acadia), 40, 53-57

Price, William, 279

Prince Edward Island, 57, 173, 196-203, 453

Private property rights, 181, 237, 313-14, 351, 437-39, 462

Quebec: before 1760, 41, 43-45, 53, 67-72; after 1760, 232, 263, 265-69, 271, 273-74, 277; fall of, 122

Quebec Act, 1774, 124-25, 232, 236

Queen's Bush, 331, 356

Quinn, D.B., 34-35

Racism, 169, 413, 443-44

Radford, Ian, 370

Radisson, Pierre-Esprit, 98, 100

Railways: Lower Canada, 264-66; Maritimes, 216, 223; to Pacific, 405, 450, 452; Upper Canada, 356-57

Rangs (ranges), 239

Rawlyk, George, 310

Ray, Arthur, 2, 44, 110-11, 386, 393

Rebellion of 1837, 261-62, 354, 455

Reciprocity Treaty, 220, 225, 357, 364

Reclus, Elisée, 117, 132

Red River, 386-88, 399-405, 412-13

Refugees from Iroquois wars, 97, 113

Reid, John, 65

Religion and the construction of difference, 224, 465-66

Reserves, 179, 308, 355, 430, 437-38

Riddington, Robin, 5

Rideau Canal, 264

Riel, Louis, 451

Roads: British Columbia, 435-37; Nova
Scotia, 219; rural Lower Canada, 239;
Upper Canada, 321-23, 345

Robert, Jean-Claude, 250-51, 267

Roberval, Jean-Françoise de la Roque,
sieur de, 24

Royal Proclamation, 1763, 123-24, 165-
66, 231, 235

Rupert's Land, 100, 452

Rural industry: Eastern Townships,
289-90; Nova Scotia, 215; PEI, 210;
seigneurial lowlands, 242, 245, 251-52;
Upper Canada, 237-38

Russell, Peter, 320

Sager, Eric, 222

Saguenay: 278-79, 283-84

Saint John (New Brunswick): 173, 178,
188-89, 199, 220, 223

Saint John Valley (New Brunswick),
167, 192

Saint-Denis (Québec), 248-49

Saint-Hyacinthe (Québec), 249

Saint-Ours (Québec), 248-49

Salmon fishery, Newfoundland, 145

Samson, Roch, 253

Savignon, 43

Sawmilling: British Columbia, 442;
Lower Canada, 279; mainland NS,
215; Saint John, 188; Upper Canada,
333, 337-38

Schooling, 218, 224, 262, 362, 456

Scots: Cape Breton, 170-71, 203-5, 209;
Eastern Townships, 293-95; New
Brunswick, 193-94; Nova Scotia, 177,
212; PEI, 170, 196-97, 201; Red River,
386-88, 399, 401; Upper Canada, 326,
329

Sealing, 145, 150-51, 154

Sea otter trade. *See* Maritime fur trade

See, Scott, 195-96

Séguin, Normand, 282

Seigneurial system: Acadia, 56, 60-61;
early Canada, 73, 82, 85; Lower
Canada, 235-37, 241-42, 253, 255-56

Selkirk, Lord, 197, 386, 388, 390

Seven Oaks, 388-89

Seven Year's War, 119-21

Shamans, 15

Shelburne (Nova Scotia), 167, 169, 173

Shipbuilding: early Canada, 68; Cape
Breton, 208; Lower Canada, 253, 271-
72, 278; Maritimes, 1860s, 220; Nova
Scotia, 214-15; PEI, 200, 202

Shoshone (peoples), 112, 379, 385

Simcoe, John Graves, 321-22

Similarity (construction of), 467-70

Simpson, George, 391-93, 424-25, 427

Smallpox, 46-48, 95, 111-12, 179, 377,
382-83, 395, 408-9

Smith, Adam, 180-81, 314,

Smith, Goldwin, 132

Smyth, William, 353

Social hierarchy: Acadia, 62; British
Columbia, 444; early Canadian
countryside, 78-80, 85-86; Eastern
Townships, 290; Halifax in 1800, 173;
Hamilton, 346-47, 360-62; Maritimes,
178, 222; Newfoundland, 156-58; PEI,
202-3; Quebec and Montreal, 70,
273-75; Red River, 402; rural Upper
Canada, 352, 365; seigneurial lowlands, 249-57; Vancouver Island, 431

Soltow, Lee, 365

Sorel (Québec), 247-48

Sovereign power, 86

Spanaxnox, 15

Spirit beings, 14-15

St. John's (Newfoundland), 142, 145,
150, 153, 158-59

Staple trades, 31, 335, 456

State power: Acadia, 56-57, 86; in Canadian tradition, 465; early Canadian countryside, 85-86; early Canadian towns, 67-68, 72, 86-87; Lower Canadian countryside, 262-64; and Maritime economy, 172-73; Maritimes, 223-24; Newfoundland, 18th century, 149-50, 158; Nova Scotia, 218

Steamboats, 264, 268, 435-37

Ste-Anne-de-la Pérade (Québec), 252

St-Hillaire, Marc

Starvation: in Ireland, 183, 310; among Native peoples, 5, 394, 412, 437; among settlers, 206, 253

Sydney (Cape Breton), 167, 173, 208

Taché, Joseph-Charles, 449

Tadoussac, 39, 40

Talon, Jean, 74

Tausig, Michael, 421

Thompson, David, 127, 418

Thompson, E.P., 314

Thoms, Michael, 308

Thule Inuit, 34, 46

Tilly, Charles, 315

Timber drives: New Brunswick, 186; Lower Canada, 281

Timber trade: New Brunswick 175-76, 184-89; Lower Canada, 277-82; Upper Canada, 339-40

Time-space compression, 314-15

Toronto, 342-43, 345-46, 356, 358-60

Tough, Frank, 409

Township surveys, 316-17

Toynbee, Arnold, 54

Treaties with Native groups: with Cree, Ojibwa, and Assiniboine at Red River, 388; with Innu and Algonquin near Tadoussac, 40; with Iroquois, 102-3; with Ojibwa in Upper Canada, 308; on Vancouver Island, 429-30

Treaty of Easton, 120, 123

Treaty of Ghent, 129

Treaty of Paris (1763): 121-23, 150; (1783): 126, 129, 166

Treaty of Saint Germain-en-Laye, 44

Treaty of Utrecht, 54, 64, 104-5, 118

Trigger, Bruce, 15, 96

Trinity (Newfoundland), 145, 147-49, 154

Trois-Rivières (Québec), 67, 267-68

Truck system, 149

Tsimshian (peoples), 15-16

Tulchinsky, Gerald, 266

Turgeon, Laurier, 34, 37, 38

Turner, Frederick Jackson, 54, 63, 133

United States (ambivalence towards), 468-69

Upton, Leslie, 15, 179

Van Kirk, Sylvia, 388-89

Vancouver, George, 131, 417-18

Vancouver Island, 429-32

Vegetation regions, 4

Verrazano, Giovanni, 23

Victoria, BC, 427, 432, 439, 443-44

Villages: early Canada, 74, 84; Eastern Townships, 292-93, 297-98; missionary, 397; seigneurial lowlands, 240-42, 260; Upper Canada, 322

Vincennes, 106

Voyageurs, 72,

Wage rates: Britain, 313; Maritimes, 222; staple trades, 456; Upper Canada, 320, 351

Wakefield, Edward Gibbon, 324, 430, 432

Wallot, Jean-Pierre, 246

War of 1812, 128-29, 423

War of the League of Augsburg, 53, 102, 142

War of the Spanish Succession, 54, 102, 104, 142

Warfare between Native groups: 11, 14, 94-97, 112-13, 379, 422

Weaver, John, 123

Webster-Ashburton Treaty, 1842, 127, 129

Whaling, Basque, 36-37, 46, 47-48, 49

Wheat-fallow-wheat farming, 333-35

White, Richard, 97, 99, 108, 111, 119, 128

Winslow (Québec), 293-95

Wood, J. David, 325

Work camps: cod fishery, 35; logging, 186-87, 282-83; in staple trades, 457; whaling, 36-37

Wynn, Graeme, 172, 177, 224

Yeo, James, 200

York (Ontario), 322

Yorkshire immigrants, 169, 172, 176

Printed and bound in Canada by Friesens
Set in Minion and GaramondAlt Italic by Artegraphica Design
Text design: Irma Rodriguez
Copy editor: Deborah Kerr